Robert J DeYoung

In memory of
William E. Pribble
1915 - 1960
given by his widow and
family.

First Congregational Church
of Hudsonville.

CALVIN AND AUGUSTINE

CALVIN AND AUGUSTINE

BY

BENJAMIN BRECKINRIDGE WARFIELD

Professor of Didactic and Polemic Theology
in the Theological Seminary of Princeton
New Jersey, 1887–1921

Edited by

SAMUEL G. CRAIG

With a Foreword by

J. MARCELLUS KIK

Published by
THE PRESBYTERIAN AND REFORMED PUBLISHING COMPANY
PHILADELPHIA, PENNSYLVANIA
1956

FOREWORD

As the Christian Church views the panorama of her history, two figures stand out in bold relief. They are Augustine and Calvin. Their influence has shaped the religious life and theological thought for centuries. For a thousand years since the fourth century the religious genius of Augustine determined the development of the Christian Church. And from the days of the Reformation to this present day it is the religious genius of Calvin, along with that of Luther, that has played such an important part in the Christian Church. To this day the "Institutes" of Calvin remains the "masterpiece of Protestant Theology." These two extraordinarily gifted men tower like pyramids over the scene of history.

To properly evaluate the work of Calvin and Augustine, requires unusual gifts. These are found in Benjamin Breckinridge Warfield. In the minds of not a few, Warfield is one of the outstanding theologians since Calvin. Because of his lucid and stately style of writing, his penetrating gift of analysis, his knowledge of the works of Calvin and Augustine, and his firm grasp of Reformed theology, there was no one better qualified to estimate and express the unique place of Calvin and Augustine in the history of the Christian Church. Christian literature has been enriched by the studies found in this book.

In reading the articles, one becomes immediately aware of the relevancy of Calvin and Augustine to the religious and theological situation of the modern day. These are not studies of museum pieces of antiquated theology. They are alive to the present ecclesiastical situation. One becomes convinced that a genuine renaissance of religion and theology must begin with a renascence of Augustinianism and Calvinism.

There is an awakening of interest in religion. Some judge this interest to be superficial and temporary because it lacks knowledge and depth. This may be true. The rubbish of neglect, misapprehension, and misunderstanding has cut off the stream of Augustinianism and Calvinism which would give vitality and permanence to this new interest in religion. Warfield removes this rubbish of misapprehension and misunderstanding. Evangelicals would be wise to deepen their movement by a study of those who inspired the true revivals of the past. As Warfield stated: "Calvinism supplied the sinew of the Evangelical Christianity in the past." What it performed in the past it can perform in the present and the future. The evangelical movement needs a theology which is true to the Scriptures. Especially in Calvin's and Augustine's doctrine of the majesty and sovereignty of God, is there found that which will inspire the evangelical movement to greater depth and permanence.

It is little realized that both Augustine and Calvin were intensely religious. Their theology sprung from the heart. It is a false representation of Calvin to picture him as a cold intellect who developed a stern logical system for theology. Both Augustine and Calvin were filled with the sense of sin and their complete dependence upon God for salvation. Their whole attitude was that of the publican: "God have mercy on me a sinner." Their religion is so well adapted for this present generation since a sense of helplessness is pervading literature, science, and even politics. There is no longer that pride that contends that man is able to save himself and the world. Pessimism and fatalism are the foul plants that grow from the cistern of despair. Only the stream of Augustinianism and Calvinism can supplant these desert plants with those of hope, knowledge, and courage. Calvinism is the theology that can fulfill the need of this world though the world knows it not. Warfield has sought in these studies to overcome this ignorance.

There is at this present time a search for authority among thinking men. Man is frightened of man. The scientist is frightened of science. They look to the Church but see no sign of authority. Even some preachers have been looking about in bewilderment for some form of authority. Some find it in tradition and the visible Church. Tradition and the ruling hierarchy become their authority for preaching and action. The question of authority was of vital importance to Augustine and Calvin. Warfield shows that with Augustine the Church was the proximate seat of authority but not the ultimate seat of authority. In and through Christ the divine revelation embodied in the Scriptures was authoritative. The Roman Catholic Church took only one aspect of the teaching of Augustine and as a result the visible Church, under the control of man, became the authority. From this perversion Calvin emancipated the Church.

From whence can man obtain knowledge of God? Warfield reveals how both Augustine and Calvin recognized the blindness of sinful man which prevented him from seeing God in nature and the written Word. There is light in nature and light in the written Word. But what is light to a blind man? Only a miracle, performed by the Holy Spirit, will enable a man to see God. To Augustine and Calvin there was a place for the supernatural in the obtaining of true knowledge. A special illumination by the Holy Spirit will enable man to obtain knowledge of God in nature and the Scriptures. Both Augustine and Calvin believed that the Bible is the objective revelation of the will of God.

Neo-orthodoxy has made much of Calvin's doctrine of the testimony of the Holy Spirit. It is maintained by dialectical theology that only that should be acknowledged as authoritative Scripture which the Holy Spirit commends to the religious judgment of the individual. This means that the judgment of man is the ultimate authority. Warfield, who wrote before Barth and Brunner and who cannot thus be accused of bias, indicates that such a view cannot be found in Calvin. Calvin establishes the canonicity and the integrity of the text of Scripture on historico-critical grounds and not by the inner voice of the Holy Spirit. Warfield proves that the objective revelation as given in Scripture was authoritative for Calvin but that it required the Holy Spirit to convince the human heart to believe and understand this objective revelation.

As one read the articles of Warfield in this book he cannot help being deeply impressed with their relevancy to the religious and theological situation of today. The problems with which the minds of Augustine and Calvin grappled are the problems which puzzle the minds of men today. Warfield has made a wonderful contribution to the Church in showing so clearly the thinking of these two great Christian intellects on the major problems of theology.

This volume is the fourth in a series of the writings of Warfield published by the Presbyterian and Reformed Publishing Company. With one exception all the articles of this volume have been taken from the two Oxford University Press volumes entitled, *Studies in Tertullian and Augustine,* and *Calvin and Calvinism.* The three previous volumes of this series contain the principal writings of Warfield dealing with *The Inspiration and Authority of the Bible, The Person and Work of Christ,* and *Biblical and Theological Studies.* All four form a classical series. It is very significant and one of the good signs of the times that the interest in the works of Warfield is greater now than when they were first published by the Oxford University Press.

J. MARCELLUS KIK
Associate Editor *Christianity Today*

CONTENTS

PART ONE

PART TWO

APPENDIX

CONTENTS

PART ONE

I

JOHN CALVIN: THE MAN AND HIS WORK

JOHN CALVIN: THE MAN AND HIS WORK[1]

JOHN CALVIN was born on the tenth of July, 1509, at Noyon, in Picardy. His boyhood was spent under the shadow of the "long, straight-backed" cathedral which dominates his native town. His mother, a woman of notable devoutness, omitted no effort to imbue her son with her own spirit. His father, a successful advocate and shrewd man of affairs, holding both ecclesiastical and civil offices, stood in close relations with the cathedral chapter, and seems to have been impressed with the advantages of a clerical life. At all events, he early devoted his promising son to it. According to the bad custom of the times, a benefice in the cathedral was assigned to the young Calvin at an early age, and to it was afterwards added a neighboring curacy; thus funds were provided for his support. His education was conducted in companionship with the youthful scions of the local noble house of Montmor, and began, therefore, with the training proper to a gentleman. As changing circumstances dictated changes of plan, he was educated, first as a churchman, then as a lawyer, and through all and most abundantly of all as a man of letters. He was an eager student, rapidly and solidly mastering the subjects to which he turned his attention, and earning such admiration from his companions as to be esteemed by them rather a teacher than a fellow-pupil. His youth was as blameless as it was strenuous. It is doubtless legendary, that the censoriousness of his bearing earned for him from his associates the nickname of " The Accusative Case." But serious-minded he undoubtedly was, dominated by a scrupulous piety and schooled in a strict morality which brooked with difficulty immorality in his associates; an open-minded, affectionate young man, of irreproachable life

[1] From *The Methodist Review*, Quarterly edited by Gross Alexander, October, 1909 (lviii. pp. 642–663). Reprinted in pamphlet form, 1909, Publishing House of the M. E. Church, South.

3

and frank manners; somewhat sensitive, perhaps, but easy to be entreated, and attracting not merely the confidence but the lasting affection of all with whom he came into contact.

At the age of twenty-two this high-minded young man is found established at Paris as a humanist scholar, with his ambition set upon literary fame. His début was made by the publication of an excellent commentary on Seneca's treatise "On Clemency" (April, 1532), in which a remarkable command of the whole mass of classical literature, a fine intelligence, and a serious interest in the higher moralities are conspicuous. A great career as a humanist seemed opening before him, when suddenly he was "converted," and his whole life revolutionized. He had always been not only of an elevated ethical temper, but of a deeply religious spirit; but now the religious motive took complete possession of him and directed all his activities. "Renouncing all other studies," says Beza, "he devoted himself to God." He did not, indeed, cease to be a "man of letters," any more than he ceased to be a man. But all his talents and acquisitions were henceforth dedicated purely to the service of God and His gospel. Instead of annotating classical texts, we find him now writing a Protestant manifesto for the use of his friend Nicholas Cop (November 1, 1533), a detailed study of the state of the soul after death (1534), and, in his enforced retirement at Angoulême (1534), making a beginning at least with a primary treatise on Christian doctrine, designed for the instruction of the people as they came out into the light of the gospel — which, however, when driven from France, he was destined to publish from his asylum at Basle (spring of 1536), in circumstances which transformed it into "at once an apology, a manifesto, and a confession of faith." It is interesting to observe the change which in the meantime had come over his attitude toward his writings. When he sent forth his commentary on Seneca's treatise — his first and last humanistic work — he was quivering with anxiety for the success of his book; he wanted to know how it was selling, whether it was being talked about, what people thought of it. He was proud of his performance; he was zealous to reap the fruits of his labor; he was eager for his legitimate reward. Only four years have passed, and he issues his first Protestant publication — it is the immortal " Institutes of the Christian Religion " in its " first state " — free from all such tremors. He is living at Basle under an assumed name, and is fully content that no one of his acquaintance shall know him for the author of the book which was creating such a stir in the world. He hears the acclamations with which it was greeted with a certain personal detachment. He has sent it forth not for his own glory, but for the glory of God; he is not seeking his own advantage or renown by it, but the strengthening and the succoring of the saints. His sole joy is that it is doing its work. He has not ceased to be a " man of letters," we repeat; but he has consecrated all his gifts and powers as a " man of letters " without reserve to the service of God and His gospel.

What we see in Calvin, thus, fundamentally is the " man of letters " as saint. He never contemplated for himself, he never desired, in all his life he never fully acquiesced in, any other vocation. He was by nature, by gifts, by training — by inborn predilection and by acquired capacities alike — a " man of letters "; and he earnestly, perhaps we may even say passionately, wished to dedicate himself as such to God. This was the life which he marked out for himself, from which he was diverted only under compulsion, and which he never in principle abandoned. It was only by " the dreadful imprecation " of Farel that he was constrained to lay aside his cherished plans and enter upon the direct work of the reformation of Geneva (autumn of 1536). And when, after two years of strenuous labor at this uncongenial employment, he was driven from that turbulent city, it came to him only as a release. Once more he settled down at Basle and applied himself to his beloved studies. It required all of Bucer's strategy as well as entreaties to entice him away from his books to an active ministry at Strasburg; and he yielded at last only when it was made clear to him that there would be leisure there for literary labors. That leisure he certainly not so much found as made for himself. His little conventicle of French refugees quickly became under his hand a model church. His lectures at the school attracted ever wider and wider attention. As time passed, he was called much away to conferences and colloquies, where as "the Theologian," as Melanchthon admiringly called him, he did important service. But it was at Strasburg that his literary activity as a Protestant man of letters really began. There he transformed his "little book" of religion — the "Institutes" of 1536, which was not much more than an extended catechetical manual — into an ample treatise on theology (August, 1539). There, too, he inaugurated the series of his epoch-making expositions of Scripture with his noble commentary on Romans (March, 1540). Thence, too, he sent out his beautiful letter to Sadoleto, the most winningly written of all his controversial treatises (September, 1539). There, too, was written that exquisite little popular tract on the Lord's Supper, which was the instruction and consolation of so many hundreds of his perplexed fellow-countrymen (published in 1541). It caused Calvin great perturbation when these fruitful labors were broken in upon by a renewed call to Geneva. It was with the profoundest reluctance that he listened to this call, and he obeyed it only under the stress of the sternest sense of duty. Returning to Geneva was to him going "straight to the cross": he went, as he said, "as a sacrifice slain unto God" — "bound and fettered to obedience to God." He was not the man to take up a cross and not bear it; and this cross, too, he bore faithfully to the end. But neither was he the man to forget the labor of love to which he had given his heart. Hence the unremitting toil of his pen, with which he wore out the days and nights at Geneva; hence the immensity of his literary output, produced in circumstances as unfavorable as any in which a rich literary output was ever produced. Even "on this rack" Calvin remained fundamentally the "man of letters."

It requires fifty-nine quarto volumes to contain the "Works of John Calvin" as collected in the great critical edition of Baum, Cunitz, and Reuss. Astonishing for their mere mass, these "works" are still more astonishing for their quality.

They are written in the best Latin of their day, elevated, crisp, energetic, eloquent with the eloquence of an earnest and sober spirit — almost too good Latin, as Joseph Scaliger said, for a theologian; or in a French which was a factor of importance in the creation of a worthy French prose for the discussion of serious themes. The variety of their literary form runs through the whole gamut of earnest discourse, from lofty discussion and pithy comment laden with meaning, to burning exhortation, vehement invective, and biting satire. The whole range of subjects proper to a teacher of fundamental truth, who was also both a churchman and a statesman, a minute observer of the life of the people, and a student of the forces by which peoples are moved, is treated, and never without that touch of illumination which we call genius.

At the head of the list of his writing stands, of course, his great dogmatic treatise — the "Institutes of the Christian Religion." In a very literal sense this book may indeed be called his life-work. It was the first book he published after he had "devoted himself to God," and thus introduces the series of his works consecrated to the propagation of religion. But from its first appearance in the spring of 1536 to the issue of its definitive edition in 1559 — throughout nearly a quarter of a century — Calvin was continually busy with it, revising, expanding, readjusting it, until from a simple little handbook, innocent of constructive principle, it had grown into a bulky but compact and thoroughly organized textbook in theology. The importance to the Protestant cause of the publication of this book can hardly be overstated. It is inadequate praise to describe it, as the Roman Catholic historian, Kampschulte, describes it, as "without doubt the most outstanding and the most influential production in the sphere of dogmatics which the Reformation literature of the sixteenth century presents." This goes without saying. What demands recognition is that the publication of the "Institutes" was not merely a literary incident but an historical event, big with issues which have not lost their importance to the present day. By it was given to perplexed, hard-bestead Protestantism an adequate positive programme for its Reformation. As even a not very friendly critic is compelled to bear witness, in this book Calvin at last raised banner against banner, and sounded out a ringing *sursum corda* which was heard and responded to wherever men were seeking the new way. " The immense service which the *Institutes* rendered to the ' Evangelicals,' " expounds this critic — it is M. Buisson in his biography of Sebastien Castellion, and he is thinking particularly of the " Evangelicals " of France though, *mutatis mutandis,* what he says has its application elsewhere too — " was to give a body to their ideas, an expression to their faith." Protesting against superstitious and materialistic interpretations of doctrine and worship, " their vague aspirations would, undoubtedly, have issued in nothing in the Church or out of it." What they needed, and what the " Institutes " did for them, was the disengagement of a principle " from this vortex of ideas," and the development of its consequences. "Such a book," continues M. Buisson, " is equally removed from a pamphlet of Ulrich von Hutten, from the satire of Erasmus, from the popular preaching, mystical and violent, of Luther: it is a work of a theologian in the most learned sense of the term, a religious work undoubtedly, penetrated with an ethical inspiration, but before all, a work of organization and concentration, a code of doctrine for the minister, an arsenal of arguments for simple believers: it is the *Summa* of Reformed Christianity." " The author's concernment is far more to bring out the logical force and the moral power of his own doctrine than to descant on the weak points of the opposing doctrine. What holds his attention is not the past but the future — it is the reconstruction of the Church." What wonder, then, that it has retained its influence through all succeeding time? As the first adequate statement of the positive programme of the Reformation movement, the " Institutes " lies at the foundation of the whole development of Protestant theology, and has left an impress on evangelical thought which is ineffaceable. After three centuries and a half, it retains its unquestioned preëminence as the greatest and most influential of all dogmatic treatises. " There," said Albrecht Ritschl, pointing to it, "There is the masterpiece of Protestant theology."

Second only to the service he rendered by his "Institutes" was the service Calvin rendered by his expositions of Scripture. These fill more than thirty volumes of his collected works, thus constituting the larger part of his total literary product. They cover the whole of the New Testament except II and III John and the Apocalypse, and the whole of the Old Testament except the Solomonic and some of the Historical books. It was doubtless in part to his humanistic training that he owed the acute philological sense and the unerring feeling for language which characterize all his expositions. A recent writer who has made a special study of Calvin's Humanism, at least, remarks: " In his sober grammatico-historical method, in the stress he laid on the natural sense of the text, by the side of his deep religious understanding of it — in his renunciation of the current allegorizing, in his felicitous, skillful dealing with difficult passages, the humanistically trained master is manifest, pouring the new wine into new bottles." Calvin was, however, a born exegete, and adds to his technical equipment of philological knowledge and trained skill in the interpretation of texts a clear and penetrating intelligence, remarkable intellectual sympathy, incorruptible honesty, unusual historical perception, and an incomparable insight into the progress of thought, while the whole is illuminated by his profound religious comprehension. His expositions of Scripture were accordingly a wholly new phenomenon, and introduced a new exegesis — the modern exegesis. He stands out in the history of biblical study as, what Diestel, for example, proclaims him, " the creator of genuine exegesis." The authority which his comments immediately acquired was immense — they " opened the Scriptures " as the Scriptures never had been opened before. Richard Hooker — " the judicious Hooker " — remarks that in the controversies of his own time, " the sense of Scripture which Calvin alloweth " was of more weight than if " ten thousand Augustines, Jeromes, Chrysostoms, Cyprians were brought forward." Nor have they lost their value even to-day. Alone of the commentaries of their age the most scientific of modern expositors still find their profit in consulting them. As Professor A. J. Baumgartner, who has set himself to investigate the quality of Calvin's Hebrew learning (which he finds quite adequate), puts it, after remarking on Calvin's "astounding, multiplied, almost superhuman activity" in his work of biblical interpretation: "And — a most remarkable thing — this work has never grown old; these commentaries whose durable merit and high value men of the most diverse tendencies have signalized, — these commentaries remain to us even to-day, an astonishingly rich, almost inexhaustible mine of profound thoughts, of solid and often ingenious interpretation, of wholesome exposition, and at the same time of profound erudition."

The Reformation was the greatest revolution of thought which the human spirit has wrought since the introduction of Christianity; and controversy is the very essence of revolutions. Of course Calvin's whole life, which was passed in the thick of things, was a continuous controversy; and directly controversial treatises necessarily form a considerable part of his literary output. We have already been taught, indeed, that his fundamental aim was constructive, not destructive: he wished to rebuild the Church on its true foundations, not to destroy its edifice. But, like certain earlier rebuilders of the Holy City, he needed to work with the trowel in one hand and the sword in the other. Probably no more effective controversialist ever wrote. "The number of Calvin's polemical treatises," remarks an unfriendly critic, "is large; and they are all masterpieces in their kind." At the head of them, in time as well as in attractiveness, stands his famous "Letter to Cardinal Sadoleto," written in his exile at Strasburg for the protection from an insidious foe of the Church which had cast him out. Courteous, even gentle and deferential in tone, and yet cogent, conclusive, in effect, it perfectly exemplifies the precept of *suaviter in modo, fortiter in re.* Others are, no doubt, set in a different key. The critic we have just quoted (E. F. Bähler) tells of the one he thinks "the harshest and bitterest of all," the " Defense Against the Calumnies of Peter Caroli." " The letter to Sadoleto," he remarks, " was certainly written in a good hour; the contrary must be said of the present book. From the point of view of literary history, the *Defense,* no doubt, merits unrestricted praise. The elegant, crisp style, the skill with which the author not only casts a moral shadow upon his opponent, but brands him as an unsavory person not to be taken seriously, while over all is poured the most sovereign disdain, brings to the reader of this book, now almost four hundred years old, such æsthetic pleasure that it is only with difficulty that he recalls himself to righteous indignation over the gross unfairness and open untruthfulness which the author permits himself against Caroli." No doubt Calvin often spoke in harsh terms of his opponents; they were harsh things they were seeking for him; and the contest in which he was engaged was not a sparring match for the amusement of the onlookers. Nor need it be asserted that he was infallible; though " even his enemies will admit," as even Mark Pattison allows, " that he knows not how to decorate or disguise a fact." Between the suavity of the " Letter to Sadoleto " and the furiousness of the " Defense Against Caroli," a long list of controversial writings of very varying manners range themselves. A frankness of speech characterizes them which never balks at calling a spade a spade; we meet in them with depreciatory, even defamatory, epithets which jar sadly on our modern sensibilities. These are faults not of the man, but of the times: as we are reminded by M. Lenient, the historian of French satire, of all figures of rhetoric euphemism was the least in use in the sixteenth century. But none of Calvin's controversial tracts fails to be informed from beginning to end with a loftiness of purpose, to be conducted with a seriousness and directness of argument, and to be filled with a solid instruction, such as raise them far above the plane of mere partisan wrangle and give them a place among the permanent possessions of the Church.

Fault was found with him in his own day — as, for example, by Castellion — for permitting himself the use of satire in religious debate. This was not merely a result of native temperament with him, but a matter of deliberate and reasoned choice. Of course he had nothing in common with the mere mockers of the time — des Périers, Marot, Rabelais — whose levity was almost as abominable to him as their coarseness. Satire to him was a weapon, not an amusement. The proper way to deal with folly, he thought, was to laugh at it. The superstitions in which the world had been so long entangled were foolish as truly as wicked; and how could it be, he demanded, that in speaking of things so ridiculous, so intrinsically funny, we should not laugh at them " with wide-open mouth " ? Of course this laugh was not the laugh of pure amusement; and as it gained in earnestness it naturally lost in lightness of touch. It was a rapier in Calvin's hands, and its use was to pierce and cut. And how well he uses it! The Sorbonne, for example, issued a series of " Articles," declaring the orthodox doctrine on the points disputed by the Protestants. Calvin republishes these " Articles," and subjoins to each of them a quite innocent-looking " Proof," conceived perfectly in the Sorbonnic manner, but issuing in each case in a hopeless *reductio ad absurdum*. Thus: " It is proved, moreover, that vows are obligatory from their being dispensed and loosed: the Pope could not dispense vows were it not for the power of the keys, and hence it follows that they bind the conscience," — truly as fine a specimen of *lucus a non lucendo* as one will find in a day's search. It is only rarely that the mask is dropped a moment and a glimpse given of the mocking eyes behind — as thus: " But that our masters, when congregated in one body, are the Church, is proved from this, that they are very like the ark of Noah — since they form a herd of all sorts of beasts." The matter is indeed in general so subtly managed that perhaps the " Antidote," which in each instance follows on the " Proof," was not altogether unnecessary. There is no such subtlety in what is, perhaps, the best known of Calvin's satirical pieces — his " Admonition, Showing the Advantage which Christendom Might Derive from an Inventory of Relics." Here we have a simple, straightforward enumeration of the relics exposed in various churches for the veneration of the people.

The effect is produced by the incongruity, which grows more and more monstrous, of the reduplication of these relics. "Everybody knows that the inhabitants of Tholouse think that they have got six of the bodies of the apostles. Now, let us attend to those who have had two or three bodies. For Andrew has another body at Malfi, Philip and James the Less have each another body at the Church of the Holy Apostles, and Simeon and Jude, in like manner, at the Church of St. Peter. Bartholomew has also another in the church dedicated to him at Rome. So here are six who each have two bodies, and also, by way of a supernumerary, Bartholomew's skin is shown at Pisa. Matthias, however, surpasses all the rest, for he has a second body at Rome, in the church of the elder Mary, and a third one at Treves. Besides, he has another head, and another arm, existing separately by themselves. There are also fragments of Andrew existing at different places, and quite sufficient to make up half a body." And so on endlessly; and of course monotonously — which, however, is part of the calculated effect. As M. Lenient remarks, " his pitiless calculations give to a mathematical operation all the piquancy of a *bon mot,* and the irony of numbers destroys the credit of the most respected pilgrimages." It is, however, in such a tract as the " Excuse of the Nicodemites " that Calvin's satire is found at its best, as he rails at those weak Protestants who were too timid to declare themselves. " His pen," says M. Lenient, " was never more light or incisive. Moralist and painter after the fashion of La Bruyère, he amuses himself sketching all these profiles of effeminate Christians, with their slacknesses, their compromises of conscience, their calculations of selfishness, and indifferent lukewarmness." Literature this all is, doubtless, and good literature; and by virtue of it " Calvinistic satire " — Calvin, Beza, and Viret were its first masters — has a recognized place in the history of French satire. But it is not primarily or chiefly literature, and it had its part to play among the moral and religious forces which Calvin liberated for the accomplishment of his reforming work.

Perhaps enough has been said to suggest how Calvin fulfilled his function as reformer by his literary labors. There were, of course, other forms of his literary product which have not been mentioned — creeds and catechisms, Church ordinances and forms of worship, popular tracts and academic consilia. We need not stop to speak of them particularly. Of one other product of his literary activity, however, a special word seems demanded. Calvin was the great letter-writer of the Reformation age. About four thousand of his letters have come down to us, some of them almost of the dimensions of treatises, many of them practically theological tractates, but many of them also of the most intimate character in which he pours out his heart. In these letters we see the real Calvin, the man of profound religious convictions and rich religious life, of high purpose and noble strenuousness, of full and freely flowing human affections and sympathies. In them he rebukes rulers and instructs statesmen, and strengthens and comforts saints. Never a perplexed pastor but has from him a word of encouragement and counsel; never a martyr but has from him a word of heartening and consolation. Perhaps no friend ever more affectionately leaned on his friends; certainly no friend ever gave himself more ungrudgingly to his friends. Had he written these letters alone, Calvin would take his place among the great Christians and the great Christian leaders of the world.

It is time, however, that we reminded ourselves that Calvin's work as a reformer is not summed up in his literary activities. A " man of letters " he was fundamentally; and a " man of letters " he remained in principle all his life. But he was something more than a " man of letters." This was his chosen sphere of service; and he counted it a cross to be compelled to expend his energies through other channels. But this cross was laid upon him, and he took it up and bore it. And the work which he did under the cross was such that had we no single word from his pen, he would still hold his rank among the greatest of the Reformers. We call him " the Reformer of Geneva." But in reforming Geneva he set forces at work which have been world-wide in their operation and are active still to-day. Were we to attempt to characterize in a phrase the peculiarity of his work as a reformer, perhaps we could not do better than to say it was the work of an idealist become a practical man of affairs. He did not lack the power to wait, to make adjustments, to advance by slow and tentative steps. He showed himself able to work with any material, to make the best of compromises, to abide patiently the coming of fitting opportunities. The ends which he set before himself as reformer he attained only in the last years of his strenuous life. But he was incapable of abandoning his ideals, of acquiescing in half measures, of drifting with the tide. Therefore his whole life in Geneva was a conflict. But in the end he made Geneva the wonder of the world, and infused into the Reformed Churches a spirit which made them not only invincible in the face of their foes, but an active ferment that has changed the face of the world. Thus this "man of letters," entering into life with his ideals, was "the means," to adopt the words of a critic whose sympathy with those ideals leaves much to be desired, "of concentrating in that narrow corner" of the world "a moral force which saved the Reformation"; or rather, to put it at its full effect, which "saved Europe." "It may be doubted," as the same critic — Mark Pattison — exclaims in extorted admiration, "if all history can furnish another instance of such a victory of moral force."

When Calvin came to Geneva, he tells us himself, he found the gospel preached there, but no Church established. "When I first came to this Church," he says, "there was as good as nothing here — *il n'y avoit quasi comme rien.* There was preaching, and that was all." He would have found much the same state of things everywhere else in the Protestant world. The "Church" in the early Protestant conception was constituted by the preaching of the Word and the right administration of the sacraments: the correction of the morals of the community was the concern not of the Church but of the civil power. As a recent historian — Professor Karl Rieker — rather flippantly expresses it: "Luther, when he had preached and sowed the seed of the Word, left to the Holy Spirit the care of producing the fruit, while with his friend Philip he peacefully drank his glass of Wittenberg beer." Calvin could not take this view of the matter. "Whatever others may hold," he observed, "we cannot think so narrowly of our office that when preaching is done our task is fulfilled, and we may take our rest." In his view the mark of a true Church is not merely that the gospel is preached in it, but that it is "followed." For him the Church is the "communion of saints," and it is incumbent upon it to see to it that it is what it professes to be. From the first he therefore set himself strenuously to attain this end, and the instrument which he sought to employ to attain it was, briefly — Church discipline. It comes to us with a surprise which is almost a shock to learn that we owe to Calvin all that is involved, for the purity and welfare of the Church, in the exercise of Church discipline. But that is the simple truth, and so sharp was the conflict by which the innovation won a place for itself, and so important did the principle seem, that it became the mark of the Reformed Churches that they made " discipline " one of the fundamental criteria of the true Church. Moreover, the application of this principle carried Calvin very far, and, indeed, in its outworking gave the world through him the principle of a free Church in a free State. It is ultimately to him, therefore, that the Church owes its emancipation from the State, and to him goes back that great battle-cry which has since fired the hearts of many saints in many crises in many lands: "The Crown Rights of King Jesus in His Church."

Censorship of manners and morals was not introduced by Calvin into Geneva. Such a censorship, often of the most petty and galling kind, was the immemorial practice not only of Geneva but of all other similarly constituted towns. It was part of the recognized police regulations of the times. Calvin's sole relation to this censorship was through his influence — he never bore civil office or exercised civil authority in Geneva, and, indeed, acquired the rights of citizenship there only late in life — gradually to bring some order and rationality into its exercise. What Calvin introduced — and it was so revolutionary with respect both to the State and to the Church that it required eighteen years of bitter struggle before it was established — was distinctively *Church* discipline. The principles on which he proceeded were already laid down in the first edition of his " Institutes " (spring of 1536). And when he came to Geneva in the autumn of 1536 he lost no time in seeking to put them into practice. Already at the opening of 1537 we find a document drawn up by him in the name of the ministers of Geneva before the Council, in which the whole new conception is briefly outlined. This great charter of the Church's liberties — for it is as truly such as the " Magna Charta " is the charter of British rights — opens with these simple and direct words: " It is certain that a Church cannot be said to be well ordered and governed unless the Holy Supper of our Lord is frequently celebrated and attended in it, and that with such good regulation that no one would dare to present himself at it except with piety and deep reverence. And it is therefore necessary for the Church to maintain in its integrity the discipline of excommunication, by which those should be corrected who are unwilling to yield themselves amiably and in all obedience to the holy Word of God." In the body of the document the matter is argued, and three things are proposed: First, that it be ascertained at the outset who of the inhabitants of the town wished " to avow themselves of the Church of Jesus Christ." For this, it is suggested that a brief and comprehensive Confession of Faith be prepared, and " all the inhabitants of your town " be required to " make confession and render reason of their faith, that it may be ascertained which accord with the Gospel, and which prefer to be of the kingdom of the Pope rather than of Jesus Christ." Secondly, that a catechism be prepared, and the children be diligently instructed in the elements of the faith. And thirdly, that provision be made by the appointment of " certain persons of good life and good repute among all the faithful, and likewise of constancy of spirit and not open to corruption," who should keep watch over the conduct of the Church members, advise with them, admonish them, and in obstinate cases bring them to the attention of the ministers, when, if they still prove unamenable, they are " to be held as rejected from the company of Christians," and " as a sign of this, rejected from the communion of the Lord's Supper, and denounced to the rest of the faithful as not to be companied with familiarly." By this programme Calvin became nothing less than the creator of the Protestant Church. The particular points to be emphasized in it are two. It is purely *Church* discipline which is contemplated, with none other but spiritual penalties. And the Church is for this purpose especially discriminated from the body of the people — the State — and a wedge is thus driven in between Church and State which was bound to separate the one from the other.

In claiming for the Church this discipline, Calvin, naturally, had no wish in any way to infringe upon the police regulations of the civil authorities. They continued, in their own sphere, to command his approval and coöperation. He has the clearest conception of the limits within which the discipline of the Church must keep itself, and expressly declares that it is confined absolutely to the spiritual penalty of excommunication. But he just as expressly suggests that the State, on its own part, might well take cognizance of spiritual offenses; and even invokes the aid of the civil magistrate in support of the authority of the Church. " This," he says to the Council, after outlining his scheme for the appointment of lay helpers — in effect elders — in the exercise of discipline, — " this seems to us a good way to introduce excommunication into our Church, and to maintain it in its entirety. And beyond this correction the Church cannot proceed. But if there are any so insolent and abandoned to all perversity that they only laugh at being excommunicated, and do not mind living and dying in such a condition of rejection, it will be for you to consider how long you will endure and leave unpunished such contempt and such mockery of God and His Gospel." This is not requiring the State to execute the Church's decrees: the Church executes her own decrees, and its extremest penalty is excommunication. It is only recognizing that the State as well as the Church may take account of spiritual offenses. And particularly it is declaring that while the Church by her own sanctions protects her own altars, it is the part of the State by its own sanctions to sustain the Church in protecting its altars. Calvin has not risen to the conception of the complete mutual independence of Church and State: his view still includes the conception of an " established Church." But the " established Church " which he pleads for is a Church absolutely autonomous in its own spiritual sphere. In asking this he was asking for something new in the Protestant world, and something in which lay the promise and potency of all the freedom which has come to the Reformed Churches since.

Of course Calvin did not get what he asked for in 1537. Nor did he get it when he returned from his banishment in 1541. But he never lost it from sight; he never ceased to contend for it; he was always ready to suffer for its assertion and defense; and at last he won it. The spiritual liberties which he demanded for the Church in 1536, for the assertion of which he was banished in 1538, for the establishment of which he ceaselessly struggled from 1541, he measurably attained at length in 1555. In the fruits of that great victory we have all had our part. And every Church in Protestant Christendom which enjoys to-day any liberty whatever, in performing its functions as a Church of Jesus Christ, owes it all to John Calvin. It was he who first asserted this liberty in his early manhood — he was only twenty-seven years of age when he presented his programme to the Council; it was he who first gained it in a lifelong struggle against a determined opposition; it was he who taught his followers to value it above life itself, and to secure it to their successors with the outpouring of their blood. And thus Calvin's great figure rises before us as not only in a true sense the creator of the Protestant Church, but the author of all the freedom it exercises in its spiritual sphere.

It is impossible to linger here on the relations of this great exploit of Calvin's, even to point out its rooting in his fundamental religious conceptions, or its issue in the creation of a spirit in his followers to the efflorescence of which this modern world of ours owes its free institutions. We cannot even stop to indicate other important claims he has upon our reverence. We say nothing here, for example, of Calvin the preacher — the "man of the Word" as Doumergue calls him, pronouncing him as such greater than he was as "man of action" or "man of thought," as both of which he was very great — who for twenty-five years stood in the pulpit of Geneva, preaching sometimes daily, sometimes twice a day, a word the echoes of which were heard to the confines of Europe. We say nothing, again, of his reorganization of the worship of the Reformed Churches, and particularly of his gift to them of the service of song: for the Reformed Churches did not sing until Calvin taught them to do it. There are many who think that he did few things greater or more far-reaching in their influence than the making of the Psalter — that Psalter of which twenty-five editions were published in the first year of its existence, and sixty-two more in the next four years; which was translated or transfused into nearly every language of Europe; and which wrought itself into the very flesh and bone of the struggling saints throughout all the "killing times" of Protestant history. The activities of Calvin were too varied and multiplex, his influence in numerous directions too enormous, to lend themselves to rapid enumeration. We can pause further only to say a necessary word of that system of divine truth which, by his winning restatement and powerful advocacy of it, he has stamped with his name, and with his eye upon which a Roman Catholic writer of our day — Canon William Barry — pronounces Calvin "undoubtedly the greatest of Protestant divines, and, perhaps, after St. Augustine, the most persistently followed by his disciples of any western writer on theology."

It has become very much the custom of modern historians to insist that Calvin's was not an original but only a systematizing genius. Thus, for example, Reinhold Seeberg remarks: "His was an acute and delicate but not a creative mind." "As a dogmatician, he furnished no new ideas; but with the most delicate sense of perception he arranged the dogmatic ideas at hand in accordance with their essential character and their historical development." " He possessed the wonderful talent of comprehending any given body of religious ideas in its most delicate refinements and giving appropriate expression to the results of his investigations." Accordingly, he did not leave behind him " uncoined gold, like Luther," or "questionable coinage, like Melanchthon," but good gold well minted — and in this lies the explanation of the greatness of his influence as a theologian. The contention may very easily be overpressed. But at its basis there lies the perception of a very important fact; perhaps we may say the most important fact in the premises.

Calvin was a thoroughly independent student of Scripture, and brought forth from that treasure-house things not only old but new; and if it was not given to him to recover for the world so revolutionizing a doctrine as that of Justification by Faith alone, the contributions of his fertile thought to doctrinal advance were neither few nor unimportant. He made an epoch in the history of the doctrine of the Trinity: by his insistence on " self-existence " as a proper attribute of Son and Spirit as well as of the Father, he drove out the lingering elements of Subordinationism, and secured to the Church a deepened consciousness of the co-equality of the Divine Persons. He introduced the presentation of the work of Christ under the rubrics of the threefold office of Prophet, Priest, and King. He created the whole discipline of Christian Ethics. But above all he gave to the Church the entire doctrine of the Work of the Holy Spirit, profoundly conceived and wrought out in its details, with its fruitful distinctions of common and efficacious grace, of noëtic, aisthetic, and thelematic effects, — a gift, we venture to think, so great, so pregnant with benefit to the Church as fairly to give him a place by the side of Augustine and Anselm and Luther, as the Theologian of the Holy Spirit, as they were respectively the Theologian of Grace, of the Atonement, and of Justification.

Nevertheless, despite such contributions — contributions

of the first order — to theological advance, it is quite true —
and it is a truth deserving the strongest emphasis — that the
system of doctrine which Calvin taught, and by his powerful
commendation of which his greatest work for the world was
wrought, was not peculiar to himself, was in no sense new, —
was, in point of fact, just " the Gospel " common to him and all
the Reformers, on the ground of which they spoke of themselves as " Evangelicals," and by the recovery of which was
wrought out the revolution which we call the Reformation.
Calvin did not originate this system of truth; as " a man of the
second generation " he inherited it, and his greatest significance as a religious teacher is that by his exact and delicate
sense of doctrinal values and relations and his genius for systematic construction, he was able, as none other was, to cast
this common doctrinal treasure of the Reformation into a well-
compacted, logically unassailable, and religiously inspiring
whole. In this sense it is as systematizer that he makes his
greatest demand on our admiration and gratitude. It was he
who gave the Evangelical movement a theology.

The system of doctrine taught by Calvin is just the Augustinianism common to the whole body of the Reformers —
for the Reformation was, as from the spiritual point of view
a great revival of religion, so from the theological point of
view a great revival of Augustinianism. And this Augustinianism is taught by him not as an independent discovery of his
own, but fundamentally as he learned it from Luther, whose
fertile conceptions he completely assimilated, and most directly
and in much detail from Martin Bucer into whose practical,
ethical point of view he perfectly entered. Many of the very
forms of statement most characteristic of Calvin — on such
topics as Predestination, Faith, the stages of Salvation, the
Church, the Sacraments — only reproduce, though of course
with that clearness and religious depth peculiar to Calvin, the
precise teachings of Bucer, who was above all others, accordingly, Calvin's master in theology. Of course he does not take
these ideas over from Bucer and repeat them by rote. They
have become his own and issue afresh from him with a new

exactness and delicacy of appreciation, in themselves and in their relations, with a new development of implications, and especially with a new richness of religious content. For the prime characteristic of Calvin as a theologian is precisely the practical interest which governs his entire thought and the religious profundity which suffuses it all. It was not the head but the heart which made him a theologian, and it is not the head but the heart which he primarily addresses in his theology.

He takes his start, of course, from God, knowledge of whom and obedience to whom he declares the sum of human wisdom. But this God he conceives as righteous love — Lord as well as Father, of course, but Father as well as Lord; whose will is, of course, the *prima causa rerum* (for is He not God?), but whose will also it will be our joy as well as our wisdom to embrace (for is He not our Father?). It was that we might know ourselves to be wholly in the hands of this God of perfect righteousness and goodness — not in those of men, whether ourselves or some other men — that he was so earnest for the doctrine of predestination: which is nothing more than the declaration of the supreme dominion of God. It was that our eternal felicity might hang wholly on God's mighty love — and not on our sinful weakness — that he was so zealous for the doctrine of election: which is nothing more than the ascription of our entire salvation to God. As he contemplated the majesty of this Sovereign Father of men, his whole being bowed in reverence before Him, and his whole heart burned with zeal for His glory. As he remembered that this great God has become in His own Son the Redeemer of sinners, he passionately gave himself to the proclamation of the glory of His grace. Into His hands he committed himself without reserve: his whole spirit panted to be in all its movement subjected to His government — or, to be more specific, to the " leading of His Spirit." All that was good in him, all the good he hoped might be formed in him, he ascribed to the almighty working of this Divine Spirit. The " glory of God alone " — the " leading of the Spirit " (or, as a bright young French student of his thought has lately expressed it, *la maitrise,* the "mastery," the control, of the Spirit), — became thus the twin principles of his whole thought and life. Or, rather, the double expression of the one principle; for — since all that God does, He does by His Spirit — the two are at bottom one.

Here we have the secret of Calvin's greatness and the source of his strength unveiled to us. No man ever had a profounder sense of God than he; no man ever more unreservedly surrendered himself to the Divine direction. "We cannot better characterize the fundamental disposition of Calvin the man and the reformer," writes a recent German student of his life — Bernhard Bess — "than in the words of the Psalm: 'What is man, that thou art mindful of him? and the son of man, that thou visitest him?' After that virtuoso in religion of ancient Israel, no one has spoken of the majesty of God and the insignificance of man with such feeling and truth as Calvin. The appearance which Luther's expressions often give, as if God exists merely for man's sake, never is given by Calvin. God is for him the almighty will which lies behind all that comes to pass. What comes to pass in the world serves no doubt man, the Church, and salvation; but this is not its ultimate end, but the revelation of the glory and the honor of God." If there is anything that will make a man great, surely it is placing himself unreservedly at the disposal of God and seeking not only to do nothing but God's will, but to do all God's will. This is what Calvin did, and it is because he did this that he was so great.

He was, of course, not without his weaknesses. He had no doubt a high temper, though to do him justice we must take the term in all its senses. He did not in all things rise superior to the best opinion of his age. We have seen, for example, that he was in full accord with his time in its extension of the cognizance of the civil courts to spiritual offenses; and it was by the consent of his mind to this universal conviction of the day that he was implicated in that unhappy occurrence — the execution of Servetus. But to do him justice here we must learn to speak both of his connection with that occurrence and of Servetus himself in quite other terms than the reckless language with which a modern writer of repute speaks when he calls Calvin " the author of the great crime of the age — the murder of the heroic Servetus." Servetus, that " fool of genius," as a recent writer, not without insight, characterizes him, was anything but an heroic figure. The "crime" of his " murder," unfortunately, had scores of fellows in that age, in which life was lightly valued, and it was agreed on all hands that grave heresy and gross blasphemy were capital offenses in well-organized states. And Servetus was condemned and executed by a tribunal of which Calvin was not a member, with which he possessed little influence, and which rejected his petition against the unnecessary cruelty of the penalty inflicted.

"There are people," remarks Paul Wernle, who is certainly under the influence of no glamour for Calvin or Calvinism — "There are people who have been told at school that Servetus was burned through Calvin's fault, and are therefore done with this man. They ought to remember that had they lived at the time, they would in all probability have joined in burning him. It is not so easy to be done with the man who was the most luminous and penetrating theologian of his time and the source from which flowed that *power* which Protestantism showed in Scotland, France, England, Holland. We are all glad, no doubt, that we did not live under his rod; but who knows what we would all be, had not this divine ardor possessed him? Concentrated, well-directed enthusiasm — that is his essence; it was himself, first of all, whom he consumed in his zeal; his rule at Geneva was no more rigorous than the heroism was glorious with which he compacted half the Protantism of Europe into a power which nothing could break. Calvin was in very truth the soul of the battling and conquering Reformed world; it was he who fought on the battlefields of the Huguenots and the Dutch, and in the hosts of the Puritans. In scarcely another of the Reformers is there to be seen such thoroughness, absoluteness. And yet what moderation, what real dread of every kind of excess;

with what deference and tact did he know how to speak to the great! If you would know the man, how he lived with and for God and the world, read first of all in the *Institutes* the section *On the Life of the Christian Man*. It is the portrait of himself. And then for his religious individuality add the sections *On Justification* and *On Predestination,* where will be found what is most profound, most moving in his life of faith."

Such a man was John Calvin; and such was the work he did for God and His Kingdom on earth. Adolf Harnack has said that between Paul the Apostle and Luther the Reformer, Augustine was the greatest man God gave His Church. We may surely add that from Luther the Reformer to our day God has given His Church no greater man than John Calvin.

II

CALVIN'S DOCTRINE OF THE KNOWLEDGE OF GOD

CALVIN'S DOCTRINE OF THE KNOWLEDGE OF GOD [1]

THE first chapters of Calvin's " Institutes " are taken up with a comprehensive exposition of the sources and guarantee of the knowledge of God and divine things (Book I. chs. i.–ix.). A systematic treatise on the knowledge of God must needs begin with such an exposition; and we require no account of the circumstance that Calvin's treatise begins with it, beyond the systematic character of his mind and the clearness and comprehensiveness of his view. This exposition therefore makes its appearance in the earliest edition of the " Institutes," which attempted " to give a summary of religion in all its parts," redacted in orderly sequence; that is to say, which was intended as a textbook in theology. This was the second edition, published in 1539, which was considered by Calvin to be the first which at all corresponded to its title. In this edition this exposition already stands practically complete. Large insertions were made into it subsequently, by which it was greatly enriched as a detailed exposition and validation of the sources of our knowledge of God; but no modifications were made in its fundamental teaching by these additions, and the ground plan of the exposition as laid down in 1539 was retained unaltered throughout the subsequent development of the treatise.

We may observe in the controversies in which Calvin had been engaged between 1536 and 1539 a certain preparation for writing this comprehensive and admirably balanced statement, with its equal repudiation of Romish and Anabaptist error and its high note of assurance in the face of the scepticism of the average man of the world. We may trace in it the fruits of his eager and exhaustive studies prosecuted in the interval,

[1] From *The Princeton Theological Review,* vii. 1909, pp. 219–325.

as pastor, professor, and Protestant statesman; and especially of his own ripening thought as he worked more and more into detail his systematic view of the body of truth. But we can attribute to nothing but his theological genius the feat by which he set a compressed apologetical treatise in the forefront of his little book — for the "Institutes" were still in 1539 a little book, although already expanded to more than double the size of their original form (edition of 1536). Thus he not only for the first time supplied the constructive basis for the Reformation movement, but even for the first time in the history of Christian theology drew in outline the plan of a complete structure of Christian Apologetics. For this is the significance in the history of thought of Calvin's exposition of the sources and guarantee of the knowledge of God, which forms the opening topic of his "Institutes." "Thus," says Julius Köstlin, after cursorily surveying the course of the exposition, "there already rises with him an edifice of Christian Apologetics, in its outlines complete (fertig). With it, he stands, already in 1539, unique (einzig) among the Reformers, and among Christian theologians in general up to his day. Only as isolated building-stones can appear in comparison with this, even what Melanchthon, for example, offered in the last elaboration of the Loci with reference to the proofs for the existence of God."[2] In point of fact, in Augustine alone among his predecessors do we find anything like the same grasp of the elements of the problem as Calvin here exhibits; and nowhere among his predecessors do we find these elements brought together in a constructive statement of anything like the completeness and systematic balance which he gave to it.

At once on its publication, however, Calvin's apologetical construction became the property of universal Christian thought, and it has entered so vitally into Protestant, and especially Reformed, thinking as to appear now-a-days very much a matter of course. It is difficult for us to appreciate

[2] Article on "Calvin's Institutio, nach Form und Inhalt, in ihrer geschichtlichen Entwickelung," printed in the Theologische Studien und Kritiken for 1868, p. 39. Köstlin's whole account of the origin of these sections in the edition of 1539 is worth reading (pp. 38–39).

its novelty in him or to realize that it is not as native to every Christian mind as it now seems to us the inevitable adjustment of the elements of the problems raised by the Christian revelation. Familiar as it seems, therefore, it is important that we should apprehend it, at least in its outlines, as it lies in its primary statement in Calvin's pages. So only can we appreciate Calvin's genius or estimate what we owe to him. A very brief abstract will probably suffice, however, to bring before us in the first instance the elements of Calvin's thought. These include the postulation of an innate knowledge of God in man, quickened and developed by a very rich manifestation of God in nature and providence, which, however, fails of its proper effect because of man's corruption in sin; so that an objective revelation of God, embodied in the Scriptures, was rendered necessary, and, as well, a subjective operation of the Spirit of God on the heart enabling sinful man to receive this revelation — by which conjoint divine action, objective and subjective, a true knowledge of God is communicated to the human soul.

Drawn out a little more into detail, this teaching is as follows. The knowledge of God is given in the very same act by which we know self. For when we know self, we must know it as it is: and that means we must know it as dependent, derived, imperfect, and responsible being. To know self implies, therefore, the co-knowledge with self of that on which it is dependent, from which it derives, by the standard of which its imperfection is revealed, to which it is responsible. Of course, such a knowledge of self postulates a knowledge of God, in contrast with whom alone do we ever truly know self: but this only the more emphasises the fact that we know God in knowing self, and the relative priority of our knowledge of two objects of knowledge which we are conscious only of knowing together may for the moment be left undetermined. Meanwhile, it is clear than man has an instinctive and ineradicable knowledge of God, which, moreover, must produce appropriate reactions in his thought, feeling, and will, whence arises what we call religion. But these reactions are conditioned by the state of the soul which reacts. Although, then, man cannot avoid possessing a knowledge of God, and this innate knowledge of God is quickened and developed by the richest manifestations of God in nature and providence, which no man can escape either perceiving or so far apprehending, yet the actual knowledge of God which is framed in the human soul is affected by the subjective condition of the soul. The soul, being corrupted by sin, is dulled in its instinctive apprehension of God; and God's manifestation in nature and history is deflected in it. Accordingly the testimony of nature to God is insufficient that sinful man should know Him aright, and God has therefore supernaturally revealed Himself to His people and deposited this revelation of Himself in written Scriptures. In these Scriptures alone, therefore, do we possess an adequate revelation of God; and this revelation is attested as such by irresistible external evidence and attests itself as such by such marks of inherent divinity that no normal mind can resist them. But the sin-darkened minds to which it appeals are not normal minds, but disordered with the awful disease of sin. What is to give subjective effect in a sin-blinded mind to even a direct revelation from God? The revelation of God is its own credential. It needs no other light to be thrown upon it but that which emanates from itself: and no other light can produce the effect which its own splendor as a revelation of God should effect. But all fails when the receptivity is destroyed by sin. For sinners, therefore, there is requisite a repairing operation upon their souls before the light of the Word itself can accredit itself to them as light. This repairing operation on the souls of sinful men by which they are enabled to perceive light is called the testimony of the Holy Ghost: which is therefore just the subjective action of the Spirit of God on the heart, by virtue of which it is opened for the perception and reception of the objective revelation of God. The testimony of the Spirit cannot, then, take the place of the objective revelation of the Word: it is no revelation in this strict sense. It presupposes the objective revelation and only prepares the heart to respond to and embrace it. But the objective revelation can take no effect on the unprepared heart.

What the operation of the Spirit on the heart does, then, is to implant, or rather to restore, a spiritual sense in the soul by which God is recognized in His Word. When this spiritual sense has been produced the necessity of external proofs that the Scriptures are the Word of God is superseded: the Word of God is as immediately perceived as such as light is perceived as light, sweetness as sweetness — as immediately and as inamissibly. The Christian's knowledge of God, therefore, rests no doubt on an instinctive perception of God native to man as man, developed in the light of a patefaction of God which pervades all nature and history; but particularly on an objective revelation of God deposited in Scriptures which bear in themselves their own evidence of their divine origin, to which every spiritual man responds with the same strength of conviction with which he recognizes light as light. This is the basis which Calvin in his " Institutes " places beneath his systematic exposition of the knowledge of God.

The elements of Calvin's thought here, it will readily be seen, reduce themselves to a few great fundamental principles. These embrace particularly the following doctrines: the doctrine of the innate knowledge of God; the doctrine of the general revelation of God in nature and history; the doctrine of the special revelation of God and its embodiment in Scriptures; the doctrine of the noëtic effects of sin; the doctrine of the testimony of the Holy Spirit. That we may do justice to his thought we must look in some detail at his treatment of each of these doctrines and of the subordinate topics which are necessarily connected with them.

I. Natural Revelation

That the knowledge of God is innate (I. iii. 3), naturally engraved on the hearts of men (I. iv. 4), and so a part of their very constitution as men (I. iii. 1), that it is a matter of instinct (I. iii. 1, I. iv. 2), and every man is self-taught it from his birth (I. iii. 3), Calvin is thoroughly assured. He lays it down as incontrovertible fact that " the human mind, by natural instinct itself, possesses some sense of a deity "

(I. iii. 1, *ad init. et ad fin.;* 3 — *sensus divinitatis* or *deitatis*),[3] and defends the corollaries which flow from this fact, that the knowledge of God is universal and indelible. All men know there is a God, who has made them, and to whom they are responsible. No savage is sunk so low as to have lost this sense of deity, which is wrought into his very constitution: and the degradation of men's worship is a proof of its ineradicableness — since even such dehumanization as this worship manifests has not obliterated it (I. iii. 1). It is the precondition of all religion, without which no religion would ever have arisen; and it forms the silent assumption of all attempts to expound the origin of religion in fraud or political artifice, as it does also of all corruptions of religion, which find their nerve in men's incurable religious propensities (I. iii. 1). The very atheists testify to its persistence in their ill-concealed dread of the deity they profess to despise (I. iv. 2); and the wicked, strive they ever so hard to banish from their consciousness the sense of an accusing deity, are not permitted by nature to forget it (I. iii. 3). Thus the cases alike of the savages, the atheists, and the wicked are made contributory to the establishment of the fact, and the discussion concludes with the declaration that it is by this innate knowledge of God that men are discriminated from the brutes, so that for men to lose it would be to fall away from the very law of their creation (I. iii. 3, *ad fin.*).[4]

[3] "Institutes," I. iii. 1: Quemdam inesse humanae menti, et quidem naturali instinctu, divinitatis sensum, extra controversiam ponimus; iii. 3, *ad init.*: "This indeed with all rightly judging men will always be assured, that there is engraved on the minds of men *divinitatis sensum, qui deleri numquam potest*"; iii. 3, *med.*: vigere tamen ac subinde emergere quem maxime extinctum cuperent, *deitatis sensum;* iv. 4, *ad fin.*: naturaliter insculptum esse deitatis sensum humanis cordibus; iv. 4, *ad fin.*: manet tamen semen illud quod revelli a radice nullo modo potest, aliquam esse divinitatem. The phraseology by which Calvin designates this "natural instinct" (*naturalis instinctus;* iii. 1, *ad init.*) varies from *sensus divinitatis* or *sensus deitatis* to such synonyms as: *numinis intelligentia, dei notio, dei notitia.* It is the basis on the one hand of whatever *cognitio dei* man attains to and on the other of whatever *religio* he reaches; whence it is called the *semen religionis.*

[4] That the knowledge of God is innate was the common property of the Reformed teachers. Peter Martyr, "Loci Communes," 1576, *praef.*, declares that *Dei cognitio omnium animis naturaliter innata*[est]. It was thrown

If the knowledge of God enters thus into the very idea of humanity and constitutes a law of its being, it follows that it is given in the same act of knowledge by which we know ourselves. This position is developed at length in the opening chapter. The discussion begins with a remark which reminds us of Augustine's familiar contention that the proper concern of mankind is the knowledge of God and the soul; to which it is added at once that these two knowledges are so interrelated that it is impossible to assign the priority to either. The knowledge of self involves the knowledge of God and also profits by the knowledge of God: the better we know ourselves the better we shall know God, but also, we shall never know ourselves as we really are save in contrast with God, by whom is supplied the only standard for the formation of an accurate judgment upon ourselves (I. i. 2). In his analysis of the mode of the implication of the knowledge of God in the knowledge of self, Calvin lays the stress upon our nature as dependent, derived, imperfect, and responsible beings, which if known at all must be known as such, and to be known as such must be known as over against that Being on whom we are dependent, to whom we owe our being, over against whom our imperfection is manifest, and to whom we are responsible (I. i. 1). As we are not self-existent, we must recognize ourselves as " living and moving" in Another. We recognize ourselves as products, and in knowing the product know the cause; thus our very endowments, seeing that they distil to us by drops from heaven, form so many streams up which our minds must needs travel to their Fountainhead. The perception of our imperfec-

---

into great prominence in the Socinian debate, as the Socinians contended that the human mind is natively a *tabula rasa* and all knowledge is acquired. But in defending the innate knowledge of God, the Reformed doctors were very careful that it should not be exaggerated. Thus Leonh. Riissen, " F. Turretini Compendium . . . auctum et illustratum," 1695, i. 8, remarks: " Some recent writers explain the natural sense of deity (*numinis*) as *an idea of God impressed on our minds.* If this idea is understood as an innate faculty for knowing God after some fashion, it should not be denied; but if it expresses an *actual and adequate representation of God from our birth,* it is to be entirely rejected." (Heppe, " Die Dogmatik der evangelisch-reformirten Kirche," 1861, p. 4.)

tions is at the same time the perception of His perfection; so that our very poverty displays to us His infinite fulness. Our sense of dissatisfaction with ourselves directs our eyes to Him whose righteous judgment we can but anticipate; and when in the presence of His majesty we realize our meanness and in the presence of His righteousness we realize our sin, our perception of God passes into consternation as we recognize in Him our just Judge.

The emphasis which Calvin places in this analysis upon the sense of sin and the part it plays in our knowledge of God, at once attracts attention. It is perhaps above everything the "miserable ruin" in which we find ourselves, which compels us, according to him, to raise our eyes towards heaven, spurred on not merely by a sense of lack but by a sense of dread: it is only, he declares, when we have begun to be displeased with ourselves that we energetically turn our thoughts Godward. This is already an indication of the engrossment of Calvin in this treatise with practical rather than merely theoretical problems. He is less concerned to show how man as man attains to a knowledge of God, than how man as he actually exists upon the earth attains to it. In the very act of declaring that this knowledge is instinctive and belongs to the very constitution of man as such, therefore, he so orders the exposition of the mode of its actual rise in the mind as to throw the emphasis on a quality which does not belong to man as such, but only to man as actually existing in the world — in that "miserable ruin into which we have been plunged by the defection of the first man" (I. i. 1). Man as unfallen, by the very necessity of his nature would have known God, the sphere of his being, the author of his existence, the standard of his excellences; but for man as fallen, Calvin seems to say, the strongest force compelling him to look upwards to the God above him, streams from his sense of sin, filling him with a fearful looking forward to judgment.

It is quite obvious that such a knowledge of God as Calvin here postulates as the unavoidable and ineradicable possession of man, is far from a mere empty conviction that such a being as God exists. The knowledge of God which is given in our knowledge of self is not a bare perception, it is a conception: it has content. " The knowledge of ourselves, therefore," says Calvin (I. i. 1, *ad fin.*), " is not only an incitement to seek after God, but becomes a considerable assistance towards finding God." The knowledge of God with which we are natively endowed is therefore more than a bare conviction that God is: it involves, more or less explicated, some understanding of what God is. Such a knowledge of God can never be otiose and inert; but must produce an effect in human souls, in the way of thinking, feeling, willing. In other words, our native endowment is not merely a *sensus deitatis,* but also a *semen religionis* (I. iii. 1, 2; iv. 1, 4; v. 1). For what we call religion is just the reaction of the human soul to what it perceives God to be. Calvin is, therefore, just as insistent that religion is universal as that the knowledge of God is universal. " The seeds of religion," he insists, " are sown in every heart " (I. iv. 1; cf. v. 1); men are propense to religion (I. iii. 2, *med.*); and always and everywhere frame to themselves a religion, consonant with their conceptions of God.

Calvin's ideas of the origin and nature of religion are set forth, if succinctly, yet with eminent clearness, in his second chapter. Wherever any knowledge of God exists, he tells us, there religion exists. He is not speaking here of a competent knowledge of God such as redeemed sinners have in Christ. But much less is he speaking of that mere notion that there is such a being as God which is sometimes called a knowledge of God. It may be possible to speculate on " the essence " of God without being moved by it. But certainly it is impossible to form any vital conception of God without some movement of intellect, feeling, and will towards Him; and any real knowledge of God is inseparable from movements of piety towards Him. Piety means reverence and love to God; and the knowledge of God tends therefore to produce in us, first, sentiments of fear and reverence; and, secondly, an attitude of receptivity and praise to Him as the fountain of all blessing. If man were not a sinner, indeed, such would be the result: men, knowing

God, would turn to Him in confidence and commit themselves without reserve to His care — not so much fearing His judgments, as making them in sympathetic loyalty their own (I. ii. 2). And herein we see what pure and genuine religion is: " it consists in faith, united with a serious fear of God, comprehending a voluntary reverence, and producing legitimate worship agreeable to the injunctions of the law " (I. ii. 2, *ad fin.*).[5]

The definition of religion to which Calvin thus attains is exceedingly interesting, and that not merely because of its vital relation to the fundamental thought of these opening chapters, but also because of its careful adjustment to the state of the controversy in which he was engaged as a leader of the Reformation. In the first of these aspects, as we have already pointed out, religion is with him the vital effect of the knowledge of God in the human soul; so that inevitably religions will differ as the conceptions of God determining our thought and feeling and directing our life differ. In the estate of purity, the knowledge of God produces reverence and trust: and the religion of sinless man will therefore exhibit no other traits but trust and love. In sinful man, the same knowledge of God must produce, rather, a reaction of fear and hate — until the grace of God intervenes with a message of mercy. Sinful man cannot be trusted, therefore, to form his own religion for himself, but must in all his religious functioning place himself unreservedly under the direction of God in His gracious revelation. In its second aspect, then, we perceive Calvin carefully framing his definition so as to exclude all " will-worship " and to prepare the way for the condemnation of the " formal worship " and " ostentation in ceremonies " which had become prevalent in the old Church. The position he takes up here is essentially that which has come down to us under the name of " the Puritan principle." Religion consists, of course, not in the externalities of worship, but in faith, united with a serious fear of God, and a willing reverence. But its

---

[5] En quid sit pura germanaque religio, nempe *fides*, cum serio *Dei timore* coniuncta; ut timor et *voluntariam reverentiam* in se contineat, et secum trahat *ligitimum cultum*, qualis in Lege praescribitur.

external expression in worship is not therefore unimportant, but is to be strictly confined to what is prescribed by God: to "legitimate worship, agreeable to the injunctions of the law" (I. ii. 2, *ad fin.*). This declaration is returned to and expounded in a striking section of the fourth chapter (I. iv. 3; cf. I. v. 13), where Calvin insists that "the divine will is the perpetual rule to which true religion is to be conformed," and asserts of newly invented modes of worshipping God, that they are tantamount to idolatry. God cannot be pleased by showing contempt for what He commands and substituting other things which He condemns; and none would dare to trifle in such a manner with Him unless they had already transformed Him in their minds into another and different Being: and in that case it is of little importance whether you worship one god or many.[6]

From this digression for the sake of asserting the "Puritan," that is, the "Reformed," principle with reference to acceptable worship, it is already apparent that Calvin did not suppose that men have been left to the *notitia Dei insita* for the framing of their religion, although he is insistent that therefrom proceeds a propensity to religion which already secures that all men shall have a religion (I. ii. 2). On the contrary, he teaches that to the ineradicable revelation of Himself which He has imprinted on human nature, God has added an equally clear and abundant revelation of Himself externally to us. As we cannot know ourselves without knowing God, so neither can we look abroad on nature or contemplate the course of

[6] The significance and relations of "the Puritan principle" of absolute dependence on the Word of God as the source of knowledge of His will, and exclusive limitation to its prescriptions of doctrine, life, and even form of Church government and worship, are suggested by J. A. Dorner, "Hist. of Protest. Theol.," 1871, i. p. 390, who criticizes it sharply from his "freer" Lutheran standpoint. But even Luther knew how, on occasion, to invoke "the Puritan principle." Writing to Bartime von Sternberg, Sept. 1, 1523, he says: "For a Christian must do nothing that God has not commanded, and there is no command as to such masses and vigils, but it is solely their own invention, which brings in money, without helping either living or dead" ("The Letters of Martin Luther" (selected and translated) by Margaret A. Currie, 1908, p. 115).

events without seeing Him in His works and deeds (I. v.). Calvin is exceedingly emphatic as to the clearness, universality, and convincingness of this natural revelation of God. The whole world is but a theatre for the display of the divine glory (I. v. 5); God manifests Himself in every part of it, and, turn our eyes whichever way we will, we cannot avoid seeing Him; for there is no atom of the world in which some sparks of His glory do not shine (I. v. 1). So pervasive is God in nature, indeed, that it may even be said by a pious mind that nature is God (I. v. 5) — though the expression is too readily misapprehended in a Pantheistic (I. v. 5) or Materialistic (I. v. 4) sense to justify its use. Accordingly, no man can escape this manifestation of God; we cannot open our eyes without seeing it, and the language in which it is delivered to us penetrates through even the densest stupidity and ignorance (I. v. 1). To every individual on earth, therefore, with the exclusion of none (I. v. 7), God abundantly manifests Himself (I. v. 2). Each of the works of God invites the whole human race to the knowledge of Him; while their contemplation in the mass offers an even more prevalent exhibition of Him (I. v. 10). And so clear are His footsteps in His providence, that even what are commonly called accidents are only so many proofs of His activity (I. v. 8).

In developing this statement of the external natural revelation of God, Calvin presents first His patefaction in creation (I. v. 1–6) and then His patefaction in providence (I. v. 7–9), and under each head lays the primary stress on the manifestations of the divine wisdom and power (I. v. 2–5, wisdom; 6, power; 8, wisdom and power). But the other attributes which enter into His glory are not neglected. Thus, under the former caption, he points out that the perception of the divine power in creation " leads us to the consideration of His eternity; because He from whom all things derive their origin must necessarily be eternal and self-existent," while we must postulate goodness and mercy as the motives of His creation and providence (I. v. 6). Under the second caption, he is particularly copious in drawing out the manifestations of the divine benignity and beneficence — of His clemency — though he does not scruple also to point to the signs of His severity (I. v. 7, cf. 10). From the particular contemplation of the divine clemency and severity in their peculiar distribution here, indeed, he pauses to draw an argument for a future life when apparent irregularities will be adjusted (I. v. 10).

The vigor and enthusiasm with which Calvin prosecutes his exposition of the patefaction of God in nature and history is worth emphasising further. He even turns aside (I. v. 9) to express his special confidence in it, in contrast to a priori reasoning, as the "right way and the best method of seeking God." A speculative inquiry into the essence of God, he suggests, merely fatigues the mind and flutters in the brain. If we would know God vitally, in our hearts, let us rather contemplate Him in His works. These, we shall find, as the Psalmist points out, declare His greatness and conduce to His praise. Once more, we may observe here the concreteness of Calvin's mind and method, and are reminded of the practical end he keeps continually in view.[7] So far is he from losing himself in merely speculative elaborations or prosecuting his inquiries under the spur of "presumptuous curiosity," that the practical religious motive is always present, dominating his thought. His special interest in the theistic argument is, accordingly, due less to the consideration that it rounds out his systematic view of truth than to the fact that it helps us to the vital knowledge of God. And therefore he is no more anxious to set it forth in its full force than he is to point out the limitations which affect its practical value.[8] In and of itself, indeed, it has

[7] Cf. P. J. Muller, "De Godsleer van Zwingli en Calvijn," 1883, p. 8: "If Zwingli follows more the a priori, Calvin follows the a posteriori method"; and E. Rabaud, "Hist. de la doctrine de l'inspiration, etc.," 1883, p. 58: "his lucid and, above everything, practical genius."

[8] It is this distribution of Calvin's interest which leads to the impression that he lays little stress on "the theistic proofs." On the contrary, he asserts their validity most strenuously: only he does not believe that any proofs can work true faith apart from "the testimony of the Spirit," and he is more interested in their value for developing the knowledge of God than for merely establishing His existence. Hence P. J. Muller is wrong when he denies the one to affirm the other, as, e.g., in his "De Godsleer van Zwingli en Calvijn," 1883, p. 11: "Neither by Zwingli nor by Calvin are

no limitations; Calvin is fully assured of its validity and analyses its data with entire confidence; to him nothing is more certain than that in the mirror of His works God gives us clear manifestations both of Himself and of His everlasting dominion (I. v. 11). But Calvin cannot content himself with an intellectualistic contemplation of the objective validity of the theistic argument. So dominated is he by practical interests that he actually attaches to the chapter in which he argues this objective validity a series of sections in which he equally strongly argues the subjective inability of man to receive its testimony. Objectively valid as the theistic proofs are, they are ineffective to produce a just knowledge of God in the sinful heart. The insertion of these sections here is the more striking in that they almost seem unnecessary in view of the clear exposition of the noëtic effects of sin which had been made in the preceding chapter (ch. iv.) — although, of course, there the immediate reference was to the *notitia Dei insita*, while here it is to the *notitia Dei acquisita*.

Thus, however, our attention is drawn very pointedly to Calvin's doctrine of the disabilities with reference to the knowl-

proofs offered for the existence of God, although some passages in their writings seem to contain suggestions of them. The proposition, ' God exists,' needed no proof either for themselves, or for their coreligionists, or even against Rome. The so-called cosmological argument has no doubt been found by some in Zwingli (Zeller, *Das theolog. Syst. Zwingli's* extracted from the *Theol. Jahrbücher,* Tübingen, 1853, p. 33; [or p. 126 in the *Th. Jahrb.*]), and the physico-theological in Calvin (Lipsius, *Lehrbuch der ev. prot. Dogmatik,* ed. 2, 1879, p. 213); but it would not be difficult to show that we have to do in neither case with a philosophical deduction, but only with a means for attaining the complete knowledge of God." Though Calvin (also Zwingli) makes use of the theistic proofs to develop the knowledge of God, it does not follow that he (or Zwingli) did not value them as proofs of the existence of God. And we do not think Muller is successful (pp. 12 *sq.*) in explaining away the implication of the latter in Zwingli's use of these theistic arguments, or in Calvin's (p. 16). Schweizer, " Glaubenslehre der ev.-ref. Kirche," 1844, i. p. 250, finds in Calvin's citation of Cicero's declaration that there is no nation so barbarous, no tribe so degraded, that it is not persuaded that a God exists, an appeal to the so-called *historical* argument for the divine existence (cf. the use of it by Zwingli, " Opera," Schuler und Schultess ed., 1832, iii. p. 156): but Calvin's real attitude to the theistic argument is rather to be sought in the implications of the notably eloquent ch. v.

edge of God which are induced in the human mind by sin. He has, as has just been noted, adverted formally to them twice in these opening chapters of his treatise — on the earlier occasion (ch. iv.) with especial reference to the revelation of God made in the constitution of human nature, and on the later occasion (ch. v. §§ 11–15) with especial reference to the revelation of God made in His works and deeds. Were man in his normal state, he could not under this double revelation, internal and external, fail to know God as God would wish to be known. If he actually comes short of an adequate knowledge of God, therefore, this cannot be attributed to any shortcomings in the revelation of God. Calvin is perfectly clear as to the objective adequacy of the general revelation of God. Men, however, do come short of an adequate knowledge of God; and that not merely some men, but all men: the failure of the general revelation of God to produce in men an adequate knowledge of Him is as universal as is the revelation itself. The explanation is to be found in the corruption of men's hearts by sin, by which not merely are they rendered incapable of reading off the revelation of God which is displayed in His works and deeds, but their very instinctive knowledge of God, embedded in their constitution as men, is dulled and almost obliterated. The energy with which Calvin asserts this is almost startling, and matches in its emphasis that which he had placed on the reality and objective validity of the revelation of God. Though the seeds of religion are sown by God in every heart, yet not one man in a hundred has preserved even these seeds sound, and in no one at all have they grown to their legitimate harvest. All have degenerated from the true knowledge of God, and genuine piety has perished from the earth (I. iv. 1). The light which God has kindled in the breasts of men has been smothered and all but extinguished by their iniquity (I. iv. 4). The manifestation which God has given of Himself in the structure and organization of the world is lost on our stupidity (I. v. 11). The rays of God's glory are diffused all around us, but do not illuminate the darkness of our mind (I. v. 14). So that in point of fact, " men who are taught only by nature, have no certain, sound or distinct knowledge, but are confined to confused principles; they worship accordingly an unknown God " (I. v. 12, *fin.*): " no man can have the least knowledge of true and sound doctrine without having been a disciple of the Scriptures " (I. vi. 2, *ad fin.*): " the human mind is through its imbecility unable to attain any knowledge of God without the assistance of the Sacred Word " (I. vi. 4, *ad fin.*).

Calvin therefore teaches with great emphasis the bankruptcy of the natural knowledge of God. We must keep fully in mind, however, that this is not due in his view to any inadequacy or ineffectiveness of natural revelation, considered objectively.[9] He continues to insist that the seeds of religion are sown in every heart (I. v. 1, *ad init.*); that through all man's corruption the instincts of nature still suggest the memory of God to his mind (I. v. 2); that it is impossible to eradicate that sense of the deity which is naturally engraved on all hearts (I. iv. 4, *ad fin.*); that the structure and organization of the world, and the things that daily happen out of the ordinary course of nature, that is under the providential government of God, bear a witness to God which the dullest ear cannot fail to hear (I. v. 1, 3, 7, esp. II. vi. 1); and that the light that shines from creation, while it may be smothered, cannot be so extinguished but that some rays of it find their way into the most darkened soul (I. v. 14). God has therefore never left Himself without a witness; but, " with various and most abundant benignity sweetly allures men to a knowledge of Him, though they persist in following their own ways, their pernicious and fatal errors " (I. v. 14). The sole cause of the failure of the natural revelation is to be found, therefore, in the corruption of the human heart. Two results flow from this fact. First, it is not a question of the extinction of the knowledge of God, but of the corruption of the knowledge of God. And secondly, men are without excuse for their cor-

---

[9] P. J. Muller, " De Godsleer van Zwingli en Calvijn," 1883, pp. 18 *sq.*, does not seem to bear this in mind, although he had clearly stated it in his " De Godsleer van Calvijn," 1881, pp. 13–25.

ruption of the knowledge of God. On both points Calvin is insistent.

He does not teach that all religion has perished out of the earth, but only that no "genuine piety" remains (I. iv. 1, *ad init.*): he does not teach that men retain no knowledge of God, but no "certain, sound or distinct knowledge" (I. v. 12, *ad fin.*). The seed of religion remains their inalienable possession, "but it is so corrupted as to produce only the worst fruits" (I. iv. 4, *ad fin.*). Here we see Calvin's judgment on natural religion. Its reality he is quick to assert: but equally quickly its inadequacy — and that because not merely of a negative incompleteness but also of a positive corruption. Men have corrupted the knowledge of God; and perhaps Calvin might even subscribe the declaration of a modern writer that men's religions are their worst crimes.[10] Certainly Calvin paints in dark colors the processes by which men form for themselves conceptions of God under the light of nature, or rather, in the darkness of their minds, from which the light of nature is as far as lies in their power excluded. "Their conceptions of God are formed, not according to the representations He gives of Himself, but by the invention of their own presumptuous imaginations" (I. iv. 1, *med.*). They set Him far off from themselves and make Him a mere idler in heaven (I. iv. 2); they invent all sorts of vague and confused notions concerning Him, until they involve themselves in such a vast accumulation of errors as almost to extinguish the light that is within them (I. iv. 4); they confuse Him with His works, until even a Plato loses himself in the round globe (I. v. 11); they even endeavor to deny His very existence (I. v. 12), and substitute demons in His place (I. v. 13). Certainly it is not surprising, then, that the Holy Spirit, speaking in Scripture, "condemns as false and lying whatever was formerly wor-

[10] Cf. F. C. Baur, "Die christliche Lehre von der Dreieinigkeit, etc.," iii. 1843, p. 41: "From this point of view" — he is expounding Calvin's doctrine — "the several manifestations in the history of religions are conceived not as stages in the gradually advancing evolution of the religious consciousness, but as inexcusable, sinful aberrations, as wilful perversions and defacements of the inborn idea of God."

shipped as divine among the Gentiles," nay, "rejects as false every form of worship which is of human contrivance," and "leaves no Deity but in Mount Zion" (I. v. 13). The religions of men differ, doubtless, among themselves: some are more, some less evil; but all are evil and the evil of none is trivial.

Are men to be excused for this, their corruption of the knowledge of God? Are we to listen with sympathy to the plea that light has been lacking? It is not a case of insufficient light, but of an evil heart. Excuses are vain, for this heart-darkness is criminal. If we speak of ignorance here, we must remember it is a guilty ignorance; an ignorance which rests on pride and vanity and contumacy (I. iv. 1), an ignorance which our own consciences will not excuse (I. v. 15). What! shall we plead that we lack ears to hear what even mute creatures proclaim? that we have no eyes to see what it needs no eyes to see? that we are mentally too weak to learn what mindless creatures teach? (I. v. 15). We are ignorant of what all things conspire to inform us of, only because we sinfully corrupt their message; their insufficiency has its roots in us, not in them; wherefore we are without excuse (I. iv. 1; v. 14–15). Our "folly is inexcusable, seeing that it originates not only in a vain curiosity, but in false confidence, and an immoderate desire to exceed the limits of human knowledge" (I. iv. 1, *fin.*). "Whatever deficiency of natural ability prevents us from attaining the pure and clear knowledge of God, yet, since that deficiency arises from our own fault, we are left without any excuse" (I. v. 15, *ad init.*).

The natural revelation of God failing thus to produce its legitimate effects of a sound knowledge of God, because of the corruption of men's hearts, we are thrown back for any adequate knowledge of God upon supernatural activities of God communicating His truth to men. It is accordingly in an assertion and validation of these supernatural revelatory operations of God that Calvin's discussion reaches its true center. To this extent his whole discussion of natural revelation — in its inception in the implantation in man of a *sensus deitatis,* in its culmination in the patefaction of God in His works and deeds, and in its failure through the sin-bred blindness of humanity —may be said to be merely introductory to and intended to prepare the way for his discussion of the supernatural operations of God by which He meets this otherwise hopeless condition of humanity sunk in its corrupt notions of God. These operations obviously must meet a twofold need. A clearer and fuller revelation of God must be brought to men than that which is afforded by nature. And the darkened minds of men must be illuminated for its reception. In other words, what is needed, is a special supernatural revelation on the one hand, and a special supernatural illumination on the other. It is to the validation of this twofold supernatural operation of God in communicating the knowledge of Himself that Calvin accordingly next addresses himself (chs. vi.–ix.).

One or two peculiarities of his treatment of them attract our notice at the outset, and seem to invite attention, before we enter into a detailed exposition of the doctrine he presents. It is noticeable that Calvin does not pretend that this supernatural provision of knowledge of God to meet men's sin-born ignorance is as universal in its reach as the natural revelation which it supplements and, so far as efficiency is concerned, supersedes. On the contrary, he draws it expressly into a narrower circle. That general revelation " presented itself to all eyes " and " is more than sufficient to deprive the ingratitude of men of every excuse, since," in it, " God, in order to involve all mankind in the same guilt, sets an exhibition of His majesty, delineated in the creatures, before them all without exception " (I. vi. 1, *init.*). But His supernatural revelation He grants only " to those whom He intends to unite in a more close and familiar connection with Himself " (*ibid.*); " to those to whom He has determined to make His instructions effectual " (I. vi. 3); in a word, to " the elect " (I. vi. 1; vii. 5 near end). In dealing with the supernatural revelation of God, therefore, Calvin is conscious of dealing with a special operation of the divine grace by means of which God is communicating to those He is choosing to be His people the saving knowledge of Himself. It is observable also that, in speaking of this supernatural revelation, he identifies it from the outset distinctly with the Scriptures (ch. vi.). This is in accordance with the practical end and engrossment which, as we have already had occasion to note, dominate his whole discussion. He was not unaware that the special revelation of God antedates the Scriptures: on occasion he speaks discriminatingly enough of this revelation in itself and the Scriptures in which it is embodied. But his mind is less on the abstract truth than on the concrete conditions which surrounded him in his work. Whatever may have been true ages gone, to-day the special revelation of God coalesces with the Scriptures, and he does not occupy himself formally with it except as it presents itself to the men of his own time. The task which he undertakes, therefore, is distinctly to show that men have in the Scriptures a special revelation of God supplementing and so far superseding the general revelation of God in nature; and that God so operates with this His special revelation of Himself as to overcome the sin-bred disabilities of man.

In this state of the case we may perhaps be justified in leaving at this point the logical development of his construction and expounding Calvin's teaching more formally under the heads of his doctrine of Holy Scripture and his doctrine of the Testimony of the Holy Spirit.

II. Holy Scripture

First, then, what was Calvin's doctrine of Holy Scripture?

Under the designation of " Scripture " or " the Scriptures " Calvin understood that body of writings which have been transmitted to us as the divinely given rule of faith and life. In this body of writings, that is to say, in " the Canon of Scripture," he included all the books of the Old Covenant which were recognized by the Jewish Church as of divine gift, and as such handed down to the Christian Church; and all the books of the New Covenant which have been given the Church by the Apostles as its authoritative law-code. Calvin's attitude towards the canon was thus somewhat more conservative than, say, Luther's. He knew of no such distinction as that between Canonical and Deutero-Canonical Books, whether in the Old or the New Testament. The so-called " Apocryphal Books " of the Old Testament, included within the canon by the decrees of Trent, he rejected out of hand: the so-called " Antilegomena " of the New Testament he accepted without exception.[11]

The representations which are sometimes made, to the effect that he felt doubts of the canonicity of some of the canonical books or even was convinced of their uncanonicity,[12] rest

[11] Cf. J. Cramer, *Nieuwe Bijdragen op het gebied van Godgeleerdheid en Wijsbegeerte,* iii. 1881, p. 102: " By the Scripture or the Scriptures he [Calvin] understood the books of the Old and New Testaments which have been transmitted to us by the Church as canonical, as the rule of faith and life. The Apocrypha of the O. T. as they were determined by the Council of Trent, he excludes. They are to him indeed *libri ecclesiastici,* in many respects good and useful to be read; but they are not *libri canonici* ' ad fidem dogmatum faciendam ' (*Acta Synodi Tridentinae, cum antidoto,* 1547)." In a later article, " De Roomsch-Katholieke en de Oud-protestantsche Schriftbeschouwing," 1883, p. 36, Cramer declares that by the Scriptures, Calvin means " nothing else than the canon, established by the Synods of Hippo and Carthage, and transmitted by the Catholic Church, with the exception of the so-called Apocrypha of the O. T.," etc. Cf. Leipoldt, " Geschichte des N. T. Kanons," ii. 1908, p. 149: " We obtain the impression that it is only for form's sake that Calvin undertakes to test whether the disputed books are canonical or not. In reality it is already a settled matter with him that they are. Calvin feels himself therefore in the matter of the N. T. canon bound to the mediæval tradition." Cf. also Otto Ritschl, " Dogmengeschichte des Protestantismus," i. 1908, pp. 70, 71, to the same effect.

[12] Cf. e.g. J. Pannier, " Le témoignage du Saint-Esprit," 1893, pp. 112 *sq.*: " One fact strikes us at first sight: not only did Calvin not comment on the Aprochryphal books, for which he wrote a very short preface, which was ever more and more abridged in the successive editions, but he did not comment on all the Canonical books. And if lack of time may explain the passing over of some of the less important historical books of the Old Testament, it was undoubtedly for a graver reason that he left to one side the three books attributed to Solomon, notably the Song of Songs. ' In the New Testament there is ordinarily mentioned only the Apocalypse, neglected by Calvin undoubtedly for critical or theological motives analogous to those which determined the most of his contemporaries, but it is necessary to note that the two lesser epistles of John are also lacking, and that in speaking of the large epistle Calvin always expresses himself as if it were the only existing one ' (Reuss, *Revue de Théologie* de Strasbourg, vi. 1853, p. 229). In effect, at the very time when he was defending particularly the au-

on a fundamental misconception of his attitude, and are wrecked on his express assertions. No doubt he has not left us commentaries on all the Biblical Books, and no doubt his omission to write or lecture on certain books is not to be explained merely by lack of time, but involves an act of selection on his part, which was not unaffected by his estimate of the relative importance of the several books or by his own spiritual sympathies.[13] He has also occasionally employed a current expres-

thority of the Scriptures against the Council of Trent, when he was dedicating to Edward VI, the King of England, his Commentaries on the 'Epistles which are accustomed to be called Canonical' (1551), he included in the Canon only the First Epistle of Peter, the First Epistle of John, James and, at the very end, the Second Epistle of Peter and Jude." — Reuss, however, in his "History of the Canon of the Holy Scriptures in the Christian Church" (1863, E. T. 1884), greatly modifies the opinion here quoted from him: "Some have believed it possible to affirm that he [Calvin] rejected the Apocalypse because it was the only book of the N. T., except the two short Epistles of John, on which he wrote no commentary. But that conclusion is too hasty. In the *Institutes*, the Apocalypse is sometimes quoted like the other Apostolic writings, and even under John's name. If there was no commentary, it was simply that the illustrious exegete, wiser in this respect than several of his contemporaries and many of his successors, understood that his vocation called him elsewhere" (p. 318). He adds, indeed, of II and III John: "It might be said with more probability that Calvin did not acknowledge the canonicity of these two writings. He never quotes them, and he quotes the First Epistle of John in a way to exclude them: *Joannes in sua canonica, Instit.* iii. 2. 21; 3. 23 (*Opp.* ii. 415, 453)." But this opinion requires revision, just as that on the Apocalypse did, as we shall see below. Cf. further, in the meantime: Reuss, "Hist. of the Sacred Scriptures of the N. T.," 1884, ii. p. 347, and S. Berger, "La Bible au seizième siècle," 1879, p. 120, who expresses himself most positively: "Calvin expresses no judgment on the lesser Epistles of St. John. But we remark that he never cites them and that he mentions the First in these terms: 'As John says in his canonical.' This word excludes, in the thought of the author, the two other Epistles attributed to this Apostle."

[13] This may have been the case with the Apocalypse, which not only Reuss, as we have seen, but Scaliger thought him wise not to have entered upon; and which he is — perhaps credibly — reported to have said in conversation he did not understand (cf. Leipoldt's "Geschichte des N. T. Kanons," ii. 1908, p. 148, note). But how impossible it is to imagine that this implies any doubt of the canonicity or authority of the book will be quickly evident to anyone who will note his frequent citation of it in the same fashion with other Scripture and alongside of other Scripture (e.g. *Opp.* i. 736 = ii. 500; i. 953 = ii. 957; i. 1033 = ii. 1063; i. 1148; ii. 88, 859; v. 191, 196, 532; vi. 176; vii.

sion, such as, for example, " the Canonical Epistle of John," [14] when speaking of I John, which, if strictly interpreted, might be thought to imply denial of the genuineness of certain books of the canon — such as II and III John — and not merely the momentary or habitual neglect of them; just as the common use of the term " the Apostle " of Paul might be said, if simi-

---

29, 118, 333; xxxi. 650), sometimes mentioning it by name (vii. 469; i. 733 = ii. 497), sometimes by the name of John (i. 715 = ii. 492, viii. 338 [along with I John]), sometimes by the name of both " John " and " the Apocalypse " (ii. 124, vii. 116, xxx. 651, xlviii. 122), and always with reverence and confidence as a Scriptural book. He even expressly cites it under the name of Scripture and explicitly as the dictation of the Spirit: vii. 559, " Fear not, says the Scripture (Eccles. xviii. 22). . . . Again (Rev. xxii. 11) . . . and (John xv. 2) "; i. 624: " Elsewhere also the Spirit testifies . . ." (along with Daniel and Paul). Cf. also such passages as ii. 734, " Nor does the Apocalypse which they quote afford them any support . . ."; xlviii. 238: " I should like to ask the Papists if they think John was so stupid that . . . etc. (Rev. xxii. 8) "; also vi. 369; v. 198.

[14] We use the simple expression " the Epistle of John "; the apparently, but only apparently, stronger and more exclusive, " the Canonical Epistle of John," which Calvin employs, although it would be misleading in our associations, is its exact synonym. Those somewhat numerous writers who have quoted the form " the *Canonical* Epistle of John " as if its use implied the denial of the *canonicity* of the other epistles of John forget that this was the ordinary designation in the West of the Catholic Epistles — " the Seven Canonical Epistles " — and that they are all currently cited by this title by Western writers. The matter has been set right by A. Lang: " Die Bekehrung Johannis Calvins " (II. i. of Bonwetsch and Seeberg's " Studien zur Geschichte der Theologie und der Kirche," 1897, pp. 26–29). On the title " Canonical Epistles " for the Catholic Epistles, see Lücke, *SK.* 1836, iii. pp. 643–650; Bleek, " Introd. to the N. T.," § 202 at end (vol. ii. 1874, p. 135); Hilgenfeld, " Einleitung in d. N. T.," 1875, p. 153; Westcott, " Epp. of St. John," 1883, p. xxix.; Salmond, Hastings' BD. i. 1898, p. 360. In 1551, Calvin published his " Commentarii in Epistolas Canonicas " — that is on the Catholic Epistles; also his " Commentaire sur l'Épistre Canonique de St. Jean," i.e. on " the Epistle of John "; also his " Commentaire sur l'Épistre Canonique de St. Jude." Calvin does not seem ever to have happened to quote from II and III John. The reference given in the Index printed in *Opp.* xxii., viz., III John 9, *Opp.* xb. 81, occurs in a letter, not by Calvin but by Christof Libertetus to Farel. Cf. J. Leipoldt, " Geschichte des N. T. Kanons " (2nd Part, Leipzig, 1908), p. 148, note 1: " The smaller Johannine Epistles Calvin seems never to have cited. He cites I John in *Inst.* III. ii. 21 by the formula: dicit Johannes in sua canonica. Nevertheless it is very questionable whether inferences can be drawn from this formula as to Calvin's attitude to II and III John." He adds a reference to Lang as above.

larly strictly pressed, to imply that there was no other Apostle
but he. It is also true that he expresses himself with moderation when adducing the evidence for the canonicity of this
book or that, and in his modes of statement quite clearly betrays his recognition that the evidence is more copious or
more weighty in some cases than in others. But he represents
the evidence as sufficient in all cases and declares with confidence his conclusion in favor of the canonicity of the whole
body of books which make up our Bible, and in all his writings
and controversies acts firmly on this presupposition. How, for
example, is it possible to contend that some grave reason connected with doubts on his part of their canonical authority
underlies the failure of Calvin to comment on " the three books
attributed to Solomon, particularly the Song of Songs," [15] in
the face of the judgment of the ministers of Geneva with regard to Castellion, which is thus reported by Calvin himself
over his signature.[16] " We unanimously judged him one who
might be appointed to the functions of the pastor, except for
a single obstacle which opposed it. When we asked him, according to custom, whether he was in accord with us on all
points of doctrine, he replied that there were two on which
he could not share our views: one of them . . . being our in-
scribing the Song of Solomon in the number of sacred books.
. . . We conjured him first of all, not to permit himself the
levity of treating as of no account the constant witness of
the universal Church; we reminded him that there is no book
the authenticity of which is doubtful, about which some discussion has not been raised; that even those to which we now
attach an undisputed authenticity were not admitted from the
beginning without controversy; that precisely this one is
one which has never been openly repudiated. We also exhorted
him against trusting unreasonably in his own judgment, espe-

---

[15] Pannier, as cited, p. 113.

[16] *Opera,* xi. 674–676: cf. Buisson, " Castellion," 1892, i. pp. 198–199.
Buisson discusses the whole incident and quotes from the minutes of the
Council before which Castellion brought the matter: the point of dispute
is there briefly expressed thus: " Moss ʳ Calvin recognizes as holy, and the
said Bastian repudiates " (p. 197) the book in question.

cially where nothing was toward which all the world had not
been aware of before he was born. . . . All these arguments
having no effect on him, we thought it necessary to consider
among ourselves what we ought to do. Our unanimous opinion
was that it would be dangerous and would set a bad precedent
to admit him to the ministry in these circumstances. . . . We
should thus condemn ourselves for the future to raise no objection to another, should one present himself and wish similarly to repudiate Ecclesiastes or Proverbs or any other book
of the Bible, without being dragged into a debate as to what
is and what is not worthy of the Holy Spirit." [17] Not merely
the firmness with which Calvin held to the canonicity of all the
books of our Bible, but the importance he attached to the acceptance of the canonical Scriptures in their integrity, is made
perfectly clear by such an incident; and indeed so also are
the grounds on which he accepted these books as canonical.

These grounds, to speak briefly, were historico-critical.
Calvin, we must bear in mind, was a Humanist before he was
a Reformer,[18] and was familiar with the whole process of determining the authenticity of ancient documents. If then he re-

[17] Calvin employs all these "three books attributed to Solomon" freely
as Scripture and deals with them precisely as he does with other Scriptures.
As was to be expected, he cites Proverbs most frequently, Canticles least: but
he cites them all as Solomon's and as authoritative Scripture. "'I have washed
my feet' says the believing soul in Solomon . . ." is the way he cites Canticles
(*Opp.* i. 778, ii. 589). "They make a buckler of a sentence of Solomon's, which
is as contrary to them as is no other that is in the Scriptures" (vii. 130) is the
way he cites Ecclesiastes. He indeed expressly contrasts Ecclesiastes as genuine
Scripture with the Apocryphal books: "As the soul has an origin apart, it has
also another preëminence, and this is what Solomon means when he says that
at death the body returns to the earth from which it was taken and the soul
returns to God who gave it (Eccl. xii. 7). For this reason it is said in the
Book of Wisdom (ii. 23) that man is immortal, seeing that he was created
in the image of God. This is not an authentic book of Holy Scripture, but
it is not improper to avail ourselves of its testimony as of an ancient teacher
(*Docteur ancien*) — although the single reason ought to be enough for us
that the image of God, as it has been placed in man, can reside only in an
immortal soul, etc." (vii. 112, written in 1544).

[18] Cf. A. Bossert, "Calvin," 1906, p. 6: "Humanist himself as well as
profound theologian . . ."; Charles Borgeaud, "Histoire de l'Université de
Genève," 1900, p. 21: "Before he was a theologian, Calvin was a Humanist. . . ."

ceived the Scriptures from the hands of the Church, not in-
dulging himself in the levity of treating the constant witness
of the universal Church as of no account, he was nevertheless
not disposed to take "tradition" uncritically at its face value.
His acceptance of the canon of the Church was therefore not
a blind but a critically mediated acceptance. Therefore he discarded the Aprocrypha: and if he accepted the Antilegomena
it was because they commended themselves to his historico-
critical judgment as holding of right a place in the canon. The
organon of his critical investigation of the canon was in effect
twofold. He inquired into the history of the books in question.
He inquired into their internal characteristics. Have they
come down to us from the Apostolic Church, commanding
either unbrokenly or on the whole the suffrages of those best
informed or best qualified to judge of their canonical claims?
Are they in themselves conformable to the claims made for
them of apostolic, which is as much as to say, divine origin?
It was by the application of this twofold test that he excluded
the Apocrypha of the Old Testament from the canon. They
had in all ages been discriminated from the canonical books,
and differ from them as the writing of an individual differs
from an instrument which has passed under the eye of a notary
and been sealed to be received of all.[19] Some Fathers, it is true,

[19] Cf. the Preface he prefixed to the Apocryphal Books (for the history
of which, see *Opera*, ix. 827, note): "These books which are called Apocryphal have in all ages been discriminated from those which are without
difficulty shown to be of the Sacred Scriptures. For the ancients, wishing to
anticipate the danger that any profane books should be mixed with those
which certainly proceeded from the Holy Spirit, made a roll of these latter
which they called 'Canon'; meaning by this word that all that was comprehended under it was the assured rule to which we should attach ourselves.
Upon the others they imposed the name of Apocrypha; denoting that they
were to be held as private writings and not authenticated, like public documents. Accordingly the difference between the former and latter is the
same as that between an instrument, passed before a notary, and sealed
to be received by all, and the writing of some particular man. It is true
they are not to be despised, seeing that they contain good and useful doctrine. Nevertheless it is only right that what we have been given by the
Holy Spirit should have preëminence above all that has come from men."
Cf., in his earliest theological treatise, the "Psychopannychia" of 1534–1542
(*Opp.* v. 182), where, after quoting Ecclus. xvii. 1 and Wisd. ii. 23 as "two

deemed them canonical; even Augustine was of that way of
thinking, although he had to allow that opinions differed
widely upon the matter. Others, however, could admit them
to no higher rank than that of "ecclesiastical books," which
might be useful to read but could not supply a foundation for
doctrine; among such were Jerome and Rufinus.[20] And, when
we observe their contents, no sane mind will fail to pass judgment against them.[21] Rome may, indeed, find her interest in
defending them, for she may discover support in them for some
of her false teachings. But this very fact is their condemnation. "I beg you to observe," he says of the closing words of
II Maccabees, where the writer sets his hope in his own works:
"I beg you to observe how far this confession falls away from
the majesty of the Holy Spirit"[22] — that is to say, from the
constant teaching of Holy Scripture.

And it was by the application of the same two-fold test
that he accredited the Antilegomena of the New Testament
as integral parts of the canon. In the Preface which he has
prefixed to II Peter, for example, he notes that Eusebius speaks
of some who rejected it. "If it is a question," he adds, "of
yielding to the simple authority of men, since he [Eusebius]
does not name those who brought the matter into doubt, no
necessity seems to be laid on us to credit these unknown

sacred writers," he adds: "I would not urge the authority of these writers
strongly on our adversaries, did they not oppose them to us. They may be
allowed, however, some weight, if not as canonical, yet certainly as ancient,
as pious, and as received by the suffrages of many. But let us omit them and
let us retain . . ." etc. In the "Psychopannychia" his dealing with Baruch
on the other hand is more wavering. On one occasion (p. 205) it is quoted
with the formula, "sic enim loquitur propheta," and on another (p. 227),
"in prophetia Baruch" corrected in 1542. In the "Institutes" of 1536 he
quotes it as Scripture: "alter vero propheta scribit" (*Opp.* i. 82) — referring
back to Daniel. This is already corrected in 1539 (i. 906; cf. ii. 632). In 1534–
1536, then, he considered Baruch canonical: afterwards not so. His dealing
with it in v. 271 (1537), vi. 560 (1545), vi. 638 (1546) is *ad hominem*.

[20] "Acta Synodi Tridentinae, cum antidoto" (1547), *Opp.* vii. 365–506.

[21] "Vera ecclesiae reformandae ratio," *Opp.* vii. 613: quae divinitus non
esse prodita, sani omnes, saltem ubi moniti fuerint, iudicabunt.

[22] "Acta Synodi Tridentinae, cum antidoto," *Opp.* vii. 413: Quantum,
obsecro, a Spiritus Sancti maiestati aliena est haec confessio!

people. And, moreover, he adds that afterwards it was generally received without contradiction. . . . It is a matter agreed
upon by all, of common accord, that there is nothing in this
Epistle unworthy of Saint Peter, but that, on the contrary,
from one end of it to the other, there are apparent the force,
vehemence and grace of the Spirit with which the Apostles were
endowed. . . . Since, then, in all parts of the Epistle the majesty of the Spirit of Christ is clearly manifest, I cannot reject
it entirely, although I do not recognize in it the true and natural phrase of Saint Peter." [23] To meet the difficulty arising
from the difference of the style from that of I Peter, he therefore supposed that the Epistle is indeed certainly Peter's, since
otherwise it would be a forgery, a thing inconceivable in a book
of its high character,[24] but was dictated in his old age to some
one of his disciples, to whom it owes its peculiarities of diction.
Here we have an argument conducted on the two grounds of
the external witness of the Church and the internal testimony
of the contents of the book: and these are the two grounds on
which he everywhere depends. Of the Epistle of Jude he says: [25]
"Because the reading of it is very useful, and it contains nothing that is not in accord with the purity of the Apostolic doctrine; because also it has long been held to be authentic by
all the best men, for my part, I willingly place it in the number
of the other epistles." In other cases the external evidence of
the Church is not explicitly mentioned and the stress of the
argument is laid on the Apostolic character of the writing as
witnessed by its contents. He receives Hebrews among the
Apostolic Epistles without difficulty, because nowhere else
is the sacrifice of Christ more clearly or simply declared and
other evangelical doctrines taught: surely it must have been
due to the wiles of Satan that the Western Church so long

[23] This is translated from the French version, ed. Meyrueis, iv. 1855, p. 743.
The Latin is the same, though somewhat more concise: nihil habet Petro
indignum, ut vim spiritus apostolici et gratiam ubique exprimat . . . eam
prorsus repudiare mihi religio est.

[24] Haec autem fictio indigna esset ministro Christi, obtendere alienam
personam.

[25] Ed. Meyrueis, iv. p. 780.

doubted its canonicity.[26] James seems to him to contain nothing unworthy of an Apostle of Christ, but to be on the contrary full of good teaching, valuable for all departments of
Christian living.[27] For the application of this argument he of
course takes his start from the Homologoumena, which gave
him the norm of Apostolic teaching which he used for testing
the other books. It must not be supposed that he received even
these books, however, without critico-historical inquiry: but
only that the uniform witness of the Church to their authority
weighed with him above all grounds of doubt. It was, in a
word, on the ground of a purely scientific investigation that
Calvin accredited to himself the canon. It had come down to
him through the ages, accredited as such by the constant testimony of its proper witnesses: and it accredited itself to critical scrutiny by its contents.[28]

[26] *Ibid.*, iv. p. 362.

[27] *Ibid.*, iv. p. 694. Latin: mihi ad epistolam hanc recipiendam satis est,
quod nihil continet Christi apostolo indignum.

[28] Cf. J. Cramer, as cited, p. 126: " It was thus, in the first place, as the
result of scientific investigations that Calvin fixed the limits of the canon
. . . not *a priori*, but *a posteriori*, that he came to the recognition of the
canonicity of the Biblical books." But especially see the excellently conceived
passage on pp. 155–6, to the following effect: " What great importance Calvin
attaches to the question whether a Biblical book is *apostolic!* If it is not
apostolic, he does not recognize it as canonical. To determine its apostolicity,
he appeals not merely to the ecclesiastical tradition of its origin, but also
and principally to its contents. This is what he does in the case of all the
antilegomena. The touchstone for this is found in the homologoumena. That
he undertakes no investigation of the apostolic origin of these latter is a
matter of course. This, for him and for all his contemporaries, stood irrevers-
ibly settled. The touchstone employed by Calvin is a scientific one. The *testimonium Spiritus Sancti* no doubt made its influence felt. But without the
help of the scientific investigation, this internal testimony would not have
the power to elevate the book into a canonical book. That Calvin was tread-
ing here in the footprints of the ancient Church will be understood. The complaint sometimes brought against the Christians of the earliest centuries is
unfounded, that they held all writings canonical in which they found their own
dogmatics. No doubt they attached in their criticism great weight to this.
But not less to the question whether the origin of the books was traceable
back to the apostolical age, and their contents accorded with apostolic doctrine, as it might be learned from the indubitably apostolic writings. So far
as science had been developed in their day, they employed it in the formation of the canon. . . ." In a later article Cramer says: " In the determina-

The same scientific spirit attended Calvin in his dealing with the text of Scripture. As a Humanist he was familiar with the processes employed in settling the texts of classical authors; and naturally he used the same methods in his determination of the text of the Biblical books. His practice here is marked by a combination of freedom and sobriety; and his decisions, though often wrong, as they could not but be in the state of the knowledge of the transmission of the New Testament text at the time, always manifest good sense, balance, and trained judgment. In his remarks on the pericope of the adulteress (John viii. 1–11), we meet the same circle of ideas with which we are familiar from his remarks on the Antilegomena: "because it has always been received by the Latin Churches and is found in many of the Greek copies and old writers, and contains nothing which would be unworthy of an apostolical spirit, there is no reason why we should refuse to take our profit from it." [29] He accepts the three-witness passage of I John v. 7. "Since the Greek codices do not agree with themselves," he says, "I scarcely dare reach a conclusion. Yet, as the context flows most smoothly if this clause is added, and I see that it stands in the best codices and those of the most approved credit, I also willingly adopt it." [30] When puzzled by

---

tion of the compass of Scripture, he [Calvin], like Luther, took his start from the writings which more than the others communicated the knowledge of Christ in His kingdom and had been recognized always by the Church as genuine and trustworthy. Even if the results of his criticism were more in harmony than was the case with those of the German reformer with the ecclesiastical tradition, he yet walked in the self-same critical pathway. He took over the canon of the Church just as little as its version and its exegesis without scrutiny " (" De Roomsch-Katholieke en de Oud-protestansche Schriftbeschouwing," 1883, pp. 31–32). Cramer considers this critical procedure on Calvin's part inconsistent with his doctrine of the testimony of the Spirit, but (p. 38) he recognizes that we cannot speak of it as the nodding of Homer: " It is not here and there, but throughout; not in his exegetical writings alone, but in his dogmatic ones, too, that he walks in this critical path. We never find the faintest trace of hesitation."

[29] Comment on John viii. 1 (Meyrueis' ed. of the Commentaries, ii. 1854, p. 169).

[30] Comment on I John v. 7 (Meyrueis' ed. of the Commentaries, iv. 1855, p. 682).

difficulties, he, quite like the Humanist dealing with a classical text, feels free to suggest that there may be a " mendum in voce." This he does, for example, in Mat. xxiii. 35, where he adduces this possibility among others; and still more instructively in Mat. xxvii. 9, where he just as simply assumes " Jeremiah " to be a corrupt reading [31] as his own editors assume that the " Apius " which occurs in the French version of the " Institutes " in connection with Josephus is due to a slip of his translators, not of his own — remarking: " It is evident that it cannot be Calvin who translated this passage." [32] His assurance that it cannot be the Biblical writer who stumbles leads him similarly to attribute what seems to him a manifest error to the copyists. It is only, however, in such passages as these that he engages formally in textual emendation. Ordinarily he simply follows the current text, although he is, of course, not without an intelligent ground for his confidence in it.[33] As we cursorily read his commentaries we feel ourselves in the hands of one who is sanely and sagely scrutinizing the text with which he is dealing from the point of view of a scholar accustomed to deal with ancient texts, whose confidence in its general integrity represents the well-grounded conclusion of a trained judgment. His occasional remarks on the text, and his rare suggestion of a corruption, are indicia of the alertness of his general scrutiny of the text and serve to assure us that his acceptance of it as a whole as sound is not merely inert ac-

[31] Quomodo Jeremiae nomen obrepserit, me nescire fateor, nec anxie laboro; certe Jeremiae nomen errore positum esse pro Zacharia res ipsa ostendit; quia nihil tale apud Jeremiam legitur (*Opera*, xlv. 749).

[32] *Opera*, iii. 100, note 3.

[33] Cf. J. Cramer, as cited, pp. 116–117: " Calvin does not largely busy himself with textual criticism. He follows the text which was generally received in his day. It deserves notice only that he exercises a free and independent judgment and recognizes the rights of science." Cramer adduces his treatment of I John v. 7 and proceeds: " He comes forward on scientific grounds against the Vulgate. The decree of Trent that this version must be followed as 'authentical,' he finds silly; and reverence for it as if it had fallen down from heaven, ludicrous. ' How can anyone dispute the right to appeal to the original text? And what a bad version this is! There are scarcely three verses in any page well rendered' (*Acta Synod. Trident.*, etc., pp. 414–416)."

quiescence in tradition, but represents the calm judgment of an instructed intelligence.

INSPIRATION OF SCRIPTURE

Now, these sixty-six books of canonical Scriptures handed down to us, in the singular providence of God,[34] in a sound text which meets the test of critical scrutiny, Calvin held to be the very Word of God. This assertion he intended in its simplest and most literal sense. He was far from overlooking the fact that the Scriptures were written by human hands: he expressly declares that, though we have received them from God's own mouth, we have nevertheless received them " through the ministry of men." [35] But he was equally far from conceiving that the relation of their human authors to their divine author resembled in any degree that of free intermediaries, who, after receiving the divine word, could do with it what they listed.[36]

[34] "Institutes," I. viii. 10. Cf. I. vi. 2–3.

[35] I. vii. 5, *ad init.*: " We have received it from God's own mouth by the ministry of men."

[36] It is quite common to represent Calvin as without a theory, at least an expressed theory, of the relation of the divine and human authors of Scripture. Thus J. Cramer, as cited, p. 103, says: " How we are to understand the relation of the divine and human activities through which the Scriptures were produced is not exactly defined by Calvin. A precise theory of inspiration such as we meet with in the later dogmaticians is not found in him." Cramer is only sure that Calvin did not hold to the theory which later Protestants upheld: " It is true that Calvin gave the impulse [from which the later dogmatic view of Scripture grew up], more than any other of the Reformers. But we must not forget that here we can speak of nothing more than the impulse. We nowhere find in Calvin such a magical conception of the Bible as we find in the later dogmaticians. It is true he used the term ' dictare ' and other expressions which he employs under the influence of the terminology of his day, but on the other hand — in how many respects does he recognize the *human* factor in the Scriptures! " (p. 142). Similarly Pannier, as cited, p. 200: " In any case Calvin has not written a single word which can be appealed to in favor of *literal* inspiration. What is divine for him, if there is anything specifically divine beyond the contents, the brightness of which is reflected upon the container, is the *sense* of each book, or at most of each phrase, — never the employment of each word. Calvin would have deplored the petty dogmatics of the *Consensus Helveticus,* which declares the vowel points of the Hebrew text inspired, and the exaggerations of the

On the contrary, he thought of them rather as notaries (IV. viii. 9), who set down in authentic registers (I. vi. 3) what was dictated to them (*Argumentum in Ev. Joh.*).[37] They wrote, therefore, merely as the organs of the Holy Ghost, and did not speak *ex suo sensu*, not *humano impulsu*, not *sponte sua*, not *arbitrio suo*, but set out only *quae coelitus mandata fuerant*.[38] The diversity of the human authors thus disappears for Calvin before the unity of the Spirit, the sole responsible author of Scripture, which is to him therefore not the *verba Dei*, but emphatically the *verbum Dei*.[39] It is *a Deo* ("Institutes," I. vii. 5); it has "come down to us from the very mouth of God" (I. vii. 5); [40] it has "come down from heaven as if the living words of God themselves were heard in it" (I. vii. 1); [41] and "we owe it therefore the same reverence which we owe to God Himself, since it has proceeded from Him alone, and there is nothing human mixed with it" (Com. on II Tim. iii. 16).[42] According to this declaration the Scriptures are altogether divine, and in them, as he puts it energetically in another place, "it is God who speaks with us and not mortal

---

theopneusty of the nineteenth century." Yet nothing is more certain than that Calvin held both to "verbal inspiration" and to "the inerrancy of Scripture," however he may have conceived the action of God which secured these things.

[37] Cf. Otto Ritschl, "Dogmengeschichte des Protestantismus," 1908, i. p. 63: "If we may still entertain doubts whether Bullinger really defended the stricter doctrine of inspiration, it certainly is found in Calvin after 1543. He may have merely taken over from Butzer the expression *Spiritus Sancti amanuenses*; but it is peculiar to him that he conceives both the books of the Old Testament inclusively as contained in the historical enumerations, and those of the New Testament, as arising out of a verbal dictation of the Holy Spirit."

[38] These phrases are brought together by J. Cramer (as cited, pp. 102-3) from the Comments on II Tim. iii. 16 and II Pet. i. 20.

[39] Cf. Pannier, as cited, p. 203: "The Word of God is for him one, *verbum Dei*, and not *verba Dei*. The diversity of authors disappears before the unity of the Spirit." [40] Ab ipsissimo Dei ore ad nos fluxisse.

[41] E coelo fluxisse acsi vivae ipsae Dei voces illic exaudirentur.

[42] Hoc prius est membrum, eandem scripturae reverentiam deberi quam Deo deferimus, quia ad eo solo manavit, nec quidquam humani habet admistum.

men " (Com. on II Pet. i. 20).[43] Accordingly, he cites Scripture everywhere not as the word of man but as the pure word of God. His "holy word" is "the scepter of God"; every statement in which is "a heavenly oracle" which "cannot fail" (Dedicatory Epistle to the "Institutes," *Opp.* ii. 12): in it God "opens His own sacred mouth" to add His direct word to the voice of His mute creatures (I. vi. 1). To say "Scripture says" and to say "the Holy Ghost says" is all one. We contradict the Holy Spirit, says Calvin — meaning the Scriptures — when we deny to Christ the name of Jehovah or anything which belongs to the majesty of Jehovah (I. xiii. 23). "The Holy Spirit pronounces," says he, . . . "Paul declares . . . the Scripture condemns . . . wherefore it is not surprising if the Holy Spirit reject" — all in one running context, meaning ever the same thing (I. v. 13): just as in another context he uses interchangeably the "commandments of Christ" and the "authority of Scripture" of the same thing (Dedicatory Letter).

It may be that Calvin has nowhere given us a detailed discussion of the mode of the divine operation in giving the Scriptures. He is sure that they owe their origin to the divine gift (I. vi. 1, 2, 3) and that God has so given them that they are emphatically His word, as truly as if we were listening to His living voice speaking from heaven (I. vii. 1): and, as we have seen, he is somewhat addicted to the use of language which, strictly taken, would imply that the mode of their gift was "dictation." The Scriptures are "public records" (I. vi. 2), their human authors have acted as "notaries" (IV. viii. 9), who have set down nothing of their own, but only what has been dictated to them, so that there appears no admixture of what is human in their product (on II Tim. iii. 16).[44] It is not

[43] Justa reverentia inde nascitur, quum statuimus, Deum nobiscum loqui, non homines mortales.

[44] The account of Calvin's doctrine of inspiration given by E. Rabaud, "Histoire de la doctrine de l'inspiration . . . dans les pays de langue française," 1883, pp. 52 *sq.*, is worth comparing. Calvin's thought on this subject, he tells us, was more precise and compact than that of the other Reformers, although even his conception of inspiration was far from possessing perfectly firm contours or supplying the elements of a really systematic view (p. 52). He

unfair to urge, however, that this language is figurative; and
that what Calvin has in mind is not to insist that the mode of
inspiration was dictation, but that the result of inspiration is

---

was the first, nevertheless, to give the subject of Sacred Scripture a fundamental, theoretic treatment, led thereto not by the pressure of controversy,
but by the logic of his systematic thought: for his doctrine of inspiration (not
yet distinguished from revelation) is one of the essential bases, if not the very
point of departure of his dogmatics (p. 55). To him "the Bible is manifestly
the word of God, in which He reveals Himself to men," and as such "proceeds
from God." "But" (pp. 56 sq.) "the action of God does not, in Calvin's
view, transform the sacred authors into machines. Jewish verbalism, Scriptural materialism, may be present in germ in the ideas of the *Institutes*
— and the cold intellects of certain doctors of the Protestant scholasticism
of the next century developed them — but they are very remote from the
thought of the Reformer. Chosen and ordained by God, the Biblical writers
were subject to a higher impulse; they received a divine illumination which
increased the energy of their natural faculties; they understood the Revelation better and transmitted it more faithfully. It was scarcely requisite for
this, however, that they should be passive instruments, simple secretaries,
pens moved by the Holy Spirit. Appointed but intelligent organs of the
divine thought, far from being subject to a dictation, in complete obedience to
the immediate will of God, they acted under the impulsion of a personal
faith which God communicated to them. 'Now, whether God was manifested
to men by visions or oracles, what is called celestial witnesses, or ordained
men as His ministers who taught their successors by tradition, it is in every
case certain that He impressed on their hearts such a certitude of the doctrine,
that they were persuaded and convinced that what had been revealed and
preached to them proceeded from the true God: for He always ratified His
word so as to secure for it a credit above all human opinion. Finally, that the
truth might uninterruptedly remain continually in vigor from age to age, and
be known in the world, He willed that the revelations which He had committed to the hands of the Fathers as a deposit, should be put on record: and
it was with this design that He had the Law published, to which He afterwards added the Prophets as its expositors' (*Institutes*, I. vi. 2). These
few lines resume in summary form the very substance of Calvin's doctrine
of inspiration. We may conclude from it that he did not give himself to the
elaboration of this dogma, with the tenacity and logical rigor which his clear
and above all practical genius employed in the study and systematization
of other points of the new doctrine. We shall seek in vain a precise declaration on the mode of revelation, on the extent and intensity of inspiration, on
the relation of the book and the doctrine. None of these questions, as we
have already had occasion to remark, had as yet been raised: the doctors
gave themselves to what was urgent and did not undertake to prove or
discuss what was not yet either under discussion or attacked. The principle
which was laid down sufficed them. God had spoken — this was the faith which
every consciousness of the time received without repugnance, and against

as if it were by dictation, viz., the production of a pure word of God free from all human admixtures. The term "dictation" was no doubt in current use at the time to express rather the effects than the mode of inspiration.[45] This being allowed, it is all the more unfair to urge that, Calvin's language being in this sense figurative, he is not to be understood as teaching that the effect of inspiration was the production of a pure word of God, free from all admixture of human error. This, on the contrary, is precisely what Calvin does teach, and that with the greatest strenuousness. He everywhere asserts that the effects of inspiration are such that God alone is the responsible author of the inspired product, that we owe the same reverence to it as to Him Himself, and should esteem the words as purely His as if we heard them proclaimed with His living voice from heaven; and that there is nothing human mixed with them. And he everywhere deals with them on that assumption. It is true that men have sought to discover in Calvin, particularly in his "Harmony of the Gospels," acknowledgments of

---

which no mind raised an objection. To search out how He did it was wholly useless: to undertake to prove it, no less so " (p. 58). There is evident in this passage a desire to minimize Calvin's view of the divinity of Scripture; the use of the passage from I. vi. 2 as the basis of an exposition of his doctrine of inspiration is indicative of this — whereas it obviously is a very admirable account of how God has made known His will to man and preserved the knowledge of it through time. The double currents of desire to be true to Calvin's own exposition of his doctrine and yet to withhold his *imprimatur* from what the author believes to be an overstrained doctrine, produces some strange confusion in his further exposition.

[45] Cf. J. Cramer, as cited, p. 114: " How Calvin conceives of this *dictare* by the Holy Ghost it is difficult to say. He borrowed it from the current ecclesiastical usage, which employed it of the *auctor primarius* of Scripture, as indeed also of tradition. Thus the Council of Trent uses the expression *dictante Spiritu Sancto* of the unwritten tradition inspired by the Holy Spirit." Otto Ritschl, " Dogmengeschichte des Protestantismus," i. 1908, p. 59, argues for taking the term strictly in Calvin. It is employed, it is true, in contemporary usage in the figurative sense, of the deliverances of the natural conscience, for example; and some Reformed writers use it of the internal testimony of the Spirit. Calvin also himself speaks as if he employed it of Scripture only figuratively — e.g. *Opp.* i. 632: verba *quodammodo* dictante Christi Spiritu. Nevertheless, on the whole Ritschl thinks he meant it in the literal sense.

the presence of human errors in the fabric of Scripture.[46] But these attempts rest on very crass misapprehensions of Calvin's efforts precisely to show that there are no such errors in the fabric of Scripture. When he explains, for example, that the purpose " of the Evangelists " — or " of the Holy Spirit," for he significantly uses these designations as synonyms — was not to write a chronologically exact record, but to present the general essence of things, this is not to allow that the Scriptures err humanly in their record of the sequences of time, but to assert that they intend to give no sequences of time and therefore cannot err in this regard. When again he suggests that an " error " has found its way into the text of Mat. xxvii. 9 or possibly into Mat. xxiii. 35, he is not speaking of the original, but of the transmitted text; [47] and it would be hard if he were not permitted to make such excursions into the region of textual criticism without laying himself open to the charge of denying his most assured conviction that nothing human is mixed with Scripture. In point of fact, Calvin not only asserts the freedom of Scripture as given by God from all error, but never in his detailed dealing with Scripture allows that such errors exist in it.[48]

[46] Cf., e.g., J. Cramer, as cited, pp. 114–116, whose instances are followed in the remarks which succeed. Cf. also p. 125. How widespread this effort to discover in Calvin some acknowledgment of errors in Scripture has become may be seen by consulting the citations made by Dunlop Moore, *The Presbyterian and Reformed Review*, 1893, p. 60: he cites Cremer, van Oosterzee, Farrar. Cf. even A. H. Strong, " Syst. Theol.," ed. 1907, vol. i. p. 217, whose list of " theological writers who admit the errancy of Scripture writers as to some matters unessential to their moral and spiritual teaching " requires drastic revision. Leipoldt (" Geschichte des N. T. Kanons," ii. 1908, p. 149) says: " Fundamentally Calvin holds fast to the old doctrine of verbal inspiration. His sound historical sense leads him, here and there, it is true, to break through the bonds of this doctrine. In his harmony of the Gospels (*Commentarii in harmoniam ex Mat., Mk., et Lk. compositam*, 1555), e.g., Calvin shows that the letters are not sacred to him; he moves much more freely here than Martin Chemnitz. But in other cases again Calvin draws strict consequences from the doctrine of verbal inspiration. He ascribes, e.g., to all four Gospels precisely similar authority, although he (with Luther and Zwingli) considers John's Gospel the most beautiful of them all."

[47] This is solidly shown, e.g., by Dunlop Moore, as cited, pp. 61–62: also for Acts vii. 16.

[48] Despite his tendency to lower Calvin's doctrine of inspiration with

If we ask for the ground on which he asserts this high doctrine of inspiration, we do not see that any other reply can be given than that it was on the ground of the teaching of Scripture itself. The Scriptures were understood by Calvin to claim to be in this high sense the word of God; and a critical scrutiny of their contents brought to him nothing which seemed to him to negative this claim. There were other grounds on which he might and did base a firm confidence in the divine origin of the Scriptures and the trustworthiness of their teach-

---

respect to its effects, J. Cramer in the following passage (as cited, pp. 120–121) gives in general a very fair statement of it: "We have seen that Calvin, although he has not given us a completed theory of inspiration, yet firmly believed in the inspiration of the entirety of Scripture. It is true we do not find in him the crass expressions of the later Reformed, as well as Lutheran, theologians. But the foundation on which they subsequently built — though somewhat onesidedly — is here. We cannot infer much from such expressions as 'from God,' 'came from God,' 'flowed from God.' Just as in Zwingli, these expressions were sometimes in Calvin synonyms of 'true.' Thus, at Titus ii. 12, he says he cannot understand why so many are unwilling to draw upon profane writers, — 'for, since all truth is from God (a Deo), if anything has been said well and truly by profane men, it ought not to be rejected, for it has come from God (a Deo est profectum).' More significant are such expressions as, 'nothing human is mixed with Scripture,' 'we owe to them the same reverence as to God,' God 'is the author of Scripture' and as such has 'dictated' (dictavit) all that the Apostles and Prophets have written, so that we 'must not depart from the word of God in even the smallest particular,' etc. All this applies not only to the Scriptures as a whole, not merely to their fundamental ideas and chief contents, but to all the sixty-six books severally. In contra-distinction from the Apocrypha, they have been given by the Holy Spirit (Préface mise en tête des livres apocryphes de l'Ancien Test.: Opp. ix. 827). The book of Acts 'beyond question is the product of the Holy Spirit Himself,' Mark 'wrote nothing but what the Holy Spirit gave him to write,' etc. To think here merely of a providential direction by God, in the sense that God took care that His people should lack nothing of a Scriptural record of His revelation — is impossible. For, however often Calvin may have directed attention to such a 'singularis providentiae cura' (Inst., I. vi. 2, cf. I. viii. 10; Argumentum in Ev. Joh.) with respect to Scripture, he yet saw something over and above this in the production of the sacred books. He looked upon them as the writings of God Himself, who, through an extraordinary operation of His Spirit, guarded His amanuenses from all error as well when they transmitted histories as when they propounded the doctrine of Christ. Thus to him Scripture (naturally in its original text) was a complete work of God, to which nothing could be added and from which nothing could be taken away."

ing as a revelation from God. But there were no other grounds on which he could or did rest his conviction that these Scriptures are so from God that there is nothing human mixed with them, and their every affirmation is to be received with the deference which is due to the living voice of God speaking from heaven. On these other grounds Calvin was led to trust the teaching of the Scriptures as a divine revelation: and he therefore naturally trusted their teaching as to their own nature and inspiration.

Such, then, are the Scriptures as conceived by Calvin: sixty-six sacred books, "dictated" by God to His "notaries" that they might, in this "public record," stand as a perpetual special revelation of Himself to His people, to supplement or to supersede in their case the general revelation which He gives of Himself in His works and deeds, but which is rendered ineffective by the sin-bred disabilities of the human soul. For this, according to Calvin, is the account to give of the origin of Scripture, and this the account to give of the function it serves in the world. It was because man in his sinful imbecility was unable to profit by the general revelation which God has spread before all eyes, so that they are all without excuse (I. vi. 1), that God in His goodness gave to " those whom He intended to unite in a more close and familiar connection with Himself," a special revelation in open speech (I. vi. 1). And it was because of the mutability of the human mind, prone to errors of all kinds, corrupting the truth, that He committed this His special revelation to writing, that it might never be inaccessible to " those to whom He determined to make His instructions effectual " (I. vi. 3). In Calvin's view, therefore, the Scriptures are a documentation of God's special revelation of Himself unto salvation (I. vi. 1, *ad init.*); but a documentation cared for by God Himself, so that they are, in fine, themselves the special revelation of God unto salvation in documentary form (I. vi. 2, 3). The necessity for the revelation documented in them arises from the blindness of men in their sin: the necessity for the documentation of this revelation arises from the instability of men, even when taught of God.

We must conceive of special revelation, and of the Scriptures as just its documentation, therefore, as not precisely a cure, but rather an assistance to man dulled in his sight so as not to be able to perceive God in His general revelation. "For," says Calvin, "as persons who are old, or whose eyes have somehow become dim, if you show them the most beautiful book, though they perceive that something is written there, can scarcely read two words together, yet by the aid of spectacles will begin to read distinctly — so the Scripture . . ." etc. (I. vi. 1). The function of Scripture thus, as special revelation documented, is to serve as spiritual spectacles to enable those of dulled spiritual sight to see God.

Of course, the Scriptures do more than this. They not only reveal the God of Nature more brightly to the sin-darkened eye; they reveal also the God of Grace, who may not be found in nature. Calvin does not overlook this wider revelation embodied in them: he particularly adverts to it (I. vi. 1). But he turns from it for the moment as less directly germane to his present object, which is to show that without the "spectacles" of Scripture, sinful man would not be able to attain to a sound knowledge of even God the Creator. It is on this, therefore, that he now insists. It was only because God revealed Himself in this special, supernatural way to them, that our first fathers — "Adam, Noah, Abraham and the rest of the patriarchs" — were able to retain Him in their knowledge (I. vi. 1). It was only through this special revelation, whether renewed to them by God, or handed down in tradition, "by the ministry of men," that their posterity continued in the knowledge of God (I. vi. 2). "At length, that the truth might remain in the world in a continual course of instruction to all ages, God determined that the same oracles which He deposited with the patriarchs, should be committed to public records" — first the Law, then the Prophets, and then the books of the New Covenant (I. vi. 2). It is now, therefore, only through these Scriptures that man can attain to a true knowledge of God. The revelation of God in His works is not useless: it makes all men without excuse; it provides an additional though lower and less certain revelation of God to His people — to a consideration of which all should seriously apply themselves, though they should principally attend to the Word (I. vi. 2). But experience shows that without the Word the sinful human mind is too weak to reach a sound knowledge of God, and therefore without it men wander in vanity and error. Calvin seems to speak sometimes almost as if the Scriptures, that is special revelation, wholly superseded general revelation (I. v. 12, *ad fin.;* vi. 2, *ad fin.;* 4, *ad fin.*). More closely scrutinized, it becomes evident, however, that he means only that in the absence of Scripture, that is of special revelation, the general revelation of God is ineffective to preserve any sound knowledge of Him in the world: but in the presence of Scripture, general revelation is not set aside, but rather brought back to its proper validity. The real relation between general and special revelation, as the matter lay in Calvin's mind, thus proves to be, not that the one supersedes the other, but that special revelation supplements general revelation indeed, but in the first instance rather repeats and by repeating vivifies and vitalizes general revelation, and flows confluently in with it to the one end of both, the knowledge of God (I. vi. 2). What special revelation is, therefore — and the Scriptures as its documentation — is very precisely represented by the figure of the spectacles. It is aid to the dulled vision of sinful man, to enable it to see God.

The question forcibly presents itself, however, whether "spectacles" will serve the purpose here. Has not Calvin painted the sin-bred blindness of men too blackly to encourage us to think it can be corrected by such an aid to any remainders of natural vision which may be accredited to them? The answer must be in the affirmative. But this only opens the way to point out that Calvin does not present special revelation, or the Scriptures as special revelation documented, as the entire cure, but places by the side of it the *testimonium Spiritus Sancti.* Special revelation, or Scripture as its documented form, provides in point of fact, in the view of Calvin, only the objective side of the cure he finds has been provided by God. The subjective side is provided by the *testimonium Spiritus Sancti.* The spectacles are provided by the Scriptures: the eyes are opened that they may see even through these spectacles, only by the witness of the Spirit in the heart. We perceive, then, that in Calvin's view the figure of the spectacles is a perfectly just one. He means to intimate that special revelation alone will not produce a knowledge of God in the human soul: that something more than external aid is needed before it can see: and to leave the way open to proceed to point out what further is required that sinful man may see God. Sinful man, we say again: for the whole crux lies there. Had there been no sin, there would have been no need of even special revelation. In the light of the splendid revelation of Himself which God has displayed in the theatre of nature, man with his native endowment of instinctive knowledge of God would have bloomed out into a full and sound knowledge of Him. But with sinful man, the matter is wholly different. He needs more light and he needs something more than light — he needs the power of sight.[49] That we may apprehend Calvin's thought, therefore, we must turn to the consideration of his doctrine of the Testimony of the Spirit.

III. The Testimony of the Spirit

What is Calvin's doctrine of the Testimony of the Spirit? The particular question which Calvin addresses himself to when he turns to the consideration of what he calls the testi-

[49] In I. v. 14 Calvin says that the Apostle in Heb. xi. 3, "By faith we understand that the worlds were framed by the Word of God" wishes to intimate that "the invisible divinity *was represented* indeed by such displays of His power, but that we have no eyes *to perceive it* unless they are illuminated through faith by the inner revelation of God" (Invisibilem divinitatem *repraesentari* quidem talibus spectaculis, sed ad illam *perspiciendam* non esse nobis oculos, nisi interiore Dei revelatione per fidem illuminentur). Here he distinguishes between the external, objective representation, and the internal, subjective preparation to perceive this representation. God is objectively revealed in His works: man in his sins is blind to this revelation: the interior operation of God is an opening of man's eyes: man then sees. The operation of God is therefore a palingenesis. This passage is already in ed. 1539 (i. 291); the last clause (nisi . . .) is not, however, reproduced in the French versions of either 1541 or 1560 (iii. 60).

mony of the Spirit concerns the accrediting of Scripture, not the assimilation of its revelatory contents. The reader cannot fail to experience some disappointment at this. The whole development of the discussion hitherto undoubtedly fosters the expectation, not, indeed, of an exclusive treatment of the assimilation of special revelation by sinful man — for both problems are raised by it and the two problems are at bottom one and their solution one — but certainly of some formal treatment of it, and indeed of such a treatment of the double problem that the stress should be laid on this. Calvin, however, is preoccupied with the problem of the accrediting of Scripture. This is due in part, doubtless, to its logical priority: as he himself remarks, we cannot be " established in the belief of the doctrine, till we are indubitably persuaded that God is its Author " (I. vii. 4, *ad init.*). But it was rendered almost inevitable by the state of the controversy with Rome, who intrenched herself in the position that the Protestant appeal to Scripture as over against the Church was inoperative, seeing that it is only by the Church that the Scriptures can be established in authority: for who but the Church can assure us that these Scriptures are from God, or indeed what books enter into the fabric of Scripture, or whether they have come down to us uncorrupted? As a practical man writing to practical men for a practical purpose, Calvin could not fail, perhaps, to give his primary attention to the aspect of the problem he had raised which was most immediately pressing. But this scarcely prepares us for the almost total neglect of its other aspect, with the effect that the construction of his general doctrine is left with a certain appearance of incompleteness. Not really incomplete; for the solution of the one problem is, as we have already suggested, the solution of the other also; and even the cursory reader — or perhaps we may say especially the cursory reader — may well be trusted to feel this as he is led on through the discussion, particularly as there are not lacking repeated suggestions of it, and the discussion closes with a direct reference to it and a formal postponement of the particular discussion of the other aspect of the double problem to a later portion of the treatise. " I pass over many things for the present," says

Calvin, "because this subject will present itself for discussion
in another place. Only, let it be known here that that alone is
true faith which the Spirit of God seals in our hearts. And
with this one reason every reader of docility and modesty will
be satisfied" (I. vii. 5, near the end). That is as much as to
say, This whole subject is only one application of the general
doctrine of faith; and as the general doctrine of faith is fully
discussed at another place in this treatise, we may content ourselves here with the somewhat incomplete remarks we have
made upon this special application of that doctrine; we only
need to remind the reader that there is no true faith except that
which is begotten in the soul by the Holy Spirit.

We can scarcely wonder that Calvin contents himself with
this simple reference of the topic now engaging his attention,
as a specific case, to the generic doctrine of faith, when we
pause to realize how nearly this simple reference of it, as a
species to its genus, comes to a sufficient exposition of it. We
shall stop now to signalize only two points which are involved
in this reference, the noting of which will greatly facilitate
our apprehension of Calvin's precise meaning in his doctrine
of the testimony of the Spirit to the divinity of Scripture. This
doctrine is no isolated doctrine with Calvin, standing out of
relation with the other doctrines of his system: it is but one
application of his general doctrine of faith; or to be more
specific, one application of his general doctrine of the function
of the Holy Spirit in the production of faith. Given Calvin's
general doctrine of the work of the Holy Spirit in applying
salvation, and his specific doctrine of the *testimonium Spiritus
Sancti* in the attestation of Scripture, and in the applying of its
doctrine as well, was inevitable. It is but one application of the
general doctrine that there is no true faith except that which
the Spirit of God seals in our hearts. For Calvin in this doctrine
— and this is the second point we wish to signalize — has in
mind specifically "true faith." He is not asking here how the
Scriptures may be proved to be from God. If that had been the
question he was asking, he would not have hesitated to say that
the testimony of the Church is conclusive of the fact. He does

say so. " The universal judgment of the Church " (I. vii. 3, *fin.*)
he represents as a very useful argument, " the consent of the
Church " (I. viii. 12, *init.*) as a very important consideration,
in establishing the divine origin of the Scriptures: although, of
course, he does not conceive the Church as lending her authority to Scripture " when she receives and seals it with her suffrage," but rather as performing a duty of piety to herself in
recognizing what is true apart from her authentication, and
treating it with due veneration (I. vii. 2, *ad fin.*). For what is
more her duty than " obediently to embrace what is from God
as the sheep hear the voice of the shepherd " ? [50] Were it a
matter of proving the Scriptures to be the Word of God, Calvin would, again, have been at no loss for rational arguments
which he was ready to pronounce irresistible. He does adduce
such arguments and he does pronounce them irresistible. He
devotes a whole chapter to the adduction of these arguments
(ch. viii.) — such arguments as these: the dignity of the
subject-matter of Scripture — the heavenliness of its doctrine
and the consent of all its parts — (§ 1), the majesty of its
style (§ 2), the antiquity of its teaching (§ 3), the sincerity of its
narrative (§ 4), its miraculous accompaniment, circumstan-
tially confirmed (§§ 5, 6), its predictive contents authenticated
by fulfilment (§§ 7, 8), its continuous use through so many
ages (§§ 9–12), its sealing by martyr blood (§ 13): and these
arguments he is so far from considering weak and inconclusive
(I. viii. 13, *med.*) that he represents them rather as capable
of completely vindicating the Scriptures against all the subtleties of their calumniators (*ibid.*). Nay, he declares that the
proofs of the divine origin of the Scriptures are so cogent, as
" certainly to evince, if there is a God in heaven, that He is the

[50] In his response to the Augsburg Interim (" Vera Ecclesiae reformandae
ratio," 1549, *Opp.* vii. 591–674) he allows it to be the *proprium ecclesiae officium*
to *scripturas veras a suppositiis discernere;* but only that *obedienter amplecti-
tur, quicquid Dei est,* as the sheep hear the voice of the shepherd. It is nevertheless *sacrilega impietas ecclesiae judicio submittere sacrosancta Dei oracula.*
See J. Cramer, as cited, p. 104, note 3. Cramer remarks in expounding Calvin's
view: " By the approbation she gives to them " — the books of Scripture —
" the Church does not make them authentic, but only yields her homage to
the truth of God."

author of the Law, and the Prophecies, and the Gospel " (I. vii.
4, near the beginning); as to extort with certainty from all
who are not wholly lost to shame, the confession of the divine
gift of the Scriptures (ibid.).[51] " Though I am far from possessing any peculiar dexterity " in argument " or eloquence," he
says, " yet were I to contend with the most subtle despisers of
God, who are ambitious to display their wit and their skill in
weakening the authority of Scripture, I trust I should be able
without difficulty to silence their obstreperous clamor " (ibid.).
But objective proofs — whether the conclusive testimony of
witnesses, or the overwhelming evidence of rational considerations — be they never so cogent,[52] he does not consider of
themselves capable of producing " true faith." And it is " true
faith," we repeat, that Calvin has in mind in his doctrine of
the testimonium Spiritus Sancti. If it seemed to him a small
matter that man should know that God is if he did not know
what God is, it equally seemed to him a small matter that man
should know what God is, in the paradigms of the intellect, if
he did not really know this God in the intimacy of communion
which that phrase imports. And equally it seemed to him utterly unimportant that a man should be convinced by stress of

[51] It would require that we should be wholly hardened (nisi ad perdi-
tam impudentiam obduruerint) that we should not perceive that the doctrine of Scripture is heavenly, that we should not have the confession wrung
from us that there are manifest signs in Scripture that it is God who speaks
in and through it (extorquebitur illis haec confessio, manifesta signa loquentis
Dei conspici in Scriptura ex quibus pateat coelestem esse eius doctrinam) —
I. vii. 4.

[52] The exact relations of the " proofs " to the divinity of Scripture,
which Calvin teaches, was sufficiently clear to be caught by his successors.
It is admirably stated in the Westminster Confession of Faith, i. 5. And we
may add that the same conception is stated also very precisely by Quenstedt:
" These motives, as well internal as external, by which we are led to the
knowledge of the authority of Scripture, make the theopneusty of Sacred
Scripture probable, and produce a certitude which is not merely conjectural
but moral . . . they do not make the divinity of Scripture infallible and
altogether indubitable." (" Theologia didactico-polemica, sive Systema theologicum,". Lipsiae, 1715, Pars prima, pp. 141–2.) That is to say, they are not
of the nature of demonstration, but nevertheless give moral certitude: the
testimony of the Spirit is equivalent to demonstration — as is the deliverance of any simply acting sense.

rational evidence that the Scriptures are the Word of God, unless he practically embraced these Scriptures as the Word of God and stayed his soul upon them. The knowledge of God which Calvin has in mind in this whole discussion is, thus, a vital and vitalizing knowledge of God, and the attestation of Scripture which he is seeking is not an attestation merely to the intelligence of men, compelling from them perhaps a reluctant judgment of the intellect alone (since those convinced against their will, as the proverb has it, are very apt to remain of the same opinion still), but such an attestation as takes hold of the whole man in the roots of his activities and controls all the movements of his soul.

This is so important a consideration for the exact apprehension of Calvin's doctrine that it may become us to pause and assure ourselves of the simple matter of fact from the language which Calvin employs of it in the course of the discussion. We shall recall that from the introduction of the topic of special revelation he has in mind and keeps before his readers' mind its destination for the people of God alone. The provisions for producing a knowledge of God, consequent on the inefficiency of natural revelation, Calvin is careful to explain, are not for all men, but for " the elect " (I. vi. 1), or, as they are more fully described, " those whom God intends to unite in a more close and familiar connection with Himself " (*ibid.*), " those to whom He determines to make His instructions effectual " (I. vi. 3). From the first provisions of His supernatural dealings, therefore, He " intends to make His instructions effectual." More pointedly still he speaks of the *testimonium Spiritus Sancti* as an act in which " God deigns to confer a singular power on His elect, whom He distinguishes from the rest of mankind " (I. vii. 5).[53] This singular power, now, is

[53] Cf. Pannier, as cited, pp. 207–8: " We see that this understanding of the Scriptures, this capacity to receive the testimony of the Spirit, is not, according to Calvin, possible for all; and that, less and less . . . He continually emphasises more and more the incapacity of man to persuade another of it, without the aid of God; but he emphasises still more progressively the impossibility of obtaining this aid if God does not accord it first. 1550 (I. viii. at end): ' Those who wish to prove to unbelievers by arguments

nothing else but " saving faith," and Calvin speaks of it in all the synonymy of " saving faith." He calls it " true faith " (I. vii. 5), " sound faith " (I. vii. 4), " firm faith " (I. viii. 13), " the faith of the pious " (I. vii. 3), " the certainty of the pious " (I. vii. 3), " that assurance which is essential to true piety " (I. vii. 4), " saving knowledge " (I. viii. 13), " a solid assurance of eternal life " (I. vii. 1). It is the thing which is naturally described by this synonymy which Calvin declares is not produced in the soul except by the testimony of the Holy Spirit. This obviously is nothing more than to declare that that faith which lays hold of Christ unto eternal life is the product of the Holy Spirit in the heart, and that it is one of the exercises of this faith to lay hold of the revelation of this Christ in the Scriptures with assured confidence, so that it is only he who is led by the Spirit who embraces these Scriptures with " sound faith," that is, " with that assurance which is essential to true piety " (I. vii. 4). What Calvin has in mind, in a word, is simply an extended comment on Paul's words: " the natural man receiveth not the things of the Spirit of God . . . but he that is spiritual judgeth all things " (I Cor. ii. 14, 15).[54]

---

that the Scriptures are from God are inconsiderate; for this is known *only to faith.*' 1559 (I. vii. *in fine*): The mysteries of God are not understood, *except by those to whom it is given.* . . . It is quite certain that the witness of the Spirit does not make itself felt except to believers, and is not *in itself* an apologetic means with respect to unbelievers. . . . The *natural* man receiveth not spiritual things."

[54] Cf. Pannier, as cited, pp. 195–6: " First let us recall this, — for Calvin this testimony of the Holy Spirit is only one act of the great drama which is enacted in the entire soul of the religious man, and in which the Holy Spirit holds always the principal rôle. While the later dogmatists make the Holy Spirit, so to speak, function mechanically, at a given moment, in the pen of the prophets or in the brain of the readers, Calvin sees the Holy Spirit constantly active in the man whom He wishes to sanctify, and the fact that He leads him to recognize the divinity and the canonicity of the sacred books is only one manifestation, — a very important one, no doubt, but only a particular one, — of His general work." It is only, of course, the Lutheran and Rationalizing dogmatists who, constructively, subject the action of the Spirit to the direction of man — whether by making it rest on the application of the " means of grace " or on the action of the human will. Calvin and his followers — the Reformed — make the act of man depend on the free and sovereign action of the Spirit.

Calvin does not leave us, however, to gather from general remarks referring it to its class or to infer from its general effects, what he means by the testimony of the Spirit of God to the divinity of Scripture, but describes for us its nature and indicates the mode of its operation and specific effects with great exactitude.[55] He tells us that it is a " secret " (I. vii. 4),

[55] J. Cramer, as cited, pp. 122–3, somewhat understates this, but in the main catches Calvin's meaning: " Calvin does not, it is true, tell us in so many words precisely what this *testimonium Sp. S.* is, but it is easy to gather it from the whole discussion. He is thinking of the Holy Spirit, who, as the Spirit of our adoption as children, leads us to say Amen to the Word which the Father speaks in the Holy Scriptures to His children. He even says expressly in *Inst.* I. vii. 4: ' As if the Spirit was not called " seal " and " earnest " just because He confers faith on the pious.' But more plainly still, and indeed so that no doubt can remain, we find it in Beza, the most beloved and talented pupil of Calvin, who assuredly also in his conception of Scripture was the most thoroughly imbued with the spirit of his teacher. In his reply to Castellion, Beza says: ' The testimony of the Spirit of adoption does not lie properly in this, that we believe to be true what the Scriptures testify (for this is known also to the devils and to many of the lost), but rather in this, — that each applies to himself the promise of salvation in Christ of which Paul speaks in Rom. viii. 15, 16.' Accordingly a few lines further down he speaks of a ' testimony of adoption and free justification in Christ.' In the essence of the matter Calvin will have meant just this by his testimony of the Holy Spirit. . . ." Beza's words are in his " Ad defensiones et reprehensiones Seb. Castellionis " (" Th. Bezae Vezelii Opera," i. Geneva, 1582, p. 503): Testimonium Spiritus adoptionis non in eo proprie positum est ut credamus verum esse quod Scriptura testatur (nam hoc ipsum quoque sciunt diaboli et reprobi multi), sed in eo potius ut quisque sibi salutis in Christo promissionem applicet, de qua re agit Paulus, Rom. viii. 15, 16. . . . That it was generally understood in the first age that this was the precise nature of the witness of the Spirit is shown by its definition in this sense not only by the Reformed, but by the Lutherans. For example, Hollaz defines thus: " The testimony of the Holy Spirit is the supernatural act (*actus supernaturalis*) of the Holy Spirit by means of the Word of God attentively read or heard (His own divine power having been communicated to the Scriptures) by which the heart of man is moved, opened, illuminated, turned to the obedience of faith, so that the illuminated man out of these internal spiritual movements truly perceives the Word which is propounded to him to have proceeded from God, and gives it therefore his unwavering assent." (" Examinis theologici acroamatici univers. theologiam thet. polem.," Holmiae et Lipsiae, 1741, p. 125.) The Lutheranism of this definition resides in the clauses: " By means of the Word of God " . . . " His own divine power having been communicated to the Scriptures " . . . which make the action of the Holy Spirit to be from out of the Word, in which He dwells *intrinsicus*. But the nature of the testi-

"internal" (I. vii. 4; viii. 13), "inward" (I. vii. 5) action of the Holy Spirit on the soul, by which the soul is " illuminated " (I. vii. 3, 4, 5), so as to perceive their true quality in the Scriptures as a divine book. We may call this " an inward teaching " of the Spirit which produces " entire acquiescence in the Scriptures," so that they are self-authenticating to the mind and heart (I. vii. 5) ; or we may call it a " secret testimony of the Spirit," by which our minds and hearts are convinced with a firmness superior to all reason that the Scriptures are from God (I. vii. 4). In both instances we are using figurative language. Precisely what is produced by the hidden internal operation of the Spirit on the soul is a new spiritual sense (*sensus*, I. vii. 5, *med.*), by which the divinity of Scripture is perceived as by an intuitive perception. " For the Scripture exhibits as clear evidence of its truth, as white and black things do of their color, and sweet and bitter things of their taste " (I. vii. 2, end) ; and we need only a sense to discern its divine quality to be convinced of it with the same immediacy and finality as we are convinced by their mere perception of light or darkness, of whiteness or blackness, of sweetness or bitterness (*ibid.*). No conclusions based on " reasoning " or " proofs " or founded on human judgment can compare in clearness or force with such a conviction, which is instinctive and immediate, and finds its ultimate ground and sanction in the Holy Spirit who has wrought in the heart this spiritual sense which so functions in recognizing the divine quality of Scripture. Illuminated by the Spirit of God, we believe, therefore, not on the ground of our own judgment, or on the ground of the judgment of others, but with a certainty above all human judgment, by a spiritual intuition.[56] With the utmost explicitness Calvin so describes this instinctive conviction in a passage of great vigor: " It is, therefore," says he, " such a persuasion as re-

_____

mony of the Spirit is purely conceived as an act of the Holy Spirit by which the heart of man is renewed to spiritual perception, in the employment of which he perceives the divine quality of Scripture.

[56] Supra humanum iudicium, certo certius constituimus (non secus ac si ipsius Dei numen illic intueremur) hominum ministerio, ab ipsissimo Dei ore ad nos fluxisse (I. vii. 5).

quires no reasons; such a knowledge as is supported by the
highest reason and in which the mind rests with greater security and constancy than in any reasons; in fine, such a sense as
cannot be produced but by a revelation from heaven " (I. vii.
5).[57] Here we are told that it is a *persuasio*, or rather a *notitia*,
or rather a *sensus*. It is a persuasion which does not require
reasons — that is to say, it is a state of conviction not induced
by arguments, but by direct perception: it is, that is to say, a
knowledge, a direct perception in accord with the highest reason, in which the mind rests, with an assurance not attainable
by reasoning; or to be more explicit still, it is a sense which
comes only from divine gift. As we have implanted in us by
nature a sense which distinguishes between light and darkness, a sense which distinguishes between sweet and bitter,
and the verdict of these senses is immediate and final; so
we have planted in us by the creative action of the Holy
Spirit a sense for the divine, and its verdict, too, is immediate and final: the spiritual man discerneth all things. Such, in
briefest outline, is Calvin's famous doctrine of the testimony
of the Spirit.

MODE OF THIS TESTIMONY

Certain further elucidations of its real meaning and bearing appear, however, to be necessary, to guard against misapprehension of it. When we speak of an internal testimony of
the Holy Spirit, it is evident that we must conceive it as presenting itself in one of three ways. It may be conceived as of
the nature of an immediate revelation to each man to whom
it is given. It may be conceived as of the nature of a blind
conviction produced in the minds of its recipients. It may be
conceived as of the nature of a grounded conviction, formed
in their minds by the Spirit, by an act which rather terminates immediately on the faculties, enabling and effectively
persuading them to reach a conviction on grounds presented

[57] Talis ergo est persuasio quae rationes non requirat; talis notitia, cui
optima ratio constet: nempe in qua securius constantiusque mens quiescit
quam in ullis rationibus; talis denique sensus, qui nisi ex coelesti revelatione
nasci nequeat (I. vii. 5).

to them, than produces the conviction itself, apart from or without grounds. In which of these ways did Calvin conceive the testimony of the Spirit as presenting itself? As revelation, or as ungrounded faith, or as grounded faith?

Certainly not the first. The testimony of the Spirit was not to Calvin of the nature of a propositional "revelation" to its recipients. Of this he speaks perfectly explicitly, and indeed in his polemic against Anabaptist mysticism insistently. He does indeed connect the term "revelation" with the testimony of the Spirit, declaring it, for example, such a sense (*sensus*) as can be produced by nothing short of "a revelation from heaven" (I. vii. 5, *med.*). But his purpose in the employment of this language is not to describe it according to its nature, but to claim for it with emphasis a heavenly source: he means merely to assert that it is not earth-born, but God-wrought, while at the same time he intimates that in its nature it is not a propositional revelation, but an instinctive "sense." That he did not conceive of it as a propositional revelation is made perfectly clear by his explicit assertions at the opening of the discussion (I. vii. 1, *init.*), that we "are not favored with daily oracles from heaven," and that the Scriptures constitute the sole body of extant revelations from God. It is not to supersede nor yet to supplement these recorded revelations that the testimony of the Spirit is given us, he insists, but to confirm them (I. ix. 3): or, as he puts it in his polemic against the Anabaptists, "The office of the Spirit which is promised us is not to feign new and unheard-of revelations, or to coin a new system of doctrine, which would seduce us from the received doctrine of the Gospel, but to seal to our minds the same doctrine which the Gospel delivers" (I. ix. 1, *fin.*).

In this polemic against the Anabaptists (ch. ix.) he gives us an especially well-balanced account of the relations which in his view obtain between the revelation of God and the witness of the Spirit. If he holds that the revelation of God is ineffective without the testimony of the Spirit, he holds equally that the testimony of the Spirit is inconceivable without the revelation of God embodied in the Word. He even declares that the Spirit is no more the agent by which the Word is impressed on the heart than the Word is the means by which the illumination of the Spirit takes effect. " If apart from the Spirit of God " we " are utterly destitute of the light of truth," he says (I. ix. 3, *ad fin.*), equally " the Word is the instrument by which the Lord dispenses to believers the illumination of the Spirit." So far as the knowledge of the truth is concerned, we are as helpless, then, without the Word as we are without the Spirit, for the whole function of the Spirit with respect to the truth is, not to reveal to us the truth anew, much less to reveal to us new truth, but efficaciously to confirm the Word, revealed in the Scriptures, to us, and efficaciously to impress it on our hearts (I. ix. 3). This Calvin makes superabundantly plain by an illustration and a didactic statement of great clearness. The illustration (I. ix. 3) is drawn from our Lord's dealings with His two disciples with whom after His rising He walked to Emmaus. "He opened their understandings," Calvin explains, "not that rejecting the Scriptures they might be wise of themselves, but that they might understand the Scriptures." Such also, he says, is the testimony of the Spirit to-day: for what is it — and this is the didactic statement to which we have referred — but an enabling of us by the light of the Spirit to behold the divine countenance in the Scriptures that so our minds may be filled with a solid reverence for the Word (I. ix. 3)? Here we have the nature of the testimony of the Spirit, and its manner of working and its effects, announced to us in a single clause. It is an illumination of our minds, by which we are enabled to see God in the Scriptures, so that we may reverence them as from Him.

Other effect than this Calvin explicitly denies to the testimony of the Spirit, and he defends his denial from the charge of inconsistency with the stress he has previously laid upon the necessity of this testimony (I. ix. 3). It is not to deny the necessity of this work of the Spirit, he argues, to confine it to the express confirmation of the Word and of the revelation contained therein. Nor is it derogatory to the Spirit to confine His operations now to the confirmation of the revealed Word. While on the other hand to attribute to Him repeated or new revelations to each of the children of God, as the mystics do, is derogatory to the Word, which is His inspired product. To lay claim to the possession of such a Spirit as this, he declares, is to lay claim to the possession of a different Spirit from that which dwelt in Christ and the Apostles — for their Spirit honored the Word — and a different Spirit from that which was promised by Christ to His disciples — for this Spirit was " not to speak of Himself." It is to lay claim to a Spirit for whose divine mission and character, moreover, we lack all criterion — for how can we know that the Spirit that speaks in us is from God, save as He honors the Word of God (I. ix. 1 and 2)? From all which it is perfectly plain not only that Calvin did not conceive the testimony of the Spirit as taking effect in the form of propositional revelations, but that he did conceive it as an operation of God the Holy Spirit in the heart of man which is so connected with the revelation of God in His Word, that it manifests itself only in conjunction with that revelation.

Calvin's formula here is, The Word and Spirit.[58] Only in the conjunction of the two can an effective revelation be made to the sin-darkened mind of man.[59] The Word supplies the ob-

[58] Köstlin, as cited, pp. 412–13, especially 413, note a, adverts to this with a reference to Dorner, " Gesch. d. protest. Theologie," p. 377, who makes it characteristic of Calvin in distinction from Zwingli to draw the outer and inner Word more closely together. The justice of Dorner's view, which would seem to assign to Calvin in his doctrine of the Word as a means of grace a position somewhere between Zwingli and Luther, may well be doubted. According to Dorner, Calvin " modified the looser connection between the outward and inward Word held by Zwingli and connected the two sides more closely together." " In reference, therefore, to the principle of the Reformation," he continues, " with its two sides, Calvin is still more than Zwingli, of one mind and spirit with the German Lutheran Reformation " (E. T. i. 1871, p. 387). Again (i. p. 390) : " The double form of the Verbum Dei externum and internum, held by Zwingli, gives place indeed in Calvin to a more inward connecting of the two sides; the Scriptures are according to him not merely the sign of an absent thing, but have in themselves divine matter and breath, which makes itself actively felt." We do not find that Calvin and Zwingli differ in this matter appreciably.

[59] Cf. his response to Sadolet (1539), Opp. v. 393: tuo igitur experimento

jective factor; the Spirit the subjective factor; and only in the union of the objective and subjective factors is the result accomplished. The whole objective revelation of God lies, thus, in the Word. But the whole subjective capacitating for the reception of this revelation lies in the will of the Spirit. Either, by itself, is wholly ineffective to the result aimed at — the production of knowledge in the human mind. But when they unite, knowledge is not only rendered possible to man: it is rendered certain. And therefore it is that Calvin represents the provision for the knowledge of God both in the objective revelation in the Word and in the subjective testimony of the Spirit as destined by God not for men at large, but specifically for His people, His elect, those " to whom He determined to make His instructions effectual" (I. vi. 3). The Calvinism of Calvin's doctrine of religious knowledge comes to clear manifestation here; and that not merely because of its implication of the doctrine of election, but also because of its implication of Calvin's specific doctrine of the means of grace. Already in his doctrine of religious knowledge, we find Calvin teaching that God is known not by those who choose to know Him, but by those by whom He chooses to be known: and this simply because the knowledge of God is God-given, and is therefore given to whom He will. Men do not wring the knowledge of God from a Deity reluctant to be known: God imparts the knowledge of Himself to men reluctant to know Him: and therefore none know Him save those to whom He efficaciously imparts, by His Word and Spirit, the knowledge of Himself. " By His Word and Spirit " — therein is expressed already the fundamental formula of the Calvinistic doctrine of the " means of grace." In that doctrine the Spirit is not, with the Lutherans, conceived as in the Word, conveyed and applied wherever the Word goes: nor is the Word, with the mystics, conceived as in the Spirit always essentially present wherever He is present in His power as a Spirit of revelation and truth. The two are severally contemplated, as separable factors, in the

---

disce non minus importunum esse spiritum iactare sine verbo, quam futurum sit insulsum, sine spiritu verbum ipsum obtendere.

one work of God in producing the knowledge of Himself which is eternal life in the souls of His people; separable factors which must both, however, be present if this knowledge of God is to be produced. For it is the function of the Word to set before the soul the object to be believed; and it is the function of the Spirit to quicken in the soul belief in this object: and neither performs the work of the other or its own work apart from the other.

It still remains, however, to inquire precisely how Calvin conceived the Spirit to operate in bringing the soul to a hearty faith in the Word as a revelation from God. Are we to understand him as teaching that the Holy Spirit by His almighty power creates, in the souls of those whom God has set upon to bring to a knowledge of Him, an entirely ungrounded faith in the divinity of the Scriptures and the truth of their contents, so that the soul embraces them and their contents with firm confidence as a revelation from God wholly apart from and in the absence of all *indicia* of their divinity or of the truth of their contents? So it has come to be very widely believed; and indeed it may even be said that it has become the prevalent representation that Calvin taught that believers have within themselves a witness of the Spirit by which they are assured of the divinity of Scripture and the truth of its contents quite apart from all other evidence. The very term, " the testimony of the Spirit," is adduced in support of this representation, as setting a divine witness to the divinity of Scripture over against other sources of evidence, and of course superseding them: and appeal is made along with this to Calvin's strong assertions of the uselessness and even folly of plying men with " the proofs " of the divine origin of Scripture, seeing that, it is said, in the absence of the testimony of the Spirit such " proofs " must needs be ineffective, and in the presence of that effective testimony they cannot but be adjudged unnecessary. What can he mean, then, it is asked, but that the testimony of the Holy Spirit is sufficient to assure us of the divinity of Scripture apart from all *indicia,* and does its work entirely independently of them?

The sufficient answer to this question is that he can mean — and in point of fact does mean — that the *indicia* are wholly insufficient to assure us of the divinity of Scripture apart from the testimony of the Spirit; and effect no result independently of it. This is quite a different proposition and gives rise to quite a different series of corollaries. Calvin's dealing with the *indicia* of the divinity of Scripture has already attracted our attention in one of its aspects, and it is quite worthy of renewed scrutiny. We have seen that he devotes a whole chapter to their exposition (chap. viii.) and strongly asserts their objective conclusiveness to the fact of the divine origin of Scripture (I. vii. 4). Nor does he doubt their usefulness whether to the believer or the unbeliever. The fulness and force of his exposition of them is the index to his sense of their value to the believer: for he adduces them distinctly as confirmations of believers in their faith in the Scriptures (I. viii. 1, 13), and betrays in every line of their treatment the high significance he attaches to them as such. And he explicitly declares that they not only maintain in the minds of the pious the native dignity and authority of Scripture, but completely vindicate it against all the subtleties of calumniators (I. viii. 13). No man of sound mind can fail to confess on their basis that it is God who speaks in Scripture and that its doctrine is divine (I. vii. 4). It is a complete misapprehension of Calvin's meaning, then, when it is suggested that he represents the *indicia* of the divinity of Scripture as inconclusive or even as ineffective.[60] Their

[60] There is a certain misapprehension involved, also, in speaking of Calvin *subordinating* the *indicia* to the witness of the Spirit, as if he conceived them on the same plane, but occupying relatively lower and higher positions on this plane. The witness of the Spirit and the *indicia* move in different orbits. We find Köstlin, as cited, p. 413, accordingly speaking not quite to the point, when he says: " He subordinated to the power of this one, immediate, divine testimony, all those several criteria by the pious and thoughtful consideration of which our faith in the Scriptures and their contents may and should be further mediated. Even miracles, as Niedner has rightly remarked (*Philosophie- und Theologiegeschichte*, p. 341, note 2), take among the evidences for the divinity of the Biblical revelation, ' nothing more than a coördinate ' place: we add in passing that Calvin introduces them here only in the edition of 1550, and then enlarges the section which treats of them in the edition of 1559. He does not, however, put a low estimate on

conclusiveness could not be asserted with more energy than he asserts it: nor indeed could their effectiveness — their effectiveness in extorting from the unbeliever the confession of the divinity of Scripture and in rendering him without excuse in refusing the homage of his mind and heart to it — in a word, will he, nill he, convincing his intellect of its divinity; their effectiveness also in confirming the believer in his faith and maintaining his confidence intact. This prevalent misapprehension of Calvin's meaning is due to neglect to observe the precise thing for which he affirms the *indicia* to be ineffective

---

such criteria; he would trust himself — as he says in an addition made in the edition of 1559 (xxx. 59) — to silence with them even stiff-necked opponents; but this certainty which faith should have, can never be attained, says he, by disputation, but can be wrought only by the testimony of the Spirit." The question between the testimony of the Spirit and the *indicia* is not a question of which gives the strongest evidence; it is a question of what each is fitted to do. The *indicia* are supreme in their sphere; they and they alone give objective evidence. But objective evidence is inoperative when the subjective condition is such that it cannot penetrate and affect the mind. All objective evidence is in this sense subordinate to the subjective change wrought by the Spirit: but considered as objective evidence it is supreme in its own sphere. The term "subordinate" is accordingly misleading here. For the rest, it is true that Calvin places the miracles by which the giving of Scripture was accompanied rather among the objective evidences of their divinity than at their apex: but this is due not to an underestimation of the value of miracles as evidence, but to the very high estimate he placed on the internal criteria of divinity, by which the Scriptures evidence themselves to be divine. And above all we must not be misled into supposing that he places miracles below the testimony of the Spirit in importance. Such a comparison is outside his argument: miracles are part of the objective evidence of the deity of Scripture; the testimony of the Spirit is the subjective preparation of the heart to receive the objective evidence in a sympathetic embrace. He would have said, of course — he does say — that no miracle, and no body of miracles, could or can produce "true faith": the internal creative operation of the Spirit is necessary for that. And in that sense the evidence of miracles is subordinated to the testimony of the Spirit. But this is not because of any depreciation of the evidential value of miracles; but because of the full appreciation of the deadness of the human soul in sin. The evidential value of miracles, and their place in the objective evidences of the divine origin of the Scriptures, are wholly unaffected by the doctrine of the testimony of the Spirit; and the strongest assertions of their valuelessness in the production of faith, apart from the testimony of the Spirit, do not in the least affect the estimate we put on them, as objective evidences.

and the precise reason he assigns for this ineffectiveness. There is only one thing which he says they cannot do: that is to produce "sound faith" (I. vii. 4), "firm faith" (I. viii. 13) — that assurance which is essential to "true piety" (I. vii. 4). And their failure to produce "sound faith" is due solely to the subjective condition of man, which is such that a creative operation of the Holy Spirit on the soul is requisite before he can exercise "sound faith" (I. vii. 4; I. viii. 13). It is the attempt to produce this "sound faith" in the heart of man, not renewed for believing by the creative operation of the Holy Spirit, which Calvin pronounces preposterous and foolish. "It is acting a preposterous part," he says, "to endeavor to produce *sound faith* in the Scriptures by disputations": objections may be silenced by such disputations, "but this will not fix in men's hearts *that assurance which is essential to true piety*"; for religion is not a matter of mere opinion, but a fundamental change of attitude towards God (I. vii. 4). It betrays, therefore, great folly to wish to demonstrate to infidels that the Scriptures are the Word of God, he repeats in another place, obviously with no other meaning, "since this cannot be known without faith," that is, as the context shows, without the internal working of the Spirit of God (I. viii. 13, end).

That Calvin should thus teach that the *indicia* are incapable of producing "firm faith" in the human heart, disabled by sin, is a matter of course: and therefore it is a matter of course that he should teach that the *indicia* are ineffective for the production of "sound faith" apart from the internal operation of the Spirit correcting the sin-bred disabilities of man, that is to say, apart from the testimony of the Spirit. But what about the *indicia* in conjunction with the testimony of the Spirit? It would seem to be evident that, on Calvin's ground, they would have their full part to play here, and that we must say that, when the soul is renewed by the Holy Spirit to a sense for the divinity of Scripture, it is through the *indicia* of that divinity that it is brought into its proper confidence in the divinity of Scripture. In treating of the *indicia*, Calvin does not, however, declare this in so many words. He sometimes even appears to speak of them rather as if they lay side by side with the testimony of the Spirit than acted along with it as co-factors in the production of the supreme effect. He speaks of their ineffectiveness in producing sound faith in the unbeliever: and of their value as corroboratives to the believer: and his language would sometimes seem to suggest that therefore it were just as well not to employ them until after faith had formed itself under the testimony of the Spirit (I. viii. 1, 13). Of their part in forming faith under the operation of the testimony of the Spirit he does not appear explicitly to speak.[61]

[61] Cf. Köstlin, as cited, pp. 413–415: "We find in Calvin the aforementioned several criteria set alongside of this witness of the Spirit, and indeed especially those which are internal to the Scriptures themselves, such as their elevation above all merely human products, which cannot fail to impress every reader, etc. It would certainly be desirable to trace an inner connection between this impression made by the character, by the style of speech, by the contents of Scripture, and that supreme immediate testimony of the Spirit for it. Assuredly God Himself, the Author of Scripture, works upon us also in such impressions, which we analyse in our reflecting human consideration, and in our debates strive to set before opponents; and we feel, on the other side, a need to analyse, as far as is possible for us, even the supreme witness of the Spirit, in spite of its immediacy, and to relate it with our other experiences and observations with respect to Scripture, so as to become conscious of the course by which God passes from one to the other. Calvin, however, does not enter into this; he sets the two side by side and over against one another: 'Although (Scripture) conciliates reverence to itself by its own supreme majesty, it does not seriously affect us, until it is sealed to our hearts by the Spirit' (XXIX. 295; XXX. 60; ed. 3, I. vii. 5): he does not show the inner relation of one to the other. He does not do this even in the edition of 1559, where he with great eloquence speaks more fully of the power with which the Word of the New Testament witnesses manifests its divine majesty. The witness of the Spirit comes forward with Calvin thus somewhat abruptly. By means of it the Spirit works true faith, which the Scripture, even through its internal criteria, cannot establish in divine certainty; and indeed He does not work it in the case of all those — and has no intention of working it in the case of all those — to whom the Scripture is conveyed with its criteria, but, as the section on Predestination further shows, only in the case of those who have been elected thereto from all eternity. Here we are already passing over into the relation of the Calvinistic conception of the Formal Principle or the Authority of Scripture, to its conception of the means of grace. In this matter the Lutheran doctrine stands in conflict with it. But with reference to what we have been discussing, we

Nevertheless, there are not lacking convincing hints that there was lying in his mind all the time the implicit understanding that it is through these *indicia* of the divinity of Scripture that the soul, under the operation of the testimony of the Spirit, reaches its sound faith in Scripture, and that he has been withheld from more explicitly stating this only by the warmth of his zeal for the necessity of the testimony of the Spirit which has led him to a constant contrasting of this divine with those human "testimonies." Thus we find him repeatedly affirming that these *indicia* will produce no fruit *until* they be confirmed by the internal testimony of the Spirit (I. vii. 4, 5; viii. 1, 13): " Our reverence may be conciliated by its internal majesty [the Scripture's], but it never seriously affects us, *till* it is confirmed by the Spirit in our hearts " (I. vii. 5). " *Without this certainty*, . . . in vain will the authority of Scripture be either defended by arguments or established by the consent of the Church, or of any other supports: since, unless the foundation be laid, it remains in perpetual suspense " (I. viii. 1). The *indicia* " are *alone* not sufficient to produce firm faith in it [the Scriptures], *till* the heavenly Father, discovering His own power therein, places its authority above all controversy " (I. viii. 13). It is, however, in his general teaching as to the formation of sound faith in the divinity of Scripture that we find the surest indication that he thought of the *indicia* as co-working with the testimony of the Spirit to this result. This is already given, indeed, in his strenuous insistence that the work of the Spirit is not of the nature of a revelation, but of a confirmation of the revelation deposited in the Scriptures, especially when this is taken in connection with his teaching that Scripture is self-authenticating. What the Spirit of God imparts to us, he says, is a *sense* of divinity: such a sense discovers divinity only where

---

do not find that the Lutheran dogmaticians, when they come to occupy themselves more particularly with the *testimonium Spiritus Sancti* to the Scriptures, dealt more vitally with its relation to the operation of these criteria on the human spirit. No doubt, in Luther's own conception this was more the case: but he gave no scientific elaboration of it."

divinity is and only by a perception of it — a perception which of course rests on its proper *indicia*. It is because Scripture "exhibits the plainest evidence that it is God who speaks in it" that the newly awakened *sense* of divinity, quickened in the soul, recognizes it as divine (I. vii. 4). The senses do not distinguish light from darkness, white from black, sweet from bitter — to use Calvin's own illustration (I. vii. 2) — save by the mediation of those *indicia* of light and darkness, whiteness and blackness, sweetness and bitterness, by which these qualities manifest themselves to the natural senses; and by parity of reasoning we must accredit Calvin as thinking of the newly implanted spiritual sense discerning the divinity of Scripture only through the mediation of the *indicia* of divinity manifested in Scripture. To taste and see that the Scriptures are divine is to recognize a divinity actually present in Scripture; and of course recognition implies perception of *indicia*, not attribution of a divinity not recognized as inherent. Meanwhile it must be admitted that Calvin has not at this point developed this side of his subject with the fulness which might be wished, but has left it to the general implications of the argument.

OBJECT TESTIFIED TO

Closely connected with the question of the mode in which Calvin conceived the testimony of the Spirit to be delivered, is the further question of the matters for which he conceived that testimony to be available. On the face of it it would seem that he conceived it directly available solely for the divinity of the Scriptures and therefore for the revelatory character of their contents. So he seems to imply throughout the discussion, and, indeed, to assert repeatedly. Nevertheless, there is a widespread impression abroad that he appealed to it to determine the canon of Scripture too,[62] and indeed also to estab-

[62] Cf. Köstlin, as cited, p. 417: "The certainty that the Scriptures really possess such authority, rests for us not on the authority of the Church, but just on this testimony of the Spirit. Calvin's reference here is even to the several books of Scripture: he is aware that the opponents ask how, without a decree of the Church, we are to be convinced what book should be re-

lish the integrity of its text. This impression is generally, though not always, connected with the view that Calvin conceived the mode of delivery of the testimony of the Spirit to be the creation in the soul of a blind faith, unmotived by reasons and without rooting in grounds; and it has been much exploited of late years in the interests of a so-called " free " attitude towards Scripture, which announces itself as following Calvin

---

ceived with reverence, what should be excluded from the canon; he himself adduces in opposition to this, even here, nothing else except the *testimonium Spiritus:* the entirety of Scripture seems to him to be equally, so to say, *en bloc*, divinely legitimated by this." So also Pannier, as cited, p. 202: " The question of canonicity never presented itself to the thought of Calvin, except in the second place as a corollary of the problem of the divinity (I. vii. 1). If the Holy Spirit attests to us that a given book is divine, He in that very act attests that it forms a part of the rule of faith, that it is canonical. Nowhere has Calvin permitted, as his successors have done, a primary place to be taken by a theological doctrine which became less capable of resisting the assaults of adversaries when isolated from the practical question. Perhaps, moreover, he did not render as exact an account as we are able to render after the lapse of two centuries, of the wholly new situation in which the Reformation found itself with respect to the canon, or of the new way in which he personally resolved the question." Accordingly, at an earlier point Pannier says: " It is true that the faculty of recognizing the Word of God under the human forms included for Calvin, and especially according to the Confession of Faith of 1559, the faculty of determining the canonicity of the books. This is a consequence secondary but natural, and so long as they maintained the principle, the Reformed doctors placed themselves in a false position when they showed themselves disposed to abandon the consequences to the criticisms of their opponents " (p. 164). Cf. J. Cramer, *Nieuwe Bijdragen*, iii. p. 140: " But you must not think . . . of an *immediate* witness of the Spirit to the particular parts of the Holy Scriptures. The old theologians did not think of that. They conceived the matter thus: The *testimonium Spiritus Sancti* gives witness *directly* to the religio-moral contents of Scripture only. Since, however, the religio-moral contents must necessarily have a particular form, and the dogmatic content is closely bound up with the historical, neither the chronological nor the topographical element can be separated out, etc.— therefore the *testimonium Spiritus Sancti* gives to the total content of Scripture witness that it is from God." This, after all, then, is not to appeal to the *testimonium Spiritus Sancti,* directly to authenticate the canon; but to construct a canon on the basis of a testimony of the Spirit given solely to the divinity of Scripture, the movement of thought being this: All Scripture given by inspiration of God is profitable; this Scripture is given by inspiration of God; accordingly this Scripture belongs to the category of profitable Scripture, that is to the canon.

when it refuses to acknowledge as authoritative Scripture any portion of or element in the traditionally transmitted Scriptures which does not spontaneously commend itself to the immediate religious judgment as divine. Undoubtedly this is to reverse the attitude of Calvin towards the traditionally transmitted Scriptures, and it is difficult to believe that two such diametrically contradictory attitudes towards the Scriptures can be outgrowths of the same principal root. In point of fact, moreover, as we have already seen, not only does Calvin not conceive the mode of the delivery of the testimony of the Spirit to be by the creation of a blind and unmotived faith, but, to come at once to the matter more particularly in hand, he does not depend on the testimony of the Spirit for the determination of canonicity or for the establishment of the integrity of the text of Scripture. So far from discarding the *via rationalis* here, he determines the limits of the canon and establishes the integrity of the transmission of Scripture distinctly on scientific, that is to say, historico-critical grounds. In no case of his frequent discussion of such subjects does he appeal to the testimony of the Spirit and set aside the employment of rational and historical argumentation as invalid or inconclusive; always, on the contrary, he adduces the evidence of valid tradition and apostolicity of contents as conclusive of the fact. It is hard to believe that such a consequent mind could have lived unconsciously in such an inconsistent attitude towards a question so vital to him and his cause.[63]

[63] Reuss, in the sixteenth chapter of his "History of the Canon of the Holy Scriptures," E. T. 1884, expounds Calvin, with his usual learning and persuasiveness, as basing the determination of the canon solely on the testimony of the Spirit. But the exposition falls into two confusions: a confusion of the authority of Scripture with its canonicity, and a confusion of the divine with the apostolic origin of Scripture. Of course, Calvin repelled the Romish conception that the authority of Scripture rests on its authentication by the Church and its tradition (p. 294), but that did not deter him from seeking by a historical investigation to discover what especial books had been committed by the apostles to the Church as authoritative. Of course, he founded the sure conviction of the divine origin of the Scriptures on the witness of the Spirit of God by and with them in the heart, but that did not prevent his appealing to history to determine what these Scriptures which were so witnessed were in their compass. Accordingly even Reuss has to admit that it

So far as support for the impression that Calvin looked to the testimony of the Spirit to determine for him the canon of Scripture and to assure him of its integrity is derived from his writings, it rests on a manifest misapprehension of a single passage in the " Institutes," and what seems to be a misassignment to him of a passage in the old French Confession of Faith.

The passage in the " Institutes " is a portion of the paragraphs which are devoted to repelling the Romish contention that " the Scriptures have only so much weight as is conceded to them by the suffrages of the Church; as though the eternal and inviolable truth of God depended on the arbitrary will of men " (I. vii. 1). " For thus," Calvin says — and this is the passage which is appealed to — " For thus, dealing with the Holy Spirit as a mere laughing stock (*ludibrio*), they ask, Who shall give us confidence that these [Scriptures] have come from God, — who assure us that they have reached our time safe and intact, — who persuade us that one book should be received reverently, another expunged from the number (*numero*) — if the Church should not prescribe a certain rule for all these things? It depends, therefore, they say, on the Church, both what reverence is due to Scripture, and what books should be inscribed (*censendi sint*) in its catalogue (*in eius catalogo*) " (I. vii. 1). This passage certainly shows that the Romish controversialists in endeavoring to prove that the authority of Scripture is dependent on the Church's suffrage, argued that it is only by the Church that we can be assured even of the contents of Scripture and of its integrity — that its very

is exceedingly difficult to carry through his theory of Calvin's theoretical procedure consistently with Calvin's observed practice. In point of fact, the Reformers, and Calvin among them, did not separate the Apocrypha from the Old Testament on the sole basis of the testimony of the Spirit: they appealed to the evidence of the Jewish Church (p. 312). Nor did they determine the question of the New Testament antilegomena on this principle: this, too, was with them " a simple question of historical criticism " (p. 316) — although Reuss here (p. 318) confuses Calvin's appeal to the internal evidence of apostolicity with appeal to " religious intuition." In a word, Reuss's exposition of Calvin's procedure in determining the canon rests on a fundamental misconception of that procedure.

canon and text rest on the Church's determination. But how can it be inferred that Calvin's response to this argument would take the form: No, of these things we can be assured by the immediate testimony of the Spirit? In point of fact, he says nothing of the kind, and the inference does not lie in the argument. What he says is that the Romish method of arguing is as absurd as it is blasphemous, a mere cavil (I. vii. 2), as well as derogatory to the Holy Spirit. The Holy Spirit, he says, assures us that in the Scriptures God speaks to us. To bid us pause on the ground that it is only the Church who can assure us that this or that book belongs to the body of the Scriptures, that the text has been preserved to us intact and the like, is to interpose frivolous objections, and can have no other end than to glorify the Church at the expense of souls. Accordingly, he remarks that these objectors are without concern what logical difficulties they may cast themselves into: they wish only to prevent men taking their comfort out of the direct assurance by the Spirit of the divinity of the Scriptures. He repudiates, in a word, the entire Romish argument: but we can scarcely infer from this, that his response to it would be that the immediate witness of the Spirit provides us with direct answers to their carping questions. It is at least equally likely from the mere fact that he speaks of these objections as cavils (I. vii. 2) and girds at the logic of the Romish controversialists as absurd, that his response would be that the testimony of the Spirit for which he was contending had no direct concernment with questions of canon and text.

The passage in the Confession of La Rochelle, on the other hand, does certainly attribute the discrimination of the canonical books in some sense — in what sense may admit of debate — to the testimony of the Spirit. In the third article of this Confession there is given a list of the canonical books.[64] The fourth article, then, runs as follows: "We recognize these

---

[64] "All this Holy Scripture is comprised in the canonical books of the Old and New Testaments, the number (le nombre) of which is as follows" . . . the list ensuing. See Opp. ix. 741.

books to be canonical and the very certain rule of our faith, not so much by the common accord and consent of the Church, as by the inward witness and persuasion of the Holy Spirit, who makes us distinguish them from the other ecclesiastical books, upon which, though they may be useful, no article of faith can be founded." This article, however, was not the composition of Calvin, but was among those added by the Synod of Paris to the draft submitted by Calvin.[65] Calvin's own article "On the Books of Holy Scripture," which was expanded by the Synod into several, reads only: " This doctrine does not derive its authority from men, nor from angels, but from God alone; we believe, too (seeing that it is a thing surpassing all human sense to discern that it is God who speaks), that He Himself gives the certitude of it to His elect, and seals it in their hearts by His Spirit." [66] In this fine statement we find the very essence of the teaching of the " Institutes " on this subject; the ideas and even the phraseology of which are reproduced.

We may learn, therefore, at most, from the Confession of La Rochelle, not that Calvin, but that some of his immediate followers attributed in some sense the discrimination of the canonical books to the witness of the Spirit. Other evidences of this fact are not lacking. The Belgian Confession, for example, much like that of La Rochelle, declares of the Scriptural books, just enumerated (Art. v.): " We receive all these books alone, as holy and canonical, for the regulation, foundation and establishment of our faith, and we fully believe all that they contain, not so much because the Church receives and approves them, but principally because the Spirit gives witness to them in our hearts that they are from God, and also because they are approved by themselves; for the very blind can perceive that the things come to pass which they predict." Perhaps, however, we may find a more instructive instance still in the words of one of the Protestant disputants in a con-

---

[65] *Opp.* ix., *prolg.*, pp. lvii.–lx.: cf. Dieterlen, " Le Synode général de Paris," 1873, pp. 77, 89; Pannier, as cited, pp. 126–7; and for a brief précis, Müller, " Bekenntnisschriften der reform. Kirche," 1903, p. xxxiii.

[66] *Opp.* ix. 741.

ference held at Paris in 1566 between two Protestant ministers and two doctors of the Sorbonne.[67] To the inquiry, How do you know that some books are canonical and others Apocryphal, the Protestant disputant (M. Lespine) answers: " By the Spirit of God which is a Spirit of discrimination, by whom all those to whom He is communicated are illuminated, so as to be made capable of judging and discerning spiritual things and of recognizing (*cognoistre*) and apprehending the truth (when it is proposed to them), by the witness and assurance which He gives to them in their hearts. And as we discriminate light and darkness by the faculty of sight which is in the eye; so, we can easily separate and recognize (*recognoistre*) truth from falsehood, and from all things in general which can be false, absurd, doubtful or indifferent, when we are invested with the Spirit of God and guided by the light which He lights in our hearts." M. Lespine had evidently read his Calvin; though there is a certain lack of crisp exactness in his language which may raise doubt whether he has necessarily reproduced him with precision. Clearly his idea is that the Spirit of God in His creative operation on the hearts of Christ's people has implanted in them — or quickened in them — a spiritual sense, which recognizes the stamp of divinity upon the books which God has given to the Church, and so separates them out from all others and thus constitutes the canon. This is to attribute the discrimination of the canonical books to the witness of the Spirit not directly but indirectly, namely, through the intermediation of the determination of the books which are of divine origin, which, then, being gathered together, constitute the canon, or divinely given rule of our faith and life. This conception of the movement of the mind in this matter became very common, and was given very clear expression, for example, by Jurieu, in a context which bears as evident marks of reminiscences of Calvin as do M. Lespine's remarks. " That grace which produces faith in a soul,"

[67] " Actes de la dispute et conference tenue à Paris ès mois de juillet et aoust 1566 " (Strasbourg, 1566), printed in the *Biblioth. de la Soc. de l'Hist. du Prot. franc.* We draw from the account of it in Pannier, as cited, pp. 141 *sq.*

says he,[68] " does not begin . . . by persuading it that a given book is canonical. This persuasion comes only afterwards and as a consequence. It gives to the consciousness a taste for the truth: it applies this truth to the mind and heart; it proceeds from this subsequently that the believer believes that a given book is canonical, because the truths which ' find ' him are found in it. In a word, we do not believe that which is contained in a book to be divine because this book is canonical. But we believe that a given book is canonical because we have perceived that what it contains is divine. And we have perceived this as we perceive the light when we look on the fire, sweetness and bitterness when we eat." Whether we are to attribute this movement of thought, however, to Calvin, is another question.[69] There is no hint òf it in his writings.

It is not even obvious that this precise movement of thought is the conception which lay in the mind of the authors of the additional articles in the Confession of La Rochelle and of the similar statement in the Belgian Confession. The interpretation of these articles is particularly interesting, as they both undoubtedly came under the eye of Calvin and their doctrine was never disavowed by him. It is not, however, altogether easy, because of a certain ambiguity in the use of the term " canonical." It is on account of the ambiguity which attends the use of this term that in speaking of their teaching we have guardedly said that they appear to suspend the canonicity of the Scriptural books in some sense directly on the testimony

[68] " Le vray systeme de l'Eglise et la véritable analyse de la foy," 1686, III. ii. 453. Pannier, as cited, quotes this, pp. 167–168.

[69] As we have seen, it is attributed to Calvin by both Pannier and Cramer. Pannier (p. 203) remarks that " if Calvin was not able to appreciate in all its purity " the new situation with regard to the canon into which the Reformation brought men, " it was even less incumbent on him to render account of the personal attitude which he himself took up with reference to it." " It is his successors only who, in adopting his conclusions (except that they apply them more or less), have asked themselves how they reached them, and have reconstructed the reasoning which no doubt Calvin himself had unconsciously followed." Is not this a confession that after all the view in question was not Calvin's own view? At least not consciously to himself? But Pannier would say, no doubt, either this was Calvin's view or he appealed to the testimony of the Spirit directly to authenticate the canon.

of the Spirit. This ambiguity may be brought sharply before us by placing in juxtaposition two sentences from Quenstedt in which the term "canonical" is employed, obviously, in two differing senses. "We deny," says he, "that the catalogue of canonical books is an article of faith, superadded to the others [articles of faith] contained in Scripture. Many have faith and may attain salvation who do not hold the number of canonical books. If the word 'canon' be understood of the *number* of the books, we concede that such a catalogue is not contained in Scripture." "These are two different questions," says he again, "whether the Gospel of Matthew is canonical, and whether it was written by Matthew. The former belongs to saving faith; the latter to historical knowledge. For if the Gospel which has come down to us under the name of Matthew had been written by Philip or Bartholomew, it would make no difference to saving faith." In the former extract the question of canonicity is removed from the category of articles of faith; in the latter it is made an integral element of saving faith. The contradiction is glaring — unless there be an undistributed middle. And this is what there really is. In the former passage, where Quenstedt is engaged in repelling the contention that there are articles of faith that must be accepted by all, which are not contained in Scripture — in defending, in a word, the Protestant doctrine of the sufficiency or perfection of Scripture — he uses the terms "canon," "canonical" in the purely technical sense of the extent of Scripture. In the latter passage, where he is insisting that the authority of Scripture as the Word of God hangs on its divine, not on its human, author, he uses the term "canonical" in the sense of "divinely given." The term "canonical" was current, then, in the two senses of "belonging to the list of authoritative Scriptures," "entering into the body of the Scriptures," and "God-given," "divine." In which of these two senses is it used in the Gallican and Belgian Confessions? If in the former, then these Confessions teach that the testimony of the Spirit is available directly for the determination of the canon: if in the latter, then they teach no such thing, but only that it is on the testimony of the Spirit that we are assured of the divine origin and character of these books.

That the Gallican Confession employs the term in the latter of these senses, seems at least possible when once attention is called to it, although regard for the last clause of the statement, "who makes us distinguish them from the other ecclesiastical books," etc., prevents the representation of this interpretation as certain. Its declaration, succeeding the catalogue of the books given in the third section, is obviously intended to affirm something that is true of them already as a definite body of books before the mind. "We recognize *these* books," it says, "to be canonical and the very certain rule of our faith." That is to say, to this body of books we ascribe the quality of canonicity and recognize their regulative character. What would seem, then, to be in question is a quality belonging to a list of books already determined and in the mind of the framer of the statement as a whole. The same may be said of the Belgian Confession. It, too, has already given a list of the canonical books, and now proceeds to affirm something that is true of "all of these books and them only." The thing affirmed is that they are "holy and canonical," where the collocation suggests that "canonical" expresses a quality which ranges with "holy." We cannot help suspecting, then, that these early confessions use the term "canonical" not quantitatively but qualitatively, not extensively but intensively; and in that sense it is the equivalent of "divine." [70]

[70] The following is the account of the treatment of the question of the canon in these creeds, given by J. Cramer ("De Roomsch-Katholieke en de Oud-protestantsche Schriftbeschouwing," 1883, pp. 48 *sq.*): "And on what now, does that authority rest? This question, too, is amply discussed in the Reformed Confessions, and that, as concerns the principal matter, wholly in the spirit of Calvin. Only, more value is ascribed to the testimony of the Church. No doubt the authority of the Scriptures is not made to rest on it; but it is permitted an important voice in the question of the canon. When it is said that 'all that is said in the Holy Scriptures is to be believed *not so much* because the Church receives them and holds them as canonical, but especially because the Holy Spirit bears witness to them in our heart that they are from God,' a certain weight is attributed to the judgment of the Church. This appears particularly from the way in which the canonical books are spoken of

Even the inference back from them to Calvin that he may have supposed that the testimony of the Spirit is available to determine the canon becomes therefore doubtful: and no other reason exists why we should attribute this view to him. We cannot affirm that the movement of his thought was never from the divinity of Scripture, assured to us by the testimony of the Spirit, to the determination of the limits of the canon: but we have no reason to ascribe this movement of thought to him except that it was adopted by some of his successors.

On the other hand, Calvin constantly speaks as if the only thing which the testimony of the Spirit assures us of in the case of the Scriptures is the divinity of their origin and contents: and he always treats Scripture when so speaking of it as a definite entity, held before his mind as a whole.[71] In these

---

in distinction from the Apocryphal books. In enumerating the Bible books, the Belgian Confession prefixes the words: 'Against which nothing can be said' (Art. iv.). By this apparently is meant, that against the canonicity of these books, from a historical standpoint, with the eye on the witness of the Church, nothing can be alleged (a thing not to be said of the Apocrypha). In the same spirit the Anglican Articles, when speaking of the books of the Old and New Testaments, says that 'Of their authority there has never been any doubt in the Church.' I will not raise the question here how that can be affirmed with the eye on the Antilegomena. It shows, however, certainly that much importance is attached to the ecclesiastical tradition. The fundamental ground, however, why the Scriptures of the Old and New Testaments are to be held to be the Word of God is sought in the Scriptures themselves, and, assuredly, in the testimony which the Holy Spirit bears to their divinity in the hearts of believers. Like Calvin, the Confessions suppose that thus they have given an immovable foundation to the divine authority of the Scriptures, and have taken an impregnable position over against Rome, which appealed to the witness of the Catholic Church. . . ." Calvin, however, allowed as much to the testimony of the Church — external evidence — as is here allowed, and the very adduction of its testimony shows that sole dependence was not placed on the testimony of the Spirit for the canonicity of a book: what it is appealed to for is the divinity of the canonical books.

[71] So even Köstlin perceives, as cited, p. 417: "The entirety of Scripture appeared to him divinely legitimated by the *testimonium Spiritus,* altogether, so to say, *en bloc.* . . . The declarations of Calvin as to the Word spoken by the prophets and apostles, which they rightly asserted to be God's Word, pass without hesitation over into declarations as to the Holy Scriptures, as such, and that in their entirety; with the proposition 'the Law and the Prophets and the Gospel have emanated from God' is interchanged the proposition 'the Scripture is from God,' — and the witness of the Spirit assures us of it." So also Pan-

circumstances his own practice in dealing with the question of canonicity and text, makes it sufficiently clear that he held their settlement to depend on scientific investigation, and appealed to the testimony of the Spirit only to accredit the divine origin of the concrete volume thus put into his hands. The movement of his thought was therefore along this course:

---

nier (pp. 203–204): " Everything goes back to his considering things not in detail but *en bloc.* The Word of God is for him one, *verbum Dei,* not *verba Dei.* The diversity of the authors disappears before the unity of the Spirit. The same reasoning applies to each single book as to the whole collection. All the verses hold together; and if one introduces us to the knowledge of salvation we may conclude that the book is canonical. Given the collection, it is enough in practice, since all the parts are of a sort, to establish the value of one of them to guarantee the value of all the others. It is certain that the critical theologian and the simple believer even yet proceed somewhat differently in this matter; the simplest and surest method is that of the humble saint, and Calvin was very right not to range himself among the theologians at this point. ' The just shall live by faith.' This affirmation seemed to him a revealed truth: he concluded from it that the whole epistle to the Romans is inspired; some remarks of this kind in other passages of the Epistles, of the Gospels, and the canonicity of the New Testament is established. The same for the Old Testament. The Second Epistle of Peter and the Song of Songs thus go with the rest. The human testimonies, internal and external criteria, useful for confirming the other parts of a book of which a passage has been recognized as inspired, are insufficient to expel from the canon a book which the witness of the Spirit has not recognized as opposed to the doctrine of salvation." We quote the whole passage to give Pannier's whole thought: but what we adduce it for is at present merely to signalize the admission it contains that Calvin dealt with the Scriptures in the matter of the testimony of the Spirit, so to speak, " in the lump " — as a whole. Pannier cites apparently as similar to Calvin's view, Gaussen, " Canon," ii. p. 10: " This testimony, which every Christian has recognized when he has read his Bible with vital efficacy, may be recognized by him only in a single page; but this page is enough to spread over the book which contains it an incomparable brightness." That is, Calvin, like the simple believer, has a definite book — the Bible — in his hands and treats it as all of a piece — of course, in Calvin's case, not without reasonable grounds for treating it as all of a piece: in other words, the canon was already determined for him before he appealed to the testimony of the Spirit to attest its divinity. Cf. Cramer (p. 140) as quoted above. Cramer is quite right *so far,* therefore, when he says (pp. 156–157): " Although we determine securely by means of the historical-critical method what must be carried back to the apostolical age and what accords with the apostolical doctrine, we have not yet proved the divine authority of these writings. This hangs on this, — whether the Holy Spirit gives us His witness to them. On this witness alone rests our assurance of faith, not on the force of a historical-critical demonstration." This, so far as appears, was Calvin's method.

first, the ascertainment, on scientific grounds, of the body of books handed down from the Apostles as the rule of faith and practice; secondly, the vindication, on the same class of grounds, of the integrity of their transmission; thirdly, the accrediting of them as divine on the testimony of the Spirit. It is not involved in this that he is to be considered to have supposed that a man must be a scholar before he can be a Christian. He supposed we become Christians not by scholarship but by the testimony of the Spirit in the heart, and he had no inclination to demand scholarship as the basis of our Christianity. It is only involved in the position we ascribe to him that he must be credited with recognizing that questions of scholarship are for scholars and questions of religion only for Christians as such. He would have said — he does say — that he in whose heart the Spirit bears His testimony will recognize the Scriptures whenever presented to his contemplation as divine, will depend on them with sound trust and will embrace with true faith all that they propound to him. He would doubtless have said that this act of faith logically implicates the determination of the " canon." But he would also have said — he does in effect say — that this determination of the canon is a separable act and is to be prosecuted on its own appropriate grounds of scientific evidence. It involves indeed a fundamental misapprehension of Calvin's whole attitude to attribute to him the view that the testimony of the Spirit determines immediately such scientific questions as those of the canon and text of Scripture. The testimony of the Spirit was to him emphatically an operation of the Spirit of God on the heart, which produced distinctively a spiritual effect: it was directed to making men Christians,[72] not to making them theologians. The testimony of the Spirit was, in effect, in his view, just what we in modern times have learned to call " regenera-

[72] Calvin would certainly have subscribed to these words of Pannier, as cited, p. 164: The most of the Catholics " have always strangely misapprehended the illumination which, according to the Reformed, the least of believers is capable of receiving and of applying to the reading of the Bible. It is a question, not as they suppose, of becoming theologians, but of becoming believers, of having not the plenitude of knowledge, but the certitude of faith."

tion" considered in its noëtic effects. That "regeneration" has noëtic effects he is explicit and iterative in affirming: but that these noëtic effects of "regeneration" could supersede the necessity of scientific investigation in questions which rest for their determination on matters of fact — Calvin would be the last to imagine. He who recognized that the conviction of the divinity of Scripture wrought by the testimony of the Spirit rests as its ground on the *indicia* of the divinity of Scripture spiritually discerned in their true weight, could not imagine that the determination of the canon of Scripture or the establishment of its text could be wholly separated from their proper basis in evidence and grounded solely in a blind testimony of the Spirit alone: which indeed in that case would be fundamentally indistinguishable from that "revelation" which he rebuked the Anabaptists for claiming to be the recipients of.

THE TESTIMONY AND THE RELIGIOUS LIFE

When we clearly apprehend the essence of Calvin's doctrine of the testimony of the Spirit to the divinity of Scripture to be the noëtic effects of "regeneration" we shall know what estimate to place upon the criticism which is sometimes passed upon him that he has insufficiently correlated his doctrine of the testimony of the Spirit with the inner [73] religious

[73] Cf. Köstlin, as cited, pp. 415–416. After raising the question of the relation of the witness of the Spirit to the inner experience of the Christian, and the relative priority of the two — and remarking that in case the vital process is conceived as preceding the witness of the Spirit to the divinity of the Scriptures, it will be hard not to allow to the Christianized heart the right and duty of criticism of the Scriptures (where the fault in reasoning lies in the term *process*), Köstlin continues: "We touch here on the relation between the formal and material sides of the fundamental evangelical principle. And we think at once of the relation in which they stood to one another in Luther's representation, by which his well-known critical attitude, with respect, say, to the Epistle of James, was rendered possible. Calvin, too, now has no wish to speak of a witness of the Spirit merely with reference to the Scriptures, and is far from desiring to isolate that witness of the Spirit for the Scriptures. He comes back to it subsequently, when speaking of faith in the saving content of the Gospel, declaring that the Spirit seals the contents

life of the Christian, has given too separate a place to the
Spirit's witness to Scripture, and thus has overestimated the
formal principle of Protestantism in comparison with the material principle,[74] with the effect of giving a hard, dry, and

of the Word in our hearts (1539, XXIX. 456 *sq.*, 468 *sq.*; further in 1559, III. 2
[In Köstlin's pagination, given here, XXIX. refers to the "Corpus Ref." as a
whole; III. 2 stands for "Institutes," Book III. chap. ii., or XXX. 397 *sq.*]). He
also inserted in the section on the Holy Scriptures and the witness of the Spirit
to them, in 1550, an additional special sentence, in which he expressly refers to
his intention to speak further on such a witness of the Spirit in a later portion of the treatise, and declares of faith in general, that there belongs to it
a sealing of the divine Spirit (XXIX. 296 [1559, I. vii. 5, near end]). In any
event he must have recurred to such a Spiritual testimony for the assurance of
individual Christians of their personal election. But in the first instance —
and this again is precisely what is characteristic for Calvin — he nevertheless
treats of the doctrine of the divine origin and the divine authority of the
Scriptures, and of the witness of the Spirit for them, wholly apart. The presentation proceeds with him in such a manner, that the Spirit first of all fully
produces faith in this character of the Scriptures, and only then the Bible-
believing Christian has to receive from the Scriptures its contents, in all its
several parts, as divinely true, — though, no doubt, this reception and this
faith in the several elements of the truth are by no means matters of human thought, but are rather to be performed under the progressive illumination and the progressive sealing of these contents in the heart by the Holy
Spirit. Even though he, meanwhile, calls that the 'truth' of the Scriptures,
which we come to feel in the power of the Spirit, he means by this in the section before us, an absolute truth-character, which must from the start be
attributed to the Scriptures as a whole, and will be experienced in and with
the divinity of the Scriptures in general. So the matter already stands in the
edition of 1539 . . . (XXIX. 292 *sq.*)." Accordingly Calvin teaches that the
Scriptures in all their parts are of indefectible authority, and should be met
in all their prescriptions with unlimited obedience (p. 418), because it is just
God who speaks in them. Then: "With Dorner (*Geschichte der protest. Theologie*, p. 380) — and even more decisively than he does it — we must remark on all this: 'The formal side of the protestant principle remains with
Calvin an over-emphasis, in comparison with the material, and with this is
connected that he sees in the Holy Scriptures above all else the revelation
of the will of God which he has dictated to man through the sacred writers.'
And this tendency came ever more strongly forward with him in the successive revisions of the *Institutes.* His conception of the formal principle thus
left no room for such a criticism as Luther employed on the several parts of
the canon." Later Lutheranism, however, Köstlin concludes by saying, adopted
Calvin's point of view here and even exaggerated it.

[74] "The formal side of the Protestant principle retains with Calvin the
ascendency over the material; and with this is connected the fact that he
sees in the Holy Scriptures chiefly the revelation of the will of God, which

legalistic aspect to Christianity as expounded by him. With Luther, it is said, everything is made of Justification and the liberty of the Christian man fills the horizon of thought; and this is because his mind is set on the "faith" out of which all good things flow and by which everything — Scripture itself — is dominated. With Calvin, on the other hand, with his primary emphasis on the authority of Scripture, accredited to us by a distinct act of the Holy Spirit, the watchword becomes obedience; and the horizon of thought is filled with a sense of obligation and legalistic anxiety as to conduct.

How Calvin could have failed to correlate sufficiently closely the testimony of the Spirit with the inner Christian life, or could have emphasized the formal principle of Protestantism at the expense of the material, when he conceived of the witness of the Spirit as just one of the effects of "regeneration," it is difficult to see. So to conceive the testimony of the Spirit is on the contrary to make the formal principle of Protestantism just an outgrowth of the material. It is only because our spirits have been renewed by the Holy Spirit that we see with convincing clearness the *indicia* of God in Scripture, that is, have the Scriptures sealed to us by the Spirit as divine. It is quite possible that Calvin may have particularly emphasized the obligations which grow out of our renewal by the Holy Spirit and the implantation in us of the Spirit of Adoption whereby we become the sons of God — obligations to comport ourselves as the sons of God and to govern our-

---

he has prescribed to men through the sacred writers." — Dorner, " Hist. of Protest. Theology," i. 1871, p. 390. Cf. p. 387: "The formal principle is, according to him, the norm and source of dogma, whilst he does not treat faith, in the same way as Luther, as a source of knowledge for the dogmatical structure, that is to say, as the mediative principle of knowledge." Hence Dorner complains (p. 390) of the more restricted freedom which Calvin left "for the free productions of the faith of the Church in legislation and dogma," and instances his treatment of "the Apostolic Age as normative for all times, even for questions of Church constitution," and the little room he left for destructive Biblical criticism. Cf. what is said above of Calvin's adoption of "the Puritan principle " (pp. 38 *sq.*).

selves by the law of God's house as given us in His Word; while Luther may have emphasized more the liberty of the Christian man who is emancipated from the law as a condition of salvation and is ushered into the freedom of life which belongs to the children of God. And it is quite possible that in this difference we may find a fundamental distinction between the two types of Protestantism — Lutheran and Reformed — by virtue of which the Reformed have always been characterized by a strong ethical tendency — in thought and in practice. But it is misleading to represent this as due to an insufficient correlation on Calvin's part of the testimony of the Spirit to the divinity of Scripture with the inner Christian life. It would be more exact to say that Calvin in this correlation thinks especially of what in our modern nomenclature we call "regeneration," while the mind of his Lutheran critics is set more upon justification and that "faith" which is connected with justification. With Calvin, at all events, the recognition of the Scriptures as divine and the hearty adoption of them as the divine rule of our faith and life is just one of the effects of the gracious operation of the Spirit of God on the heart, renewing it into spiritual life, or, what comes to the same thing, one of the gracious activities into which the newly implanted spiritual life effloresces.

Whether we should say also that it was with him the first effect of the creative operation of the Spirit on the heart, the first act of the newly renewed soul, requires some discrimination. If we mean logically first, there is a sense in which we should probably answer this question also in the affirmative. Calvin would doubtless have said that it is in the Scriptures that Christ is proposed to our faith, or, to put it more broadly, that Christ is the very substance of the special revelation documented in the Scriptures, and that the laying hold of Christ by faith presupposes therefore confidence in the revelation the substance of which He is — which is as much as to say the embracing of the Scriptures in firm faith as a revelation from God. If the Word is the vehicle through which the knowledge of Christ is brought to the soul, it follows of itself that it is only when our minds are filled with a solid reverence for the Word, when by the light of the Spirit we are enabled and prevalently led to see Christ therein, that we can embrace Christ with a sound faith: so that it may truly be said that no man can have the least true and sound knowledge of Christ without learning from Scripture (cf. I. ix. 3; I. vi. 2). In this sense Calvin would certainly have said that our faith in Christ presupposes faith in the Scriptures, rather than that we believe in the Scriptures for Christ's sake. But if our minds are set on chronological sequences, the response to the question which is raised is more doubtful. Faith in the revelation the substance of which is Christ and faith in Christ the substance of this revelation are logical implicates which involve one another: and we should probably be nearest to Calvin's thought if, without raising questions of chronological succession, we should recognize them as arising together in the soul. The real difference between Calvin's and the ordinary Lutheran conception at this point lies in the greater profundity of Calvin's insight and the greater exactness of his analysis. The Lutheran is prone to begin with faith, which is naturally conceived at its apex, as faith in Jesus Christ our Redeemer; and to make everything else flow from this faith as its ultimate root. For what comes before faith, out of which faith itself flows, he has little impulse accurately to inquire. Calvin penetrates behind faith to the creative action of the Holy Spirit on the heart and the new creature which results therefrom, whose act faith is; and is therefore compelled by an impulse derived from the matter itself to consider the relations in which the several activities of this new creature stand to one another and to analyse the faith itself which holds the primacy among them (for trust is the essence of religion, chap. ii.), into its several movements. The effect of this is that " efficacious grace " — what we call in modern speech " regeneration " — takes the place of fundamental principle in Calvin's soteriology and he becomes preëminently the theologian of the Holy Spirit. In point of fact it is from him accordingly that the effective study of the work of the Holy Spirit takes its rise, and it is only in the channels cut by him and at the hands of thinkers taught by him that the theology of the Holy Spirit has been richly developed.[75]

[75] Cf. the Introduction to the English Translation of Kuyper's "The Work of the Holy Spirit," 1900, especially pp. xxxiii.-iv. Cf. what Pannier, pp. 102–104, says of Calvin's general doctrine of the work of the Spirit and the relation borne to it by his particular doctrine of the testimony of the Spirit to Scripture. "If we pass beyond the two particular chapters whose contents we have been analysing and seek in the *Institutes* from 1536 to 1560 for other passages relating to the Holy Spirit, we shall see Calvin insisting ever more and more and on all occasions — as in the Commentaries — upon these diverse manifestations of the Holy Spirit, and presenting them all more or less as *testimonies*. He constantly recurs to the natural incapacity of man and the necessity of divine illumination in his mind, and especially in his heart, for the act of faith. It is from this point of view that he brings together the ideas of the Spirit and the Word of God in the definition of faith: 'It is a firm and certain knowledge of the good will of God towards us: which, being grounded in the free promise given in Jesus Christ, is revealed to our heart by the Holy Spirit.' He introduces the same ideas in his introductory remarks on the Apostles' Creed, and they lie at the basis of the explication he gives of the Third Article in all its forms, . . . e.g., in the ed. of 1560: 'In sum, He is set before us as the sole fountain from which all the celestial riches flow down to us. . . . For it is by His inspiration that we are regenerated into celestial life, so as no longer to govern or guide ourselves, but to be ruled by His movement and operation; so that if there is any good in us, it is only the fruit of His grace. . . : But since *faith is His prime master-piece*, the most of what we read in the Scriptures of His virtue and operation relates itself to this faith, by which He brings us to the brightness of the Gospel, in a manner which justifies calling Him the King by whom the treasures of the kingdom of heaven are offered to us, and His illumination may be called the longing of our souls.' From these quotations it is made plain that the witness of the Holy Spirit which at the opening of the *Institutes* in 1539 appeared as the *means of knowledge*, was thenceforward nevertheless considered, in the progress of the work, as the *means of grace*, and that taking his start from this point of view, Calvin discovered ever more widely extending horizons, so as at the end to speak particularly of the Holy Spirit in at least four different connections, but always — even in the first — in direct and constant relation to faith, with respect to its origin, and with respect to its consequences; and by no means almost exclusively with respect to assurance of the authority of the Scriptures." The progress which Pannier supposes he traces in Calvin's doctrine of the work of the Spirit seems illusory: the general doctrine of the work of the Spirit is already pretty fully outlined in 1536. But the relating of the testimony of the Spirit to Scripture to Calvin's general doctrine of faith as the product of the Spirit is exact and important for the understanding of his teaching. From beginning to end, Calvin conceived the confidence of the Christian in Scripture, wrought by the Holy Spirit, as one of the exercises of saving faith. Calvin is ever insistent that all that is good in man comes from the Spirit — whether in the sphere of thought, feeling, or act. " It is a notion

It is his profound sense of the supernatural origin of all that is good in the manifestations of human life which constitutes the characteristic mark of Calvin's thinking: and it is this which lies at the bottom of and determines his doctrine of the witness of the Holy Spirit. He did not doubt that the act of faith by which the child of God embraees the Scriptures as a revelation of God is his own act and the expression of his innermost consciousness. But neither did he doubt that this consciousness is itself the expression of a creative act of the Spirit of God. And it was on this account that he represented to himself the act of faith performed as resting ultimately on " the testimony of the Spirit." Its supernatural origin was to him the most certain thing about it. That language very much resembling his own might be employed in a naturalistic sense was, no doubt, made startlingly plain in his own day by the teaching of Castellion. Out of his pantheising rationalism Castellion found it possible to speak almost in Calvin's words. " It is evident," says he, " that the intention and secret counsels of God, hidden in the Scriptures, are revealed only to believers, the humble, the pious, who fear God and have the Spirit of God." If the wicked have sometimes spoken like prophets, they have nevertheless not really understood what they said, but are like magpies in a cage going through the forms of speech without inner apprehension of its meaning.[76] But Castellion meant by this nothing more than that sympathy is requisite to understanding. Since his day multitudes more have employed Calvin's language to express little more than this; and

---

of the natural man," he says on John xiv. 17 (1553: xlvii. 329–330), " to despise all that the Sacred Scriptures say of the Holy Spirit, depending rather on his own reason, and to reject the celestial illumination. . . . For ourselves, feeling our penury, we know that all we have of sound knowledge comes from no other fountain. Nevertheless the words of the Lord Jesus show clearly that nothing can be known of what concerns the Holy Spirit by human sense, but He is known only by the experience of faith." " No one," says he again (" Institutes " of 1543, i. 330), " should hesitate to confess that he attains the knowledge of the mysteries of God only so far as he has been illuminated by God's grace. He that attributes more knowledge to himself is only the more blind that he does not recognize his blindness."

[76] *Opp.* xiv. 727–733 (Pannier, as cited, p. 120).

have even represented Calvin's own meaning as nothing more than that the human consciousness acquires by association with God in Christ the power of discriminating the truth of God from falsehood. Nothing could more fundamentally subvert Calvin's whole teaching. The very nerve of his thought is, that the confidence of the Christian in the divine origin and authority of Scripture and the revelatory nature of its contents is of distinctively supernatural origin, is God-wrought. The testimony of the Spirit may be delivered through the forms of our consciousness, but it remains distinctively the testimony of God the Holy Spirit and is not to be confused with the testimony of our consciousness.[77] Resting on the language of Rom. viii. 16, from which the term "testimony of the Spirit" was derived, he conceived it as a co-witness along with the witness of our spirit indeed, but on that very account distinguishable from the witness of our spirit. This particular point is nowhere discussed by him at large, but Calvin's general sense is perfectly plain. That there is a double testimony he is entirely sure — the testimony of our own spirit and that of the Holy Spirit: that these are though distinguishable yet inseparable, he is equally clear: his conception is therefore that this double testimony runs confluently together into one. This is only as much as to say afresh that the testimony of the Holy Spirit is not delivered to us in a propositional revelation, nor by the creating in us of a blind conviction, but

[77] The classical instance of this confusion is supplied by the teaching of Claude Pajon (1626–1685), who, in accordance with his general doctrine that "without any other grace than that of the Word, God changes the whole man, from his intellect to his passions," explained the "testimony of the Spirit" as nothing else than the effect of the *indicia* of divinity in Scripture on the mind. The effect of these "marks" is a divine effect, because it is wrought in prearranged circumstances prepared for this effect: *facit per alium facit per se*. The conception is essentially deistic. It is no small testimony to the cardinal place which the doctrine of "the testimony of the Spirit" held in the Reformed system of the seventeenth century that Pajon still taught it; and it is no small testimony to its current conception as just "regeneration" that Pajon too identified it with regeneration, explained, of course, in accordance with his fundamental principle that all that God works He works through means. See on the whole matter Jurieu, "Traitté de la Nature et de la Grace," 1688, pp. 25, 26, who quotes alike from Pajon and his followers.

along the lines of our own consciousness. In its essence, the act of the Spirit in delivering His testimony, terminates on our nature, or faculties, quickening them so that we feel, judge, and act differently from what we otherwise should. In this sense, the testimony of the Spirit coalesces with our consciousness. We cannot separate it out as a factor in our conclusions, judgments, feelings, actions, consciously experienced as coming from without. But we function differently from before: we recognize God where before we did not perceive Him; we trust and love Him where before we feared and hated Him; we firmly embrace Him in His Word where before we turned indifferently away. This change needs accounting for. We account for it by the action of the Holy Spirit on our hearts; and we call this His "testimony." But we cannot separate His action from our recognition of God, our turning in trust and love to Him and the like. For this is the very form in which the testimony of the Spirit takes effect, into which it flows, by which it is recognized. We are profoundly conscious that of ourselves we never would have seen thus, and that our seeing thus can never find its account in anything in us by nature. We are sure, therefore, that there has come upon us a revolutionary influence from without; and we are sure that this is the act of God. Calvin would certainly have cried as one of his most eloquent disciples cries to-day: "The Holy Spirit is God, and not we ourselves. What we are speaking of is a Spirit which illuminates our spirit, which purifies our spirit, which strives against our spirit, which triumphs over our spirit. And you say this Spirit is nothing but our spirit? By no means. The Holy Spirit, the Spirit of God — this is God coming into us, not coming from us." [78] It is with equal energy that Calvin declares the supernaturalness of the testimony of the Spirit and repels every attempt to confound it with the human consciousness through which it works. To him this testimony is just God Himself in His intimate working in the human heart, opening it to the light of

[78] Doumergue, "Le problème protestant," 1892, p. 46 (Pannier, as cited, p. 192).

the truth, that by this illumination it may see things as they really are and so recognize God in the Scriptures with the same directness and surety as men recognize sweetness in what is sweet and brightness in what is bright. Here indeed lies the very hinge of his doctrine.[79]

It has seemed desirable to enter into some detail with respect to Calvin's doctrine of the testimony of the Spirit, not only because of its intrinsic interest, but also because of its importance for understanding Calvin's doctrine of the knowledge of God and indeed his whole system of truth, and for a

[79] Pannier, as cited, pp. 188 *sq.*, is quite right in insisting on this. After quoting D. H. Meyer (" De la place et du rôle de l'apologétique dans la théologie protestante," in the *Revue de théologie et des quest. relig.*, Jan., 1893, p. 1) to the effect that " the witness of the Holy Spirit in the heart of Christians is not a subjective phenomenon . . . it is an objective thing and comes from God," — he continues: " Now this objective character of the witness of the Holy Spirit is precisely what appears to make it 'incomprehensible' to our modern theologians (so A. E. Martin, *La Polemique de R. Simon et de J. Le Clerc*, 1880, p. 29: 'This intervention of the Holy Spirit distinct from the individual consciousness appears to us incomprehensible '). We are not speaking of those who venture to pretend that Calvin identifies the witness of the Holy Spirit with 'the intimate feeling' of each Christian. When one takes his place by the side of Castellion he may lawfully say, For me as for him 'the inspiration of the Holy Ghost confounds itself with consciousness; these revelations made to the humble are nothing more than the intuitions of a moral and religious sense fortified by meditation' (Buisson, *Castellion*, i. p. 304, cf. p. 201: ' Castellion placed above the tradition of the universal Church his own sense, his own reason, or rather, let us say it all at once, for it is the foundation of the debate, his consciousness '). But when one invokes the real fathers of the real Reformation, ah, please do not take for theirs the very opinions they combat. To make of the testimony of the Holy Spirit the equivalent of the testimony of the human spirit, of the individual consciousness, is to deny the real existence and the distinct rôle of the Holy Spirit, is to show that we have nothing in common with the faith expounded by Calvin so clearly, and defended through a century against the attacks of the Catholics as one of the essential bases of the Reformed theology and piety." Again, Pannier is quite right in his declaration (p. 214): " What we deny is that our reason — moral consciousness, religious consciousness, the term is of no importance — can, of itself, *make us see* the divinity of the Scriptures. It is this which *sees* it; but it is the Holy Spirit which *makes us see it*. He is not the inner eye for seeing the truth which is outside of us, but the supernatural hand which comes to open the eye of our consciousness — an eye which is, no doubt, divine in the sense that it too was created by God, but which has been blinded by the consequences of sin."

proper estimate of his place in the history of thought. His
doctrine of the testimony of the Spirit is the keystone of his
doctrine of the knowledge of God. Men endowed by nature
with an ineradicable *sensus deitatis,* which is quickened into
action and informed by a rich revelation of God spread upon
His works and embodied in His deeds, are yet held back from
attaining a sound knowledge of God by the corruption of their
hearts, which dulls their instinctive sense of God and blinds
them to His revelation in works and deeds. That His people
may know Him, therefore, God lovingly intervenes by an objective revelation of Himself in His Word, and a subjective
correction of their sin-bred dullness of apprehension of Him
through the operation of His Spirit in their hearts, which
Calvin calls the Testimony of the Holy Spirit. Obviously it
is only through this testimony of the Holy Spirit that the
revelation of God, whether in works or Word, is given efficacy:
it is God, then, who, through His Spirit, reveals Himself
to His people, and they know Him only as taught by Himself.
But also on this very account the knowledge they have of Him
is trustworthy in its character and complete for its purpose;
being God-given, it is safeguarded to us by the dreadful sanction of deity itself. This being made clear, Calvin has laid a
foundation for the theological structure — the scientific statement and elaboration of the knowledge of God — than which
nothing could be conceived more firm. There remained nothing more for him to do before proceeding at once to draw out
the elements of the knowledge of God as they lie in the revelation so assured to us, except to elucidate the *indicia* by which
the Christian under the influence of the testimony of the
Spirit is strengthened in his confidence that the Scriptures are
the very Word of God, and to repudiate the tendency to neglect these Scriptures so authenticated to us in favor of fancied
continuous revelations of the Spirit. The former he does in a
chapter (chap. viii.) of considerable length and great eloquence, which constitutes one of the fullest and most powerful expositions of the evidence for the divine origin of the
Scriptures which have come down to us from the Reforma-

tion age. The latter he does in a briefer chapter (chap. ix.), of crisp polemic quality, the upshot of which is to leave it strongly impressed on the reader's mind that the whole knowledge of God available to us, as the whole knowledge of God needful for us, lies objectively displayed in the pages of Scripture, which, therefore, becomes the sole source of a sound exposition of the knowledge of God.

This strong statement is not intended, however, to imply that the Spirit-led man can learn nothing from the more general revelation of God in His works and deeds. Calvin is so far from denying the possibility of a " Natural Theology," in this sense of the word, that he devotes a whole chapter (chap. v.) to vindicating the rich revelation of God made in His works and deeds: though, of course, he does deny that any theology worthy of the name can be derived from this natural revelation by the " natural man," that is, by the man the eyes of whose mind and heart are not opened by the Spirit of God — who is not under the influence of the testimony of the Spirit; and in this sense he denies the possibility of a " Natural Theology." What the strong statement in question is intended to convey is that there is nothing to be derived from natural revelation which is not also to be found in Scripture, whether as necessary presupposition, involved implication or clear statement; and that beside that documented in Scripture there is no supernatural revelation accessible to men. The work of the Spirit of God is not to supplement the revelation made in Scripture, far less to supersede it, but distinctively to authenticate it. It remains true, then, that the whole matter of a sound theology lies objectively revealed to us in the pages of Scripture; and this is the main result to which his whole discussion tends. But side by side with it requires to be placed as a result of his discussion secondary only to this, this further conclusion, directly given in his doctrine of the testimony of the Spirit — that only a Christian man can profitably theologize. It is in the union of these two great principles that we find Calvin's view of the bases of a true theology. This he conceives as the product of the systematic investigation and logical elaboration of the contents of Scripture by a mind quickened to the apprehension of these contents through the inward operations of the Spirit of God. It is on this basis and in this spirit that Calvin undertakes his task as a theologian; and what he professes to give us in his "Institutes" is thus, to put it simply, just a Christian man's reading of the Scriptures of God.

The Protestantism of this conception of the task of the theologian is apparent on the face of it. It is probably, however, still worth while to point out that its Protestantism does not lie solely or chiefly in the postulate that the Scriptures are the sole authoritative source of the knowledge of God — "formal principle" of the Reformation though that postulate be, and true, therefore, as Chillingworth's famous declaration that "the Bible and the Bible only is the religion of Protestants" would be, if only Chillingworth had kept it to this sense. It lies more fundamentally still in the postulate that these Scriptures are accredited to us as the revelation of God solely by the testimony of the Holy Spirit — that without this testimony they lie before us inert and without effect on our hearts and minds, while with it they become not merely the power of God unto salvation, but also the vitalizing source of all our knowledge of God. There is embodied in this the true Protestant principle, superior to both the so-called formal and the so-called material principles — both of which are in point of fact but corollaries of it. For it takes the soul completely and forcibly out of the hands of the Church and from under its domination, and casts it wholly upon the grace of God. In its formulation Calvin gave to Protestantism for the first time, accordingly, logical stability and an inward sense of security. Men were no more puzzled by the polemics of Rome when they were asked, You rest on Scripture alone, you say: but on what does your Scripture rest? Calvin's development of the doctrine of the testimony of the Spirit provided them with their sufficient answer: "On the testimony of the Spirit of God in the heart." Here we see the historical importance of Calvin's formulation of this doctrine. And here we see the explanation of the two great facts which reveal its historical importance, the facts, to wit, that Calvin had no predecessors in the formulation of the doctrine, and that at once upon his formulation of it it became the common doctrine of universal Protestantism.

IV. Historical Relations

The search for anticipations of the doctrine of the testimony of the Spirit among the Fathers and Scholastics [80] reveals only such sporadic assertions of the dependence of man on the inward teaching of the Holy Spirit for the knowledge or the saving knowledge of God as could not fail in the speech of a series of Christian men who had read their Bibles. A sentence of this kind from Justin Martyr,[81] another from Chrysostom,[82] two or three from Hilary of Poitiers,[83] almost exhaust

[80] See especially P. Du Moulin, " Du Iuge des controverses traitté," 1636, pp. 294 sq., and cf. Pannier, as cited, pp. 64–68.

[81] " Dialogue with Trypho," vii. (" Opera," ed. Otto. I. ii. 32): οὐ γὰρ συνοπτὰ οὐδὲ ʽσυννοητὰ πᾶσίν ἐστιν, εἰ μή τῳ θεὸς δῷ συνιέναι, καὶ ὁ Χριστὸς αὐτοῦ: " these things cannot be perceived or understood by all, but only by the man to whom God and His Christ have given it to understand them."

[82] " In Cap. v. et vi. Genes. homil. xxi." (Migne, liii. 175): Διάτοι τοῦτο προσήκει ἡμᾶς ὑπὸ τῆς ἄνωθεν χάριτος ὁδηγουμένους, καὶ τὴν παρὰ τοῦ ἁγίου Πνεύματος ἔλλαμψιν δεξαμένους οὕτως ἐπιέναι τὰ θεῖα λόγια. Οὐδὲ γὰρ σοφίας ἀνθρωπίνης δεῖται ἡ θεία Γραφὴ πρὸς τὴν κατανόησιν τῶν γεγραμμένων, ἀλλὰ τῆς τοῦ Πνεύματος ἀποκαλύψεως . . . : " For we must be led by the grace from above, and must receive the illumination of the Holy Spirit, to approach the divine oracles; for it is not human wisdom but the revelation of the Holy Spirit that is needed for understanding the Holy Scriptures." It will be perceived that it is more distinctly the understanding of the Scriptures than the reception of them as from God which is in question with both Justin and Chrysostom.

[83] " De Trinitate," ii. 34: Animus humanus, nisi per fidem donum Spiritus hauserit, habebit quidem naturam Deum intelligendi, sed lumen scientiae non habebit; iii. 24: non enim concipiunt imperfecta perfectum, neque quod ex alio subsistit, absolute vel auctoris sui potest intelligentiam obtinere, vel propriam; v. 21: neque enim nobis ea natura est, ut se in coelestem cognitionem suis viribus efferat. A Deo discendum est quid de Deo intelligendum sit; quia non nisi se auctore cognoscitur. . . . Loquendum ergo non aliter de Deo est, quam ut ipse ad intelligentiam nostram de se locutus est. (For these citations see Migne, " Patro. Lat.," x. 74–75; x. 92; x. 143.) Hilary certainly teaches that for such creatures as men there can be no knowledge of God except it be God-taught: but it is not so clear that he teaches that for sinful

what the first age yields. It is different with Augustine. With
his profound sense of dependence on God and his vital conviction of the necessity of grace for all that is good in man, in
the whole circle of his activities, he could not fail to work out
a general doctrine of the knowledge of God in all essentials
the same as Calvin's. In point of fact, as we have already
pointed out, he did so. There remain, however, some very interesting and some very significant differences between the
two.[84] It is interesting to note, for instance, that where Calvin
speaks of an innate *sensus deitatis* in man, as lying at the root
of all his knowledge of God, Augustine, with a more profound
ontology of this knowledge, as at least made explicit in the
statement, speaks of a continuous reflection of a knowledge of
Himself by God in the human mind.[85] There is here, however,
probably only a difference in fulness of statement, or at most
only of emphasized aspect. On the other hand, it is highly
significant that, instead of Calvin's doctrine of the testimony
of the Spirit, Augustine, in conformity with the stress he laid
upon the " Church " and the " means of grace " in the conference of grace, speaks of the knowledge of God as attainable
only " in the Church." [86] Accordingly, in him also and his successors there are to be found only such anticipations specifically
of the doctrine of the testimony of the Spirit as are afforded
by the increased frequency of their references to the dependence of man for all knowledge of God and divine things on
grace and the inward teaching of the heavenly Instructor. The
voice of men may assail our ears, says Augustine, for instance,
but those remain untaught " to whom that inward unction
does not speak, whom the Holy Spirit does not inwardly

---

creatures there must be a special illapse of the Spirit that such as they may
know God — may perceive Him in His Word and so recognize that Word as
from Him and derive a true knowledge of Him from it. It is this soteriological doctrine which is Calvin's doctrine of the Holy Spirit's testimony:
not that ontological one.

[84] Cf. article: " Augustine's Doctrine of Knowledge and Authority " in
this volume.

[85] *Ibid.*

[86] *Ibid.*

teach ": for " He who teaches the heart has His seat in heaven." [87] Moses himself, yea, even if he spoke to us not in Hebrew but in our own tongue, could convey to us only the knowledge of what he said: of the truth of what he said, only the Truth Himself, speaking within us, in the secret chamber of our thought, can assure us though He speaks neither in Hebrew nor in Greek nor in Latin, nor yet in any tongue of the barbarians, but without organs of voice or tongue and with no least syllabic sound.[88] Further than this men did not get before the Reformation: [89] nor did the first Reformers themselves get further. No doubt they discerned the voice of the Spirit in the Scriptures, as the Fathers did before them; and in a single sentence, written, however, after the " Institutes " of 1539 (viz., in 1555), Melanchthon notes with the Fathers that the mind is " aided in giving its assent " to divine things " by the Holy Spirit." [90] Zwingli here stands on the same plane with his brethren. He strongly repels the Romish establishment of confidence in the Scriptures on the *ipse dixit* of the Church, indeed: and asserts that those who sincerely search the Scriptures are taught by God, and even that none acquire faith in the Word except as drawn by the Father, admonished

[87] " Tract. iii. in Ep. Joan. ad Parthos," ii. 13 (Migne, xxxv. 2004). Again: " There is, then, I say, a Master within that teacheth: Christ teacheth; His inspiration teacheth. Where His inspiration and His unction are not, in vain do words make a noise from without."

[88] " Confessions," xi. 3 (Migne, xxxii. 811). Cf. vi. 5 (Migne, xxxii. 723).

[89] Pannier, *loc. cit.*, says: " The whole of the testimony of the Holy Spirit is not yet here. Only once is the Holy Spirit Himself named [in these passages from Augustine] in a formal way. But Augustine has the intuition of a mysterious work wrought in the soul of the Christian, of an understanding of the Bible which comes not from man but from a power exterior and superior to him; and he sets forth the rôle which this direct correspondence between the book and the reader may play in the foundation of Christian certitude. In this, as in so many other points, Augustine was the precursor of the Reformation, and a precursor without immediate followers: for except a couple of very vague and isolated hints in Salvianus (*De Provid.*, iii. 1) and Gregory the Great († 604, *Homil. in Ezek.*, I. x.), nothing further is found on this subject through ten centuries: it comes into view again at the approach of the new age, when thought aspired to free itself from the Scholastic ruts, with Biel († 1495, *Lib. iii. Sent.* dist. 25, dub. 3) and Cajetan († 1534, *Opera*, II. i. 1)."

[90] " Loci," ed. 1555 (" Corpus Ref.," xxi. 605).

by the Spirit, taught by the unction — as, says he, all pious men have found.[91] But such occasional remarks as this could not fail wherever the Augustinian conception of grace was vitally felt; and show only that the doctrine of the testimony of the Spirit was always implicit in that doctrine.[92]

[91] " De vera et falsa religione ": Cum constet verbo nusquam fidem haberi quam ubi Pater traxit, Spiritus monuit, unctio docuit . . . hanc rem solae piae mentes norunt. Neque enim ab hominum disceptatione pendet, sed in animis hominum tenacissime sedet. Experientia est, nam pii omnes eam experti sunt. " Articles of 1523 " (Niemeyer, " Collectio confessionum in eccles. ref. publ.," 1840, p. 5) : Art. xiii. Verbo Dei quum auscultant homines pure et sinceriter voluntatem Dei discunt. Deinde per Spiritum Dei in Deum trahuntur et veluti transformantur. " Von Klarheit und Gewüsse des Worts Gottes " (" Werke," Schuler und Schulthess, 1828, i. 81; or " Werke " in " Corp. Ref.," i. 382): " The Scriptures . . . came from God, not from man; . . . and the God who has shined into them will Himself give you to understand that their speech comes from God." Cf. the interesting biographical account of how he came to depend on the Scriptures only, on p. 79 (or " Corp. Ref.," i. 379).

[92] E. Rabaud, " Hist. de la doctr. de l'inspiration," etc., 1883, pp. 32–33, 42–43, 47 sq., 50, expounds the earlier Reformers as in principle standing on the doctrine of the testimony of the Spirit. With respect to the interpretation of Scripture he remarks: " The hermeneutical principle of the witness of the Holy Spirit (if we may speak of it as a principle) is common to all the Reformers. Luther only, without being ignorant of it, makes no use of it. Besides responding to the polemic needs, it responded to the aspirations of the faith and of the piety of simple men, better than rational demonstrations " (p. 50, note 4). " In a general way," he remarks, pp. 32–33, " Luther considered the Bible as the sole incontestable and absolute authority. Here is the solid foundation of the edifice, the impregnable citadel in which he shut himself in order to repel victoriously all attacks. It is for him, in truth, a religious axiom, a postulate of faith, and not a dogma or a theory; it is revealed to his believing soul independently of all intellectual activity. Thus Luther, trusting in the action of the Holy Spirit, operating through the Scriptures, does not pause to prove its authority, nor to establish it dialectically: it imposes itself; a systematic treatment is not needed. More and more as circumstances demanded it, he gave reasons for his faith and his submission. Poor arguments to modern thinking, but in his times, and commended by his vibrant eloquence and powerful personality, possessing a power of persuasion very impressive. . . . It seemed idle to Luther, we may say, to enter into an argument to establish what was evident to him. He did not attempt, therefore, to prove the authority of the Bible — he asserted it repeatedly in warm words, . . . in passionate declarations, but rarely if ever proceeds by a formal demonstration." Raising the question of Zwingli's doctrine of the mode and extent of inspiration (p. 47), he remarks: " No more than the others does Zwingli respond to these questions, which had not yet been raised. God has spoken: the Bible contains His word: that is enough. The divinity of

The same remark applies to the first edition of Calvin's "Institutes" (1536) also, though with a difference. This difference — that, if we cannot say that the doctrine of the internal testimony of the Spirit to the divinity of the Scriptures is found there already in germ [93] any more than we can say the same of the Augustinian Fathers, and the criticism passed [94] on the adduction of Melanchthon's single sentence in this reference to the effect that he speaks rather " of the action of the Holy Spirit with reference to the object of faith, that is to say, to the contents of the Word of God " than " with reference to the divinity of the Scriptures themselves," is valid also for Calvin's first edition; yet it is certainly true that the general doctrine of the internal testimony of the Spirit comes much more prominently forward in even the first edition of the "Institutes" than in any preceding treatise of the sort — that much more is made in it than in any of its predecessors of the poverty of the human spirit and the need and actuality of the prevalent influence of the Spirit of God that man may have — whether in knowledge or act — any good thing. We shall have to go back to Augustine to find anything comparable to the conviction and insight with which even in this his earliest work Calvin urges these things. Calvin's whole thought is already dominated by the conception of the powerlessness of the human soul in its sin in all that belongs to the knowledge

---

the Bible is once more a fact, an axiom, so much so that he does not dream of establishing it dialectically or of defending it."

[93] So Pannier, as cited, p. 63: " Like all the other essential parts of the Reformed Dogmatics, the doctrine of the internal testimony of the Holy Spirit is found in germ in the first edition of the *Institutes,* although still without any development. It is almost possible to deny that it exists there, as has been done with predestination. Nevertheless, if the doctrine is not yet scientifically formulated, it may yet be perceived to preëxist necessarily as an essential member of the complete body of doctrine which is slowly to grow up." When Pannier comes, however (pp. 72-77), to expound in detail the germs of the doctrine as they lie in the edition of 1536, it turns out that there is not only no full development of the doctrine in that edition, but also no explicit mention of it, as it is applied to the conviction which the Christian has of the divinity of Scripture; so that it preëxists in this edition only as implicit in its general doctrine of the Spirit and His work.

[94] By Pannier, p. 69.

of God which is salvation, and its entire dependence on the
sovereign operations of the Holy Spirit: and in this sense it
may be said that the chapters in the new "Institutes" of
1539 in which he develops this doctrine of the noëtic effects of
sin and their cure by objective revelation, documented in
Scripture, and subjective illumination wrought by the Holy
Spirit, lay implicitly in his doctrine of man's need and its
cure by the indwelling Spirit which pervades the "Institutes"
of 1536. There he already teaches that the written law was
required by the decay of our consciousness of the law written on the heart; that to know God and His will we have
need to surpass ourselves; that it is the Spirit dwelling in us
that is the source of all our right knowledge of God; and
that it is due to the power of the Spirit alone "that we hear
the word of the Holy Gospel, that we accept it by faith, and
that we abide in this faith" (p. 137, or *Opp.* i. 72). With
eminent directness and simplicity he already there tells us that
"our Lord first teaches and instructs us by His Word; seconda-
rily confirms us by His Sacraments; and thirdly by the light
of His Holy Spirit illuminates our understandings and gives
entrance into our hearts both to the Word and to the Sacraments, which otherwise would only beat upon our ears and
stand before our eyes, without penetrating or operating beneath them" (p. 206, or *Opp.* i. 104). There is, in other words,
very rich teaching in the "Institutes" of 1536 of the entire
dependence of sinful man on the Spirit of God for every sound
religious movement of the soul: but there is no development
of the precise doctrine of the testimony of the Holy Spirit to
the divinity of the Scriptures. It is not merely that the term
testimonium Spiritus Sancti does not occur in this early draft,
or occurs only once, and then not in this sense: [95] it is that the

[95] Pannier, as cited, p. 77, notes that "the words: *testimonio Spiritus
Sancti* occur only a single time, at the end, and in the old sense of — 'by the
divinely inspired Scriptures.'" He refers to the ed. of 1536, p. 470, that is,
Opp. i. 228: and notes that this passage was dropped in the edition of 1559
(*Opp.* iv. 796, note 5). The passage runs: "Thus Hezekiah is praised *by the
testimony of the Holy Spirit*" — that is, obviously, "by the inspired Scriptures" — "for having broken up the brazen serpent which Moses had made
by Divine command."

thing is not explicated and is present only as implicated in the general doctrine of grace, which is very purely conceived.

It was left, then, to the edition of 1539 to create the whole doctrine at, as it were, a single stroke.[96] For, as we have already had occasion to note, Calvin's whole exposition of the doctrine of the testimony of the Spirit to the divinity of Scripture appears all at once in its completeness in the second edition of the "Institutes," the first edition which he issued as a textbook on theology, that of 1539. This exposition was reproduced without curtailment or alteration in all subsequent editions, and is thereby given the great endorsement of Calvin's permanent approval: while the additions which are made to it in the progressive expansion of the treatise, while large in amount, are devoted to guarding it from the misapprehension that the necessity it asserted for the testimony of the Spirit in any way detracted from the objective value of the *indicia* of the divinity of Scripture, rather than to modifying the positive doctrine expounded. The additions within the limits of chapter vii. consist essentially of the insertion of the discussion of Augustine's doctrine in § 3 and of the caveat with reference to the underestimation of the *indicia* in § 4, while practically the whole of chapter viii. — all except the opening sentence — is of later origin. If we will omit the first sentence of chapter vii., the whole of §§ 3 and 4, with the exception of the sentence near the beginning of the latter, which begins: " Now if we wish to consult the true intent of our conscience " — and the beginning and end of § 5, retaining only the central passage beginning: " For though it conciliate our reverence . . ." down to the words: " Superior to the power of any human will or knowledge," and also the two striking sentences, beginning with: " It is such a persuasion " and ending with " a just ex-

[96] Köstlin, as cited, p. 411, strongly states these facts. The whole of the discussion on the sources and norms of religious truth " is altogether lacking in the original form " of the " Institutes ": " Calvin worked out this section for the first time for the edition of 1539 ": but it is found here already thoroughly done, " in all its fundamental traits already complete and mature." He adds that the Lutheran dogmatists (as well as the Reformed) at once, however, took up the construction of Calvin and made it their own.

plication of the subject" — we shall have substantially the
text of the edition of 1539, needing only to add the two opening sentences of chapter viii. and the major part of chapter
ix. It will at once be seen that the edition of 1539 contains the
entire positive exposition of the doctrine of the testimony of
the Spirit as retained by Calvin to the end.

The formulation of this principle of the testimony of the
Spirit by Calvin in 1539 had an extraordinary effect both immediate and permanent.[97] Universal Protestantism perceived
in it at sight the pure expression of the Protestant principle
and the sheet-anchor of its position. The Lutherans as well as
the Reformed adopted it at once and made it the basis not
only of their reasoned defence of Protestantism, but also of
their structure of Christian doctrine and of their confidence
in Christian living.[98] To it they both continued to cling so
long and so far as they continued faithful to the Protestant
principle itself. It has given way only as the structure of Protestantism has itself given way in reaction to the Romish position, or, more widely, as the structure of Christian thought has
given way in rationalizing disintegration. No doubt it has
undergone at the hands of its various expounders, from time to
time, more or less modification, and in its journeyings to the

[97] The history of the doctrine among the Reformed is touched on by
A. Schweizer, "Glaubenslehre," i. § 32; among the old Lutherans by Klaiber,
"Die Lehre der altprotestantischen Dogmatiker von dem test. Sp. Sancti" in
the *Jahrbücher für d. Theologie*, 1857, pp. 1–54. Its history among French
theologians is traced by Pannier, as cited, Part iii. pp. 139–181, cf. 186–193:
his notes on the history outside of France (pp. 181–185) are very slight. On
pp. 161–163 Pannier essays to gather together, chiefly, as it appears, from the
scattered citations in the Protestant controversialists of the seventeenth century (p. 162, note 2), the hints which appear in the Romish writers, mainly
Jesuits of the early seventeenth century, of recognition of the internal work
of the Holy Spirit illuminating the soul. These bear more or less resemblance
to the Protestant doctrine of the testimony of the Spirit. Some of the passages he cites are quite striking, but do not go beyond the common boundaries of universal Christian supernaturalism.

[98] In his brief remarks on the subject in his "Dogmengeschichte des Protestantismus," i. 1908, pp. 178 *sq.*, Otto Ritschl seeks to discriminate between
the Reformed and Lutherans in their conception of the testimony of the
Spirit; but his discrimination touches rather the application than the essence
of the matter.

ends of the earth, has suffered now and again some sea-change — sometimes through sheer misapprehension, sometimes through sheer misrepresentation, sometimes through more or less admixture of both. A spurious revival of the doctrine was, for example, set on foot by Schleiermacher in his strong revulsion from the cold rationalism which had so long reigned in Germany to a more vital religious faith; and sentences may be quoted from his writings which, when removed out of the context of his system of thought, almost give expression to it.[99] But after all, his revival of it was rather the revival of sub-

[99] Some of them are cited, e.g., by Schweizer, *op. cit.*, followed, e.g., by Pannier, as cited (p. 186, note 1) — such as: " Faith is already presupposed when a peculiar authority is conceded to Scripture," — " The recognition of what is canonical comes into existence only gradually and progressively, since the sense for the truly Apostolic is a gracious gift which grows up only gradually in the Church," — " Faith cannot be established in unbelievers by the Scriptures, so that their divine authority is in the first instance proved from merely rational considerations." — There is much that is true and well said in such remarks, and they enrich the writings of Schleiermacher and his followers with a truly spiritual element. But at bottom the central position occupied is vitiated by the use of " faith " as an " undistributed middle," and the remarks of writers of this type do not so much tend to exalt the place of saving faith as to depress the authority of Scripture, by practically denying the existence or validity of *fides humana*. That attitude towards the Scriptures which gladly and heartily recognizes them as the Word of the Living God, and with all delight in them as such, seeks to subject all thought and feeling and action to their direction, certainly is, if not exactly a product of " true faith," yet (as the Westminster Confession defines it) an exercise of true faith, and a product of that inward creative operation of the Holy Spirit from which all true faith comes: that keen taste for the divine which is the outgrowth of the spiritual gift of discrimination — the " distinguishing of things that differ " which Paul gives a place among Christian graces — is assuredly a " gift of grace " which may grow more and more strong as the Christian life effloresces; and such a taste for the divine cannot be awakened in unbelievers by the natural action of the Scriptures or any rational arguments whatever, but requires for its production the work of the Spirit of God *ab extra accidens*. But it is a totally different question whether the peculiarity of Scripture as a divine revelation can call out no intellectual recognition in the minds of inquiring men, but must remain wholly hidden and produce no mental reaction conformable to its nature, until true faith has already been born in the heart: whether there are no valid tests of what is apostolical except a spiritual sense for the truly apostolical which can only gradually grow up in the Church; whether the unbeliever may not be given a well-grounded intellectual conviction of the apostolic origin, the canonical author-

jectivity in religion than of the doctrine of the testimony of the Spirit as the basis of all faith: and it has borne bitter fruit in a widespread subjectivism, the mark of which is that it discards (as " external ") the authority of those very Scriptures to which the testimony of the Spirit is borne. Not in such circles is the continued influence of the doctrine of the testimony of the Spirit to be sought or its continued advocacy to be found. If we would see it in its purity in the modern Church we must look for it in the hands of true successors of Calvin — in the writings, to name only men of our own time, of William Cunningham [100] and Charles Hodge [101] and Abraham Kuyper [102] and Herman Bavinck.[103]

As we have already had occasion to note, the principle of the testimony of the Spirit as the true basis of our confidence in the Scriptures as the Word of God was almost from the hands of Calvin himself incorporated into the Reformed Creeds. We have already pointed out the sharpness and strength of its expression in the Gallican (1557–1571) and Belgian (1501–1571)

---

ity, and the divine character of Scripture by the presentation to him of rational evidence which, however unwillingly on his part, will compel his assent. The question here is not whether this *fides humana* is of any great use in the spiritual life: the question is whether it is possible and actual. We may argue, if we will, that it is not worth while to awake it — though opinions may differ there: but how can we argue that it is a thing inherently impossible? To say this is not merely to say that reason cannot save, which is what Calvin said and all his followers: it is to say that salvation is intrinsically unreasonable — which neither Calvin nor any of his true followers could for a moment allow. Sin may harden the heart so that it will not admit, weigh, or yield to evidence: but sin, which affects only the heart subjectively, and not the process of reasoning objectively, cannot alter the relations of evidence to conclusions. Sin does not in the least degree affect the cogency of any rightly constructed syllogism. No man, no doubt, was ever reasoned into the kingdom of heaven: it is the Holy Spirit alone who can translate us into the kingdom of God's dear Son. But there are excellent reasons why every man should enter the kingdom of heaven; and these reasons are valid in the forum of every rational mind, and their validity can and should be made manifest to all.

100 " Theological Lectures," etc., New York, 1878, pp. 317, 320 *sq.*
101 " The Way of Life," 1841; also " Systematic Theology," as per Index.
102 " Encyclopædie, etc.," ii. 1894, pp. 505 *sqq.*
103 " Gereformeerde Dogmatiek," ed. 1, i. pp. 142–145, 420–422, 490–491.

Confessions, and it finds at least the expression of suggestion in the Second Helvetic Confession (1562). It was not, however, merely into the Confessions of the Reformation age that it was incorporated. It is given an expression as clear as it is prudent, as decided as it is comprehensive, in that confession of their faith which the persecuted Waldenses issued after the massacres of 1655; [104] and it is incorporated into the Westminster Confession of Faith (1646) in perhaps the best and most balanced statement it has ever received — the phraseology of which is obviously derived in large part from Calvin, either directly or through the intermediation of George Gillespie,[105]

[104] Written, no doubt, by Léger, moderator at the time of "the Table," and preserved for us in his "Histoire générale des églises évangéliques des vallées de Piédmont," 1669, i. p. 112 (cf. p. 92). See Pannier, as cited, p. 133.

[105] Dr. A. F. Mitchell ("The Westminster Assembly, its History and Standards," the Baird Lecture for 1882, ed. 2, 1897, p. 441, note), following Prof. J. S. Candlish (Brit. and For. Ev. Rev., 1877, p. 173), is "very sure" that Gillespie has here "left his mark on the Confession." The "Miscellany Questions," in the xxi. of which occurs the passage from Gillespie from which the Confession is supposed to have drawn, was a posthumous work, published in 1649; but a number of the papers of which it is made up have the appearance of being briefs drawn up by Gillespie for his own satisfaction, or as preparations for speeches, or possibly even as papers handed in to committees, during the discussions of the Westminster Assembly. The language in question, however, whether in Gillespie or in the Confession, is so strongly reminiscent of Calvin, that the possibility seems to remain open that the resemblance between Gillespie and the Confession is due to their common relation to Calvin. Here is the passage in Gillespie ("Presbyterian Armoury" ed., vol. ii. pp. 105–106): "The Scripture is known to be indeed the Word of God by the beams of divine authority it hath in itself, and by certain distinguishing characters, which do infallibly prove it to be the Word of God; such as the heavenliness of the matter; the majesty of the style; the irresistible power over the conscience; the general scope, to abase man and to exalt God; nothing driven at but God's glory and man's salvation; the extraordinary holiness of the penmen of the Holy Ghost, without respect to any particular interests of their own, or of others of their nearest relations (which is manifest by their writings); the supernatural mysteries revealed therein, which could never have entered into the reason of men; the marvellous consent of all parts and passages (though written by divers and several penmen), even where there is some appearance of difference; the fulfilling of prophecies; the miracles wrought by Christ, by the prophets and apostles; the conservation of the Scriptures against the malice of Satan and fury of persecutors; — these and the like are characters and marks which evidence the Scriptures to be the Word of God; yet all these cannot beget in the soul a full persua-

but the substance of which was but the expression of the firmly held faith of the whole body of the framers of that culminating Confession of the Reformed Churches.

"We recognize the divinity of these sacred books," says the Waldensian Confession (chap. iv.), "not only through the

---

sion of faith that the Scriptures are the Word of God; this persuasion is from the Holy Ghost in our hearts. And it hath been the common resolution of sound Protestant writers (though now called in question by the sceptics of this age [the allusion being to "Mr. J. Godwin in his Hagiomastix"]) that these arguments and infallible characters in the Scripture itself, which most certainly prove it to be the Word of God, cannot produce a certainty of persuasion in our hearts, but this is done by the Spirit of God within us, according to these Scriptures, I Cor. ii. 10–15; I Thes. i. 5; I John ii. 27; v. 6–8, 10; John vi. 45."—Whatever may be the immediate source of the Confessional statement, Calvin is clearly the real source of Gillespie's statement.—For the essence of the matter Gillespie's discussion is notably clear and exact, particularly with reference to the relation of the *indicia* to the testimony of the Spirit, a matter which he strangely declares had not to his knowledge been discussed before. The clarity of his determinations here is doubtless due to the specific topic which he is in this Question investigating, viz., the validity of the argument from marks and fruits of sanctification to our interest in Christ: a parallel question in the broader soteriological sphere to the place of *indicia* in our conviction of the divinity of Scripture, which he therefore uses illustratively for his main problem. "It may be asked," he remarks, "and it is a question worthy to be looked into (though I must confess I have not read it, nor heard it, handled before), How doth this assurance by marks agree with or differ from assurance by the testimony of the Holy Spirit? May the soul have assurance either way, or must there be a concurrence of both (for I suppose they are not one and the same thing) to make up the assurance?" (p. 105). He proves that they are "not one and the same thing"; and then shows solidly that for assurance there "must be a concurrence of both." "To make no trial by marks," he says, "and to trust an inward testimony, under the notion of the Holy Ghost's testimony, when it is without the least evidence of any true gracious marks, this way (of its own nature, and intrinsically, or in itself) is a deluding and ensnaring of the conscience" (p. 105). That is to say, a blind confidence and conviction, without cognizable grounds in evidence cannot be trusted. Again and very clearly: "So that, in the business of assurance and full persuasion, the evidences of graces and the testimony of the Spirit, are two concurrent causes or helps, both of them necessary. Without the evidence of graces, it is not a safe nor a well-grounded assurance" (p. 106). It remains only to add that while arguing this out in the wider soteriological sphere, Gillespie appears to take it as a matter of course in the accrediting of the Scriptures as divine—giving that case, in the course of his argument, as an illustration to aid in determining his conclusion.

testimony of the Church, but principally through the eternal and indubitable truth of the doctrine which is contained in them, through the excellence, sublimity, and majesty of the pure divinity (*du tout divine*) which are apparent in them, and through the operation of the Holy Spirit which makes us receive with deference the testimony which the Church gives to them, which opens our eyes to receive the rays of the celestial light which shines in the Scriptures, and so corrects our taste that we discern this food by the divine savor which it possesses." The dependence of this fine statement on Calvin's exposition is evident; but what is most striking about it is the clarity with which it conceives and the fulness with which it expounds the exact mode of working of the testimony of the Spirit and its relation to the *indicia* of divinity in Scripture, through which, and not apart from or in opposition to which, it performs its work. So far from supposing that the witness of the Spirit is of the nature of a new and independent revelation from heaven or works only a blind faith in us, setting thus aside all evidences of the divinity of Scripture, external and internal alike, this careful statement particularly explains that our faith in the divinity of Scripture rests, under the testimony of the Spirit, on these evidences as its ground, but not on these evidences by themselves, but on them as apprehended by a Spirit-led mind and heart — the work of the Spirit consisting in so dealing with our spirit that these evidences are, under His influence, perceived and felt in their real bearing and full strength.

An even more notable statement of the whole doctrine is that incorporated into the Westminster Confession (i. 4, 5), and in a more compressed form into the Larger Catechism (Q. 4). "The authority of the Holy Scripture, for which it ought to be believed and obeyed," says the Confession, " dependeth not upon the testimony of any man or church, but wholly upon God (who is truth itself) the author thereof; and therefore it is to be received, because it is the Word of God. We may be moved and induced by the testimony of the Church to a high and reverent esteem of the Holy Scripture;

and the heavenliness of the matter, the efficacy of the doctrine, the majesty of the style, the consent of all the parts, the scope of the whole (which is to give all glory to God), the full discovery it makes of the only way of man's salvation, the many other incomparable excellencies, and the entire perfection thereof, are arguments whereby it doth abundantly evidence itself to be the Word of God; yet notwithstanding, our full persuasion and assurance of the infallible truth, and divine authority thereof, is from the inward work of the Holy Spirit, bearing witness by and with the Word in our heart." In the Larger Catechism this is reduced to the form: " The Scriptures manifest themselves to be the Word of God, by their majesty and purity; by the consent of all the parts, and the scope of the whole, which is to give all glory to God; by their light and power to convince and convert sinners, to comfort and build up believers unto salvation; but the Spirit of God bearing witness by and with the Scriptures in the heart of man, is alone able fully to persuade it that they are the very Word of God." The fundamental excellence of this remarkable statement (for the full understanding of which what is said of " faith " in chapter xiv. of the Confession and Question 72 of the Catechism should be compared with it — just as Calvin referred his readers to his later discussion of " faith " for further information on the topic of the testimony of the Spirit) is the care with which the several grounds on which we recognize the Scriptures to be from God are noted and their value appraised, and that yet the supreme importance of the witness of the Spirit is safe-guarded.[106] The external testimony of the Church is noted and its value pointed out: it moves and induces us to a high and reverent esteem for Scripture. The internal testimony of the characteristics of the Scriptures themselves is noted and its higher value pointed out: they " abundantly evidence " or " manifest " the Scriptures " to be the

---

[106] For the meaning of the Confession's statement, supported by illustrative excerpts from its authors, see *The Presbyterian and Reformed Review*, iv. 1893, pp. 624–32; and cf. W. Cunningham, " Theological Lectures," New York, 1878, pp. 320 *sq.*, and *The Presbyterian Quarterly*, January, 1894, pp. 19 *sq.*

Word of God." The need and place of the testimony of the Spirit is then pointed out in the presence of this "abundant evidencing" or "manifesting": it is not to add new evidence — which is not needed — but to secure deeper conviction — which is needed; and not independently of the Word with its evidencing characteristics, but "by and with the Word" or "the Scriptures." What this evidence of the Spirit does is "*fully* to persuade us" that "the Scriptures are the very Word of God," — to work in us "*full* persuasion and assurance of the infallible truth and divine authority" of the Word of God. It is a matter of completeness of conviction, not of grounds of conviction; and the testimony of the Spirit works, therefore, not by adding additional grounds of conviction, but by an inward work on the heart, enabling it to react upon the already "abundant evidence" with a really "full persuasion and assurance." Here we have the very essence of Calvin's doctrine, almost in his own words, and with even more than his own eloquence and precision of statement.

What Calvin has given to the Reformed Churches, therefore, in his formulation of the doctrine of the Testimony of the Spirit is a fundamental doctrine, which has been as such expounded by the whole body of their theologians, and incorporated into the fabric of their public Confessions, so that it has been made and continues to be until to-day the officially declared faith of the Reformed Churches in France and Holland, Switzerland, Italy, Scotland, and America, wherever the fundamental Reformed Creeds are still professed.

III

CALVIN'S DOCTRINE OF GOD

CALVIN'S DOCTRINE OF GOD [1]

HAVING expounded in the opening chapters of the " Institutes " the sources and means of the knowledge of God, Calvin naturally proceeds in the next series of chapters (I. x. xi. xii. xiii.) to set forth the nature of the God who, by the revelation of Himself in His Word and by the prevalent internal operation of His Spirit, frames the knowledge of Himself in the hearts of His people. He who expects to find in these chapters, however, an orderly discussion of the several topics which make up the *locus de Deo* in our formal dogmatics, will meet with disappointment. Calvin is not writing out of an abstract scientific impulse, but with the needs of souls, and, indeed, also with the special demands of the day in mind. And as his purpose is distinctively religious, so his method is literary rather than scholastic. In the freedom of his literary manner, he had permitted himself in the preceding chapters repeated excursions into regions which, in an exact arrangement of the material, might well have been reserved for exploration at this later point. To take up these topics again, now, for fuller and more orderly exposition, would involve much repetition without substantially advancing the practical purpose for which the " Institutes " were written. Calvin was not a man to confound formal correctness of arrangement with substantial completeness of treatment; nor was he at a loss for new topics of pressing importance for discussion. He skillfully interposes at this point, therefore, a short chapter (chap. x.) in which under the form of pointing out the complete harmony with the revelation of God in nature of the revelation of God in the Scriptures — the divine authority of which in the communication of the knowledge of God he had just demonstrated — he reminds his readers of all that he had formerly said of the nature

1 From *The Princeton Theological Review,* vii. 1909, pp. 381–436.

and attributes of God on the basis of natural revelation, and takes occasion to say what it remained necessary to say of the same topics on the basis of supernatural revelation. Thus he briefly but effectively brings together under the reader's eye the whole body of his exposition of these topics and frees his hands to give himself, under the guidance of his practical bent and purpose, to the two topics falling under the rubric of the doctrine of God which were at the moment of the most pressing importance. His actual formal treatment of the doctrine of God thus divides itself into two parts, the former of which (chaps. xi. xii.), in strong Anti-Romish polemic is devoted to the uprooting of every refuge of idolatry, while the latter (chap. xiii.), in equally strong polemic against the Anti-trinitarianism of the day, develops with theological acumen and vital faith the doctrine of Trinity in Unity.

It is quite true, then, as has often been remarked, that the "Institutes" contain no systematic discussion of the existence, the nature, and the attributes of God.[2] And the lack of formal, systematic discussion of these fundamental topics, may, no doubt, be accounted a flaw, if we are to conceive the "Institutes" as a formal treatise in systematic theology. But it is not at all true that the "Institutes" contain no sufficient indication of Calvin's conceptions on these subjects: nor is it possible to refer the absence of formal discussion of them

---

[2] Cf. Köstlin, "Calvin's Institutio," etc., in *Studien und Kritiken*, 1868, i. pp. 61–2: "On the other hand — and this is for us the most important matter, — there is not given there any comprehensive exposition of the attributes, especially not of the ethical attributes of God, nor is any such afterwards attempted." Again, iii. p. 423: "We cannot present and follow out the doctrine of the *Institutio* on the divine nature and the divine attributes, and their relations, as a whole, as we can its doctrine of the Trinity, because Calvin himself, as we have mentioned already, has nowhere presented them as a whole." Cf. also P. J. Muller, "De Godsleer van Zwingli en Calvijn," 1883, p. 11: "Neither by Zwingli nor by Calvin are there offered proofs of the existence of God" (cf. p. 16). Again, "De Godsleer van Calvijn," 1881, p. 26: "A doctrine of the nature of God as such we do not find in Calvin." *Ibid.*, p. 38: "We find nowhere in Calvin a special section which is devoted particularly to the treatment of God's attributes"; "since he gives no formal doctrine of the attributes, we find in him also no classification of the attributes."

either to indifference to them on Calvin's part or to any peculiarity of his dogmatic standpoint,[3] or even of his theological method.[4] The omission belongs rather to the peculiarity of this treatise as a literary product. Calvin does not pass over all systematic discussion of the existence, nature, and attributes of God because from his theological standpoint there was nothing to say upon these topics, nor because, in his theological method, they were insignificant for his system; but simply because he had been led already to say informally about them all that was necessary for the religious, practical purpose he had in view in writing this treatise. For here as elsewhere the key to the understanding of the " Institutes " lies in recognizing their fundamental purpose to have been religious, and their whole, not coloring merely, but substance, to be profoundly religious — in this only reflecting indeed the most determinative trait of Calvin's character.

It is important to emphasize this, for there seems to be still an impression abroad that Calvin's nature was at bottom cold and hard and dry, and his life-manifestation but a piece of incarnated logic: while the " Institutes " themselves are frequently represented, or rather misrepresented — it is difficult to believe that those who so speak of them can have read them — as a body of purely formal reasoning by which intolerable conclusions are remorselessly deduced from a set of metaphysical assumptions.[5] Perhaps M. Ferdinand Brune-

[3] As Köstlin, for example, has suggested, as cited, p. 423, followed by P. J. Muller in his earlier work, " De Godsleer van Calvijn," 1881, pp. 10, 46.

[4] So P. J. Muller expresses himself in his later volume — " De Godsleer van Zwingli en Calvijn," 1883, p. 46 — modifying his earlier view: " Köstlin asks if it does not belong to Calvin's dogmatic standpoint that he does not venture to seek after a bond between the several elements which come forward in God's many-sided relation to men. This question can undoubtedly be answered in the affirmative, although we should rather speak here of the peculiarity of Calvin's *method*." That is to say, Muller here prefers to refer the phenomenon in question to Calvin's *a posteriori* method rather than to his theological standpoint.

[5] André Duran, " Le Mysticisme de Calvin," 1900, p. 8, justly says: " The *Institutes* are remarkable precisely for this: the absence of speculation. It is especially with the heart that Calvin studies God in His relations with men; and it is by the heart that he attains to complete union of man with God."

tiere may be looked upon as a not unfair representative of the
class of writers who are wont so to speak of the "Institutes." [6]
According to him, Calvin has "intellectualized" religion and
reduced it to a form which can appeal only to the "reasonable," or rather to the "reasoning" man. "In that oratorical
work which he called *The Institutes*," M. Brunetière says,
"if there is any movement . . . it is not one which comes
from the heart . . . and — I am speaking here only of the
writer or the religious theorizer, not of the man — the insensi-
bility of Calvin is equalled only by the rigor of his reasoning.
. . ." The religion Calvin sets forth is "a religion which consists essentially, almost exclusively, in the adhesion of the intellect to truths all but demonstrated," and commends itself
by nothing "except by the literalness of its agreement with a
text — which is a matter of pure philology — and by the solid-
ity of its logical edifice — which is nothing but a matter of pure
reasoning." To Calvin, he adds, "religious truth attests itself
in no other manner and by no other means than mathematical
truth. As he would reason on the properties of a triangle, or of
a sphere, so Calvin reasons on the attributes of God. All that
will not adjust itself to the exigencies of his dialectic, he contests or he rejects . . . Cartesian before Descartes, rational
evidence, logical incontradiction are for him the test or the
proof of truth. He would not believe if faith did not stay itself
on a formal syllogism. . . . From a 'matter of the heart,' if
I may so say, Calvin transformed religion into an 'affair of
the intellect.'"

We must not fail to observe, in passing, that even M. Brunetière refrains from attributing to Calvin's person the hard in-
sensibility which he represents as the characteristic of his religious writings — a tribute, we may suppose, to the religious
impression which is made by Calvin's personality upon all

For a satisfactory discussion of the "heart in Calvin's theology" see E. Doumergue, "Jean Calvin," etc., iii. 1905, pp. 560–563. Compare also the third address in Doumergue's "L'Art et le sentiment dans l'oeuvre de Calvin," Geneva,
1902.

[6] "Discours de combat," 1903, pp. 135–140.

who come into his presence, and which led even M. Ernest Renan, who otherwise shares very largely M. Brunetière's estimate of him, to declare him "the most Christian man of his age."[7] Nor can we help suspecting that the violence of the invectives launched against the remorseless logic of the "Institutes" and of Calvin's religious reasoning in general, is but the index of the difficulty felt by M. Brunetière and those who share his point of view, in sustaining themselves against the force of Calvin's argumentative presentation of his religious conceptions. It is surely no discredit to a religious reasoner that his presentation commends his system irresistibly to all "reasonable," or let us even say "reasoning" men. A religious system which cannot sustain itself in the presence of "reasonable" or "reasoning" men, is not likely to remain permanently in existence, or at least in power among reasonable or reasoning men; and one would think that the logical irresistibility of a system of religious truth would be distinctly a count in its favor. The bite of M. Brunetière's assault is found, therefore, purely in its negative side. He would condemn Calvin's system of religion as nothing but a system of logic; and the "Institutes," the most systematic presentation of it, as in essence nothing but a congeries of syllogisms, issuing in nothing but a set of logical propositions, with no religious quality or uplift in them. In this, however, he worst of all misses the mark; and we must add he was peculiarly unfortunate in fixing, in illustration of his meaning, on the two matters of the "attributes of God" as the point of departure for Calvin's dialectic and of the intellectualizing of "faith" as the height of his offending.

In Calvin's treatment of faith there is nothing more striking than his determination to make it clear that it is a matter not of the understanding but of the heart; and he reproaches

[7] "Études d'histoire religieuse," ed. 7, 1864, p. 342: "l'homme le plus chrétien de son siècle." It must be borne in mind that this is not very high praise on M. Renan's lips; and was indeed intended by him to be depreciatory. We need not put an excessive estimate on Calvin's greatness, he says in effect; he lived in an age of reaction towards Christianity and he was the most Christian man of his age: his preëminence is thus accounted for.

the Romish conception of faith precisely because it magnifies the intellectual side to the neglect of the fiducial. " We must not suppose," it is said in the Confession of Faith drawn up for the Genevan Church,[8] either by himself or by his colleagues under his eye, " that Christian faith is a naked and mere knowledge of God or understanding of the Scriptures, which floats in the brain without touching the heart. . . . It is a firm and solid confidence of the heart." Or, as he repeats this elsewhere,[9] " It is an error to suppose that faith is a naked and cold knowledge.[10] . . . Faith is not a naked knowledge,[11] which floats in the brain, but draws with it a living affection of the heart." [12] " True Christian faith," he expounds in the second edition of the " Institutes," [13] . . . " is not content with a simple historical knowledge, but takes its seat in the heart of man." " It does not suffice that the understanding should be illuminated by the Spirit of God if the heart be not strengthened by His power. In this matter the theologians of the Sorbonne very grossly err, — thinking that faith is a simple consent to the Word of God, which consists in understanding, and leaving out the confidence and assurance of the heart." " What the understanding has received must be planted in the heart. For if the Word of God floats in the head only, it has not yet been received by faith; it has its true reception only when it has taken root in the depths of the heart." Again, to cite a couple of passages in which the less pungent statement of the earlier editions has been given new point and force in the final edition of the " Institutes ": " It must here be again observed," says he,[14] " that we are invited to the knowledge of

[8] " Instruction et confession de foy dont on use en l'eglise de Genève " (Opp. xxii. 47). The Strasburg editors assign it to Calvin's colleagues; Doumergue (" Jean Calvin," ii. 1902, pp. 236–251) to Calvin.

[9] " Vera Christianae pacificationis et ecclesiae reformandae ratio," 1549 (Opp. vii. 598–600).

[10] nudam frigidamque notitiam.

[11] nudam notitiam.

[12] vivum affectum qui cordi insideat.

[13] Ed. of 1539: the quotations are made from the French version of 1541, pp. 189, 202, 204. See Opp. iii. 15, 53, 57.

[14] I. v. 9.

God — not a knowledge which, content with empty speculation, floats only in the brain, but one which shall be solid and fruitful, if rightly received by us, and rooted in the heart." " The assent we give to God," he says again,[15] " as I have already indicated and shall show more largely later — is rather of the heart than of the brain, and rather of the affections than of the understanding." [16] It is quite clear, then, that Calvin did not consciously address himself merely to the securing of an intellectual assent to his teaching, but sought to move men's hearts. His whole conception of religion turned, indeed, on this: religion, he explained, to be pleasing to God, must be a matter of the heart,[17] and God requires in His worshippers precisely heart and affection.[18] All the arguments in the world, he insists, if unaccompanied by the work of the Holy Spirit on the heart, will fail to produce the faith which piety requires.[19]

This scarcely sounds like a man to whom religion was simply a matter of logical proof.

And so far is he from making the attributes of God, metaphysically determined, the starting-point of a body of teaching deduced from them by quasi-mathematical reasoning — as one would deduce the properties of a triangle from its nature as a triangle — that it has been made his reproach that he has so little to say of the divine nature and attributes, and in this little confines himself so strictly to the manifest *indicia* of God in His works and the direct teaching of Scripture, refusing utterly to follow " the high priori " road either in determining the divine attributes or from them determining the divine activities. Thus, his doctrine of God is, it is said, no doubt notably sober and restrained, but also, when compared with Zwingli's, for example — equally notably unimportant.[20]

---

[15] III. ii. 8.

[16] Cordis esse magis quam cerebri, et affectus magis quam intelligentiae.

[17] fidem et veritatem cordis.

[18] cor et animum (*Opp.* vi. 477, 479).

[19] I. vii. 4.

[20] Cf. P. J. Muller, " De Godsleer van Zwingli en Calvijn," 1883, p. 111: " A theologian like Calvin, Zwingli was not; but still in the history of the doctrine of God the pages devoted to Zwingli are more important than

It is confessed, however, that it is at least thoroughly religious; and in this is found, indeed, its fundamental characteristic. Precisely where Calvin's doctrine differs from Zwingli's markedly is that he constantly contemplated God religiously, while Zwingli contemplated him philosophically — that to him God was above and before all things the object of religious reverence, while to Zwingli he was predominatingly the First Cause, from whom all things proceed.[21] " It is not with the doctrine of God," says the historian whose representations we have been summarizing, " but with the *worship* of God that Calvin's first concern was engaged. Even in his doctrine of God — as we may perceive from his remarks upon it — religion

those devoted to Calvin. The *loci de Trinitate, de Creatione,* and *de Lapso* apart, Zwingli's system is undeniably more coherent than that of Calvin, in which we miss the bond by which the several parts are joined. On the other hand, however, we miss in Zwingli's doctrine of God precisely what constitutes the value of a doctrine of God for the *theologian,* that is to say, its religious character. We do not find in Zwingli as in Calvin a recoil from the consequences of his own reasoning, which leads necessarily to the ascription to God of the origination of evil, or sin, just because God is *not* with him as with Calvin conceived above everything as the object of religious reverence, but rather as the object of speculative thought."

[21] Cf. P. J. Muller, " De Godsleer van Zwingli en Calvijn," 1883, p. 6: " If the doctrine of God for the theologian is determined by its religious character, the contemplation of God as the object of religious reverence will take a higher place with him than the merely philosophical contemplation of God as the ultimate cause. Since it is not to be denied — as the following exposition will show — that with Zwingli God is speculatively contemplated much more as the ultimate cause than as the object of religious reverence, we may conclude that — so far as religious value is concerned — Zwingli's doctrine of God must be ranked below Calvin's." Again (p. 21): " In the nature of the case Calvin's conceptions of the nature of God must be very sober. For to him, God was very predominantly the object of religious reverence, and he could not therefore do otherwise than disapprove of the attempt to penetrate into the nature of the Godhead (I. v. 9). With Zwingli, on the contrary, in whose system God is preëminently conceived as the ultimate cause, the doctrine of the nature of God must form one of the most important sections of the doctrine of God." Once more (p. 23): " Calvin, whose pride it was to be a 'Biblical theologian,' does not follow the method of the philosophers, — the aprioristic method. He is therefore sober in his conceptions of the nature of God, since he had noted that in the Scriptures God speaks little of His nature, that He may teach us sobriety " — quoting I. xiii. 1: *ut nos in sobrietate contineat, parce de sua essentia [Deus] disserit.*

stands ever in the foreground (I. ii. 1). Before everything else Calvin is a religious personality. The Reformation confronts Catholicism with a zeal to live for God. With striking justice Calvin remarked that 'all alike engaged in the worship of God, but few really reverenced Him, — that there was everywhere great ostentation in ceremonies but sincerity of heart was rare' (I. ii. 2). *Reverence* for God was the great thing for Calvin. If we lose sight of this a personality like Calvin cannot be understood; and it is only by recognizing the religious principle by which he was governed, that a just judgment can be formed of his work as a dogmatician. . . ." [22] Again, Calvin " considers the knowledge of the nature and of the attributes of God more a matter of the heart than of the understanding; and such a knowledge, he says, must not only arouse us to ' the service of God, but must also awake in us the hope of a future life ' (I. v. 10). In his extreme practicality — as the last remark shows us — Calvin rejected the philosophical treatment of the question. The Scriptures, for him the source of the knowledge of God, he takes as his guide in his remarks on the attributes. . . ." [23] Still again, " Already more than once have we had occasion to note that when Calvin treats of God, he does this as a *believer,* for whom the existence of God stands as a fixed fact; and what he says of God, he draws from the Scriptures as his fundamental source, finding his pride in remaining a *Biblical* theologian, and whenever he can, taking the field against the *philosophico more interpretari* of the Scriptural texts (see e.g. I. xvi. 3). His doctrine of God has the *practical* end of serving the needs of his fellow-believers. It is also noteworthy that he closes every stage of the consideration with an exhortation to the adoration of God or to the sur-

[22] Cf. P. J. Muller, " De Godsleer van Calvijn," 1881, p. 117.

[23] Cf. P. J. Muller, " De Godsleer van Zwingli en Calvijn," 1883, pp. 46, 47. The author of the anonymous Introduction to the edition of the " Institutes " in French, published by Meyrueis et Cie, Paris, 1859, p. xii., says similarly: " Of a mind positive, grave, practical, removed from all need of speculation, very circumspect, not expressing its thought until its conviction had attained maturity, taking the fact of a divine revelation seriously, Calvin learned his faith at the feet of the Holy Scriptures . . ."

render of the heart to Him. Of the doctrine of the Trinity he
declares that he will hold himself ever truly to the Scriptures,
because he desires to do nothing more than to make what
the Scriptures teach accessible to our conceptions *planioribus
verbis*, and this will apply equally to the *whole* of his doctrine
of God." [24] In a word, nothing can be clearer than that in his
specific doctrine of God as well as in his general attitude to religious truth Calvin is as far as possible from being satisfied
with a merely logical effect. When we listen to him on these
high themes we are listening less to the play of his dialectic
than to the throbbing of his heart.

It was due to this his controlling religious purpose, and to
his dominating religious interest, that Calvin was able to
leave the great topics of the existence, the nature, and the attributes of God, without formal and detailed discussion in his
"Institutes." It is only a matter, we must reiterate, of the
omission of formal and detailed discussion; for it involves not
merely a gross exaggeration but a grave misapprehension to
represent him as leaving these topics wholly to one side, and
much more to seek to account for this assumed fact from some
equally assumed peculiarity of Calvin's theological point of
view or method. Under the impulse of his governing religious
interest, he was able to content himself with such an exposition of the nature and attributes of God, in matter and form,
as served his ends of religious impression, and was under no
compulsion to expand this into such details and order it into
such a methodical mode of presentation as would satisfy the
demands of scholastic treatment. But to omit what would be
for his purpose adequate treatment of these fundamental elements of a complete doctrine of God would have been impossible, we do not say merely to a thinker of his systematic
genius, but to a religious teacher of his earnestness of spirit. In
point of fact, we do not find lacking to the "Institutes" such
a fundamental treatment of these great topics as would be appropriate in such a treatise. We only find their formal and
separate treatment lacking. All that it is needful for the Chris-

[24] P. J. Muller, "De Godsleer van Calvijn," 1881, pp. 103–104.

tian man to know on these great themes is here present. Only, it is present so to speak in solution, rather than in precipitate: distributed through the general discussion of the knowledge of God rather than gathered together into one place and apportioned to formal rubrics. It is communicated moreover in a literary and concrete rather than in an abstract and scholastic manner.

It will repay us to gather out from their matrix in the flowing discourse the elements of Calvin's doctrine of God, that we may form some fair estimate of the precise nature and amount of actual instruction he gives regarding it. We shall attempt this by considering in turn Calvin's doctrine of the existence, knowableness, nature, and attributes of God.

We do not read far into the "Institutes" before we find Calvin presenting proofs of the existence of God. It is quite true that this book, being written by a Christian for Christians, rather assumes the divine existence than undertakes to prove it, and concerns itself with the so-called proofs of the divine existence as means through which we rather obtain knowledge of what God is, than merely attain to knowledge that God is. But this only renders it the more significant of Calvin's attitude towards these so-called proofs that he repeatedly lapses in his discussion from their use for the former into their use for the latter and logically prior purpose. That he thus actually presents these proofs as evidences specifically of the existence of God can admit of no doubt.[25]

[25] P. J. Muller's view is different, as may be seen from the following extracts: "Neither by Zwingli nor by Calvin are there offered proofs of the existence of God, although there are particular passages in their writings which seem to recall them. The proposition 'That God exists' needed neither for themselves nor for their fellow-believers, nor even against Rome, any proof. It has been thought indeed that the so-called cosmological argument is found in Zwingli, the physico-theological argument in Calvin (Lipsius, *Lehrb. der ev. prot. Dogmatik*, ed. 2, 1879, p. 213). But it would not be difficult to show that in the case of neither have we to do with a philosophical deduction, but only with an aid for attaining a complete knowledge of God" ("De Godsleer van Z. en C.," 1883, p. 11, cf. p. 14). In a note Prof. Muller adverts to the possible use by Calvin, I. iii. 1, of "the so-called historical argument." "If Zwingli gives us no proof of God's existence, the same is true of Calvin. It is true that the physico-theological argument has been discovered

If, for example, he adduces that *sensus deitatis* with which all men, he asserts, are natively endowed, primarily as the germ which may be developed into a profound knowledge of God, he yet does not fail explicitly to appeal to it also as the source of an ineradicable conviction, embedded in the very structure of human nature and therefore present in all men alike, of the existence of God. He tells us expressly that because of this *sensus divinitatis*, present in the human mind by natural instinct, all men without exception (*ad unum omnes*) know (*intelligant*, perceive, understand) "that God exists" (*Deum esse*), and are therefore without excuse if they do not worship Him and willingly consecrate their lives to Him (I. iii. 1). It is to buttress this assertion that he cites with approval Cicero's declaration [26] that "there is no nation so barbarous, no tribe so savage, that there is not stamped on it the conviction that there is a God." [27] Thus he adduces the argument of the *consensus gentium* — the so-called "historical" argument — with exact appreciation of its true bearing, not directly as a proof of the existence of God, but directly as a proof that the conviction of the divine existence is a native endowment of human nature, and only through that indirectly as a proof of the existence of God. This position is developed in the succeed-

in the *Institutes*. Yet as he wrote over the fifth chapter of the first book, 'That the knowledge of God is manifested in the making and continuous government of the world,' — it is already evident from this that he did not intend to argue from the teleology of the world to the existence of God as its Creator, Sustainer, and Governor, but that he wished merely to point to the world as to 'a beautiful book,' — to speak in the words of our [Netherlandish] Confession (Art. ii.), — 'in which all creatures, small and great, serve as letters to declare to us the invisible things of God.' Here, too, we have accordingly to do simply with a means for a rise to a fuller *knowledge* of God" (*Do.*, p. 16). "The Scholastics may indeed — although answering the inquiry affirmatively — begin with the question, Is there a God? Such a question cannot rise with Calvin. The Reformer, assured of his personal salvation, the ground of which lay in God Himself, could also for his co-believers leave this question to one side. Practical value attached only to the inquiry how men can come to know God, of whose existence Calvin entertained no doubt" ("De Godsleer van Calvijn," 1881, p. 11).

[26] ut ethnicus ille ait (the allusion is to Cicero, "De natura deorum," i. 16).

[27] Deum esse.

ing paragraph into a distinct anti-atheistic argument. The existence of religion, he says, presupposes, and cannot be accounted for except by, the presence in man of this " constant persuasion of God " from which as a seed the propensity to religion proceeds: men may deny " that God exists," [28] " but will they, nill they, what they wish not to know they continually are aware of." [29] It is a persuasion ingenerated naturally into all, that " some God exists " [30] (I. iii. 3), and therefore this does not need to be inculcated in the schools, but every man is from the womb his own master in this learning, and cannot by any means forget it. It is therefore mere detestable madness to deny that " God exists " (I. iv. 2).[31] In all these passages Calvin is dealing explicitly, not with the knowledge of what God is, but with the knowledge that God is. It is quite incontrovertible, therefore, that he grounds an argument — or rather the argument — for the existence of God in the very constitution of man. The existence of God is, in other words, with him an " intuition," and he makes this quite as plain as if he had devoted a separate section to its exposition.

Similarly, although he writes at the head of the chapter in which he expounds the revelation which God makes of Himself in His works and deeds: " That the knowledge of God is manifested in the making of the world and its continuous government " (chap. v.), he is not able to carry through his exposition without occasional lapses into an appeal to the patefaction of God in His works as a proof of His existence, rather than as a revelation of His nature. The most notable of these lapses occurs in the course of his development of the manifestation of God made by the nature of man himself (I. v. 4), where once more he gives us an express anti-atheistic argument. " Yea," he cries, " the earth is supporting to-day many monstrous beings, who without hesitation employ the very seed of divinity which has been sown in human nature

[28] qui Deum esse negent.

[29] velint tamen nolint, quod nescire cupiunt, subinde sentiscunt.

[30] imo et naturaliter ingenitam esse omnibus hanc persuasionem, esse aliquem Deum.

[31] negantes Deum esse.

for eclipsing of the name of God. How detestable, I protest, is this insanity, that a man, discovering God a hundred times in his body and soul, should on this very pretext of excellence deny that God exists! [32] They will not say that it is by chance that they are different from brute beasts; they only draw over God the veil of 'nature,' which they declare the maker of all things, and thus abolish (*subducunt*) Him. They perceive the most exquisite workmanship in all their members, from their countenances and eyes to their very finger nails. Here, too, they substitute 'nature' in the place of God. But above all how agile are the movements of the soul, how noble its faculties, how rare its gifts, discovering a divinity which does not easily permit itself to be concealed: unless the Epicureans, from this eminence, should like the Cyclops audaciously make war against God. Is it true that all the treasures of heavenly wisdom concur for the government of a worm five feet long, and the universe lacks this prerogative? To establish the existence of a kind of machinery in the soul, correspondent to each several part of the body, makes so little to the obscuring of the glory of God that it rather illustrates it. Let Epicurus tell what concourse of atoms in the preparation of food and drink distributes part to the excrements, part to the blood, and brings it about that the several members perform their offices with as much diligence as if so many souls by common consent were governing one body." " The manifold agility of the soul," he eloquently adds (I. v. 5, *med.*), " by which it surveys the heavens and the earth, joins the past to the future, retains in memory what it once has heard, figures to itself whatever it chooses; its ingenuity, too, by which it excogitates incredible things and which is the mother of so many wonderful arts; are certain insignia in man of divinity. . . . Now what reason exists that man should be of divine origin and not acknowledge the Creator? Shall we, forsooth, discriminate between right and wrong by a judgment which has been given to us, and yet there be no Judge in heaven? . . . Shall we be thought the inventors of so many useful arts, that we may defraud

---

[32] Deum esse neget.

God of His praise — although experience sufficiently teaches us that all that we have is distributed to us severally from else-where? . . ." Calvin, of course, knows that he is digressing in a passage like this — that "his present business is not with that sty of swine," as he calls the Epicureans. But digression or not, the passage is distinctly an employment of the so-called physico-theological proof for the existence of God, and advises us that Calvin held that argument sound and would certainly employ it whenever it became his business to develop the arguments for the existence of God.

The proofs for the existence of God on which we perceive Calvin thus to rely had been traditional in the Church from its first age. It was precisely upon these two lines of argument that the earliest Fathers rested. "He who knows himself," says Clement of Alexandria, quite in Calvin's manner, "will know God." [33] "The knowledge of God," exclaims Tertullian, "is the dowry of the soul." [34] "If you say, 'Show me thy God,'" Theophilus retorts to the heathen challenge, "I reply, 'Show me your man and I will show you my God.'" [35] The God who cannot be seen by human eyes, declares Theophilus,[36] "is beheld and perceived through His providence and works": we can no more surely infer a pilot for the ship we see making straight for the harbor, than we can infer a divine governor for the universe tending straight on its course. "Those who deny that this furniture of the whole world was perfected by the divine reason," argues the Octavius of Minucius Felix,[37] "and assert that it was heaped together by certain fragments casually adhering to each other, seem to me to have neither mind, nor sense, nor, in fact, even sight itself." "Whence comes it," asks Dionysius of Alexandria, criticizing the atomic theory

[33] "Paed.," III. i. ed. Stählin, i. 1905, p. 235; cf. E. T. in the "Ante-Nicene Christian Library": "Clement of Alexandria," i. 1867, p. 273. Cf. "Strom.," V. xiii.; "Protrep.," vi.

[34] "Adv. Marc.," i. 10: E. T. "The Ante-Nicene Fathers," iii. 1903, p. 278. Cf. "De test. animae," vi.: E. T. op. cit., p. 179.

[35] "Ad Autol.," i. 2: E. T. "Ante-Nicene Fathers," ii. 1903, p. 89.

[36] Do., i. 5: E. T. op. cit., p. 90.

[37] Chap. xvii.: E. T. "Ante-Nicene Fathers," iv. 1902, p. 182.

quite in Calvin's manner,[38] that the starry hosts — " this multitude of fellow-travellers, all unmarshalled by any captain, all ungifted with any determination of will, and all unendowed with any knowledge of each other, have nevertheless held their course in perfect harmony? " Like these early Fathers, Calvin adduces only these two lines of evidence: the existence of God is already given in our knowledge of self, and it is solidly attested by His works and deeds. Whether, had we from him a professed instead of a merely incidental treatment of the topic, the metaphysical arguments would have remained lacking in his case as in theirs,[39] we can only conjecture; but it seems very possible that as foreign to his *a posteriori* method (cf. I. v. 9) they lay outside of his scheme of proofs. Meanwhile, he has in point of fact adverted, in the course of this discussion, only to the two arguments on which the Church teachers at large had depended from the beginning of Christianity. He states these with his accustomed clearness and force, and he illuminates them with his genius for exposition and illustration; but he gives them only incidental treatment after all. In richness as well as in fulness of presentation he is surpassed here by Zwingli,[40] and it is to Melanchthon that we shall have to go

[38] " Adv. Epic.," iii.: E. T. " Ante-Nicene Fathers," vi. 1899, p. 88.

[39] H. C. Sheldon, " History of Christian Doctrine," i. 1886, p. 56: " Metaphysical proofs of the existence of God, such as those adduced by Augustine, Anselm, and Descartes, were quite foreign to the theology of the first three centuries." But in the next age they had already come in; cf. Sheldon, p. 187: " We find a new class of arguments, something more in the line of the metaphysical than anything which the previous centuries brought forward. Three writers in particular aspired to this order of proofs; viz., Diodorus of Tarsus, Augustine, and Boëthius." Augustine is the real father of the ontological argument: but Augustine only chronologically belonged to the old world; as Siebeck puts it, he was " the first modern man."

[40] Cf. P. J. Muller, " De Godsleer van Zwingli en Calvijn," 1883, pp. 11–16, where a very interesting account is given of Zwingli's handling of the theistic proofs — though Prof. Muller thinks that Zwingli employs them not to establish the existence of God but to increase our knowledge of God. With Zwingli all knowledge of God rests at bottom on Revelation, which is his way of saying what Calvin means by his universal *sensus deitatis*. Zwingli says, on his part, that " a certain seed of knowledge of God is sown [by God] also among the Gentiles " (iii. 158). But he argues with great force and in very striking language, that all creation proclaims its maker. Cf. A. Baur, " Zwinglis

to find among the Reformers a formal enumeration of the proofs for the divine existence.[41]

Theologie," i. 1885, pp. 382–383: "In the doctrine of God, Zwingli distinguishes two questions: first that of the nature, and secondly that of the existence of God. The answer to the first question surpasses the powers of the human mind; that of the second, does not." That the knowledge of the existence of God, which "may be justified before the understanding" (Muller, p. 13), does not involve a knowledge of His nature, Zwingli holds, is proved by the wide fact of polytheism on the one hand and the accompanying fact, on the other, that natural theism is always purely theoretical (Baur, p. 383).

[41] In the earliest "Loci Communes" (1521) there was no *locus de Deo* at all. In the second form (1535–1541) there was a *locus de Deo,* but it was not to it but to the *locus de Creatione* that Melanchthon appended some arguments for the existence of God, remarking ("Corp. Ref.," xxi. 369): "After the mind has been confirmed in the true and right opinion of God and of Creation by the Word of God itself, it is then both useful and pleasant to seek out also the vestiges of God in nature and to collect the arguments (*rationes*) which testify that there is a God." These remarks are expanded in the final form (1542 +) and reduced to a formal order, for the benefit of "good morals." The list ("Corp. Ref.," xxi. 641–643) consists of nine "demonstrations, the consideration of which is useful for discipline and for confirming honest opinions in minds." "The first is drawn from the order of nature itself, that is from the effects arguing a maker. . . . The second, from the nature of the human mind. A brute thing is not the cause of an intelligent nature. . . . The third, from the distinction between good and evil . . . and the sense of order and number. . . . Fourthly: natural ideas are true: that there is a God, all confess naturally: therefore this idea is true. . . . The fifth is taken, in Xenophanes, from the terrors of conscience. . . . The sixth from political society. . . . The seventh is . . . drawn from the series of efficient causes. There cannot be an infinite recession of efficient causes. . . . The eighth from final causes. . . . The ninth from prediction of future events." "These arguments," he adds, "not only testify that there is a God, but are also *indicia* of providence. . . . They are perspicuous and always affect good minds. Many others also could certainly be collected; but because they are more obscure, I leave off." . . . G. H. Lamers, "Geschiedenis der Leer aangande God," 1897, p. 179 [687], remarks: "It should be noted that Melanchthon always when speaking of God, whether as *Spirit* or as *Love,* wishes everywhere to ascribe the highest value to God's ethical characteristics. Even the particulars, nine in number, to which he (Doedes, *Inleiding tot de Leer van God,* p. 191) points as proofs that God's existence must be recognized, show that ethical considerations especially attract him." More justly Herrlinger, "Die Theologie Melanchthons," 1879, comments on Melanchthon's use of the "proofs" as follows: "The natural knowledge of God, resting on an innate idea and awakened especially by teleological contemplation of the world, Melanchthon makes in his philosophical writings, particularly in his physics, the object of consideration, so that we may speak of the elements of a natural theology

That this God, the conviction of whose existence is part
of the very constitution of the human mind and is justified by
abundant manifestations of Himself in His works and deeds,
is knowable by man, lies on the face of Calvin's entire discussion. The whole argument of the opening chapters of the
" Institutes " is directed precisely to the establishment of this
knowledge of God on an irrefragable basis: and the emphasis
with which the reality and trustworthiness of our knowledge
of God is asserted is equalled only by the skill with which the
development of our native instinct to know God into an actual
knowledge of Him is traced (in chap. i.), and the richness with
which His revelation of Himself in His works and deeds is illustrated by well-chosen and strikingly elaborated instances
(in chap. v.). Of course, Calvin does not teach that sinful man
can of himself attain to the knowledge of God. The noëtic
effects of sin he takes very seriously, and he teaches without
ambiguity that all men have grossly degenerated from the true
knowledge of God (chap. iv.). But this is not a doctrine of the
unknowableness of God, but rather of the incapacitating effects
of sin. Accordingly he teaches that the inadequateness of the
knowledge of God to which alone sinners can attain is itself a
sin. Men's natures prepare them to serve God, God's revelations
of Himself display Him before men's eyes: if men do not know
God they are without excuse and cannot plead their inculpat-
ing sinfulness as exculpation. God remains, then, knowable

---

in him " (p. 168). Melanchthon heaps up these arguments, enumerating nine
of them, in the conviction that they will mutually strengthen one another.
Herrlinger thinks that, as they occur in much the same order in more of
Melanchthon's writings than one, they may be arranged on some principle —
possibly beginning with particulars in nature and man, proceeding to human
association, and rising to the entirety of nature (p. 392). He continues (p. 393):
" Clearly enough it is the teleological argument which in all these proofs is
the real nerve of the proof. Melanchthon accords with Kant, as in the high
place he gives this proof, so also in perceiving that all these proofs find their
strength in the ontological argument, in the innate idea of God, which is the
most direct witness for God's existence. 15. 564; ' The mind reasons of God
from a multitude of vestiges. But this reasoning would not be made if there
were not infused (insita) into the mind a certain knowledge (notitia) or
πρόληψις of God.' Similarly, De Anima, 13. 144, 169." The relation of the proofs
to the innate sensus deitatis here indicated, holds good also for Calvin.

to normal man: it is natural to man to know Him. And if in point of fact He cannot be known save by a supernatural action of the Holy Spirit on the heart, this is because man is not in his normal state and it requires this supernatural action of the Spirit on his heart to restore him to his proper natural powers as man. The " testimony of the Holy Spirit in the heart " does not communicate to man any new powers, powers alien to him as man: it is restorative in its nature and in principle merely recovers his powers from their deadness induced by sin. The knowledge of God to which man attains through the testimony of the Spirit is therefore the knowledge which belongs to him as normal man: although now secured by him only in a supernatural manner, it is in kind, and, so far as it is the product of his innate *sensus deitatis* and the revelation of God in His works and deeds, it is in mode also, natural knowledge of God. Calvin's doctrine of the noëtic effects of sin and their removal by the " testimony of the Spirit," that is to say, by what we call " regeneration," must not then be taken as a doctrine of the unknowableness of God. On the contrary it is a doctrine of the knowableness of God, and supplies only an account of why men in their present condition fail to know Him, and an exposition of how and in what conditions the knowableness of God may manifest itself in man as now constituted in an actually known God. When the Spirit of God enters the heart with recreative power, he says, then even sinful man, his blurred eyes opened, may see God, not merely that there is a God, but what kind of being this God is (I. i. 1; ii. 1; v. 1).

Of course, Calvin does not mean that God can be known to perfection, whether by renewed man, or by sinless man with all his native powers uninjured by sin. In the depths of His being God is to him past finding out; the human intelligence has no plumbet to sound those profound deeps. " His essence " (*essentia*), he says, " is incomprehensible (*incomprehensibilis*); so that His divinity (*numen*) wholly escapes all human senses " (I. v. 1, cf. I. xi. 3); and though His works and the signs by which He manifests Himself may " admonish men of His incomprehensible essence " (I. xi. 3), yet, being men, we are not *capax Dei;* as Augustine says somewhere, we stand disheartened before His greatness and are unable to take Him in (I. v. 9).[42] We can know then only God's glory (I. v. 1), that is to say, His manifested perfections (I. v. 9), by which what He is to us is revealed to us (I. x. 2). What He is in Himself, we cannot know, and all attempts to penetrate into His essence are but cold and frigid speculations which can lead to no useful knowledge. "They are merely toying with frigid speculations," he says (I. ii. 2), "whose mind is set on the question of what God is (*quid sit Deus*), when what it really concerns us to know is rather what kind of a person He is (*qualis sit*) and what is appropriate to His nature (*natura*)" (I. ii. 2).[43] We are to seek God, therefore, "not with audacious inquisitiveness by attempting to search into His essence (*essentia*), which is rather to be adored than curiously investigated; but by contemplating Him in His works, in which He brings Himself near to us and makes Himself familiar and in some measure communicates Himself to us" (I. v. 9). For if we seek to know what He is in Himself (*quis sit apud se*) rather than what kind of a person He is to us (*qualis erga nos*) — which is revealed to us in His attributes (*virtutes*) — we simply lose ourselves in empty and meteoric speculation (I. x. 2).

The distinction which Calvin is here drawing between the knowledge of the *quid* and the knowledge of the *qualis* of God; the knowledge of what He is in Himself and the knowledge of what He is to us, is the ordinary scholastic one and fairly repeats what Thomas Aquinas contends for ("Summa Theol.," i. qu. 12, art. 12), when he tells us that there is no knowledge of God *per essentiam,* no knowledge of His nature, of His *quidditas per speciem propriam;* but we know only *habitudinem ipsius ad creaturas.* There is no implication of nominalism here; nothing, for example, similar to Occam's declaration that we can know neither the divine essence, nor

---

[42] "In Psalmos," 144: illum non possumus capere, velut sub eius magnitudine deficientes.

[43] We cannot know the quiddity of God: we can only know His quality: that is, to say what His essence is, is beyond our comprehension, but we may know Him in His attributes.

the divine quiddity, nor anything intrinsic to God, nor anything that God is *realiter*. When Calvin says that the Divine attributes describe not what God is *apud se*, but what kind of a person He is *erga nos*,[44] he is not intending to deny that His attributes are true determinations of the divine nature and truly reveal to us the kind of a person He is; he is only refusing to speculate on what God is apart from His attributes by which He reveals Himself to us, and insisting that it is only in these attributes that we know Him at all. He is refusing all *a priori* methods of determining the nature of God and requiring of us to form our knowledge of Him *a posteriori* from the revelation He gives us of Himself in His activities. This He insists is the only knowledge we can have of God, and this the only way we can attain to any knowledge of Him at all. Of what value is it to us, he asks (I. v. 9), to imagine a God of whose working we have had no experience? Such a knowledge only floats in the brain as an empty speculation. It is by His attributes (*virtutes*) that God is manifested; it is only through them that we can acquire a solid and fruitful knowledge of Him. The only right way and suitable method of seeking Him, accordingly, is through His works, in which He draws near to us and familiarizes Himself to us and in some degree communicates Himself to us. Here is not an assertion that we learn nothing of God through His attributes, which represent only determinations of our own. On the contrary, here is an assertion that we obtain through the attributes a solid and fruitful knowledge of God. Only it is not pretended that the attributes of God as revealed in His activities tell us all that God is, or anything that He is in Himself: they only tell us, in the nature of the case, what He is to us. Fortunately, says Calvin, this is what we need to know concerning God, and we may well eschew all speculation concerning His intrinsic nature and content ourselves with knowing what He is in His relation to His

---

[44] Cf. the passage in ed. 2 and other middle editions in which, refuting the Sabellians, he says that such attributes as strength, goodness, wisdom, mercy, are "epithets" which "show *qualis erga nos sit Deus*," while the personal names, Father, Son, Spirit, are "names" which "declare *qualis apud semetipsum vere sit*" (*Opp.* i. 491).

creatures. His object is, not to deny that God is what He seems — that His attributes revealed in His dealings with His creatures represent true determination of His nature. His object is to affirm that these determinations of His nature, revealed in His dealings with His creatures, constitute the sum of our real knowledge of God; and that apart from them speculation will lead to no solid results. He is calling us back, not from a fancied knowledge of God through His activities to the recognition that we know nothing of Him, that what we call His attributes are only effects in us: but from an *a priori* construction of an imaginary deity to an *a posteriori* knowledge of the Deity which really is and really acts. This much we know, he says, that God is what His works and acts reveal Him to be; though it must be admitted that His works and acts reveal not His metaphysical Being but His personal relations — not what He is *apud se,* but what He is *quoad nos.*

Of the nature of God in the abstract sense, thus — the *quiddity* of God, in scholastic phrase — Calvin has little to say.[45]

[45] Cf. P. J. Muller, " De Godsleer van Calvijn," 1881, p. 26: " A doctrine of the nature of God as such we do not find in Calvin." To teach us modesty, Calvin says, God says little of His nature in Scripture, but to teach us what we ought to know of Him he gives us two epithets — immensity and spirituality (p. 29). Again, " De Godsleer van Zwingli en Calvijn," 1883, pp. 30–31: " The little that Calvin gives us on this subject (the Divine Essence) limits itself to the remark that God's essence is ' immense and spiritual ' (I. xiii. 1), ' incomprehensible to us ' (I. v. 1)." Again, p. 38: " If the aprioristic method [as employed by Zwingli] is thus not favorable to the development of a doctrine of the Trinity, Calvin's aposterioristic method is on the other hand the reason that his conceptions of the nature of God — apart from the Trinity — are of less significance than Zwingli's. Since our understanding, according to Calvin, is incapable of grasping *what* God is, it is folly to seek with arrogant curiosity to investigate God's nature, ' which is much rather to be adored than anxiously to be inquired into ' (*On Romans,* i. 19: ' They are mad who seek to discover what God is '; *Institutes,* I. ii. 2: ' The essence of God is rather to be adored than inquired into '). If we nevertheless wish to solve the problem up to a certain point, let this be done only by means of the Scriptures in which God has revealed His nature to us so far as it is needful for us to know it. The warning he gives us is therefore certainly fully comprehensible, — that ' those who devote themselves to the solving of the problem of what God is should hold their speculations within bounds; since it is of much more importance for us to know *what kind of a being God is* ' (I. ii. 2). How can a man who cannot understand his own nature be able

But his refusal to go behind the attributes which are revealed to us in God's works and deeds, affords no justification to us for going behind them for him and attributing to him against his protest developed conceptions of the nature of the divine essence, which he vigorously repudiates. Calvin has suffered more than most men from such gratuitous attributions to him of doctrines which he emphatically disclaims. Thus, not only has it been persistently asserted that he reduced God, after the manner of the Scotists, to the bare notion of arbitrary Will, without ethical content or determination,[46] but the con-

---

to comprehend God's nature? ' Let us then leave to God the knowledge of Himself: and ' — so Calvin says — ' we leave it to Him when we conceive Him as He has revealed Himself to us, and when we seek to inquire with reference to Him nowhere else than in His Word ' (I. xiii. 21). . . ."

[46] This is fast becoming the popular representation. Cf. e.g. Williston Walker, " John Calvin," 1906, p. 149: " Thus he owed to Scotus, doubtless without realizing the obligation, the thought of God as almighty will, for motives behind whose choice it is as absurd as it is impious to inquire." Again, p. 418: " Whether this Scotist doctrine of the rightfulness of all that God wills by the mere fact of His willing it, leaves God a moral character, it is perhaps useless to inquire." But Calvin does not borrow unconsciously from Scotus: he openly repudiates Scotus. And Calvin is so far from representing the will of God to be independent of His moral character, that he makes it merely the expression of His moral character, and only inscrutable to us. Cf. also C. H. Irwin, " John Calvin," 1909, p. 179: " Holding as he did the theory of Duns Scotus, that a thing is right by the mere fact of God willing it, he never questioned whether a course was or was not in harmony with the Divine character, if he was once convinced that it was a course attributed to God in Scripture." But Calvin did not hold that a thing is made right by the mere fact that God wills it but that the fact that God wills it (which fact Scripture may witness to us) is proof enough to us that it is right. The vogue of this remarkable misrepresentation of Calvin's doctrine of God is doubtless due to its enunciation (though in a somewhat more guarded form) by Ritschl (Jahrbb. für deutsche Theologie, 1868, xiii. pp. 104 sq.). Ritschl's fundamental contention is that the Nominalistic conception of God, crowded out of the Roman Church by Thomism, yet survived in Luther's doctrine of the enslaved will and Calvin's doctrine of twofold predestination (p. 68), which presuppose the idea of " the groundless arbitrariness of God " in His actions. Calvin was far from adopting this principle in theory or applying it consistently. He is aware of and seeks to guard against its dangers (p. 106); but his doctrine of a double predestination (in Ritschl's opinion) proceeds on its assumption: " In spite of Calvin's reluctance, we must judge that the idea of God which governs this doctrine comes to the same thing as the Nominalistic potentia absoluta" (p. 107). The same line of reasoning may be read also

tradictory conceptions of a virtual Deism [47] and a developed
Pantheism [48] have with equal confidence been attributed to
him. To instance but a single example, Principal A. M. Fairbairn permits himself to say that " Calvin was as pure, though
not as conscious and consistent a Pantheist as Spinoza." [49] As-

in Seeberg, " Text-Book of the History of Doctrines," § 79, 4 (E. T. ii. 1905,
p. 397), who also is compelled to admit that this conception of God is both
repudiated by Calvin and is destructive of his " logical structure "! For a
sufficient refutation of this whole notion see Max Scheibe's " Calvin's Prädes-
tinationslehre," 1897, pp. 113 *sq.* " Calvin," says Scheibe, " could therefore very
properly repudiate the charge of proceeding on the Scoto-nominalistic idea
of the *potentia absoluta* of God. . . . With Calvin, on the contrary, the conception of the will of God as the highest causality has the particular meaning
that God is not determined in His actions by anything lying outside of Himself, . . . while it is distinctly not excluded that God acts by virtue of an inner
necessity, accordant with His nature."

[47] Cf. e.g. A. V. G. Allen, " The Continuity of Christian Thought," 1884,
p. 299: " The God who is thus revealed is a being outside the framework of
the universe, who called the world into existence by the power of His will.
Calvin positively rejected the doctrine of the divine immanence. When he
spoke of that ' dog of a Lucretius ' who mingles God and nature, he may have
also had Zwingli in his mind. In order to separate more completely between
God and man, he interposed ranks of mediators. . . ." Also, p. 302: " In
some respects the system of Calvin not merely repeats but exaggerates the
leading ideas of Latin Christianity. In no Latin writer is found such a determined purpose to reject the immanence of Deity and assert His transcendence
and His isolation from the world. In his conception of God, as absolute arbitrary will, he surpasses Duns Scotus. . . . The separation between God and
humanity is emphasized as it has never been before, for Calvin insists, dogmatically and formally, upon that which had been, to a large extent, hitherto,
an unconscious though controlling sentiment." Prof. Allen had already represented the Augustinian theology as " resting upon the transcendence of
Deity as its controlling principle," — which he explains as a " tacit assumption " of Deism (pp. 3, 171).

[48] Cf. Principal D. W. Simon, " Reconciliation by Incarnation," 1898, p.
282, where he speaks of " the Pantheism . . . with which Calvin is logically
chargeable — strongly as he might resent the imputation — when he says:
' Nothing happens but what He has knowingly and willingly decreed '; ' All
the changes which take place in the world are produced by the secret agency
of the hand of God '; ' Not heaven and earth and inanimate creatures only,
but also the counsels and wills of men are so governed as to move exactly in
the course which He has destined.' " To Dr. Simon providential government of
the world implies pantheism!

[49] " The Place of Christ in Modern Theology," 1893, p. 164. Even H. M.
Gwatkin, " The Knowledge of God," etc., 1906, ii. p. 226, having spoken of

tonishing as such a declaration is in itself, it becomes more astonishing still when we observe the ground on which it is based. This consists essentially in the discovery that the fundamental conception of Calvinism is that " God's is the only efficient will in the universe, and so He is the one ultimate causal reality " [50] — upon which the certainly very true remark is made that " the universalized Divine will is an even more decisive and comprehensive Pantheism than the universalized Divine substance." [51] The logical process by which the Calvinistic conception of the sovereign will of God as the *prima causa rerum* — where the very term *prima* implies the existence and reality of " second causes " — is transmuted into the Pantheising notion that the will of God is the sole efficient cause in the universe; or by which the Calvinistic conception of God as the sovereign ruler of the universe whose " will is the necessity of things " is transmuted into the reduction of God, Hegelian-wise, into pure and naked will [52] — although it has apparently appealed to many, is certainly very obscure. In point of fact, when the Calvinist spoke of God as the *prima causa rerum* (the phrase is cited from William Ames [53]) he meant by it only that all that takes place takes place in accordance with the divine will, not that the divine will is the only efficient cause in the universe; and when Calvin quotes

---

Calvin as " taking over from the Scotists " his conception of God as " sovereign and inscrutable will," adds that he needed only to suppose further that " the divine will " is " necessitated as well as inscrutable " to have taught a Pantheistic system. But as he thus allows Calvin did not suppose this, and had just pointed out that Calvin explains that God is not an " absolute and arbitrary power," we probably need not look upon this language as other than rhetorical: it certainly is not true to the facts in either of its members.

[50] P. 164. Cf. p. 430. It is Amesius to whom Dr. Fairbairn appeals to justify this statement: but he misinterprets Amesius.

[51] P. 168.

[52] Cf. Baur, " Die christliche Lehre von der Dreieinigkeit," iii. 1843, pp. 35 *sq.*

[53] " Medulla," I. vii. 38: " Hence the will of God is the first cause of things. ' By thy will they are and were created ' (Apoc. iv. 11). But the will of God, as He wills to operate *ad extra,* does not presuppose the goodness of the object, but by willing posits and makes it good."

approvingly from Augustine — for the words are Augustine's [54] — that " the will of God is the necessity of things," so little is either he or Augustine making use of the words in a Pantheistic sense that he hastens to explain that what he means is only that whatever God has willed will certainly come to pass, although it comes to pass in " such a manner that the cause and matter of it are found in " the second causes (*ut causa et materia in ipsis reperiatur*).[55]

Calvin beyond all question did cherish a very robust faith in the immanence of God. " Our very existence," he says, " is subsistence in God alone " (I. i. 1). He even allows, as Dr. Fairbairn does not fail to inform us, that it may be said with a pious meaning — so only it be the expression of a pious mind — that "nature is God" (I. v. 5, end).[56] But Dr. Fairbairn

[54] The phrase is quoted by Dr. Fairbairn (p. 164) as Calvin's, to support the assertion that he was " as pure . . . a pantheist as Spinoza." But it is cited by Calvin (III. xxiii. 8) from Augustine. The matter in immediate discussion is the perdition of the reprobate.

[55] III. xxiii. 8.

[56] Cf. Muller, " De Godsleer van Zwingli en Calvijn," 1883, p. 26: "Accordingly also Pliny was right — according to Zwingli (*De Provid. Dei Anamnema*, iv. 90) — in calling what he calls God, nature, since the learned cannot adjust themselves to the conceptions of God of the ununderstanding multitude; inasmuch as by nature he meant the power which moves and holds together all things, and that is nothing else but God." Again, on the general question of the charge of Pantheism brought against Zwingli, pp. 26–28: " As is well known, it has been supposed that there is a pantheistic element in Zwingli's *Anamnema*. It cannot be denied that there are some expressions which sound Spinozistic; and for those who see Pantheism in every controversion of fortuitism, Zwingli must of necessity be a Pantheist. Yet if we are to discover Spinozism in Zwingli, we can with little difficulty point to traces of Spinozism also in Paul. Such a passage as the following, for example, would certainly have been subscribed by Paul: ' If anything comes to pass by its own power or counsel, then the wisdom and power of our Deity would be superfluous there. And if that were true, then the wisdom of the Deity would not be supreme, because it would not comprehend and take in all things; and his power would not be omnipotent, because then there would exist power independent of God's power, and in that case there would be another power which would not be the power of the Deity ' (*Opp.* vi. 85). In any case, Zwingli cannot be given the blame of standing apart from the other Reformers on this point. Calvin certainly recognizes (*Inst.* I. v. 5) that — so it occurs, simply — ' it may be said out of a pious mind that nature is God '; (cf. *Zwingli*, vi. a. 619: ' Call God Himself Nature, with the philosophers, the principle from

neglects to mention that Calvin adds at once, that the expression is " crude and unsuitable " (*dura et impropria*), since " nature is rather the order prescribed by God "; and, moreover, noxious, because tending to " involve God confusedly with the inferior course of His works." He neglects also to mention that the statement occurs at the end of a long discussion, in which, after rebuking those who throw an obscuring veil over God, retire Him behind nature, and so substitute nature for Him — Calvin inveighs against the " babble about some sort of hidden inspiration which actuates the whole world," as not only " weak " but " altogether profane," and brands the speculation of a universal mind animating and actuating the world as simply jejune (I. v. 4 and 5). Even his beloved Seneca is reproved for " imagining a divinity transfused through all parts of the world " so that God is all that we see and all that we do not see as well (I. xiii. 1), while the Pantheistic scheme of Servetus is made the object of an extended refutation (II. xiv. 5–8). To ascribe an essentially Pantheistic conception of God to Calvin in the face of such frequent and energetic repudiations of it on his own part [57] is obviously to miss his meaning altogether. If he " may be said to have anticipated Spinoza in his notion of God as *causa immanens*," and " Spinoza may be said . . . to have perfected and reduced to philosophical consistency the Calvinistic conception of Deity " [58] — this can mean nothing more than that Calvin was not a Deist. And in point of fact he repudiated Deism with a vehemence equal to that which he displays against Pantheism. To rob God of the active exercise of His judgment and providence, shutting Him up as an

---

which all things take their origin, from which the soul begins to be '); although he adds the warning that in matters of such importance ' no expressions should be employed likely to cause confusion.' Danaeus (*Lib.* i. 11 of his *Ethices Christ. lib. tres*) marvels that those who would fain bear the name of Christians, should conceive of God and nature as two different hypostases, since even the heathen philosophers (and like Zwingli, he names Seneca) more truly taught that ' the nature by which we have been brought forth is nothing else than God. . . .' "

[57] Cf. instances in addition at I. xiv. 1, I. xv. 5.

[58] Fairbairn, *op. cit.*, pp. 165–166.

idler (*otiosum*) in heaven, he characterizes as nothing less than
"detestable frenzy," since, says he, "nothing could less comport with God than to commit to fortune the abandoned government of the world, shut His eyes to the iniquities of men
and let them wanton with impunity" (I. iv. 2).[59]

Calvin's conception of God is that of a pure and clear
Theism, in which stress is laid at once on His transcendence
and His immanence, and emphasis is thrown on His righteous government of the world. "Let us bear in mind, then,"
he says as he passes from his repudiation of Pantheism, "that
there is one God, who governs all natures" (I. v. 6, *ad init.*),
"and wishes us to look to Him, — to put our trust in Him, to
worship and call upon Him" (I. v. 6); to whom we can look
up as to a Father from whom we expect and receive tokens of
love (I. v. 3). So little is he inclined to reduce this divine
Father to bare will, that he takes repeated occasion expressly
to denounce this Scotist conception. The will of God, he says,
is to us indeed the unique rule of righteousness and the supremely just cause of all things; but we are not like the
sophists to prate about some sort of "absolute will" of God,
"profanely separating His righteousness from His power,"
but rather to adore the governing providence which presides
over all things and from which nothing can proceed which is
not right, though the reasons for it may be hidden from us
(I. xvii. 2, end). "Nevertheless," he remarks in another place,
after having exhorted his readers to find in the will of God a
sufficient account of things — "nevertheless, we do not be-
take ourselves to the fiction of absolute power, which, as it is
profane, so ought to be deservedly detestable to us; we do not
imagine that the God who is a law to Himself is *exlegem*, . . .
the will of God is not only pure from all fault, but is the su-

---

[59] Cf. I. xvi. 1: "To make God a momentaneous creator, who entirely
finished all His work at once, were frigid and jejune," etc. Also the Genevan
Catechism of 1545 (*Opp.* vi. 15–18): The particularization of God's creator-
ship in the creed is not to be taken as indicating that God so created His
works at once that afterwards He rejects the care of them. It is rather so to
be held that the world as it was made by Him at once, so now is conserved
by Him; and He is to remain their supreme governor, etc.

preme rule of perfection, even the law of all laws " (III. xxiii. 2, end).[60] In a word, the will of God is to Calvin the supreme rule for us, because it is the perfect expression of the divine perfections.[61]

Calvin thus refuses to be classified as either Deist, Pantheist, or Scotist; and those who would fain make him one or the other of these have nothing to go upon except that on the one hand he does proclaim the transcendence of God and speaks with contempt of men who imagine that divinity is transfused into every part of the world, and that there is a portion of God not only in us but even in wood and stone (I. xiii. 1, 22); and on the other he does proclaim the immanence of God and invites us to look upon His works or to descend within ourselves to find Him who " everywhere diffuses, sustains, animates and quickens all things in heaven and in earth," who,

[60] It is not uncommon for historians of doctrine who are inclined to represent Calvin as enunciating the Scotist principle, therefore, to suggest that he is scarcely consistent with himself. Thus, e.g., H. C. Sheldon, " History of Christian Doctrine," 1886, ii. pp. 93–94: " Some, who were inclined to extreme views of the divine sovereignty, asserted the Scotist maxim that the will of God is the absolute rule of right. Luther's words are quite as explicit as those of Scotus. . . . ' The will of God,' says Calvin . . . (*Inst.* III. xxiii. 2). . . . Calvin, however, notwithstanding this strong statement, suggests after all that he meant not so much that God's will is absolutely the highest rule of right, as that it is one which we cannot transcend, and must regard as binding on our own judgment; for he adds, ' We represent not God as lawless, who is a law to Himself.' " Cf. Victor Monod, " Le problème de Dieu," 1910, p. 44: " Calvin was assuredly not himself a Scotist; but his disciples were." Again: " It was in the Calvinistic logic to place God above the moral law itself, and Calvin was not always able to resist this tendency."

[61] " The goodness of God," says Calvin (" Institutes," II. iii. 5), " is so united with His divinity that it is as much a necessity to Him to be good as to be God." Again (*Opp.* viii. 361) : " It would be easier to separate the light of the sun from its heat, or its heat from its fire, than to separate the power of God from His righteousness." Cf. Bavinck, " Geref. Dogmatiek," ii. 1897, p. 226, who, after remarking on Calvin's rejection of the Scotist notion of *potentia absoluta*, as a " profane invention " — adducing " Institutes," III. xxiii. 1, 5; I. xvi. 3; II. vii. 5; IV. xvii. 24; " Comm. in Jes.," xxiii. 9, " in Luk.," i. 18, adds: " The Romanists on this account charge Calvin with limiting and therefore denying God's omnipotence (Bellarmine, *De gratia et lib. arbitrio*, iii. chap. 15). But Calvin is not denying that God can do more than He actually does, but only opposing such a *potentia absoluta* as is not connected with His Being or Virtues, and can therefore do all kinds of inconsistent things."

"circumscribed by no boundaries, by transfusing His own vigor into all things, breathes into them being, life and motion" (I. xiii. 14); while still again he does proclaim the will of God to be inscrutable by such creatures as we are and to constitute to us the law of righteousness, to be accepted as such without murmurings or questionings. In point of fact, all these charges are but several modes of expressing the dislike their authors feel for Calvin's doctrine of the sovereignty of the divine will, which, following Augustine, he declares to be " the necessity of things": they would fain brand this hated conception with some name of opprobrium, and, therefore, seek to represent Calvin now as hiding God deistically behind His own law, and now as reducing Him to a mere stream of causality, or at least to mere naked will.[62] By thus declining alternately to contradictories they show sufficiently clearly that in reality Calvin's doctrine of God coincides with none of these characterizations.

The peculiarity of Calvin's conception of God, we perceive, is not indefiniteness, but reverential sobriety. Clearing his skirts of all Pantheistic, Deistic, Scotist notions — and turning aside even to repudiate Manichaeism and Anthropomorphism (I. xiii. 1) — he teaches a pure Theism which he looks upon as native to men (I. x. 3). The nature of this one God, he con-

[62] A flagrant example may be found in the long argument of F. C. Baur, "Die christl. Lehre von der Dreieinigkeit," iii. 1843, pp. 35 ff., where he represents the Calvinistic doctrine of election and reprobation as postulating in God a schism between mercy and justice which can be reduced only by thinking of Him as wholly indifferent to good and evil, and indeed of good and evil as a non-existent opposition. If justice is an equally absolute attribute with God as grace, he argues, then evil and good are at one, in that reality cannot be given to the attribute in which the absolute being of God consists without evil. Evil has the same relation to the absolute being of God as good; and " God is in the same sense the principle of evil as of good "; and " as God's justice cannot be without its object, God must provide this object " (pp. 37–38). " But if evil as well as the good is from God, then on that very account evil is good: thus good and evil are entirely indifferent with respect to each other, and the absolute Dualism is resolved into the same absolute arbitrariness (*Willkür*) in which Duns Scotus had placed the absolute Being of God " (p. 38). This, however, is not represented as Calvin's view, but as the consequence of Calvin's view — as drawn out in the Hegelianizing dialectic of Baur.

ceives, can be known to us only as He manifests it in His works (I. v. 9); that is to say, only in His perfections. What we call the attributes of God thus become to Calvin the sum of our knowledge of Him. In these manifestations of His character we see not indeed what He is in Himself, but what He is to us (I. x. 2); but what we see Him to be thus to us, He truly is, and this is all we can know about Him. We might expect to find in the " Institutes," therefore, a comprehensive formal discussion of the attributes, by means of which what God is to us should be fully set before us. This, however, as we have already seen, we do not get.[63] And much less do we get any metaphysical discussion of the nature of the attributes of God, their relation to one another, or to the divine essence of which they are determinations. We must not therefore suppose, however, that we get little or nothing of them, or little or nothing to the point. On the contrary, besides incidental allusions to them throughout the discussion, from which we may glean much of Calvin's conceptions of them, they are made the main subject of two whole chapters, the one of which discusses in considerable detail the revelation of the divine perfections in His works and deeds, the other the revelation made of them in His Word. We have already remarked upon the skill with which Calvin, at the opening of his discussion of the doctrine of God (chap. x.), manages, under color of pointing out the harmony of the description of God given in the Scriptures with the conception of Him we may draw from His works, to bring all he had to say of the divine attributes at once before the reader's eye. The Scriptures, says he, are in essence here merely a plainer (I. x. 1) republication of the general revelation given of God in His works and deeds: they " contain nothing " in their descriptions of God, " but what may be known from the contemplation of the creatures " (I. x. 2, *med.*). And he illustrates this remark by quoting from Moses (Ex. xxxiv. 6), the

---

[63] Cf. P. J. Muller, " De Godsleer van Zwingli en Calvijn," 1883, p. 40: " Neither in Zwingli nor in Calvin do we meet with a formal ' doctrine of the attributes ' or with a classification of the attributes. No doubt it happens that both occasionally name a number of attributes together; and have something to say of each attribute in particular."

Psalms (cxlv.) and the prophets (Jer. ix. 24), passages in which God is richly described, and remarking on the harmony of the perfections enumerated with those which he had in the earlier chapter (v.) pointed out as illustrated in the divine works and deeds. This comparison involves a tolerably full enumeration and some discussion of the several attributes, here on the basis of Scripture, as formerly (chap. v.) on the basis of nature. He does not, therefore, neglect the attributes so much as deal with them in a somewhat indirect manner. And, we may add, in a highly practical way: for here too his zeal is to avoid " airy and vain speculations " of what God is in Himself and to focus attention upon what He is to us, that our knowledge of Him may be of the nature of a lively perception and religious reaction (I. x. 2, *ad init. et ad fin.*).

In a number of passages Calvin brings together a plurality of the attributes — his name for them is " virtues " [64] — and even hints at a certain classification of them. One of the most beautiful of these passages formed the opening words of the first draft of the " Institutes," but fell out in the subsequent revisions — to the regret of some, who consider it, on the whole, the most comprehensive description of God Calvin has given us.[65] It runs as follows: " The sum of holy doc-

[64] *Virtutes Dei,* I. ii. 1; v. 7, 9, 10; x. 2. In xiii. 4, *med.,* he uses the term *attributa.* In xiii. 1, speaking of the divine spirituality and immensity, he used *epitheta.*

[65] Köstlin, as cited, pp. 61–62: " On the other hand, — and this is the most important for us, — there is not given in the *Institutes* any comprehensive presentation of the attributes, especially of the ethical attributes of God, nor is any such attempted anywhere afterwards; the first edition, which began with some comprehensive propositions about God as infinite wisdom, righteousness, mercy, etc., rather raises an expectation of something more in the later, more thoroughly worked out editions of the work: but these propositions fell out of the first edition and were never afterward developed." In the intermediate editions (1543–1550) this paragraph has taken the form of: " Nearly the whole sum of our wisdom — and this certainly should be esteemed true and solid wisdom — consists in two facts: the knowledge of God and of ourselves. The one, now, not only shows that there is one God whom all ought to worship and adore, but at the same time teaches also that this one God is the source of all truth, wisdom, goodness, righteousness, justice, mercy, power, holiness, so that we are taught that we ought to expect and seek all these things from Him, and when we receive them to refer them to Him with

trine consists of just these two points, — the knowledge of God and the knowledge of ourselves. These, now, are the things which we must keep in mind concerning God. First, we should hold fixed in firm faith that He is infinite wisdom, righteousness, goodness, mercy, truth, power (*virtus*), and life, so that there exists no other wisdom, righteousness, goodness, mercy, truth, power, and life (Baruch iii.; James i.), and wheresoever any of these things is seen, it is from Him (Prov. xvi.). Secondly, that all that is in heaven or on earth has been created for His glory (Ps. cxlviii.; Dan. iii.; and it is justly due to Him that everything, according to its own nature, should serve Him, acknowledge His authority, seek His glory, and obediently accept Him as Lord and King (Rom. i.). Thirdly, that He is Himself a just judge, and will therefore be severely avenged on those who depart from His commandments, and are not in all things subject to His will; who in thought, word, and deed have not sought His glory (Ps. vii.; Rom. ii.). In the fourth place that He is merciful and long-suffering, and will receive into His kingdom, the miserable and despised who take refuge in His clemency and trust in His faithfulness; and is ready to spare and forgive those who ask His favor, to succor and help those who seek His aid, and desirous of saving those who put their trust in Him (Ps. ciii.; Is. lv.; Ps. xxv., lxxxv.)." In the first clause of this striking paragraph we have a formal enumeration of God's ethical attributes, which is apparently meant to be generically complete — although in the course of the paragraph other specific forms of attributes here enumerated occur; and all of them are declared to exist in God in an infinite mode. The list contains seven items: wisdom; righteousness; goodness (clemency); mercy (long-sufferingness); truth; power; life.[66] If we compare this list with the enumera-

---

praise and gratitude. The other, however, by manifesting to us our weakness, misery, vanity and foulness, first brings us into serious humility, dejection, diffidence and hatred of ourselves, and then kindles a longing in us to seek God, in whom is to be found every good thing of which we discover ourselves to be so empty and lacking."

[66] In the list which takes the place of this in the middle editions of the "Institutes," the order is different (and scarcely so regular), and "life" is

tion in the famous definition of God in the Westminster
"Shorter Catechism" (Q. 4),[67] we shall see that it is practically the same: the only difference being that Calvin adds to
the general term "goodness" the more specific "mercy," af-
fixes "life" at the end, and omits "holiness," doubtless considering it to be covered by the general term "righteousness."

If just this enumeration does not recur in the "Institutes"
as finally revised, something very like it evidently underlies
more passages than one. Even in the first section of the first
chapter, which has taken its place, we have an enumeration
of the "good things" (*bona*) in God which stand opposed to
our "evil things" (*mala*), that brings together wisdom, power,
goodness, and righteousness: for in God alone, we are told, can
be found "the true light of *wisdom*, solid *power* (*virtus*),
a perfect affluence of all *good* things, and the purity of *righteousness*" (I. i. 1). In the opening section of the next chapter we have two enumerations of the divine perfections, obviously rhetorical, and yet betraying an underlying basis of
systematic arrangement: the later and fuller of these brings together power, wisdom, goodness, righteousness, justice, mercy
— closing with a reference to God's powerful "protection."
God, we are told, "sustains this world by His immense *power*
(*immensa potentia*), governs it by His *wisdom*, preserves it by
His *goodness*, rules over the human race especially by His
righteousness and *justice* (*iudicium*), bears with it in His
mercy, defends it by His *protection* (*praesidium*)." The most
complete enumerations of all, however, are given, when, leaving the intimations of nature, Calvin analyses some Scriptural
passages with a view to drawing out their descriptions of the
divine perfections. His analysis of Exod. xxxiv. 6 is particularly
full (I. x. 2). He finds the divine eternity and self-existence
embodied in the name Jehovah; the divine strength and power
(*virtus et potentia*) expressed in the name Elohim; and in the

omitted, while "justice" is added to "righteousness," and "sanctity" appended at the end, and "potentia" substituted for "virtus": "truth; wisdom; goodness; righteousness; *justice;* mercy; (power); *holiness*."
    [67] "Wisdom, power, holiness, justice, goodness, and truth."

description itself an enumeration of those virtues which describe God not indeed as He is *apud se,* but as He is *erga nos* — to wit, His clemency, goodness, mercy, righteousness, justice, truth. The strongest claim which this passage has on our interest, however, is the suggestion it bears of a classification of the attributes. The predication to God of eternity and self-existence (*αὐτουσία*) evidently is for Calvin something specifically different from the ascription to Him of those virtues by which are described not what He is *apud se,* but what He shows Himself to be *erga nos.* They in a word belong rather to the quiddity of God than to His *qualitas.* In a subsequent passage (xiii. 1) we have a plainer hint to the same effect. There we are given " two epithets " which we are told are applied by Scripture to the very " essence " of God, in its rare speech concerning His essence — immensity and spirituality.[68] It seems quite clear, then, that Calvin was accustomed to distinguish in his thought between such epithets, describing what God is *apud se,* and those virtues by which He is manifested to us in His relations *erga nos.* That is to say, he distinguishes between what are sometimes called His physical or metaphysical and His ethical attributes: that is to say, between the fundamental modes of the Divine Being and the constitutive qualities of the Divine Person.[69]

If we profit by this hint and then collect the attributes of the two classes as Calvin occasionally mentions them, we shall in effect reconstruct Calvin's definition of God.[70] This

---

[68] Quod de immensa et spirituali Dei essentia traditur in Scripturis . . . parce de sua essentia disserit, duobus tamen illis quae dixi epithetis. . . .

[69] See the distinction very luminously drawn out by J. H. Thornwell, " Works," i. 1871, pp. 168–169.

[70] Perhaps as near as Calvin ever came to framing an exact definition of God *apud se,* is the description of God in the middle edd. of the " Institutes," vi. 7 (*Opp.* i. 480), summed up in the opening words: " That there is one God of eternal, infinite and spiritual essence, the Scriptures currently declare with plainness." The *essence* of God then is eternal, infinite and spiritual. Cf. " Adv. P. Caroli Calumnias " (*Opp.* vii. 312): " The one God which the Scriptures preach to us we believe in and adore, and we think of Him as He is described to us by them, to wit, as of eternal, infinite and spiritual essence, who also alone has in Himself the power of existence from Himself and bestows it upon His creatures."

would run somewhat as follows: There is but one only true God,[71] a self-existent,[72] simple,[73] invisible,[74] incomprehensible[75] Spirit,[76] infinite,[77] immense,[78] eternal,[79] perfect,[80] in His Being, power,[81] knowledge,[82] wisdom,[83] righteousness,[84] justice,[85] holiness,[86] goodness,[87] and truth.[88] In addition to these more general designations, Calvin employs a considerable number of more specific terms, by which he more precisely expresses his thought and more fully explicates the contents of the several attributes. Thus, for example, he is fond of the term "severity"[89] when he is endeavoring to give expression to God's attitude as a just judge to the wicked; and he is fond of setting in contrast with it the corresponding term "clemency"[90] to express His attitude towards the repentant sinner. It is especially the idea of "goodness" which he thus draws out into its several particular manifestations. Beside the term

[71] unicus et verus Deus, I. ii. 2; unicus Deus, xii. 1; xiii. 2; xiv. 2; unus Deus, ii. 1; v. 6; x. 3; xii. 1; verus Deus, x. 3; xiii. 2; unitas Dei, xiii. 1, etc.

[72] a se ipso principium habens, v. 6; αὐτουσία, x. 2; αὐτουσία, id est a se ipso existentia, xiv. 3.

[73] simplex Dei essentia, xiii. 2; simplex et individua essentia Dei, xiii. 2; una simplexque Deitas, "Adv. Val. Gent." (*Opp.* ix. 365).

[74] invisibilis Deus, I. v. 1; II. vi. 4 (made visible in Christ, so also II. ix. 1); invisibilis I. xi. 3 (of Holy Spirit).

[75] incomprehensibilis, v. 1; xi. 3 (in xiii. 1 apparently used for immensa).

[76] spiritualis Dei essentia, xiii. 1; spiritualis natura, xiii. 1.

[77] in Deo residet bonorum infinitas, i. 1 (cf. ed. 1, i. *ad init.* [p. 42], infinitas).

[78] eius immensitas, xiii. 1; immensitas, xiii. 1; immensa Dei essentia, xiii. 1.

[79] aeternitas, v. 6; x. 2; xiii. 18; xiv. 3; aeternus [Deus], v. 6.

[80] exacta iusticiae, sapientiae, virtutis eius perfectio, i. 2.

[81] potentia, ii. 1; v. 3, 6, 8; x. 2; immensa potentia, ii. 1; omnipotentia, xvi. 3; omnipotens, xvi. 3; virtus, i. 1, 3; v. 1, 6, 10; x. 2; virtus et potentia, x. 2.

[82] notitia, III. xxi. 5; praescientia, III. xxi. 5.

[83] sapientia, i. 1, 3; ii. 1; v. 1, 2, 3, 8, 10; mirifica sapientia, v. 2.

[84] iustitia, ii. 1; v. 10; x. 2; xv. 1; III. xxiii. 4; iustitiae puritas, i. 1; iustitia iudiciumque, ii. 1.

[85] iudicium, ii. 2; x. 2; iustitia iudiciumque, ii. 1; iustus iudex, ii. 2.

[86] sanctitas, x. 2; puritas, i. 3; divina puritas, i. 2.

[87] bonitas, ii. 1; v. 3, 6, 9, 10; x. 1, 2; xv. 1; bonus, ii. 2.

[88] veritas, x. 2; Deus verax, III. xx. 26.

[89] severitas, ii. 2; v. 7, 10; xvii. 1.

[90] clementia, v. 7, 8, 10; x. 2.

"clemency" he sets the still greater word "mercy," or "pity,"[91] and by the side of this again he sets the even greater word "grace,"[92] while the more general idea of "goodness" he develops by the aid of such synonyms as "beneficence"[93] and "benignity,"[94] and almost exhausts the capacity of the language to give expression to his sense of the richness of the Divine goodness.[95] God is "good and merciful" (ii. 2), "benign and beneficent" (v. 7), "the fount and source of all good" (ii. 2), their fecund "author" (ii. 2), whose "will is prone to beneficence" (x. 1), and in whom dwells a "perfect affluence," nothing less than an "infinity," of good things. And therefore he looks upwards to this God not only as our Lord (ii. 1) the Creator (ii. 1), Sustainer (ii. 1), and Governor (ii. 1) of the world — and more particularly its moral governor (ii. 2), its "just judge" (ii. 2) — but more especially as our "defender and protector,"[96] our Father[97] who is also our Lord, in whose "fatherly indulgence"[98] we may trust.

There is in the "Institutes" little specific exposition of the manner in which we arrive at the knowledge of these attributes. The works of God, we are told, illustrate particularly His wisdom (v. 2) and His power (v. 6). But His power, we are further told, leads us on to think of His eternity and His self-existence, "because it is necessary that He from whom everything derives its origin, should Himself be eternal and have the ground of His being in Himself": [99] while we must

[91] misericordia, ii. 1; x. 2; misericors, ii. 2 (bonus et misericors).

[92] gratia, v. 3.

[93] beneficus, v. 7; voluntas ad beneficentiam proclivis, x. 1; Dei favor et beneficentia, xvii. 1.

[94] benignitas, v. 7; benignus et beneficus, v. 7.

[95] bonus et misericors, ii. 2; benignus et beneficus, v. 7; bonorum omnium fons et origo, ii. 2; bonorum omnium autor, ii. 2; voluntas ad beneficentiam proclivis, x. 1; bonorum omnium perfecta affluentia, i. 1; in Deo residet bonorum infinitas, i. 1.

[96] tutor et protector, ii. 2.

[97] Dominus et Pater, ii. 2.

[98] paterna indulgentia, v. 7.

[99] v. 6: iam ipsa potentia nos ad cogitandam eius aeternitatem deducit; quia aeternum esse, et a se ipso principium habere necesse est unde omnium trahunt originem.

posit His goodness to account for His will to create and preserve the world.[100] By the works of providence God manifests
primarily His benignity and beneficence; and in His dealing
with the pious, His clemency, with the wicked His severity [101]
— which are but the two sides of His righteousness: although,
of course, " His power and wisdom are equally conspicuous." [102]
It is precisely the same body of attributes which are ascribed
to God in the Scriptures,[103] and that not merely in such a passage as Ex. xxxiv. 6, to which we have already alluded, but
everywhere throughout their course (x. 1, *ad fin.*). Psalm cxlv.,
for example, so exactly enumerates the whole list of God's perfections that scarcely one is lacking. Jeremiah ix. 24, while not
so full, is to the same effect. Certainly the three perfections
there mentioned are the most necessary of all for us to know —
the divine " mercy in which alone consists all our salvation;
His justice, which is exercised on the wicked every day, and
awaits them more grievously still in eternal destruction; His
righteousness, by which the faithful are preserved and most
lovingly supported." Nor, adds Calvin, is there any real omission here of the other perfections — " either of His truth, or
power, or holiness, or goodness." " For how could we be assured, as is here required, of His righteousness, mercy and
justice, unless we were supported by His inflexible veracity?
And how could we believe that He governs the world in justice
and righteousness unless we acknowledged His power? And
whence proceeds His mercy but from His goodness? And if all
His ways are justice, mercy, righteousness, certainly holiness
also is conspicuous in them." The divine power, righteousness,
justice, holiness, goodness, mercy, and truth are here brought
together and concatenated one with the others, with some indication of their mutual relations, and with a clear intimation
that God is not properly conceived unless He is conceived in
all His perfections. Any description of Him which omits more
or fewer of these perfections, it is intimated, is justly chargeable with defect. Similarly when dealing with those more fundamental " epithets " by which His essence is described (xiii.

[100] *Do.*   [101] v. 7.   [102] v. 8.   [103] x. 2.

1), he makes it plain that not to embrace them all in our thought of God, and that in their integrity, is to invade His majesty: the fault of the Manichaeans was that they broke up the unity of God and restricted His immensity.[104]

There is no lack in Calvin's treatment of the attributes, then, of a just sense of their variety or of the necessity of holding them all together in a single composite conception that we may do justice in our thought to God. He obviously has in mind the whole series of the divine perfections in clear and just discrimination, and he accurately conceives them as falling apart into two classes, the one qualities of the divine essence, the other characteristics of the divine person — in a word, essential and personal attributes: and he fully realizes the relation of these two classes to each other, and as well the necessity of embracing each of the attributes in its integrity in our conception of God, if we are to do any justice whatever to that conception.

What seems to be lacking in Calvin's treatment of the attributes is detailed discussion of the notion imbedded in each several attribute and elaboration of this notion as a necessary element in our conception of God. Calvin employs the terms unity, simplicity, self-existence, incomprehensibility, spirituality, infinity, immensity, eternity, immutability, perfection, power, wisdom, righteousness, justice, holiness, goodness, benignity, beneficence, clemency, mercy, grace,[105] as current terms

104 I. xiii. 1: Certe hoc fuit et Dei unitatem abrumpere, et restringere immensitatem.

105 These are fairly brought together by P. J. Muller, " De Godsleer van Calvijn," 1881, pp. 39–44. The third section of the " Instruction " (French, 1537) or " Catechism " (Latin, 1538) is almost a complete treatise in brief on the attributes. As in the " Institutes," on which this " Catechism " is based, the attributes derived from the study of the Divine Works are first enumerated and then those derived from the Word. As to the former, Calvin says: " For we contemplate in this universe of things, the *immortality* of our God, from which has proceeded the commencement and origin of all things; His *power* (*potentia*) which has both made and now sustains so great a structure (*moles*, machine); His *wisdom*, which has composed and perpetually governs so great and confused a variety in an order so distinct; His *goodness*, which has been the cause to itself that all these things were created and now exist; His *justice*, which wonderfully manifests itself in the defense of the

bearing well-understood meanings, and does not stop to develop their significance except by incidental remarks.[106] The
confidence which he places in their conveyance of their meaning seems to be justified by the event; although, no doubt,
much of the effect of their mere enumeration is due to the remarkable lucidity of Calvin's thought and style: he uses his
terms with such consistency and exactness, that they become
self-defining in their context. We are far, then, from saying
that his method of dealing with the attributes, by mere allusion as we might almost call it, is inadequate for the practical
religious purpose for which he was writing: and certainly it
is far more consonant with the literary rather than scholastic
form he gives his treatise. When we suggest, then, that from
the scholastic point of view it seems that it is precisely at this
point that Calvin's treatment of the attributes falls somewhat
short of what we might desire, we must not permit to slip
out of our memory that Calvin expressly repudiates the scholastic point of view and is of set purpose simple and practical.[107]

---

good and the punishment of the wicked; His *mercy*, which, that we may be
called to repentance, endures our wickedness with so great a clemency " (*Opp.*
v. 324–325).

[106] Observe the admirable discussion of the omnipotence of God after
this incidental fashion in " Institutes," I. xvi. 3.

[107] Cf. P. J. Muller, " De Godsleer van Calvijn," 1881, p. 45: " No doubt
we should expect a doctrine of the attributes, when we hear him say that
God has revealed Himself in His *virtutes*, but we should bear in mind
that Calvin (although not always free himself from philosophical influences)
renounces philosophical treatment of theological questions, and is extremely
practical, so that it is to him, for example, less important to seek a connection between the several attributes, than to point out what we may learn
from them not so much of God, as for ourselves and our lives." — So, also,
" De Godsleer van Zwingli en Calvijn," 1883, pp. 46–47: " Calvin does not recommend such a ' knowledge of God ' as merely ' raises an idle speculation in
the brain,' but such an one ' as should be firm and fruitful also in consequences,
which can be expected only of the knowledge which has its seat in the
heart ' (I. v. 9). He considers the knowledge of the nature and of the attributes of God more a matter of the heart than of the understanding; and such
knowledge not only must arouse us to ' the service of God, but must also
plant in us the hope of a future life ' (I. v. 10). In his extreme practicality —
as the last remark shows us — Calvin rejected the philosophical treatment of
the question. The Scriptures, for him the fountain of the knowledge of God,
he takes as his guide in his remarks on the attributes." Compare what Lob-

He does not seek to obtain for himself or to recommend to others such a knowledge of God as merely "raises idle speculation in the brain"; but such as "shall be firm and fruitful" and have its seat in the heart. He purposely rejects, therefore, the philosophical mode of dealing with the attributes and devotes himself to awakening in the hearts of his readers a practical knowledge of God, a knowledge which functions first in the fear (*timor*) of God and then in trust (*fiducia*) in Him.

And here we must pause to take note of this two-fold characterization of the religious emotion, corresponding, as it does in Calvin's conception, to the double aspect in which God is contemplated by those who know Him. God is our Lord, in whose presence awe and reverence become us; God is our Father, to whom we owe trust and love. Fear and love — both must be present where true piety is: for, says Calvin, what " I call piety (*pietas*) is that reverence combined with love of God, which a knowledge of His benefits produces " (I. ii. 1). In the form he has given this statement the element of reverence (*reverentia*) appears to be made the formative element: piety is reverence, although it is not reverence without love. But if it is not reverence in and of itself but only the reverence which is informed by love, love after all may be held to become the determining element of true piety. And Calvin does not hesitate to declare with the greatest emphasis that the apprehension of God as deserving of our worship and adoration — in a word as our Lord — *simpliciter*, does not suffice to produce true piety: that is not born, he says, until " we are persuaded that God is the fountain of all that is good and cease to seek for good elsewhere than in Him " (*ibid.*); that is to say, until we apprehend Him as our Father as well as our Lord. " For," adds he, " until men feel that they owe everything to God,

---

stein says in his " Études sur la doctrine Chrétienne de Dieu," 1907, p. 113: " The passages of Calvin's *Institutes* devoted to the idea of the divine omnipotence are inspired and dominated by the living interest of piety, which gives to their discussions a restrained emotion and a warmth to which no reader can remain insensible."

that they are cherished by His paternal care, that He is the author to them of all good things and nothing is to be sought out of Him, they will never subject themselves to Him in willing obedience (*observantia, reverent* obedience); or rather I should say, unless they establish for themselves a solid happiness in Him they will never devote themselves to Him without reserve truly and heartily (*vere et ex animo totos*)." And then he proceeds (I. ii. 2) to expound at length how the knowledge of God should first inspire us with fear and reverence and then lead us to look to Him for good. The first thought of Him awakes us to our dependence on Him as our Lord: any clear view of Him begets in us a sense of Him as the fountain and origin of all that is good — such as in anyone not depraved by sin must inevitably arouse a desire to adhere to Him and put his trust (*fiducia*) in Him — because he must recognize in Him a guardian and protector worthy of complete confidence (*fides*). "Because he perceives Him to be the author of all good, in trial or in need," he proceeds, still expounding the state of mind of the truly pious man, " he at once commits himself to His protection, expectant of His help; because he is convinced that He is good and merciful, he rests on Him in assured trust (*fiducia*), never doubting that a remedy is prepared in His clemency for all his ills; because he recognizes Him as Lord and Father, he is sure that he ought to regard His government in all things, revere His majesty, seek His glory, and obey His behests; because he perceives Him to be a just judge, armed with severity for punishing iniquities, he keeps His tribunal always in view, and in fear restrains and checks himself from provoking His wrath. And yet, he is not so terrified by the sense of His justice, that he wishes to escape from it, even if flight were possible: rather he embraces Him not less as the avenger of the wicked than as the benefactor of the pious, since he perceives it to belong to His glory not less that there should be meted out by Him punishment to the impious and iniquitous, than the reward of eternal life to the righteous. Moreover, he restrains himself from sinning not merely from fear of punishment, but because he loves and reverences God as a father (*loco patris*) and honors and worships Him as Lord (*loco domini*), and even though there were no hell he would quake to offend Him."

We have quoted this eloquent passage at length because it throws into prominence, as few others do, Calvin's deep sense not merely of reverence but of love towards God. To him true religion always involves the recognition of God not only as Lord but also as Father. And this double conception of God is present whether this religion be conceived as natural or as revealed. "The knowledge of God," says he (I. x. 2, *ad fin.*), "which is proposed to us in the Scriptures is directed to no other end than that which is manifested to us in the creation: to wit, it invites us first to the fear of God, then to trust in Him; so that we may learn both to serve Him in perfect innocence of life and sincere obedience, and as well to rest wholly in His goodness." That is, in a word, the sense of the divine Fatherhood is as fundamental to Calvin's conception of God as the sense of His sovereignty. Of course, he throws the strongest conceivable emphasis on God's Lordship: the sovereignty of God is the hinge of His thought of God. But this sovereignty is ever conceived by him as the sovereignty of God our Father. The distinguishing feature of Calvin's doctrine of God is, in a word, precisely the prevailing stress he casts on this aspect of the conception of God. It is a Lutheran theologian who takes the trouble to make this plain to us. "The chief elements which are dealt with by Calvin in the matter of the religious relation," he says, "are summed up in the proposition: God is our Lord, who has made us, and our Father from whom all good comes; we owe Him, therefore, honor and glory, love and trust. We must, so we are told in the exposition of the Decalogue in the first edition of the *Institutes,* just as we are told in Luther's Catechism — we must ' fear and love ' God. . . . [But] we find in the *Institutes,* and, indeed, particularly in the final edition, expressions in which the second of these elements is given the preference. . . . We may find, indeed, in Luther and the Lutherans, the element of fear in piety still more emphasized

than in Calvin. . . ." [108] In a word, with all his emphasis on
the sovereignty of God, Calvin throws an even stronger emphasis on His love: and his doctrine of God is preëminent
among the doctrines of God given expression in the Reformation age in the commanding place it gives to the Divine
Fatherhood. " Lord and Father " — fatherly Sovereign, or sovereign Father — that is how Calvin conceived God.

It was precisely because Calvin conceived of God not only
as Lord, but also as Father, and gave Him not merely his
obedience but his love, that he burned with such jealousy for
His honor. Everything that tended to rob God of the honor due
Him was accordingly peculiarly abhorrent to him. We cannot
feel surprised, therefore, that he devotes so large a portion of
his discussion of the doctrine of God to repelling that invasion of the divine rights which was wrought by giving the
worship due to Him alone to others, and particularly to idols,
the work of man's own hand. His soul filled with the vision of
the majesty of a God who will not give His glory to another,
and his heart aflame with a sense of the Fatherly love he was
receiving from this great God, the Lord of heaven and earth,
he turned with passionate hatred from the idolatrous rites into
which the worship of the old Church had so largely degenerated, and felt nothing so pressingly his duty as to trace out the
fallacies in the subtle pleas by which men sought to justify
them to themselves, and so far as lay within him to rescue
those who looked to him for guidance from such dreadful profa-
nation of the divine majesty. As a practical man, with his
mind on the practical religious needs of the time, this " brutal
stupidity " of men, desiring visible figures of God — who is an
invisible Spirit — corrupting the divine glory by fabricating
for themselves gods out of wood, or stone, or gold, or silver, or
any other dead stuff, seemed to him to call for rebuke as little
else could. The principle on which he proceeds in his rebuke
of idolatry is expressed by himself in the words, that to attribute to anything else than to the one true God, anything that
is proper to divinity is " to despoil God of His honor and to

[108] Köstlin, as cited, pp. 424–425.

violate His worship." [109] So deeply rooted is the jealousy for
the divine honor given expression in this principle not only in
Calvin's thought, but in that of the whole tendency of thought
which he represents, that it may well be looked upon as a determinative trait of the Reformed attitude — which has therefore been described as characterized by a determined protest
against all that is pagan in life and worship.[110]

Certainly the zeal of Calvin burned warmly against the
dishonor he felt was done to God by the methods of worshipping Him prevalent in the old Church. God has revealed Himself not only in His Word, but also in His works, as the one
only true God. But the vanity of man has ever tended to corrupt the knowledge of God and to invent gods many and lords
many, and not content with that, has sunk even to the degradation of idolatry — fabricating gods of wood or stone,

[109] I. xii. 1: Quod autem priore loco posui, tenendum est, nisi in uno
Deo resideat quidquid proprium est divinitatis, honore suo ipsum spoliari,
violarique eius cultum.

[110] Cf. Schweizer, "Glaubenslehre d. rf. Kirche," i. 1844, p. 16: "Only an
essentially complete survey of the particular Reformed dogmas can lead to
the fundamental tendency to which they all belong. This can be represented
as a dominating protest against all that is pagan." P. 25: "Protestation against
the deification of the creature is therefore everywhere the dominating, all-
determining impulse of Reformed Protestantism." (Cf. pp. 40, 59, and the
exposition there of how this principle worked to prevent all half-measures
and inconsequences in the development of Reformed thought.) Cf. also
Scholten, "De Leer der Hervormde Kerk," 1870, ii. pp. 12, 13: "Schweizer
finds the characteristic of the Reformed doctrine in the Biblical principle of
man's entire dependence on God, together with protestation on the ground
of original Christianity against any heathenish elements which had seeped
into the Church and its teaching. That in the opposition of the Reformed to
Rome, such an aversion to all that is heathenish exhibited itself, history tells
us, and cannot be denied." P. 17: "The maintenance of the sovereignty of
God is the point from which, with the Reformed, everything proceeds. Hence
as well their protest against the pagan element in the Romish worship. . . ."
Pp. 150–151: "What led Luther to repudiate the intercession and adoration
of Mary and the saints was primarily the conviction that the saints are sinners and their intercession and merits, therefore, cannot avail us, cannot cover
our sins before God. Zwingli and Calvin take their starting point here, from
the conception of *God* and deny that the love of *God* can be dependent
on any intercession, and reject the worship of Mary and the honoring of the
saints as a deification of creatures, and an injury to the sovereignty of God"
(cf. also pp. 139–140; 16 *sq.*).

gold or silver, or some other dead stuff. It is, of course, not idolatry in general, but the idolatry of the Church of Rome that Calvin has his eye particularly upon, as became him as a practical man, absorbed in the real problems of his time. He therefore particularly animadverts upon the more refined forms of idolatry, ruthlessly reducing them to the same level in principle with the grossest. God does not compare idols with idols, he says, as if one were better and another worse: He repudiates all without exception — all images, pictures, or any other kind of tokens by which superstitious people have imagined He could be brought near to them (I. xi. 1, end). He embraces all forms of idolatry, however, in his comprehensive refutation; he even expressly adverts to the "foolish subterfuge" (*inepta cautio*) of the Greeks, who allow painted but not graven images (I. xi. 4, end). Or rather he broadens his condemnation until it covers even the false conceptions of God which we frame in our imaginations (I. xi. 4, *ad init.*), substituting them for the revelations He makes of Himself: for the "mind of man," he says, "is, if I may be allowed the expression, a perpetual factory of idols" (I. xi. 8). Thus he returns to "the Puritan conception" which we have seen him already announcing in former chapters, and proclaims as his governing principle (I. xi. 4, *med.*) that "all modes of worship which men excogitate from themselves are detestable." [111]

He does not content himself, however, with proclaiming and establishing this principle. He follows the argument for the use of images in worship into its details and refutes it item by item. To the plea that "images are the books of the illiterate" and by banishing them he is depriving the people of their best means of instruction, he replies that no doubt they do teach something, but what they teach is falsehood: God is not as they represent Him (§§ 5–7). To the caveat that no one worships the idols, but the deity through the idols, that they are never called "gods" and that what is offered them is δουλεία, not λατρεία — he replies that all this is distinction

[111] Ut hoc fixum sit, detestabiles esse omnes cultus quos a se ipsis homines excogitant.

without difference; the Jews in their idolatry reasoned in a similar manner, and it is easy to erect a distinction between words, but somewhat more difficult to establish a real difference in fact (§§ 9–11). To the reproach that he is exhibiting a fanaticism against the representative arts, he rejoins that such is far from the case; he is only seeking to protect these arts from abusive application to wrong purposes (§§ 12, 13). And finally to the appeal to the decisions of the Council of Nice of 786–787 favorable to image-worship, he replies by an exposure of the " disgusting insipidities " and " portentous impiety " of the image-worshipping Fathers at that Council (§§ 14 *sq.*). The discussion is then closed (chap. xii.), with a chapter in which he urges that God alone is to be worshipped and only in the way of His own appointment; and above all that His glory is not to be given to another. Thus the ever-present danger of idolatry, as evidenced in the gross practices of Rome, is itself invoked to curb speculation on the nature of the Godhead and to throw men back on the simple and vitalizing revelation of the word of a God like us in that He is a spiritual person, but unlike us in that He is clothed in inconceivable majesty. These two epithets — immensity and spirituality — thus stand out as expressing the fundamental characteristics of the divine essence to Calvin's thinking: His immensity driving us away in terror from any attempt to measure Him by our sense; His spirituality prohibiting the entertainment of any earthly or carnal speculation concerning Him (I. xiii. 1).

In the course of this discussion there are three matters on which Calvin somewhat incidentally touches which seem too interesting to be passed over unremarked. These are what we may call his philosophy of idolatry, his praise of preaching, and his recommendation of art.

His philosophy of idolatry (I. xi. 8, 9) takes the form of a psychological theory of its origin. While allowing an important place in the fostering and spread of idolatry to the ancient customs of honoring the dead and superstitiously respecting their memory, he considers idolatry more ancient than these customs, and the product of debased thoughts of God. He enumerates four stages in its evolution. First, the mind of man, filled with pride and rashness, dares to imagine a god after its own notion; [112] and laboring in its dullness and sunk in the crassest ignorance, naturally conceives a vain and empty spectre for God. Next, man attempts to give an outward form to the god he has thus inwardly excogitated; so that the hand brings forth the idol which the mind begets. Worship follows hard on this figment; for, when they suppose they see God in the images, men naturally worship Him in them. Finally, their minds and eyes alike being fixed upon the images, men begin to become more imbruted, and stand amazed and lost in wonder before the images, as if there were something of divinity inherent in them. Thus easy Calvin supposes to be the descent from false notions of deity to the superstitious adoration of stocks and stones, and thus clearly and reiteratedly he discovers the roots of idolatry in false conceptions of God and proclaims its presence in principle wherever men permit themselves to think of God otherwise, in any particular, than He has revealed Himself in His works and Word.

As we read Calvin's energetic arraignments of the sinfulness of our deflected conceptions of God — the essential idolatry of the imaginary images we form of Him — and our duty diligently to conform our ideas of God to the revelations of Himself He has graciously given us, we are reminded of an eloquent picture which the late Professor A. Sabatier once drew [113] of a concourse of professing Christians coming together to worship in common a God whom each conceives after his own fashion. Anthropomorphists, Deists, Agnostics, Pantheists — all bow alike before God and worship, says Prof. Sabatier; and the worship of one and all is acceptable, equally acceptable, to God. Not so, rejoins M. Bois: [114] and there is not a less admirable spectacle in the world than this. Calvin was of M. Bois's opinion. To his thinking we have before us in such a

[112] pro captu suo.

[113] In his "Esquisse d'une philosophie de la religion," 1897, pp. 303–304. The chapter of which this is a part was published separately in a slightly different form in 1888, with the title: " La vie intime des dogmes et leur puissance d'évolution."   [114] H. Bois: " De la connaissance religieuse," 1894, p. 36.

concourse only a company of idolaters — each worshipping not
the God that is but the god who in the pride of his heart he
has made himself. And to each and all Calvin sends out the
cry of, Repent! turn from the god you have made yourself and
serve the God that is!

It is in the midst of his response to the specious plea that
images are the books of the illiterate and the only means of
instruction available for them that Calvin breaks out into a
notable eulogy on preaching as God's ordained means of instructing His people (I. xi. 7). Even though images, he remarks, were so framed that they bore to the people a message
which might be properly called divine — which too frequently
is very far from the case — their childish suggestions (*naeniae*)
are little adapted to convey the special teaching which God
wishes to be taught His people in their solemn congregations,
and has made the common burden of His Word and Sacraments — from which it is to be feared, however, the minds of
the people are fatally distracted as their eyes roam around to
gaze on their idols. Do you say the people are too rude and
ignorant to profit by the heavenly message and can be reached
only by means of the images? Yet these are those whom the
Lord receives as His own disciples, honors with the revelation
of His celestial philosophy, and has commanded to be instructed in the saving mysteries of His kingdom! If they have
fallen so low as not to be able to do without such " books " as
images supply, is not that only because they have been de-
frauded of the teaching which they required? The invention of
images, in a word, is an expedient demanded not by the rude-
ness of the people so much as by the dumbness of the priests.
It is in the true preaching of the Gospel that Christ is really
depicted — crucified before our eyes openly, as Paul testifies:
and there can be no reason to crowd the churches with cruci-
fixes of wood and stone and silver and gold, if Christ is faithfully preached as dying on the cross to bear our curse, expiating
our sins by the sacrifice of His body, cleansing us by His blood
and reconciling us to God the Father. From this simple proclamation more may be learned than from a thousand crosses.

Thus Calvin vindicates to the people of God their dignity as God's children taught by His Spirit, their right to the Gospel of grace, their capacity under the instruction of the Spirit to receive the divine message, and the central place of the preaching of the atonement of Christ in the ordinances of the sanctuary.

It seems the more needful that we should pause upon Calvin's remarks on art in this discussion long enough to take in their full significance, that this is one of the matters on which he has been made the object of persistent misrepresentation. It has been made the reproach of the Reformation in general and of Calvinism in particular that they have morosely set themselves in opposition to all artistic development, while Calvin himself has been inveighed against as the declared enemy of all that is beautiful in life. Thus, for example, Voltaire in his biting verse has explained that the only art which flourished at Geneva (where men cyphered but could not laugh) was that of the money-reckoners: and that nothing was sung there but the antique concerts of " the good David " in the belief " that God liked bad verses." Even professed students of the subject have passionately assailed Calvin as insensible to the charms of art and inimical to all forms of artistic expression. Thus, M. D. Courtois, the historian of sacred music among the French Reformed, permits himself, quite contrary to the facts in the sphere of his own especial form of art, to say that Calvin " nourished a holy horror for all that could resemble an intrusion of art into the religious domain "; and M. E. Müntz, who writes on " Protestantism and Art," exclaims that " in Calvin's eyes beauty is tantamount to idolatry "; while M. O. Douen, the biographer of Clément Marot, brands Calvin as " anti-liberal, anti-artistic, anti-human, anti-Christian." The subject is too wide to be entered upon here in its general aspects. Professor E. Doumergue and Dr. A. Kuyper have made all lovers of truth their debtors by exposing to the full the grossness of such calumnies.[115]

[115] See: A. Kuyper, " Calvinisme en de Kunst," 1888; " Calvinism," Stone Lectures for 1898–1899, Lecture v.; E. Doumergue, " L'Art et le sentiment dans

In point of fact Calvin was a lover and fosterer of the arts, counting them all divine gifts which should be cherished, and expressly declaring even of those which minister only to pleasure that they are by no means to be reckoned superfluous and are certainly not to be condemned as if forsooth they were inimical to piety. Even in the heat of this arraignment of the misuse of art-representations in idolatry which is at present before us, we observe that he turns aside to guard himself against being misunderstood as condemning art-representations in general (§ 12). The notion that all representative images are to be avoided he brands as superstition and declares of the products both of the pictorial and of the sculptural arts that they are the gifts of God granted to us for His own glory and our good. " I am not held," he says, " in that superstition, which considers that no images at all are to be endured. I only require that since sculptures and pictures are gifts of God, the use of them should be pure and legitimate; lest what has been conferred on us by God for His own glory and for our good, should not only be polluted by preposterous abuse, but even turned to our injury." Here is no fanatical suspicion of beauty: no harsh assault upon art. Here is rather the noblest possible estimate of art as conducive in its right employment to the profit of man and the glory of the God who gives it. Here is only an anxiety manifested to protect such a noble gift of God from abuse to wrong ends. Accordingly in the " Table or brief summary of the principal matters contained in this Institution of the Christian religion," which was affixed to the French edition of 1560, the contents of this section are described as follows: " That when idolatry is condemned, this is not to abolish the arts of painting and sculpture, but to require that the use of both shall be pure and legitimate; and we are not to amuse ourselves by representing God by some

---

l'oeuvre de Calvin," 1902 (the second " Conference " is on " Painting in the Work of Calvin "); " Jean Calvin," etc., ii. 1902, pp. 479–487; " Calvin et l'art " in *Foi et Vie*, 16 March, 1900. Cf. also H. Bavinck, " De Algemeene Genade," 1894; also article " Calvin and Common Grace " in *The Princeton Theological Review*, 1909, vii. pp. 437–465.

visible figure, but only such things as may be objects of sight." [116] Calvin, then, does not at all condemn art, but only pleads for a pure and reverent employment of art as a high gift of God, to be used like all others of God's gifts so as to profit man and glorify the Great Giver.

If we inquire more closely what he held to be a legitimate use of the pictorial arts, we must note first of all that he utterly forbids all representations of God in visible figures.[117] This prohibition he rests on two grounds: first, God Himself forbids it; and secondly, " it cannot be done without some deformation of His glory," — in which we catch again the note of zeal against everything which detracts from the honor of God. To attempt the portraiture of God is, thus, to Calvin, not merely to disobey God's express command, but also to dishonor Him by an unworthy representation of Him, which is essential idolatry. Highly as he esteemed the pictorial arts, as worthy of all admiration in their true sphere, he condemned utterly pressing them beyond their mark, lest even they should become procurers to the Lords of Hell. We note secondly that he dissuaded from the ornamentation of the churches with the products of the representative arts (I. xi. 13); but this on the ground not of the express commandment of God or of an inherent incapacity of art to serve the purposes contemplated, but of simple expediency.[118] Experience teaches us, he says, that to set up images in the churches is tantamount to raising the standard of.idolatry, because the folly of man is so great that it immediately falls to offering them superstitious worship. And a deeper reason lies behind, which would determine his judgment even if this peril were not so great. The Lord has Himself ordained living and expressive images of His grace for His temples, by which our eyes should be caught and held — such ceremonies as Baptism and the Lord's Sup-

[116] *Opp.* iv. 1195. Cf. the parallel remark in the " Genevan Catechism " of 1545 (*Opp.* vi. 55) : " It is not to be understood then, that all sculpture and painting are forbidden, in general; but only all images which are made for divine service or for honoring Him in things visible, or in any way abusing them in idolatry. . . ."

[117] Deum effingi visibile specie nefas esse putamus.   [118] expediat.

per — and we cannot require others fabricated by human ingenuity; and it seems unworthy of the sanctity of the place to intrude them. There is, of course, an echo here of Calvin's fundamental " Puritan principle " with reference to the worship of God: his constant and unhesitating contention that only that worship which is ordained by Himself is acceptable to God. Had God desired the aid of pictorial representations to quicken the devotions of His people He would have ordained them: to employ them is in principle to despise the provisions He has made and to invent others — and we may be sure inadequate if not misleading ones — for ourselves.

This is not the place to inquire into Calvin's positive theory of art-representation. It is worth while, however, as illustrating the wide interests of the man, to note that he has such a theory and betrays the fact that he has it and somewhat of the lines on which it runs, in incidental remarks, even in such a discussion as this. It emerges, for example, that he would confine the sphere of the representative arts to the depicting of objects of sight (*ea sola quorum sint capaces oculi*) — of such things as the eye sees. Of these, however, he discovers two classes — " histories and transactions " on the one side, " images and forms of bodies " on the other.[119] The former may be made useful for purposes of instruction or admonition, he thinks; the latter, so far as he sees, serve only the ends of delectation. Both are, however, alike legitimate, if only they be kept to their proper places and used for their proper ends; for the delectation of man is as really a human need as his instruction. So little does Calvin then set himself with stern moroseness against all art-representation, that he is found actually forming a comprehensive theory of art-representation and pleading for its use, not only for the profit, but also for the pleasure of man.

It remains to speak of Calvin's doctrine of the Trinity.

[119] A. Bossert, " Calvin," 1906, pp. 203–204, after quoting this statement of Calvin's adds: " It is the program of Dutch painting," in this repeating what E. Doumergue in his " Conference " on " Painting in the Work of Calvin " (as cited, pp. 36–51) had fully set forth.

IV
CALVIN'S DOCTRINE OF THE TRINITY

CALVIN'S DOCTRINE OF THE TRINITY [1]

WHEN Calvin turns, in his discussion of the doctrine of
God, from the Divine Being in general to the Trinity (chap.
xiii.), he makes the transition most skillfully by a paragraph
(§ 1) which doubtless has the design, as it certainly has the
effect, of quickening in his readers a sense of the mystery of
the divine mode of existence.[2] The Scriptures, he tells us,
speak sparingly of the divine essence. Yet by two " epithets "
which they apply to it, they effectually rebuke not only the
follies of the vulgar but also the subtleties of the learned
in their thought of God. These epithets are " immensity " and
" spirituality "; and they alone suffice at once to check the
crass and to curb the audacious imaginations of men. How
dare we invade in our speculations concerning Him either the
spirituality or the immensity of this infinite Spirit, conceiving
Him like the Pantheists as an impersonal diffused force, or like
the Manichæans limiting His immensity or dividing His unity?
Or how can we think of the infinite Spirit as altogether like
ourselves? Do we not see that when the Scriptures speak of

[1] From *The Princeton Theological Review*, vii. 1909, pp. 553–652.

[2] Something like Calvin's mode of transition here is repeated by Triglandius when he arrives at this topic in his " Antapologia " (c. v.). " That God
is most simple in His essence," writes Triglandius, " eternal, infinite, and
therefore of infinite knowledge and power, has been sufficiently demonstrated
in the preceding chapter. Whence it is clear that He is one and unique. But
Scripture sets before us here a great mystery, namely that in the one unique
essence of God, there subsist three hypostases, the first of which is called the
Father, the second the Son, the third the Holy Spirit. An arduous mystery
indeed, and one simply incomprehensible to the human intellect; one, therefore, not to be measured by human reason, nor to be investigated by reasons drawn from human wisdom, but to be accredited solely from the Word
of God; by going forward as far as it leads us, and stopping where it stops.
Whenever this rule is neglected the human reason wanders in a labyrinth and
cannot discern either end or exit " (in " Refutatio Apologiae Remonstran-
tium," p. 76).

Him under human forms they are merely employing the art-less art of nurses as they speak to children? All that we can either say or think concerning God descends equally below His real altitude. Calvin thus prepares us to expect depths in the Divine Being beyond our sounding, and then turns at once to speak of the divine tripersonality, which he represents as a mysterious characteristic of the divine mode of existence by which God is marked off from all else that is. " But " — this is the way he puts it (xiii. 2, *ad init.*) — " He points Himself out by another special note also, by which He may be more par-ticularly defined: for He so predicates unity of Himself that He propones Himself to be considered distinctively in three Persons; and unless we hold to these there is nothing but a bare and empty name of God, by no means (*sine*) the true God, floating in our brain."

That we may catch the full significance of this remarkable sentence we should attend to several of its elements. We must observe, for example, that it ranges the tripersonality of God alongside of His immensity and spirituality as another special " note " by which He is more exactly defined. The words are: " But He designates Himself also by *another* special note, by which He may be more particularly distinguished," — the *an-other* referring back to the " epithets " of immensity and spir-ituality.[3] The tripersonality of God is conceived by Calvin,

---

[3] We must not fancy, however, that Calvin conceived the personal dis-tinctions in the Godhead as mere " epithets," that is, that he conceived the Trinity Sabellianwise as merely three classes of attributes or modes of mani-festation of God. He does not say that the tripersonality of God is another " epithet " but another " note " along with His immensity and spirituality — that is to say, another characteristic fact defining God as differing from all other beings. He explicitly denies that the personal distinctions are analogous in kind to the qualities of the divine essence. He says: " Yet in that one essence of God we acknowledge the Father, with His eternal Word and Spirit. In using this distinction, however, we do not imagine three Gods, as if the Father were some other entity (*aliud quiddam*) than the Word, nor yet do we understand them to be mere epithets (*nuda epitheta*) by which God is variously designated, according to His operations; but, in common with the ecclesiastical writers, we perceive in the simple unity of God these three hypostases, that is, subsistences, which, although they coexist in one essence, are not to be confused with one another. Accordingly, though the Father is

therefore, not as something added to the complete idea of God, or as something into which God develops in the process of His existing, but as something which enters into the very idea of God, without which He cannot be conceived in the truth of His being. This is rendered clearer and more emphatic by an additional statement which he adjoins — surely for no other purpose than to strengthen this implication — to the effect that " if we do not hold to these [the three Persons in the divine unity], we have nothing but a naked and empty name of God, by no means the true God, floating in our brain." According to Calvin, then, it would seem, there can be no such thing as a monadistic God; the idea of multiformity enters into the very notion of God.[4] The alternative is to suppose that he is speaking here purely *a posteriori* and with his mind

one God with His Word and Spirit, the Father is not the Word, nor the Word the Spirit." — "Adversus P. Caroli Calumnias," *Opp.* vii. 312. And again in refuting the Sabellians he expressly draws the distinction: " The Sabellians do indeed raise the cavil that God is called now Father, now Son, now Spirit in no other sense than He is spoken of as both strong and good, and wise and merciful; but they are easily refuted by this, — that it is clear that these latter are epithets which manifest what God is *erga nos,* while the others are names which declare what God really is *apud semetipsum.*" — "Institutes," ed. 2, and other middle edd., *Opp.* i. 491.

    [4] The idea of " multiformity," not of " multiplicity " — which would imply *composition.* Hence Calvin, I. xiii. 2, *ad fin.,* declares that it is impious to represent the essence of God as " multiplex "; and at the beginning of that section he warns against vainly dreaming of " a triplex God," and defines that as meaning the division of the simple essence of God among three Persons. The same warning had been given by Augustine, " De Trinitate," VI. vii. 9: " Neither, because He is a Trinity, is He to be therefore thought to be triplex; otherwise the Father alone, or the Son alone, would be less than the Father and Son together, — although it is hard to see how we can say, either the Father alone, or the Son alone, since both the Father is with the Son and the Son with the Father always inseparably." That is to say, God is not a compound of three deities, but a single deity which is essentially trinal. This mode of statement became traditional. Thus Hollaz says: " That is triune which, one in essence, has three modes of subsistence; that is triplex which is compounded of three. We say God is triune; but we are forbidden by the Christian religion to say He is triplex " (in " Examinis Theol. Acroam.," 1741, p. 297). Again: " We may speak of the trinal, but not of the triple deity." Note also Hase's " Hutterus Redivivus," 1848, pp. 166–167; and Keckermann, " Syst. S. S. Theol.," 1615, p. 21.

absorbed in the simple fact that the only true God is actually
a Trinity: so that he means only to say that since the only
God that is, is, in point of fact, a Trinity, when we think of
a divine monad we are, as a mere matter of fact, thinking of
a God which has no existence — which is a mere naked and
empty name, and not the true God at all. The simplicity of
Calvin's speech favors this supposition; and the stress he has
laid in the preceding discussion upon the necessity of conceiving God only as He reveals Himself, on pain of the idolatry of inventing unreal gods for ourselves, adds weight to it.
But it scarcely seems to satisfy the whole emphasis of the statement. The vigor of the assertion appears rather to invite us to
understand that in Calvin's view a divine monad would be less
conceivable than a divine Trinity, and certainly suggests to us
that to him the conception of the Trinity gave vitality to the
idea of God.[5]

This suggestion acquires importance from the circumstance
that the Reformers in general and Calvin in particular have
been sometimes represented as feeling little or no interest in
such doctrines as that of the Trinity. Such doctrines, we are
told, they merely took over by tradition from the old Church,
if indeed they did not by the transference of their interest to
a principle of doctrinal crystallization to which such doctrines
were matters of more or less indifference, positively prepare for
their ultimate discarding. Ferdinand Christian Baur, for example, points out that the distinctive mark of the Reformation, in contrast with Scholasticism with its prevailing dialectic
or intellectualistic tendency, was that it was a deeply religious
movement, in which the heart came to its rights and everything was therefore viewed from the standpoint of the great

---

[5] So in his "Instruction" or "Catechism" of 1537 and 1538 (*Opp.* v.
337 or xxii. 52), Calvin says: "The Scriptures, and pious experience itself,
show us in the absolutely simple essence of God, the Father, the Son, and the
Holy Spirit; so that our intelligence is not able to conceive the Father without at the same time comprehending the Son in whom His living image is
repeated, and the Spirit in whom His power and virtue are manifested." Cf.
the Commentary on Gen. i. 26: "I acknowledge that there is something in
man which refers to the Father and the Son and the Spirit"—the exact
meaning of which, however, is not apparent (see below, note 54, p. 225).

doctrines of sin and grace.[6] He then seeks to apply this observation as follows: " The more decisively Protestantism set the central point of its dogmatic consciousness in this portion of the system, the more natural was the consequence that even such doctrines as that of the Trinity were no longer able to maintain the preponderating significance which they possessed in the old system; and although men were not at once clearly conscious of the altered relation — as, in point of fact, they were not and could not be — it is nevertheless the fact that the doctrines which belong to this category attracted the interest of the Reformers only in a subordinate degree; and, without giving themselves an exact account of why it was so, men merely retained with reference to them the traditional modes of teaching — abiding by these all the more willingly that they could not conceal from themselves the greatness of the difference which existed between them and their opponents in so many essential points." [7] They no doubt set themselves in opposition to the more radical spirits of their time who, taking their starting point from the same general principles, were led by their peculiarities of individuality and relations, of standpoint and tendency, to discard the doctrine of the Trinity altogether. But they could not stem the natural drift of things. " How could the Protestant principle work so thoroughgoing an alteration in one part of the system, and leave the rest of it unaffected? " [8] And what was to be expected except that the polemic attitude with reference to the ecclesiastical doctrine of the Trinity, which was at first confined to small parties outside the limits of recognized Protestantism, should ultimately become a part of Protestantism itself? [9]

In accordance with this schematization, Baur represents Melanchthon as, in the first freshness of his Reformation-consciousness, passing over in his " Loci " such doctrines as that of the Trinity altogether as incomprehensible mysteries of God which call rather for adoration than scrutiny; [10] and,

---

[6] " Die christliche Lehre von der Dreieinigkeit," iii. 1843, pp. 6–7.

[7] Pp. 9–10.   [9] Pp. 10–11.

[8] P. 10.   [10] P. 20.

though he returned to them subsequently, doing so with a difference, a difference which emphasized their subordinate and indeed largely formal place in his system of thought.[11] While as regards Calvin, he sees in him the beginnings of a radical transformation of the doctrine of the Trinity. Calvin does, indeed, like Melanchthon, present the doctrine as the teaching of Scripture, and attaches himself to the ecclesiastical definitions of it as merely a republication of the Scriptural doctrine in clearer words. "We perceive, however, that he does not know how to bring the doctrine itself out of its transcendental remoteness into closer relations with his religious and dogmatic consciousness. Instead, therefore, of speculatively developing the Trinitarian relation as the objective content of the idea of God, out of itself, he rather repels the whole conception as a superfluity which leads to empty speculation (*Inst.*, I. xiii. 19 and 20), or else where he enters most precisely into it, inclines to a mode of apprehending it in which the ecclesiastical *homoousia* is transmuted into a rational relation of subordination." [12] "The intention was to retain the old orthodox doctrine unchanged; but it was internally, in the new consciousness of the times, already undermined, since there was no longer felt for it the same religious and dogmatic interest, as may be seen from the whole manner in which it is dealt with in these oldest Protestant theologians. Men could no longer find their way in the old, abstract form of the dogma. A new motive impulse must first proceed from the central point of the Protestant consciousness. The first beginnings of a transformation of the dogma are already discoverable in Calvin, when he locates the chief element of the doctrine of the Trinity in the practical consciousness of the operations in which the Son and Spirit make themselves known as the peculiar principles of the divine life (I. xiii. 13, 14), and finds the assurance of the election in which the finite subject has the consciousness of his unity with God solely in the relation in which the individual stands to Christ." [13] That is to say, if we understand Baur aright, the new construction of the Trinity already foreshadowed in Calvin was

[11] Pp. 24 *sq.*   [12] Pp. 42–43.   [13] Pp. 44–45.

to revolve around Christ; but around Christ as God-man conceived as the mediating principle between God and man, the unity of the finite and infinite, bearing to us the assurance that what God is in Himself that also He must be for the finite consciousness — in which mode of statement we see, however, a great deal more of Baur's Hegelianism than of Calvin's Protestantism.

So far as this representation implies that Calvin's interest in the doctrine of the Trinity was remote and purely traditional, it is already contradicted, as we have seen, by the first five lines of his discussion of the subject (I. xiii. 2, *ad init.*) — if, that is, as we have seen some reason to believe, he really declares there that vitality is given to the idea of God only by the Trinitarian conception of Him. It is indeed contradicted by itself. For the real meaning of the constitutive place given in Calvin's thought of the Trinity to " the practical consciousness of the operations in which the Son and Spirit make themselves known as the peculiar principles of the divine life," is that the doctrine of the Trinity did not for him stand out of relation to his religious consciousness but was a postulate of his profoundest religious emotions; was given, indeed, in his experience of salvation itself.[14] For him, thus, certainly in no less measure than it had been from the beginning of Christianity, the nerve of the doctrine was its implication in the experience of salvation, in the Christian's certainty that the Redeeming Christ and Sanctifying Spirit are each Divine Persons. Nor did he differ in this from the other Reformers. The Reformation movement was, of course, at bottom a great revival of religion. But this does not mean that its revolt from Scholasticism was from the doctrines " of God, of His unity and His trinity, of the mystery of creation, of the mode of the incarnation "[15]

[14] In the " Catechism " of 1537, 1538 (*Opp.* v. 337 or xxii. 52) he says: " Scripture and *pious experience itself* show us in the absolutely simple essence of God, the Father, the Son and the Holy Spirit."

[15] This is Melanchthon's enumeration of the doctrines which he will not enter into largely in his " Loci." Cf. Augusti's ed. of 1821, p. 8, as quoted by Baur, p. 20: " Proinde non est, cur multum operae ponamus in locis supremis de Deo, de unitate, de trinitate Dei, de mysterio creationis, de modo incarna-

themselves, but from the formalism and intellectualism of the treatment of these doctrines at the hands of the Scholastic theologians. When Melanchthon demands whether, when Paul set down a compendium of Christian doctrine in his Epistle to the Romans, he gave himself over to philosophical disquisitions (*philosophabatur*) " on the mysteries of the Trinity, on the mode of the incarnation, on active and passive creation," and the like, we must not neglect the emphasis on the term "*philosophical disquisitions.*" [16] Melanchthon was as far as possible from wishing to throw doubt upon either the truth or the importance of the doctrines of the Trinity, the Incarnation, Creation. He only wished to recall men from useless speculations upon the mysterious features of these doctrines and to focus their attention no doubt on the great central doctrines of sin and grace, but also on the vital relations of such doctrines as the Trinity, the Incarnation, and Creation to human needs and the divine provision for meeting them. The demand of the Reformers, in a word, was not that men should turn away from these doctrines, but that they should accord their deepest interest to those elements and aspects of them which minister to edification rather

---

tionis." How little Melanchthon was intending to manifest indifference to these doctrines is already apparent from the word *supremis* here. Baur's comment is: " It is precisely with these doctrines which the dialectic spirit of speculation of the Scholastics regarded as its peculiar object, and on which it expended itself with the greatest subtlety and thoroughness, — with the doctrines of God, of His unity and trinity, of creation, incarnation, etc., — that Melanchthon would have so little to do, that he did not even make a place for them in his *Loci,* and that not on the ground that it did not belong to the plan of that first sketch of Protestant dogmatics to cover the whole system, but on the ground of the objective character of those doctrines, as they appeared to him from the standpoint determined by the Reformation " (p. 20). Even so, however, there is not involved any real underestimate of the importance of these doctrines, but only a reference of them to a place in the system less immediately related to the experience of salvation. Nor must we forget the origin of the " Loci " in an exposition of the Epistle to the Romans and its consequent lack of all systematic form, or completeness.

[16] " Loci," as above, p. 9, quoted by Baur, p. 21. The point of Melanchthon's remark is that Paul did not give himself over to philosophical disquisition on abstruse topics, but devoted himself single-heartedly to applying the salvation of Christ to sinning souls.

than to curious questions that furnish exercise only to intellectual subtlety. Any apparent neglect of these doctrines which may seem to be traceable in the earliest writings of the Reformers was, moreover, due not merely to their absorption in the proclamation of the doctrine of grace, but also to the broad fact that these doctrines were not in dispute in their great controversy with Rome, and therefore did not require insisting upon in the stress of their primary conflict. So soon as they were brought into dispute by the radicals of the age, we find the Reformers reverting to them and reasserting them with vigor: and that is the real account to be given of the increased attention given to them in the later writings of the Reformers, which seems to those historians who have misinterpreted the relatively small amount of discussion devoted to them in the earlier years of the movement, symptomatic of a lapse from the purity of their first love and of a reëntanglement in the Scholastic intellectualism from which the Reformation, as a religious movement, was a revolt. In point of fact, it marks only the abiding faith of the Reformers in doctrines essential to the Christian system, but not hitherto largely asserted and defended by them because, shortly, there was not hitherto occasion for extended assertion and defense of them.

In no one is the general attitude of the Reformers to the doctrine of the Trinity more clearly illustrated than in Calvin. The historian of Protestant Dogmatics, Wilhelm Gass, tells us that " Calvin's exposition of the Trinity is certainly the best and most circumspect which the writings of the Reformers give us: surveying as it does the whole compass of the dogma and without any loss to the thing itself wisely avoiding all stickling for words." [17] That this judgment is quoted by subsequent expounders of Calvin's doctrine of the Trinity,[18] surprises us only in so far as so obvious a fact seems not to need the authority of Gass to support it. Apart, however, from the superiority

[17] " Geschichte der protestantischen Dogmatik," i. 1854, p. 105.
[18] Köstlin, *Theologische Studien und Kritiken*, 1868, p. 420; Muller, " De Godsleer van Zwingli en Calvijn," 1883, p. 31.

of Calvin's theological insight, by which his treatment of the doctrine of the Trinity is made not only " the best and most circumspect which the writings of the Reformers have given us," but even one of the epoch-making discussions of this great theme, Calvin's whole dealing with the doctrine of the Trinity supplies an exceptionally perfect reflection of the attitude of the Reformers at large to it. At one with them in his general point of view, the circumstances of his life forced him into a fulness and emphasis in the exposition of this doctrine to which they were not compelled. The more comprehensive character of the work, even in its earliest form, coöperated with the comparative lateness of the time of its publication [19] and his higher systematic genius, to secure the incorporation into even the first edition of Calvin's " Institutes " (1536) not only of a Biblical proof of the doctrine of the Trinity, argued with exceptional originality and force, but also of a strongly worded assertion and defense of the correctness and indispensableness of the current ecclesiastical formulation of it. No more than the earlier Reformers, however, was Calvin inclined to confound the essence of the doctrine with a particular mode of stating it; nor was he willing to confuse the minds of infantile Christians with the subtleties of its logical exposition. The main thing was, he insisted, that men should heartily believe that there is but one God, whom only they should serve; but also that Jesus Christ our Redeemer and the Holy Spirit our Sanctifier is each no less this one God than God the Father to whom we owe our being; while yet these three are distinct personal objects of our love and adoration.[20] He was wholly agreed with his colleagues at Geneva in holding that " in the beginning of the preaching of the Gospel," it conduced more to edification and readiness of comprehension to refrain from

[19] For example, Servetus' " De Trinitatis erroribus " appeared in 1531, and his " Dialogi de Trinitate " in 1532.

[20] " Institutes," I. xiii. 5, *ad init.:* " I could wish that they [the technical terms by which the Trinity is expressed and guarded] were buried, indeed, if only this faith stood fast among all: that the Father and the Son and the Spirit are one God; and yet neither is the Son the Father, nor the Spirit the Son, but they are distinct by a certain property."

the explanation of the mysteries of the Trinity, and even from the constant employment of those technical terms in which these mysteries are best expressed, and to be content with declaring clearly the divinity of Christ in all its fulness, and with giving some simple exposition of the true distinction between the Father, Son, and Holy Spirit.[21] He acted on this principle in drawing up the formularies of faith with which he provided the Church at Geneva immediately after his settlement there, and he vigorously defended this procedure when it was called in question by that " theological adventurer," as he has been not unjustly called,[22] Peter Caroli. This, of course, does not mean that he was under any illusions as to the indispensableness to the Christian faith of a clear as well as a firm belief in the doctrine of the Trinity, or as to the value for the protection of that doctrine of the technical terms which had been wrought out for its more exact expression and defense in the controversies of the past. He was already committed to an opposite opinion by his strong assertions in the first edition of his " Institutes " (1536), which he retained unaltered through all the subsequent editions; and the controversies in which he was contemporaneously embroiled — with Anabaptists, Anti-

---

[21] Cf. their defense of themselves, *Opp.* xi. 6.

[22] Philip Schaff, " History of the Christian Church," vii. 1892, p. 351: " A more serious trouble was created by Peter Caroli, a doctor of the Sorbonne, an unprincipled, vain, and quarrelsome theological adventurer and turncoat. . . . He [Caroli] raised the charge of Arianism against Farel and Calvin at a synod in Lausanne, May, 1537, because they avoided in the Confession the metaphysical terms *Trinity* and *Person*, (though Calvin did use them in his *Institutio* and his Catechism,) and because they refused, at Caroli's dictation, to sign the Athanasian Creed with its damnatory clauses, which are unjust and uncharitable." See also Schaff's " Creeds of Christendom," i. 1881, p. 27, note 1: " Calvin, who had a very high opinion of the Apostles' Creed, depreciates the Nicene Creed, as a ' *carmen cantillando magis aptum, quam confessionis formula* ' (*De Reform. Eccles.*)." It would not, however, be easy to crowd more erroneous suggestions into so few words than Dr. Schaff manages to do here. Calvin did not have difficulty with the metaphysical terminology of the doctrine of the Trinity; he did not object to the damnatory clauses in the Athanasian Creed; he did not depreciate the Nicene Creed. Nor is the passage in which he speaks of the Nicene Creed as more suitable for a song than a creed to be found in the tract, " De vera ecclesiae reformatione."

trinitarians, "theological quacks" — were well calculated to
fix in his mind a very profound sense of the importance of stating this doctrine exactly and defending it with vigor. He was
only asserting, as strongly as he knew how, the right of a
Christian teacher, holding the truth, to avoid strife about words
and to use his best endeavors to "handle aright the word of
truth." He never for one moment doubted, we do not say the
truth merely, but also the importance for the Christian system,
of the doctrine of the Trinity. He held this doctrine with a
purity and high austerity of apprehension singular among its
most devoted adherents. As we have seen, he conceived it not
only as the essential foundation of the whole doctrine of redemption, but as indispensable even to a vital and vitalizing
conception of the Being of God itself. He did not question even
the importance of the technical phraseology which had been
invented for the expression and defense of this doctrine, in
order to protect it from fatal misrepresentation. He freely confessed that by this phraseology alone could the subtleties of
heresy aiming at its disintegration be adequately met. But he
asserted and tenaciously maintained the liberty of the Christian teacher, holding this doctrine in its integrity, to use it
in his wisdom as he saw was most profitable for the instruction of his flock — not with a view to withdrawing it in its entirety or in part from their contemplation or to minimizing its
importance in their sight or to corrupting their apprehension
of it, but with a view to making it a vital element in their faith;
first perhaps more or less implicitly — as implied in the very
core of their creed — and then more or less explicitly, as they
were able to apprehend it; but never as a mere set of more or
less uncomprehended traditional phrases. To him it was a great
and inspiring reality: and as such he taught it to the babes of
the flock in its most essential and vital elements, and defended
it against gainsayers in its most complete and strict formulation.

The illusion into which it is perhaps possible to fall in the
case of the earlier Reformers, by which this double treatment
of the doctrine of the Trinity is supposed to represent consecu-

tive states of mind, is impossible in the case of Calvin. Circumstances compelled him to deal with the doctrine after both fashions contemporaneously. None can say of him, as Baur says of Melanchthon — in our belief wrongly interpreting the phenomena — that he first passed by the doctrine of the Trinity unconcernedly and afterwards reverted to the Scholastic statement of it. At the very moment that Calvin was insisting on teaching the doctrine vitally rather than scholastically, he was equally insisting that it must be held in its entirety as it had been brought into exact expression by the ecclesiastical writers.

Calvin began his work at Geneva on the fifth day of September, 1536, and among the other fundamental tasks with which he engaged himself during the winter of 1536 and 1537 was the drawing up of his first catechism, the " *Instruction* used in the Church at Geneva," as it is called in its French form, which was published in 1537, or the " Catechismus sive Christianae Religionis Institutio," as it is called in the Latin form, which was published early (March) in 1538. Along with this Catechism, there had been prepared in both languages also a briefer " Confession of Faith," written, possibly, not by Calvin himself, but by his colleagues in the Genevan ministry, or, to be more specific, by Farel,[23] but certainly in essence Calvin's, and related to the Catechism very much as the Catechism was related to the " Institutes " of 1536; that is to say, it is a free condensation of the Catechism. In this Confession of Faith, although it was the fundamental documentation of the faith of the Genevan Church to which all citizens were required to subscribe, there is no formal exposition of the doctrine of the Trinity at all: the unity of God alone is asserted (§ 2), and it is left to the mere recitation of the Apostles' Creed, which is incorporated into it (§ 6), supported only by a rare (§ 15) reference to Jesus as God's Son, to suggest the Trinity. Even in

[23] So the Strasburg editors and also A. Lang (" Die Heidelberger Katechismus," 1907, pp. xxxv.–xxxvi.; " Johannes Calvin," 1909, pp. 38 and 208). Doumergue (" Jean Calvin," ii. 1902, pp. 236–251) agrees with Rilliet (" Le Cat. fran. de Calvin, publié en 1537," 1878, pp. lii.–lvii.) in assigning it to Calvin himself.

the Catechism [24] the statement of the doctrine, although explicit and precise, and supported by equally explicit assertions of the uniqueness of our Lord's Sonship ("He is called Son of God, not like believers, by adoption and grace, but true and natural and therefore sole and unique, so as to be distinguished from the others," p. 53, cf. pp. 45-46, 53, 60, 62), and of His true divinity ("His divinity, which He had from all eternity with the Father," p. 53), is far from elaborate. It is confined indeed very much to the assertion of the fact of the Trinity — although even here it is suggested that it enters by necessity into our conception of God; and even this assertion is made apparently only because it seemed to be needed for the understanding of the Apostles' Creed. In the general remarks on this Creed, before the exposition of its several clauses is taken up (p. 52), we read as follows: " But in order that this our confession of faith in the Father, Son and Holy Spirit may trouble no one, it is necessary first of all to say a little about it. When we name the Father, Son and Holy Spirit we by no means imagine three Gods; but the Scriptures and pious experience itself show us in the absolutely simple (*tres-simple*) essence of God, the Father, His Son and His Spirit. So that our intelligence is not able to conceive the Father without at the same time comprehending the Son in whom His living image is repeated, and the Spirit, in whom His power and virtue are manifested. Accordingly, we adhere with the whole thought of our heart to one sole God; but we contemplate nevertheless the Father with the Son and His Spirit." There is certainly here a clear and firm assertion of the fact of the Trinity; we may even admire the force with which, in so few words, the substance of the doctrine is proclaimed, and it is also suggested that it has its roots planted not only in Scripture but in Christian experience, and indeed is involved in a vital conception of God. Calvin assuredly was justified in pointing to it, when

[24] *Opp.* xxii. 33-74. The Latin edition of this Catechism (*Opp.* v. 317-354) was not printed until 1538, but it must have been prepared contemporaneously with the French, since it was quoted by Calvin in the debate with Caroli as early as February, 1537 (see Bähler, "Petrus Caroli und Johannes Calvin," in the *Jahrbuch für schweizerische Geschichte*, xxix. 1904, p. 64, note).

the calumnies raised by Caroli were spread abroad and men were acquiring a suspicion that his " opinion concerning the personal distinctions in the one God dissented somewhat (*non nihil*) from the orthodox consent of the Church," as a proof that he had from the first taught the Church at Geneva " a trinity of persons in the one essence of God." [25] But it is perhaps not strange that this should seem to some very little to say on the fundamental doctrine of the Trinity in a statement of fundamental doctrines which extends to some forty-two pages in length.[26] In its brevity it may perhaps illustrate almost as strikingly as the entire omission of all statement of the doctrine from the accompanying Confession (except as implied in the repetition of the Apostles' Creed) the feeling of Calvin and his colleagues that the elaboration of this doctrine belongs rather to the later stages of Christian instruction, while for babes in Christ it were better to leave it implicit in their general religious standpoint (seeing that it is implicated in the experience of piety itself) than to clog the unformed Christian mind with subtle disputations about it. Meanwhile, at the very moment when Calvin and his colleagues were preparing these primary statements of faith, in which no or so small a space was given to the doctrine of the Trinity, they were also vigorously engaged in confuting and excluding from the Genevan Church impugners of that doctrine. For from the very beginning of his work at Geneva Calvin was brought into conflict with that anti-trinitarian radicalism the confutation of which was to draw so heavily upon his strength in the future. There were already in the early spring of 1537 Anabaptists to confute and banish, among whom was that John Stordeur whose widow was afterwards to become Calvin's wife.[27] And there was to

[25] Preface to the Latin Translation, which was issued, in fact, precisely to meet these calumnies, which had obtained an incredible vogue (*Opp.* v. 318).

[26] We may compare, however, the brevity with which the doctrine of the Trinity is dealt with in the Westminster Confession and Shorter Catechism.

[27] So Colladon tells us, *Opp. Calvini*, xxi. 59; the registers of the Council of Geneva read the name, " Jehan Tordeur." See N. Weiss, *Bulletin de la société de l'histoire du protestantisme français*, lvi. 1907, pp. 228–229.

deal with just before their appearance that poor half-crazy fanatic Claude Aliodi — once Farel's colleague at Neuchâtel — who had as early as 1534 been denying the preëxistence of Christ, and was in the spring of 1537 at Geneva, teaching his anti-trinitarian heresies.[28]

Calvin's exact attitude on the doctrine of the Trinity and its teaching was, moreover, just at this time forced into great publicity by the assaults made upon the Genevan pastors by one of the most frivolous characters brought to the surface by the upheaval of the Reformation.[29] It was precisely at this

[28] Cf. Doumergue, "Jean Calvin," ii. 1902, pp. 241–242. Herminjard, "Correspondance," etc., ed.•2, iii. 1878, Index (note especially pp. 172–175, notes 1, 5, 7). Cf. also the clear brief account of E. Bähler, "Petrus Caroli und Johannes Calvin" (in the *Jahrbuch für schweizerische Geschichte*, xxix. 1904), pp. 73 *sq.*

[29] The Strasburg editors (*Calvini Opera*, vii. p. xxx.) characterize Caroli as "vir vana ambitione agitatus, opinionibus inconstans, moribus levis." Doumergue's judgment upon him is embodied in these words: "Unhappily his character was not as high as his intelligence, and if the new ideas attracted him they did not transform him" (ii. 1902, p. 252). He quotes Douen's characterization of him as "a bold and adventurous spirit badly balanced, and more distinguished by talents than by rectitude of conduct" (p. 253, note 2). Kampschulte ("Johann Calvin," i. 1869, p. 162) contents himself with calling him "a man of restless spirit and changeable principles" — who (p. 295) was not above playing on occasion a dishonorable part. A. Lang's ("Johannes Calvin," 1909, p. 40) characterization runs: "Acute but also weak in character and self-seeking." The inevitable rehabilitation of Caroli has been undertaken by Eduard Bähler, Pastor at Thierachern in Switzerland, in a long article entitled "Petrus Caroli und Johannes Calvin: Ein Beitrag zur Geschichte und Kultur der Reformationszeit," published in the twenty-ninth volume of the *Jahrbuch für schweizerische Geschichte* (1904, pp. 39–168). Bähler's thesis is that Caroli belonged really to that large semi-Protestant party in the French Church which found its inspiration in Faber Stapulensis and its spiritual head in William Briçonnet, Bishop of Meaux; occupying thus a middle ground he could rest content neither in the Roman nor in the Protestant camp — and from this ambiguous position is to be explained all his vacillations and treacheries. Granting the general contention and its explanatory value up to a certain point, it supplies no defense of Caroli's character and conduct, which Bähler's rehabilitation leaves where it found them. Cf. A. Lang's estimate of Bähler's lack of success: "There remains clinging to Caroli enough of wretched frivolity and of the most deplorable inconstancy. How great over against him stands out particularly Farel!" ("Johannes Calvin," 1909, p. 209). On Caroli the historians of the Protestant movement in Metz should be consulted, e.g., Dietsch, "Die evang. Kirche von

time (January, 1537) that Peter Caroli, who was at the moment giving himself the airs of a bishop as "first pastor" at Lausanne, conceived the idea of avenging himself upon the pastors of Geneva for what he thought personal injuries by bringing against them the charge of virtual Arianism. That the charge received an attention which it did not deserve was, no doubt, due in part to an old suspicion which had been aroused against Farel by the calumnies of Claude Aliodi.[30] These were founded on the circumstance that in his "Sommaire" (1524–1525), Farel — with a purely paedagogical intent, as he explained in a preface prefixed to the edition of 1537–1538, because he believed the doctrine of the Trinity too difficult a topic for babes in faith — had passed over the doctrine of the Trinity, just as the Genevan pastors did again in their Confession of 1537.[31] It is difficult for us, in any event, however, at this late date, to understand the hearing which a man like Caroli obtained for his calumnies. The whole Protestant world was filled with suspicions of the orthodoxy of the Genevan pastors. It was whispered from one to another — at Bern, Basle, Zurich, Strasburg, Wittenberg — that they were strangely chary of using the terms "Trinity," "Person," — that they were even "heady" in their refusal to employ them in their popular formularies. It was widely reported that they were beginning to fall into Arianism, or rather into that worst of all errors (*pessimus error*) which Servetus the Spaniard was spreading abroad. Not only was a local crisis thus created, which entailed personal controversies and synods and decisions, but a widely spread atmosphere of distrust was produced, which demanded the most careful and prompt attention. All the spring and summer Calvin was occupied in writing letters hither and thither, correcting the harmful rumors

Metz," pp. 68–77, and Winkelmann, "Der Anteil der deutschen Protestanten an den kirchlichen Reformbestrebungen in Metz bis 1543," in the *Jahrbuch der Gesellschaft für lothringische Geschichte und Altertumskunde*, ix. 1897, pp. 229 *sq.*

30 Cf. Doumergue, "Jean Calvin," ii. 1902, p. 258, note; and Bähler, "Petrus Caroli und Johannes Calvin," p. 73.

31 Cf. Bähler, as cited, p. 71.

which had, as he said, been set going by "a mere nobody" (*homo nihili*), urged on by "futile vanity." [32] And after the conferences and synods and letters, there came at length treatises. The result is that all excuse is taken away for any misapprehension of Calvin's precise position.

Throughout the whole controversy — in which Calvin was ever the chief spokesman, coming forward loyally to the defense of his colleagues, who, rather than he, were primarily struck at — two currents run, as they run through all his writings on the Trinity, and not least through his chapter (I. xiii.) on that subject in the "Institutes." There is everywhere manifested not only a clear and firm grasp of the doctrine, but also a very deep insight into it, accompanied by a determination to assert it at its height. Along with this there is also manifest an equally constant and firm determination to preserve full liberty to deal with the doctrine free from all dictation from without or even prescription of traditional modes of statement. There is nothing inconsistent in these two positions. Rather are they outgrowths of the same fundamental conviction: but the obverse and reverse of the same mental attitude. At the root of all lies Calvin's profound persuasion that this is a subject too high for human speculation and his consequent fixed resolve to eschew all theoretical constructions upon it, and to confine himself strictly to the revelations of Scripture. On the one hand, therefore, because he appealed to Scripture only, he refused to be coerced in his expression of the doctrine by present authority or even the formularies of the past; on the other, because he trusted Scripture wholly, he was insistent in giving full validity to all that he found there. It was the purity of his Protestantism, in other words, which governed Calvin's dealing with this doctrine; giving it an independence which is not yet always understood and has afforded occasion once and again for comment upon his attitude which betrays a somewhat surprising inability to enter into his mind. [33]

[32] Doumergue, ii. 1902, pp. 266–268.

[33] An old instance is supplied by Bellarmine, who, on Caroli's testimony, seeks to intimate that Calvin's refusal at the Council of Lausanne to sign the

For the matter, which has been thus vexed, was perfectly simple. Calvin refused to subscribe the ancient creeds at Caroli's dictation, not in the least because he did not find himself in accord with their teaching, but solely because he was determined to preserve for himself and his colleagues the liberties belonging to Christian men, subject in matters of faith to no other authority than that of God speaking in the Scriptures. He tells us himself that it was never his purpose to reject these creeds or to detract from their credit;[34] and he points out that he was not misunderstood even by Caroli to be repudiating their teaching; but Caroli conceded that what he did was — in Caroli's bad Latin, or as Calvin facetiously calls it, "his

---

Creeds resembled the conduct of the Arians at the Council of Aquileia (" Controversia de Christo," ii. 19, near middle, in " Opp. Omnia," Paris, i. 1870, p. 335). " Calvin," he says, " is not unlike the Arians in this: for at the Council of Aquileia, St. Ambrose never could extort from the two Arian heretics that they should say that the Son is very God of very God; for they always responded that the Son is the very Only-begotten, Son of the very God, and the like, but never that He is very God of very God, although they were asked perhaps a hundred times. And that from Calvin at the Council of Lausanne, it could never be extorted that he should confess that the Son is God of God, Petrus Caroli, who was present, reports in his letter to the Cardinal of Lorraine." Bellarmine is blind to the fact that Calvin was ready to confess all that the Creeds contained to the exaltation of the Son and *more,* while the Arians would not confess so much. Even F. W. Kampschulte (" Johann Calvin," u. s. w., ii. 1899, p. 171) permits himself to say that Calvin " in the controversy with Caroli expresses himself on the Athanasian symbol in a very dubious way (*in sehr bedenklichem Masse*)," and adds in a note: " It was not groundlessly that he was upbraided with this by his later opponents. ' Calvin waxes angry and employs the same taunts as the anti-trinitarians against the Symbol of Athanasius and the Council of Nice, when his opinion touching the Trinity is brought under discussion.' Cf. F. Claude de Saintes, *Declaration d'aucuns atheismes de la doctrine de Calvin,* Paris, 1568, p. 108." Cf. on Kampschulte, Doumergue, " Jean Calvin," ii. 1902, p. 266. We have already had occasion to point out the uncomprehending way in which Dr. Schaff speaks of the matter (above, p. 199, note 22), in which, however, he is only the type of a great crowd of writers.

[34] " Adv. P. Caroli calumnias," *Opp.* vii. 315: Calvino quidem et aliis propositum nequaque erat symbola abiicere aut illis derogare fidem. Compare what he writes on Oct. 8, 1539, to Farel of the discussion at Strasburg: Quamquam id quoque diluere promtum erat, nos non respuisse, multo minus improbasse, sed ideo tantum detrectasse subscriptionem, ne ille, quod captaverat, de ministerio nostro triumpharet (Herminjard, vi. 1883, p. 53).

Sorbonnic elegance " — " neither to credit nor to discredit them." [35] He considered it intolerable that the Christian teacher's faith should be subjected to the authority of any traditional modes of statement, however venerable, or however true; and he refused to be the instrument of creating a precedent for such tyranny in the Reformed Churches by seeming to allow that a teacher might be justly treated as a heretic until he cleared himself by subscribing ancient symbols thrust before him by this or that disturber of the peace. There were his writings, and there was his public teaching, and he was ready to declare plainly what he believed: let him be judged by these expressions of his faith in accordance with the Word of God alone as the standard of truth. Accordingly, when he first confronted Caroli in behalf of the Genevan ministers, he read the passage on the Trinity from the new Catechism as the suitable expression of their belief. And when Caroli cried out, " Away with these new Confessions; and let us sign the three ancient Creeds," Calvin, not without some show of pride, refused, on the ground that he accorded authority in divine things to the Word of God alone.[36] " We have professed faith in God alone," he said, " not in Athanasius, whose Creed has not been

[35] " Adv. P. Caroli calumnias," *Opp.* vii. 316: ego neque credo neque discredo. So Calvin tells Farel that Caroli had reported at Strasburg, not that Calvin and his colleagues had denied the teaching of the three Symbols, but: nos vero non tantum detrectasse [subscriptionem], sed vexasse multis cachinnis symbola illa quae perpetua bonorum consensione authoritatem firmam in Ecclesia semper habuerunt (Herminjard, vi. 1883, p. 52). And, when writing to the Pope, what Caroli charges the Protestant preachers with doing is " ridiculing, satirizing, defaming " the symbols and denying not their truth but their authority: eoque devenisse ut concilii Niceni et divi Athanasii symbola maiori ex parte riderent, proscinderent, proculcarent, et ab ecclesia legitima umquam fuisse recepta negarent (Herminjard, iv. ed. 2, 1878, p. 249). Compare below, note 37, p. 209.

[36] Cf. A. Lang (" Johannes Calvin," 1909, p. 41): " There shows itself here Calvin's self-reliance and independence as over against every kind of ecclesiastical tradition. . . . Thus, in the Confession which he adduced at Lausanne in his and his colleagues' names, he explains: ' We cannot seek God's majesty anywhere except in His Word; nor can we think anything about Him except with His Word, or say anything of Him except through His Word.' . . . ' A religious Confession is nothing but a witness to the faith which abides in us; . . . therefore it must be drawn only from the pure fountain of Scripture.' "

approved by any properly constituted Church." [37] His meaning
is that he refused to treat any human composition as an authoritative determination of doctrine, from which we may decline only on pain of heresy: that belongs to the Word of God
alone. At the subsequent Council of Lausanne he took up precisely the same position, and addressing himself more, as he
says,[38] *ad hominem* than *ad rem*, turned the demand that he

[37] *Opp.* xb. 83–84 (Herminjard, iv. ed. 2, 1878, pp. 185–186): " Ad haec Calvinus, nos in Dei unius fidem iurasse respondit, non Athanasii cuius Symbolum
nulla unquam legitima ecclesia approbasset." Doumergue (" Jean Calvin," ii.
1902, p. 256) renders correctly: " Nous avons jure la foi en un seul Dieu, et non
en Athanase, dont le symbole n'a été approuvé par aucune Église légitime."
Williston Walker (" John Calvin," 1906, p. 197), missing the construction, renders misleadingly: " We swear in the faith of the one God, not of Athanasius,
whose creed no true church would ever have approved." So also A. Lang
(" Johannes Calvin," 1909, p. 40): " Wir haben den Glauben an den einen Gott
beschworen, aber nicht an Athanasius, dessen Symbol eine wahre Kirche nie
gebilligt haben würde." Perhaps worst of all, James Orr, " The Christian View
of God and the World," 1893, p. 309, note: " We have sworn to the belief in
One God, and not to the creed of Athanasius, whose symbol a true Church
would never have had admitted." Calvin is not declaring the Athanasian Creed
unworthy of the approbation of any true church; he is recalling the fact that it
is a private document authorized by no valid ecclesiastical enactment. For
Caroli's account of what Calvin said, see above, note 35, end. Nevertheless,
the Athanasian Creed had attained throughout the Western Church a position of the highest reverence (for the extent of its " reception and use " see
Ommaney, " A Critical Dissertation on the Athanasian Creed," 1897, pp. 420
sq.), and was soon to be " approbated " by the Protestant Churches at large.
Zwingli in the " Fidei Ratio " (1530) and Luther in the Smalcald Articles (1537)
had already placed it among the Symbols of the Churches, whose authority
they recognized: and the " Formula Concordiae " and many Reformed Confessions, beginning with the Gallican, were soon formally to accord it a place
of authority in the Protestant Churches. See Loofs, " Athanasianum," in Herzog, " Realencyklopädie," ed. 3, ii. p. 179; Schaff, " Creeds of Christendom,"
ed. 1, i. p. 40; E. F. Karl Müller, " Die Bekenntnisschriften der reformierten
Kirche," Index *sub voc.*, " Athanasianum "; Ménégoz, as cited in note 42.
Calvin found at Strasburg that the manner in which he had spoken of the
Creeds was offensive to his colleagues there. He writes to Farel (Herminjard,
vi. 1883, p. 53): " It was somewhat harder to purge ourselves in the matter
of the Symbols: for this was what was offensive (*odiosum*), that we repudiated them, though they ought to be beyond controversy, since they were
received by the suffrages of the whole Church. It was easy to explain that
we did not disapprove, much less reject them, but only declined to subscribe
them that he [Caroli] might not enjoy the triumph over our ministry which
he longed for. Some odium, however, always remained."

[38] *Opp.* vii. 316: non tam ad rem quam ad hominem.

should express his faith in the exact words of former formularies into ridicule. He was, he tells us, in what he said about the Creeds just " gibing " [39] Caroli. Caroli had attempted to recite the Creeds and had broken down at the fourth clause of the Athanasian Symbol.[40] You assert, Calvin said, that we cannot acceptably confess our faith except in the exact words of these ancient symbols. You have just pronounced these words from the Athanasian Creed: "Which faith whosoever doth not hold cannot be saved." You do not yourself hold this faith: and if you did, you could not express it in the exact words of the Creed. Try to repeat those words: you will infallibly again stick fast before you get through the fourth clause. Now what would you do, if you should suddenly come to die and the Devil should demand that you go to the eternal destruction which you confess awaits those who do not hold this faith whole and entire, meaning unless you express this your faith in these exact terms? And as for the Nicene Creed — is it so very certain it was composed by that Council? One would surely suppose those holy Fathers would study conciseness in so serious a matter as a creed. But see the battology here: "God of God, Light of Light, very God of very God." Why this repetition — which adds neither to the emphasis nor to the expressiveness of the document? Don't you see that this is a song, more suitable for singing than to serve as a formula of confession? [41] We may or may not think Calvin's pleasantry happy. But we certainly cannot fail to marvel when we read in even recent writers that Calvin refused to sign the Athanasian Creed because of its damnatory clauses, " which are unjust and uncharitable," and that he " depreciated the Nicene Creed." [42]

[39] iocatus est (ibid., p. 315).

[40] " When he had recited three clauses of the Athanasian Symbol, he was not able to recite the fourth . . ." (ibid., p. 311, top).

[41] Ibid., pp. 315–316. This manner of speaking of the Nicene Creed also impressed the Strasburg theologians unfavorably. Calvin writes to Farel Oct. 8, 1539 (Herminjard, vi. 1883, p. 54) : " I had to give satisfaction about the battologies. I could not by any effort convince them that there is any battology there. I admitted, however, that I should not have so spoken if I had not been compelled by that man's wickedness."

[42] Schaff: see p. 199 above, note 22. E. Ménégoz is therefore in the essen-

According to his own testimony, he did nothing of the kind: he "never had any intention of depreciating (*abiicere*) these creeds or of derogating from their credit." [43] His sole design was to make it apparent that Caroli's insistence that only in the words of these creeds could faith in the Trinity be fitly expressed was ridiculous.

Calvin's refusal to be confined to the very words of the old formulas in his expression of the doctrine of the Trinity did not carry with it, therefore, any unwillingness to employ in his definition of the doctrine the terms which had been beaten out in the Trinitarian controversies of the past. These terms he considered rather the best expressions for stating and defending the doctrine. That they were unwilling to employ them had indeed been made the substance of one of the charges brought by Caroli against the Genevan pastors. But the refutation of this calumny, so far as Calvin himself was concerned, was easy. He had only to point to the first edition of the " Institutes " (1536), in which he had not only freely used the terms in question, but had defended at large the right and asserted the duty of employing them, as the technical language by which alone the doctrine of the Trinity can be so expressed as to confound heretical misconstructions. When, then, Caroli expressed his wonder at " the pertinacity with which

tials of the matter right, when he expresses his wonder that men can suppose that the circumstances that Calvin " once refused to obey an injunction to sign the Symbol," or " pronounced a judgment unfavorable to the literary form of this document " — M. Ménégoz is confusing for the moment the Athanasian and Nicene Creeds — prove that " in the depths of his heart he held these anathemas in aversion " (" Publications diverses sur le Fidéisme," 1900, pp. 276–277). He adds with equal justice: " It is an infelicitous idea to appeal to Calvin as a witness that Protestantism, though receiving the Catholic Symbols, had no intention of approving their anathemas. And it is a historical error to imagine that the Reformers would have accepted these Symbols, if they had not firmly believed them, if they had felt any scruples, or cherished any mental reservations regarding the damnatory clauses. There was no paltering in a double sense in that age. There was no practice of ' economy.' . . . If the Protestants had felt any hesitation about the anathemas, they would have said so without ambiguity, and they would have purely and simply discarded the Symbols. Nothing would have been easier."

[43] *Opp.* vii. 315.

Calvin refused the terms ' Person,' ' Trinity,' '' Calvin replied flatly that neither he nor Farel nor Viret ever had the smallest objection to these terms. " The writings of Calvin," he adds, " testify to the whole world that he always employed them freely, and even reprehended the superstition of those who either disliked or avoided them." [44] That the Genevan pastors passed them by in their Confession, and refused to employ them when this was violently demanded of them, he explains, was due to two reasons. They were unwilling to consent to such tyranny as that when a matter has been sufficiently and more than sufficiently established, credit should be bound to words and syllables. But their more particular reason was, he adds, that they might " deprive that madman of the boast he had insolently made." " For Caroli's purpose was to cast suspicion on the entire doctrine of men of piety and to destroy their influence." [45] Though they felt to the full, therefore, the value of these terms, not only for confounding heresy, but also for consolidating churches in a common confession, when their use was contentiously demanded of them they followed a high example and refused to give place, in the way of subjection, even for an hour.

Calvin's attitude to the employment of this technical language is sufficiently interesting in itself to repay a pause to observe it. As we have intimated, it is fully set forth already in the first edition of the " Institutes " (1536) in a very interesting passage, which is retained without substantial alteration throughout all the subsequent editions. The position of this passage in the discussion of the doctrine of the Trinity, however, is changed in the final edition from its end (as in all the earlier editions) to its beginning. In the final edition, therefore, it appears as a preface to the discussion of the substance of the doctrine (I. xiii. 3–5), and it is strengthened in this edition by an introductory paragraph (§ 2), in which an attempt is made to vindicate for one of these technical terms direct Biblical authority. Calvin finds the term " Person " in the ὑπόστασις of Heb. i. 3; and insists, therefore, that it, at

[44] *Opp.* vii. 318.   [45] " Adv. P. Caroli calumnias ": *Opp.* vii. 318.

least, is not of human invention (*humanitus inventa*). The argument in which he does this is too characteristic of him and too instructive, not only as to his attitude towards the terms in question, but also as to his doctrine of the Trinity and his exegetical methods, to be passed over in silence. We must permit ourselves so much of a digression, therefore, as will enable us to attend to it.

What Calvin does, in this argument, is in essence to subject the statement of Heb. i. 3 that the Son is " the very image of the hypostasis of God " — the χαρακτὴρ τῆς ὑποστάσεως αὐτοῦ — to a strict logical analysis. The term ὑπόστασις, he argues, must designate something the Son is not: for He could scarcely be said to be the *image* of something He is. When we say *image,* we postulate two distinct things: the thing imaged and the thing imaging it. If the Son is the *image* of God's hypostasis, then, the hypostasis of God must be something which the Son does not *share;* it must be rather something which He is *like.* The Son *shares* the Divine essence: hence hypostasis here cannot mean essence. It must be taken then in its alternative sense of " person ": and what the author of the Epistle says, therefore, is that the Son is exactly like the Father in person; His double, so to speak. This Epistle, therefore, expressly speaks here of two Persons in the Godhead, one Person which is imaged, another which precisely images it. And the same reasoning may be applied to the Holy Spirit. There is Biblical warrant, therefore, for teaching that there are three hypostases in the one essence of God — " therefore, if we will give credit to the Apostle's testimony, there are in God three hypostases, " — and since the Latin " person " is but the translation of the Greek " hypostasis," it is mere fastidiousness to balk at the term " person." If anyone prefers the term " subsistence " as a more literal rendering, why, let him use it: or even " substance," if it be taken in the same sense. The point is not the vocable but the meaning, and we do not change the meaning by varying the synonyms. Even the Greeks use " person " (πρόσωπον) interchangeably with " subsistence " (ὑπόστασις) in this connection.

It is not likely that this piece of exegesis will commend itself to us. Nor indeed is it likely that we shall feel perfect satisfaction in the logical analysis, even as a piece of logical analysis. After all, the Son is not the image of the Father in His Personality — if we are, like Calvin, to take the Personality here in strict distinction from the Essence. What the Son differs from the Father in is, rather, just in His " Personality," in this sense: as Person He is the Son, the Father the Father, and what we sum up under this " Fatherhood " and " Sonship " is just the distinguishing " properties " by which the two are differentiated from each other. That concrete Person we call the Son is exactly like that concrete Person we call the Father; but the likeness is due to the fact that each is sharer in the identical essence. After all, therefore, the reason why the Son is the express image of the Father is because, sharing the divine essence, He is in His essence all that the Father is. He is the repetition of the Father: but the repetition in such a sense that the one essence in which the likeness consists is common to the two, and not merely of like character in the two. The fundamental trouble with Calvin's argument is that it seeks a direct proof for the Trinitarian constitution of the Godhead from a passage which was intended as a direct proof only of the essential deity of the Son. What the author of the Epistle to the Hebrews had in mind was not to reveal the relation of the Son to the Father in the Trinity — as a distinct hypostasis in the unity of the essence; but to set forth the absolute deity of the Son, to declare that He is all that God is, the perfect reflection of God, giving back to God when set over against Him His consummate image. The term " hypostasis " is not indeed to be taken here, in the narrow sense, as " essence ": but neither is it to be taken, in the abstract sense, as " person." It means the concrete person, that is to say, the whole substantial entity we call God; which whole substantial entity is said to be in the Son exactly what it is in the Father. Nothing is said directly as to the relation of the Son to the Father, as distinct persons in the Trinity; the whole direct significance of the declaration is exhausted in the assertion that this "Son" differs in no single particular from "God": He is God in the full height of the conception of God.

It is not, however, the success or lack of success of Calvin's exegesis which most interests us at present. It is rather two facts which his exegetical argument brings before us with peculiar force. The one of them is that the developed doctrine of the Trinity lay so firmly entrenched in his mind that he makes it, almost or perhaps quite unconsciously, the major premise of his argument. And the other is that he was so little averse to designating the distinctions in the Godhead by the term "persons" that that term was rather held by him to have definite Biblical warrant. His argument that ὑπόστασις in this passage cannot mean "essence," but must mean "person," turns on this precise hinge — that the Father and Son are numerically one in essence, and can be represented as distinct only in person: "For since the essence of God is simple and indivisible (*simplex et individua*) Him — who contains in Himself the whole of it, not in apportionment or in deflection, but in unbroken perfection (*integra perfectione*) — it would be improper or rather inept to call its image." In other words, the doctrine of the Trinity in its complete formulation is the postulate of his argument. And the outcome of the argument is that the Epistle to the Hebrews distinctly sets the Father and Son over against each other as distinguishable "Persons," employing this precise term, ὑπόστασις, to designate them in their distinction. "Accordingly," says Calvin, "if the testimony of the Apostle obtains credit, it follows that there are in God three hypostases." This term as the expression of the nature of the distinctions in the Godhead is therefore not a "human invention" (*humanitus inventa*) to Calvin, but a divine revelation.

Since, then, the Bible had obtained credit with Calvin, he could not object to the use of the term "person" to express the distinctions in the Trinity. But he nevertheless takes over from the earlier editions, in which the discovery of the term in Heb. i. 3 is not yet to be found, a defense of the use of this term on the assumption that it is not Biblical. And this defense is in essence the assertion of the right and the exposition of a theory of interpretation. There are men, says Calvin, who cry out against every term framed according to human judgment (*hominum arbitrio confictum nomen*) and demand that our words as well as our thoughts concerning divine things shall be kept within the limits of Scripture example. If we use only the words of Scripture we shall, say they, avoid many dissensions and disputes, and preserve the charity so frequently broken in strifes over "exotic words." Certainly, responds Calvin, we ought to speak of God with not less religion than we think of Him. But why should we be required to confine ourselves to the exact words of Scripture if we give the exact sense of Scripture? To condemn as "exotic" every word not found in so many syllables in Scripture, is at once to put under a ban all interpretation which is not a mere stringing together of Scriptural phrases. There are some things in Scripture which are to our apprehension intricate and difficult. What forbids our explaining them in simpler terms — if these terms are held religiously and faithfully to the true sense of Scripture, and are used carefully and modestly and not without occasion? Is it not an improbity to reprobate words which express nothing but what is testified and recorded by the Scriptures? And when these words are a necessity, if the truth is to be plainly and unambiguously expressed — may we not suspect that the real quarrel of those who object to their use is with the truth they express; and that what they are offended by is that by their use the truth has been made clear and unmistakable (*plana et dilucida*)? As to the terms in which the mystery of the Trinity is expressed — the term Trinity itself, the term Person, and those other terms which the tergiversations of heretics have compelled believers to frame and employ that the truth may be asserted and guarded — such as *homoousios*, for example — no one would care to draw sword for them as mere naked words. Calvin himself would be altogether pleased to see them buried wholly out of sight — if only all men would heartily receive the simple faith, that the

Father, Son, and Spirit are one God and yet neither is the Son the Father, nor the Spirit the Son, but they are each distinguished by a certain property (I. xiii. 5). But that is just the trouble. Men will not accept the simple faith, but palter in a double sense. Arius was loud enough in declaring Christ to be God — but wished to teach also that He is a creature and has had a beginning: he was willing to say Christ is one with the Father, if he were permitted to add that His oneness is the same in kind as our own oneness with God. Say, however, the one word ὁμοούσιος — "consubstantial" — and the mask is torn from the face of dissimulation and yet nothing whatever is added to the Scriptures. Sabellius was in no way loath to admit that there are in the Godhead these three — Father, Son, and Holy Spirit; but he really distinguished them only as attributes are distinguished. Say simply that in "the unity of God a trinity of persons subsists," and you have at once quenched his inane loquacity. Now, if anyone who does not like the words will ingenuously [46] confess the things the words stand for — *cadit quaestio:* we shall not worry over the words. "But," adds Calvin significantly, "I have long since learned by experience, and that over and over again, that those who contend thus pertinaciously about terms, are really cherishing a secret poison; so that it is much better to bear their resentment than to consent to use less precise and clear language for their behoof" (I. xiii. 5, *ad fin.*). Golden words! How often since Calvin has the Church had bitter cause to repeat them! When we read, for example, William Chillingworth's subtle pleas for the use of Scriptural language only in matters of faith; his eloquent asseverations — "The Bible, I say, the Bible only is the religion of Protestants"; his loud railing at "the vain conceit, that we can speak of the things of God better than in the words of God," "thus deifying our own interpretations and tyrannously enforcing them upon others" — we know what it all means: that under this cloak of charity are to lie hidden a multitude of sins. When we hear Calvin refusing to swear in the words of another, we must not

[46] non fraudulenter.

confuse his defense of personal right with a latitudinarianism like Chillingworth's. If he said, It is the Word of God, not the word of Athanasius, to which I submit my judgment, he said equally, The sense of Scripture, not its words, is Scripture. No ambiguous meanings should be permitted to hide behind a mere repetition of the simple words of Scripture, but all that the Scripture teaches shall be clearly and without equivocation brought out and given expression in the least indeterminate language.[47]

Calvin's interest was, in other words, distinctly in the substance of the doctrine of the Trinity rather than in any particular mode of formulating it. It rested on the terms in which it was formulated only because, and so far as, they seemed essential to the precise expression and effective guarding of the doctrine. This was consistently his attitude from the beginning. Already in the " Institutes " of 1536, as we have seen, he had given this attitude an expression so satisfactory to himself that he retained the sections devoted to it until the end. It is indeed astonishing how complete a statement of the doctrine of the Trinity itself was already incorporated into this earliest edition of the " Institutes," and how clearly in that statement all the characteristic features of Calvin's treatment of the doctrine already appear. The discussion was no doubt greatly expanded in its passage from the first to the last edition. In the

[47] Dorner's account of Calvin's attitude to these questions is not quite exact either in the motive suggested, or in the precise action ascribed to him, though it recognizes Calvin's contribution to a better understanding of the doctrine ("Doctrine of the Person of Christ," E. T. II. ii. 1862, p. 158, note 1): "Even Calvin, about the time of his dispute with Caroli, asserted the necessity of a developing revision of the doctrine of the Trinity. On this ground he declined pledging himself to the Athanasian Creed, and wished to cast aside the terms 'persona,' 'Trinitas,' as scholastic expressions. At the same time he was so far from being inclined towards the Antitrinitarians, that he wished to carry out the doctrine of the Trinity still more completely. He saw clearly that in the traditional form of the doctrine, the Son had not full deity, because aseity (aseitas) was reserved to the Father alone, who thus received a preponderance over the Son, and was identified with the Monas, or the Divine essence. The Antitrinitarians, with whom he had to struggle, usually directed their attacks on this weak point of the dogma, and deduced therefrom the Antitrinitarian conclusions."

first edition (1536) it occupies only five columns in the Strasburg edition; these have grown to fifteen and a half columns in the middle editions and to twenty-seven and a half (of which eleven and a half are retained from the earlier editions and sixteen are new) in the final edition of 1559. That is to say, its original compass was tripled in the middle editions and almost doubled again in the final edition, where it has become between five and six times as long as in the first draft.[48] And in this process of expansion it has not only gathered increment but has suffered change. This change is not, however, in the substance of the doctrine taught or even in the mode of its formulation or the language in which it is couched or in the general tone which informs it. It is only in the range and the governing aim of the discussion.

The statement in the first edition is dominated by a simple desire to give guidance to docile believers, and therefore declines formal controversy and seeks merely to set down briefly what is to be followed, what is to be avoided on this great subject. Positing, therefore, at the outset that the Scriptures teach one God, not many, but yet not obscurely assert that the Father is God and the Son is God and the Holy Spirit is God; Calvin here at once develops, by combining Eph. iv. 5 and Mat. xxviii. 19, a Biblical proof of the Trinity which in its strenuous logic reminds us of the analytical examination of Heb. i. 3 which we have already noted. Paul, he says, connects together one baptism, one faith and one God; but in Matthew we read that we are to be baptized in the name of the Father and of the Son and of the Holy Spirit — and what is that but to say that the Father and the Son and the Holy Spirit are together the one God of which Paul speaks? [49] This is supported

[48] The "Institutes" as a whole were about doubled in length from the first edition (1536) to the second (1539), and again about doubled in the last edition (1559), so that the last edition (1559) is about four times as long as the first (1536). The treatment of the Trinity was, therefore, a little more expanded than the volume as a whole.

[49] This argument is retained in the later editions and appears in its final form in the ed. of 1559, I. xiii. 16. In its earliest statement it runs thus (1536, pp. 107–108: Strasburg ed., p. 58): "Paul so connects these three things, God, faith and baptism, that he reasons from one to the other (Eph. 4). So that,

by Jeremiah's (xxiii. 33) designation of the Son by " that name which the Jews call ineffable " [50] and other Scriptural evidence

---

because there is one faith, thence he demonstrates that there is one God; because there is one baptism, thence he shows that there is one faith. For since faith ought not to be looking about hither and thither, neither wandering through various things, but should direct its view towards the one God, be fixed on Him and adhere to Him; it may be easily proved from these premises that if there be many faiths there should be many Gods. Again because baptism is the sacrament of faith, it confirms to us His unity, seeing that it is one. But no one can profess faith except in the one God. Therefore as we are baptized into the one faith, so our faith believes in the one God. Both that therefore is one and this is one, because each is of one God. Hence also it follows that it is not lawful to be baptized except into the one God, because we are baptized into faith in Him, in whose name we are baptized. Now, the Scriptures have wished (Mat. at end) that we should be baptized into the name of the Father and of the Son and of the Holy Ghost, at the same time that it wishes all to believe with one faith in the Father, the Son and the Holy Spirit. What is that, truly, except a plain testimony that the Father, Son and Holy Spirit are one God? For if we are baptized in their name, we are baptized into faith in them. They are therefore one God, if they are worshipped in one faith."

[50] *Opp.* i. 58. This awkward periphrasis suggests that, when the " Institutes " were written — in 1534–1535 — Calvin had no convenient expression at hand for the Tetragrammaton. This conjecture is supported by the circumstance that " Jehovah " does not seem to occur in the first edition; it is lacking even in the Preface to the First Commandment, where the customary *Dominus* takes its place. Already in the spring of 1537, however (*Opp.* vii. 314; ix. 704, 708, 709; xb. 107, 121) it is used familiarly; and thenceforward throughout Calvin's life. During his sojourn at Basle (1535) Calvin had studied Hebrew with Sebastian Münster (Baumgartner, " Calvin Hébraïsant," 1889, p. 18), and it was doubtless from him that he acquired the pronunciation " Jehovah " (see Münster on Ex. vi. 3 in " Critici Sacri," Amsterdam ed., 1698, i. 107, 108; Frankfort ed., i. 447; cf. 32). From his own comment on Ex. vi. 3 we may learn the clearness of Calvin's conviction that " Jehovah " is the right pronunciation: " It would be tedious to enumerate all the opinions on the name 'Jehovah.' It is certainly a foul superstition of the Jews that they dare not either pronounce or write it, but substitute 'Adonai' for it. It is no more probable that, as many teach, it is unpronounceable because it is not written according to grammatical rule. . . . Nor do I assent to the grammarians who will not have it pronounced because its inflection is irregular. . . ." How fixed the pronunciation " Jehovah " had become at Geneva by 1570 is revealed by an incident which occurred at the " Promotions " at the Academy that year. The Hebrew Professor, Corneille Bertram, having declared in response to an inquiry that " Adonai " not " Jehovah " was to be read, was rebuked therefor and compelled to apologize: " This M. de Bèze and all the Company found ill-said, and remonstrated with him for agitating

that our Lord is one God with the Father and the Spirit. He has in mind to prove both elements in the doctrine of the Trinity, the unity of God and the true distinction of persons, and therefore introduces these citations with the words: " There are extant also other clear (*luculenta*) testimonies, which assert, in part, the one divinity of the three, and in part their personal

---

this curious and idle question, and for affirming an opinion which very many great men of this age, of good knowledge, piety, and judgment, have held to be absurd, superstitious and merely Rabbinic " (*Reg. Comp.*, 31 May, 1570, cited by Charles Borgeaud, " Histoire de l'Université de Genève," 1900, p. 228). — The history of the pronunciation " Jehovah " has not been adequately investigated. See, however, G. F. Moore, " Notes on the Name יהוה," A. J. T., 1908, xii. pp. 34–52; A. J. S. L., 1909, xxv. pp. 312–318; 1911, xxviii. pp. 56–62. It has become the scholastic tradition to say that it was introduced by Peter Galatin, confessor of Leo X, and first appears in his " De Arcanis Catholicae Veritatis," ii. 10 (the first of two chapters so numbered) which was first published in 1516 (cf. Buhl's " Gesenius' Lexicon," ed. 13, 1899, p. 311, "about 1520 "; Brown, Driver, Briggs, " Hebrew and English Lexicon," 1906, p. 218a, 1520; Kittel, " Herzog," [3] viii. pp. 530–531, 1518; Davidson, Hastings' B. D., art. " God," 1520; A. J. Maclean, Hastings' One Vol. B. D., 1909, p. 300a, 1518; A. H. McNeile, " Westminster Commentary on Exodus," 1908, p. 23, 1518; Oxford English Dictionary, *sub voc.*, 1516; and Moore, *op. cit.*, 1518: cf. the very strong statement of Dillmann, " Alttest. Theologie," 1895, p. 215). But this tradition is simply reported from mouth to mouth, from Drusius' tract on the Tetragrammaton (" Critici Sacri," Amsterdam ed., vol. I. part ii. pp. 322 *sq.*: also in Reland, " Decas. Exercitationum . . . de vera pronuntiatione nominis Jehova," 1707). Since Drusius no one seems to have made any independent effort to ascertain the facts, except F. Böttcher, " Ausführliches Lehrbuch der Hebräischen Sprache," i. 1866, § 88 (p. 49, note 2). In copying Drusius the scholars have failed to note that he himself points out in a later note, inserted on p. 355, that the form " Jehovah " (Porchetus' form is Johova, not Jehova) occurs already in Porchetus, A.D. 1303: and it has been pointed out also that it occurs in Raimund Martini's " Pugio Fidei," which was written about 1270 (Böttcher's suggestion that it may be an interpolation in the " Pugio Fidei " does not seem convincing, although Moore agrees with him here, *op. cit.*). It is not unlikely that Galatin, who draws heavily on Martini either directly or through Porchetti, may have derived it from him: and in any event he uses it not as a novel invention of his own, but as a well-known form. The origin and age of the pronunciation are accordingly yet to seek. The words of Dr. F. Chance (*The Athenæum*, No. 2119, June 6, 1868, p. 796) are here in point: " There is no doubt, I think, that the letters *jhvh* were from the very introduction of the Hebrew points pointed as they now are . . . and if so, surely anybody that read what he had before him must have *read* Jehovah. If the word were never so *written* before the sixteenth century, it was probably because up to that time Hebrew was studied by very few people, except by

distinctions." [51] Then comes the defense of the technical words
by which the truth of the Trinity is expressed and protected,
of which we have already spoken. The enlarged and readjusted
treatment of the topic for the second edition of 1539 seems to
have been composed under the influence of the controversy
with Caroli. It is marked at least by the incorporation of a
thorough proof of the Godhead of the Father, Son and Spirit,
of the unity of their essence, and of the distinction between
them, and a coloring apparently derived from this controversy is thrown over the whole discussion, in which liberty to
formulate the doctrine in our own words and the value of the
technical terms already in use are equally vigorously asserted.
The material of 1539 remains intact throughout the middle
editions (1543, 1550), although some short quotations from
Augustine (§§ 16, 20) and from Jerome and Hilary (§ 24)
were introduced in 1543. But it is very freely dealt with in the
final edition (1559). Only some two-thirds of it (eleven and
a half columns out of fifteen and a half) is preserved in that
edition, while sixteen new columns are added: about three-
fifths of the whole is thus new.[52] Moreover, whole sections are

---

Jews who could not write this holiest of God's names, and by Gentiles who,
having learned their Hebrew from Jews, followed their example in substituting for it in reading and writing, Adonai, the Lord, etc." — No doubt the
vogue of the form in the middle of the sixteenth century is due, not to its
accidental occurrences in Galatin's book, but to the progress of Hebrew scholarship in sequence to the revival of letters, which looked upon the Jewish refusal to pronounce the name as mere superstition and attached an exaggerated importance to the Massoretic pointing. The debate about the proper
pronunciation of the name is, in any event, a Humanistic phenomenon, and
the form "Jehovah" is found in use everywhere where Hebrew scholarship
penetrated, until it was corrected by this scholarship itself. Reuchlin indeed
appears not to have used it; nor Melanchthon. But it is used by Luther
(1526–1527 and 1543, though not in his Bible), and by Matthew Tyndale in
his Pentateuch of 1530, and so prevailingly by Protestant scholars that Romish
controversialists were tempted to represent it as an impiety (so Genebrardus)
of the "Calviniani et Bezani" following the example of Sanctes Pagninus
(who, according to MS. but not printed copies did indeed use it).

[51] *Opp.* i. 58.
[52] The most notable additions are the argument on ὑπόστασις in Heb. i. 3
(§ 2); the definition of "person" (§ 6); and the whole polemic against Servetus and Gentilis (§§ 22 to end). These sections contain nine of the sixteen
new columns.

omitted (§§ 10 and 15), a new order of arrangement is adopted, and much minor alteration is introduced. In this recasting and expansion of the discussion the chief place in the formative forces determining its form and tone is taken by the attack of the radical Antitrinitarians. The existence of these Antitrinitarian scoffers is recognized, indeed, from the first: they are explicitly adverted to already in the edition of 1536 as "certain impious men, who wish to tear our faith up by the roots": it is quite clear, indeed, that Servetus' teachings were already before his mind at this date. But it is only for the final edition (1559) that their assault assumes the determining position at the basis of the whole treatment: and it is only in this edition that Servetus, for example, is named. Now, Calvin not only arrays against them the testimony of Scripture in a developed polemic, but adjusts the whole positive exposition of the doctrine to its new purpose, shaping and phrasing its statements and modifying them by added sentences and clauses. The result is a polemic the edge of which is turned no longer against those who may have doubted Calvin's orthodoxy, as was the case in 1539, but rather against those who have essayed to bring into doubt or even openly to deny the mysteries which enter into the Christian doctrine of the Trinity. The sharp anti-scholastic sentences which are permitted to remain, serve to give a singular balance to the discussion, and to make it clear that the polemic against the Antitrinitarians has in view vital interests and not mere matters of phraseology.

The disposition of the material in this its final form follows the lines of its new dominant interest. The discussion opens, as we have seen, with a paragraph designed to bear in on the mind a sense of the mystery which must characterize the divine mode of existence (§ 1). This is immediately followed by an announcement of the Trinitarian fact and a defense of the technical terms used to express and protect it (§§ 2-5). After this introduction the subject itself is taken up (§ 6, *ad init.*) and treated in two great divisions, by way first of positive statement and proof (§§ 6-20) and by way secondly of polemic defense (§§ 21 to end). The positive portion opens with a careful definition of what is meant by the " Trinity " (§ 6) and is prosecuted by an exhibition of the Scriptural proof of the doctrine in three sections: first the proof of the complete deity of the Son (§§ 7–13), then the proof of the deity of the Spirit (§§ 14–15), and then the proof of the Trinitarian distinctions, which includes a dissertation on the nature of these distinctions on the basis of Scripture (§§ 16–20). The polemic phase of the discussion begins with some introductory remarks (§ 21) and then defends in turn the true personality of the Son against Servetus (§ 22) and His complete deity against its modern impugners, Valentinus Gentilis being chiefly in mind (§§ 23–29).

This comprehensive outline is richly filled in with details, all of which are treated, however, with a circumspection and moderation which illustrate Calvin's determination to eschew human speculations upon this high theme and to confine himself to the revelations of Scripture, only so far explicated in human language as is necessary for their pure expression and protection.[53] We observe, for example, that he introduces no proofs or illustrations of the Trinity derived from metaphysical reasoning or natural analogies. From the example of Augustine it had been the habit throughout the Middle Ages to make much of these proofs or illustrations, and the habit had passed over into the Protestant usage. Melanchthon, for example, gave new currency alike to the old ontological speculations which under the forms of subject and object sought to conceive the Logos as the image of Himself which the thinking Father set over against Himself, and to the human analogies by which the Trinitarian distinctions were fancied to be illustrated, such, for example, as the distinctions between the intellect, sensibility and will in man. Calvin held himself aloof from all

[53] Cf. Köstlin, *Studien und Kritiken,* 1868, p. 419, who speaks of "the circumspect, cautious moderation with which Calvin confines himself to the simplest principles of the Church conception and refuses to pass beyond the simple declarations of Scripture to a dogmatic formulation, much more to scholastic questions and answers, one step farther than seemed to him to be demanded for the protection of the Godhead of the Redeemer and of the Holy Spirit from the assaults of old and new enemies."

such reasoning, doubting, as he says (§ 18), "the value of similitudes from human things for expressing the force of the Trinitarian distinction," and fearing that their employment might afford only occasion to those evil disposed for calumny and to those little instructed for error.[54] What he desired was a plain proof from Scripture itself of the elements of the doctrine, freed from all additions from human speculation. This proof he attempted, in outline at least, to set down in his pages. It is interesting to observe how he conducts it.

He begins, as we have already pointed out, with a plain statement of what he means by the Trinity (§ 6). Such a "short and easy definition" (*brevis et facilis definitio*) had been his object from the outset (§ 2, *ad init.*), and it was in fact in order to obtain it that he entered upon the defense, which fills the first sections, of the term and conception of "Person" as applied to the distinctions in the Godhead. Reverting to it after this defense, he carefully defines (§ 6) what he means by "Person" in this connection, viz., "a subsistence in the Divine essence, which, related to the others, is yet distinguished by an incommunicable property." What he has to prove, therefore, he conceives to be that in the unity of the Godhead there is such a distinction of persons; or, as he phrases it, in a statement derived from Tertullian, that "there is in God a certain disposition or economy, which makes no difference, however, to the unity of the essence"; or, as he puts it himself a little later on (§ 20, *ad init.*), that "there is understood under the name of God, a unitary and simple essence,

[54] Cf. I. xv. 4, *ad fin.* Cf. Commentary on Genesis, i. 26, where, speaking of the human faculties, he remarks: "But Augustine, beyond all others, speculates with excessive refinement for the purpose of fabricating a trinity in man. For in laying hold of the three faculties of the soul enumerated by Aristotle, the intellect, the memory and the will, he afterwards out of one trinity derives many. If any reader, having leisure, wishes to enjoy such speculations, let him read the tenth and fourteenth books of *The Trinity*, also the eleventh book of *The City of God*. I acknowledge indeed that there is something in man which refers to the Father, and the Son, and the Spirit; and I have no difficulty in admitting the above distribution of the faculties, . . . but a definition of the image of God ought to rest on a firmer basis than such subtleties." For the later Reformed attitude, see Heppe, "Die Dogmatik der ev.-ref. Kirche," 1861, pp. 85 *sqq.*

in which we comprise three persons or hypostases." In order to prove this doctrine, it would be necessary to prove that while God is one, there are three persons who are God, and Calvin undertakes the proof on that understanding. He does not pause here, however, to argue the unity of God at length, taking that for the moment for granted, though he reverts to it in the sequel to show that the distinction of persons which he conceives himself to have established in no respect infringes on it (§ 19), and indeed in his polemic against Valentinus Gentilis very fully vindicates it from the objections of the Arianisers and Tritheists (§§ 23 *sq.*). His proof resolves itself, therefore, into the establishment of the distinctions in the Godhead; and in order to do this he undertakes to prove first that the Son and the Holy Spirit are each God, and then to show that the Scriptures explicitly recognize that there is such a distinction in the Godhead as their divinity (taken in connection with the Divine unity) implies.

The proof of the deity of the Son is very comprehensive and detailed, and is drawn from each Testament alike. The Word of God, by which, as God " spake," He made the worlds, it is argued, must be understood of the substantial Word, which is also called in Proverbs, Wisdom (§ 7); and must accordingly be understood as eternal. In connection with this, the whole scheme of temporal prolation as applied to the Son is sharply assaulted. It is impious to suppose that anything new can ever have happened to God in Himself (*in se ipso*), and there is " nothing less tolerable than to invent a beginning for that Word, who both was always God and afterwards became the maker of the world " (§ 8). To this more general argument is brought the support of a number of Old Testament passages, which, it is contended, advert to the Son with declarations of His deity: such as the Forty-fifth Psalm, " Thy throne, O God, is for ever and ever "; Is. ix. 6, " His Name shall be called Mighty God, Father of Eternity "; Jer. xxiii. 6, " The Branch of David shall be called Jehovah our Righteousness " (§ 9). And then the phenomena connected with the manifestations of the Angel of Jehovah are adduced in corroboration

(§ 10). The New Testament evidence is marshalled under two heads: the divine names are applied to Christ by the New Testament writers (§ 11), and divine works and functions are assigned to Him (§§ 12–13). Not only are Old Testament passages which speak of Jehovah applied to Christ in the New Testament (Is. viii. 14, Rom. ix. 33; Is. xlv. 23, Rom. xiv. 10, 11; Ps. lxviii. 18, Eph. iv. 8; Is. vi. 1, Jno. xii. 41), but these writers themselves employ the term "God" in speaking of Christ (Jno. i. 1, 14; Rom. ix. 5; I Tim. iii. 16; I Jno. v. 20; Acts xx. 28; Jno. xx. 28), and the like. And what divine work do not the New Testament writers credit Him with, either from His own lips or theirs? They represent Him as having been co-worker with God from all eternity (Jno. v. 17), as the upholder and governor of the world (Heb. i. 3), as the forgiver of iniquities (Mat. ix. 6) and the searcher of hearts (Mat. ix. 4). They not only accredit Him with mighty works, but distinguish Him from others who have wrought miracles, precisely by this — these others wrought them by the power of God, He by His own power (§ 13a). They represent Him as the dispenser of salvation, the source of eternal life and the fountain of all that is good: they present Him as the proper object of saving faith and trust, and even of worship and prayer (§ 13b).

The deity of the Spirit is similarly argued on the ground of certain Old Testament passages (Genesis i. 2; Is. xlviii. 16) where the Spirit of God seems to be hypostatized; of the divine works attributed to Him, such as ubiquitous activity, regeneration, and the searching of the deep things of God on the one hand and the bestowing of wisdom, speech and all other blessings on men on the other; and finally of the application of the name God to Him in the New Testament writings (e.g., I Cor. iii. 16, vi. 19; II Cor. vi. 16; Acts v. 3; xxviii. 25; Mat. xii. 31).

Having thus established the deity of the Son and the Spirit, Calvin turns to the passages which elucidate their deity to us by presenting to us the doctrine of the Trinity. These are all in the New Testament, as was natural (suggests Calvin), because the advent of Christ involved a clearer revelation of God and therefore a fuller knowledge of the personal distinc-

tions in His being (§ 16). The stress of the argument here is
laid upon Eph. iv. 5 in connection with Mat. xxviii. 19, which
were already expounded at length, as we have seen, in the first
edition of the " Institutes," and are here only strengthened
and clarified by a better statement. As we are initiated by
baptism into faith in the one God and yet baptism is in the
name of the Father, the Son and the Holy Spirit, argues Calvin,
it is " solidly clear " that the Father, Son and Spirit are this
one God; whence it is perfectly obvious that " there reside
(*residere*) in the essence of God three Persons, in whom the
one God is cognized" (*cognoscitur*); and " since it remains
fixed that God is one not many, we can only conclude that the
Word and the Spirit are nothing other than the essence of
God itself." The Scriptures, however, he proceeds (§ 17), no
more thus identify the Son and Spirit with God than they distinguish them — distinguish, not divide them. He appeals to
such passages as Jno. v. 32, viii. 16, 18, xiv. 16, " another "; [55]
xv. 26, viii. 16, " proceeding," " being sent ": but this part of
the subject is lightly passed over on the ground that the passages already adduced themselves sufficiently show that the
Son possesses a " distinct property " by which He is not the
Father — for, says he, " the Word could not have been *with*
God unless He had been another than the Father, neither could
He have had His glory *with* the Father, unless He was distinct
from Him ": the distinction noted in which passages it is plain,
further, is not one which could have begun at the incarnation,
but must date from whatever point He may be thought to have
begun to be " in the bosom of the Father " (Jno. i. 18). The
determination that there is a personal distinction between
Father and Son and Holy Spirit leads Calvin to inquire what
this distinction carries with it. He finds it to be Scriptural to
say that " to the Father is attributed the *principium agendi*,
as fountain and source of all things; to the Son, wisdom, counsel and the actual dispensation of things to be done; but to the

---

[55] In ed. 1 (1536) he remarks (*Opp.* i. 59) that " that the Holy Spirit is
' another ' than Christ is proved by more than ten passages from the Gospel of
John (John xiv. xv.)."

Spirit is assigned the power and efficiency (*virtus et efficacia*) of the action " — that is to say, if we may be permitted to reduce the definitions to single words, the Father is conceived as the Source, the Son as the Director, the Spirit as the Executor of all the divine activities; the Father as the Fountain, the Son as the Wisdom emerging from Him, the Spirit as the Power by which the wise counsels of God are effectuated (§ 18).[56] Only now when this argument is finished and his conclusion drawn (§ 19) does Calvin pause formally to point out that " this distinction in no way impedes the absolutely simple unity of God " — since the conception is that the " whole nature (*natura*) is in each hypostasis," while " each has its own propriety." " The Father," he adds, " is *totus* in the Son, and the Son *totus* in the Father " — as Christ Himself teaches in Jno. xiv. 10. We are here, however, obviously passing beyond the proof to the exposition of the Trinity — a topic which occupies some later sections (§§ 19 and 20).

It will have already become apparent from the citations incidentally adduced that in his doctrine of the Trinity Calvin departed in nothing from the doctrine which had been handed down from the orthodox Fathers. If distinctions must be drawn, he is unmistakably Western rather than Eastern in his conception of the doctrine, an Augustinian rather than an Athanasian.[57] That is to say, the principle of his construction of the

[56] This passage is already found in ed. 1 (1536) (*Opp.* i. 62): " The Persons are so distinguished by the Scriptures that they assign to the Father the *principium agendi*, and the fountain and origin of all things; to the Son the wisdom and *consilium agendi;* to the Spirit the *virtus et efficacia actionis;* whence also the Son is called the Word of God, not such as men speak or think, but eternal and unchangeable, as emerging in an ineffable manner from the Father."

[57] Cf. L. L. Paine, " The Evolution of Trinitarianism," 1900, p. 95: " It is a remarkable fact that the Protestant Reformation only increased the prestige of Augustine. . . . The question of the Trinity was not a subject of controversy and the Augustinian form of trinitarian doctrine became a fixed tradition. The Nicene Creed, as interpreted by the Pseudo-Athanasian Creed, was accepted on all sides and passed into all the Protestant Confessions. It is to be noted that Calvin insisted on the use of the term ' person ' as the only word that would unmask Sabellianism. He also held to numerical unity of essence. This would seem to indicate that Calvin believed that God was

Trinitarian distinctions is equalization rather than subordination. He does, indeed, still speak in the old language of refined subordinationism which had been fixed in the Church by the Nicene formularies; and he expressly allows an " order " of first, second and third in the Trinitarian relations. But he conceives more clearly and applies more purely than had ever previously been done the principle of equalization in his thought of the relation of the Persons to one another, and thereby, as we have already hinted, marks an epoch in the history of the doctrine of the Trinity. That he was enabled to do this was a result, no doubt, at least in part, of his determination to preserve the highest attainable simplicity in his thought of the Trinity. Sweeping his mind free from subtleties in minor matters, he perceived with unwonted lucidity the main things, and thus was led to insist upon them with a force and clearness of exposition which throw them out into unmistakable emphasis. If we look for the prime characteristics of Calvin's doctrine of the Trinity, accordingly, we shall undoubtedly fix first upon its simplicity, then upon it consequent lucidity, and finally upon its elimination of the last remnants of subordinationism, so as to do full justice to the deity of Christ. Simplification, clarification, equalization — these three terms are the notes of Calvin's conception of the Trinity. And, of course, it is the last of these notes which gives above all else its character to his construction.[58]

---

one Being in three real persons, and, if so, he must have allowed that in God nature and person are not coincident. Yet he nowhere raises the question, and I am inclined to think he was not conscious of any departure from the views of Augustine." Calvin does, however, repeatedly raise the question whether " nature " and " person " are coincident and repeatedly decides that they are, in the sense that the person is the whole nature in a personal distinction. " The whole nature (tota natura) " is affirmed to be " in each hypostasis (in unaquaque hypostasi)," though there is present to each one its own propriety (I. xiii. 19). Hence there is no such thing as " a triplex God," as " the simple essence of God being divided among the three Persons " (xiii. 2); the essence is not multiplex, and the Son contains the whole of it in Himself (totam in se), etc. (ibid.).

[58] It is the same thing that is meant by G. A. Meier, " Lehre von der Trinität, etc.," 1844, ii. pp. 58–59, where, after remarking that the Reformed were prone to emphasize especially the unity of God (which involves what

The note of simplification is struck at the outset of the discussion when Calvin announces it as his intention to seek "a short and easy definition which shall preserve us from all error" (I. xiii. 2, *ad init.*). What the short and easy definition which he had in mind included is suggested when he tells us later (20) that "when we profess to believe in one God, under the name of God is to be understood the single and simple essence in which we comprehend three persons or hypostases." He accordingly expresses pleasure in the definition of Tertullian, when properly understood, that "there is in God a certain disposition or economy, which in no respect derogates from the unity of the essence" (6, *ad fin.*); and frankly declares that for him the whole substance of the doctrine is included in the simple statement "that the Father and the Son and the Spirit are one God; and yet neither is the Son the Father nor the Spirit the Son, but they are distinct by a certain property" (5). Similar simple forms of statement are thickly scattered through the discussion. "God so predicates Himself to be one," he says at its outset, "that He propones Himself to be dis-

---

we have called "equalization"), he proceeds: "External circumstances early led to the sharp emergence of this peculiarity. In the controversy with Gentilis, who maintained that the essential being of the Son was from the Father, Calvin was compelled to contend that in His Godhead and in His nature, the Son is of Himself, and without principium, and only in His personal subsistence, has His principium in the Father.[1] Catholic theologians, especially Petau, have charged him with heresy for this, though he was only enunciating with increased sharpness the conviction of the Church, and rightly recalling that otherwise a plurality of Gods would be introduced.[2]" At the points indicated the following notes are added. "1. 'Since the name Jehovah is used in the passages cited above, it follows that the Son of God is with respect to His deity solely of Himself.' *Val. Gentilis impietatum brevis explic.* (*Calv. Opp.,* Amstel. 1667, viii. p. 572). 'The essence of the Son has no principium, but the principium of the Person is God Himself' (*loc. cit.,* p. 573). 'We concede that the Son takes origin from the Father, so far as He is Son, but it is an origin not of time, nor of essence, . . . but of order only' (*l. c.,* p. 580)." "2. 'Unless moreover the Son is God along with the Father, a plurality of Gods will necessarily be brought in' (*Ep. ad Fratres Polonos,* p. 591). Accordingly Calvin called the "Deus de Deo" a "hard saying." Against him see Petau, *De theol. dogm.,* II. *lib.* iii. c. 3, §§ 2, 3. On the other hand, Bellarmine acknowledges that in the maintenance of the αὐτοθεότης of the Son there is no real departure from the doctrine of the Church."

tinctly considered in three Persons " (2, *ad init.*). " There truly
subsist in the one God, or what is the same thing, in the unity
of God," he says again, "a trinity of Persons" (4, *ad fin.*).
" There are three *proprietates* in God" (*ibid.*). " In the one
essence of God, there is a Trinity of Persons," and these are
"consubstantial" (5, *ad fin.*). " In the divine essence there
exist three Persons, in whom the one God is cognized" (16).
" There is a Trinity of Persons contained in the one God, not
a trinity of Gods " (25). It is quite clear, not only from the
frequency with which he lapses into such brief formulas, but
also from the distinctness with which he declares that they contain all that is essential to the doctrine of the Trinity (e.g., § 5),
that in Calvin's habitual thought of the Trinity it lay summed
up in his mind in these simple facts: there is but one God; the
Father, the Son, the Spirit is each this one God, the entire divine essence being in each; these three are three Persons, distinguished one from another by an incommunicable property.[59]

Calvin's main interest among the elements of this simple
doctrine of the Trinity obviously lay in his profound sense
of the consubstantiality of the Persons. Whatever the Father
is as God, that the Son and the Spirit are also. The Son — and,
of course, also the Spirit — contains in Himself the whole essence of God, not part of it only nor by deflection, but in complete perfection (§ 2). What the Father is, reappears therefore
in its totality (*se totum*) in the Son and in the Spirit. This is
a mere corollary of their community in the numerically one
essence. If the "entire nature" (*tota natura*, § 19) is included
in each, it necessarily carries with it all the qualities by which
it is made this particular nature which we call divine. Calvin

[59] Cf. "Adv. P. Caroli calumnias" (*Opp.* vii. 312): "Yet in that one
essence of God we acknowledge the Father with His eternal Word and
Spirit. In using this distinction, however, we do not imagine three Gods, as
if the Father were some other thing than the Son, nor yet do we understand
them to be naked epithets, by which God is variously designated from His
actions; but, along with the ecclesiastical writers, we perceive in the simple
unity of God these three hypostases, that is subsistences, which although
they coexist in one essence are not to be confused with each other. Accordingly, though the Father is one God with His Word and Spirit, the Father is
not the Word, nor the Word the Spirit."

is accordingly never weary of asserting that every divine attribute, in the height of its meaning, is manifested as fully in the Son — and, of course, also in the Spirit — as in the Father. In this indeed lay for him the very nerve of the doctrine of the Trinity. And in it, consistently carried out, lies the contribution which he made to the clear apprehension and formulation of that doctrine. For, strange as it may seem, theologians at large had been accustomed to apply the principle of consubstantiality to the Persons of the Trinity up to Calvin's vigorous assertion of it, with some at least apparent reserves. And when he applied it without reserve it struck many as a startling novelty if not a heretical pravity. The reason why the consubstantiality of the Persons of the Trinity, despite its establishment in the Arian controversy and its incorporation in the Nicene formulary as the very hinge of orthodoxy, was so long in coming fully to its rights in the general apprehension was no doubt that Nicene orthodoxy preserved in its modes of stating the doctrine of the Trinity some remnants of the conceptions and phraseology proper to the older prolationism of the Logos Christology, and these, although rendered innocuous by the explanations of the Nicene Fathers and practically antiquated since Augustine, still held their place formally and more or less conditioned the thought of men — especially those who held the doctrine of the Trinity in a more or less traditional manner. The consequence was that when Calvin taught the doctrine in its purity and free from the leaven of subordinationism which still found a lurking place in current thought and speech, he seemed violently revolutionary to men trained in the old forms of speech and imbued with the old modes of conception, and called out reprobation in the most unexpected quarters.

Particular occasion of offense was given by Calvin's ascription of " self-existence " (aseity, $\alpha\dot{v}\tauoov\sigma\acute{\iota}\alpha$) to the Son, and the consequent designation of Him by the term $\alpha\dot{v}\tau\acuteo\theta\epsilon os$. This term, which became famous in later controversy as designating Calvin's doctrine of Christ, seems, however, to have come forward only in the latest years of his life, in the dispute with Valentinus Gentilis (1558, 1561); and indeed to be rather Gentilis' word than Calvin's. Calvin, indeed, does not appear to have himself employed it, but only to have reclaimed it for Christ (and the Spirit) when Gentilis asserted that it was exclusively God the Father who could be so designated. " The Father alone," said Gentilis, " is αὐτόθεος, that is, essentiated by no superior divinity; but is God *a se ipso* "; " the λόγος of God is not that one αὐτόθεος whose λόγος it is; neither is the Spirit of God that immense and eternal Spirit whose Spirit it is." [60] Such assertions, declares Calvin, are against all Scripture, which makes Christ very God: for " what is more proper to God than to exist (*vivere*), and what else is αὐτοουσία than this? " [61] But the thing represented by the term — " self-existence " — Calvin asserts of Christ from the beginning of his activity as a Christian teacher. It does not seem to be explicitly declared of Christ that He is self-existent, indeed, in the first edition of the " Institutes " (1536), although it is already implied there too, not only in the general vigor with which the absolute deity of Christ is asserted with all its implications, but also in the identification of Christ with Jehovah, which was to Calvin the especial vehicle of his representation of Him as the self-existent God. " That name which the Jews call ineffable is attributed to the Son in Jeremiah " (Jer. xxiii. 33),[62] he already here tells us. In the spring of the following year,[63] however, at the councils held within a few days of one another respectively at Lausanne and Bern, our Lord's self-existence was fairly enunciated in so many words in the statement of his faith which Calvin made in rebuttal of the charges of Caroli. He begins with a very clear exposition of the doctrine of the Trinity, and then comes to speak of what peculiarly concerns

---

[60] " Expositio impietatis Valentini Gentilis," 1561 (*Opp.* ix. 374, 380).

[61] *Ibid.*, Preface, p. 368. Cf. Beza in his Life of Calvin, who speaks of Gentilis under the year 1558 and describes him as wishing to make the Father alone αὐτόθεος (*Opp.* xxi. 154). These four references (ix. 368, 374, 380; xxi. 154) are all that are given in the Index to the Strasburg ed. (xxii. 493 — this word does not occur in the Index of xxiii. *sq.*) of Calvin's works under the word αὐτόθεος.

[62] *Opp.* i. 58, at bottom of column.   [63] May 14 and 31, 1537.

Christ, adverting especially to His two natures. "For," he continues, "before He assumed flesh He was the eternal Word itself, begotten by the Father before the ages, very God, of one essence, power, majesty with the Father, and indeed Jehovah Himself, *who has always had it of Himself that He should be and has inspired the power of subsisting in others.*" [64] Caroli at once seized upon this declaration, and complained that therein "Christ was set forth as Jehovah, as if He had His essence of Himself (*a se ipso*)." [65] From this beginning rose the controversy. For in this one of his "calumnies" Caroli found some following, and Calvin was worried by petty attacks upon this element of his teaching through a series of years.[66]

Calvin apparently was somewhat astonished by the pother which was raised over an assertion which seemed to him not only a very natural one to make, but also a very necessary one to make if the true deity of our Lord is to be defended. He calls this particular one of Caroli's assaults the "most atrocious" of all his calumnies, and he betrays some irritation at the repetition of it by others. One effect of it was, however, to make him see that, although it might seem to him a matter of course to speak of Christ as the self-existent God, it was not a matter which could be taken for granted, but needed assertion and defense. He inserted, therefore, in the "Institutes" of 1539 (second edition) a clear declaration on the subject, which, with only the adduction of some additional support chiefly drawn from Augustine (inserted in 1543 and 1559), was retained throughout the subsequent editions. "More-

[64] *Opp.* vii. 314: qui a se ipso semper habuit ut esset, et aliis subsistendi virtutem inspiravit. Cf. ix. 707; xb. 107, 121. Cf. Ruchat, "Histoire de la reformation de la Suisse," 1835 *sq.*, v. pp. 27–28; Bähler, as cited, p. 78; and also Merle D'Aubigné, "History of the Reformation in Europe in the Time of Calvin," E. T. vi. 1877, p. 316.

[65] *Ibid.*, p. 315.

[66] *Ibid.*, p. 322: "But the most atrocious calumny of all is where he impugns this statement: that Christ always had it of Himself that He should be; in which he has been followed by some others, men of no account, who, however, worry good men with their improbity; in the number of whom is a certain rogue (*furcifer*) very like himself (Caroli), who calls himself Cortesius."

over," says he in this passage, " the absolutely simple unity of
God is so far from being impeded by this distinction, that it
rather affords a proof that the Son is one God with the Father,
because He possesses one and the same Spirit with Him: while
the Spirit is not another Being diverse from the Father and the
Son, because He is the Spirit of the Father and of the Son. For
in each hypostasis the whole nature is understood, along with
that which is present to each one as His propriety. The Father
is as a whole (*totus*) in the Son, the Son as a whole in the
Father, as He Himself also asserts: ' I in the Father and the
Father in me '; and that one is not separated from another by
any difference of essence is conceded by the ecclesiastical writers.[67] By this understanding the opinions of the fathers are to
be conciliated, which otherwise would seem altogether at odds
with one another. For they teach now that the Father is the
principium of the Son; and now they assert that the Son has
from Himself (*a se ipso*) both divinity and essence.[68] When,
however, the Sabellians raise a cavil that God is called now
Father, now Son, now Spirit, in no way differently from His
being named both strong and good and wise and merciful, they
may easily be refuted from this, — that these manifestly are

[67] References to Augustine and Cyril are given in the margin: and in
1543 the following is inserted here in the text: " ' By these appellations which
denote distinctions,' says Augustine, ' what is signified is a reciprocal relation;
not the substance itself which is one.' "

[68] In 1543 there was added: " and therefore is one principium with the
Father. The cause of this diversity, Augustine explains well and perspicuously in another place, speaking as follows: ' Christ with reference to Himself
(*ad se*) is called God; with reference to the Father (*ad patrem*) is called
Son.' And again ' The Father *ad se* is called God, *ad filium* is called Father.
What is called Father *ad filium* is not the Son; what is called Son *ad patrem*
is not the Father: what is called Father *ad se*, and Son *ad se* is the same God.'
When therefore we speak *simpliciter* of the Son without respect to the Father,
we well and properly assert Him to be *a se,* and therefore call Him the unique
principium. When, however, we are noting the. relation in which He stands
to the Father, we properly make the Father the principium of the Son."
To this there is further added in 1559: " To the explication of this matter
the fifth book of Augustine's *De Trinitate,* is wholly devoted. It is far safer
to rest in that relation which he teaches, than by more subtly penetrating
into the divine mystery to wander through many vain speculations." And
with these words the paragraph closes in 1559.

epithets which show what God is with respect to us, while the others are names which declare what He is really with respect to Himself. Neither ought anyone to be moved to confound the Spirit with the Father and the Son, because God announces Himself as a whole to be a Spirit (Jno. iv. 24). For there is no reason why the whole essence of God should not be spiritual, and in that essence the Father, Son and Spirit be comprehended. And this very thing is made clear by the Scriptures. For as we hear God called a Spirit in them, so also we hear the Holy Spirit spoken of, and that both as God's Spirit and as from God." [69]

Calvin was not permitted, however, to content himself with this brief positive declaration. A running fire was kept up upon his assertion of self-existence for Christ by two pastors of Neuchâtel and its neighboring country, Jean Chaponneau (Capunculus) and Jean Courtois (Cortesius) — the latter of whom had married the daughter of Chaponneau's wife.[70] Calvin was disposed at first to treat their criticism lightly, but was ultimately driven to give it serious attention. Writing to the Neuchâtel ministers regarding certain articles which Courtois had drawn up — with the help, as was understood, of Chaponneau — Calvin remarks that he sees no reason for supposing them directed as a whole against him. One of them, however, he recognizes as having him in view — that one in which, " as from a tripod," the writer pronounces heretics those who say that " Christ, as He is God, is *a se ipso.*" " The answer," he declares, " is easy. First let him tell me whether Christ is true and perfect God. Unless he wishes to parcel out the essence of God, he must confess that the whole of it is in Christ. And Paul's words are express: that ' in Him dwelleth the fulness of the Godhead.' Again I ask, ' Is that fulness of

[69] *Opp.* i. 490–491.

[70] See Haag, " La France protestante," *sub nom.,* " Chaponneau," ed. 2, iii. p. 1084: " Shortly afterwards Chaponneau married; he married a widow whose daughter soon became the wife in turn of the Pastor John Courtois, known by some disputes that he had with Calvin. Chaponneau no more than his son-in-law hesitated to enter the lists with Calvin. The quarrel had its rise from a question relating to the person of Jesus. . . ."

the Godhead from Himself or from some other source?' But
he will object that the Son is of the Father. Who denies it?
That I, for one, have not only always acknowledged, but even
proclaimed. But this is where these donkeys deceive themselves: because they do not consider that the name of Son
is spoken of the Person, and therefore is included in the pre-
dicament of relation, which relation has no place where we are
speaking simply (*simpliciter*) of the divinity of Christ." [71]
In support of this distinction he then quotes Augustine, and
proceeds to cite Cyril on the main point at issue — passages to
which we shall revert in the sequel. This letter was written at
the end of May, 1543, and later in the year we find Calvin
holding a conference with Courtois, the course of which he reports to the Neuchâtel ministers in a letter written in November.[72] Courtois went away, however, still unconvinced, and
Calvin found himself compelled not many months later (opening of 1545) to write to the Neuchâtel pastors again at length
on the subject, under considerable irritation.[73] " This," he here
declares, " is the state of the controversy (*status controver-
siae*): Whether it may be truly predicated of Christ, that He is,
as He is God, *a se ipso?* This Capunculus denies. Why? Because the name of Christ designates the Second Person in the
Godhead, who stands in relation to the Father. I confess that
if respect be had to the Person, we ought not so to speak. But
I say we are not speaking of the Person but of the essence. I
hold that the Holy Spirit is the real (*idoneum* = proper) author of this manner of speaking, since He refers to Christ all
the declarations in which αὐτοουσία is predicated of God, as
in other passages, so in the first chapter of the Epistle to the
Hebrews. . . . He [Capunculus] contends that Christ, because He is of the substance of the Father, is not *a se ipso*,
since He has a principium from another. This I allow to him
of the Person. What more does he want? . . . I confess that

<hr>

[71] *Opp.* xi. 560, Letter 474.

[72] *Opp.* xi. 652, Letter 521.

[73] *Opp.* xii. 16, Letter 607; cf. the letter of Capunculus, *Opp.* xi. 781, Letter
590.

the Son of God is of the Father. Accordingly, since the Person
has a cause (*ratio*), I confess that He is not *a se ipso*. But when
we are speaking, apart from consideration of the Person, of
His divinity or simply of the essence, which is the same thing,
I say that it is rightly predicated of Him that He is *a se ipso*.
For who, heretofore, has denied that under the name of Jehovah, there is included the declaration of αὐτοουσία? . . ."

It was, however, in his " Defense Against the Calumnies of
Peter Caroli," which was sent out in 1545 in reply to a new
" libel " put forth by Caroli early that year,[74] that Calvin
speaks most at large on this subject, gathering up into this
one defense, indeed, all the modes of statement and forms of
argument he had hitherto worked out. He regards Caroli's
strictures upon his assertion of Christ's self-existence as the
most atrocious of all his calumnies, and prefixes to his discussion of them a citation of his own explanation of the matter,
which he calls a " brief and naked explication." This runs as
follows: " When we are speaking of the divinity of Christ all

---

[74] The " Defensio " was pseudonymously published under the name of
Nicholas des Gallars, Calvin's secretary. Bähler, as cited, pp. 153 *sq.*, judges
it very unfavorably and sharply criticises the advantage taken of its pseudony-
mity and its inaccuracies, as well as its harshness of tone. " The number of
Calvin's polemical writings," says he, " is great, and they are all master-
works of their order. No other, however, surpasses the *Defensio* in harshness
and bitterness. It is all in all, scarcely a happy creation of Calvin's. . . . From
the standpoint of literary history the *Defensio* indisputably deserves unrestricted praise. The elegant, crisp style, the skill with which the author
not only morally annihilates his opponent, but puts upon him the stamp of
an impertinent person not to be taken seriously, and permeates all with the
most sovereign scorn, makes the reading of this book, now nearly four hundred
years old, an aesthetic enjoyment, which obscures the protest of righteous
indignation at the startling injustices and glaring untruths which the author
has permitted himself against Caroli. No doubt Calvin's conduct, if it cannot
be excused, may yet to a certain degree be understood, when we reflect that
Caroli, through almost ten years, had brought to the Reformer of Geneva in-
cessant annoyances and the most bitter mortification, and by his accusations
had imperilled his life-work as perhaps no other antagonist had been able to
do " (p. 159). Compare the more measured censure of A. Lang (" Johannes
Calvin," 1909, p. 42) of the harshness of tone and opprobrious language used
towards Caroli, in contrast with the high praise given the three Reformers
— " when, although it was questionless written by Calvin himself, it was published in the name of his amanuensis, Nicholas des Gallars."

that is proper to God is rightly ascribed to Him, because respect is there had to the Divine essence and no question is raised as to the distinction which exists between the Father and the Son. In this sense it is true to say that Christ is the One and Eternal God, existing of Himself (*a se ipso existentem*). Nor can it be objected to this statement — what certainly is also taught by the ecclesiastical writers — that the Word or Son of God is of the Father (*a Patre*), even with respect to His eternal essence; since there is a notation of Persons, when there is commemorated a distinction of the Son from the Father. But what I have been speaking of is the divinity, in which is embraced not less the Father and the Spirit than the Son. So Cyril, who is often wont to call the Father the principium of the Son, holds it in the highest degree absurd for the Son not to be believed to have life and immortality of Himself (*a se ipso*). He also teaches that if it is proper to the ineffable nature to be self-existent (*a se ipsa*), this is rightly ascribed to the Son. And moreover in the tenth book of his *Thesaurus,* he argues that the Father has nothing of Himself (*a se ipso*) which the Son does not have of Himself (*a se ipso*)." [75] From this beginning, he proceeds to elucidate the whole subject, drawing freely upon all that he had previously written upon it. The note of the discussion is given in the words: "I assert both truths — both that Christ is of the Father as He is the second Person, and that He is of Himself (*a se ipso*) if we have respect to the Divine essence *simpliciter* " [76] — a declaration which he supports from the Fathers, particularly Augustine, thus: "Similarly Augustine (*Sermo* 38 'de tempore'): 'Those names which signify the substance . . . or essence of God, or whatever God is said to be in Himself (*ad se*), belong equally to all the Persons. There is not, therefore, any name of nature which can so belong to the Father that it may not belong also to the Son, or Holy Spirit.' " The whole is brought to a conclusion by a passage the substance of which we have already had before us, but which seems worth quoting again that its force may be appreciated in its new

[75] *Opp.* vii. 322.   [76] *Opp.* vii. 323.

setting: " I confess that if respect be had to the Person we ought not so to speak, but I say we are not speaking of the Person but of the essence. I hold that the Holy Spirit is the real author of this manner of speaking, since He refers to Christ all the declarations in which αὐτοουσία is predicated of God, as well in other passages, as in the first chapter of the Epistle to the Hebrews. . . . They contend that Christ, because He is of (ex) the substance of the Father, is not of Himself (a se ipso), since He has His principium from another. This I allow to them of the Person. What more do they ask? I acknowledge, then, that the Son of God is of the Father, and when we are speaking of the Person I acknowledge that He is not of Himself. But when, apart from consideration of the Person, we are speaking of His divinity, or which is the same thing simpliciter of the essence, I say that it is truly predicated of it that it is a se ipso. For who hitherto has denied of the name Jehovah, that it includes the declaration of αὐτοουσία? When, then, they object that the Son is of the Father, that I not only willingly acknowledge, but have even continually proclaimed. But here is where these donkeys are in error — that they do not consider that the name of Son is spoken of the Person, and is therefore contained in the predication of relation; which relation has no place when we are talking of Christ's divinity simpliciter. And Augustine discourses eloquently on this matter " . . . quoting the passages from Augustine to which we have already made reference.[77]

That Calvin let the paragraph he had prepared on this subject for the second edition of his " Institutes " (1539) stand practically unchanged — strengthened only by a couple of passages cited from Augustine — in the editions of 1543 and 1550, may be taken as indication that he supposed that what he had brought together in his " Defense Against the Calumnies of Caroli " (1545), incorporating as it does the essence of former expositions and defenses, was a sufficient exposition of the subject and defense of his point of view. In the meantime, how-

[77] *Opp.* vii. 323–324.

ever, the troubles in the Italian church in Geneva had broken
out, culminating after a while in the controversies with Valentinus Gentilis (1558), in which new occasion was given for
asserting the self-existence of Christ, and this brought it
about that something more on this subject was incorporated
into the "Institutes" of 1559. The positive statement was
left, indeed, much as it had been given form in the "Institutes"
of 1539 (§ 19): but in the long defense of the doctrine of the
Trinity against Gentilis and his congeners with which the discussion of the doctrine closes in this edition much more is
added on the self-existence of Christ. As over against these
opponents the especial point in the doctrine of the Trinity
which required defense was the true deity of the second and
third Persons. On this defense Calvin entered *con amore,* for he
ever showed himself, as he had himself expressed it, a "detester
as sacrilegious of all who have sought to overturn or to mini-
mise or to obscure the truth of the divine majesty which is in
Christ." [78] The God whom Isaiah saw in the Temple (vi. 1), he
says, John (xii. 41) declares to have been Christ; the God
whom the same Isaiah declares shall be a rock of offense to the
Jews (viii. 14) Paul pronounces to be Christ (Rom. ix. 33); the
God to whom the same Isaiah asserts every knee shall bow
(xlv. 23), Paul tells us is Christ (Rom. xiv. 11); the God whom
the Psalmist proclaims as laying the foundations of the earth
and whom all angels shall worship (Ps. cii. 25, xcvii. 7) the
Epistle to the Hebrews identifies with Christ (i. 6, 10). Now,
continues Calvin, in every one of these passages it is the name
"Jehovah" which is used, and that carries with it the self-
existence of Christ with respect to His deity. [79] "For if He is
Jehovah, it cannot be denied that He is the same God who elsewhere cries through Isaiah (xliv. 6), 'I, I am, and besides me
there is no God.' We must also weigh," he adds, "that declaration of Jeremiah (x. 11): 'the gods which have not made
the heaven and the earth shall perish from the earth which is

---

[78] *Opp.* vii. 314.

[79] *Opp.* ii. 110; "Institutes," 1559, I. xiii. 23: nam quum ubique ponatur
nomen Iehovae, sequitur deitatis respectu ex se ipso esse.

under heaven '; while on the other hand it must be acknowledged that it is the Son of God whose deity is often proved by Isaiah from the creation of the world. But how shall the Creator who gives being to all things not be self-existent (*ex se ipso*) but derive His essence from another? For whoever says the Son is essentiated by the Father, denies that He is of Himself (*a se ipso*). But the Holy Spirit cries out against this by naming Him Jehovah." " The deity, therefore, we affirm," he says a little later,[80] " to be absolutely self-existent (*ex se ipsa*). Whence we acknowledge the Son, too, as He is God, to be self-existent (*ex se ipso*), when reference to His Person is not present: while, as He is Son, we say He is of the Father. Thus the essence is without principium; but the principium of the Person is God Himself."

It does not seem necessary, however, to multiply citations. Enough have already been adduced, doubtless, to illustrate the clearness, iterance and emphasis with which Calvin asserted the self-existence of Christ as essential to His complete deity; and at least to suggest his mode of conceiving the Trinity in accordance with this emphasis on the absolute equality, or rather, let us say, identity of the three Persons of the Godhead in their deity. His conception involved, of course, a strongly emphasized distinction between the essence and the Personality. In essence the three Persons are numerically one: the whole essence belongs to each Person:[81] the whole essence, of course, with all its properties, which are only its peculiarities as an essence and are inseparable from it just because they are not other substances but only qualities. In person, however, the three Persons are numerically three, and are as distinct from one another as the distinguishing qualities by which one is the Father, another the Son and the third the Spirit. In these facts Calvin found the essence of the doctrine of the Trinity, and in accordance with his professed purpose to find a brief and easy definition of the

[80] P. 113: I. xiii. 25.
[81] Cf. I. xiii. 2: The Son contains in Himself the whole essence of God: not a part of it only, nor by deflection only, but in *integra perfectione*.

Trinity we may say that in these facts are summed up all he held to be necessary to a doctrine of the Trinity.

Nevertheless Calvin's conception of the Trinity, if we cannot exactly say necessarily included, yet in point of fact included, more than this. It included the postulation of an " order " in the Persons of the Trinity, by which the Father is first, the Son second, and the Spirit third. And it included a doctrine of generation and procession by virtue of which the Son as Son derives from the Father, and the Spirit as Spirit derives from the Father and the Son. Perhaps this aspect of his conception of the Trinity is nowhere more succinctly expressed than in a passage in the eighteenth section of this chapter (xiii.). Here he explicitly declares that " although the eternity of the Father is the eternity of the Son and Spirit also, since God could never be without His Wisdom and Power, — and in eternity there is no question of first and last — it is nevertheless not vain or superfluous to observe an *order* [in the three Persons], since the Father is enumerated as the first, next the Son *ex eo,* and afterwards the Spirit *ex utroque.* For everyone's mind instinctively inclines to consider God first, then the Wisdom emerging from Him, and finally the Power by which He executes the decrees of His counsel. For this reason the Son is said to come forth (*exsistere*) from the Father (*a Patre*), the Spirit alike from the Father and the Son." The intimations which are here brought together are often repeated. Thus, for example: " For since the properties in the Persons bear an order, so that in the Father is the *principium et origo* . . . the *ratio ordinis* is held, which, however, in no respect derogates from the deity of the Son and Spirit " (§ 20). Again: " But from the Scriptures we teach that *essentialiter* there is but one God, and therefore the essence as well of the Son as of the Spirit is unbegotten (*ingenitam*). Yet inasmuch as (*quatenus*) the Father is first in order and has begotten His own Wisdom *ex se,* He is justly (as we have just said) considered the *principium et fons* of the whole divinity " (§ 25). Again, although he " pronounces it a detestable figment that the essence is the property of the Father alone as if He were the *deificator* of the Son," he yet " acknowledges that *ratione ordinis et gradus,* the *principium divinitatis* is in the Father " (§ 24). " The Father is the fountain of the deity, not with respect of the essence, but the order " (§ 26). And because the Father is thus the *fons et principium deitatis* (§ 23) from whom (*ex eo,* § 18) there have come forth (*exsistere,* § 18) the Son and afterwards from the Son along with the Father the Spirit (§ 18, *ex utroque*), there is involved here a doctrine of an eternal generation of the Son and procession of the Spirit. Both are repeatedly asserted. Of the Son, for example, we read: " It is necessary to understand that the Word was begotten of the Father (*genitum ex Patre*) before time (*ante saecula*) " (§ 7); " we conclude again, therefore, that the Word, before the beginning of time, was conceived (*conceptum*) by God " (§ 8); " He is the Son of God, because He is the Word begotten of the Father (*genitus a Patre*) before the ages (*saecula*) " (§ 23); " He is called the Son of God, . . . inasmuch as He was begotten of the Father (*genitus ex Patre*) before the ages (*saecula*) " (§ 24).[82]

Although such passages, however — and they are very numerous, or we may perhaps better say, pervasive, in Calvin's discussion of the Trinity — make it perfectly plain that he taught a doctrine of order and grade in the Persons of the Trinity, involving a doctrine of the derivation — and that, of course, before all time — of the second and third Persons from the first as the fountain and origin of deity, it is important for a correct understanding of his conception that we should attend to the distinctions by which he guarded his meaning. Of course, he did not teach that the essence of the Son or of the Spirit is the product of their generation or procession. It had been traditional in the Church from the begin-

[82] Already in the *first* edition of the " Institutes " this phraseology is fixed; *Opp.* i. 64: " By which we confess that we believe in Jesus Christ, who, we are convinced, is the unique Son of God the Father, not like believers by adoption and grace only, but naturally as begotten from eternity by the Father." So p. 62: " The Word of the Father — not such as men speak or think, but eternal and unchangeable, as emerging in an ineffable manner from the Father."

ning of the Trinitarian controversies to explain that generation and procession concerned only the Persons of the Son and
Spirit; [83] and Calvin availed himself of this traditional understanding. " The essence, as well of the Son as of the Spirit, is
unbegotten (*ingenitam*) " (§ 25). " The essence of the Son has
no *principium*, but God Himself is the *principium* of His Person " (§ 25). The matter does not require elaboration here,
both because this is obviously the natural view for Calvin to
present and hence goes without saying, and because his mode
of presenting and arguing it has been sufficiently illustrated
in passages already cited.[84] There is another distinction he ap-

[83] Cf. De Moor, " In Marckii Compend.," i. 1761, p. 775: " The Nicene
fathers had reference to nothing but the personal order of subsistence when they
said the Son is ' God of God, Light of Light '; while, considered absolutely
and essentially, the Son is the same God with the Father." This is expressed
by Dr. Shedd with his wonted clearness and emphasis as follows (" A History
of Christian Doctrine," 1873, i. pp. 339 *sq*.): " The Nicene Trinitarians rigorously confined the ideas of ' Sonship ' and ' generation ' to the hypostatical
character. It is not the essence of the Deity that is generated, but a *distinction* in that essence. And, in like manner, the term ' procession ' applied to
the Holy Spirit pertains exclusively to the third hypostasis, and has no application to the substance of the Godhead. The term ' begotten ' in the Nicene
trinitarianism is descriptive only of *that which is peculiar to the second Person, and confined to Him*. The Son is generated with respect only to His
Sonship, or, so to speak, His individuality (ἰδιότης), but is not generated
with respect to His essence or nature. . . . The same *mutatis mutandis* is true
of the term ' procession.' . . . Thus, from first to last, in the Nicene construction of the doctrine of the Trinity, the terms ' beget,' ' begotten,' and ' proceed,' are confined to the hypostatical distinctions, and have no legitimate
or technical meaning, when applied to the Trinity as a whole, or, in other
words, to the Essence in distinction from the hypostasis." . . . Calvin was
fully entitled to avail himself of this distinction, as he fully did so.

[84] His later Trinitarian controversies with Gentilis and his companions
brought out many strong assertions precisely in point. For example, in the
discussion in the " Institutes " (I. xiii. 23 *sq*.), he defines the precise thing he
wishes to refute as the representation of the Father as " the sole essentiator "
who " in forming the Son and the Spirit has transfused His own deity into
them " (§ 23) ; to whom therefore alone the " essence of God belongs " and to
whom as " essentiator " the Son and Spirit owe their essence. In opposition
to this he declares that " although we confess that in point of order and
degree the *principium divinitatis* is in the Father, we nevertheless pronounce
it a detestable figment that the essence is the property of the Father alone,
as if He were the deificator of the Son; because in this way either the essence
would be multiplex or the Son would be called God only in a titular and

pears to have made, however, which is not so clear. Although he taught that the Son was begotten of the Father, and of course begotten before all time, or as we say from all eternity, he seems to have drawn back from the doctrine of " eternal generation " as it was expounded by the Nicene Fathers. They were accustomed to explain " eternal generation " (in accordance with its very nature as " eternal "), not as something which has occurred once for all at some point of time in the past — however far back in the past — but as something which is always occurring, a perpetual movement of the divine essence from the first Person to the second, always complete, never completed.[85] Calvin seems to have found this conception difficult, if not meaningless. In the closing words of the discussion of the Trinity in the " Institutes " (I. xiii. 29, *ad fin.*) he classes it among the speculations which impose unnecessary burdens on the mind. " For what is the profit," he asks, " of disputing whether the Father always generates (*semper generet*), seeing that it is fatuous to imagine a continuous act of generating (*continuus actus generandi*) when it is evident that

---

imaginary sense. If they allow that the Son is God but second from the Father, then the essence will be in Him *genita et formata,* which is in the Father *ingenita et informis*" (§ 24, near end). " We teach from the Scriptures," he explains (§ 25, beginning) " that there is one God in point of essence (*essentialiter*), and therefore the essence of both Son and Spirit is *ingenita*. But inasmuch as the Father is first in order and has begotten from Himself (*genuit ex se*) His own Wisdom, He is rightly considered, as I have just said, the *principium et fons totius divinitatis*. Thus God indefinitely is *ingenitus;* and the Father with regard to His Person also is *ingenitus*." Calvin's weapon against the tritheists, therefore, was precisely that the essence of God, whether in the first, second or third Person, is not generated: that it is only the Person which is generated, and that, strictly speaking, only the Person of the Son — the Person of the Father being ingenerate, and it being more proper to speak of the Person of the Spirit as " proceeding." This is merely, however, the traditional representation, utilized by Calvin, not a new view of his own.

[85] Cf. Sheldon, " History of Christian Doctrine," 1886, i. p. 202: " Like Origen, the Nicene fathers seem to have conceived of the generation, not as something accomplished once for all, but as something parallel with the eternal life of the Son, ever complete and ever continued." Also, Shedd, " A History of Christian Doctrine," i. 1864, p. 317: " Eternal generation is an immanent perpetual activity in an ever existing essence."

three Persons have subsisted in God from eternity?" His meaning appears to be that the act of generation must have been completed from all eternity, since its product has existed complete from all eternity, and therefore it is meaningless to speak of it as continually proceeding. If this is the meaning of his remark, it is a definite rejection of the Nicene speculation of " eternal generation." But this is very far from saying that it is a rejection of the Nicene Creed — or even of the assertion in this Creed to the effect that the Son is " God of God." We have just seen that Calvin explicitly teaches the " eternal generation " of the Son, in the sense that He was begotten by the Father before all time. It manifestly was a matter of fixed belief with him. He does indeed refuse to find proof texts for it in many of the passages which it had been the custom to cite in evidence of it.[86] But he does not therefore feel that he lacks adequate proof of it. There is one argument for it, he tells us, which seems to him worth a thousand distorted texts. " It is certain that God is not a Father to men except through the intercession of that only begotten Son, who alone rightly vindicates to Himself this prerogative, and by whose beneficence it derives to us. But God always wished to be called upon by His people by His name of Father: whence it follows that there was already then in existence the Son through whom that relationship was established." [87] That the Son is " God of God "

---

[86] Of this Scholten, " De Leer der Hervormde Kerk," ed. 4, ii. p. 237 (cf. i. p. 24, ii. p. 229) makes great capital. In the middle edd. of the " Institutes," i. 483, however, Calvin in the very act of discarding these texts as proof asserts his firm belief in the fact of the Divine Sonship of our Lord, as is immediately to be shown. On Calvin's clear-sightedness and critical honesty in dealing with such texts Baumgartner has some good remarks (" Calvin Hébraïsant," 1889, pp. 37, 38). He illustrates the scandal it created at the time among those accustomed to rely on these texts by citing Aegidius Hunnius' book with the portentous title: Calvinus judaizans, hoc est: Judaicae glossae et corruptelae quibus Johannes Calvinus illustrissima Scripturae sacrae loca et testimonia de gloriosa trinitate, deitate Christi et Spiritus Sancti, cumprimis autem vaticinia prophetarum de adventu Messiae, nativitate ejus passione et resurrectione, ascensione in coelos et sessione ad dextram Dei, detestandum in modum corrumpere non exhorruit. Addita est corruptelarum confutatio (Wittemberg: 1593).

[87] Middle edd. of " Institutes," Opp. i. 483.

he is therefore as fully convinced as the Nicene Fathers themselves. When, then, he criticises the formulas of the Nicene
Creed, " God of God, Light of Light, very God of very God,"
as repetitious, this is a criticism of the form, not of the content of this statement.[88] And when he speaks of the " Deus de
Deo " of the Creed as a " hard saying " (dura locutio), he by
no means denies that it is " true and useful," in the sense its
framers put on it, in the sense, that is, that the Son has His
principium merely as Son in the Father, but only means that
the form of the statement is inexact — the term " Deus " requiring to be taken in each case of its occurrence in a non-
natural personal sense — and that, being inexact, it is liable
to be misused in the interests of a created God, in the sense
of Gentilis, and must therefore be carefully explained.[89] His

[88] *Opp.* vii. 315, where it is explicitly declared that he had no intention
of derogating from the symbol: cf. p. 316.

[89] Preface to the " Expositio impietatis Valen. Gentilis," 1561 (*Opp.* ix.
368): " But the words of the Council of Nice run: Deum esse de Deo. A hard
saying (*dura locutio*), I confess; but for removing its ambiguity no one can be
a more suitable interpreter than Athanasius, who dictated it. And certainly
the design of the fathers was none other than to maintain the origin which
the Son draws from the Father in respect of Person, without in any way opposing the sameness of the essence and deity in the two, so that as to essence the
Word is God *absque principio,* while in Person the Son has His principium
from the Father." Petavius' criticism is therefore wide of the mark when (" De
Trinitate," III. iii. 2, ed. Paris, 1865, pt. ii. p. 523; cf. also Bellarmine, " De
Christo," Preface of his " Opera," i. p. 244) he declares that Calvin " speaks
rashly and altogether untheologically (temere et prorus ἀθεολογήτως) when
he calls this locution ' *hard,*' because he supposes that Christ, as He is God
is *a se ipso,* i.e., αὐτόθεος." But Calvin (who certainly does believe that Christ
is self-existent God and therefore may properly be called αὐτόθεος), does
not find the locution *Deus de* (or *ex*) *Deo* " hard " (*dura*) on that account:
he thoroughly believes both in the θεός ἐκ θεοῦ of the Creed and in the
αὐτοθεότης of Christ, and found no difficulty whatever in harmonizing them.
When he pronounces this locution " harsh " his mind is on the possibility of
its misuse by the Antitrinitarians as if it meant that the Son was *made God*
by the Father. When, therefore, Petavius adds (§ 3, p. 524): " So then, the
locution, *God is from God,* is not only true but useful (*proba*) and con-
sentaneous to Christian teaching; not as the Autotheani and Calvinists igno-
rantly babble, *hard* " — he says no more for the substance of it than Calvin
had himself said in the very passage in which he called the locution " harsh,"
— that is to say, that it expresses an important truth; this, to wit, that the
Son draws His origin, with respect to His Person, from the Father. No doubt

position is, in a word, that of one who affirms the eternal generation of the Son, but who rejects the speculations of the
Nicene Fathers respecting the nature of the act which they
called "eternal generation." It is enough, he says in effect, to
believe that the Son derives from the Father, the Spirit from
the Father and the Son, without encumbering ourselves with
a speculation upon the nature of the eternally generating act
to which these hypostases are referred. It is interesting to observe that Calvin's attitude upon these matters is precisely repeated by Dr. Charles Hodge in his discussion in his "Systematic Theology." [90] It seems to be exactly Calvin's point of
view to which Dr. Hodge gives expression when he writes: " A
distinction must be made between the Nicene Creed (as ampli-
fied in that of Constantinople) and the doctrine of the Nicene
Fathers. The creeds are nothing more than the well-ordered arrangement of the facts of Scripture which concern the doctrine
of the Trinity. They assert the distinct personality of the
Father, Son and Spirit; their mutual relation as expressed by
these terms; their absolute unity as to substance or essence,
and their consequent perfect equality; and the subordination
of the Son to the Father, and of the Spirit to the Father and
the Son, as to the mode of subsistence and operation. These
are Scriptural facts, to which the creeds in question add nothing; and it is in this sense that they have been accepted by the
Church Universal. But the Nicene Fathers did undertake in
a greater or less degree to explain these facts. These explanations relate principally to the subordination of the Son and
Spirit to the Father, and to what is meant by generation, or
the relation between the Father and the Son. . . . As in reference to the subordination of the Son and Spirit to the Father,
as asserted in the ancient creeds, it is not to the fact that ex-

---

Calvin may also suggest that there might wisely have been chosen a less
ambiguous way of saying this than the "harsh" locution *Deus de Deo* — which
certainly is capable of being misunderstood as teaching that the Son owes His
divinity to the Father — as Gentilis taught. See below, note 94.

[90] "Systematic Theology," i. 1874, pp. 462 *sq.* On pp. 466, 467 he gives
a very clear statement of Calvin's position, of which he expresses full approval.

ception is taken, but to the explanation of that fact, as given
by the Nicene Fathers, the same is true with regard to the doctrine of Eternal Generation."

The circumstance that Dr. Charles Hodge, writing three
centuries afterwards (1559–1871), reproduces precisely Calvin's position may intimate to us something of the historical
significance of Calvin's discussion of the Trinity. Clearly Calvin's position did not seem a matter of course, when he first
enunciated it. It roused opposition and created a party. But
it did create a party: and that party was shortly the Reformed
Churches, of which it became characteristic that they held and
taught the self-existence of Christ as God and defended therefore the application to Him of the term αὐτόθεος; that is to
say, in the doctrine of the Trinity they laid the stress upon the
equality of the Persons sharing in the same essence, and thus
set themselves with more or less absoluteness against all subordinationism in the explanation of the relations of the Persons to one another. When Calvin asserted, with the emphasis
which he threw upon it, the self-existence of Christ, he unavoidably did three things. First and foremost, he declared
the full and perfect deity of our Lord, in terms which could
not be mistaken and could not be explained away. The term
αὐτόθεος served the same purpose in this regard that the term
ὁμοούσιος had served against the Arians and the term ὑπόστασις
against the Sabellians. No minimizing conception of the deity
of Christ could live in the face of the assertion of aseity or
αὐτοθεότης of Him. This was Calvin's purpose in asserting
aseity of Christ and it completely fulfilled itself in the event.
In thus fulfilling itself, however, two further effects were unavoidably wrought by it. The inexpugnable opposition of subordinationists of all types was incurred: all who were for any
reason or in any degree unable or unwilling to allow to Christ
a deity in every respect equal to that of the Father were necessarily offended by the vindication to Him of the ultimate Divine quality of self-existence. And all those who, while prepared to allow true deity to Christ, yet were accustomed to
think of the Trinitarian relations along the lines of the tradi-

tional Nicene orthodoxy, with its assertion of a certain subordination of the Son to the Father, at least in mode of subsistence, were thrown into more or less confusion of mind and compelled to resort to nice distinctions in order to reconcile the two apparently contradictory confessions of αὐτοθεότης and of θεὸς ἐκ θεοῦ of our Lord. It is not surprising, then, that the controversy roused by Caroli and carried on by Chaponneau and Courtois did not die out with their refutation; but prolonged itself through the years and has indeed come down even to our own day. Calvin's so-called innovation with regard to the Trinity has, in point of fact, been made the object of attack through three centuries, not only by Unitarians of all types, nor only by professed Subordinationists, but also by Athanasians, puzzled to adjust their confession of Christ as "God of God, Light of Light, very God of very God" to the at least verbally contradictory assertion that in respect of His deity He is not of another but of Himself.

The attack has been especially sharp naturally where the assailants were predisposed to criticism of Calvin on other grounds, as was the case, for example, with Romanists, Lutherans and afterward with Arminians. As was to be expected, it is found in its most decisive form among the Romanists, and we are afraid we must say with Gomarus that with them it seems to have been urged in the first instance, rather because of a desire to disparage Calvin and the Calvinists than in any distinct doctrinal interest.[91] The beginning of the assault seems to have been made by Genebrardus, who "in the first book of his treatise on the Trinity, refutes what he calls the heresy of those denominated *Autotheanites,* that is of those who say that Christ is God of Himself *(a se ipso),* not of the Father, attributing this heresy to Calvin and Beza and in the Preface to his work [mistakenly] surmising that Francis Stancarus was the originator of it."[92] The way thus opened, however, was

[91] "Diatribe de Christo αὐτοθεῷ," printed by Voetius, in "Selectae Disputationes Theologicae," Part i. 1648, p. 445: calumniandi potius libidine quam erroris cum Arianis societate.

[92] We are quoting from Bellarmine, "De Christo," II. cap. xix. *ad init.* (his "Opera," i. p. 333). Cf. the opening words of Petavius' discussion, "De

largely followed by the whole crowd of Romish controversialists, the most notable of whom in the first age were probably Anthony Possevinus, Alphonsus Salmeron, William Lindanus, Peter Canisius, Dionysius Petavius,[93] all of whom exhaust the resources of dialectics in the endeavor to fix upon Calvin and his followers a stigma of heresy in the fundamental doctrine of the Trinity. A more honorable course was pursued by probably the two greatest Romish theologians of the time, Gregory of Valentia and Robert Bellarmine. Although in no way disinclined to find error in the teaching of Calvin and the Calvinists, these more cautious writers feel compelled to allow that Calvin in his zeal to do full justice to the deity of Christ has not passed beyond Catholic truth, and blame him therefore only for inaccuracy of phrase. Gregory of Valentia, whom Gomarus calls " the Coryphaeus of Papal theologians," speaking of the error of the Autotheanites, remarks: " Genebrardus has attributed this error to Calvin (*Inst.*, I. xiii), but, in point of fact, if he be read attentively, it will be seen that he [Calvin] meant merely that the Son, as He is indeed essentially God, is *ex se*, and is *ex Patre* only as He is a Person: and that is true. For although the Fathers and Councils assert that He is *Deus ex Deo* most truly, by taking the term [God] personally, so that it signifies the Person itself at once of the Father and of

---

Trinitate," VI. xi. 5 (his " Opera," iii. p. 251): " With respect to more recent writers, there exists a far from small altercation of the Catholics with heretics, especially with Calvin, Beza and their crew (*asseclis*). For Genebrardus in the first book of his " De Trinitate " very sharply upbraids (*insectatur*) them and gives them the name *autotheanites,* because they say the Son has His divinity and essence of Himself; an error mentioned also by William Lindanus."

93 Voetius, " Dispt.," i. pp. 453, 454, gives an account of the opponents of the Reformed ascription of αὐτοθεότης to Christ. There are three classes: Romanists, Lutherans, and Arminians, to which he adds as fourth and fifth classes Peter Caroli, and the Antitrinitarians (Crell and Schlichting). The Romanists he subdivides into two classes, those who find that Calvin taught heresy and those who object to his language only. The latter sub-class includes only Bellarmine and Gregory of Valentia. Under the former, however, he enumerates a long list of writers with exact references. Cf. also De Moor, " In Marck. Comp.," i. 1761, pp. 773–774 (V. x.).

the Son; [94] nevertheless the Son, as He is essentially God, that is, as He is that one, most simple Being which is God, is not from another, because as such He is an absolute somewhat. If this were all that were meant by the other heretics who are called 'Autotheanites,' there would be no occasion for contending with them. For it was in this sense that Epiphanius, *Haer.* 69, seems to have called the Son αὐτοθεός." [95] Bellarmine's candor scarcely stretches so far as Gregory's. While he too feels compelled to allow that Calvin's meaning is catholic, he yet very strongly reprobates his mode of stating that meaning and declares that it gives fair occasion for the strictures which have been passed upon him. " When," says he, " I narrowly look into the matter itself, and carefully consider Calvin's opinions, I find it difficult to declare that he was in this error. For he teaches that the Son is of Himself (*a se*), in respect of essence, not in respect of Person, and seems to wish to say that the Person is begotten by the Father [but] the essence is not begotten or produced, but is of itself (*a se ipsa*); so that if you abstract from the Person of the Son the relation to the Father, the essence alone remains, and that is of itself (*a se ipsa*)." But on the other hand Bellarmine thinks " that Calvin has undoubtedly erred in his manner of expressing himself, and given occasion to be spoken of as he has been spoken of by our [the Romish] writers." This judgment is supported by the following specifications: " For he [Calvin] says, *Inst.*, I. xiii. 19: 'The ecclesiastical writers now teach that the Father

[94] That is to say, the phrase " God of God " is interpreted to mean " God the Son, of God the Father "—God in the first instance meaning (not the essence but) the Person of the Son, and in the second instance (not the essence but) the Person of the Father. Only on this supposition, as Gregory allows, can the phrase " God of God " be applied to Christ in exactness of speech. That is to say, Gregory finds the phrase as inexact as Calvin does when he calls it a *dura locutio*.

[95] We repeat the passage from Gomarus' citation in Voetius' " Disputat.," i. 1648, p. 448. Gomarus cites Gregory, " Ad summae Thomae," part i. disp. 2, quaest. 1, punct. 1, p. 718. The passage is found also, however, in Gregory's treatise " De Trinitate," ii. 1 (to which Voetius refers us, p. 454, adding appropriate references also to i. 22 and ii. 17). See Gregorii de Valentia " . . . de rebus fidei hoc tempore controversis Libri," Paris, 1610, p. 205, first column, B and C.

is the principium of the Son, now assert that the Son has both divinity and essence of Himself (*a se ipso*).' And below this: ' Accordingly, when we speak of the Son *simpliciter* without respect to the Father, we may well and properly assert that He is of Himself (*a se*).' And in the twenty-third section, speaking of the Son, ' How,' he asks, ' shall the creator who gives being to all things not be of Himself (*a se ipso*), but derive His essence from another? ' And in his letter to the Poles and in his work against Gentilis, Calvin frequently asserts that the Son is αὐτόθεος, that is, God of Himself (*a se ipso*), and [declares] the expression in the Creed ' God of God, Light of Light ' an improper and hard saying." [96]

The gravamen of Bellarmine's charges we see from a later passage (p. 334b, near bottom) turns on Calvin's assertion that " the Son has [His] essence from Himself (*a se*)." This, Bellarmine declares, is to be " repudiated *simpliciter*," as he undertakes to demonstrate, on the grounds that it is repugnant to Scripture, the definitions of the Councils, the teaching of the Fathers, and reason itself, and as well to Calvin's own opinions; and is not established by the arguments which Calvin adduces in its behalf. In Bellarmine's view, however, in so speaking Calvin merely expressed himself badly: he really meant nothing more than that the Son with respect to His essence, which is His as truly as it is the Father's, is of Himself (*a se ipso*). He thinks this is proved by the fact that Calvin elsewhere speaks in terms which infer his orthodoxy in the point at issue. He speaks of the Son, for example, as begotten of the Father, which would be meaningless, if He does not receive His nature, or essence, from the Father, since " it is not a mere relation which is called the Son, but a real somewhat subsisting in the divine nature," and the Son is " not a mere propriety but an *integra hypostasis*." He even plainly says in so many words (I. xiii. 28) that the essence is communicated from the Father to the Son: " If the difference is in the essence, let them reply whether He has not shared it (*communicaverit*) with the Son. . . . It follows that it is wholly and al-

[96] *Op. cit.*, p. 334a.

together (*tota et in solidum*) common to the Father and Son."
And he does not embrace the errors which would flow from
ascribing to the Son His essence of Himself: for example, he
ascribes but a single essence to the Persons of the Trinity, and
he does not distinguish the essence from the Persons *realiter*
but only *ratione*.

Petavius does not find it possible to follow Bellarmine in
this exculpating judgment. For his part, he willingly admits
that Calvin sometimes speaks inconsistently with himself,
but he cannot doubt that he means what he says, when he
declares that the Son has His essence not from the Father but
from Himself — and this is a thing which, says he, is not only
false, but impious to say, and cannot be affirmed by any Catholic. For it stands to reason, he argues, that everyone "has his
essence from him by whom he is begotten; since generation is
just the communication of the nature, — whether, as in created things, in kind, or, as in the divine production of the
Word, in number. It is indeed impossible to form any conception of generation without the nature, and some communication of the essence, occurring to the mind." [97] The whole question of Calvin's orthodoxy, between these writers, it will be
seen, turns on their judgment as to his attitude towards the
doctrine of "eternal generation." Bellarmine judges that, on
the whole, though he has sometimes expressed himself inconsistently with regard to it, Calvin soundly believes in the doctrine of "eternal generation"; and therefore he pronounces
him orthodox. Petavius judges that, though he sometimes expresses himself in the terms of the doctrine of "eternal generation," Calvin does not really believe in it; and therefore he
pronounces him heretical. To both authors alike the test of
orthodoxy lies in conformity of thought to the Nicene speculation, and they cannot conceive of a sound doctrine of the Trinity apart from this speculation and all the nice discrimina-
tions and adjustments which result from it.[98] And it can

[97] *Op. cit.*, p. 252a.
[98] It is interesting to observe how constantly the argument hangs formally on the suppressed premise of the Nicene doctrine of generation.

scarcely be denied that Calvin laid himself open to suspicion from this point of view. The principle of his doctrine of the Trinity was not the conception he formed of the relation of the Son to the Father and of the Spirit to the Father and Son, expressed respectively by the two terms " generation " and " procession ": but the force of his conviction of the absolute equality of the Persons. The point of view which adjusted everything to the conception of " generation " and " procession " as worked out by the Nicene Fathers was entirely alien to him. The conception itself he found difficult, if not unthinkable; and although he admitted the facts of " generation " and " procession," he treated them as bare facts, and refused to make them constitutive of the doctrine of the Trinity. He rather adjusted everything to the absolute divinity of each Person, their community in the one only true Deity; and to this we cannot doubt that he was ready not only to subordinate, but even to sacrifice, if need be, the entire body of Nicene speculations. Moreover, it would seem at least very doubtful if Calvin, while he retained the conception of " generation " and " procession," strongly asserting that the Father is the *principium divinitatis*, that the Son was " begotten " by Him before all ages and that the Spirit " proceeded " from the Father

---

Thus Bellarmine argues (p. 334b) that " those who assert that the Son has His essense *a se ipso* err because they are compelled either (1) to make the Son ingenerate *and the same person with the Father*, or (2) to mulply the essences, or at least (3) to distinguish the essence from the person *realiter* and so introduce a quaternity." As Calvin does none of these things, he is pronounced orthodox in meaning. But the point now to be illustrated lies in the assumption under (1) that to make the Son ingenerate is to make Him the same person with the Father. It does not occur to Bellarmine as possible that one should deny the Son to be generated and yet not make Him the same person with the Father, while holding free from (2) and (3). Similarly, when replying to Danaeus, who asks: " If He is not God *a se*, how is He God? " Petavius (p. 256) declares that so to speak is perfidious and ignorant — " for," says he, " it either robs the Son of His deity or denies that He is God begotten of the Father." The one seems to him as intolerable as the other. Neither Bellarmine nor Petavius seems fairly to have faced the possibility of a doctrine of a true Trinity of Persons in one essence which did not hang on the doctrine of " eternal generation," which seemed to them, thus, equipollent with the doctrine of the Trinity.

and Son before time began, thought of this begetting and procession as involving any communication of essence. His conception was that, because it is the Person of the Father which begets the Person of the Son, and the Person of the Spirit which proceeds from the Persons of the Father and Son, it is precisely the distinguishing property of the Son which is the thing begotten, not the essence common to Father and Son, and the distinguishing property of the Spirit which is the product of the procession, not the essence which is common to all three persons. Of course, he did not hold, as Bellarmine phrases it, that " the Son is a mere relation," " a mere property ": the Son was to him too, as a matter of course, " *aliquid subsistens in natura divina,*" " *integra hypostasis.*" But he did hold that Sonship is a relation and that the Son differs from the Father only by this property of Sonship which is expressed as a relation (I. xiii. 6); and it looks very much as if his thought was that it is only in what is expressed by the term Sonship that the second Person of the Trinity is the Son of the Father, or, what comes to the same thing, has been begotten of the Father. His idea seems to be that the Father, Son and Spirit are one in essence, and differ from one another only in that property peculiar to each, which, added to the common essence, constitutes them respectively Father, Son and Spirit; and that the Father is Father only as Father, the Son, Son only as Son, or what comes to the same thing, the Father begets the Son only as Son, or produces by the act of generation only that by virtue of which He is the Son, which is, of course, what constitutes just His Sonship.

The evidence on which Bellarmine relies for his view that Calvin taught a communication of essence from Father to Son is certainly somewhat slender. If we put to one side Bellarmine's inability to conceive that Calvin could really believe in a true generation of the Son by the Father without holding that the Son receives His essence from the Father, and his natural presumption that Calvin's associates and pupils accurately reproduced the teaching of their master — for there is no doubt that Beza and Simler, for example, understood by

generation a communication of essence — the evidence which
Bellarmine relies on reduces to a single passage in the " Institutes " (I. xiii. 23). Calvin there, arguing with Gentilis, opposes to the notion that the Father and Son differ in essence,
the declaration that the Father " shares " the essence together
with the Son, so that it is common, *tota et in solidum*, to the
Father and the Son. It may be possible to take the verb " communicate " here in the sense of " impart " rather than in that of
" have in common," but it certainly is not necessary and it
seems scarcely natural; and there is little elsewhere in Calvin's
discussion to require it of us. Petavius points out that the sentence is repeated in the tract against Gentilis — but that carries us but a little way. It is quite true that there is nothing
absolutely clear to be found to the opposite effect either. But
there are several passages which may be thought to suggest a
denial that the Son derives His essence from the Father. Precisely what is meant, for example, when we are told that the
Son " contains in Himself the simple and indivisible essence
of God in integral perfection, not *portione aut deflexu*," is no
doubt not clear: but by *deflexu* it seems possible that Calvin
meant to deny that the Son possessed the divine essence by im-
partation from another (I. xiii. 2). It is perhaps equally questionable what weight should be placed on the form of the statement (§ 20) that the order among the Persons by which the
principium and *origo* is in the Father, is produced (*fero*) by
the " proprieties "; or on the suggestion that the more exact
way of speaking of the Son is to call Him " the Son of the
Person " (§ 23) — the Father being meant — the term God
in the phrase " Son of God " requiring to be taken of the Person of the Father. When it is argued that " whoever asserts
that the Son is essentiated by the Father denies that He is self-
existent " (§ 23), and "makes His divinity a something ab-
stracted from the essence of God, or a derivation of a part from
the whole," the reference to Gentilis' peculiar views of the
essentiation of the Son by the Father, i.e., His creation by the
Father, seems to preclude a confident use of the phrase in the
present connection. Nor does the exposition of the unbegot-

tenness of the essence of the Son and Spirit as well as of the Father, so that it is only as respects His Person that the Son is of the Father (§ 25) lend itself any more certainly to our use. A survey of the material in the " Institutes " leads to the impression thus that there is singularly little to bring us to a confident decision whether Calvin conceived the essence of God to be communicated from the Father to the Son in " generation " and from the Father and Son to the Spirit in " procession." And outside the " Institutes" the same ambiguity seems to follow us. If we read that Christ has " the fulness of the Godhead " of Himself (*Opp.* xi. 560), we read equally that the Fathers taught that the Son is " of the Father even with respect to His eternal essence " (vii. 322), and is of the substance of the Father (vii. 324). In this state of the case opinions may lawfully differ. But on the whole we are inclined to think that Calvin, although perhaps not always speaking perfectly consistently, seeks to avoid speaking of generation and procession as importing the communication of the Divine essence; so that Petavius appears to be right in contending that Calvin meant what he says when he represents the Son as " having from Himself both divinity and essence " (I. xiii. 19).

We have thought it worth while to dwell with some fulness on this matter, because, as we have suggested already, it is precisely in this peculiarity of Calvin's doctrine of the Trinity that the explanation is found of the widespread offense which was taken at it. Men whose whole thought of the Trinity lived, moved and had its being in the ideas of generation and procession, that is, in the notion of a perpetual communication of the Divine essence from the Father as the *fons deitatis* to the Son, who is thereby constituted the Son, and from the Father and Son to the Spirit, who is thereby constituted the Spirit, could not but feel that the Trinity they had known and confessed was taken away when this conception was conspicuous only by its absence, or was at best but remotely suggested, and all the stress was laid on the absolute equality of the Father, Son and Holy Spirit. Such a conception of the

Trinity would inevitably appear to them to savor of Sabellianism or of Tritheism, according as their minds dwelt more on the emphasis which was laid upon the numerical unity of the essence common to all the Persons or on that which was laid upon the distinctness of the Persons. Dissatisfaction with Calvin's Trinitarian teaching was therefore not confined to Romish controversialists seeking ground of complaint against him, but was repeated in all whose thought had run strictly in the moulds of Nicene speculation. Despite an occasional defender like Meisner or Tarnov,[99] the Lutheran theologians, for example, generally condemned it. Many, like Tilemann Heshusius and Aegidius Hunnius and, later, Stechmannus, hotly assailed it, and the best that could be hoped for at Lutheran hands was some such firm though moderately worded refusal of it as is found, for example, in John Gerhard's " Loci Theologici." " The Greek doctors," he tells us,[100] " call only the Father αὐτόθεος καὶ αὐτοούσιος, not because there is a greater perfection of essence in the Father than in the Son, but because He is ἀγένητος and a se ipso and does not have deity through generation or spiration. Bucanus, Loc. i, De Deo, p. 6, responds thus: ' The Son is a se ipso as He is God; from the Father as He is Son.' This he got from Calvin, who, Book I, c. xiii, § 25, writes: ' The Son as He is God we confess is ex se ipso, considered apart from His Person, but as He is Son we say that He is of the Father; thus His essence is without principium, but of His Person God is Himself the principium.' We are not able, however, to approve these words, but confess rather with the

[99] It is to be hoped that modern Lutherans in general will subscribe the excellent remarks of Prof. Milton Valentine, " Christian Theology," 1906, i. 309: " Emphasis must . . . be laid on the attribute of aseity as belonging to the whole Godhead, to the divine Being as such. . . . It cannot therefore be allowable to think of God as originating the Trinality of the Godhead, as though there was a time when He was not Tripersonal in His Being. . . ." Accordingly he ascribes self-existence to the Son (pp. 321–322). A. Ritschl, " Justification and Reconciliation," iii. E. T. 1900, p. 470, represents " theological tradition," which at least includes Lutheran tradition, as " expressly excluding aseity " in its representations of the Deity of Christ.

[100] Ed. Cotta, i. Tubingen, 1762, pp. 291–292 (Loc. IV. pars ii. cap. v. § 179).

Nicene Creed that 'the Son is begotten of the Father, God of God, Light of Light,' and follow the saying of Christ, Jno. v. 26 . . . Prov. viii. 24. . . . Zacharias Ursinus [101] therefore is right to separate from his preceptor here, writing in *Catech.*, p. II. q. 25, p. 179: 'The Son is begotten of the Father; that is, He has the Divine Essence in an ineffable manner communicated to Him from the Father.' D. Lobechius, *disp.* 3 *in Augustinum Conf.* th. 26, says: 'The essence should be considered in a two-fold way, either with respect to itself or with respect to its own being, or else with respect to its communication: it has no principium with respect to its own being; but with respect to its communication we say that the essence has as its principium, to be from the Father in the Son, for it has been communicated from the Father to the Son.'" Nevertheless, Gerhard, of course, does not deny that, when properly explained, the Son may fitly be called αὐτόθεος; since that would be tantamount to denying His true divinity. Accordingly he writes elsewhere: [102] "The term is ambiguous: for it is either opposed to communication of the divine essence and in that sense we deny that Christ is αὐτόθεος, because He receives the essence by eternal generation from the Father; or it is opposed to the inequality of the Divine essence, and in that sense we concede that Christ is αὐτόθεος. Gregory of Valentia, *De Trinitate*, i. 22: 'The Son as He is a Person is from another; as the most simple being, is not from another.' Christ is verily and in Himself God (*vere et se ipso Deus*), but He is not of Himself (*a se ipso*) God." One would think Gerhard was skating on very thin ice to agree with Gregory of Valentia — who agrees with Calvin and uses his very mode of statement — and yet not agree with Calvin.

---

[101] It must not be supposed, however, that Ursinus separated himself from Calvin as to the self-existence of the Son as He is God: his language is: "the Son is begotten of the Father, of the essence of the Father, but the essence of the Son is not begotten, but, existent of itself (*a se ipsa existens*), is communicated to the Son at His begetting (*nascenti*) by (*a*) the Father." "And what is said concerning the generation of the Son," he adds, "is to be understood also of the procession of the Spirit" ("Loci," p. 542).   [102] iii. Tubingen, 1764, p. 395 (Locus IV. cap. v. § 67).

The subordinationism [103] of the Arminians was of quite a different quality from that of the Lutherans. The dominant note which the Lutheran Christology sounded was the majesty of Christ; nothing that tended to exalt Christ could be without its appeal to Lutherans; they drew back from Calvin's assertion of His αὐτοθεότης only in the interests of the traditional Nicene construction of the Trinity. The Arminians had, on the other hand, a distinct tendency to the proper subordinationism of the Origenists; and in the later members of the school, indeed, there was present a strong influence from the Socinians. To them, of course, the Father alone could be thought of as αὐτόθεος and the Son was conceived as in His very nature, because God only by derivation, less than the Father. As in his whole theological outlook, Arminius himself was here better than his successors. He fairly saves his orthodoxy, indeed; but he emphatically denies the αὐτοθεότης of the Son. The Son

[103] Cf. H. Bavinck, "Geref. Dogmatiek," ed. 1, ii. p. 263. Remarking that the tendency which finds its typical form in Arianism, has manifested itself in various forms in the Church for centuries: "First of all in the form of Subordinationism: the Son is to be sure eternal, generated out of the essence of the Father, no creature, and not made of nothing; but He is nevertheless inferior to or subordinated to the Father. The Father alone is ὁ θεός, πηγή θεότητος, the Son is θεός, receives His nature by communication from the Father. This was the teaching of Justin, Tertullian, Clement, Origen, etc., also of the Semi-Arians, Eusebius of Caesarea and Eusebius of Nicomedia, who placed the Son ἐκτὸς τοῦ πατρός and declared Him ὁμοιοούσιος with the Father; and later of the Remonstrants (Conf. Art. 3; Arminus *Op. theol.* 1629, pp. 232 *sq.;* Episcopius, *Instit. theol.* IV. sect. ii. c. 32; Limborch, *Theol. Christ.* II. c. xvii. § 25), of the Supranaturalists (Bretschneider, *Dogm.,* i.⁴ pp. 602 *sq.;* Knapp, *Glaubenslehre,* i. p. 260; Muntinghe, *Theol. Christ.* pars theor. § 134 *sq.,* etc.), and of very many theologians of recent times (Frank, *Syst. d. chr. Wahr.,* i. pp. 207 *sq.;* Beck, *Chr. Gl.* ii. pp. 123 *sq.;* Twesten, ii. p. 254; Kahnis, i. pp. 353, 398; van Oosterzee, ii. § 52; Doedes, *Ned. Gel.* 71 *sq.*)." Cf. also H. C. Sheldon, "History of Christian Doctrine," ii. 1886, p. 97: "The Arminians, while they held to the doctrine of three Divine Persons in the Godhead, diverged from the current teaching on the subject by an express emphasis upon the subordination of the Son and the Spirit. Arminius was not specially related to this development, and contented himself with denying, in opposition to Calvin's phraseology, the propriety of attributing self-existence to the Son. But Episcopius, Curcellaeus, and Limborch were very pronounced in the opinion that a certain preëminence must be assigned to the Father over the Son and the Spirit."

may just as well be called Father, he intimates, as be represented as " having His essence *a se ipso* or *a nullo* "; and the employment of such language cannot be justified by saying that to affirm that the Son of God, as God, has His essence *a se ipso,* is only to say that the divine essence is not *ab aliquo:* there can, in fact, be no reason for calling the Son αὐτόθεος.[104] On the other hand, nevertheless, he recognizes that the word αὐτόθεος may be taken in two senses. It may describe the one to whom it is applied either merely as *vere et se ipso* God, or else as God *a se.* In the former usage it is as applied to the Son tolerable; in the latter not.[105] He argues that we must distinguish between saying that the essence which the Son has is from none, and that the Son which has this essence is from none: " for," says he, " the Son is the name of a person, which has a relation to the Father, and therefore cannot be defined or contemplated apart from this relation; while the essence, on the other hand, is an absolute somewhat." [106] " To contend," he urges, " that to say ' He is God ' and ' He has His essence from none ' are equivalent statements, is to say either that the Father alone is God, or else that there are three collateral Gods." He cheerfully allows that neither of these assertions expresses the meaning of Calvin or Beza: but he contends that they use misleading language when they call Christ αὐτόθεος and he appeals to Beza's admission, when excusing Calvin, that " Calvin had not strictly observed the discrimination between the particles *a se* and *per se.*"

The gravitation of Arminianism was, however, downward; and we find already taught by Episcopius, no longer a certain subordination in order among the Persons of the Trinity in the interests of the Nicene doctrine of " eternal generation " and " procession," but rather a generation and procession in the interests of a subordination in nature among the Persons of the

[104] " Declaratio sententiae suae ad ordines Holl. et Westfr.," in " Opera Theol.," 1635, pp. 100–101. See E. T. " Works," translated by James Nichols, London, i. 1825, pp. 627–631.

[105] " Resp. ad xxxi. Articulos," in " Opera," p. 131 (E. T. " Works," ii. 1828, pp. 29–32).

[106] *Ibid.,* p. 132.

Trinity. " It is certain " from Scripture, says he, " that this divinity and the divine perfections are to be attributed to these three persons, not collaterally and coördinately, but subordinately." " This subordination," he adds, " should be carefully attended to, because of its extremely great usefulness, since by it not only is there fundamentally overthrown the τριθεότης which collateralism almost necessarily involves, but also the Father's glory is preserved to Him unimpaired." Wherefore, he continues, " they fall into perilous error who contend that the Son is αὐτόθεος, in such a manner that as He is God He is of Himself, as He is Son of the Father; because from this point of view, the true subordination between the Father and the Son is taken away." [107] It is scarcely necessary to pause to point out with Triglandius [108] that to say that the Son and Spirit are not collaterally or coördinally divine with the Father is to say they are not equally divine with Him, and to say that it is injurious to the Father's glory to call the Son αὐτόθεος, even as He is God, is to say that He is inferior to the Father even in His essence. No doubt Episcopius says in the same breath that " one and the same divine nature " is to be attributed to the three Persons. But this is not easy to conciliate with his argument, except on the supposition that in saying " one and the same nature," his thought wavered somewhat between numerical oneness and specific oneness,[109] or else that he conceived the relation of the several Persons to this one nature to differ among themselves — one possessing it of Himself, the others by derivation from — shall we even suggest, by favor of? — another.

The path thus opened by Episcopius was eagerly walked in by his successors. All that may be thought to be latent in Episcopius came to light in Curcellaeus. We will, however, permit another hand to describe to us his teaching with regard to the Trinity. " If you take his own account," writes Robert

[107] Cf. Episcopius' theologial works, printed at Amsterdam, 1650–1665; espec. his " Instit. Theolog.," lib. iv. § 11, de Deo, capp. 32–36. But we cite from Triglandius.

[108] Triglandius, " Antapologia," cap. v. pp. 77 sq.

[109] Cf. Triglandius, pp. 579, 580.

Nelson, in his " Life of Dr. George Bull," [110] there would be no man more orthodox and catholic " than Curcellaeus is " in the doctrine of the Trinity, as also in that of the Incarnation of Christ. And he insisted, that both from the pulpit and from the chair, he had always taught and vindicated that faith, into which he had been baptized, and which he had publicly professed in the congregation, according to the form generally received; and did even teach and vindicate the same at that very time, when the charge of Anti-trinitarianism was brought against him. Yea, he expressed so great a zeal for the orthodox doctrine in this great fundamental, as he would seem forward to seal the truth thereof, even with his blood; if, as he said, God would vouchsafe him this honor. Notwithstanding all this, it is notoriously known, and that from his own very Apology, that he was no less an enemy to the Council of Nice than his master before him, if not more than he; that he was no friend at all to the use of the word ' Trinity '; that he so explained himself concerning that mystery as to assert no more than a ' specifical unity ' in the divine Persons; that he defended the cause of Valentinus Gentilis, beheaded at Bern in Switzerland for Tritheism, maintaining his doctrine to have been the same with that of the primitive Fathers, particularly of Ignatius, Justin Martyr, Irenaeus, Athenagoras, Tertullian, and Clemens Alexandrinus; that he impeached the common (which he called the Modern and Scholastic) doctrine of the Trinity for approaching so very near Sabellianism, as hardly to be distinguished from it, and charged it to be a thousand years younger than that which was taught by Christ and His apostles; that he exploded the notion of consubstantiality, in the sense in which it is now generally taken, when applied to the Father and Son; that he was very much afraid to have his mind perplexed with the ' divine relations,' or with the manner of ' generation ' and ' procession ' in the Deity, or with modes of ' subsistence ' and ' personalities,' or with ' mutual consciousness,' and the like; and therefore was for discarding at once all such terms and phrases as are not ' expressly legiti-

[110] London, 1713, pp. 290 *sq.*

mated' by the sacred writers; that he fully believed the Godhead of the Father to be more excellent than that of the Son,
or of the Holy Ghost, even so far as to look upon this superiority as a thing unquestionable, and to appeal to the consentient
testimony of the primitive Church for evidence; and lastly
that he took care to recommend Petavius, and the author of
Irenicum Irenicorum,[111] a learned physician of Dantzick . . .
to the perusal of his readers, for the sake of that collection of
testimonies which is to be found in them, as wherein they
might easily find ' an account of the primitive faith' concerning these great articles." A subordinationism like this, of course,
could not endure Calvin's Trinitarianism, of which the corner-
stone was the equality of the Persons in the Trinity — which
equality it was that was safeguarded by the ascription of
αὐτοθεότης to Christ.

Indeed, this ascription was equally unacceptable to a subordinationism of far less extreme a type than that of Curcellaeus and his Remonstrant successors. It is the biographer of
George Bull to whom we have appealed to bring Curcellaeus'
trinitarian teaching before us: and George Bull is perhaps the
best example of that less extreme, convinced, no doubt, but
well-guarded, subordinationism which we have now in mind
— the subordinationism which entrenched itself in the Nicene
definitions and the explanations of the Nicene Fathers, interpreted, however, rather from the tentative and inadequate constructions out of which they were advancing to a sounder and
truer trinitarianism, than from this sounder and truer trinitarianism of which they were the expression. It can scarcely
be doubted that Bull's subordinationism owed much to the
Arminian movement, from the extremes of which, on this
point at least, he drew back. The Arminianism flowing in from
the continent had been a powerful co-factor in the production
of that Catholic reaction of seventeenth century England of
which Bull was, in its post-Restoration days of triumph, one of
the representatives and ornaments. It is interesting to note
that the " Theological Institutes " of Episcopius, at the time

[111] Daniel Zwicker. See "Allgem. deutsche Biog.," xlv. 1900, p. 533.

that Bull was contemplating writing his " Defence of the Nicene Creed," was " generally in the hands of students of divinity in both universities, as the best system of Divinity that had
appeared," [112] and that Bull himself speaks of Episcopius with
high respect in all except his attitude towards the Nicene Fathers.[113] Indeed, when he comes to state the subordinationism
which he professes to defend as commended by Catholic antiquity, he avails himself of Episcopius' precise phrase, declaring that all " the Catholic Doctors, those that lived before and
those that lived after the Council of Nice," " with one consent
have taught that the divine Nature and Perfections do agree
to the Father and Son, not collaterally or coördinately, but
subordinately." [114] But the particular form which Bull's subordinationism took was determined, naturally, by that special
appeal which the neo-Catholic party to which he belonged
made to primitive antiquity, by which he was led — with some
insular exaggeration of the importance of his own position —
to suppose that the design of Petavius in his exposition of the
unformed trinitarianism of the ante-Nicene Fathers was to
help " the cause of the Pope " by showing that " there is very
little regard to be had to the Fathers of the three first ages, to
whom the Reformed Catholics " — that is to say, the Catholiz-
ing party of the Church of England — " generally do appeal." [115] Whatever may be said of this conjecture, it cannot
be doubted that Bull's design was to show that the appeal to
the " first three ages " yielded in the matter of the Trinity the
self-same doctrine which the Nicene Fathers formulated. In
order to do this, however, he was compelled to saddle upon the
Nicene doctrine a subordinationism which, of the very essence
of the Logos Christology of the second and third centuries, was
in the Nicene construction happily in the act of being tran-

[112] Nelson, as cited, p. 301.

[113] " Defence," Proem., § 5. Ralph Cudworth was at the moment teaching
a doctrine of the Trinity indistinguishable from that of Episcopius and his
followers.

[114] Nelson, p. 315, Bull, Sect. iv. cap. i. § 1 (E. T. Oxford, 1852, p. 557, in
the " Library of Anglo-Catholic Theology ").

[115] Nelson, p. 287: Bull, Proem, § 8.

scended. In the interests of this subordinationism Calvin's equalization of the Son with the Father through the ascription to Him of αὐτοθεότης was necessarily distasteful to Bull. That the Son is "very God" and in that sense may fitly be called αὐτοθεός he is, indeed, frank to allow, for he is himself, with all the Fathers, a true and firm believer in the Godhead of Christ: but that the Son is αὐτόθεος, "God of Himself," he repudiates with decision as inconsistent with "catholic consent" which pronounces Him rather θεὸς ἐκ θεοῦ. For, depending here on Petavius, he will not allow that it is possible to say "that the Son is from God the Father, as He is Son, and not as He is God; that He received His Person, not His essence, or Divine Nature, from the Father"; on the ground that begetting means just communication of essence.[116] It is a little amusing to see Bull, from his Anglican tripod, as Calvin would himself have said, patronizing Calvin. He graciously allows that Calvin has deserved well of us "for the good service which he rendered in purging the Church of Christ from the superstition of popery"; but he "earnestly exhorts pious and studious youths to beware of a spirit from which have proceeded such things" as Calvin's unreverential allusions to the Nicene Creed, which he had dared to speak of as containing harsh expressions and "vain repetitions."[117] "Even the zeal of Mr. Bull" thus, as his admiring biographer tells us, "hath not here hindered him from treating with esteem the author of so dangerous an opinion" as that Christ is God of Himself, the self-existent God, "while at the same time he is confuting it, for the sake of some laudable qualifications which he discerned in him, and was endeavoring to excuse him as well as the matter could bear, against the insults of the most learned writer of his whole order, so famous for learning"[118] — by which we suppose Nelson means to intimate that Bull defended Calvin against injurious imputations of Petavius; though we have failed to observe this feature of Bull's discussion.

In England, too, however, the downward movement ful-

---

[116] "Defence of the Nicene Faith," IV. i. 7 *sq.*
[117] *Ibid.*, § 8.   [118] Nelson, pp. 319 *sq.*

filled itself. After Bull came Samuel Clarke and his fellow
Arians in the established Church, matched by the Socinian
drift among the dissenters. To these, naturally, Calvin's αὐτόθεος was as far beyond the range of practical consideration as it
was to Crell [119] or Schlichting,[120] who did him the honor to express their dissent from it. Clarke, however, may claim from us
a moment's notice, not so much on his own account, as for the
sake of a distinction which Waterland was led to make in refuting him. Clarke was willing to admit that the Son may have
been begotten of the essence of the Father, though he wished
it to be allowed that it was equally possible that He may have
been made out of nothing. "Both are worthy of censure," he
said,[121] "who on the one hand affirm that the Son was made
out of nothing, or on the other affirm that He is self-existent
substance." In his response, Waterland exhibits afresh the difficulties which lie in wait for those who take their starting-
point from even the measure of subordinationism which is em-
balmed in the language of the Nicene formularies, when they
seek to do justice to the full deity of Christ. In the interests of
the Nicene doctrine of eternal generation, he proposes to distinguish between necessary existence and self-existence, and,
denying the latter, to claim only the former for the Son. The
Second Person of the Godhead, he says, participates in the one
substance of the Godhead, and is therefore necessarily existent; but He participates in it by communication from the
Father, not of Himself, and therefore He is not self-existent.
"*We* say," he explains,[122] "the Son is not self-existent, meaning He is not unoriginate. *You*" — that is, Clarke — "not only
say the same, but contend for it, meaning not *necessarily existing*." "*Self*-existence as distinct from *necessary* existence, is
expressive only of the *order* and *manner* in which the perfections are in the Father, and not of any distinct perfection." [123]

[119] "Tract. de uno Deo Patre," Book I. sect. ii. cap. 2.
[120] "Contra Meisnerum."
[121] "On the Trinity," 1712, Part ii. § 14, p. 276. Cf. ii. § 5. An interesting
account of Clarke may be found in Nelson, as cited, pp. 322 *sq.*
[122] "Vindication," etc., Q. xiii. (Cambridge, 1721, p. 207).
[123] "Second Defense," Q. iii. (London, 1723, p. 172).

That is to say, in Waterland's view, the Son is all that the Father is, but not in the same manner: the Father is all that He is in this manner, viz., that He is it of Himself; the Son, in this manner, viz., that He is it of the Father. Both are necessarily all that they are, and therefore both are necessarily existent: but only the Father is all that He is of Himself, and therefore self-existence can be predicated of Him alone. What is really declared here is obviously only that the generation of the Son is a necessary and not a voluntary movement in the divine nature: and all that is affirmed is therefore merely that the existence of the Son is not dependent on the divine will. Is this all that need be affirmed, however, in order to vindicate to the Son true deity? We must bear in mind that it is not impossible to conceive creation itself as necessary: the history of theology has not been a stranger to the idea that the world is the eternal and necessary product of the divine activity. In order to vindicate true deity to the Son it is not sufficient, therefore, to affirm that He is equally with the Father " necessary in respect of existence." [124] That might be true of Him even were He a creature. What must be affirmed of Him if we would recognize His true deity is not merely that He could not but exist, but that the ground of His existence is in Himself. It is self-existence, not necessary existence, in other words, which really imports deity, and it is a degradation of this great and fundamental attribute to attempt to reduce it to a mere synonym of " ingenerate." It is rather the synonym of necessary existence as applied to deity, describing this necessary existence in its deeper significance and implications. The artificial distinction which Waterland wishes to make between the two as applied to the Son, seems thus merely an invention to " save the face " of the Nicene doctrine of " generation." Let us admit, says he, in effect, that the Son is equally with the Father " necessary in respect of existence." That is, of course, " self-existent " according to the proper significance of the term in its application to a Divine Being. But let us agree to say that we will not use the term " self-existence " but " neces-

[124] *Ibid.*

sarily existing " in this sense, and will reserve " self-existence "
for another sense, distinct from " necessary existence." Now,
" *as distinct from necessary existence*," " self-existence " can
express only " the order and manner in which the perfections
are in the Father " and not " any distinct perfection." Granted.
If we are to use the term " self-existence " to express some other
idea than self-existence — then it may express something
which the self-existing, i.e., necessarily existing God who is the
Son is not. But then it remains true that this necessarily existing God who is the Son is at this very moment confessed to be
the self-existent God — under its synonym of " necessarily
existent." In a word, if we will agree to use the term " self-
existent " in the sense of " ingenerate " — which it does not in
the least mean — we may, of course, deny that the Son who
is " generate " is " self-existent ": but if we employ that term
in the sense of " necessarily existent," — which is just what it
means in the full reach of that term as applied to God — why,
then we must say that the Son is " self-existent." To put the
thing in a nutshell: the Nicene doctrine that the generation of
the Son and the procession of the Spirit are necessary movements in the divine essence and not voluntary acts of God the
Father, carries with it the ascription of necessary existence, in
the sense of that term applicable to God, that is of " self-
existence," to the Son and Spirit and requires that each
be spoken of as αὐτόθεος. To deny to them the quality of
αὐτοθεότης is thus logically to make them creatures of the Father's power, if not of His will; by which their true deity is
destroyed. Thus the tendency among the so-called strict Nicenists to deny to our Lord that He is, as God, *a se ipso* betrays
a lurking leaven of subordinationism in their thought. It indicates a tendency to treat the Nicene doctrine of eternal generation, not, as it was intended by its framers, as the safeguard of the absolute equality of the Son with the Father, but
rather as the proclamation of the inferiority of the Son to the
Father: the Son because generate must differ from the ingenerate Father — must differ in this, that He cannot be, as
is the Father, self-existent God, which is, of course, all one

with saying that He is not God at all, since the very idea of
God includes the idea of self-existence.[125]

It was, therefore, a very great service to Christian theology
which Calvin rendered when he firmly asserted for the second
and third persons of the Trinity their αὐτοθεότης. It has never
since been possible for men to escape facing the question
whether they really do justice to the true and complete deity
of the Son and Spirit in their thought of the Trinitarian distinctions. It has not even been possible since for men who
heartily believe in the deity of the Son and Spirit to refuse
to them the designation of αὐτοθεός. They may have distinguished, indeed, between αὐτόθεος and αὐτοθεός — Self-
Existent God and Very God — and allowed the latter to the
second and third Persons while withholding the former.[126] But

---

[125] De Moor, " In Marck. Compend.," i. 1761, p. 772, seems to prefer the
word " independence " for the expression of the aseity of God and of the Son
as God: " By parity of reasoning, it is certain that if the Son be *true* God, He is
independent God; for independence is easily first among the attributes of
God, and is inseparable from the essence of God. . . . And this being true, the
title αὐτόθεος or αὐτοθεός (for the theologians accent it differently) cannot be
denied to the Son, nor to the Spirit, as if this title were suitable to the Father
only." . . . " By independence," he continues, " God is, as we have seen at
chap. iv. § 20, *a se* in the negative sense, not in the sense of a proper causality of
Himself, and it is this that the title αὐτοθεός expresses. 1. If then the Son is the
supreme and independent God He is αὐτοθεός. 2. And since the reality of the
Divine essence cannot exist without independence, the Son would not be true
God unless He was at the same time αὐτοθεός. 3. If the Father be acknowledged
to be αὐτοθεός, the Son must also be such, unless the Son be denied to be
the same God with the Father and a plurality of Gods is erected, a numerical
plurality of divine essences. For the same God and the same Divine essence
cannot at the same time be *a se ipso* and not *a se ipso*. The Son is not, of course,
αὐτουἱός, *Son a se ipso;* but He certainly is αὐτοθεός, *God a se ipso*. He is of
the Father relatively to His being Son, but He is *a se* considered absolutely as
He is God: as He has the Divine essence existing *a se,* and not divided or produced by another essence; but not as if having that essence *a se ipso*. He is
' God *a se* '; not, ' He is *a se,* God,' or, what is the same thing, He is not Son
a se."

[126] The debate on the αὐτοθεότης of the Son caused the theologians to enter
into long disquisitions on the force of αὐτός in composition and the proper
sense or senses of αὐτόθεος. Voetius, for example (pp. 449–451) argues that
αὐτός in composition has five senses. It either (1) emphasises singularity; or
(2) distinguishes as κατ' ἐξοχήν; or (3) means *a se;* or (4) *per se,* intrinsically,
essentially; or (5) *per se* and operating with a proper and sufficient principial

in the very act of drawing such a distinction, they have emphasized the true deity of the second and third Persons, and have been deterred from ascribing αὐτοθεότης to them in the sense of self-existence only by confusing it with " ingeneration." It is, however, a part of the heritage, particularly of the Reformed Churches, that they have learned from Calvin to claim for Christ the great epithet of αὐτόθεος: [127] and their characteristic mark has therefore become the strength of the emphasis which they throw on the complete deity of the Lord. Whatever differences may have existed among them have not concerned the true deity of Christ, but rather the attitude taken by their teachers towards the Nicene speculation of " eternal generation." Concerning this speculation differences early manifested themselves. Immediate successors of Calvin, such as Theodore Beza and Josiah Simler, were as firm and exact in their adhesion to it as Calvin was dubious with reference to it. " The Son," says Beza, " is of the Father by an ineffable communication from eternity of the whole nature." [128] " We deny not," says Simler, " that the Son has His essence

---

force, producing somewhat. Accordingly it is improper to assume that theologians always mean the *third* sense, when they employ the term αὐτόθεος. Any one of five senses may be intended: (1) God κατ' ἐξοχήν; (2) The only, sole God; (3) God essentially, not by participation, *per se* and not *per accidens, in se* and essentially, not in some external respect or denomination; (4) God *a se* and not *ab alio*, ἄναρχος, that is to say, καὶ ἀναίτιος; (5) God, the *primus agens, primus motor,* dependent on none, but the first cause.

[127] Voetius, " Disp.," i. 1648, p. 460, gives a characteristic list of Reformed doctors who previous to himself (1648) had taught that Christ is properly to be called αὐτόθεος — lest anyone should think that the αὐτοθεότης of Christ had been proclaimed only by one here and there, zealous for their own notion or loving novelty, rather than by all in the necessary defense of the common truth. His list includes, besides Calvin, Beza, Simler, the whole mass of representative Reformed teachers: Danaeus, Perkins, Keckermann, Trelcatius, Tilenus, Polanus, Wollebius, Scalcobrigius, Altingius, Grynaeus, Schriverius, Zanchius, Chamierus, Zadeel, Lectius, Pareus, Mortonus, Whittaker, Junius, Vorstius, Amesius, Rivetus. Heppe, " Dogmat. d. ev.-ref. Kirche," 1861, p. 84, records: " And moreover the Son is as such not created or made by God, or adopted out of favor or on account of desert, but He is according to His nature God the Son, and is therefore like the Father and the Holy Spirit veritably αὐτόθεος."

[128] " Axiomat. de Trinitate," Axiom 14.

from God the Father; what we deny is a begotten essence." [129]
And no less or less prejudiced an authority than Bellarmine
pronounces these declarations "Catholic." [130] Indeed, despite
the influence of Calvin, the great body of the Reformed teachers remained good Nicenists. But they were none the less, as
they were fully entitled to be, good "Autotheanites" also.
They saw clearly that a relation within the Godhead between
Persons to each of whom the entire Godhead belongs, cannot
deprive any of these Persons of any essential quality of the
Godhead common to them all.[131] And they were determined
to assert the full and complete Godhead of them all. Of course,
there have been others, on the other hand, who have followed
Calvin in sitting rather loosely to the Nicene tradition. Examples of this class are furnished by Trelcatius, Keckermann,
Maccovius.[132] Keckermann, for example, while not denying
that many have preferred to say that " the Son has His essence
communicated from the Father," yet considers that this can
be said only in a modified sense and must be accompanied by
certain important explanations — for, says he, " it is false if
spoken of the essence considered absolutely, since the Son (as
also the Holy Spirit) has this *a se ipso*." For himself he prefers,

[129] " Epist. ad Polon." or " Lib. de Filio Dei."

[130] *Op. cit.,* p. 334b.

[131] Cf. the remark of De Moor, " In Marck. Compend.," i. 1761, p. 775:
" Distinctions in *mode of subsistence,* and the personal order which flows from
this, cannot affect the equality of essence; and inferiority and inequality cannot consist with numerical oneness of essence."

[132] Cf. Voetius, as cited, p. 465: " Trelcatius, *Loc. Com.,* and Keckermann, *Syst. Theol.,* seem to deny the communication of the essence: and
Maccovius, in his *Metaphysica,* c. 8, follows them, when, against Arminius,
he determines that not the essence, but the personality, is communicated from
the Father." " Strictly speaking, however, we must say," adds Voetius, " that
the Person is begotten by the communication of the essence: though these
authors are to be excused because they took the word ' communication ' too
physically and had Valentinus Gentilis in view." Voetius' own view is expressed
in the " maxims " (p. 461) that: " The essence *in divinis* neither begets nor is
begotten, but the person of the Father begets *in, de* and *ex* His essence which
is the same with the essence of the Son ": " the essence may therefore be said
to be communicated, given, by the Father, and received, and had, by the Son
from that communication or gift. Briefly, the Person of the Father begets the
Person of the Son by the communication of the essence."

therefore, to say that " the second mode of existence in the Trinity, which is called the Son, . . . is communicated from the Father." [133] This is, as we have seen, apparently Calvin's own view, while the more advanced position still which rejects, or at least neglects, the conception of " communication " altogether, whether of essence or of mode of existence,[134] although

[133] " Systema SS. Theologiae," Hanoviae, 1615, p. 54.

[134] This position was taken by Herman Alexander Roëll, professor at Franeker, at the end of the seventeenth century. The idea of " eternal generation " he held to be wholly unscriptural and at war with the perfect nature of God — whether as Father or as Son. The designation of the Second Person of the Trinity as Son he at first found to rest on His consubstantiality with the Father (" By the words ' Son ' and ' Generation ' is signified, in emphasis, that the Second Person has the same essence and nature with the First, and has coëxisted with Him from eternity," — " De Generatione Filii," 1689, p. 5), but afterwards to be expressive rather of His divine mission, and the clear relation existing between God the Sender and God the Sent. A good account is given of his views by Ypeij and Dermout, " Geschiedenis der Nederlandsche Hervormde Kerk," ii. 1822, pp. 544 sq. The idea of Herman Muntinghe, professor at Hardewijk and later at Groningen, at the end of the next century (see Ypeij and Dermout, iv. 1827, pp. 271 sq.) was similar. Much the same notions were introduced into the Congregational churches of New England by Nathaniel Emmons. " We feel constrained to reject the eternal generation of the Son, and the eternal procession of the Holy Ghost, as such mysteries as cannot be distinguished from real absurdities, and as such doctrines as strike at the foundation of the true doctrine of three equally divine persons in one God " (" Works," iv. 1842, p. 114). " The Scripture teaches us that each of the divine persons takes His peculiar *name* from the peculiar *office* which He sustains in the economy of redemption. . . . The first person assumes the name of Father, because He is by office the Creator or Author of all things, and especially of the human nature of Christ. The second person assumes the name of Son and Word, by virtue of His incarnation and mediatorial conduct. . . . The third person in the Trinity is called the Holy Ghost on account of His peculiar office as Sanctifier " (p. 109). This view became thereafter the common view among the New England churches, finding its complete expression in Moses Stuart (" Letters on the Eternal Generation of the Son," 1822) and Horace Bushnell (" God in Christ," 1849). Cf. George P. Fisher, " Discussions in History and Theology," 1880, p. 273 : " Hopkins was the last to hold to the Nicene doctrine of the primacy of the Father and the eternal Sonship of Christ. The whole philosophy of the Trinity, as that doctrine was conceived by its great defenders in the age of Athanasius, when the doctrine was formulated, had been set aside. It was even derided; and this chiefly for the reason that it was not studied. Professor Stuart had no sympathy with or just appreciation of the Nicene doctrine of the generation of the Son." It should be noted, however, that the " eternal primacy " of the Father and the " eternal generation " of the Son do not necessarily go together. Neither Roëll nor

it cannot find an example in Calvin, may yet be said to have had its way prepared for it by him. The direct Scriptural proof which had been customarily relied upon for its establishment he destroyed, refusing to rest a doctrinal determination on " distorted texts." He left, therefore, little Biblical basis for the doctrine of " eternal generation" except what might be inferred from the mere terms " Father," " Son " and " Spirit," and the general consideration that our own adoption into the relation of sons of God in Christ implies for Him a Sonship of a higher and more immanent character, which is His by nature and into participation in the relation of which we are admitted only by grace.[135] Certainly other explanations of these facts are

---

Emmons, for example, while decidedly denying the " eternal generation" of the Son, doubted that the Father is first in the Trinity, not only in office but also in order — as Emmons (p. 137) expresses it, is " the head of the sacred Trinity." They do deny, however, that the Father is superior to the Son in nature; and they take their starting point from the absolute deity of the Son, in the interests of which it is largely that they deny the doctrine of " eternal generation." When Dr. Fisher (p. 273) says, " The eternal fatherhood of God, the precedence of the Father, is as much a part of the orthodox doctrine of the Trinity as is the divinity of the Son," by the orthodox doctrine of the Trinity he means the doctrine as it was formulated by " the Nicene Fathers who framed the orthodox creed." The rejoinder lies ready at hand that the Nicene Fathers overdid the matter from the point of view of " the precedence of the Father," and left the way open for doing less than justice to " the divinity of the Son " — which therefore requires reassertion and better guarding. In point of fact, it is around these two foci — " the precedence of the Father," which in its exaggeration becomes Arianism, and " the divinity of the Son," which in its exaggeration becomes Sabellianism — that the Trinitarian constructions have revolved. The Trinitarian problem is, to find a mode of statement that does full justice to both. To do this it must of course be carefully ascertained from Scripture in what sense " the Father " has " precedence " of the Son; and in what sense the Son is God. Roëll and Emmons deny that the Scriptures accord such " precedence " to the Father as is expressed by the phrase " God of God": they affirm that the Scriptures ascribe absolute deity to the Son. On the New England doctrine of the Trinity from Emmons down see L. L. Paine, " The Evolution of Trinitarianism," 1900, pp. 104 sq.

135 Cf. the striking passage, already alluded to in part, which is found in the middle editions of the " Institutes," at the opening of the discussion (Opp. i. 482–483) : " But since everything follows from the proof of the divinity [of the Son], we shall lay our chief stress on the assertion of that. The Ancients, whose idea was that the Son existed (exstitisse) by eternal generation from the Father, endeavored to prove it by the testimony of Isaiah (Is. liii. 8), ' Who shall declare His generation? ' But it is clear that they were under an illusion

possible; [136] and the possibility — or preferability — of other explanations was certain sooner or later to commend itself to some. Nothing, meanwhile, could illustrate more strikingly the

in citing this text. For the prophet does not speak there of how the Father generated the Son but by how numerous a posterity His kingdom should be increased [so 1539: but 1550 *sq.*: " but through how long a period His kingdom should endure "]. Neither is there much force in what they take from the Psalms: ' from the womb before the morning star have I begotten Thee '; for that version is by no means consonant with the Hebrew, which runs thus (Ps. cx. 3): ' From the womb of the morning is to thee the dew of thy nativity.' The argument, then, which seems to have special plausibility, is taken from the words of the Apostle in which it is taught that the worlds were made by the Son; for unless there had already been a Son, His power could not have been put forth. But little weight can attach to this argument either, as appears from similar formulas. For none of us would be affected if anybody sought to take the word ' Christ ' back to that time, in which Paul says that ' Christ ' was tempted by the Jews (I Cor. x. 9) [where Calvin evidently reads " Christ "]. For its particular application belongs properly to the humanity [of Christ]. Similarly, because it is said (Heb. xiii. 8) that ' Jesus Christ ' was yesterday, is to-day, and shall be forever, if anybody should contend that the name of ' Christ ' belonged to Him always, he has accomplished nothing. What do we do but expose the holy and orthodox doctrines of religion to the cavils of heretics, when we contort texts after this fashion, which, when taken in their proper sense, serve our cause either not at all or very little? To me, however, this one argument is worth a thousand for confirming my faith in the eternity of the Son of God. For it is certain that God is not a Father to men, except through the intercession of that only begotten Son, who alone rightly vindicates this prerogative to Himself, and by whose favor it comes to us. But God always wished to be worshipped by His people under the name of Father; from which it follows that already then [i.e., *semper*] He was Son, through whom that relationship is established." Similarly in his Commentaries he explains Micah v. 1, 2 of the eternal decree of God, not of the eternity of the generation of Christ: and on Ps. ii. 7 prefers to follow Paul (Acts xiii. 33) to referring it to the eternal generation of Christ by " subtly philosophizing on the word ' to-day.'" In the New Testament he follows the rule (with few exceptions) " that the writers of the New Testament, and especially Jesus Himself, speak of Christ not as the absolute Logos but as the God-man. . . . Especially in the Gospel of John, the declarations of Jesus concerning Himself are expounded not out of an absolute logos-consciousness but out of the theanthropic consciousness of Jesus, so that after John i. 14 there is no further reference to the Logos ἄσαρκος or to the *nuda divinitas Christi* except only in Jno. viii. 58 and xvii. 5 " (Scholten, " De Leer der Hervormde Kerk," ed. 4, ii. p. 231; cf. p. 229 and i. p. 24). Similarly of the Holy Spirit (p. 236) he refuses to get proof for His trinitarian relation either from Jno. xiv. 16 or I Cor. ii. 10.

[136] As, for example, that the terms " Son," " Spirit " are not expressive

vitality of the ecclesiastical tradition than that in such a state of the case the Nicene construction of the Trinity held its ground: held its ground with Calvin himself in its substantial core, and with the majority of his followers in its complete speculative elaboration. We are astonished at the persistence of so large an infusion of the Nicene phraseology in the expositions of Augustine, after that phraseology had really been antiquated by his fundamental principle of equalization in his construction of the Trinitarian relations: we are more astonished at the effort which Calvin made to adduce Nicene support for his own conceptions: and we are more astonished still at the tenacity with which his followers cling to all the old speculations.[137]

The repeated appeals which he makes to the Fathers is, as we have just hinted, a notable feature of Calvin's discussion of the Trinity and especially of his defense of his construction of the Trinitarian relationships. The citations he drew from the

---

of " derivation " (by " generation " or " spiration ") but just of " consubstantiality." The Son is the repetition of the Father; the Spirit is the expression of God. So Roëll in his first view; and even Stuart remarks, justly: " The Hebrew idiom calls him the son of any person or thing, who exhibits a resemblance in disposition or character " (*op. cit.*, p. 105). More broadly, W. Robertson Smith (" The O. T. in the Jewish Church," ed. 1, p. 427) remarks: " Among all Semites membership in a guild is figured as sonship." That is to say, in the Semitic view, sonship denotes broadly oneness of kind, class; more specifically likeness; at the height of its meaning, consubstantiality; and does not suggest derivation. As the son of a man is a man, the Son of God is God. It is the Indo-European consciousness which imparts to the terms Son, Spirit the idea of derivation.

[137] When during the first weeks of its sessions, the Westminster Assembly was engaged on the revision of the Thirty-nine Articles, and Article viii. on the Three Creeds came up for discussion, objection was made to the ἐκ θεοῦ clauses. It does not appear that there was any pleading for the subordinationist position: the advocates for retaining the Creeds rather expended their strength in voiding the credal statement of any subordinationist implications. Thus Dr. Featley's reply to the current objection was that " although Christ is God of God, it doth not therefore follow that the deity of the Son is from the deity of the Father, . . . as it does not follow *quia Deus passus est ergo Deitas passa est*, or *quia Maria mater Dei, ergo est Maria mater deitatis* " (see his speech printed in his " Dippers Dipt," London, 1651, pp. 187–189). Were this taken literally it would explain the Sonship of our Lord wholly from the side of His humiliation and identify His filiation with the incarnation.

Fathers for this purpose were naturally much striven over. One instance seems worth scrutinizing, as on it was founded an accusation that Calvin did not know the difference between the two Latin prepositions " *ad* " and " *a*," or else chose to "play to the gallery," which he counted upon not to know it. That the best Latinist of his day, whose Latin style is rather classical than mediæval, could fail to feel the force of the common prepositions of that language is, of course, absurd: that a reasoner conspicuous for his fair-mindedness in his argumentation could have juggled with ambiguous phrases is even more impossible. An attentive reading of the passages in question will, as was to be expected, quickly make it clear that it is not Calvin but his critics who are at fault. Bellarmine, arguing that the reasons which Calvin assigns for calling our Lord αὐτόθεος are not valid, adduces his appeal to the passages in which Augustine remarks that our Lord " is called Son, with reference to the Father (*ad patrem*) and God with reference to Himself (*ad seipsum*)." " But," he adds, in rebuttal, " it is not the same thing to say that the Son is God *ad se*, and that He is God *a se*." " For," he somewhat superfluously argues, " the first signifies that the name of God is not relative and yet belongs to the Son: and this Augustine says and says truly, for although the Son is a relative, it is nevertheless a relative which exists, is divine, and accordingly includes the essence which is absolute. But [to say] that the Son is God *a se* signifies that the Son of God is not the Son of God, but is unbegotten, which Augustine never said, but Calvin falsely attributes to him." [138] " It is either," writes Petavius,[139] improving even on Bellarmine, " a remarkable piece of chicanery or else a remarkable hallucination in Calvin, when he seems to take as equivalents these two terms *ad se* and *a se*: as also these two, *ad alium* and *ab alio*, which " [i.e., *ad se* and *ad alium*] " Augustine makes free use of in explaining the mystery of the Trinity." Then, after quoting Calvin's citation of Augustine, he concludes: " Unless Calvin had supposed *ad se* to be the same as *a se*, and *ad alium* to be the same as *ab alio*, he would not have employed

138 *Op. cit.*, p. 335.   139 *Op. cit.*, p. 252.

these passages from Augustine." [140] In point of fact, however, Calvin does not confuse "*ad*" and "*a*" and he does not cite Augustine's use of the one as if he had employed the other. His citations are not intended to show that Augustine taught that the Son is not of the Father but of Himself: but only to show that we may — or rather must — speak in a twofold

[140] We suppose Arminius scarcely intended to repeat Bellarmine's and Petavius' accusation of confusion between *a se* and *ad se* when (" Works," E. T. ii. 1828, p. 32) he remarks on the modified manner in which αὐτοθεός is used when applied to Christ, and adds: " But their explanation does not agree with the phraseology they employ. For this reason Beza excuses Calvin, and openly confesses ' that he had not with sufficient strictness observed the difference between these particles *a se* and *per se.*' " The remark of Beza is referred to his " Praef. in Dialog. Athanasii." We have not access to Beza's edition of this Pseudo-Athanasian tractate and cannot assure ourselves of his meaning. We assume that he was not criticizing Calvin's philological equipment but his doctrinal construction; and we suspect that what he says is that Calvin in insisting that Christ is God *a se ipso* was not sufficiently carefully distinguishing between saying He is God *per se* — in and of Himself, and that He is God *a se* — from Himself. In that likely case Beza is only explaining the differences between himself and Calvin which are expressed in Calvin's denial that the Son has His essence from the Father and Beza's affirmation that He has His essence from the Father. Calvin here, he says, is not sufficiently considering the difference between being God *a se* and being God *per se*. In this case Beza's distinction is much like Waterland's between self-existent and necessarily-existent God and makes αὐτοθεότης mean merely ingenerateness; and we note that if our conjecture is right, there is involved a testimony from Beza that Calvin's real thought of the Trinity denied the communication of essence from Father to Son. In his letter to Prince Radziwil on " The Unity of the Divine Essence and the three Persons subsisting in it," against the Polish Unitarians, Beza declares (" Tractat. Theolog.," 1582, i. p. 647) that it is inept to say that " the Father alone is αὐτόθεος, that is, as they interpret it, has His Being *a se ipso* and therefore can be called God," — and gives his reason: " For to be *a se* and *ab alio,* do not constitute different kinds of nature; and therefore the Father cannot on that ground be said to be the sole and unique God, nor ought He to be, but rather the sole and unique Father, as the Son is sole and unique because ' only-begotten.' " Can we really say that " to be *a se* and *ab alio* do not constitute different kinds of nature (*aliam naturae speciem*)? If the contrast is that of self-existing and derived Being it can scarcely be said. But if the contrast is between ingenerate and generate Being — it is true enough. Every father and son are consubstantial, and the very point of the usage of Father and Son in this connection seems to be to assert their consubstantiality. Beza has this latter contrast in view and only means to say that the ascription of αὐτοθεότης to the Son is in no way interfered with by the fact that He is " generate " — for the generate and the generator are ever the same in kind.

way of the Son, absolutely, to wit, as He is in Himself and relatively, as He is with reference to the Father. It is his own statement, not Augustine's, when he proceeds to say that when we thus speak of our Lord absolutely as He is in Himself, we are to say that He is *a se,* and only when we speak of Him relatively as He is with reference to the Father are we to speak of Him as *a Patre.* It is marvellous that anyone could confuse this perfectly clear argument: more marvellous still that, on the ground of such a confusion, anyone should venture to charge Calvin with gross ignorance of the meaning of the simplest Latin words or else of " remarkable chicanery " in his use of Latin texts. Here is what Calvin actually says: " By these appellations, which denote distinction, says Augustine, that is signified by which they are mutually related to one another: not the substance itself by which they are one. By which explanation, the sentiments of the ancients which otherwise might seem contradictory may be reconciled with one another. For now they teach that the Father is the principium of the Son; and now they assert that the Son has His divinity and essence alike of Himself, and is therefore one principium with the Father. The cause of this diversity is elsewhere well and perspicuously explained by Augustine when he speaks as follows: Christ is called God with respect to Himself, He is called Son with respect to the Father. And again, the Father is called God with respect to Himself, with respect to the Son He is called Father. What is called Father with respect to the Son is not the Son; what is called Son with respect to the Father is not the Father: what is called Father with respect to Himself and Son with respect to Himself is God. When, then, we speak of the Son, simply, without respect to the Father, we rightly and properly assert that He is of Himself; and we therefore call Him the sole (*unicum*) principium; but when we are noting the relation in which He stands to the Father, we justly make the Father the principium of the Son." [141] A simple reading of the passage is enough to refute the suggestion that Calvin makes Augustine assert that Christ is " of Him-

[141] " Institutes," I. xiii. 19.

self " when he is merely asserting that Christ is God when considered with respect to Himself and not relatively to the Father. If a matter so clear in itself, however, can be made clearer by further evidence, it is easy enough to adduce direct evidence. For Calvin has incorporated into the " Institutes " here material he uses often elsewhere. And in more than one of these instances of its use elsewhere, he distinctly tells us that he did not understand Augustine in these passages to be asserting the aseity of the Son. We may take, for example, a letter to the Neuchâtel pastors, written in November, 1543, with respect to Cortesius, with whom he had been having a discussion on our Lord's aseity — or as Calvin puts it, περὶ αὐτοουσίας Christi. In the course of the discussion, he says, " we came to that difficulty that he did not think he could speak of the essence of Christ without mention of the person. I opposed to this first the authority of Augustine, who testifies that we can speak in a twofold way (bifariam) of Christ, as He is God — according to relation, that is, and simply (simpliciter). And that the discussion might not be prolonged, I adduced certain passages of Cyril, where in so many words (dissertis verbis) he pronounces on what we were discussing." [142] That is to say, the passages of Augustine were appealed to not as direct witness to the αὐτοουσία of Christ, but only to prove the subordinate point that we can speak of our Lord in a twofold way: the passages from Cyril alone " expressly " declare on the point at issue. The declaration that Cyril was adduced as pronouncing on the point itself in so many words, is a declaration that Augustine was not so adduced.

In his assertion of the αὐτοθεότης of the Son Calvin, then, was so far from supposing that he was enunciating a novelty that he was able to quote the Nicene Fathers themselves as asserting it " in so many words." And yet in his assertion of it he marks an epoch in the history of the doctrine of the Trinity. Not that men had not before believed in the self-existence of the Son as He is God: but that the current modes of stating

[142] Opp. xi. 653.

the doctrine of the Trinity left a door open for the entrance of defective modes of conceiving the deity of the Son, to close which there was needed some such sharp assertion of His absolute deity as was supplied by the assertion of His αὐτοθεότης. If we will glance over the history of the efforts of the Church to work out for itself an acceptable statement of the great mystery of the Trinity, we shall perceive that it is dominated from the beginning to the end by a single motive — to do full justice to the absolute deity of Christ. And we shall perceive that among the multitudes of great thinkers who under the pressure of this motive have labored upon the problem, and to whom the Church looks back with gratitude for great services, in the better formulation of the doctrine or the better commendation of it to the people, three names stand out in high relief, as marking epochs in the advance towards the end in view. These three names are those of Tertullian, Augustine and Calvin. It is into this narrow circle of elect spirits that Calvin enters by the contribution he made to the right understanding of the doctrine of the Trinity. That contribution is summed up in his clear, firm and unwavering assertion of the αὐτοθεότης of the Son. By this assertion the ὁμοουσιότης of the Nicene Fathers at last came to its full right, and became in its fullest sense the hinge of the doctrine.

VI
CALVINISM

CALVINISM [1]

1. MEANING AND USES OF THE TERM

CALVINISM is an ambiguous term in so far as it is currently employed in two or three senses, closely related indeed, and passing insensibly into one another, but of varying latitudes of connotation. Sometimes it designates merely the individual teaching of John Calvin. Sometimes it designates, more broadly, the doctrinal system confessed by that body of Protestant Churches known historically, in distinction from the Lutheran Churches, as "the Reformed Churches"; but also quite commonly called "the Calvinistic Churches" because the greatest scientific exposition of their faith in the Reformation age, and perhaps the most influential of any age, was given by John Calvin. Sometimes it designates, more broadly still, the entire body of conceptions, theological, ethical, philosophical, social, political, which, under the influence of the master mind of John Calvin, raised itself to dominance in the Protestant lands of the post-Reformation age, and has left a permanent mark not only upon the thought of mankind, but upon the life-history of men, the social order of civilized peoples, and even the political organization of states. In the present article, the term will be taken, for obvious reasons, in the second of these senses. Fortunately this is also its central sense; and there is little danger that its other connotations will fall out of mind while attention is concentrated upon this.

On the one hand, John Calvin, though always looked upon by the Reformed Churches as an exponent rather than as the creator of their doctrinal system, has nevertheless been both

[1] From "The New Schaff-Herzog Encyclopedia of Religious Knowledge," edited by Samuel Macauley Jackson, D.D., LL.D., ii. pp. 359–364 (copyright by Funk and Wagnalls Company, New York, 1908).

287

reverenced as one of their founders, and deferred to as that particular one of their founders to whose formative hand and systematizing talent their doctrinal system has perhaps owed most. In any exposition of the Reformed theology, therefore, the teaching of John Calvin must always take a high, and, indeed, determinative place. On the other hand, although Calvinism has dug a channel through which not merely flows a stream of theologial thought, but also surges a great wave of human life — filling the heart with fresh ideals and conceptions which have revolutionized the conditions of existence — yet its fountain-head lies in its theological system; or rather, to be perfectly exact, one step behind even that, in its religious consciousness. For the roots of Calvinism are planted in a specific religious attitude, out of which is unfolded first a particular theology, from which springs on the one hand a special church organization, and on the other a social order, involving a given political arrangement. The whole outworking of Calvinism in life is thus but the efflorescence of its fundamental religious consciousness, which finds its scientific statement in its theological system.

2. Fundamental Principle

The exact formulation of the fundamental principle of Calvinism has indeed taxed the acumen of a long series of thinkers for the last hundred years (e.g., Ullmann, Semisch, Hagenbach, Ebrard, Herzog, Schweizer, Baur, Schneckenburger, Güder, Schenkel, Schöberlein, Stahl, Hundeshagen; for a discussion of the several views cf. H. Voigt, " Fundamentaldogmatik," Gotha, 1874, pp. 397–480; W. Hastie, " The Theology of the Reformed Church in its Fundamental Principles," Edinburgh, 1904, pp. 129–177). Perhaps the simplest statement of it is the best: that it lies in a profound apprehension of God in His majesty, with the inevitably accompanying poignant realization of the exact nature of the relation sustained to Him by the creature as such, and particularly by the sinful creature. He who believes in God without reserve, and is determined

that God shall be God to him in all his thinking, feeling, willing — in the entire compass of his life-activities, intellectual,
moral, spiritual, throughout all his individual, social, religious
relations — is, by the force of that strictest of all logic which
presides over the outworking of principles into thought and
life, by the very necessity of the case, a Calvinist. In Calvinism, then, objectively speaking, theism comes to its rights;
subjectively speaking, the religious relation attains its purity;
soteriologically speaking, evangelical religion finds at length its
full expression and its secure stability. Theism comes to its
rights only in a teleological conception of the universe, which
perceives in the entire course of events the orderly outworking of the plan of God, who is the author, preserver, and governor of all things, whose will is consequently the ultimate
cause of all. The religious relation attains its purity only when
an attitude of absolute dependence on God is not merely tem-
porarily assumed in the act, say, of prayer, but is sustained
through all the activities of life, intellectual, emotional, executive. And evangelical religion reaches stability only when the
sinful soul rests in humble, self-emptying trust purely on the
God of grace as the immediate and sole source of all the efficiency which enters into its salvation. And these things are the
formative principles of Calvinism.

3. RELATION TO OTHER SYSTEMS

The difference between Calvinism and other forms of theistic thought, religious experience, evangelical theology is a
difference not of kind but of degree. Calvinism is not a specific
variety of theism, religion, evangelicalism, set over against
other specific varieties, which along with it constitute these
several genera, and which possess equal rights of existence with
it and make similar claims to perfection, each after its own
kind. It differs from them not as one species differs from other
species; but as a perfectly developed representative differs
from an imperfectly developed representative of the same species. There are not many kinds of theism, religion, evangeli-

calism, among which men are at liberty to choose to suit at will their individual taste or meet their special need, all of which may be presumed to serve each its own specific uses equally worthily. There is but one kind of theism, religion, evangelicalism; and the several constructions laying claim to these names differ from each other not as correlative species of a broader class, but as more or less perfect, or more or less defective, exemplifications of a single species. Calvinism conceives of itself as simply the more pure theism, religion, evangelicalism, superseding as such the less pure. It has no difficulty, therefore, in recognizing the theistic character of all truly theistic thought, the religious note in all actual religious activity, the evangelical quality of all really evangelical faith. It refuses to be set antagonistically over against any of these things, wherever or in whatever degree of imperfection they may be manifested; it claims them in every instance of their emergence as its own, and essays only to point out the way in which they may be given their just place in thought and life. Whoever believes in God; whoever recognizes in the recesses of his soul his utter dependence on God; whoever in all his thought of salvation hears in his heart of hearts the echo of the *soli Deo gloria* of the evangelical profession — by whatever name he may call himself, or by whatever intellectual puzzles his logical understanding may be confused — Calvinism recognizes as implicitly a Calvinist, and as only requiring to permit these fundamental principles — which underlie and give its body to all true religion — to work themselves freely and fully out in thought and feeling and action, to become explicitly a Calvinist.

4. CALVINISM AND LUTHERANISM

It is unfortunate that a great body of the scientific discussion which, since Max Goebel (" Die religiöse Eigenthümlichkeit der lutherischen und der reformirten Kirchen," Bonn, 1837) first clearly posited the problem, has been carried on somewhat vigorously with a view to determining the fundamental principle of Calvinism, has sought particularly to bring out its contrast with some other theological tendency, commonly with the sister Protestant tendency of Lutheranism. Undoubtedly somewhat different spirits inform Calvinism and Lutheranism. And undoubtedly the distinguishing spirit of Calvinism is rooted not in some extraneous circumstance of its antecedents or origin — as, for example, Zwingli's tendency to intellectualism, or the superior humanistic culture and predilections of Zwingli and Calvin, or the democratic instincts of the Swiss, or the radical rationalism of the Reformed leaders as distinguished from the merely modified traditionalism of the Lutherans — but in its formative principle. But it is misleading to find the formative principle of either type of Protestantism in its difference from the other; they have infinitely more in common than in distinction. And certainly nothing could be more misleading than to represent them (as is often done) as owing their differences to their more pure embodiment respectively of the principle of predestination and that of justification by faith. The doctrine of predestination is not the formative principle of Calvinism, the root from which it springs. It is one of its logical consequences, one of the branches which it has inevitably thrown out. It has been firmly embraced and consistently proclaimed by Calvinists because it is an implicate of theism, is directly given in the religious consciousness, and is an absolutely essential element in evangelical religion, without which its central truth of complete dependence upon the free mercy of a saving God can not be maintained. And so little is it a peculiarity of the Reformed theology, that it underlay and gave its form and power to the whole Reformation movement; which was, as from the spiritual point of view, a great revival of religion, so, from the doctrinal point of view, a great revival of Augustinianism. There was accordingly no difference among the Reformers on this point: Luther and Melanchthon and the compromising Butzer were no less jealous for absolute predestination than Zwingli and Calvin. Even Zwingli could not surpass Luther in sharp and unqualified assertion of it: and it was not Calvin but Melanchthon who gave it a formal place in his primary scientific statement of the elements of the Protestant faith (cf. Schaff, "Creeds," i. 1877, p. 451; E. F. Karl Müller, "Symbolik," Erlangen and Leipzig, 1896, p. 75; C. J. Niemijer, "De Strijd over de Leer der Praedestinatie in de IXde Eeuw," Groningen, 1889, p. 21; H. Voigt, "Fundamentaldogmatik," Gotha, 1874, pp. 469–470). Just as little can the doctrine of justification by faith be represented as specifically Lutheran. Not merely has it from the beginning been a substantial element in the Reformed faith, but it is only among the Reformed that it has retained or can retain its purity, free from the tendency to become a doctrine of justification on account of faith (cf. E. Böhl, "Von der Rechtfertigung durch den Glauben," Leipzig, 1890). Here, too, the difference between the two types of Protestantism is one of degree, not of kind (cf. C. P. Krauth, "The Conservative Reformation and its Theology," Philadelphia, 1872). Lutheranism, the product of a poignant sense of sin, born from the throes of a guilt-burdened soul which can not be stilled until it finds peace in God's decree of justification, is apt to rest in this peace; while Calvinism, the product of an overwhelming vision of God, born from the reflection in the heart of man of the majesty of a God who will not give His glory to another, can not pause until it places the scheme of salvation itself in relation to a complete world-view, in which it becomes subsidiary to the glory of the Lord God Almighty. Calvinism asks with Lutheranism, indeed, that most poignant of all questions, What shall I do to be saved? and answers it as Lutheranism answers it. But the great question which presses upon it is, How shall God be glorified? It is the contemplation of God and zeal for His honor which in it draws out the emotions and absorbs endeavor; and the end of human as of all other existence, of salvation as of all other attainment, is to it the glory of the Lord of all. Full justice is done in it to the scheme of redemption and the experience of salvation, because full justice is done in it to religion itself which underlies these elements of it. It begins, it centers, it ends with the vision of God in His glory: and it sets itself before all things to render to God His rights in every sphere of life-activity.

5. Soteriology of Calvinism

One of the consequences flowing from this fundamental attitude of Calvinistic feeling and thought is the high supernaturalism which informs alike its religious consciousness and its doctrinal construction. Calvinism would not be badly defined, indeed, as the tendency which is determined to do justice to the immediately supernatural, as in the first, so also in the second creation. The strength and purity of its belief in the supernatural Fact (which is God) saves it from all embarrassment in the face of the supernatural act (which is miracle). In everything which enters into the process of redemption it is impelled by the force of its first principle to place the initiative in God. A supernatural revelation, in which God makes known to man His will and His purposes of grace; a supernatural record of this revelation in a supernaturally given book, in which God gives His revelation permanency and extension — such things are to the Calvinist almost matters of course. And, above all, he can but insist with the utmost strenuousness on the immediate supernaturalness of the actual work of redemption itself, and that no less in its application than in its impetration. Thus it comes about that the doctrine of monergistic regeneration — or as it was phrased by the older theologians, of " irresistible grace " or " effectual calling " — is the hinge of the Calvinistic soteriology, and lies much more deeply embedded in the system than the doctrine of predestination itself which is popularly looked upon as its hall-mark. Indeed, the soteriological significance of predestination to the Calvinist consists in the safeguard it affords to monergistic regeneration — to purely supernatural salvation. What lies at the heart of his soteriology is the absolute exclusion of the creaturely element in the initiation of the saving process, that so the pure grace of God may be magnified. Only so could he express his sense of man's complete dependence as sinner on the free mercy of a saving God; or extrude the evil leaven of Synergism by which, as he clearly sees, God is robbed of His glory and man is encouraged to think that he owes to some power, some act of choice, some initiative of his own, his participation in that salvation which is in reality all of grace. There is accordingly nothing against which Calvinism sets its face with more firmness than every form and degree of autosoterism. Above everything else, it is determined that God, in His Son Jesus Christ, acting through the Holy Spirit whom He has sent, shall be recognized as our veritable Saviour. To it sinful man stands in need not of inducements or assistance to save himself, but of actual saving; and Jesus Christ has come not to advise, or urge, or induce, or aid him to save himself, but to save him. This is the root of Calvinistic soteriology; and it is because this deep sense of human helplessness and this profound consciousness of indebtedness for all that enters into salvation to the free grace of God is the root of its soteriology that to it the doctrine of election becomes the *cor cordis* of the Gospel. He who knows that it is God who has chosen him and not he who has chosen God, and that he owes his entire salvation in all its processes and in every one of its stages to this choice of God, would be an ingrate indeed if he gave not the glory of his salvation solely to the inexplicable elective love of God.

6. CONSISTENT DEVELOPMENT OF CALVINISM

Historically the Reformed theology finds its origin in the reforming movement begun in Switzerland under the leadership of Zwingli (1516). Its fundamental principles are already present in Zwingli's teaching, though it was not until Calvin's profound and penetrating genius was called to their exposition that they took their ultimate form or received systematic development. From Switzerland Calvinism spread outward to France, and along the Rhine through Germany to Holland, eastward to Bohemia and Hungary, and westward, across the Channel, to Great Britain. In this broad expansion through so many lands its voice was raised in a multitude of confessions; and in the course of the four hundred years which have elapsed since its first formulation, it has been expounded in a vast

body of dogmatic treatises. Its development has naturally been
much richer and far more many-sided than that of the sister
system of Lutheranism in its more confined and homogeneous
environment; and yet it has retained its distinctive character
and preserved its fundamental features with marvelous consistency throughout its entire history. It may be possible to
distinguish among the Reformed confessions, between those
which bear more and those which bear less strongly the stamp
of Calvin's personal influence; and they part into two broad
classes, according as they were composed before or after the
Arminian defection (*ca.* 1618) and demanded sharper definitions on the points of controversy raised by that movement. A
few of them written on German soil also bear traces of the influence of Lutheran conceptions. And, of course, no more
among the Reformed than elsewhere have all the professed expounders of the system of doctrine been true to the faith they
professed to expound. Nevertheless, it is precisely the same
system of truth which is embodied in all the great historic Reformed confessions; it matters not whether the document emanates from Zurich or Bern or Basel or Geneva, whether it sums
up the Swiss development as in the second Helvetic Confession, or publishes the faith of the National Reformed Churches
of France, or Scotland, or Holland, or the Palatinate, or Hungary, Poland, Bohemia, or England; or republishes the established Reformed doctrine in opposition to new contradictions,
as in the Canons of Dort (in which the entire Reformed world
concurred), or the Westminster Confession (to which the whole
of Puritan Britain gave its assent), or the Swiss Form of Consent (which represents the mature judgment of Switzerland
upon the recently proposed novelties of doctrine). And despite
the inevitable variety of individual points of view, as well as
the unavoidable differences in ability, learning, grasp, in the
multitude of writers who have sought to expound the Reformed faith through these four centuries — and the grave de-
partures from that faith made here and there among them —
the great stream of Reformed dogmatics has flowed essentially

unsullied, straight from its origin in Zwingli and Calvin to its debouchure, say, in Chalmers and Cunningham and Crawford, in Hodge and Thornwell and Shedd.

7. VARIETIES OF CALVINISM

It is true an attempt has been made to distinguish two types of Reformed teaching from the beginning; a more radical type developed under the influence of the peculiar teachings of Calvin, and a (so-called) more moderate type, chiefly propagating itself in Germany, which exhibits rather the influence, as was at first said (Hofstede de Groot, Ebrard, Heppe), of Melanchthon, or, in its more recent statement (Gooszen), of Bullinger. In all that concerns the essence of Calvinism, however, there was no difference between Bullinger and Calvin, German and Swiss: the Heidelberg Catechism is no doubt a catechism and not a confession, but in its presuppositions and inculcations it is as purely Calvinistic as the Genevan Catechism or the catechisms of the Westminster Assembly. Nor was the substance of doctrine touched by the peculiarities of method which marked such schools as the so-called Scholastics (showing themselves already in Zanchius, d. 1590, and culminating in theologians like Alsted, d. 1638, and Voetius, d. 1676); or by the special modes of statement which were developed by such schools as the so-called Federalists (e.g., Cocceius, d. 1669, Burman, d. 1679, Wittsius, d. 1708; cf. Diestel, "Studien zur Föderaltheologie," in *Jahrbücher für deutsche Theologie*, x. 1865, pp. 209–276; G. Vos, " De Verbondsleer in de Gereformeerde Theologie," Grand Rapids, 1891; W. Hastie, " The Theology of the Reformed Church," Edinburgh, 1904, pp. 189–210). The first serious defection from the fundamental conceptions of the Reformed system came with the rise of Arminianism in the early years of the seventeenth century (Arminius, Uytenbogaert, Episcopius, Limborch, Curcellæus); and the Arminian party was quickly sloughed off under the condemnation of the whole Reformed world. The five points of its "Remonstrance" against the Calvinistic system were met by the reassertion of the fundamental doctrines of absolute predestination, particular redemption, total depravity, irresistible grace, and the perseverance of the saints (Canons of the Synod of Dort). The first important modification of the Calvinistic system which has retained a position within its limits was made in the middle of the seventeenth century by the professors of the French school at Saumur, and is hence called Salmurianism; otherwise Amyraldism, or hypothetical universalism (Cameron, d. 1625, Amyraut, d. 1664, Placæus, d. 1655, Testardus, d. *ca.* 1650. This modification also received the condemnation of the contemporary Reformed world, which reasserted with emphasis the importance of the doctrine that Christ actually saves by His spirit all for whom He offers the sacrifice of His blood (e.g. Westminster Confession, Swiss Form of Consent).

8. Supralapsarianism and Infralapsarianism

If " varieties of Calvinism " are to be spoken of with reference to anything more than details, of importance in themselves no doubt, but of little significance for the systematic development of the type of doctrine, there seem not more than three which require mention: supralapsarianism, infralapsarianism, and what may perhaps be called in this reference, postredemptionism; all of which (as indeed their very names import) take their start from a fundamental agreement in the principles which govern the system. The difference between these various tendencies of thought within the limits of the system turns on the place given by each to the decree of election, in the logical ordering of the " decrees of God." The supralapsarians suppose that election underlies the decree of the fall itself; and conceive the decree of the fall as a means for carrying out the decree of election. The infralapsarians, on the other hand, consider that election presupposes the decree of the fall, and hold, therefore, that in electing some to life God has mankind as a *massa perditionis* in mind. The extent of the

difference between these parties is often, indeed usually, grossly
exaggerated: and even historians of repute are found representing infralapsarianism as involving, or at least permitting,
denial that the fall has a place in the decree of God at all: as if
election could be postposited in the *ordo decretorum* to the de-
decree of the fall, while it was doubted whether there were any
decree of the fall; or as if indeed God could be held to conceive men, in His electing decree, as fallen, without by that
very act fixing the presupposed fall in His eternal decree. In
point of fact there is and can be no difference among Calvinists
as to the inclusion of the fall in the decree of God: to doubt
this inclusion is to place oneself at once at variance with the
fundamental Calvinistic principle which conceives all that
comes to pass teleologically and ascribes everything that actu-

9. Postredemptionism

ally occurs ultimately to the will of God. Accordingly even the
postredemptionists (that is to say the Salmurians or Amyrald-
ians) find no difficulty at this point. Their peculiarity consists
in insisting that election succeeds, in the order of thought, not
merely the decree of the fall but that of redemption as well,
taking the term redemption here in the narrower sense of the
impetration of redemption by Christ. They thus suppose that
in His electing decree God conceived man not merely as fallen
but as already redeemed. This involves a modified doctrine of
the atonement from which the party has received the name
of Hypothetical Universalism, holding as it does that Christ
died to make satisfaction for the sins of all men without exception *if* — if, that is, they believe: but that, foreseeing that
none would believe, God elected some to be granted faith
through the effectual operation of the Holy Spirit. The indifferent standing of the postredemptionists in historical Calvinism is indicated by the treatment accorded it in the historical
confessions. It alone of the " varieties of Calvinism " here mentioned has been made the object of formal confessional condemnation; and it received condemnation in every important

Reformed confession written after its development. There are, it is true, no supralapsarian confessions: many, however, leave the questions which divide supralapsarian and infralapsarian wholly to one side and thus avoid pronouncing for either; and none is polemically directed against supralapsarianism. On the other hand, not only does no confession close the door to infralapsarianism, but a considerable number explicitly teach infralapsarianism which thus emerges as the typical form of Calvinism. That, despite its confessional condemnation, post-redemptionism has remained a recognized form of Calvinism and has worked out a history for itself in the Calvinistic Churches (especially in America) may be taken as evidence that its advocates, while departing, in some important particulars, from typical Calvinism, have nevertheless remained, in the main, true to the fundamental postulates of the system. There is another variety of postredemptionism, however, of which this can scarcely be said. This variety, which became dominant among the New England Congregationalist churches about the second third of the nineteenth century (e.g., N. W. Taylor, d. 1858; C. G. Finney, d. 1875; E. A. Park, d. 1900), attempted, much after the manner of the "Congruists" of the Church of Rome, to unite a Pelagian doctrine of the will with the Calvinistic doctrine of absolute predestination. The result was, of course, to destroy the Calvinistic doctrine of "irresistible grace," and as the Calvinistic doctrine of the "satisfaction of Christ" was also set aside in favor of the Grotian or governmental theory of atonement, little was left of Calvinism except the bare doctrine of predestination. Perhaps it is not strange, therefore, that this "improved Calvinism" has crumbled away and given place to newer and explicitly anti-Calvinistic constructions of doctrine (cf. Williston Walker, in *AJT*, April, 1906, pp. 204*sqq.*).

10. Present Fortunes of Calvinism

It must be confessed that the fortunes of Calvinism in general are not at present at their flood. In America, to be sure, the controversies of the earlier half of the nineteenth century compacted a body of Calvinistic thought which gives way but slowly: and the influence of the great theologians who adorned the Churches during that period is still felt (especially Charles Hodge, 1797–1878, Robert J. Breckinridge, 1800–1871, James H. Thornwell, 1812–1862, Henry B. Smith, 1815–1877, W. G. T. Shedd, 1820–1894, Robert L. Dabney, 1820–1898, Archibald Alexander Hodge, 1823–1886). And in Holland recent years have seen a notable revival of the Reformed consciousness, especially among the adherents of the Free Churches, which has been felt as widely as Dutch influence extends, and which is at present represented in Abraham Kuyper and Herman Bavinck, by a theologian of genius and a theologian of erudition worthy of the best Reformed traditions. But it is probable that few " Calvinists without reserve " exist at the moment in French-speaking lands: and those who exist in lands of German speech and Eastern Europe appear to owe their inspiration directly to the teaching of Kohlbrügge. Even in Scotland there has been a remarkable decline in strictness of construction ever since the days of William Cunningham and Thomas J. Crawford (cf. W. Hastie, " The Theology of the Reformed Church," Edinburgh, 1904, p. 228). Nevertheless, it may be contended that the future, as the past, of Christianity itself is bound up with the fortunes of Calvinism. The system of doctrine founded on the idea of God which has been explicated by Calvinism, strikingly remarks W. Hastie (" Theology as Science," Glasgow, 1899, pp. 97–98), " is the only system in which the whole order of the world is brought into a rational unity with the doctrine of grace. . . . It is only with such a universal conception of God, established in a living way, that we can face, with hope of complete conquest, all the spiritual dangers and terrors of our time. . . . But it is deep enough and large enough and divine enough, rightly understood, to confront them and do battle with them all in vindication of the Creator, Preserver, and Governor of the world, and of the Justice and Love of the Divine Personality."

PART TWO

I

AUGUSTINE

AUGUSTINE [1]

1. LIFE. — Aurelius Augustine (the prænomen " Aurelius "
is attested by contemporaries but does not occur in his own
works or in his correspondence) was born of mixed heathen
and Christian parentage November 13, 354 A.D., at Tagaste, a
small municipality in proconsular Numidia. He was taught in
his childhood the principles of Christianity, and great sacrifices
were made to give him a liberal education. From his youth he
was consumed by an insatiable thirst for knowledge, and was
so inflamed by the reading of Cicero's " Hortensius " in his
nineteenth year that he thenceforth devoted his life to the
pursuit of truth. The profession to which he was bred was that
of rhetorician, and this profession he practiced first at Tagaste,
and then successively at Carthage, Rome, and Milan up to the
great crisis of his life (386). In his early manhood he had fallen
away from his Christian training to the Manichæans, who were
the rationalists of the age (373) ; and subsequently (383) had
lapsed into a general skepticism ; but he had already fought his
way out of this, under the influence of the Neo-Platonists, before his conversion to Catholic Christianity took place at Milan
in the late summer of 386. He spent the interval between this
crisis and his baptism (Easter, 387) in philosophical retirement at Cassiciacum, and then, after a short sojourn at Rome,
returned to Africa (autumn, 388) and established at his native
town a sort of religio-philosophical retreat for himself and his
friends. Early in 391 he was almost forcibly ordained presbyter
at Hippo Regius, and nearly five years later (shortly before
Christmas, 395) was raised to the rank of coadjutor-bishop.
From the first he sustained practically the entire burden of the
administration, and, soon succeeding to its sole responsibility,

[1] From " Encyclopaedia of Religion and Ethics," ed. by James Hastings,
ii. pp. 219–224 Used by permission of the publishers, Charles Scribner's Sons.

continued bishop of that second-rate diocese until his death, August 28, 430.

In this simple framework was lived out the life of one who has been strikingly called incomparably the greatest man whom, "between Paul the Apostle and Luther the Reformer, the Christian Church has possessed." [2] We cannot date from him, it is true, an epoch in the external fortunes of the Church in the same sense in which we may from, say, Gregory the Great or Hildebrand. He was not, indeed, without ecclesiastico-political significance. He did much to heal the schisms which tore the African Church. He regenerated the clergy of Africa by his monastic training school. And it must not be forgotten that the two great Gregorys stood upon his shoulders. But his direct work as a reformer of Church life was done in a corner, and its results were immediately swept away by the flood of the Vandal invasion.

2. WRITINGS. — It was through his voluminous writings, by which his wider influence was exerted, that he entered both the Church and the world as a revolutionary force, and not merely created an epoch in the history of the Church, but has determined the course of its history in the West up to the present day. He was already an author when he became a Christian, having published (about 380) an æsthetical study (now lost), on " De pulchro et apto." But his amazing literary productivity began with his conversion. His first Christian writings were a series of religio-philosophical treatises, in which he sought to lay the foundations of a specifically Christian philosophy. These were followed by a great number of controversial works against the Manichæans, Donatists, Pelagians, interspersed with Biblical expositions and dogmatic and ethical studies. The whole was crowned by four or five great books in which his genius finds perhaps its fullest expression. These are his " Confessiones " (397–400), in which he gives an analysis of his religious experience and creates a new *genre* in literary form; the " de Doctrina Christiana " (397–426), in which the

2 Harnack, " Monasticism and the Confessions of St. Augustine," p. 123.

principles of his Biblical exposition are expounded; the "Enchiridion ad Laurentium" on Faith, Hope, and Charity (421), which contains his most serious attempt to systematize his thought; the "De Trinitate (395–420), in which its final formulation was given to the Christian doctrine of the Trinity; and the "De Civitate Dei" (413–426), in which are laid the foundations of a rational philosophy of history.

He seems to have been himself aware of the significance of the writings into which he had so unstintedly poured himself, and he devoted some of his last years to a careful survey and revision of them in his unique "Retractationes" (426–428), in which he seeks to compact them into an ultimate whole. The influence which they exerted from the beginning is attested no less by the spiteful comments on their volume which escaped from those less well affected to them (e.g., the interpolators of Gennadius), than by the wondering admiration of the better disposed (already, Possidius, "Vita," chap. vii.). In point of fact they entered the Church as a leaven which has ever since wrought powerfully towards leavening the whole mass.

3. INFLUENCE. — (a) *Its extent.* — The greatness of the influence exerted by Augustine is fairly intimated by the suggestion that the division between the Eastern and Western Churches may properly be represented as having been " prepared " by him.[3] No doubt, according to Renan's saying, the building of Constantinople contained in it the prophecy of the division of the Empire, and the division of the Empire the prophecy of the division of the Church. But it was Augustine who imprinted upon the Western section of the Church a character so specific as naturally to bring the separation of the Churches in its train. It must not be inferred, however, that his influence was felt only in the West. The prevailing impression to this effect implies some failure to appreciate not only the extent of the intercourse between the East and the West in Augustine's day, but also the indebtedness of the East to the West for its theological constructions. The interest of the An-

[3] Reuter, " Augustinische Studien," vii. p. 499.

tiochenes in Western Christological thought, as illustrated, for instance, in the "Eranistes" and the correspondence of Theodoret, is only one example of a much wider fact; and in any event, the great doctrines of the Trinity and the Person of Christ, which form almost the entirety of "dogma" in the East, so far from being a gift from the East to the West, as often represented, had their origin in the West, and were thence communicated to the East — the former through the intermediation of "the great Hosius," and the latter through that of Leo the Great. Augustine, through whom — working, no doubt, in full knowledge of what had been done by the Greeks, but in entire independence of them — the doctrine of the Trinity received its completed statement, came too late to affect the Greek construction of this doctrine, and accordingly gave form on this great topic only to the thought of the West. But his Christological conceptions underlay the formulations of Leo, as those of Ambrose underlay his, and through Leo determined the Christological definitions of the East as well as of the West. Accordingly, while the doctrines of the East and the West on the Person of Christ have remained identical, in their doctrines of the Trinity the two sections draw somewhat apart, not only with respect to that perennial bone of contention, the *filioque* clause in the definition of the procession of the Spirit, but in what underlies this difference — their general conception of the relations of the Trinitarian Persons. This in the East is ruled by subtle subordinational inheritances (embedded in the Nicene formulary in the phrase θεὸς ἐκ θεοῦ and its equivalents), while in the West it is dominated by that principle of equalization which found its sharpest assertion in the ascription of αὐτοθεότης to Christ by Calvin, whose construction marks the only new (subordinate) epoch in the development of the doctrine of the Trinity after Augustine. This complete determination of Western thought on the fundamental Christian doctrine of the Trinity fairly illustrates at once the place of Augustine in Western Christian thought, and the effect of his supreme influence there in creating a specifically Western type of Christianity.

It is worth while, no doubt, to distinguish between the actual influence exerted by Augustine in the West, and what may perhaps, in a more external sense, be called the authority enjoyed by his name in the Latin Church. To no other doctor of the Church has anything like the same authority been accorded, and it seemed for long as if his doctrine of grace at least was to be treated as a definitely defined dogma, *de fide* in the Church. Already in 431 Celestine sharply reproved the bishops of Gaul for permitting Augustine's authority to be questioned in their dioceses; and soon afterwards, Gelasius (493) addressed to the bishop of Picenum a similar letter of rebuke for the like carelessness. Subsequent deliverances of Hormisdas (520), and Boniface II (530–531), and John II (534) confirmed the authority thus assigned him; and their encomiums were repeated by many later Roman bishops. It very naturally became, therefore, the custom of the " Augustinians " in the Church of Rome — like Diego Alvarez, Jansen, Noris — to ascribe " irrefragable authority " to his teaching; and the question was gravely debated among the theologians whether a truly plenary authority were really to be attributed to him, or whether he were only to rank as the first of the Church's authorized teachers. The result was very naturally that every tendency of thought in the Church was eager to claim for itself the support of his name; and the extraordinary richness of his mind, and the remarkable variety of, so to say, the facets of his teaching, lent him more than ordinarily to the appeal of numerous and even divergent points of view. The possibility of this was increased by the long period of time covered by his literary activity, and the only gradual crystallization of his thought around his really formative ideas. The Augustine of Cassiciacum or even of the presbyterate was a somewhat different Augustine from the Augustine of the episcopate; and not even at his death had perfect consistency been attained in his teaching. Accordingly the most amazing variety of doctrine, on almost every conceivable subject, throughout the Middle Ages, and later in the Church of Rome, has sought support for itself in some saying or other of his; and both sides of almost every controversy have appealed with confidence to his teaching. Schools of thought which had drifted entirely away from his most fundamental postulates still regarded and represented themselves as " Augustinian "; and the Church of Rome itself, whose whole history since the second Council of Orange (529) has been marked by the progressive elimination of Augustinianism from its teaching, is still able to look upon him as the chief doctor of the Church, upon whom its fabric is especially built. Confusion became so confounded that the Confession of Faith which Pelagius presented to Innocent was inserted quite innocently into the " Libri Carolini," and was even produced by the Sorbonne in 1521 against Luther as Augustine's own.

Obviously this universal deference to the name of Augustine furnishes no accurate measure of his real influence. It supplies, however, a fair general reflection of its extent. In point of fact the whole development of Western life, in all its phases, was powerfully affected by his teaching. This, his unique ascendancy in the direction of the thought and life of the West, is due in part to the particular period in history in which his work was done, in part to the richness and depth of his mind and the force of his individuality, and in part to the special circumstances of his conversion to Christianity. He stood on the watershed of two worlds. The old world was passing away; the new world was entering upon its heritage; and it fell to him to mediate the transference of the culture of the one to the other. It has been strikingly remarked that the miserable existence of the Roman Empire in the West almost seems to have been prolonged for the express purpose of affording an opportunity for the influence of Augustine to be exerted on universal history.[4] He was fortunate even in the place of his birth and formative years; although on the very eve of its destruction, Africa was at this precise moment, in the midst of the universal decadence, the scene of intense intellectual activity — into which he entered with all the force of his ardent

<hr />

[4] Harnack, " Grundriss der Dogmengeschichte," E. T. " Outlines of the History of Dogma," p. 335.

nature. He gathered up into himself all that the old world had to offer, and re-coining it sent it forth again bearing the stamp of his profound character. It belonged to the peculiarity of his genius that he embraced all that he took up into himself " with all the fibres of his soul "; not, as has been said, " with his heart alone, for the heart does not think, nor with the mind only; he never grasps truth in the abstract, and as if it were dead," [5] but with his whole being, giving himself to it and sending it forth from himself as living truth, driven on by all the force of his great and inspiring personality. Accordingly, when, having tested everything that the old world had to offer and found it wanting, he gave himself at last to Catholic Christianity, it was with no reserves. Catholicism, frankly accepted as such, became his passion, and into the enthusiastic maintenance of it he threw all his forces. It was primarily as a Catholic Christian, therefore, that he thought, and worked, and lived. But the man who threw himself with such zeal into the service of Catholic Christianity was a man who had already lived through many experiences and had gathered much spoil in the process. He had sounded the depths of heresy in its most attractive form and had drunk the waters of philosophy in its culminating development; life in the conventicles of the sects and in the circle of cultured heathenism was alike familiar to him. But, above all the spoil he brought from without, he brought with him himself. He was a man of the highest and most individual genius — intellectual, but far beyond that, religious — who had his own personal contribution to make to thought and life. If we cannot quite allow that there were in very truth many Augustines, we must at least recognize that within the one Augustine there were very various and not always consistent currents flowing, each of which had its part to play in the future. Within the Catholic Christian a philosopher of the first rank was restlessly active; and within both a religious genius of the highest order was working; while for the expression of the resulting complex of feelings and ideas a lit-

[5] Portalié, in Vacant-Mangenot, " Dictionnaire de la Théologie Catholique," i. col. 2453.

erary talent was available second to none in the annals of the
Church.

It is no wonder, therefore, that the Western Church has
felt the force of his influence in all the main lines of its development, and in no one of its prominent characteristics could it
have been without him what it has become. In him are found
at once the seed out of which the tree that we know as the
Roman Catholic Church has grown; the spring or strength of
all the leading anti-hierarchical and mystical movements which
succeeded one another through the Middle Ages; at least the
promise and pre-formation of the great types of Western philosophical thought; and, above all, the potent leaven of vital
religion. Beginning in the first force of its fresh promulgation
by overcoming the ingrained rationalism of the popular Christianity expressed in Pelagianism and its daughter movements,
it refused to be bound by the compromises of the Council of
Orange, compacted though they were into a system by the
genius of a Thomas, and given irrefragable authority in the
Church of Rome by the decrees of Trent, but manifested its
power by outbreak after outbreak, from Gottschalk in the
ninth to Jansen in the seventeenth century; and then burst all
bonds and issued in the Protestant Reformation in the sixteenth century.

(b) *Augustine as a Church-teacher.* — No doubt it is pre-
eminently as the great Catholic doctor that Augustine stands
out on the page of history. To his own consciousness he was
just a Catholic Christian; and the whole mass of his teaching
was conceived by him as simply the body of Catholic doctrine.
It is, accordingly, interesting to observe that it is precisely as
the Catholic doctor that he has lived in the hearts of the people. The legends which have gathered around his name picture
him preëminently as the expounder of the *principia* of the
Christian faith, particularly of the mysteries of the Godhead,
who abode continually *in excelsis disputans de gloria excel-
lentissimæ Trinitatis,* and communicated to the Church the results of his high meditations "as he was able" — a note of
humility caught from his own habitual tone when speaking of

himself.[6] The task to which he consciously gave himself was to apprehend, so far as it was given to him to apprehend, to proclaim, maintain, and defend the Catholic truth; and from this task he never swerved. It was no empty formula with him when he declared, as he repeatedly declared, " This is the Catholic faith, and it is therefore also my faith "; and he was altogether in earnest when he exhorted his readers not to love him more than the Catholic faith, and his critics not to love themselves more than the Catholic truth.[7] The body of Catholic doctrine constitutes thus the traditional element in Augustine's teaching. But, of course, it by no means left his hands precisely as it entered them. Nor did he contribute to it merely intellectual precision and logical completeness; he impressed on it the stamp of his religious fervor, and transmuted its elements into religious entities.

It was particularly in the doctrine of the Church, which he thus took up and transfigured, that he became in a true sense the founder of Roman Catholicism, and thus called into being a new type of Christianity, in which " the idea of the Church became the central power in the religious feeling " and " in ecclesiastical activity," " in a fashion which has remained unknown to the East." [8] This idea of the Church was, to be sure, so little the creation of Augustine that he took it over whole from his predecessors, and in his innermost thought, indeed, never thoroughly homologated it. It was Cyprian, not Augustine, who identified the Church with the episcopate, and to whom the Church outside which there is no salvation was fundamentally the hierarchical institution. It was Gregory the Great who first spoke of the organized Church as the divine *civitas*. To Augustine the Church was fundamentally the *congregatio sanctorum,* the Body of Christ, and it is this Church which he has in mind when he calls it the *civitas Dei,* or the Kingdom of God on earth. He is, however, not carefully observant of the distinction between the empirical and the ideal

---

[6] Cf. Stilting, " Acta Sanctorum," Aug. vi.

[7] " De Trinitate," I. iv. 7; III. *præf.* 2.

[8] Reuter, *op. cit.,* p. 499.

Church, and repeatedly — often apparently quite unconsciously — carries over to the one the predicates which in his
fundamental thought, belonged properly to the other. Thus
the hierarchically organized Church tends ever with him to
take the place of the *congregatio sanctorum,* even when he is
speaking of it as the Kingdom or City of God in which alone
any communion with God is possible here, and through which
alone eternal blessedness with God is attainable hereafter.

In the Donatist controversy, although the distinction between *habere* and *utiliter* or *salubriter habere* is made to do
yeoman service, the conception of the Church as the sole
sphere of salvation, passing into the conception of the Church
as the sole mediatrix of grace, and therefore the sole distribu-
tor of salvation, was necessarily thrown into high emphasis;
and the logic of the situation too directly and too powerfully
identified this Church with the empirical Church for the
deeper-lying conception of the *congregatio sanctorum* to remain in sight. Thus Augustine, almost against his will, became the stay of that doctrine of the Church as the sole instrument at once of true knowledge of the divine revelation and
of saving grace which provides the two *foci* about which the
ellipse of Roman Catholic doctrine revolves. What before him
was matter of assertion became in his hands a religion and
went forth to conquer the world. His profounder conception
of the Church as the *congregatio sanctorum,* and the consequent distinction between the empirical and the ideal Church,
with all its implications with respect to the action of the Sacraments and the effect of ecclesiastical decrees, and even of excommunication, did not indeed remain unobserved or unutil-
ized when occasion demanded. Thus, for example, they came
forward in their completeness in the arguments of the Im-
perialists in the great controversies of the later eleventh century.[9] These also, and in a truer sense than the Papalists in
that debate, were " Augustinians." But the main stream of
Augustine's influence flowed meanwhile in the traditionalist

[9] Mirbt, " Die Stellung Augustins in der Publicistik des gregorianischen
Kirchenstreits," p. 80.

channel, and gave the world the Church as the authoritative
organ of divine truth and the miraculous vehicle of saving
grace, through which alone the assured knowledge of the revelation of God could be attained, or the effective operations of
His redeeming love experienced. Many of the subsidiary conceptions which fill out the system of Roman Catholic doctrine
also find their direct prop in his teaching — its doctrine of
merit, the distinctions between precepts and counsels, mortal
and venial sins, and particularly the elaborate sacramental
system, with its distinction between matter and form, its assertion of *ex opere operato* action, and of the indelible character
of baptism and ordination, and even the doctrine of intention.
On this side of his teaching the Roman Catholic Church may
well be accounted Augustine's monument.

(c) *As a thinker*. — But beneath Augustine the traditionalist lay Augustine the thinker, and as a thinker he gave law
not only to the Church but to the world. From the moment of
his conversion, to be sure, religion became paramount with
him. But this did not quench his philosophical impulse; it only
made his specifically a religious philosophy, and himself, to
adopt Rudolph Eucken's more precise definition,[10] " the single
great philosopher on the basis of Christianity proper the world
has had " — in the richness of his thought and poetry of his expression alike, not unworthy of comparison even with his great
master Plato.[11] He brought with him into Catholic Christianity
not only a sufficient equipment of philosophical knowledge,
but a powerful and trained intelligence, and an intellectual
instinct which had to find scope. It was in the rôle of Christian philosopher, seeking to give form and substance to fundamental verities from the Christian standpoint, that he first
came forward in the service of faith; and though later the religious teacher and defender of the faith seemed likely to swal-
low up the philosophical inquirer, they never really did so, but

[10] Eucken, " Die Lebensanschauungen der grossen Denker [2], p. 216.

[11] Cf. E. Norden, in " Die Kultur der Gegenwart, i. 8, 1905, p. 394: " Augustine was the great poet of the ancient Church, though just as little as
Plato did he write in verse. These two go together as the great poet-philoso-
phers of all time."

his rich and active mind kept continually at work sounding all depths. Thus not only was there imparted to all his teaching an unwonted vitality, originality, and profundity, but "the activities set in motion were not confined to the narrow circle of theological science, but extended, directly or indirectly, to all forms of human life." [12] In every department of philosophical inquiry he became normative for the succeeding centuries; and until the rise of Aristotelianism in the twelfth century and its establishment in influence by the advocacy of such teachers as Albertus Magnus and Thomas Aquinas, Augustinianism reigned supreme. Throughout the remainder of the Middle Ages it contended masterfully with its great rival, forming many compromises with it, and tending to offset the rationalism into which Aristotelianism was ever degenerating by itself falling into mysticism. It thus became the support of the tendency towards mysticism which prevailed through the Middle Ages, or rather its protection from the pantheism into which, when drawing more directly from Neo-Platonic sources, it was ever liable to deteriorate. From it every Catholic reformer drew his strength, and to it the whole body of reformers before the Reformation made their appeal. From its partial obscuration it emerged at the Renaissance, and burst again into full view in the seventeenth century to lay the foundations of modern thought. Siebeck accordingly bids us see in Augustine "the first modern man"; [13] and, if Eucken questions the exactness of the designation, he is free to allow that the modern world finds in Augustine many points of contact, and, not only in questions of religious philosophy may wisely take its start from him rather than from Luther or Thomas, Schleiermacher or Kant, but in purely philosophical matters will find him in many respects more modern than Hegel or Schopenhauer. [14]

It was in the spheres of psychology and metaphysics that the dominion of Augustine was most complete. He aspired to

[12] Mirbt, *op. cit.,* p. 1.
[13] *Zeitschrift für Philosophie und Pädagogik,* 1888, p. 190.
[14] Eucken, *op. cit.,* p. 249.

know nothing, he tells us, but God and the soul; but these he
strove with all his might to know altogether. His characteristic
mark as a thinker was the inward gaze; the realities of consciousness were the primary objects of his contemplation; and
from them he took his starting point for reflection on the
world. Antiquity supplies no second to him in the breadth and
acuteness of his psychological observation. And in his establishment of "immediate certainty of inner experience," as
Windelband calls it,[15] in "the controlling central position of
philosophic thought" he transcended his times and became
"one of the founders of modern thought." If he may truly be
said to have derived from Plato and Plotinus, in a far truer
sense he stood above his Neo-Platonic teachers, and of his line-
age have come Descartes and Malebranche and all that has
proceeded from the movements of thought inaugurated by
them. Even the famous ontological argument for the being
of God, and, indeed, the very *cogito, ergo sum* of Descartes,
have not merely their material but their formal pre-formation
in him. It was not, however, in abstract thought alone, or
chiefly, that he made his mark on the ages; his own thinking
was markedly concrete, and nothing characterized it more
strongly than the firmness of its grasp upon the realities of life,
to the understanding and direction of which it was held strictly
ancillary.

His impact upon the world might accordingly not unfairly
be summed up, from one point of view, in the ethical revolution which he wrought. "In essence," remarks Harnack,[16] "Augustine's importance in the history of the Church and dogma
lies in his giving to the West in the place of the Stoic-Christian
popular morals, as that was recapitulated in Pelagianism, a religious, specifically Christian ethics, and so strongly impressing
this on the Church that at least its formulas maintain up to
to-day their supremacy in the whole extent of Western Chris-

15 "A History of Philosophy," pp. 264, 270, 276.
16 "Dogmengeschichte" [E. T. v. p. 30]; cf. on Augustine's place in the
history of ethics, Joseph Mausbach, in "Die Kultur der Gegenwart," i. 4,
1906, p. 526.

tianity." Indeed, we might do worse, in seeking an index of his influence as a thinker, than fix upon the place he has occupied in political theory and practice. The entire political development of the Middle Ages was dominated by him; and he was in a true sense the creator of the Holy Roman Empire. It was no accident that the *De civitate Dei* was the favorite reading of Charlemagne: " he delighted," Einhard tells us (*Vita Caroli,* 24), " in the books of St. Augustine, and especially in those that bear the title ' Of the City of God.' " And in the great struggle between the Empire and the Papacy in the later eleventh century it was expressly to him that the controversialists on both sides made their appeal. No Father is quoted by them as often as he, except, perhaps, Gregory the Great; and no series of documents is cited more frequently than his writings, except, perhaps, the pseudo-Isidorian decretals.[17] Not only do writers like Walram of Naumburg and Wido of Ferrara reflect accurately his conception of the Church, with its emphasis on unity and its vacillation between the ideas of the *congregatio sanctorum* and a hierarchical organization — echoes of which still sound in William of Occam's " Defensor Pacis " and the discussions of the conciliatory party in the Roman Church whose ornament was Gerson — but they made their appeal to Augustine in their endeavors to give validity to their defense " of the State as a Divine institution, of the moral significance and relative independence of the earthly sovereignty, of the necessary concordance of the *Sacerdotium* and *Imperium*," and the like.[18]

On the theoretical side he must be accredited, in this aspect of his thought, with the creation of the science of the Philosophy of History. For the primary significance of the *De civitate Dei* lies in the fact that " in it for the first time an ideal consideration, a comprehensive survey of human history found its expression." [19] No doubt his external position at the division of the ages, when the Old World was dying and the New

---

[17] Mirbt, *op. cit.,* p. 75.
[18] Reuter, *op. cit.,* p. 508.
[19] Seyrich, " Die Geschichtsphilosophie Augustins," 1891, p. 68.

World, under the dominion of Christianity, was struggling into its place, supplied him with incitement for the creation of this new science; and the demands which the times, in the crash of the secular order, made for an apology for Christianity, powerfully determined him to a general historical philosophy. But it was Christianity itself, as the entrance into the world of a renovating force, and his own particular conception of Christianity (leading him to conceive the history of human society no less than the course of the individual life, as the continuous evolution of the divine purpose, and impeling him to interpret all the forces of time as working harmoniously onward towards that faroff divine event to which all creation moves) that gave him not only the impulse to work out a philosophy of history, but the elements of the particular philosophy of history which he actually presents in his epoch-making treatise, which, incomplete and perhaps one-sided as it is, still retains full validity in its fundamental traits.

(d) *As a regilious genius.* — Not even, however, in Augustine the philosopher do we find the Augustine whose influence has wrought most powerfully in the world. The crisis through which he passed at his conversion was a profound religious revolution; and if he gave himself at once to the task of constructing a philosophy, it was distinctively a Christian philosophy he sought to construct, built though it was largely out of Platonic materials: the authority of Christ, he tells us in the earliest of the writings in which this task was prosecuted, ranked with him even above that of reason. And if he devoted all his powers to the exposition and defense of the Catholic faith, it was because he saw in the Catholic faith the pure expression of religion, and poured into the Catholic faith all the fulness of his religious emotion. It is not Augustine the traditionalist, or Augustine the thinker, but Augustine the religious genius, who has most profoundly influenced the world. The most significant fact about him is that he, first among Church teachers, gave adequate expression to that type of religion which has since attached to itself the name of " evangelical "; the religion, that is to say, of faith, as distinct from the religion of works; the religion which, despairing of self, casts all its hope on God, as opposed to the religion which, in a greater or less degree, trusts in itself; in a word — since religion in its very nature is dependence on God — religion in the purity of its conception, as over against a *quasi*-religious moralism. What requires particularly to be noted is that he gave full expression to this type of religion both in its vital and in its thetical aspects — the former most adequately in that unique book in which he reveals his soul, and admits us as spectators to the struggles of his great heart as it seeks to cleanse itself of all trust in itself and to lay hold with the grasp, first of despair, next of discerning trust, and then of grateful love, on the God who was its salvation; and the latter most adequately in that long series of writings in which he expounds, defends, and enforces with logical argument and moving exhortation the fundamental elements of the theology of grace, as against the most direct assailants which that theology has been called upon to meet in the whole history of Christian thought. The great contribution which Augustine has made to the world's life and thought is embodied in the theology of grace, which he has presented with remarkable clearness and force, vitally in his "Confessions," and thetically in his anti-Pelagian treatises.

It would be altogether a mistake to suppose that Augustine consciously discriminated between the theology of grace, which was his personal contribution to Christian thought, and the traditional Catholicism, which he gave his life to defend and propagate. In his own consciousness, the two were one: in his theology of grace he was in his own apprehension only giving voice to the Catholic faith in its purity. Nevertheless, however unconsciously, he worked with it a revolution both in Christian teaching and in Christian life, second in its depth and its far-reaching results to no revolution which has been wrought in Christian feeling and thought in the whole course of its history. A new Christian piety dates from him, in which, in place of the alternations of hope and fear which vex the lives of those who, in whatever degree, hang their hopes on their own merits, a mood of assured trust in the mercy of a gracious God is substituted as the spring of Christian life. And a new theology corresponding to this new type of piety dates from him; a theology which, recalling man from all dependence on his own powers or merits, casts him decisively on the grace of God alone for his salvation. Of course, this doctrine was not new in the sense that it was Augustine's invention; it was the doctrine of Paul, for example, before it was the doctrine of Augustine, and was only recovered for the Church by Augustine, though in that age, dominated in all its thinking by the dregs of Stoic rationalism, it came with all the force of a new discovery. And, of course, Augustine did not discover it all at once. Because his conversion was a vital religious experience, in which the religious relation was realized in thought and life in unwonted purity and power, the fundamental elements of his religious revolution were from the first present in his mind and heart; in his earliest Christian writings he already gives expression to both the formal and the material principles, as we may term them, of the theology of grace. The authority of the divine revelation in and through Christ, embodied in the Scriptures, and the utter dependence of man on God for all good (*potestas nostra Ipse est, da fidem*), are already the most intimate expression of his thought and life. But just because the religious system to which he gave himself on his conversion was taken over by him as a whole, time was requisite for the transfusion of the whole mass by the consistent explication and conscious exposition of the " Augustinianism " implicitly summed up in such maxims. The adjustment went on slowly, although it went on unbrokenly. It required ten years before the revived Paulinism attained even a fully consistent positive enunciation (first in the work, " De diversis quæstionibus ad Simplicianum," A.D. 396); and, though the leaven worked steadily thereafter more and more deeply and widely into his thought, death intervened before all the elements of his thinking were completely leavened. That is the reason why Augustine was both the founder of Roman Catholicism and the author of that doctrine of grace which it has been the constantly pursued effort of Roman Catholicism to neutralize, and which in very fact either must be neutralized by, or will neutralize, Roman Catholicism. Two children were struggling in the womb of his mind. There can be no doubt which was the child of his heart. His doctrine of the Church he had received whole from his predecessors, and he gave it merely the precision and vitality which insured its persistence. His doctrine of grace was all his own: it represented the very core of his being; and his whole progress in Christian thinking consists in the growing completeness with which its fundamental principles applied themselves in his mind to every department of life and thought. In this gradual subjection to them of every element of his inherited teaching, it was inevitable, had time been allowed, that his inherited doctrine of the Church, too, with all its implications, would have gone down before it, and Augustine would have bequeathed to the Church, not " problems," but a thoroughly worked out system of evangelical religion.

(e) *Augustine and Protestantism.* — The problem which Augustine bequeathed to the Church for solution, the Church required a thousand years to solve. But even so, it is Augustine who gave us the Reformation. For the Reformation, inwardly considered, was just the ultimate triumph of Augustine's doctrine of grace over Augustine's doctrine of the Church. This doctrine of grace came from Augustine's hands in its positive outline completely formulated: sinful man depends, for his recovery to good and to God, entirely on the free grace of God; this grace is therefore indispensable, prevenient, irresistible, indefectible; and, being thus the free grace of God, must have lain, in all the details of its conference and working, in the intention of God from all eternity. But, however clearly announced and forcefully commended by him, it required to make its way against great obstacles in the Church. As over against the Pelagians, the indispensableness of grace was quickly established; as over against the Semi-Pelagians, its prevenience was with almost equal rapidity made good. But there advance paused. If the necessity of prevenient grace was thereafter (after the second Council of Orange, 529) the established doctrine of the Church, the irresistibility of this prevenient grace was put under the ban, and there remained no place for a complete " Augustinianism " within the Church, as Gottschalk and Jansen were fully to discover. Therefore, when the great revival of religion which we call the Reformation came, seeing that it was, on its theological side, a revival of " Augustinianism," as all great revivals of religion must be (for " Augustinianism " is but the thetical expression of religion in its purity), there was nothing for it but the rending of the Church. And therefore also the greatest peril to the Reformation was and remains the diffused anti-" Augustinianism " in the world; and, by a curious combination of circumstances, this, its greatest enemy, showed itself most dangerous in the hands of what we must otherwise look upon as the chief ally of the Reformation — that is to say, Humanism. Humanism was the ally of the Reformation in so far as it, too, worked for the emancipation of the human spirit; and, wherever it was religious, it became the seed-plot of the Reformation. But there was a strong anti-" Augustinian " party among the Humanists, and from it emanated the gravest danger which threatened the Reformation. Where this tone of thought was dominant the Reformation failed, because religious depth was wanting. What Spain, for example, lacked, says R. Saint-Hilaire justly, was not freedom of thought, but the Gospel. In the first stages of the Reformation movement in the North, this anti-" Augustinianism " may be looked upon as summed up in Erasmus; and Erasmus, on this very ground, held himself aloof from the Reformation movement, and that movement held itself aloof from him. " I am at present reading our Erasmus," wrote Luther six months before he nailed his theses on the door of the Schloss-Kirche at Wittenberg, " but my heart recoils more and more from him. . . . Those who ascribe something to man's freedom of will regard these things differently from those who know only God's free grace." Do we realize how much we owe to Erasmus and his friends that they remained Roman Catholics, and thus permitted the " Augustinianism " of the Reformation to plant its seed and to bear its fruit?

LITERATURE. — The literature upon Augustine is immense.

An excellent selection from it is given by Loofs at the head of the article " Augustinus " in Herzog, " Realencyklopädie für protestantische Theologie und Kirche," [3] ii. pp. 257 ff., with which should be compared that given by Harnack, "History of Dogma," v. pp. 61 f. The following deal directly with the influence of Augustine: Feuerlein, " Ueber die Stellung Augustins in der Kirchen- und Kulturgeschichte," in von Sybel's " Historische Zeitschrift," 1869, xxii. pp. 270–313; Reuter, " Augustinische Studien," Gotha, 1887, vii. pp. 479–516; Cunningham, " S. Austin and his place in the History of Christian Thought " (Hulsean Lectures for 1885), London, 1886; Schaff, " History of the Christian Church," iii., New York, 1884, § 180, pp. 1016–1028; Eucken, " Die Lebensanschauungen der grossen Denker," Leipzig, 1890 (2nd ed. 1897, pp. 216–250; 4th ed. 1902, pp. 210, etc.) ; Nourrisson, " La Philosophie de Sant Augustin," Paris, 1866, ii. pp. 147–276; Werner, " Die Scholastik des späteren Mittelalters," iii., Vienna, 1883, and " Die Augustinische Psychologie in ihrer mittelalterlich-scholastischen Einkleidung und Gestaltung," *Sitzungsberichte der phil.-hist. Classe der kais. Akademie der Wissenschaften*, Vienna, 1882, pp. 435–494; Siebeck, " Die Anfänge der neueren Psychologie," in *Zeitschrift für Philosophie und Pädagogik*, 1888, pp. 161 f., cf. his " Geschichte der Psychologie "; Ehrle, " Der Augustinismus und der Aristotelismus in der Scholastik gegen Ende des xiii. Jahrhundert," " Archiv für Literatur- und Kirchengeschichte des Mittelalters," 1889, v. pp. 603–635, cf. also *Zeitschrift für Katholische Theologie*, Innsbruck, 1889, xiii. pp. 172–193; Mirbt, " Die Stellung Augustins in der Publicistik des gregorianischen Kirchenstreits," Leipzig, 1888; Koch, " Der heilige Faustus, Bischof von Riez," Stuttgart, 1895, pp. 129–191; Gwatkin, " The Knowledge of God," [2] 1908, ii. p. 179; Portalié, " Augustine," in " Catholic Encyclopædia," ii. pp. 84–104, New York, 1907. The text of Augustine is most generally accessible in " Patrologia Latina," xxxii.-xlvii.; and his chief writings are translated in " Nicene and Post-Nicene Fathers," First Series i.–viii., Oxford and New York, 1886–1888.

II

AUGUSTINE AND HIS " CONFESSIONS "

AUGUSTINE AND HIS " CONFESSIONS "[1]

THERE is probably no man of the ancient world, of whose outward and inward life alike we possess such full and instructive knowledge as of Augustine's. His extraordinarily voluminous literary product teems with information about himself: and the writings of his contemporaries and successors provide at least the usual quota of allusions. But in his case these are supplemented by two remarkable books. For the whole earlier portion of his experiences, up to and including the great crisis of his conversion, we have from his own hand a work of unique self-revelation, in which he becomes something more than his own Boswell. And for the rest of his career, comprising the entire period of his activity as a leader in the Church, we have an exceptionally sober and trustworthy narrative from the hand of a pupil and friend who enjoyed a close intimacy with him for an unbroken stretch of nearly forty years. He is accordingly the first of the Christian fathers, the dates of whose birth and death we can exactly determine, and whose entire development we can follow from — as we say — the cradle to the grave.

The simple facts of his uneventful external life are soon told. He was born of mixed heathen and Christian parentage, in the small African municipality of Thagaste, on the thirteenth of November, 354. Receiving a good education, he was trained to the profession of rhetorician and practiced that profession successively at Thagaste, Carthage, Rome, and Milan, until his conversion, which took place at the last-named city in the late summer of 386. Baptized at Easter, 387, he returned to Africa in the autumn of 388, and established at his native town a sort of religio-philosophical retreat for himself and his friends. Here he lived in learned retirement until early in 391,

---

[1] From *The Princeton Theological Review*, iii. 1905, pp. 81–126.

when he was ordained a presbyter at Hippo — the sacred office being thrust upon him against his will, as it was later upon his followers, John Calvin and John Knox. Five years later (shortly before Christmas, 395), he was made coadjutor-bishop of Hippo, and from the first sustained practically the entire burden of its administration. He continued bishop of that second-rate sea-side town, until his death on August 28, 430, meanwhile having revolutionized the Church of Africa by his ceaseless labors and illuminated the world by his abundant writings. In this humble framework was lived a life the immediate products of which seemed washed out at once by the flood of disasters which instantly overwhelmed the African provinces, and with them the African Church which it had regenerated; but the influence of which is, nevertheless, not yet exhausted after a millennium and a half of years.

I. Possidius' Portrait of Augustine

The "Life" by Possidius is much briefer than we could have wished, but it presents a clear outline of Augustine's life drawn by the hand of one who worked in the full consciousness that he was handing down to posterity the record of a career which was of the first importance to the world. Augustine's literary activity by means of which he freed the Church from her enemies and built her up in the knowledge and service of God; Augustine's labors for the Church's peace by means of which he healed the schisms that divided the African community; Augustine's regeneration of the clergy of Africa through his monastic training-school: these are the points on which Possidius lays the greatest stress. In the meanwhile, however, he does much more than sum up for us what Augustine was doing for the Church and the world; though in doing this, he was speaking with a wisdom beyond his own knowledge, inasmuch as in a broader field than Africa Augustine has been a determining factor in precisely the matters here emphasized. He also paints for us a touchingly sincere portrait of the personality of his beloved master and enables us to see him at his daily work, submerged under superabundant labors, but always able to lift his heart to God, and already enjoying his rest with Him even in the midst of the clangor of the warfare he was ever waging for His Church and His truth.

Even as a presbyter, we read, he began to reap the fruit of his labors:

Alike at home and in the Church, he gave himself unstintedly to teaching and preaching the word of salvation with all confidence, in opposition to the heresies prevalent in Africa, especially to the Donatists, Manicheans and Pagans — now in elaborated books, and again in unstudied sermons — to the unspeakable admiration and delight of the Christians who as far as in them lay spread abroad his words. And thus, by God's help, the Catholic Church began to lift up its head in Africa, where it had long lain oppressed under luxuriating heresies, and especially under the Donatists, who had rebaptized the greater part of the people. And these books and tractates of his, flowing forth by the wonderful grace of God in the greatest profusion, instinct with sweet reasonableness and the authority of Holy Scripture, the heretics themselves, with the greatest ardor, vied with the Catholics in hearkening to, and moreover every one who wished and could do so brought stenographers and took notes even of what was spoken. Thus the precious doctrine and sweet savour of Christ was diffused throughout all Africa, and even the Church across the sea rejoiced when she heard it — for, even as when one member suffers all the members suffer with it, so when one member is exalted all the members rejoice with it.[2]

The labors he thus began as a presbyter, we are told, he but completed as bishop, the Lord crowning his work for the peace of the Church with the most astonishing success:

And more and more, by the help of Christ, was increased and multiplied the unity of peace and the fraternity of the Church of God. . . . And all this good, as I have said, was both begun and brought to a completion by this holy man, with the aid of our bishops.[3]

But alas! while man may propose it is God that disposes. Scarcely had this hard-won *pax ecclesiæ* been attained, when

2 " Sancti Augustini Vita Scripta a Possidio Episcopo," chap. vii .

3 Chap. xiii.

the Vandal invasion came and with it the ruin of the land. As the fabric he had built up fell about him, the great builder passes away also, and Possidius draws for us the picture of his last days with a tenderness of touch which only a true friend could show: [4]

We talked together very frequently and discussed the tremendous judgment of God enacted under our eyes, saying, " Just art Thou, O God, and Thy judgment is righteous." Mingling our grief and groans and tears we prayed the Father of mercies and Lord of all consolation to vouchsafe to help us in our trouble. And it chanced on a day as we sat at the table with him and conversed, that he said, " Bear in mind that I am asking God in this our hour of tribulation, either to deign to deliver this town from the enemy that is investing it, or, if that seems not good to Him, to strengthen His servants to submit themselves to His will, and in any event to take me away from this world to Himself." Under his instruction it became therefore our custom thereafter, and that of all connected with us, and of those who were in the town, to join with him in such a prayer to God Almighty. And behold, in the third month of the siege, he took to his bed, afflicted with a fever; and thus fell into his last illness. Nor did the Lord disappoint His servant of the fruit of his prayer. . . . Thus did this holy man, his path prolonged by the Divine bounty for the advantage and happiness of the Church, live seventy and six years, almost forty of which were spent in the priesthood and bishopric. He had been accustomed to say to us in familiar conversation, that no baptised person, even though he were a notable Christian and a priest, should depart from the body without fitting and sufficient penitence. So he looked to this in his last sickness, of which he died. For he ordered that those few Psalms of David called Penitential should be written out, and the sheets containing them hung upon the wall where he could see them as he lay in bed, in his weakness; and as he read them he wept constantly and abundantly. And that he might not be disturbed, he asked of us who were present, some ten days before he departed from the body, that no one should come in except at those hours when the physicians visited him or when food was brought him. This wish was, of course, observed, and he thus had all his time free for prayer. Unintermittently, up to the outbreak of this last illness, he had zealously and energetically preached

[4] Chaps. xxviii. xxix. xxxi.

in the church the Word of God, with sanity of mind and soundness of judgment. And now, preserved to a good old age, sound in all the members of his body, and with unimpaired sight and hearing, and with us, as it is written, standing by and watching and praying, he fell asleep with his fathers, having been preserved to a good old age: and we offered a sacrifice to God for the peaceful repose of his body and buried him.

His library, the biography proceeds, he left to the Church; and his own books, who that reads them can fail to read in them the manner of man he was? He adds: [5]

But I think that those could profit more from him who could hear and see him speaking as he stood in the church, especially if they were not ignorant of his walk among men. For he was not merely a learned scribe in the kingdom of heaven, bringing out from his treasury things new and old, and one of those merchantmen who, having found a pearl of great price, went and sold all that he had and bought it; but he was also of those to whom it is written, " So speak and so do," and of whom the Saviour says, " Whosoever shall do and teach men thus, he shall be called great in the kingdom of heaven.

What a testimony is this to Augustine's daily life before his companions! And how pathetic is this companion's parting request of his readers:

Pray with me and for me, that I may both in this world become the emulator and imitator of this man with whom for almost forty years, by God's grace, I lived in intimacy and happiness, without any unpleasant disagreement, and in the future may enjoy with him the promises of God Almighty.

II. The " Confessions " of Augustine

It is, however, to his own " Confessions," of course, that we will turn if we would know Augustine through and through. This unique book was written about 397–400, say about a dozen years after Augustine's conversion and shortly after his ordination as bishop of Hippo — at a time when he was al-

[5] Chap. xxxi.

ready thoroughly formed in both life and thought. There is laid bare to us in it a human heart with a completeness of self-revelation probably unparalleled in literature.

Jean Jacques Rousseau, to be sure, claims this distinction for his own " Confessions." " I have entered on a performance," says he, " which is without example, whose accomplishment will have no imitator. I mean to present my fellow-mortals with a man in all the integrity of nature; and this man shall be myself." Rousseau has at least the merit of perceiving what many have not recognized, that his book cannot be considered to belong to the same class of literature with Augustine's. But what we wish now to emphasize is that even as an unveiling of the soul of a man, which it makes its sole object, Rousseau's performance falls far behind Augustine's searching pages, although, as we shall see, self-revelation was in these merely an incidental effect. The truth is, Rousseau did not see deeply enough and could not command a prospect sufficiently wide to paint all that is in man, even all that is in such a man as he essayed to portray. Quite apart from the interval that separates the two souls depicted, Rousseau's conception of self-revelation rose little above exhibiting himself with his clothes off. To his prurient imagination nakedness, certainly unadorned and all the better if it were unadorning, appeared the most poignant possible revelation of humanity. It seemed to him, essential scandal-monger that he was, that he needed but to publish on the housetop all his " adventures " to enable the whole world to say of him in the Roman proverb, *Ego te intus et in cute novi;* and he was only too pleased to believe that the world, on so seeing his inward disposition at least if not his outward life, would be convinced that it agreed well with " loose Natta's." [6] He could feel no sympathy with Augustine's cry, " I became a mighty puzzle to myself." [7] The shallow self he knew only too well absorbed his entire attention and his one engagement was in presenting this self to the gaze of the public. What lay beneath the surface he passed by with

[6] Persius, " Satt.," iii. 30.
[7] " Confessiones," iv. 4. 9.: " factus eram ipse mihi magna quæstio."

the unconsciousness of an essentially frivolous nature.[8] No wonder that an air of insincerity hangs over the picture he has drawn. There will be few readers who will easily persuade themselves that what they read all happened, or happened as it is set down; they will rather be continually haunted with the suspicion that they are perusing not a veracious autobiography but a piccaroon novel. The interval that divides the " Confessions " of Rousseau from the " Adventures of Gil Blas of Santillane " is, in any case, narrower than that which separates it from the " Confessions " of Augustine.

It must be confessed, it is true, that, if not the sincerity, at least the trustworthiness of the portrait Augustine draws of himself also has not passed wholly unquestioned. It has of late become quite the mode, indeed, to remind us that the " Confessions " were written a dozen years after the conversion up to which their narrative leads; and that in the meanwhile the preceding period of darkness had grown over-black in Augustine's eyes, and as he looked back upon it through the intervening years he saw it in distorted form and exaggerated colors.[9] His is accordingly represented as " a prominent example

---

[8] James Russell Lowell, " Prose Works," 1891, ii. p. 261: " Rousseau cries, ' I will bare my heart to you! ' and throwing open his waistcoat, makes us the confidants of his dirty linen."

[9] See, e.g., Boissier, " La Fin du Paganisme," i. p. 293; Harnack, " Monasticism and the Confessions of Augustine," pp. 132, 141; Reuter, " Augustinische Studien," p. 4; Loofs, Herzog " Realencyklopädie für protestantische Theologie und Kirche," [3] ii. pp. 260–261, and especially pp. 266–267. Cf. also Gourdon, " Essai sur la Conversion de Saint Augustin," Cahors, 1900. R. Schmid in an article entitled " Zur Bebehrungsgeschichte Augustins " in the *Zeitschrift für Theologie und Kirche*, 1897, vii. pp. 80–96, has made the fact and extent of failure of the " Confessions" in trustworthiness the subject of a special study. No one doubts, he remarks, the subjective sincerity of the " Confessions"; and its objective trustworthiness can come into question only in minutiæ. The conclusion at which he arrives is that only in two points are the " Confessions " open to correction in their representation. Augustine was not led to give up his professorship by his conversion, but these two things fell together only by accident; and he still wished after conversion for a comfortable life, an *otium cum dignitate,* and loved to teach. " Thus in reality there remains, so far as the ' Confessions' do not correct themselves — that is, permit the history to be seen through the veil of later reflections thrown over it — very little over. But even a little is, here, much. . . . In the main matter, however, the ' Con-

of a tendency frequently found in religionists of an effusive type, to exaggerate their infirmities in order to enhance their merits in having escaped them, or by way of contrasting present attainment with former unworthiness, just as a successful merchant sometimes boasts that he began his career with only sixpence in his pocket." [10] We are warned, therefore, not to take his descriptions of his youthful errors and of his fruitless wanderings in search of truth at the foot of the letter. A recent writer, for example, condemns all current biographies of Augustine because, as he says, they "all are constructed on the perverse type which is followed by Augustine himself in his seductive 'Confessions,'" in which he "is sternly bent on magnifying his misdeeds." Blinded by "the glare of his new ideal," as leading ecclesiastic and theologian of the West, his psychic perspective was foreshortened and he hopelessly misrepresented his unregenerate youth. "The truth seems to be," we are told, "that the book is a kind of theological treatise and work of edification. The Bishop of Hippo takes the rhetorician as an 'awful example' of nature without God. To point his dogmatic antithesis of nature and grace, philosophy and Christianity, nothing could be more forceful than his own career painted as darkly as conscience would permit. . . . But the fallacy of it all for us, reducing its value as a human document, is that Augustine examines his earlier life from a false point of view." [11]

Despite the modicum of truth resident in the recognition by the writer last quoted that the book is not formally an autobiography, but, as he terms it, "a kind of theological treatise and work of edification," this whole representation is fundamentally wrong. The judgment that Augustine passed on the misdeeds not merely, but the whole course, of his youth was

---

fessions' remain in the right — that it was a revolutionary inward experience, which brought him completely into the road on which he sought and found God and himself" (p. 96).

[10] See John Owen, "Evenings with the Sceptics," ii. p. 139.

[11] Joseph McCabe, "St. Augustine and His Age," pp. v., 24, 39, 41, 54, 69, 70, 195–198.

naturally essentially different at the time when he wrote his
" Confessions " from what it had been during the life which is
passed in review in them. He does not leave us to infer this —
he openly declares it; or rather it is precisely this change of
judgment which it is one of the chief purposes of the " Confessions " to signalize. We could hardly ask a man after he has
escaped from what he has come to look upon as the sty to write
of his mode of life in it from the point of view of one who loves
to wallow in the mire. It is, however, something very like this
that is suggested by our critics as the ideal of autobiographical
narration. At least we read: " About the year 400, when they
[the " Confessions "] were written, Augustine had arrived at a
most lofty conception of duty and life; he commits the usual
and inevitable fallacy of taking this later standard back to il-
lumine the ground of his early career. In the glare of his new
ideal, actions which probably implied no moral resistance at
the time they were performed, cast an appalling shadow." [12]
And again: " There is no trace in the ' Confessions ' that his
conscience had anything to say at the time." [13]

Surely there is laid here a most unreasonable requirement
upon the historian. We may or may not accord with the judgment that Augustine passes upon his early life. We may or
may not consider that he who takes his knowledge of Augustine's youth from the " Confessions " must guard himself from
accepting from them also the judgment they pass on the course
of that youth as well as on the separate events that entered
into it. For example, we may or may not believe that Augustine was right in attributing the passions of anger and jealousy manifesting themselves in infancy to the movements of
inherent corruption derived from our first parents, or in representing the childish escapade of robbing a pear tree as an exhibition of a pure love of evil, native in men as men. But any
such differences of moral standpoint of which we may be conscious, between ourselves and the Augustine who wrote the
" Confessions," are one thing; and the trustworthiness of the
record he has given us, whether of the external occurrences of

[12] *Op. cit.,* p. 24.   [13] *Ibid.,* p. 41.

his youth or of the inner movements of his soul during that period of restless search, which knew no rest because it had not yet found rest in God, is quite another thing. It is not merely the transparent sincerity of the " Confessions" which impresses every reader; it is the close and keen observation, the sound and tenacious memory, the sane and searching analysis that equally characterize them. " Observation, indeed," says Harnack, with eminent justice, " is the strong point of Augustine. . . . What is *characteristic* never escapes him " — and that is especially true of the secret movements of the heart.[14] The reader feels himself in the hands of a narrator not only whose will but whose capacity as well both to see and to tell the truth he cannot doubt. There is spread over the whole the evidence no more of the most absolute good faith than of the utmost care to distinguish between fact and opinion — between what really was and what the writer could wish had been. You may think " there is a morbid strain in the book"; you may accuse its author of "making a stage-play of his bleeding heart "; you may judge him " in many places overstrained, unhealthy, or even false." [15] All this will depend on the degree in which you feel yourself in sympathy with his standpoint. But " there is a look of intense reality on every page," as a careful student has put it; [16] and as you read you cannot doubt that here is not merely a sincere but a true record of the experiences of a soul, which you may — nay, must — trust as such without reserve.

It is important, however, in order that we may appraise the book properly, to apprehend somewhat more exactly than perhaps is common precisely what Augustine proposed to himself in it. It is inadequate to speak of it simply either broadly as an autobiography, or more precisely as a *vie intime*. Not to emphasize just here the decisive consideration that only nine of

[14] *Op. cit.,* pp. 128, 131. Cf. also T. R. Glover, " Life and Letters in the Fourth Century," p. 195.

[15] Harnack, *op. cit.,* p. 132.

[16] A. F. West, " Roman Autobiography, Particularly Augustine's Confessions," in *The Presbyterian and Reformed Review,* xii. No. 46 (April 1901) p. 183.

its thirteen books have any biographical content, it lies quite on the face of the narrative that even the biographical material provided .in these nine books is not given with a purely biographical intent. Augustine is not the proper subject either of the work as a whole, or even of those portions of it in which his life-history is depicted. What he tells us about himself, full and rich and searching as it is, nevertheless is incidental to another end than self-portraiture, and is determined both in its selection and in its mode of treatment by this end. In sending a copy of the book, almost a generation later, to a distinguished and admiring friend who had asked him for it, he does indeed speak of it frankly as a mirror in which he himself could be seen; and, be it duly noted, he affirms that he is to be seen in this mirror truly, just as he was. " Accept," he writes to his correspondent [17] — " accept the books of my Confessions which you have asked for. Behold me therein, that you may not praise me above what I am. Believe there not others about me, but me myself, and see by means of myself what I was in myself; and if there is anything in me that pleases you, praise with me there Him whom I wish to be praised for me — for that One is not myself. Because it is He that made us and not we ourselves; nay, we have destroyed ourselves, but He that made us has remade us. And when you find me there, pray for me that I be not defective but perfected." Similarly in his " Retractations," [18] he says simply that the first ten books were " written about himself "; but he does not fail to declare also of the whole thirteen that " they praise the just and good God with respect both of his evil and his good and excite the human intellect and affection toward Him." This, he says, was their effect on himself as he wrote them, and this has been their effect on those that have read them.

From such passages as these we perceive how Augustine uniformly thought of his " Confessions " — not as a biography of himself, but, as we have commended a rather blind com-

[17] " Epist." 231, to Count Darius (§ 6).
[18] ii. 6: " a primo usque ad decimum de me scripti sunt."

mentator for seeing, rather as a book of edification, or, if you will, a theological treatise. His actual subject is not himself, but the goodness of God; and he introduces his own experiences only as the most lively of illustrations of the dealings of God with the human soul as He makes it restless until it finds its rest in Him. Such being the case the congeners of the book are not to be found in simple autobiographies even of the most introspective variety. The " Confessions " of Rousseau, of Hamann, of Alfred de Musset — such books have so little in common with it that they do not belong even in the same literary class with it. Even the similarity of their titles to its is an accident. For Augustine does not use the term " Confessions " here in the debased sense in which these writers use it; the sense of unveiling, uncovering to the sight of the world what were better perhaps hidden from all eyes but God's which see all things; but in that higher double sense in which we may speak of confessing the grace of God and our humble dependence on Him, a sense compounded of mingled humility and praise.

The real analogues of Augustine's " Confessions " are to be found not then in introspective biographies whose sole purpose is to depict a human soul, but in such accounts of spiritual experiences as are given us in books like John Newton's " Authentic Narrative," although the scope of this particular narrative is too narrow to furnish a perfect analogy. At the head of his narrative Newton has written this text: " Thou shalt remember all the way, by which the Lord thy God led thee through this wildness "; and the same text might equally well be written at the head of Augustine's " Confessions." We might almost fancy we hear Augustine explaining his own purpose when we hear Newton declaring that with him it was a question " only concerning the patience and long-suffering of God, the wonderful interposition of His providence in favor of an unworthy sinner, the power of His grace in softening the hardest heart, and the riches of His mercy in pardoning the most enormous and aggravated transgressions." Perhaps, however, the closest analogy to Augustine's " Confessions," among books, at least, which have attained anything like the same popular influence, is furnished by John Bunyan's " Grace Abounding to the Chief of Sinners." Bunyan's purpose is precisely the same as Augustine's — to glorify the grace of God. He employs also the same means of securing this end — an autobiographical account of the dealings of God with his soul. " In this relation of the merciful working of God upon my soul," says Bunyan, " it will not be amiss if, in the first place, I do, in a few words, give you a hint of my pedigree and manner of bringing up; that thereby the goodness and bounty of God toward me may be the more advanced and magnified before the sons of men." Just so Augustine, also, gave what he gave of " his pedigree and manner of bringing up"; and what he gave of his youthful wanderings in error and in sin; and what he gave of his struggles to find and grasp, to grasp and cling to what of good he saw and loved: only that " the goodness and bounty of God toward him might be the more advanced and magnified before the sons of men." We have said that the interval that divides Rousseau's " Confessions " from the " Adventures of Gil Blas of Santillane," is less than that which separates them from Augustine's. We may now say that the interval that divides Augustine's " Confessions " from the " Pilgrim's Progress " is less than that which separates them from any simple autobiography — veracious and searching autobiography though a great portion of it is. For the whole concernment of the book is with the grace of God to a lost sinner. It is this, and not himself, that is its theme.

This fundamental fact is, of course, written large over the whole work, and comes not rarely to explicit assertion. " I wish to record my past foulnesses and the carnal corruptions of my soul," says Augustine, " not because I love them, but in order that I may love Thee, O my God. For love of Thy love do I do this thing, — recollecting my most vicious ways in the bitterness of my remembrance, that Thou mayest become my Joy, Thou never-failing Joy, Thou blessed and sacred Joy; and collecting myself from the dissipation in which I was torn to pieces, when turned from Thee, the One, I was lost among the many." [19] " To whom do I relate this? . . . And why? Just that I and whosoever may read this may consider out of what depths we are to cry unto Thee. And what is nearer to Thy ears than a confessing heart and a life of faith? " [20] " Accept the sacrifice of my confessions from the hand of my tongue which Thou didst form and hast prompted that it may confess to Thy name. Heal all my bones and let them say, Lord, who is like unto Thee? . . . Let my soul praise Thee that it may love Thee, and let it confess to Thee Thy mercies that it may praise Thee." [21] " Why, then, do I array before Thee the narrations of so many things? . . . That I may excite my affection toward Thee, and that of those who read these things, so that we all may say, ' Great is the Lord and highly to be praised.' " [22] In these last words we observe that as he approaches the end of the book, he is still bearing in mind the words which he set at its beginning; [23] and by thus reverting to the beginning, he binds the whole together as one great volume of praise to the Lord for His goodness to him in leading him to His salvation. Accordingly he adds at once: " Therefore, we are manifesting our affection to Thee, in confessing to Thee our miseries and Thy mercies toward us, in order that Thou mayest deliver us altogether since Thou hast made a beginning, and we may cease to be miserable in ourselves and become blessed in Thee, since Thou hast called us to be poor in spirit, and meek and mourners, and hungerers, and thirsters after righteousness, and merciful and pure in heart and peacemakers." [24] Here the theme of the " Confessions " is clearly set before us. It is the ineffable goodness of God, which is illustrated by what He has done for Augustine's miserable soul, in delivering it from its sins and distresses and bringing it out into the largeness of the divine life and knowledge.

It is, obviously, only from this point of view that the unity of the book becomes apparent. For we must not fancy that

[19] ii. 1. 1.
[20] ii. 3. 5.
[21] v. 1. 1.

[22] xi. 1. 1.
[23] i. 1. 1.
[24] xi. 1. 1.

when Augustine has brought to a completion the narrative of the wonderful dealings of God with him, by which he was led to repentance, he has ended his " confessions "; to which he attaches the last four books therefore purely mechanically, without any rational bond of connection with their predecessors. To his consciousness, throughout the whole extent of these books, he continues to sound the voice of his confessions: and if we search in them for it we shall find the same note ringing in them as in the others. " Behold," he cries,[25] " Thy voice is my joy: Thy voice surpasses the abundance of pleasures. . . . Let me confess unto Thee whatsoever I have found in Thy books, and let me hear the voice of praise and drink Thee in and consider the wonderful things of Thy law, even from the beginning, in the which Thou didst make the heaven and the earth, down to the everlasting kingdom of Thy Holy City, that is with Thee." Not the least of the mercies that Augustine wished to confess to God that he had received from His hand was the emancipation of His intellect, and the freeing of his mind from the crudities with which it had been stuffed; and it is this confession that he makes, with praises on his lips, in these concluding books. The construction of the work, then, is something like the following: first Augustine recounts how God has dealt with him in bringing him to salvation (books i.–ix.); then what he has under the divine grace become, as a saved child of God (book x.); and finally what reaches of sound and satisfying knowledge have been granted to him in the divine revelation (books xi.–xiii.): and all to the praise of the glory of His grace. Body, heart, mind, all were made for God: all were incited to seek Him and to praise Him: and all were restless, therefore, until at last they found their rest in Him. Elsewhere than in Him had happiness, peace, knowledge been sought, but nowhere else had they been found. The proud was cast down: and he that exalted himself inevitably fell. But they whose exaltation God becomes — they fall not any more forever. This is the concluding word of the " Confessions."

[25] xi. 2. 3, *ad fin.*

Only in proportion as this, the true character of the book, is apprehended, moreover, does its true originality become evident. Even were it possible to think of it merely as an introspective autobiography, it would no doubt be epoch-making in the history of literary form. In an interesting paper on " Roman Autobiography," [26] Prof. A. F. West points out that this species of composition was especially Roman. " Autobiography, as well as satire," he remarks, " should be credited to the Romans as their own independent invention." " The appearance of Augustine's 'Confessions,' in 399 or 400," he continues, " dates the entrance of a new kind of autobiography into Latin literature — the autobiography of introspection, the self-registered record of the development of a human soul." It was characteristic of Augustine's genius that, in a purely incidental use of it, he invented an entirely new literary form and carried it at a stroke to its highest development. No wonder that Harnack falls into something like enthusiasm over this accomplishment.

The significance of the " Confessions," says he, " is as great on the side of form as on that of content. Before all, they were a literary achievement. No poet, no philosopher before him undertook what he here performed; and I may add that almost a thousand years had to pass before a similar thing was done. It was the poets of the Renascence, who formed themselves on Augustine, that first gained from his example the daring to depict themselves and to present their personality to the world. For what do the " Confessions " of Augustine contain? The portrait of a soul — not psychological disquisitions on the Understanding, the Will, and the Emotions in Man, not abstract investigations into the nature of the soul, not superficial reasonings and moralizing introspections like the " Meditations " of Marcus Aurelius, but the most exact portraiture of a distinct human personality, in his development from childhood to full age, with all his propensities, feelings, aims, mistakes; a portrait of a soul, in fact, drawn with a perfection of observation that leaves on one side the mechanical devices of psychology, and pursues the methods of the physician and the physiologist.[27]

[26] *Presbyterian and Reformed Review*, xii. No. 46 (April, 1901), p. 183.
[27] *Op. cit.*, pp. 127–128.

Obviously Harnack is thinking of the first nine books only. Otherwise he could scarcely speak so absolutely of the absence from the "Confessions" of "psychological disquisitions." For what is the great discourse on "Memory," embodied in the tenth book, but a psychological disquisition of the most penetrating kind, to say nothing now of the analysis of the idea of "Time," broached in the eleventh book? The achievement which he signalizes is, therefore, only part of the achievement of the book, and if Augustine in it has incidentally become the father of all those who have sought to paint the portrait of a human soul, what must be said of the originality of his performance when understood in its real peculiarity — as the dramatic portraiture of the dealing of divine grace with a sinful soul in leading it through all its devious wanderings into the harbor of salvation? Not in the poets of the Renascence — not even in Goethe's "Faust" in which Harnack strangely seeks the nearest literary parallel to the "Confessions" — can it now find its tardy successors. We must come down to the Reformation — perhaps to the "second Reformation" as the men of the seventeenth century loved to call their own times, and after that to that almost third Revolution which was wrought by the "Evangelical Revival" or "Great Awakening" — before we discover its real successors; and we must look through all the years, perhaps in vain, to find any successor worthy to be placed on a level with it.

We must avoid exaggeration, however, even with respect to the novelty of the book. Perhaps if we eliminate the question of value and think merely of the literary species which it so uniquely represents, it can scarcely be said that Augustine's performance was absolutely without forerunners, or remained absolutely without successors "for a thousand years." The greatness of its shining may blind our eyes unduly to lesser points of light, which, except for the glare of its brilliancy, might be seen to stud the heavens about it. A recent writer, for example, claims for a tractate of Cyprian's — the treatise or letter "To Donatus" — the honor of having pointed out the way in which Augustine afterward walked. He says:

Finally,[28] a great novelty appears in this little book. The pages on the conversion of Cyprian, which mark almost the advent of a new species of literature, directly herald the "Confessions" of St. Augustine. For a long time, a very profane manner of life, a passionate taste for pleasure, along with a sort of instinctive defiance of Christianity; subsequently, up to the very eve of the decisive event, incapacity to believe in the renewal promised in baptism, a very clear perception of the obstacles which a life so worldly opposed to so sudden a revolution; then, after many hesitations, grace, as startling as a clap of thunder, revolutionizing the whole being in its profoundest depths, to turn it toward a new destiny; and in the recollection left by this miraculous transformation, a fixed determination to refer all to God, to turn confession into acts of thankfulness: such are in Cyprian the essential traits that mark the steps of conversion. And these are precisely the ideas that dominate the "Confessions" of Augustine.

In effect, we have in this affected, mincing tract of Cyprian's, hidden as its lessons well-nigh are under the shadow of its rhetorical virtuosity, what may be called the beginnings of the Autobiography of Conversion — unless we prefer to penetrate yet a hundred years further back and see its beginnings in the beautiful description with which Justin Martyr opens his "Dialogue with Trypho" of how he found his way through philosophy to Christ. Both narratives have much in their substance that is fitted to remind of Augustine's. But both are too brief; the one is too objective and the other too affected; neither is sufficiently introspective or sufficiently searching to justify their inclusion in the same class with their great successor. A better claim, many will think, might be put in for the spiritual history which Hilary of Poictiers gives of his own former life in the splendid Latin of the first fifteen sections of his treatise "On the Faith" or, as it is commonly called, "On the Trinity." It is the story of a naturally noble soul, seeking and gradually finding more and more perfectly the proper aim of life as it rises to the knowledge first of the God of philosophy and then of the God of revelation, and ulti-

28 Monceaux, "Hist. Lit. de l'Afrique Chrét.," II., "S. Cyprien et son temps," p. 266.

mately attains assured faith in the God and Father of our
Lord Jesus Christ. Did it not move so exclusively on the intellectualistic plane, without depth of experimental coloring, its
dignity of language and high eloquence might, despite its brevity, justify us in esteeming it no unworthy forerunner of the
" Confessions."

Such predecessors, interesting as they are and valuable as
marking the channels in which the new Christian literature
naturally flowed, can hardly be thought of as having opened
the way for Augustine — partly because their motive is too
primarily autobiographical. Similarly he had few immediate
successors who can be said to follow closely in his steps. Perhaps the " Eucharisticos Deo " of Paulinus of Pella — in which
he essays to praise God for His preservation of him and for
His numerous kindnesses through a long and eventful life —
may not unfairly be considered a typical instance of such
spiritual autobiographies as the next age produced. This poem
is assuredly not uninteresting, and to the student of manners
it has its own importance; but as a history of a soul it lacks
nearly everything that gives to the " Confessions " their charm.
That some resemblance should be discernible between the
picture Augustine draws of his life and that which such writers
draw of their own was unavoidable, since he and they were
alike men and Christians and were prepared to thank God
for making them both. But the resemblance ends very much
at that point. The sublime depths and heights of Augustine
and all that has made him the teacher of the world in this
his most individual book is wanting, as well in his successors
as in his predecessors. He had to wait for Bunyan before there
was written another such spiritual " autobiography," or to be
more precise, another such history of God's dealings with a
soul: and even the " Grace Abounding " stands beside the
" Confessions " only *longe intervallo*.

The attractiveness of the " Confessions " obviously lurks,
not in its style, but in its matter — or rather in the personality
that lies behind both style and matter and gives unity, freshness, depth, brilliancy to both matter and style. Harnack is

quite right when he remarks that the key to the enduring influence of the book is found in the fact that we meet a person in it — a person " everywhere richer than his expression ": [29] that we feel a heart beating behind its words and perceive that this is a great heart, to whose beating we cannot but attend. Nevertheless the form of the " Confessions " is itself not without its fascination, and its very style has also its allurement. His rhetorical training had entered, to be sure, into Augustine's very substance and the false taste with which he had been imbued had become a second nature with him. Even in such heart-throes as express themselves in this book, he could not away with the frivolous word-plays, affected assonances, elaborate balancing of clauses and the like that form the hallmark of the sophistic rhetoric of the times. It has been remarked that " rhetorician as Augustine was, and master of several styles, he had a curious power of dropping his rhetoric when he undertook in homilies and commentaries to interpret Scripture." [30] Unfortunately, he also had a curious facility of dropping into offensive rhetorical tricks in the midst of the most serious discussions, or the most moving revelations of feeling. Apart from these occasional lapses — if lapses so frequent can be called occasional — the very form given this book as a sustained address to God is wearisome to many. M. Boissier [31] remarks that the transports and effusions with which Augustine addresses himself to God " end by seeming to us monotonous." Harnack thinks the book too long and too alien to modern thought ever to enter into really literary use in its entirety: and therefore welcomes the preparation of abridgements of it. [32] Prof. West [33] finds in it " ineptitudes and infelicities " which can be expected to shrink and permit " the central power " of the book to appear only for him who reads it in its original Latin. The merely English reader, he remarks, can

[29] *Op. cit.*, i. p. 136.

[30] E. W. Watson, *Classical Review*, February, 1901, p. 65, quoted in Glover, *op. cit.*, p. 195, note.

[31] *Op. cit.*, p. 292.

[32] *Theolog. Literaturzeitung*, 1903, No. 1, 12.

[33] As cited, pp. 184–185.

scarcely hope to find it very interesting. "The unchecked rhetoric, the reiterated calls on God, varied and wearisome, the shrewd curiosity in hunting down subtleties to their last hiding-places, the streaks of inane allegorizing,[34] and sometimes the violent bursts of feeling, — these are the things that frighten away readers and prevent them from reaching the real delights of the book."

It is difficult to draw up a catalogue of such defects without exaggeration: and in the present case an exaggerated impression, both with respect to quantity and quality, is almost certain to be conveyed. After all said, the "Confessions" are an eminently well and winningly written book. There is even in the mere style a certain poetic quality that gives it not merely character but beauty. Harnack justly speaks of "the lyricism of the style." There is certainly present in it, as Dr. Bigg points out,[35] something of "the same musical flow, the same spiritual refinement and distinction" that characterizes the "Imitation of Christ." It is not, indeed, as Dr. Bigg justly adds, either "so compact or so highly polished" as the "Imitation of Christ": "St. Augustine cannot give the time to cut each word as if it were an individual diamond, as a Kempis did." But Augustine more than compensates for this deficiency in preciosity by his greater richness, depth, and variety. There is nothing effeminate in Augustine's style, nothing over-filed, nothing cloying or wearisome. Here, too, indeed, it is true, as it generally is, that the style is the man. And Augustine is never an uninteresting person to meet, even through the medium of the written, or even of the translated, page. No more individual writer ever lived: and the individuality which was his was not only powerful and impressive, but to an almost unexampled degree profound, rich, and attractive. Harnack is right; the charm of the "Confessions" is that they are Augustine's and that he draws his readers into his life by

[34] Are these found to any appreciable extent outside the Thirteenth Book?

[35] Introduction to his version, published in Methuen's series, called the "Library of Devotion," 3d ed., 1900, p. 5.

them. Here are reflected, as in a mirror, the depth and tenderness of his ardent nature, the quickness and mobility of his emotions and yet, underlying all, his sublime repose. He who reads shares the conflicts and the turmoils depicted: but he enters also into the rest the writer has found with God.

It is in this fact that the unique attractiveness of the book as a " work of edification " resides — an attractiveness which has made it through a millennium and a half the most widely read of all books written in Latin, with the possible exception of the " Æneid " of Virgil.[36] He who reads these pages enters as in none other into the struggles of a great soul as it fights its way to God, shares with it all its conflict, and participates at last with it in the immensity of its repose. As he reads, that great sentence that sounds the keynote of the book and echoes through all its pages, echoes also in his soul: " Thou hast made us for Thyself, O Lord, and our heart is restless till it finds its rest in Thee." The agonizing cry becomes his also, " O by Thy loving-kindness, tell me, O Lord my God, what Thou art to me: say unto my soul, *I am thy Salvation.*" And there likewise becomes his the childlike prattle of the same soul, stilled in praise now that it has found God its salvation, as it names over to itself as its dearest possession the sweet names by which its God has become precious to it, " O Lord, my God, my Light, my Wealth, my Salvation! " What is apt to escape us who have, after so many years, entered into the heritage which Augustine has won for us is that it was really he who won it for us — that in these groans and tears into which we so readily enter with him as we read, and in this hard-earned rest in God into which we so easily follow him, he was breaking out a pathway not only for his own but for our feet. For here is the astonishing fact that gives its supreme significance to this book: it is the earliest adequate expression of that type of religion which has since attached to itself the name of " evangelical "; and, though the earliest, it is one of the fullest, richest, and most perfect expressions of this type of religion

[36] Glover, *op. cit.*, p. 195.

which has ever been written. Adolf Harnack, realizing the immense significance of the appearance in Augustine of this new type of religion, consecrates a whole chapter in his " History of Dogma " to " The Historical Position of Augustine as Reformer of Christian Piety," as a preparation for the due exposition of his doctrinal teaching. In this chapter he makes many true and striking remarks; but he hardly exhibits a just appreciation of the intimate relation which subsists between Augustine's peculiar type of piety and his peculiar type of doctrine. Harnack, in fact, speaks almost as if it were conceivable that one of these could have come into existence apart from the other. The truth is, of course, that they are but the joint products in the two spheres of life and thought of the same body of conceptions, and neither could possibly have arisen without the other. If before Augustine alternating hope and fear were the characteristic sentiments of Christians and the psychological form of their piety was therefore unrest, while in Augustine the place of hope and fear is taken by trust and love, and unrest gives way to profound rest in God, this was because pre-Augustinian Christianity was prevailingly legalistic, and there entered into it a greater or less infusion of the evil leaven of self-salvation, while Augustine, with his doctrine of grace, cast himself wholly on the mercy of God, and so, as the poet expresses it,

> Turned fear and hope to love of God.
> Who loveth us.

The fact of the matter is that pre-Augustinian Christian thinking was largely engrossed with Theological and Christological problems and with Augustine first did Christian Soteriology begin to come to its rights. It was not he first, of course, who discovered that man is a sinner and therefore depends for his salvation on the grace of God; but in him first did these fundamental Christian truths find a soil in which they could come to their richest fruitage in heart and life, in thought and teaching. And here lies the secret of his profound realization (on which Harnack lays so much stress) that Christian happiness consists in "comforted remorse" (getrösteter Sünden-schmerz).[37] Before him men were prone to conceive them-selves essentially God's creatures, whose business it was to commend themselves to their Maker: no doubt they recognized that they had sinned, and that provision had been made to relieve them of the penalty of their sins; but they built their real hope of acceptance in God's sight more or less upon their own conduct. Augustine realized to the bottom of his soul that he was a sinner and what it is to be a sinner, and therefore sought at God's hands not acceptance but salvation. And this is the reason why he never thought of God without thinking of sin and never thought of sin without thinking of Christ. Be-cause he took his sin seriously, his thought and feeling alike traveled continually in this circle, and could not but travel in this circle. He thus was constantly verifying afresh the truth of the Savior's declaration that he to whom little is forgiven loves little, while he loves much who is conscious of having received much forgiveness: and as his trust increased and his love grew ever greater he realized better and better also that other saying that there is joy in heaven over one sinner that repents more than over ninety and nine righteous persons which need no repentance. So he came to understand that the heights of joy are scaled only by him who has first been miser-able, and that the highest happiness belongs only to him who has been the object of salvation. Self-despair, humble trust, grateful love, fullness of joy — these are the steps on which his own soul climbed upward: and these steps gave their whole color and form both to his piety and to his teaching. In his doctrine we see his experience of God's seeking and saving love toward a lost sinner expressing itself in propositional form; in his piety we see his conviction that the sole hope of the sinner lies in the free grace of a loving God expressing itself in the forms of feeling. In doctrine and life alike he sets before us in that effective way which belongs to the discoverer, the religion of faith as over against the religion of works — the religion

[37] "Lehrbuch der Dogmengeschichte," iii. p. 59; E. T. "History of Dogma," v. p. 66.

which despairing of self casts all its hope on God as over against the religion that to a greater or less degree trusts in itself: in a word, since religion in its very nature is dependence on God, religion in the purity of its conception as over against a quasi-religious moralism. It is to the fact that in this book we are admitted into the very life of Augustine and are permitted to see his great heart cleansing itself of all trust in himself and laying hold with the grasp first of despair, then of discerning trust and then of grateful love upon the God who was his salvation, that the "Confessions" owe their perennial attractiveness and their supreme position among books of edification. In them Augustine uncovers his heart and lets us see what religion is in its essence as it works in the soul of one who has, as few have, experienced its power. He has set himself determinedly in this book to exhibit the grace of God in action. Elsewhere he has expounded it in theory, defended it against its assailants, enforced it with logical argument and moving exhortation. Here he shows it at work, and at work in his own soul.

It was only in his effort to show us the grace of God as it worked upon his own soul, that Augustine was led to set before us his life-history through all the formative years of his career — until, after long wandering, he at last had found his rest in God. This is the meaning and this is the extent of the autobiographical element in the "Confessions." Nine of the thirteen books are devoted to this religious analysis of his life-history; and although, of course, the matter admitted and its treatment alike are determined by the end in view, yet Augustine's analysis is very searching and the end in view involves a very complete survey of all that was especially determining in his life-development. In these pages we can see, therefore, just what Augustine was, and just how he became what he became. And the picture, almost extreme in its individuality as it is, is nevertheless as typical as it is individual. It is typical of the life of the ancient world at its best: for in his comprehensive nature Augustine had gathered up into himself and given full play to all that was good in the culture of the ancient world. And it is typical of what Christian experience is at its best: for in Augustine there met in unusual fullness and fought themselves out to a finish all the fundamental currents of thought and feeling that strive together in the human heart when it is invaded by divine grace, and is slowly but surely conquered by it to good and to God. It may repay us to run over the salient elements in this life-history as here depicted for us.

III. The Augustine of the "Confessions"

Augustine came into being at the "turn of the ages," just as the old world was dying, and the new was being born. He was the offspring of a mixed marriage, itself typical of the mixed state of the society of the times. His father, a citizen of importance but of straitened means, in a small African town, remained a heathen until his gifted son had attained his middle youth: [38] he appears to have been a man of generally jovial disposition, liable to fits of violent temper, possessing neither intellectual endowments nor moral attainments to distinguish him from the mass of his contemporaries: but he appreciated the promise of his son, and was prepared to make sacrifices that opportunity might be given for his development. His mother, on the other hand, was one of nature's noblewomen, whose naturally fine disposition had been further beautified by grace. Bred a Christian from her infancy, her native sensibility had been heightened by a warm piety: and her clear and quick intellect had been illuminated by an equally firm and direct conscience. Under her teaching her son was imbued from his infancy with a sense of divine things which never permitted him to forget that there is a God who governs all things and who is unchangeably good, or to find satisfaction in any teaching in which the name of Jesus Christ was not honored. He thus grew up in the nurture of the Lord,[39] but with the divided mind

[38] He became a catechumen shortly before Augustine's sixteenth year ("Confessiones," ii. 3. 6. Cf. ix. 9. 22). He died soon afterward.

[39] Cf. "De duabus anim.," i. 1: "The seeds of the true religion wholesomely implanted in me from boyhood."

which almost inevitably results from the divided counsels of a mixed parentage.

As his gifts more and more exhibited themselves worldly ambition took the helm and every nerve was strained to advance him in his preparation for a great career. His early piety, which had been exhibited in frequent prayer as a schoolboy [40] and in an ardent desire for baptism during an attack of dangerous illness,[41] more and more fell away from him, and left him, with his passionate temperament inherited from his father, a prey to youthful vices. An interval of idleness at home, in his sixteenth year (A.D. 370), brought him his great temptation, and he fell into evil ways; and these were naturally continued when, to complete his education, he went next year up to Carthage, that great and wicked city. But this period of unclean life was happily of short duration, lasting at the most only a couple of years. By the time Augustine had reached his seventeenth birthday (autumn of 371) we find him already attached to her who was to be the companion of his life for the next fourteen years, in a union which, though not marriage in the highest sense, differed from technical marriage rather in a legal than in a moral point of view. Though he himself, later at least, did not look upon such a union as true marriage,[42] it was esteemed its equivalent not only in the best heathen society of the time, but even in certain portions of the Church, perhaps up to his own day by the entire Church; [43] and it served to screen him from the multitudinous temptations to vice that

[40] "Confessiones," i. 9. 14: "For even as a boy I began to pray to Thee, my Help and my Refuge; to call upon Thee I burst the bonds of my tongue and prayed to Thee — child as I was, how passionately! — that I might not be flogged at school."　　[41] "Confessiones," i. 11.

[42] "Confessiones," iv. 2. 2.: "One not joined to me in lawful wedlock"; x. 30. 41: "Thou hast commanded me to abstain from concubinage." Cf. "Apost. Constt.," viii. 32: "A believer who has a concubine — if she be a slave, let him cease, and take a wife legitimately: if she be free, let him take her as his legitimate wife; and if he does not, let him be rejected."

[43] Cf. the canons of the Council of Toledo of 400, can. 17: "Only let him be content with one woman, whether wife or concubine." Cf. Herzog, "Realencyclopädie für protestantische Theologie und Kirche [3]," x. p. 746, and The Princeton Theological Review, i. No. 2 (April, 1903), pp. 309–10.

otherwise would have beset him. " I was faithful to her,"
he says.[44]

It was an overmastering and lofty ambition, not fleshly lust,
that constituted the real power in his life, and these years of
preparation at Carthage were years of strenuous labor, during
which Augustine was ever growing toward his higher ideals.
Already in his nineteenth year (373) he was incited to lay
aside his lower ambitions by the reading of a book of Cicero's,
since lost,[45] which had been designed to inflame the heart of
the reader with a love of philosophy and which wrought so
powerfully on Augustine that he resolved at once to make pure
truth thenceforward the sole object of his pursuit.[46] During
this whole period he must be believed to have remained nomi-
nally Christian; and perhaps we may suppose him to have continued in the formal position of a catechumen.[47]

He seems to have been a frequenter of the Church services,[48]
and he speaks of himself as having been during this time under
the dominance of " a certain puerile superstition " which held
him back from the pursuit of truth.[49] Accordingly, when the
" Hortensius " stirred his heart to seek wisdom and yet left him
unsatisfied, because the name of Jesus which, as he says, he
had " sucked in with his mother's milk," was not mentioned in
it, he turned to the Scriptures in apparently the first earnest
effort to seek their guidance he had made since his earliest
youth. But the lowly Scriptures — especially as read in the
rough Old Latin Version — had nothing to offer to the finical
rhetorician, and his eyes were holden that he could not penetrate their meaning: he was offended by their servant-form
and — seeking wisdom, not salvation — turned from them in
disgust. He had reached a crisis in his life, and the result was
that he formally broke with Christianity.

[46] Cf. especially " Solil.," iv. 2. 2. 17.

[45] His " Hortensius."   [46] Cf. especially " Solil." iv. 2. 2. 17.

[47] " De utilitate credendi," i. 2: " sed de me quid dicam, qui iam catholicus
christianus eram? "

[48] " Confessiones," iii. 3. 5. According to " Contra Epist. Manich. Fundam,"
viii. 9, ad fin., he had been accustomed to enjoy the Easter festival and missed
it sadly when he became a Manichæan.   [49] " De beata vita," 4.

It was eminently characteristic of Augustine both that throughout his years of indulgence and indifference he had maintained his connection with the Church, and that he broke with it when, having sloughed off his grosser inclinations, he turned to it in vain for the satisfaction of his higher aspirations. Essential idealist that he was, throughout the years in which he was entangled in lower aims the Church had stood for him as a promise of better things: now he felt that his spirit soared above all it had to offer him. But in breaking with the Church, he could not break with his conception of God as the good Governor of the world, nor with his devotion to the name of Jesus Christ. So he threw himself into the arms of the Manichæans. The Manichæans were the rationalists of the day. Professing the highest reverence for Christ and continually bearing His name on their lips, they yet set forth, under his cloak, a purely naturalistic system. The negative side of their teaching included a most drastic criticism of the Christian Scriptures, while on the positive side they built up a doctrine of God which seemed to separate Him effectually from all complicity with evil, and a doctrine of man which relieved the conscience of all sense of unworthiness and responsibility for sin, while yet proposing a stringent ascetic ideal. In all these aspects its teaching was attractive to the young Augustine, who, on fire with a zeal for wisdom, despised all authority, and, conscious of moral weaknesses, wished to believe neither God nor himself answerable for them. He not only, therefore, heartily adopted the Manichæan system, but entered apparently with enthusiasm into its propagation.

The change nearly cost him the chief saving external influence of his life — intercourse with his godly mother. Terrified by his open repudiation of Christianity and his ardent identification of himself with one of its most dangerous rivals for the popular favor, she forbade him her house, and was only induced to receive him back into the family circle when she became convinced that his defection was not hopeless. Monnica has been made the object of much severe and, as it seems to us, scarcely intelligent criticism for her action on this occasion. It has been sneeringly remarked, for example, that she did not object very much to Augustine's cherishing a concubine, but did object violently to his cherishing a heresy. " She seems to have accepted his companion without a murmur," says a recent writer,[50] " but the descent into heresy was an unpardonable depth." We shall raise no question here of the validity of Bacon's dictum, that " it is certain that heresies and schisms are of all others the greatest scandals; yea, more than corruption of manners." In any event the antithesis is unwisely chosen. We have seen that no great moral obliquity attached to such concubinage as Augustine's, which was, in fact, only an inferior variety of marriage: and though, no doubt, this entanglement was deeply regretted by Monnica, whose ambition for her son had earlier forbidden her providing him with a wife, yet it is quite likely that she saw no reason seriously to reprobate a relation which not only the law of the State, but probably that of the Church, too, acknowledged as legitimate. On the other hand, it is unfair not to recognize the immense change which Augustine's step wrought in his attitude to the religion which was his mother's very life. He may have been up to this moment both indifferent and even of evil life. But he had remained at least formally a Christian; he was still a catechumen; and there was ever hope of repentance. Now he had formally apostatized. He had not only definitively turned his back on Christianity, but was actively assailing it with scorn and ridicule, and that with such success that he was drawing his circle of friends away with him.[51] It was, says Augustine,[52] " because she hated and detested the blasphemies of his error " that she had broken off fellowship with him. Surely his mother's horror is not inexplicable; and it is to be remembered that her attitude of renunciation of intercourse was at once reversed on the reintroduction of hope for her son into

[50] McCabe, *op. cit.*, p. 66.
[51] In the " De duabus anim.," chap. ix., Augustine tells of the effect his easy victory over the ignorant Catholics had in hardening him in his error.
[52] " Confessiones," iii. 11. 19.

her heart. Nor did she ever cease to pursue him with her tears and her prayers.[53]

Despite the eagerness with which he cast himself into the arms of the Manicheans and the zeal with which he became their advocate, Augustine had had very little grounding in the debatable questions that lay at the base of the system. His studies in literature and the rhetorical art had been formal rather than philosophical. His sudden discovery in the teachings of the Manicheans, of the " wisdom " he had been inflamed to seek, was therefore liable to a rude shock of awaking when his studies in the liberal sciences, on which he now zealously entered, should begin to bear fruit. It was not, in effect, long before the sagacity of the good bishop's advice to Monnica, that he should not be plied with argument but left to the gradual effects of his own reading and meditation to open his eyes, began to manifest itself. He remained nine years — from the end of his nineteenth to the beginning of his twenty-ninth year (373–383) — in the toils of the Manichean illusion, exercising in the interval his function of teacher, first at Thagaste and then at Carthage. But by the end of this period the doubts which had early in it began to insinuate themselves, first as to the mythological elements, and then as to the whole structure of the system, had fulfilled themselves. He seems to have been no longer inwardly a Manichean when he went to Rome in the spring of 383, though throughout his one year's stay at that city he remained in outer connection with the sect. When he left Rome for Milan in the late spring of 384, as his thirtieth year was running its course, he left his Manicheism definitively behind him. Nothing had come, however, to take its place. His

[53] It is probably not necessary to revert here to the fact that Manichæism was not merely under the ban of the Church, but also under that of the State — that it was crime as well as heresy. The " severe and bloody laws enacted against them by Valentinian, A.D. 372, Theodosius, A.D. 381," repeating, possibly, the earlier proscription of Diocletian, A.D. 287 (see Stokes, " Smith & Wace," *op. cit.*, iii. p. 799), do not seem to have been executed with sufficient vigor in Africa to have made the profession of the heresy very dangerous (cf. Stokes as above: and Loofs, Herzog, " Realencyklopädie für protestantische Theologie und Kirche,[3] " ii. pp. 262, ll. 37 ff).

own experiences combined with his philosophical reading to cast his mind into a complete state of uncertainty, not to say of developed skepticism. He was half-inclined to end the suspense by adopting out of hand the opinions of " those philosophers who are called Academics, because they taught we must doubt everything, and held that man lacks the power of comprehending any truth." [54] But he revolted from committing the sickness of his soul to them, " because they were without the saving name of Christ." [55] And so, no longer a Manichean and yet not a Catholic, he hung in the balance, and " determined therefore to be a catechumen in the Catholic Church, commended to him by his parents, until something assured should come to light by which to steer his way." [56] Thus he reverted to the condition of his youth, but in a state of mind unspeakably different.

So far as his outward fortunes were concerned Augustine was now at last in a fair way to realize the ambitions which had been the determining force in his life.[57] Driven from Thagaste by a burning heart, racked with grief for a lost friend; and then successively from Carthage and Rome by chagrin over the misbehavior of his pupils; he cannot be said hitherto to have attained a position of solid consequence. Whatever reputation he may have acquired as a teacher, whatever applause he may have gained in the practice of his art, whatever triumphs he may have secured in public contests,[58] all were by the way, and left him still a " viator " rather than a " consummator." At Milan, however, as Government Professor of Rhetoric, he had at last secured a post which gave him assured social standing and influence, and in the fulfillment of the official duties of which he was brought into pleasant contact with the highest civic circles and even with the court itself. Now for the first time all that he had hoped and striven for seemed within his reach. His mother and brother came to him out of Africa; the circle of his old intimates gathered around him; new friends

---

[54] " Confessiones," v. 10. 19.   [57] Cf. Loofs, op. cit., pp. 265 ff.
[55] " Confessiones," v. 14. 25.   [58] Cf. " Confessiones," iv. 2. 3; iv. 3. 5.
[56] " Confessiones," v. 14. 25.

of wealth and influence attached themselves to him. It appeared no difficult matter to obtain some permanent preferment — through his host of influential friends a governorship might easily be had; and then a wife with a little money to help toward expenses could be taken; and the height of his desire would be reached.[59] Things were set in train to consummate this plan; a suitable maiden was sought and found and the betrothment concluded; [60] and everything was apparently progressing to his taste.

But, as so often happens, as the attainment of what had been so long and eagerly sought drew nigh, it was found not to possess the power to satisfy which had been attributed to it.[61] At no period of his life, in fact, was Augustine so far removed from complaceny with himself and his situation, inward and outward, as at this moment. His whole mental life had been thrown into confusion by the growth of his skeptical temper, and he had been compelled to see himself deprived of all rational basis for his intellectual pride. And now the very measures taken to carry his ambitious schemes to their fruition reacted to rob him of whatever remnants of moral self-respect may have remained to him. The presence in his household of his concubine was an impediment to the marriage he was planning: and accordingly she was, as he expresses it,[62] torn from his side, leaving a sore and wounded place in his heart where it had adhered to hers. This was bad enough: but worse was to follow. Finding the two years that were to intervene before his marriage irksome, he took another concubine to fill up the interval. He could conceal from himself no longer his abject slavery to lust. And he was more deeply shamed still by the contrast into which his degrading conduct brought him with others whom he had been accustomed to consider his inferiors. His discarded concubine to whom his heart still clung

[59] vi. 11. 19, *ad fin.*: " amicorum maiorum copia "; " præsidatus "; " cum aliqua pecunia."

[60] vi. 13. 23.

[61] Cf. Loofs, *op. cit.*, p. 265, and Bret, " La Conversion de St. Augustine," pp. 68–69.

[62] vi. 15. 25.

set him a better example; but, as he says, he could not imitate even a woman. The iron entered his soul; and his pride, intellectual and moral, was preparing for itself a most salutary fall. No doubt the precarious state of his health at this moment added something to increase his dejection. Possibly on account of the harshness of the northern climate of Milan, he had been seized with a serious affection of the chest, which required rest at least from his labors, and possibly threatened permanently his usefulness as a rhetorician. It tended at all events to cause deep searchings of heart in which he was revealed to himself in all his weakness.

Simultaneously with the growth of his better knowledge of himself, there was opening up to him also a better knowledge of Christianity. Received with distinguished kindness by Ambrose on coming to Milan and drawn by the fame of his oratory, he was accustomed to frequent the preaching services, with a view to estimating Ambrose's rhetorical ability. But as he listened, the matter of the discourses began also to reach his conscience, and he gradually learned not only that the absurdities of belief — such as, for example, that God had a physical form like a man's — which the Manicheans had charged upon the Catholics, but that the whole scheme of the baneful Biblical criticism he had learned from them lacked foundation. His prejudices having thus been removed he soon came to perceive that the Catholics had something to say for themselves worth listening to, and that there was an obvious place for authority in religion. By this discovery his mind was made accessible to the evidences of the divine authority of the Christian Scriptures, and he turned with new zest to them for instruction. Another discovery in his thirty-first year contributed powerfully to open his mind to their meaning. This was nothing less than the discovery of metaphysics. Up to this time Augustine's learning had been largely empirical and his thought was confined to crassly materialistic forms. Now the writings of the Neo-Platonists came into his hands and revealed to him an entirely new world — the world of spirit. Under these new influences his whole mental life was revolutionized: he passed from his divided mind with a bound, and embraced with all the warmth of his ardent nature the new realities assured to him at once by the authority of Scripture and the authentication of reason. To all intents and purposes he was already on the intellectual side a Christian, and needed but some determining influence to secure the decisive action of his will, for his whole life to recrystallize around this new center.

This determining influence was brought him apparently by means of a series of personal examples. These were given especial power over him by the self-contempt into which he had fallen through his discovery of his moral weakness. There was first the example of the rhetorician Victorinus, the story of whose conversion was related to him by Simplicianus, whom Augustine had consulted for direction in his spiritual distress. By this narrative Augustine was inflamed with an immense emulation to imitate his distinguished colleague, but found himself unable to break decisively with his worldly life. Then came the example of Anthony and the Egyptian monks, related to him by a fellow-countryman, Pontianus, on a chance visit; and with this the example also of their imitators in the West. This brought on the crisis. " A horrible shame," he tells us, " gnawed and confounded his soul " while Pontianus was speaking. " What is the matter with us? " he cried to Alypius. " What is it you hear? The unlearned rise and take heaven by storm, and we with all our learning, see how we are wallowing in flesh and blood! Are we ashamed to follow where they lead the way? Ought we not rather to be ashamed not to follow at once? " [63] We all know the story of the agony of remorse that seized him and how release came at length through a child's voice, by which he was led at last to take up the book that lay on the table and read; reading, he found strength to make the great decision that changed his whole life. It is a story which must not be told, however, except in Augustine's own moving words.[64]

[63] " Confessiones," viii. 8. 19.
[64] " Confessiones," viii. 8. 19; 11. 25; 12. 28–30.

There was a little garden to our lodging of which we had the use.
. . . Thither the tumult of my heart drove me, where no one could
interrupt the fierce quarrel which I was waging with myself, until it
should reach the issue known to Thee but not to me. . . . Thus was I
sick and tormented, reproaching myself more bitterly than ever,
twisting and writhing in my chain, until it should be entirely broken,
since now it held me but slightly — though it held me yet. . . . And I
kept saying in my heart, " O let it be now! let it be now! " and as I
spoke I almost resolved — I almost did it, but I did it not. . . . So
when searching reflection had drawn out from the hidden depths all
my misery and piled it up in the sight of my heart, a great tempest
broke over me, bearing with it a great flood of tears. . . . And I
went further off . . . and flung myself at random under a fig tree
there and gave free vent to tears; and the flood of my eyes broke
forth, an acceptable sacrifice to Thee. And not indeed in these words,
but to this purport, I cried to Thee incessantly, " But Thou, O Lord,
how long? How long, O Lord? Wilt Thou be angry forever? O remember not against us our iniquities of old! " I felt myself held by
them: I raised sorrowful cries: " How long, How long? To-morrow,
and to-morrow? Why not now, why not this instant, end my wickedness? "

I was speaking thus and weeping in the bitterest contrition of
heart, when lo, I heard a voice, I know not whether of boy or girl,
saying in a chant and repeating over and over: Take and read, Take
and read. At once with changed countenance I began most intently
to think whether there was any kind of game in which children
chanted such a thing, but I could not recall ever hearing it. I choked
back the rush of tears and rose, interpreting it no otherwise than as
a divine command to me to open the book and read whatever passage I first lighted upon. For I had heard of Anthony, that he had
received the admonition from the Gospel lesson which he chanced
to come in upon, as if what was read was spoken to himself: " Go,
sell all that thou hast and give to the poor, and thou shalt have treasure in heaven: and come, follow me "; and was at once converted by
this oracle to Thee. So I returned quickly to the place where Alypius
was sitting, for I had laid down the volume of the apostle there when
I left him. I seized it, opened it, and read in silence the passage on
which my eyes first fell: " Not in rioting and drunkenness, not in
chambering and wantonness, not in strife and envying; but put ye
on the Lord Jesus Christ, and make not provision for the flesh, to

fulfil the lusts thereof." No further did I wish to read: nor was there need. Instantly, as I reached the end of this sentence, it was as if the light of peace was poured into my heart and all the shades of doubt faded away. . . . . For Thou didst convert me to Thyself in such a manner that I sought neither a wife nor any hope of this world — taking my stand on that Rule of Faith on which Thou didst reveal me to my mother so many years before.

Thus there was given to the Church, as Harnack says,[65] incomparably the greatest man whom " between St. Paul the Apostle and Luther the Reformer the Christian Church has possessed "; and the thankful Church has accordingly made a festival of the day on which the great event occurred — according this honor of an annual commemoration of their conversions only to Paul and Augustine among all her saints, " thus seeming to say," as Boissier remarks,[66] " that she owes almost an equal debt of gratitude to each." But it would be more in accordance with Augustine's own heart to say, Thus a soul was brought to its God, and made so firmly His that throughout a long life of service to Him it never knew the slightest wavering of its allegiance. It is easy to make merry over the impure elements that entered into the process of his conversion. It is easy to point scornfully to the superstition which made out of the voice of a child at play a message from heaven; and which resorted to the sacred volume as to a kind of book of divination. It is easy to exclaim that after all Augustine's " conversion " was not to Christianity but to Monachism [67] — with its entire ascetic ideal, including its depreciation of woman and its perversion of the whole sexual relation. It is easy to raise doubts whether the conversion was as sudden or as complete as Augustine represents it: to trace out the steps that led up to it with curious care and to lay stress on every hint of incompleteness of Christian knowledge or sentiment which may plausibly be brought forward from his writings of the immediately suc-

[65] " Monasticism and the Confessions of Augustine," E. T. p. 123.

[66] " La Fin du Paganisme," i. p. 291.

[67] Loofs says Augustine " was converted, because he permitted himself to be shamed — by Monachism " (op. cit., p. 267, l. 31).

ceeding months.[68] But surely all this is to confuse the kernel with the husk. Of course, the conversion was led up to by a gradual approach, and Augustine himself analyzes for us with incomparable skill the progress of this preparation through all the preceding years. And, equally of course, there was left a great deal for him to learn after the crisis was past: and he does not conceal from us how much of a babe in Christ he was and felt himself to be as he emerged new-born from the stress of the conflict. And of course, in the preparation for it and in the gradual realization of its effects in his thought and life alike, and even in the very act itself by which he gave himself to God, there were mingled elements derived from his stage of Christian knowledge and feeling, from the common sentiments of the time, which powerfully affected him, and from his own personality and ingrained tendencies. But these things, which could not by any possibility have been absent, not only do not in any respect derogate from the reality or the profundity of the revolution then accomplished — the reality and profundity of which are attested by his whole subsequent life [69] — but do not even detract from the humanity or attractiveness of the narrative or of the personality presented to us in it. He must be sadly lacking not only in dramatic imagination, but in human sympathy as well, who can find it strange that in the stress of his great crisis, when his sensibilities were strained to the breaking point, Augustine could see the voice of heaven in the

[68] So especially Harnack and Boissier: they are sufficiently though briefly answered by Wörter, " Die Geistesentwickelung des hl. Aurelius Augustinus bis zu seiner Taufe," Paderborn, 1892, pp. 63 *sq.*

[69] Even Loofs, who is quite ready to correct the " Confessions " by what he deems the testimony of the treatises emanating from the period just after the conversion, is free to admit that a revolutionary crisis did take place in Augustine's life at this time, and that, therefore, the " Confessions," in describing such a crisis, give us a necessary complement to what we could derive from these treatises. He says (Herzog, " Realencyclopädie für protestantische Theologie und Kirche [3]," p. 267) that there must have happened *something* between Augustine's adoption of Neo-Platonism at a time when he still lived in concubinage and his decisive revulsion from all sexual life, witnessed in the " Soliloquies " (i. 17), which will account for the great change: and this *something* the " Confessions " alone give us. This is a testimony to the historicity of the " Confessions " of the first value.

vagrant voice of a child; or should have followed out the hint
thus received into his heated imagination and committed his
life, as it were, to the throw of a die. Surely this is as psycho-
logically true to life as it is touching to the sensibilities: and
in no way, in the circumstances, can it be thought derogatory
to either the seriousness of his mind or the greatness of his
character. And how could he, in the revulsion from what he
felt his special sin, fail to be carried in the swing of the pendu-
lum far beyond the point of rest, in his estimate of the relation
that could safely obtain between the sexes? The appearance of
such touches of human weakness in the story contributes not
only to the narrative the transparent traits of absolute truth
and to the scene depicted a reality which deeply affects the
heart of the reader, but to the man himself just that touch of
nature which " makes the whole world kin." In such traits as
these we perceive indeed one of the chief elements of the charm
of the " Confessions." The person we meet in them is a person,
we perceive, who towers in greatness of mind and heart, in the
loftiness of his thought and in his soaring aspirations, far above
ordinary mortals: and yet he is felt to be compacted of the
same clay from which we have ourselves been molded. If it
were not so obviously merely the art of artless truth, we should
say that herein lies, more than in anything else, the art of the
" Confessions." For it is the very purpose of this book to give
the impression that Augustine himself was a weak and erring
sinner, and that all of good that came into his life was of God.

It is especially important for us precisely at this point to recall our minds to the fact that to give such an impression is the
supreme purpose of the " Confessions." This whole account of
his life-history which we have tried to follow up to its crisis in
his conversion is written, let us remind ourselves, not that we
may know Augustine, but that we may know God: and it shows
us Augustine only that we may see God. The seeking and saving grace of God is the fundamental theme throughout. The
events of Augustine's life are not, then, set forth in it *simpliciter*. Only such events of his life are set down as manifest how
much he needed the salvation of God and how God gradually

brought him to that salvation: and they are so set down and so dealt with as to make them take their places, rightly marshaled, in this great argument. This is the account to give of that coloring of self-accusation that is thrown over the narrative which is so offensive to some of its readers; as if Augustine were set upon painting his life in the blackest tints imaginable, and wished us to believe that his " quiet and honest youth " and strenuous and laborious manhood, marked as they really were by noble aspiration and adequate performance, were rather " all sin ": nay, that the half-instinctive acts of his infancy itself and the very vitality of his boyish spirits were but the vents which a peculiarly sinful nature formed for itself. In these traits of the narrative, however, Augustine is not passing judgment on himself alone, but in himself on humanity at large in its state of sin and misery. By an analysis of his own life-history he realizes for himself, and wishes to make us realize with him, what man is in his sinful development on the earth, that our eyes may be raised from man to see what God is in His loving dealing with the children of men. We err, if from the strong, dark lines in which he paints his picture we should infer that he would have us believe that in his infancy, youth, or manhood he was a sinner far beyond the sinfulness of other men. Rather would he say to us in his Savior's words: " Nay, but except ye repent ye shall all likewise perish." But we should err still more deeply, should we fancy that he meant us to suppose that it was due to any superiority to other men on his part that God had sought him out and granted to him His saving grace. He knew his own sinfulness as he knew the sinfulness of no other man, and it was his one burning desire that he should in his recovery to God recognize and celebrate the ineffableness of the grace of God. The pure grace of God is thus his theme throughout, and nowhere is it more completely so than in this culminating scene of his conversion. The human elements that enter into the process, or even into the act itself by which he came to God, only heightened the clearness of his own perception that it was to the grace of God alone that he owed his recovery, and he would have them similarly heighten the clearness with which his readers perceive it with him.[70]

With his conversion, therefore, the narrative of the "Confessions" culminates and practically ends. There follows, indeed, another book of narration in which he tells us briefly of his preparation for baptism and of the baptism itself and its meaning to him; but chiefly of his mother and of that remarkable conversation he held with her at Ostia in which they fairly scaled heaven together in their ardent aspirations; and then of how he laid her away with a heart full of appreciation of her goodness and of his loss. And then, in yet another book, he undertakes to tell us not what he was, but what he had become, but quickly passes into such searching psychological and ethical analyses that the note of autobiography is lost. Not in this book, then, is the revelation of what Augustine had become to be found; it is rather given us by means of the narrative which fills the first nine books, in the judgment he passes there on his former self and in the cries of gratitude he raises there to God for the great deliverance he had wrought in his soul. We see without difficulty that this new Augustine who is writing is a different Augustine from him whom he depicts in the narrative: we see that it is even a different Augustine from him whom he leaves with us at the end of the narrative — after his conversion, and his emergence from his country retreat for baptism, and his return to his native Africa. And yet we see also that the making of this new Augustine was in essence completed at the point where the narrative leaves him. Whatever development came after this came in the processes of natural growth, and argues no essential change.

IV. The Development of Augustine

It is convenient to draw a distinction between what we may call, by a somewhat artificial application of the terms, the

---

[70] Augustine's testimony that it was to the grace of God that he owed his conversion is drawn out at some length by T. Bret, "La Conv. d. St. Augustine," pp. 60–66. See also Wörter, *op. cit.*, especially the summary, pp. 62 ff.

making and the development of Augustine. Under the former term we may sum up the factors that coöperated to make the man who emerged from the crisis of his conversion just the man he was; and by the latter we may designate the gradual ripening of his thought and life after he had become a Christian to their final completeness. The factors that enter into his " making," in this sense, are exhibited to us in his own marvelous analysis in the vital narrative of the " Confessions." It is in the mirror of the works which he composed through the course of his busy life that we must seek the manner of man he was when he entered upon his Christian race and the man he became as he pressed forward steadily to his goal. Soundly converted though he was, it was yet the man who had been formed by the influences which had worked upon him through those thirty eager years who was converted: and his Christianity took form and color from the elements he brought with him to it.

An interesting indication of the continued significance to him of those old phases of his experience is discoverable in his setting about, at once upon his conversion, to refute precisely those systems of error in the toils of which he had himself been holden, and that in the reverse order in which he had passed through them. And that is as much as to say that he attacked them in the order in which they may be supposed to have been still living memories to him. It was during the very first months after his conversion, and even before his baptism, that his treatise " Against the Academics " was written. And before the year was out his first work against the Manichæans was published, inaugurating a controversy which was to engage much of his time and powers for the next ten years.[71] This very polemic reveals the completeness with which he had outgrown these phases of belief, or rather of unbelief: there is no trace in it of remaining sympathy with them, and his entanglement in them is obviously purely a matter of memory.

[71] On the place in his works of a polemic against Polytheism — which would be going back to the very beginning — see Naville, " Saint-Augustin," etc., pp. 70–71, note.

He entered at this time into no such refutation of Neo-platonism: this was reserved for the teeming pages of the "City of God." Rather it was as a Neo-platonic thinker that Augustine became a Christian; and he carried his Neo-platonic conceptions over into Christianity with him. This is not to say, however, as has been said, that his thinking "was still essentially Neo-platonic," and "his Christianity during this period was merely Neo-platonism with a Christian stain and a Christian veneering." [72] Much less is it to say, as also has been said, that what we call his "conversion" was a conversion not to Christianity but merely to Neo-platonic spiritualism, while actual Christianity was embraced by him only some years later on [73] — if indeed it was ever fully assimilated, for still others insist that his thinking remained "essentially Neo-platonic" throughout his life, or at least a complete Neo-platonic system lay always in his mind alongside his superinduced Christianity, unassimilated and unassimilable by it.[74] All this is the gravest kind of exaggeration. An analysis of Augustine's writings composed during his retreat at Cassiciacum while he was awaiting baptism, presents to our observation already a deeply devout and truly Christian thinker, although it reveals the persistence in his thought and in his modes of expression alike, of conceptions and terms derived from his engrossment with Neo-platonic forms of thought and speech, which in his later writings no longer appear.[75]

The reality of a gradual development of Augustine's thought is already indicated by this circumstance, and it remains only to fix its course with such precision as may be attainable and to determine its stages and its rate of progress. It has become quite common to mark off in it quite a series of definite changes.

---

[72] Loofs, Herzog, "Realencyclopädie für protestantische Theologie und Kirche [8]," p. 270, l. 31.

[73] L. Gourdon, *op. cit.*, pp. 45–50, 83.

[74] Harnack, "History of Dogma" (E. T.), V. chap. iv.

[75] Such an analysis, brief but admirably done (except that justice is not done to the *Christianity* of this period of Augustine's life), may be found in Loofs' article, Herzog, "Realencyclopädie für protestantische Theologie und Kirche [8]," pp. 270, line 11; 274, line 8. See also Wörter, *op. cit.*

Thus we read [76] that it was only "on his entrance upon a clerical career," that is, only on his ordination as presbyter in 391, that Augustine entered upon a new phase of thought, marked by increasing knowledge of the Scriptures and deepening Church feeling; and only on his consecration as bishop, late in 395, that he at length attained in principle that complete system of thought which we know as " Augustinianism." Even greater detail is sometimes attempted with respect to the development of the preëpiscopal period. The presbyterial period (391–395) is appropriately called " the last section of his apprenticeship," and the preceding four or five years are subdivided into the period between conversion and baptism in which the first place is given to reason and the effort is to conciliate religion with philosophy; and the period from baptism to ordination in which the first place is given to Scripture and the effort has come to be to conciliate philosophy with religion.[77] Four successive epochs in Augustine's thought are thus distinguished, marked by the progressive retirement of philosophy — Neo-platonism in this case — and the progressive advancement of Scripture to its rightful place as primary source of divine knowledge: and these four epochs are sharply divided from one another by external occurrences in Augustine's life — his baptism, ordination as presbyter, and consecration as bishop.

It is scarcely possible to avoid the impression that the scheme of development thus outlined suffers from over-precision and undue elaboration. We are struck at once by the rapidity of the movement which is supposed to have taken place. Augustine's conversion occurred in the late summer of 386: the treatise "On Divers Questions to Simplicianus," in which it is allowed on all hands that "Augustinianism" appears, in principle, in its completeness, was written before the end of 396. Only ten years are available, then, for a development which is supposed to run through four well-marked

[76] Loofs, Herzog, " Realencyclopädie für protestanische Theologie und Kirche ³," loc. cit., pp. 270, 279.

[77] Nourisson, " La philos. de St. Augustine," i. pp. 33–34.

stages. The exact synchronism of the periods of development with changes of importance in the external conditions of Augustine's life raises further suspicion: there seems to be nothing either in the external changes fitted to produce the internal ones, or in the internal changes to produce the external ones. We begin to wonder whether the assumed internal " development " may not be largely an illusion produced merely by the gradual shifting of interest, accompanied by the natural adjustments of emphasis, which was inevitable in the passage of a layman to official positions in the Church of increasing responsibility. Color is given to this suggestion by the actual series of treatises proceeding from each of these periods of Augustine's life. When Augustine connected himself with the Church in 386, and entered the arena of discussion, he entered it not as an accredited teacher clothed with ecclesiastical authority, but in the rôle of Christian philosopher. His earliest writings bear entirely this character; and it does not appear that writings on the same themes and with the same end in view, if proceeding from him later in life, would not have assimilated themselves closely to these in tone and character. The shifting of the emphasis to more positive Christian elements in the later treatises belonging to his lay period, follows closely the change in the subjects which he treated. His polemic against the Manichæans, already begun in Rome, continued during his residence in Thagaste to absorb his attention. This controversy still largely occupied him through his presbyterial period: but already not only was the Donatist conflict commenced, but his positive expositions of Scripture began to take a large place in his literary product. Speaking now from the point of view of an official teacher of the Church, it is not strange that a stronger infusion of positive elements found their way into his works. In his episcopal period purely thetical treatises enter into the product in important proportions, and the anti-Manichæan polemic gave way first to the anti-Donatist, and after 412 to the anti-Pelagian, both of which were favorable to the fuller expression of the positive elements of his Christian doctrine — the one in its ecclesiastical and the other in its individualistic aspects. On a survey of the succession of treatises we acquire a conviction that such a series of treatises could not fail to give the impression of a developing doctrinal position such as is outlined by the expositors, whether such a development was actual or not. In other words, the doctrinal development of Augustine as drawn out by the expositors may very well be and probably is largely illusory. Its main elements may be fully accounted for by the different occasions and differing purposes on and for which the successive treatises were written.

We must, then, look deeper than this gradual change from treatises of thoroughly philosophical tenor to treatises of thoroughly Christian contents before. we can venture to affirm a marked doctrinal growth in Augustine from 386 to 396 and beyond. On seeking to take this deeper view we are at once struck by two things. The first of these is that the essence of "Augustinianism" as expounded in the treatises of the episcopal period is already present in principle in the earliest of Augustine's writings and, indeed, from the first constitutes the heart of his teaching. The second is that the working of this "Augustinianism" outwards, so as to bring all the details of teaching into harmony with itself, was, nevertheless, a matter of growth — and a growth, we may add, which had not reached absolute completeness, we do not say merely, until Augustine had obtained his episcopacy in 396, but when he laid down his pen and died in 430. Augustine's great idea was the guiding star of his life from the very beginning of his Christian career. It more and more took hold of his being and extruded more and more perfectly the remainders of inconsistent thinking. But up to the end it had not, with absolute completeness, adjusted to itself his whole circle of ideas. An attempt must now be made at least to illustrate this suggestion.

What is the essence of "Augustinianism"? Is it not that sense of absolute dependence on God which, conditioning all the life and echoing through all the thought, produces the type of religion we call "evangelical" and the type of theology we call "Augustinian"? This is the keynote of the "Confessions," and gives it at once its evangelical character and its

appeal to the heart of the sinner. It is summed up in the famous prayer: "Command what Thou wilt, and give what Thou
commandest " — hearing which, Pelagius, representative of
anti-Augustinianism at its height, recognized in it the very
heart of Augustinianism and was so incensed as to come nearly
to blows with him who had rashly repeated it to him. Now it
is notable that this note is already struck in the earliest class
of Augustine's writings. " Command, I beg," he prays in the
" Soliloquies " (i. 5) — " Command and ordain, I beg, whatsoever Thou wilt; but heal and open my ears. . . . If it is by
faith that those who take refuge in Thee find Thee, give faith."
When exhorted to believe — if, indeed, that is in our power —
his pious response is: " Our power He Himself is." These great
words, " *Da fidem*," " *Potestas nostra Ipse est*," sum up in
themselves implicitly the whole of "Augustinianism"; and
they need only consistent explication and conscious exposition
so as to cover the entirety of life and thought, to give us all
that " Augustinianism " ever gave us.

It may still, indeed, be asked whether the note they strike is
the fundamental note of these earlier writings and whether
such expressions constitute as large an element in them as
might be expected from Augustine. On the whole, we think,
both questions must be answered in the affirmative. But
this answer must be returned with some discrimination. It is
not meant, of course, that the substance of these books is made
up of such sentences, even in the sense in which this is true,
say, of the " Confessions." What is meant is that these books,
being of an entirely different character from, say, the " Confessions," and written to subserve an entirely different purpose,
yet betray this fundamental note throbbing behind the even
flow of their own proper discourse, and thus manifest themselves as the product of a soul which was resting wholly upon
its God. We must profess our inability fully to understand the
standpoint of those who read these earliest books as the lucu-
brations of a Neo-platonic philosopher throwing over the mere
expression of his thoughts a thin veil of Christian forms.
Plainly it is not the philosopher, only slightly touched by

Christianity, that is speaking in them, but the Christian theologian, who finds all his joy in the treasures he has discovered in his newly gained faith. Through the Socratic severity of their philosophical discourse — which is, after all, but the stillness after the storm — there continually breaks the undercurrent of suppressed emotion. The man who is writing has obviously passed through severe conflicts and has only with difficulty attained his present peace. He has escaped from the bonds of superfluous desires, and, the burden of dead cares being laid aside, now breathes again, has recovered his senses, returned to himself.[78] There is no direct reference made to the conversion that had so lately transformed him into a new man, but the consciousness of it lies ever in the background and it is out of its attainment that he now speaks.[79]

We may be sure that when this man gives himself up after passing through such a crisis to philosophical discourses, it is not because there lies nothing more than these abstract reasonings deep in his heart, but because he has a conscious end of importance to serve by them. The end he has set before him in them certainly is not, as Harnack supposes, merely to " find himself " after the turmoil of the revolution he has experienced, to clarify to his own thinking his new religio-philosophical position. There is indication enough that he does not speak his whole heart out. He is rather seeking, as Boissier hints, to serve the religion to which he has at last yielded his heart and his life. In breaking with the world had he taken an irrational step? Had he sacrificed his intellect in bowing to authority? No, he would have all men know he is rather just entering now upon the riches of his inheritance — in which, moreover, all that he has really gained from the best thought of the world has its proper place and its highest part to play. He is, in a word, not expounding here the Neo-platonic philosophy in Christian terms: he is developing the philosophy of Christianity in terms of the best philosophic thought of the day — serving himself as a Christian heir to the heritage of the ages.

[78] " Cont. Acad.," ii. 2. 4, *ad init.*
[79] Cf. " Cont. Acad.," ii. 2. 5.

The task he had set himself [80] was to construct a Christian philosophy out of Platonic materials. Nor will the notion that he was at the outset so keen an advocate of the hegemony of reason that he was unprepared to submit his thought to the authority of Christ and of the Scriptures which He has given us, bear investigation: it shatters itself not only against the whole tone of the discussion, but also against repeated express declarations. In the very earliest of his books he tells us, for example, that to him the authority of Him who says " Seek and ye shall find " is greater than that of all philosophy; [81] and he sets the authority of Christ over against that of reason with the declaration that it is certain that he shall never fall away from it, because he cannot find a stronger.[82]

Although, however, he had thus firmly from the beginning laid hold of what we may call both the formal and the material principles of his theology — the authority of the divine revelation in and through Christ, embodied in the Scriptures, and the utter dependence of man on God for all good; it does not in the least follow that he had already drawn out from Scripture all that was to be believed on its authority or worked out all the implications of his profound sense of absolute dependence on God. The explication of the teaching of Scripture and the realization of the implications of his fundamental principle of dependence on God constituted, on the contrary, precisely his life-work, on which he was just entering. As we read on from book to book we do not fail to feel, even within the limits of his lay life, a gradual deepening and widening of his knowledge of Scripture, and under the influence of this growing knowledge, a gradual modification of his opinions philosophical and theological alike, and even a gradual change in his very style.[83]

---

[80] Cf. Naville, *op. cit.*, p. 69.

[81] " Cont. Acad.," ii. 3. 9.

[82] *Ibid.*, iii. 20. 43. For this point of view see especially R. Schmid's paper in the *Zeitschrift für Theologie und Kirche*, 1897, vii. p. 94.

[83] Cf. Naville, *op. cit.*, p. 70: " Beyond doubt, when we study in their chronological succession the works of these five years, we perceive the rôle of Scripture gradually to increase. The author, we feel, has immersed himself in the study of Scripture. He has acquired a knowledge of it, of ever-increasing

His earliest writings certainly contain indications enough of crudities of thought which were subsequently transcended. We do not need to advert here to such peripheral matters as his confession that he cannot understand why infants are baptized.[84] Despite the passion of his dependence on God and the vigor of his reference to God alone of all that is good, he had not throughout this whole period learned to exclude the human initiative from the process of salvation itself. "God does not have mercy," he says,[85] "unless the will has preceded." "It belongs to us to believe and to will, but to Him to give to those that believe and will the power to do well, through the Holy Spirit, through whom love is shed abroad in our hearts."[86] "God has not predestinated any one except whom He foreknew would believe and answer His call."[87] Thus his zeal for free will which burned warmly throughout this whole period of his life, did not expend itself merely in its strong assertion over against the notion of involuntary sin,[88] but was carried over also into the matter of salvation. No doubt this zeal was in large measure due to the stress of his conflict with Manicheism, which colored the thought of the whole period: but what it concerns us here to note especially is that it was possible for him to hold and proclaim these views of human initiative in salvation although the center of his thought and feeling alike lay in the great confession: "Our power He Himself is." It is quite clear that throughout this period his most central ideas had not yet succeeded in coming fully to their rights. He had not yet attained to a thorough understanding of himself as a Christian teacher.

---

depth. His very style becomes modified under its influence. No doubt, also, the idea of the Church is more and more emphasized up to the book on the True Religion, in which Augustine expressly undertakes to expound the faith of the Catholic Church. Finally the philosophical thought itself undergoes on some points alterations, which we shall point out." This is all very justly said.

[84] "De quantitate animae," 36. 80.
[85] "De diversis quaestionibus lxxxiii." 68. 5.
[86] "Exposito quarumdam propositionum ex Epistola ad Romanos," 61.
[87] Ibid., 55.
[88] E.g., "De vera religione," 14. 27.

It is well to focus our attention on the particular instance
of as yet unformed views which we have adduced. For it happens that with reference to it we have the means of tracing the
whole process of his change of view; and it is most instructive.
It was indeed just at the opening of his episcopal period that
the change took place; but it stood in no direct connection
with this alteration in his external status. Nor was it the result
of any controversial sharpening of his sight: it is characteristic
of Augustine's life that his views were not formed through or
even in controversy, but were ready always to be utilized in
controversies which arose after their complete formation. It
was the result purely and simply of deeper and more vital
study of Scripture.

The corrected views find their first expression in the first
book of the work " On Divers Questions to Simplicianus,"
which was written in 396, the same year in which he was made
bishop. The " questions " discussed in this book were Rom. vii.
7–25 and Rom. ix. 10–29. In the "Retractations" [89] he says
relatively to the latter " question ": " Later in this book the
question is taken from that passage where it says, ' But not
only so, but Rebecca also having conceived of one, even our
father Isaac ' — down to where it says, ' Except the God of
Sabaoth had left us a seed we had been made a Sodom and
had been like unto Gomorrah.' In the solution of this question,
we struggled indeed for the free choice of the human will; [90]
but the grace of God conquered: otherwise the apostle could
not have been understood to speak with obvious truth when he
says, ' For who maketh thee to differ? and what has thou that
thou didst not receive? But if thou didst receive it why dost
thou glory, as if thou hadst not received it? ' It was because he
wished to make this clear that the martyr Cyprian set forth the
whole meaning of this passage by saying: ' We are to glory in
nothing because nothing is ours ' " (*Cypr.*, lib. 3, testim. 4).
Driven thus by purely exegetical considerations — working, no
doubt, on a heart profoundly sensible of its utter dependence

[89] ii. 1. 1.

[90] " Laboratum est quidem pro libero arbitrio voluntatis humanæ."

on God — Augustine was led somewhat against his will to recognize that the "will to believe" is itself from God. Accordingly, in this "question" he teaches at length that whether man
despises or does not despise the call does not lie in his own
power.[91] For, he reasons, "if it lies in the power of him that is
called not to obey, it is possible to say, 'Therefore it is not of
God that showeth mercy, but of man that willeth and runneth,'
because the mercy of him that calls is in that case not enough
unless it is followed by the obedience of him that is called."[92]
No, he argues, "God has mercy on no one in vain: but so calls
him on whom He has mercy — after a fashion He knows will
be congruous to him — that he does not repulse Him that
calls."[93]

At a much later time, Augustine details to us the entire
history of this change of view.[94] The whole passage is well
worth reading, but we can adduce only the salient points here.
His earlier view he speaks of as merely an unformed view. He
"had not yet very carefully inquired into or sought out the
nature of the election of grace of which the apostle speaks"
in Rom. x. 1–5. He had not yet thought of inquiring whether
faith itself is not God's gift. He did not sufficiently carefully
search into the meaning of the calling that is according to God's
purpose. It was chiefly I Cor. iv. 7 that opened his eyes. But
here we will listen to his own words: "It was especially by this
passage that I myself also was convinced, when I erred in a
similar manner" — with the Semi-Pelagians, that is — "thinking that the faith by which we believe in God is not the gift of
God, but that it is in us of ourselves, and that by it we obtain
the gifts of God whereby we may live temperately and
righteously and piously in this world. For I did not think that
faith was preceded by God's grace — so that by its means
might be given us what we might profitably ask — except in
the sense that we could not believe unless the proclamation of
the truth preceded; but to consent after the Gospel had been

[91] "De diversis quaestionibus ad Simplicianum," i. 2. 12.
[92] Ibid.
[93] Ibid., 13.
[94] "De prædest. sanctt.," iii. 7.

preached to us, I thought belonged to ourselves, and came to us from ourselves."

That it was precisely at the beginning of his episcopate that he attained to his better and more consistent doctrine on this cardinal point, thus giving its completed validity for the first time to his fundamental principle of utter dependence on God, was obviously a pure accident. And there is a single clause in the expression he gives to his new doctrine on this the first occasion of its enunciation which exhibits to us that even yet he had not worked it out in its completeness. "But him on whom He has mercy," we read, "He calls, *in the manner that He knows will be congruous to him,* so that he will not repulse the Caller." [95] About this clause there was much disputation a thousand years later between the Jansenists and the Congruists. As it stands in the text it is only a chance clause, in no way expressive of Augustine's developed thought, in which undoubtedly the grace of God is conceived as creative. Indeed, immediately before it occurs the declaration that " the effect of the Divine mercy can by no means be abandoned to the powers of man, as if, unless man willed it, God would vainly have exercised His mercy," the doctrine suggested by which is scarcely wholly congruous with the notion of " congruous grace." What the clause indicates to us is not, therefore, a determinate teaching of Augustine's, but rather the fact that he had not even yet very carefully inquired into the nature of the operation of God which he called grace, and was liable to suggest inconsistent views of its mode of operation in immediately contiguous sentences. Was it the *quâ* or merely a *sine quâ non* of salvation? To this question his fundamental principle of absolute dependence on God, that God alone is " our power," had a very decisive reply to give: and he was destined to find that reply and to announce it with great decision. But as yet he had not been led to think it out with precision. In important respects his view remained still unformed.

This instance of the gradual elaboration even of Augustine's most fundamental conceptions is only one of many that

[95] " De diversis quaestionibus ad Simplicianum," i. 2. 13.

could be adduced. Another striking illustration is offered by the slow clarification of his doctrine of predestination — purely again under the influence of deeper study of Scripture.[96] The totality of Augustine's development consists, in a word, of ever fuller and clearer evolution of the contents of his primary principle of complete dependence on God, in the light of ever richer and more profound study of Scripture: and we can follow out this development quite independently of external influences, which in his case never conditioned his thought, but only gave occasion to its fuller expression. It might fairly be said that his entire growth is simply a logical development of his fundamental material principle of dependence on God under the guidance of his formal principle of the authority of Scripture. One of the most striking results of this was that he learned little or nothing of primary moment from the controversies in which he was constantly engaged: but rather met them with already formed convictions. No doubt his conceptions were brought out in more varied and even in part clearer and stronger expression during the course of these controversies: but in point of mere fact they were in each case already formed and had been formally announced before the controversies arose. If Loofs says of Athanasius, for example, that he did not make the Nicænum, but the Nicænum made him; he is compelled to say, on the contrary, of Augustine, that he was not formed in the Pelagian controversy, but his preformation was the occasion of it. "Pelagianism," he remarks,[97] perhaps with some slight exaggeration, "was first of all nothing but a reaction of the old moralistic rationalism against the monergism of grace that was exalted by Augustine's type of piety." Of course, we are not to imagine that on this showing Augustine had from the first nothing to learn: or even that he ultimately worked out his fundamental principle perfectly into all the details of his teaching. We have already intimated that a

[96] "Expositio quarumdam propositionum, etc.," 60. The matter is sufficiently expounded by Loofs, Herzog, "Realencyclopädie für protestantische Theologie und Kirche[3]," p. 276, line 21.

[97] Leitfaden zum Studium der Dogmengeschichte[2]," § 53, p. 210.

process of growth is traceable in him and that the process of his growth to a perfect elaboration of his principle was never completed. Had it been, Harnack could not say of him that he bequeathed to posterity only "problems."

In very fact, there remained to the end, as the same writer puts it, "two Augustines," which is as much as to say, that he embraced in his public teaching inconsistent elements of doctrine.[98] It is indeed quite possible by attending alternately to one element of his teaching alone to draw out from his writings two contradictory systems: and this is just what has been done in the vital processes of historical development. To him as to their founder both Romanist and Protestant make their appeal.[99] The specific estimate which the Catholic places on the *unitas ecclesiæ* goes back to him, who it was that gave that compactness and far-reaching elaboration to the doctrine of the Church and its Sacraments which rendered the immense structure of Catholicism possible. It was equally he who by his doctrine of grace contributed the factor of positive doctrine by which the Reformation was rendered possible; for the Reformation on its theological and religious side was just an Augustinian revival. Two children were thus struggling in the womb of his mind. There can be no doubt which was the child of his heart. His doctrine of the Church he had received whole from his predecessors and himself gave it only the sharpness and depth which insured its vitality. His doctrine of grace was all his own, his greatest contribution to Christian thought. He was pleased to point out how this element of it and that had found broken expression in the pages of his great predecessors. He was successful in showing that all the true religious life of the Church from the beginning had flowed in the channels determined by it. But after all it was his, or rather it was he

[98] Harnack, "Dogmengeschichte," iii. p. 90 (E. T. "History of Dogma," v. p. 102); cf. Schaff, "Saint Chrysostom and Saint Augustin," p. 154.

[99] And not Romanist and Protestant alone: in a finely conceived passage Loofs, Herzog, "Realencyclopädie für protestantische Theologie und Kirche ³," ii. p. 277 outlines Augustine's position as the spring out of which many different waters flow. Cf. also his "Leitfaden zum Studium der Dogmengeschichte," § 46 (p. 176).

himself translated into forms of doctrine. It represented the very core of his Christian being: by it he lived; and his whole progress in Christian thinking is only the increasing perfection with which its fundamental principle applied itself in his mind to every department of Christian thought and life. Everything else gave way gradually before it, and it was thus that his thought advanced steadily toward a more and more consistent system.

But his doctrine of the Church and Sacraments had not yet given way before his doctrine of grace when he was called away from this world of partial attainment to the realms of perfect thought and life above. It still maintained a place by its side, fundamentally inconsistent with it, limited, modified by it, but retaining its own inner integrity. It is the spectacle of collectivism and individualism striving to create a *modus vivendi;* of dependence on God alone, and the intermediation of a human institution endeavoring to come to good understanding. It was not and is not possible for them to do so. Augustine had glimpses of the distinction between the invisible and the visible Church afterward elaborated by his spiritual children: he touched on the problem raised by the notions of baptismal regeneration and the necessity of the intermediation of the Church for salvation in the face of his passionately held doctrine of the free grace of God, and worked out a sort of compromise between them. In one way or another he found a measure of contentment for his double mind. But this could not last. We may say with decision that it was due only to the shortness of human life; to the distraction of his mind with multifarious cares; to the slowness of his solid advance in doctrinal development — that the two elements of his thought did not come to their fatal conflict before his death. Had they done so, there can be no question what the issue would have been. The real Augustine was the Augustine of the doctrine of grace.[100] The whole history of his inner life is a history of the

[100] Cf. Reuter, "Augustinische Studien," Studies First and Second; e.g., p. 102: "It was not the idea of the Church as the institute of grace that was dominant in his later years, but that of predestinating grace"; "the doctrine

progressive extension of the sway of this doctrine into all the chambers of his thought; of the gradual subjection to it of every element of his inherited teaching. In the course of time — had time been allowed — it was inevitable that his inherited doctrine of the Church also would have gone down before it, and he would have bequeathed to the Church not "problems" but a thoroughly worked-out system of purely evangelical religion.

No doubt it was the weakness of Augustine that this was not accomplished during the span of his six and seventy years. But it was a weakness in which there abode an element of strength. No facile theorizer he. Only as the clearly ascertained teaching of the Word slowly and painfully acquired moved him, did he move at all. Steadily and surely his thought worked its way through the problems presented to it; solidly but slowly. He left behind him, therefore, a structure which was not complete: but what he built he built to last. Had he been granted, perhaps, ten years longer of vigorous life, he might have thought his way through this problem also. He bequeathed it to the Church for solution, and the Church required a thousand years for the task. But even so, it is Augustine who gave us the Reformation. For what was the Reformation, inwardly considered, but the triumph of Augustine's doctrine of grace over Augustine's doctrine of the Church?

---

of predestinating grace was the fundamental principle of his religious consciousness. *It* must be unconditionally maintained, while all else must give way to it."

III

AUGUSTINE'S DOCTRINE OF KNOWLEDGE AND AUTHORITY

AUGUSTINE'S DOCTRINE OF KNOWLEDGE AND AUTHORITY[1]

FIRST ARTICLE

AUGUSTINE marks almost as great an epoch in the history of philosophy as in the history of theology. It was with him that the immediate assurance of consciousness first took its place as the source and warrant of truth. No doubt there had been a long preparation for the revolution which was wrought by his announcement of " the principle of the absolute and immediate certainty of consciousness," as Windelband calls it, and his establishment of it in " the controlling central position of philosophic thought." But the whole preceding development will not account for the act of genius by which he actually shifted the basis of philosophy, and in so doing became " the true teacher of the middle ages," no doubt, but above and beyond that " one of the founders of modern thought." [2] He may himself be said to have come out of Plato, or Plotinus; but in even a truer sense out of him came Descartes and his successors.[3] When he urged men to cease seeking truth without them, and to turn within, since the home of truth is inside of man, he already placed them upon the firm footing which Descartes sought with his *cogito ergo sum*.[4]

[1] From *The Princeton Theological Review*, v. 1907, pp. 353–397.

[2] Windelband, " A History of Philosophy," E. T. pp. 276, 264, 270.

[3] Leder, " Augustins Erkenntnistheorie," p. 76: " If we must see in Plotinus the father of Augustine's Platonism, we may yet recognize it as an especially original service of the Church Father, that he established over against all scepticism the first point of all certitude in self-consciousness. He found in Plotinus no guidance for this: rather by an act of genius he anticipated in it the line of thought which Descartes (1640) made in his *Meditationes* the starting point of his expositions."

[4] " De vera religione," 39.72: " Noli foras ire, in te ipsum redi, in interiore homine habitat veritas."

If Augustine can be said to have had a philosophical master before he fell under the influence of the Neo-Platonists, that master must be discerned in Cicero. And from Cicero he derived rather a burning zeal in the pursuit of truth than a definite body of philosophical tenets or even a philosophical point of view. It is a mistake to think of him as ever surrendering himself to the skepticism of the New Academy. He does, indeed, tell us that, in his disillusionment with Manichaeism and his increasing despair of attaining the truth, the notion sprang up within him that the so-called Academics might after all prove the best philosophers, contending as they did that everything hangs in doubt and truth cannot be comprehended by men.[5] It is not strange that at such moments his thoughts surged in great waves towards their teachings.[6] But he tells us also that he could not commit himself to them; not only because he was repelled by their heathenism,[7] but also because he was shocked by their skepticism.[8] His difficulty at the time lay, in fact, in another quarter. He found no obstacle in the attainment of certitude: but nothing but apodeictic certitude satisfied him. He entertained no doubt, for example, that seven and three make ten; what he demanded was the same kind and degree of certainty he had here, for everything else. In other words, he would not commit himself to any truth for which he did not have ready at hand complete demonstration.

[5] " Confessiones " v. 10. 19.

[6] " De ultilitate credendi," viii. 20: " Saepe mihi videbatur [verum] non posse inveniri, magnique fluctus cogitationum mearum in Academicorum suffragium ferebantur." He proceeds to say that so often as he was thus tempted, he reacted on considering the vivacity, sagacity, perspicacity of the human mind; he could not believe this mind so much incapable of truth as ignorant as yet of the right way of going about its discovery: thus he was led to meditate on the problem of authority. " De beata vita," i. 4: " at ubi discussos eos [Manichaeos] evasi, maxime trajecto isto mari, dui gubernacula mea repugnantia omnibus ventis in mediis fluctibus Academici tenuerunt."

[7] " Confessiones " v. 14. 25: " I utterly refused to commit the healing of my soul to these philosophers, because they knew not the saving name of Christ."

[8] " Confessiones " vi. 4. 6: " I was not so insane as to fancy that not even this " — mathematical truth — " could be comprehended."

Augustine's point of departure was therefore the precise contradictory of that of the Academics. They asserted that we can never get beyond suspense because we lack all criterion of truth. The best we can do is to say that this or that looks like truth; that it is *verisimile* or *probabile:* we can never affirm that it is truth, *verum;* though, of course, we can as little affirm that it is not truth. Lacking all *signum,* we are left in utter and hopeless uncertainty. Augustine, on the contrary, in the apodeictic certainty of, say, mathematical formulas, was in possession of a sure criterion on the basis of which he could confidently assert truth. His difficulty was that he wished to apply this *signum* mechanically to every sphere of truth alike, and could content himself with no other kind of certitude. He was tempted to declare that nothing resting on less cogent grounds is known, or can be known, at all. What he needed yet was to learn that so far from the possession of apodeictic certitude for some things throwing into the shadow of doubt all for which it cannot be adduced, it provides a basis for valid assurance with respect to them, too. On the basis of this *signum* we may obtain in every sphere at least the *verisimile,* the *probabile* — a sufficient approach to truth to serve all practical purposes; or rather truth itself though not truth in its purity, free from all admixture of error. In other words, in every department of investigation there is attainable real and clear, if somewhat roughly measured, knowledge. What we currently call a yard of muslin, for example, though shown by the application of a micrometer not to be an exact yard, is yet by the self-same test just as truly shown to be a yard for all the practical ends for which muslin is used. The possession of a criterion gives validity to the *verisimile;* for who can declare that anything is like the truth unless he has the truth itself in mind with which to compare it and by which to judge it?

It was by a line of reasoning something like this that Augustine overthrew the Academics when, in his retirement at Cassiciacum, in the interval between his conversion and his baptism, he undertook to lay the foundations of a positive

Christian philosophy. It is absurd to talk of a *verisimile*, he urged, unless the standard, the *verum*, is in our possession. And not only is this standard, this *verum*, certainly in the possession of every man and instinctively employed by him; but no one can by any means rid himself of it. Do what we will, we cannot help knowing that the world is either one or not one; [9] that three times three are nine; [10] and the like; that is to say the principles which underlie, say for example, logic and mathematics. And in knowing these things, we know them not only to be true, but to be eternally and immutably true, quite independently of our thinking minds — so that they would be equally true if no human minds had ever existed, and would remain true though the whole human race should perish.[11] With this indefectible certainty of necessary truth the mind unavoidably knows, therefore, the laws of the true, the beautiful and the good,[12] according to which, as its criterion, it judges all of the true, beautiful, and good which is brought into observation in the experience of life. Nor can doubt be thrown upon these things by calling in question the reality of the very mind itself by which they are known, and therefore the validity of its convictions. Rather, the reality of the mind is given in the very act of knowledge: for what is not cannot act. Say even that this act is an act of doubt. If the mind did not exist, it could not even doubt.[13] The act of doubt itself becomes, thus, the credential of certitude. It is impossible even to doubt unless we are, and remember, and understand, and will, and think, and know, and judge: so that he that doubts must not and cannot doubt of these things, seeing that even if he doubts he does them.[14] Even he who says, " I do not know," thereby evinces not only that he exists and that he knows that he exists, but also that he knows what knowing is and that he

[9] " Cont. Acad." iii. 10. 23.

[10] " Cont. Acad." iii. 11. 25.

[11] " Cont. Acad." iii. 11. 25: necesse est, vel genere humano stertente, sit verum. Cf. " De lib. arbit." ii. 8. 21 ; " De Trinitate, ix. 6.

[12] " De lib. arbit." ii. 8, 9, 10, 15, 16; " De Trinitate," ix. 6; viii. 3; xiv. 15.

[13] " De lib. arbit." ii. 3, 7.

[14] " De Trinitate," x. 10. 14.

knows that he knows it.[15] It is impossible to be ignorant that we are; and as this is certain, many other things are certain along with it, and the confident denial of this is only another way of demonstrating it.

What Augustine is doing in this reasoning, it will be observed, is withdrawing attention from the external world and focusing it upon the inner consciousness. There, there alone, he asserts, can truth be found. Those who seek it without, never attain to it;[16] it is in the inner man that it makes its home, and it can be discovered, therefore, only by those who look within.[17] His polemic is turned upon that Sensationalism in philosophy which had long reigned supreme in the schools, and the dominion of which he was the first to break. In this polemic, he considered himself to be building upon the New Academy, whose mordant criticism of knowledge he persuaded himself was only the negative side of a defense of an essential Platonism which they kept, in its positive side, meanwhile in reserve. In this judgment of fact he was certainly mistaken; the Academy had itself fallen into the prevalent Sensationalism and was itself, therefore, as truly as the Epicurean and Stoic schools of the time the object of his confutation.[18] But to the Sensationalistic maxim that " there is nothing in the intellect which was not beforehand in the senses," by whomsoever taught and in whatsoever forms, he opposes the direct contradiction that truth is to be sought, in the first instance, in the intellect alone. As Robert Browning phrases it, " to know rather consists in opening out a way whence the imprisoned splendor may escape, than in effecting entry for a light supposed to be without." In other words, Augustine came forward as a flaming Rationalist in the philosophical sense of that term; in the sense, that is, in which it describes those thinkers who hold that the " reason " is the fundamental source of

[15] " De Trinitate," x. 1. 3.

[16] " De vera religione," 49.94: . . . " veritas, ad quam nullo modo perveniunt qui foris eam quaerunt."

[17] " De vera religione," 39.72: " noli foras ire, in te ipsum redi, in interiore homine habitat veritas." Cf. " Retractationes," i. 13.

[18] Cf. Leder, " Augustins Erkenntnistheorie," p. 35.

knowledge; and, in opposition alike to Sensationalism and Empiricism, which teach respectively that our knowledge is derived exclusively from sensation or experience (that is, sensation and reflection), contend rather that it is the " reason," acting under laws of its own, which supplies the forms of thought without which no knowledge can be obtained either by sensation or by experience.

Arnobius, his fellow African of a hundred years before, on the basis of the popular Stoicism was as flaming a Sensationalist as Augustine was a Rationalist, and it is interesting to contrast the strong expressions which the two give, each to his own point of view. Arnobius calls to the aid of his exposition the imaginary case of a man secluded from infancy to maturity in a dark cavern, guarded from every possible commerce with the external world. Such an one, he contends, would remain mentally empty; and, if confronted, not with some complicated problem, but with even the simple twice two are four, would stand like a stock or the Marpesian rock, as the saying is, dumb and speechless, understanding nothing.[19] In staring contrast with Arnobius, Augustine sometimes speaks as if contact with the external world and the intrusion of sensible images into the mind were a positive hindrance to the acquisition of knowledge; and as if the mind would do its essential work better if it could do it free from what, in that case, would be conceived as the distractions of sense; as if, in a word, something like the condition in which Laura Bridgman or Helen Keller were found were the most favorable for the development of human intelligence. This exaggeration, however, is no part of his system; and its occasional suggestion serves only to throw into a high light the strength and seriousness of his rationalism.

This rationalism, however, it may be observed, is never pressed to the extreme of conceiving the reason as the creator of its own object. That is to say, it never passes into the Idealism which in more modern times has lain so frequently in its

[19] Arnobius, " Adv. Gent." ii. 20 (American ed. of " The Ante-Nicene Fathers," vi. p. 442).

pathway. To Augustine the world of observation was far from being merely a " psychological phenomenon." Indeed, not only does he recognize the objectivity of the world of sense, but, with all the vigor of his contention that we must look within for truth, he insists equally on the objectivity of even the intelligible world. Man no more creates the world of ideas he perceives within him, than the world of sense he perceives without him. In his assertion that the objects of sensible and intellectual perception alike have indubitable objectivity lies, indeed, one of the main features of Augustine's philosophy.[20] Perhaps we may best catch his general idea, in the distinction he made between the two modes of knowledge — sense perception and intellection — corresponding to the two worlds, sensible and intelligible — if we represent him as thinking of the human soul as existing in a double environment, with both of which it is connected by appropriate organs of perception. On the one hand, it is connected with the sensible world by the external senses; on the other hand, with the intelligible world by the *sensus intimus* which is the intellect.[21] Augustine's notion is, essentially, that the soul, by these two modes of contact with its double environment, is enabled to read off the facts of each. His mode of statement commonly takes the form that as the sensible world impresses itself upon us through the external senses, so the intelligible world impresses itself upon us through the intellect: but we must not press the passivity of the soul to its several impressions which might seem

[20] Cf. Nourrison, " La Philosophie de Sant Augustin," ii. p. 295: " To affirm the certitude of consciousness is, for him, to affirm in the same act the certitude of the external world. . . . It is well to take note of the sagacity with which he distinguishes the phenomenon from the being and thus exonerates the senses from the errors which are commonly attributed to them. Organs and witnesses of what passes, and not of what does not pass, of the phenomenal and not the real, they are not the judges of truth — *judicium veritatis non esse in sensibus.* It is the intellect that knows or the intellect that deceives itself. Its knowledge is certitude. No Scotchman of our day could express it better."

[21] " Cont. Acad." iii. 17. 37: " Platonem sensisse duos esse mundos, unum intelligibilem, in quo ipsa veritas habitaret, istum autem sensibilem, quem manifestum esse nos visu tactuque sentire. Itaque illum verum, hunc verisimilem. . . ."

to be implied in this mode of statement. If, now, these two worlds, the sensible and the intelligible, stood contradictorily over against each other, the soul of man lying between them and invaded by impressions from each, would be in parlous case. Such, however, is not Augustine's conception. The sensible world is not thought of by him as itself independent of the intelligible. It not only has its source in the intelligible world, but derives its whole support and direction from it; and reflects, after its own fashion, its content. It cannot be perceived, therefore, save, so to speak, from the angle of the intelligible world; and in order that it may be understood, the soul must bring to its perception the principles derived from the intelligible world. In a word, the soul is caparisoned for the perception and understanding of the sensible world only by prior perception and understanding of the intelligible world. That is to say, the soul brings over from the intelligible world the forms of thought under which alone the sensible world can be received by it into a mental embrace.

This is, of course, a very developed form of Intuitionalism. According to the Stoics — those Sensationalists *a outrance* — the human mind is in the first instance a *tabula rasa,* on which outer things impress themselves (τύπωσις). But even the Stoics could speak of truths of nature. In their most materialistic development they could find a place in their system for general ideas common to all men (κοιναὶ ἔννοιαι, *communes notiones*), which they not only recognized as real, but valued as the best constituents of human knowledge. As men have practically the same environment, they explained, the sum of the impressions made by surrounding nature upon each, is practically the same as the sum of the impressions made upon all. Hence, peculiar confidence should be put in the ideas common to all men: they are the general teachings of nature, that nature life in conformity with which is the wise man's mark. "Natural ideas" are not foreign, then, to the Stoic system; but when the Stoics spoke of these ideas as "natural," they did not at all mean that they constitute a part of the nature with which man is endowed. Man was not supposed to bring

them into life with him, but distinctly to acquire them in the
process of living: they are impressed by nature on his soul.
The transition is easy, however, from the conception of a body
of ideas natural to man in this sense, to a conception of a
body of ideas belonging to his nature as such, or, in other
words, innate. Along with his reason, it is now said, every man
possesses by nature, that is, by his constitution as man, a body
of ideas: they belong to his nature as a rational being. In making this step we have definitely passed over from Sensationalism to Rationalism, and have so far approached Augustine's
conception. But we have not yet reached it. The doctrine of
innate ideas, strictly construed in that form is deistic. These
ideas are ours because they have been from the beginning once
for all impressed upon our nature by our Maker, who has made
us thus and not otherwise — namely, so that by the action of
our intellect we become aware of the principles thus made a
part of our very structure. Augustine, however, was as little
deistic as Sensationalistic in his thinking, and necessarily advanced a step further to a truly theistic Intuitionalism. These
ideas, he teaches, are natural to man in the sense that they
inhere in his nature as such, and are not impressed on him
by external nature; and they are innate in the sense that they
belong to his nature from the beginning of his being. But he
cannot conceive them merely as impressed on the mind, or
rather built into its structure, once for all at its creation. He
thinks rather of the soul as constantly dependent on God, who
is no more its Creator than its Upholder and Director; and of
its intrinsic ideas as, therefore, continuously impressed on it
by God. Thus its light is God alone; and the soul, in intellection, bears the same constant relation to God the Illuminator
as in ethical action it bears to God the Sanctifier. God, he is
never weary of saying, in his own adaptation of a Platonic
formula, is at once the Author of all being, the Light of all
knowledge, and the Fountain of all good; the God of creation,
of truth, of grace: or, otherwise put, the *causa subsistendi*, the
ratio intelligendi, and the *ordo vivendi*. His ontology of "innate ideas," accordingly, is that they are the immediate prod-

uct in the soul of God the Illuminator, always present with the soul as its sole and indispensable Light, in which alone it perceives truth.

No doubt there is a Neo-Platonic factor in this construction, and possibly also the modes of expression employed may betray a reminiscence of Stoic τύπωσις — with the source of the impression elevated, however, from nature to nature's God. But we must beware of pushing it out of its theistic sobriety into the regions of an essentially pantheistic mode of thought, whether developed or only implicated. Nothing could be farther from Augustine's meaning than that God, as the Universal Reason and Sole Intelligence, comes to the knowledge of the truth in us, and we in and by Him, so that our knowledge simply coalesces with His. His doctrine of creation, by which the creature is set as an objective somewhat, with powers of its own, over against God the Creator, placed him at a whole diameter's distance from the pantheistic tendencies of Plotinus, otherwise so much his master.[22] But neither does the " ontologism " of William of Paris and Malebranche, Fenelon and Bossuet precisely reproduce his meaning. Augustine does not teach that we contemplate immediately the Divine Being, and in Him the intelligible world, that pleroma of eternal and immutable truths which constitutes the world of divine Ideas.[23] It would be much nearer his meaning to say that we see God in the eternal truths which by our *sensus intimus* we contemplate, than that we see them in Him. Undoubtedly he teaches that the soul has an immediate knowledge of God; and, in a sense, he does identify with God the intelligible world into contact with which the soul is brought by its *sensus intimus*. We should not be far from his meaning, however, if, reverting to a mode of representation we have already employed, we should say that the soul, set in its double environment, the sensible world on the one hand and the intelligible world on the

[22] Cf. Nourrison, *op. cit.*, ii. pp. 301, 334; Grandgeorge, " St. Augustine et le Néoplatonisme," p. 111; Portalié in Vacant-Mangenot, " Dictionaire de Théologie Catholique, i. col. 2330. *Per contra*, however, Ritschl, Loesche, etc.

[23] Cf. Portalié as cited, col. 2335; and Storz, " Philosophie d. hl. Aug.," pp. 65 *sq.*

other, as it knows the sensible world directly through the
senses, so knows God in the intelligible world directly through
the intellect. But God is not identified with the intelligible
world, as it appears in the soul of man, except as its immediate author. He is in the soul of man not *substantialiter* but only
effective; and it is precisely in this that the difficulty of the
conception lies. If we may be permitted to employ theological
conceptions here, we may say that Augustine's ontology of the
intuition by which man attains intelligible truth, embraced
especially two factors: the doctrine of the image of God, and
the doctrine of dependence on God. To put it briefly, man's
power of attaining truth depends, in his view, first of all upon
the fact that God has made man like Himself, Whose intellect
is the home of the intelligible world, the contents of which
may, therefore, be reflected in the human soul; and then, secondly, that God, having so made man, has not left him, deistically, to himself, but continually reflects into his soul the contents of His own eternal and immutable mind — which are
precisely those eternal and immutable truths which constitute
the intelligible world. The soul is therefore in unbroken communion with God, and in the body of intelligible truths reflected into it from God, sees God. The nerve of this view, it
will be observed, is the theistic conception of the constant dependence of the creature on God. This stands midway between
the deistic conception, on the one side, that has no need of God
except for the primal originating of the creature, and supposes
that after that the creature's own powers suffice for all its acts;
and the pantheistic view, on the other side, which substitutes
the divine action for the creature's action and, having no need
of a creature at all, transforms it into a mere simulacrum without reality of being or action. In the Theistic view, there is
postulated the creature as the product of a real creation, by
which it produced a real thing with real activities of its own;
and alongside of this, the real dependence of this creature for
the persistence and use of all its activities on the constant action of God. Applying this conception to the problem of intellection, Augustine conceives the soul as at once active and

acted upon, but as active only because acted upon. It is only in the light of God, the sun of the soul, that the soul is illuminated to see light.

There was nothing novel in the ascription of all human knowledge to the illumination of God. It was not only Numenius who declared all knowledge to be but the kindling of a little light from the great light which lightens the world.[24] Platonist and Stoic alike offered a metaphysical and epistemological basis for such a representation. According to the one, knowledge is recollection; and Cicero had explained this — or explained it away — as meaning that right knowledge is implanted in the soul by God at its creation, and is, therefore, inherent in it; while Plotinus' language on the subject is scarcely distinguishable from Augustine's.[25] According to the other, the human *logos* is but a fraction of the universal *Logos* and reproduces in its thought His normative mind. In the mere matter of forms of statement, therefore, Augustine had harbingering enough. It was, nevertheless, quite a new spirit which informed his declarations, the spirit of a pure theism, derived, not from his philosophical predecessors, but from those Scriptures which themselves also told him of the true light that lighteth every man who cometh into the world.[26] It was the personal God, therefore, whom he spoke of as the "Sun of the soul, by whose illumination alone can intelligible verities be perceived,"[27] the "Light of the truth," by which alone is knowledge of the truth awakened in the soul,[28] or — changing the figure only — the inner Monitor and Master of the soul.[29] It was the personal Logos that he had in mind, through whose immanent working all things that exist exist, all things that live live, all things that understand understand. Surely if it

[24] Eusebius, "Praep. Evang.," xi. 18.

[25] Cf. "De civitate Dei," x. 2.

[26] Cf. "Tract. in Joan." ii. 7; "Epist." 120. 4; "De pecc. merit." i. 25, 37, 48.

[27] "Solill.," i. 3.

[28] "De pecc. merit.," i. 25, 37.

[29] "De magistro."

be true even of the body that in Him we live and move and have our being,[30] it must much more be true of the mind, which, having been made in His likeness, lives and moves and has its being in Him in some more excellent, but of course not visible but intelligible way,[31] so that our spiritual illumination comes from the Word of God.[32]

We perceive that the outcome of this conception is that the condition of all knowledge is revelation. Accordingly, our action in seeking knowledge is represented as essentially a consultation of God; God's action in giving us knowledge as essentially a transference of truth to us by a divine imprinting of it on the soul. That mental act which we call understanding, Augustine explains,[33] is performed in two ways: either by the mind or reason within itself, as when we understand that the intellect itself exists; or on occasion of a suggestion from the senses, as when we understand that matter exists: in the first of which two kinds of acts we understand through ourselves, that is, by consulting God[34] concerning that which is within us; while in the second we understand by consulting God regarding that of which intimation is given us by the body and the senses. That is to say, in brief, knowledge of the sensible and of the intelligible alike is God-given, and in both instances is to be obtained only by referring to His teaching. He adds, in another place,[35] that this God who is so consulted, and who, being so consulted, teaches us, is none other than Christ, who dwells in the inner man — that is to say, "the incommutable Virtue of God, and His eternal Wisdom, which every rational soul, indeed, consults, though to each there is given only in proportion to his receptive capacity as determined by his own bad or good will." The divine act of giving, Augustine presents by predilection under the figure of an impressing as by a seal

[30] "Epist." 120. 4; "De Trinitate," xiv. 12.
[31] "De Trinitate, xiv. 12.
[32] Cf. "Tract. in Joan.," i.
[33] "Epist." xiii. (to Nebridius) 4.
[34] Deum consulendo.
[35] "De magistro," xi. 38.

or stamp, upon the soul. In what may be thought, perhaps, the classical passage on this subject,[36] he raises the question whence men obtain their knowledge of God and of the moral law. Not from memory, he answers, whether of their former existence in Adam or of any other state. Whence, then? Can we suppose that they can read off these immutable laws from their own mutable natures; these righteous laws from their own unrighteous hearts? "Where, then, do these rules stand written, whence even the unrighteous may recognize what is righteous; whence he that has not may learn what he ought to have? Where can they stand written save in the book of that Light which is called the Truth, whence every righteous law is transcribed, and transferred into the heart of the man who works righteousness, not by a process of transportation, but by a process of imprinting, as the device from a ring while it passes over into the wax, yet does not leave the ring." What the soul receives, therefore, is not the ring itself with its device; certainly not the device in the ring; but the device as impressed upon it from the ring, and the ring only in and through the device. The care which is taken here to represent the process as a transference of the laws without transfusion of the substance may be said to be the characteristic feature of this passage, as it is of the entire teaching of Augustine on the topic. The figure itself is in repeated use by him, and always with the same implication. Nowhere does he permit the reader to suppose either that God in His substance invades the soul, or that the soul sees in God the ideas which constitute the intelligible world: although he insists steadily that these ideas are the ideas that are in God and that he who sees them, therefore, so far sees God — but in a glass darkly. In a word, he preserves the distinctness of the human soul at the same time that he discovers in the intelligible world open to the soul a point of contact with God; and in the soul's perception of the intelligibles a perception at the same time of God, whose existence thus becomes to the soul as intuitively certain as is its own.

[36] "De Trinitate," xiv. 15. 21.

The effect of such an ascription of all human knowledge to a revelation from God is naturally greatly to increase the assurance with which truth is embraced. The ultimate ground of our certitude becomes our confidence in God. In the last analysis, God is our surety for the validity of our knowledge; and that, not merely remotely, as the author of our faculties of knowing, but also immediately as the author of our every act of knowing, and of the truth which is known. We must guard, indeed, against supposing that, in Augustine's view, the human mind is passive in the acquisition of knowledge, or that the acquisition of knowledge is unconditioned by the nature or state of the acquiring soul. We have already had occasion to quote passages in which the contrary is asserted, but we must now emphasize it with some energy. We have been contemplating thus far only Augustine's ontology of knowledge: that we may be sure that we understand him aright we need to attend also to his expositions of its mode. The fundamental principle which rules his thought here may be brought into relation with his favorite figure, if we bear in mind that an impression from a seal is conditioned not only by the device on the seal from which the transference is made, but also by the nature and state of the wax into which it is made — which " takes " the impression, as we say. Suppose, for example, that the wax is not of a quality, or is not in a condition, to take or to retain with exactness or with clearness the device which is impressed upon it? Augustine accordingly, insists that, although " every rational mind consults the eternal wisdom," that is to say, by virtue of its very rationality is a recipient of impressions from the divine world of ideas, and thus has the acquisition of truth opened to it, or even, rather, thrust upon it: yet this truth is " actually laid open to it ('unfolded to it,' *panditur*) in each case, only so far as it is able to lay hold of it ('receive it,' 'take it,' *capere*) by reason of (*propter*) its own will, whether evil or good." [37] In the interests of this point of

37 " De magistro," xi. 38; cf. also " De Trinitate," xiv. 15. 21, *ad finem;* " In Psalmos," iv. 8, *med. et fin.* Knowledge, therefore, with Augustine, is conditioned by the will; though we must be careful not to take the term " will "

view, Augustine made, in effect, a distinction between ideas, conceptions and perceptions. The ideas, which are reflections from the divine mind are always shining into the souls of men, unchangeable in the midst of men's multiform changes, whether these changes are due to their natural development from infancy to maturity, and on to old age, or to any other accident of life. But the perception of these ideas by the differing souls of men, or by the same soul in its varying stages or states, and, much more, the conceptions built up upon the foundation of these perceptions by the differing souls, or by the same soul in its varying states — obviously these are very different matters. In these things the soul itself comes into play, and the result will differ as soul differs from soul, or the soul in one of its states differs from itself in another of its states. If the condition of all knowledge, then, is revelation, and therefore all knowledge is in its source divine; yet it is equally true that the qualification of all knowledge is rooted in the human nature that knows, and in the specific state of the human being whose particular knowledge it is. It is in this fact that the varying degrees of purity in which knowledge is acquired by men find their explanation.

The underlying conception here is the very fruitful one that knowledge is not a function of the intellect merely but involves the whole man. There is nothing on which Augustine more strenuously insists; as, indeed, there is nothing upon which from his psychological or ethical point of view it became him more strenuously to insist. His psychological insight was too clear, and his analysis too profound, for him to lose sight of the simplicity of the soul and its consequent engagement

---

in too narrow a sense — as if it always must mean in Augustine the faculty of determination. It is, rather, quite frequently the whole voluntary nature; and what Augustine is really teaching is that the ethical state of the soul conditions knowledge. See the whole subject discussed from different points of view by W. Kahl, " Die Lehre vom Primat des Willens bei Augustinus, Duns Scotus und Descartes," 1886, and O. Zänker, " Der Primat des Willens vor dem Intellekt bei Augustin," in " Beiträge zur Förderung christlicher Theologie," xi. 1907. The literature of the subject is cited by these writers.

as a whole in all its acts; and the demands of his ethical nature
were too clamant and his religious sense too lively to permit
him to forget for an instant the determining effect upon every
movement of the soul of the influences proceeding from them.
Accordingly he does not content himself with declaring that
no one can hope to see the truth without giving to philosophy
his whole self.[38] Applying this conception in detail, he insists
that God accords the truth only to those who seek it *pie, caste
et diligenter*,[39] and urges therefore to a strenuous and devout
pursuit of it, because it is only those who so seek whom God
aids,[40] and the vision of the truth belongs only to those who
live well, pray well, and labor well.[41] The conception includes
more than a contention that for the actual framing of knowledge there is required no less than the action of God reflecting
truth into the soul, an action of the soul's own in embracing
this truth, and prior to that a preparation of the soul for embracing it. It seems to be further implied that the several orders
of truth need different kinds or at least degrees of preparation
for their reception. In proportion as we rise in the scale of
knowledge, in that proportion embracing the truth becomes
difficult and the preparation of the soul arduous. To attain the
knowledge of God, which stands at the apex of achievement,
demands therefore a very special purgation. Drawing near to
Him does not mean journeying through space, for He is everywhere; it means entering into that purity and virtue in which
He dwells.[42] " O God," he prays, " whom no one finds who is

---

[38] " Cont. Acad." ii. 3. 8: " ipsum verum non videbis, nisi in philosophiam
totus intraveris."

[39] " De quantitate animae," xiv. 24.

[40] " De vera religione," x. 20: " intende igitur . . . diligenter et pie,
quantum potes; tales enim adjuvat Deus."

[41] " De ordine," ii. 19. 51.

[42] " De doctrina Christiana," i. 10. 10: " The soul must be purified that it
may have power to perceive that light and to rest in it when it is perceived ";
this purification is journeying to God, for it is not by change of place that we
draw near to Him who is everywhere, but by becoming pure and virtuous. Cf.
" De Trinitate," iv. 18. 24: Sinful men need cleansing to be fitted to see eternal
things; " De agone Christiano," xiii. 14: A vicious life cannot see that pure
and sincere and changeless life.

not fully purged."[43] The influence of his Neo-Platonic teachers is here very apparent, and is further manifested in a tendency to represent the purgation of the soul for the higher knowledge as consisting largely in its emancipation from sense. With him as with them knowledge of the truth is constantly spoken of as hanging essentially upon the escape of the soul from entanglement with the sensible.[44] This, as we have seen, is a corollary of his rationalism and was perhaps inevitable with his training. But these expressions which might be almost exactly matched in Plotinus, have in Augustine, nevertheless, an indefinitely deeper implication than in his Neo-Platonic predecessors. With him the purely intellectualistic bearing which they have with them, has noticeably given way to a profoundly ethical one. Though he may still say that " the filth of the soul " " from which filth the more one is cleansed, the more readily he sees the truth," is shortly " the love of anything whatever except God and the soul ";[45] and though, therefore, he may still relatively depreciate all knowledge other than that of God and the soul; yet after all, as he uses these terms, it is of something far more profound than the relative intellectual rank of the several objects of knowledge that he is thinking.

The implications of this general conception carried Augustine very far. Three of the corollaries which flow from it seem especially worthy of attention here. The first of these is that, the human soul being finite, it cannot hope to attain to absolutely perfect knowledge. The second is that, the human soul being subject to development, it can hope to attain to anything like adequate knowledge only by a slow process, and by means of aid from without. The third is that, the human soul in its present condition being sinful, there is a clog upon it in its aspiration to knowledge which it can never in its own strength overcome. In order that we may apprehend Augustine's thought we must therefore attend to his doctrine of mystery as lying at the heart of all our knowledge; to his doctrine

[43] " Solil.," i. 3.   [45] " De utilitate credendi," 34.
[44] " Cont. Acad." II. ii.

of authority as the necessary pedagogue to knowledge; and to his doctrine of revelation as the palliative, and of grace as the cure, of the noetic effects of sin.

In his assertion of the certitude of human knowledge, Augustine is far from asserting that the human soul can know everything; or that it can know anything with that perfection of knowledge with which the infinite mind knows all things. It is impossible for the finite intelligence to comprehend in its mental embrace all that is the object of knowledge: it is as impossible for it to penetrate to the bottom of any object of knowledge which it embraces. For it, mystery not only surrounds the circle of knowledge illuminated by its intelligence, with a vast realm of impenetrable darkness; mystery equally underlies all that it knows as an unfathomable abyss which it cannot plumb. We know, then, and can know, only in part; only part of what there is to know, and what we do know only in part. This is true of all our knowledge alike, whether of sensible things or of intelligible things, whether of the world without us or of the world within us, or — in the highest measure — of the world above us, culminating in God, the mystery that surrounds whom dismays the intellect and compels us to exclaim that no knowledge can be had of Him beyond the knowledge of how ignorant we are of Him.[46] Of our very souls themselves, the very selves which know and which are known most intimately of all things, we know next to nothing. Augustine exhorts his somewhat bumptious young correspondent who fancied, apparently, that he knew all that was to be known of the soul, " to understand what he did not understand, lest he should understand nothing at all." [47] For who knows either how the soul comes into existence, or (that impenetrable mystery) how it is related to the body? So far is Augustine from supposing, therefore, that the soul is clothed in omniscience, or that it can know unto perfection any single object of its knowledge, that he rather teaches that all our knowledge rests

[46] " De ordine " ii. 18. 47: " cujus (Dei) nulla scientia est in anima, nisi scire quomodo eum nesciat." Cf. " De doctrina Christiana " i. 6. 6.

[47] " De anima et ejus origine," vi. 11. 15.

on mystery and runs up into mystery. What we know we know; and our certitude of that may be complete. But what we do not know surges all about us, an ocean of illimitable extent, and sinks beneath our very knowledge, a bottomless depth. We penetrate with our knowing but a very little way into the knowable before we lose ourselves in profundities which baffle all our inquisition.

The limitation which is placed upon our knowledge by our very nature as finite beings is greatly aggravated by the circumstance that we are not only finite but immature beings. We do not come into existence in the maturity of our powers; indeed, we remain throughout life, or we would better say throughout eternity, creatures whose very characteristic is change, or, to put it at its best, ever-progressing growth. At no given point in this development, of course, are we all that even we shall become. For the attainment, then, in our immaturity, of such knowledge as belongs to us as finite beings, there is obvious need of help from without. In other words, there is place for authority, and its correlate, faith. This is an ordinance of nature. Those who are first infants, then children, and only through the several stages of gradual ripening attain the maturity of their powers, will need at every step of their growth the guidance of those who are more mature than they, that they may accept on their authority, by faith, what they are not yet in a position to ascertain for themselves, by reason. And, as it is inevitable even among mature men, that some should outrun others in the attainment of knowledge; and especially that some should become particularly knowing in this or that sphere of knowledge, to which they have given unusual attention, or for which they have enjoyed uncommon facilities; there will always remain for creatures subject to change and developing progressively in their powers, not only a legitimate but a necessary place for authority on the one hand and for faith on the other. Not, of course, as if faith should, or could, supplant reason, or be set in opposition to reason. On the one hand, a right faith is always a reasonable faith; that is to say, it is accorded only to an authority which commends itself to reason as a sound authority, which it would be unreasonable not to trust. On the other hand, faith is in its idea not so much a substitute for reason as a preparation for reason; and the effort of the wise man should be to transmute his faith into knowledge, that is to say as his powers become more and more capable of the performance and opportunity offers, gradually to replace belief by sight. But in any event for such creatures as we are, our walk must largely be guided by faith, and it is only through faith that we can hope to attain to knowledge.[48]

Now add the factor of sin — sin which enters the soul of man, already, one would think, sufficiently handicapped in attaining truth by its finiteness and its immaturity, and refracts and deflects the rays of truth reflected into it from the divine source, so rendering the right perception of the truth impossible. The finiteness of the soul only so far limits it in the attainment of truth, that, being finite, it cannot know all truth nor all that is true of what it truly knows: what it does know is truth, and so far as it is known this truth is truly known. The immaturity of the soul passes gradually away as its powers develop, and therefore imposes only a temporary check upon the attainment of truth — determines that attainment to be a process of gradual advance instead of an instantaneous achievement. Neither the soul's finiteness, nor its mutability, accordingly, need more than warn us of the limitations of our powers and induce in us a becoming humility and patience. But the invasion of the soul by sin is a different matter. Here is a power which acts destructively upon the soul's native powers of apprehending truth, blinds the eyes of the mind, distorts its vision, fills it with illusions, so that it sees awry; and a power

[48] For this doctrine in its highest application, cf., e.g., " De Trinitate " xv. 27. 49: " But if they think they ought to deny that these things are, because they, with their blind minds, cannot discern them, then those who are blind from their birth, also, ought to deny that there is a sun. The light shines in darkness, and if the darkness comprehend it not, let them first be illuminated by the gift of God, that they may be believers: and let them begin to be light in comparison with unbelievers; and when this foundation has been laid, let them look up and see what they believe, that at some time they may be able to see."

which so far from passing away with time and growth, battens by what it feeds on and increases in its baleful influence until it overwhelms the soul with falsehood. No merely incomplete, or as yet uncompleted, knowledge accordingly results; but just no knowledge at all, or even anti-knowledge, positive error, vanity, and lies; and thus a condition is created which assuredly calls not for humility and patience, but for despair.

The question obtrudes itself whether such a doctrine does not render nugatory all of Augustine's carefully built up theory of the acquisition of knowledge. Granted that normal man may look within and find there impressed upon his very being the forms of thought by which God thinks, in the light of which he may see truth and know it to be divinely certain because certainly divine. Man as we know him is not normal man. Afflicted by the disease of sin which darkens the light that shines into him from God, clouding his vision of truth and deflecting all the activities of his mind — who will give him true knowledge? Surely, whatever may be true of abstract man, sinful man, which is the only man we know, is on this teaching condemned to eternal nescience. Must not Augustine, on his own showing, in the case of actual man, take his place, then, among the skeptics? It certainly is important for the understanding of Augustine's doctrine of knowledge to observe how he meets this obvious criticism.

Of the form in which the criticism itself is often urged, we may find a very instructive example in the formulation of it by Mr. John Owen, who, as an outcome of the very line of reasoning which we have suggested, formally classes Augustine not only among the skeptics, but among the skeptics of the worst order. Simple skepticism, he tells us, affects the basis of knowledge only; Augustine's variety of skepticism undermines the foundations, not only of truth but also of morals. For, according to Augustine, he continues —

By the disobedience of its ancestor the majority of the whole human race has become totally incapacitated for knowing or doing what is right and good. The faculties of every man, both of soul and body, have become perverted and misleading. It is needless to dwell on the theological aspects of this momentous doctrine; our present concern is with its philosophical bearings. We here see, as I have already suggested, the Augustinian theology in intimate relationship with Skepticism. With one voice the Greek Skeptics had declared the senses to be untrustworthy, the reason to be perverted, all the natural powers of man to be insufficient to attain knowledge, and precisely the same conclusions were arrived at by Augustine with the portentous extension of the incapacity to all right and good action. The latter fact renders, in my opinion, Augustine's theological Skepticism much more mischievous than any amount of mere speculative theoretical unbelief could possibly have been. . . . That man with all his efforts is unable to attain truth may conceivably be an unavoidable necessity of the only possible *modus operandi* of his faculties, and therefore the fact may not in the least detract from the beneficence of his Creator; but the moment we make his creation and fall, and perhaps his consequent eternal misery, indissoluble parts of the original intention of Omnipotence concerning him, that moment God is shorn of his attribute of goodness, man becomes the hapless victim of a caprice as unreasonable as it is irresistible, and the creation, so far as the majority of human beings is concerned, is a stupendous act of despotism and cruelty.[49]

We have required to quote so much of Mr. Owen's remarks in order to place his representation fully before us; and we require to say this much to exonerate ourselves from the suspicion of having quoted so much merely in order that we might stultify Mr. Owen's profession of concerning himself solely with the philosophical bearings of Augustine's doctrine of original sin. In point of fact he concerns himself with little except its theological aspects. After having barely remarked that it has philosophical bearings, he lapses at once into an assault on the doctrine on the ground that it contradicts the beneficence of God and indeed transmutes the good God into a cruel demon. We must refuse to be led off from our proper subject by this impertinent display of the *odium theologicum;* and we take note here accordingly merely of Mr. Owen's phil-

[49] John Owen, "Evenings with the Skeptics," ii. p. 196.

osophical criticism that Augustine's doctrine of original sin
brings him into intimate relations with Greek skepticism.

Apparently what Mr. Owen means to suggest is that
Augustine reached " precisely the same conclusions " with the
Greek skeptics, and differed from them only in the grounds
upon which he based these conclusions. They contended that
human faculties are, as such, incapable of ascertaining truth;
he, that human faculties have been so injured by sin as to have
become incapable of ascertaining truth. That there is a sense
in which this representation is perfectly just is obvious.
Augustine did hold that the native depravity of man has
noetic as well as thelematic and ethical effects: and that sinful
man, as such, is therefore precluded by his sinfulness from
that perception of truth which can be only *pie et caste*
attained. To him it was therefore axiomatic that the natural
man is incapable of attaining to true knowledge, at least in
its highest reaches — those reaches in which the deflection
of sin would be most apparent. But in his hatred of Augustine's
doctrine of original sin, Mr. Owen has failed to observe that
Augustine did not leave matters at that point. Where he
differs by a whole diameter from the skeptics is that he knows
a remedy for the dreadful condition in which human nature
finds itself. When the skeptics declared that it belongs to
human nature as such to be incapable of knowledge, there was
an end of the matter. The condition of man is hopeless: he
actually lacks faculty for knowing. Augustine's contention, on
the contrary, is that it is knowledge, not nescience, which
belongs to human nature as such. And if he finds human
nature in a state in which it cannot fulfill its destiny of knowing, he knows how it may be recovered to itself and to the
capacity for knowledge which properly belongs to it. In other
words, the sinful condition of human nature is viewed by
Augustine as abnormal; and all the results of this sinfulness
as abnormalities which may be and are to be overcome. That
Mr. Owen says nothing at this point of the provisions for
overcoming these abnormalities cannot be set down to the
credit of his account of Augustine's teaching.

At another point of Mr. Owen's discussion, no doubt, there does occur some suggestion of these provisions, though certainly a very insufficient one. He remarks [50] that "from the earliest history of Christianity the skeptical argument had been employed, for evidential purposes, as an à priori justification of divine revelation both in its ethical and intellectual acceptation." And he supports this by remarking further that "by the early Christian Fathers the confessions of ignorance, limitation, &c. on the part of Greek skeptics were put forward to show the necessity of superhuman knowledge." Even this suggestion is introduced, however, not to palliate but to accentuate Augustine's fault — not to point so much to the remedy which he offered for the noetic effects of sin, as to the excess of his "depreciation of human nature." Augustine had so low an opinion "of the intellectual imbecility of humanity," it seems, that he readily accepted the dogma "of the natural depravity of man" "as a complete solution of what would otherwise have been an enigma" to him. Nevertheless, it is not difficult to perceive that the postulation of a divine revelation comes in upon the conception of the sin-born "imbecility of humanity" as a mitigation of its otherwise hopeless condition. The proclamation of the provision of a divine revelation, if on the one hand it implies a need for it, on the other hand asserts a remedy for that need. Nor does the assertion of divine revelation cover the whole provision which Augustine offers for the removal of the natural incapacities of sinful man. He did not confine himself to pointing out a mitigation for the symptom; he sought and found also a remedy for the disease. If the noetic effects of sin might be neutralized by divine revelation, sin itself might be removed by divine grace. It is certainly grossly unfair to Augustine's teaching as to man's condition to focus attention upon the disease under which he holds that man suffers, and withdraw it entirely from the remedy which he asserts has been provided for this disease.

We must not, then, be misled into supposing Augustine

[50] *Op. cit.*, ii. p. 190.

to teach, even by remote implication, that man is hopelessly sunk in nescience or even in sin. Perfectly true as this is of his teaching of the condition of man considered in himself alone and so far as his own powers are concerned, it is considerably less than half the truth of Augustine's teaching of the condition of man. It means, no doubt, that Augustine, as he looked upon the virtues of the heathen as little more than *splendida vitia,* so looked upon the philosophy of the heathen as very much a farrago of nonsense. What a multitude of philosophers there have been, he exclaimed, in effect, and almost more opinions than philosophers! Who can find any two of them who perfectly agree? Varro enumerates not less than two hundred and eighty-eight possible sects. It would be easier to find a needle in a haystack than truth among these professional purveyors of truth.[51] But then Augustine knew something better than heathen thought to which to direct one in search of truth, as he knew something better than heathen ethics to which to direct one in search of holiness. His great word was *revelation;* and behind and above and all through revelation, there was the greater word still, *grace.* No doubt this means that he transferred dependence for truth, as for holiness, from man to God. He did distrust human nature as he found it. He did consider it in its own strength incapable of any good thing, and equally of any right thought. He did cast men back for all good on God's grace, for all truth on God's teaching. So far writers like Mr. Owen are quite right. Augustine did believe in the ingrained depravity of man in his present manifestation on earth; he did believe that this depravity renders him morally incapable and intellectually imbecile, if this somewhat exaggerated language pleases us. But he believed also in the goodness of God; and he believed that this good God has intervened with His grace to cure man's moral inability, and with His revelation to rescue man from his intellectual imbecility.

Nor was this doctrine of revelation and grace as remedies for man's sinful incapacities and condition a mechanical in-

[51] See " De Civitate Dei," xviii. 41.

trusion of an alien idea into Augustine's general conception.
It rather stands in the most direct analogy alike with his whole
conception of man's relation to God and with his particular
view of man's natural needs and the natural provision for
their satisfaction. Even had man not been sinful, Augustine
would never have allowed that he was in a position of himself,
apart from God, to do any good or to attain any truth. That
would have seemed to him a crass deism, of which he would
have been incapable. Even sinless man would have been to
him absolutely dependent on God, the Author of all being,
the Light of all knowledge, the Source of all good. We have
seen him openly teaching that man as man can see light only
in the Light; that all truth is the reflection into the soul of
the truth that is in God; in a word, that the condition of all
knowledge for dependent creatures is revelation, in the wider
sense of that word. When now he teaches that revelation in
a narrower sense and a more objective form is the condition
of all right knowledge of higher things for sinful man — a
revelation which is an integral part of a scheme of grace for
the recovery of sinful man, not only from the effects of his
sin but form his sin itself — he is speaking in close analogy
with his fundamental theistic conception of the universe. He
is but throwing sinful man back afresh on the God on whom
men in all states and condition are absolutely dependent.

Similarly, the provision which Augustine makes, in revelation, to meet the sin-bred inability of men to attain right
knowledge, is only an extension in a right line of the provision
he discovered for meeting man's natural weakness growing
out of his finiteness, and especially out of his only gradually
attained maturity. In that case, we remember, he pointed to
authority as the remedy for as yet ineffective reason. The child
is naturally dependent on the authority of its elders, who
offer to its faith the truth which its reason is as yet incapable
of discovering or authenticating for itself. In every sphere
of life we remain dependent on the authority of those who
are in this or that or the other department of knowledge better
instructed than we; and he who will be taught nothing, but

insists on following his reason alone, is soon at the end of living in this world. Revelation plays precisely the same rôle for the mind darkened by sin. The heavenly Father intervenes to meet the needs of sin-blinded souls by offering to their faith, on the authority of God, the truth which they are as sinners incapable of ascertaining for themselves. This is the essence of Augustine's doctrine of revelation. Of course the condition of man as sinner determines as well the nature of the truths he needs to know as the manner in which alone he can come to the knowledge of them: the whole content of revelation is determined by the needs of those to whom it is made. But that may be left to one side here. What we are at present especially concerned with is that the need of revelation and the provision of revelation for sinful man stand in perfect analogy with the need and provision of instruction for, say, the immature child. The principle which governs in both cases is, not that reason is superseded by something better, but that, in default of reason due to special circumstances, provision is taken to supply the lack of reason, until reason may come to its rights. The lame man is supplied with a crutch until his lameness is healed. Here we have in brief Augustine's whole doctrine of revelation.

Clear and reasonable, however, as is Augustine's doctrine of revelation as the remedy for man's sin-bred disability to know aright, it seems to be very difficult for some writers to believe that it could have been a reality to him. It is not rare, therefore, to hear it intimated that he passed all his days under the torture of gnawing doubt, and flung himself upon the authority of the Church as some sort of palliation of his wearing despair. His permanent state of mind regarding Christianity, we are told, is much that which is exhibited in a certain class of Romish controversial literature, in which after every other support for human trust has been sedulously removed we are ultimately invited to take refuge in the authority of the Church as the sole haven of peace. This representation is given expression, as well as elsewhere, in some remarks of Prof. Adolf Harnack's, when he comes, in his

"History of Dogma," to deal with Augustine's attitude to the authority of the Church.[52] Here we are told that Augustine had become convinced, in his conflict with himself, "of the badness of human nature," and had been left by Manichæism "in complete doubt as to the foundations and truth of the Christian faith." And then:

His confidence in the rationality of Christian truth had been shaken to the very depths, *and it was never restored.* In other words, as an individual *thinker* he never gained the subjective certitude that Christian truth, and as such everything contained in the two Testaments had to be regarded, was clear, consistent and demonstrable. When he threw himself into the arms of the Catholic Church, he was perfectly conscious that he needed its *authority* not to sink in scepticism or nihilism.

Dr. Harnack is too good a scholar to enunciate a historical judgment utterly without elements of truth. There are elements of truth of great importance even in this judgment, far from the mark as is the application which is made of them; and there are even points of great interest in the use which Dr. Harnack makes of these elements of truth. It is certainly true that in his experience with the Manichæans Augustine learned to distrust unaided reason as the source of religious truth; and discovered that there is a legitimate place for authority in religion. The Manichæans had promised him a purely rational religion; he found on testing it that what they gave him was a mass of irrationalities; and on feeling out for himself he discovered that unaided reason was inadequate to the task of meeting all the needs of man. There is truth, therefore, in saying that he once for all discarded reason as the sole instrument for the acquisition of truth in the religious sphere, and cast himself on instruction as the single hope of the soul in its longing after truth. But the sense in which this is true of Augustine is indefinitely different from the sense it takes upon itself in Dr. Harnack's representation. Beneath Dr. Harnack's representation there lies

[52] E. T. v. p. 79.

Dr. Harnack's own conception not only of the place of authority in religion, but of the nature of the Christian religion and its relation to authority, and of the nature of the particular source of authority to which he conceives that Augustine fled in his need, and of the rationality of Augustine's act in taking refuge with it. His whole statement, therefore, leaves the impression that Augustine in despair of reason renounced rationality, and gave himself over to an unreasoned authority for guidance; and never again recovered, we will not say objective rationality in his religious views, but even subjective confidence. The very interesting defense of authority in religion — from the historical point of view at least, if not from the intrinsic — with which Dr. Harnack closes his discussion [53] does nothing to modify this impression. It remains the gist of his exposition that Augustine took refuge in authority, because he despaired of reason, and therefore his attitude towards Christianity remained throughout life that of an irrationalist.

Nothing, however, could be less true than this of Augustine's real attitude. His appeal to authority was in his own mind not a desertion of reason but an advance towards reason. He sought truth through authority only because it became clear to him that this was the rational road to truth. It was thus not as an irrationalist, but as a rationalist, that he made his appeal to authority. His breach with Manichæism and his gradual establishment in Christian truth, in other words, was on this side of it merely the discovery that the Christian religion is not a natural religion and is therefore not either excogitable or immediately demonstrable by reason working solely on natural grounds; but is rather a revealed religion and therefore requires in the first instance to be told to us. It is thus in the last analysis, supernaturalism as versus naturalism that he turns to; [54] and this is far from the same

[53] Pp. 82–83.

[54] "De utilitate credendi," 29: "Therefore this so vast difficulty, since our inquiry is about religion, God alone can remedy: nor, indeed, unless we believe both that He is, and that He helps men's minds, ought we even to inquire of the true religion itself."

thing as irrationality as versus rationality — except, indeed, on the silent assumption that the supernatural is an absurdity, an assumption which was decidedly not Augustine's. In the sixth book of the " Confessions " he recounts to us the several steps by which he rose from the pure naturalism which had hitherto held him to this Christian supernaturalism. His disillusionment with Manichæism did not at once deliver him from his naturalistic point of view. He had found the tenets of the Manichæans irrational. But his rejection of them as such did not at once entail the adoption of another set of tenets as rational. His sad experience with them operated rather to make him chary of committing himself to any other body of conclusions whatever. He remained in principle a naturalist á outrance. He demanded the apodeictic certainty of mathematical demonstration for conviction; that is to say, he still depended for the discovery of truth upon immediate rational demonstration alone. This alone seemed to him adequate evidence upon which one could safely venture. All this time, says he, he was restraining his heart from believing anything, and thus in avoiding the precipice was strangling his soul: what he was demanding was that he should be made as certain of things unseen as that seven and three make ten.[55] He goes on to remark that a cure for his distress lay open before him in faith (*credendo*), had he chosen to take that road, since thus the sight of his mind might have been purged for vision of the truth. But as yet he could not enter that path. It was not long, however, before it began to invite his feet, slowly but surely. He could not avoid perceiving after a while that it is the path of nature. He reflected upon the host of things which he accepted on testimony. He reminded himself that in it lay the foundation of all history: and that life itself would soon come to a standstill if we refused to act on the credit of others. He meditated further upon the strength of the conviction which testimony produces when its validity and adequacy are beyond question. As the great place which faith fills in common life thus became more and more clear

[55] " Confessiones," vi. 4. 6.

to him, he could not escape the query why it should not serve a similar end in higher things. The principle of faith and its correlate authority, having once been recognized, it became, indeed, only a question of time before it should take its proper place in these higher concerns also. And, then, it was only a question of fact whether there existed in the world any adequate authority to guide men into the truth. Thus, says he, the Lord drew him on little by little, with a hand of infinite gentleness and mercy, and composing his heart gradually convinced him that in the Scriptures He had given to men an authority to which their faith is due, and through which they may attain by faith that knowledge of divine things to which they are as yet unable to rise through reason. "And also," he adds, "since we are too weak to search out the truth by mere (*liquida*) reason, and therefore need the authority of Holy Scriptures, I began to believe God never would have given such surpassing authority to those Scriptures throughout the whole world except that He wished to be believed through them and to be sought by their means." [56] There is depicted for us in this vital narrative, no despairing act of renunciation in which Augustine offered up his intellect a sacrifice upon the altar of faith, and sought peace from insatiable doubt in an arbitrary authority to which by an effort of sheer will he submits. What we see is a gradual advance under the leading of reason itself to a rational theory of authority in religion, on the basis of which rational certitude may be enjoyed in the midst of the weakness of this life.

What has been thus incidentally brought before us, it will be perceived, is Augustine's doctrine of faith and reason. The relations of faith and reason, as thus outlined, remained to him always a matter of sincere and reasoned conviction. We may read them so stated in the books "Against the Academics" and in the books "On the Predestination of the Saints" alike. It will be enough for our purpose, however, to observe how he deals with the matter in two or three treatises which are devoted expressly to elucidating certain aspects of it.

[56] "Confessiones," vi. 4. 8.

Take for example the treatises " On the Profit of Believing "
(A.D. 391) and " On Faith in Things Not Seen " (A.D. 400),
which were written not very far apart in time and in very
similar circumstances. In both of these treatises he begins by
setting himself sharply in opposition to the Sensationalists,
" who fancy," says he,[57] " that there is nothing else than what
they perceive by those five well-known reporters of the body,"
and " essay to measure the unsearchable resources of truth "
by " the deceitful rule " of the " impressions (*plagas*) and
images they have received from these "; whom, in a word,
" folly has so made subject to their carnal eyes that whatsoever they see not through them they think they are not to believe." [58] From this starting point, in both alike, however, the
advance is made at once to the defense of faith as a valid form
of conviction, with respect not only to things not perceived by
the bodily senses, but also to those lying beyond the reach of
the intellect itself.[59] And in both alike the stress of the argument is laid upon the naturalness of faith and its indispensableness in the common life of men.[60] Why should that act of
faith which lies at the very basis of human intercourse be excluded from the sphere of religion — especially in the case of
one, say, of weak intelligence? Must a man have no religion
because he is incapable of excogitating one for himself? [61] Certainly we must not confound faith with credulity: nobody asks
that Christ should be believed in without due evidence that he
is worthy of being believed in.[62] But, on the other hand, it is
just as certain that we shall not attain to any real religion without faith. Say you are determined to have a religion which
you can demonstrate. The very search for it presupposes a
precedent faith that there is a God and that he cares for us;
for surely no one will seek God, or inquire how we should

---

[57] " De utilitate credendi," 1.
[58] " De fide rerum quae non vid.," 1.
[59] *Ibid.* 2 *sq.*
[60] *Ibid.* 4; " De utilitate credendi," 23.
[61] " De utilitate credendi," 24.
[62] " De fide rerum quae non vid.," 5: cf. " De utilitate credendi," 22 *sq.*, and
25, where the necessary distinctions are drawn.

serve Him, without so much to go on.[63] And where and how will you seek? Perchance you will inquire the way of those who are wise? Who are the wise? How will you determine who are wise in such things? In the manifold disagreements of pretenders to wisdom, it will require a wise man to select the really wise. We are caught in a fatal circle here; we must needs be wise beforehand in order to discriminate wisdom.[64] There is but one outlet; and that outlet is, shortly, revelation. For revelation is a thing which can be validated by appropriate evidence even to those who have not yet attained wisdom; and which, when once trusted on its appropriate grounds, gradually leads us into that wisdom which before was unobtainable. Thus, to man unable to see the truth, a justified authority steps in to fit him to see it; and it is authority alone which can bring such wisdom.[65] This is the reason the Lord has chosen this method of dealing with us. Bringing us a medicine destined to heal our corrupted condition, " he procured authority by miraculous works, acquired faith by authority, drew together numbers by faith, gained antiquity by numbers, confirmed religion by antiquity: so that not only the supremely inept novelty of heresy in its deceitful working, but even the inveterate error of heathenism in its violent antagonism can never root up this religion in any way whatever." [66] Here we have Augustine's golden chain. Miracles, authority, faith, numbers, antiquity, an absolutely established religion: that is the sequence, traveling along which men arrive at a secure conviction which nothing can shake.

We may hear him argue the question with even more specific application to the Christian religion in a notable letter which he wrote about 410 to an eminent courtier and scholar.[67] " The minds of men," he tells us here, " are blinded by the pollutions of sin and the lust of the flesh "; they are therefore lost in the mazes of discussion and are unable to

---

[63] " De utilitate credendi," 29.
[64] Ibid. 28.
[65] Ibid. 34.
[66] Ibid. 32 ad fin.
[67] " Epist." 118 (to Dioscorus), 5. 32–33.

discover the truth of things by reason. Therefore, that men may have the truth, Christ came — the Truth Itself, in union with a man — to instruct them in truth. Thus men are given the truth through faith, in order that "by instruction in salutary truth they may escape from their perplexities into the atmosphere of pure and simple truth." That is to say, we are introduced to truth by Christ's authority, so that, thus receiving it by faith, we may then be able to defend it by reason. " The perfection of method in training disciples," we read, " is, that those who are weak should be encouraged to enter the citadel of authority, in order that, when they have been safely placed there, the conflict necessary for their defence may be maintained by the most strenuous use of reason." " Thus," he adds, " the whole supremacy of authority and light of reason for regenerating and reforming the human race has been made to reside in the one saving Name, and in His one Church." For Christ has " both secured the Church in the citadel of authority . . . and supplied it with the abundant armor of equally invincible reason." The former He has done by means of the " highly celebrated ecumenical councils, and the Apostolic sees themselves " — which is as much as to say, apparently, that the authority of the Church finds expression through these organs. And the latter He has done " by means of a few men of pious learning and unfeigned spirituality " — that is to say, apparently, these are the organs through which the inherent rationality of Church teaching evinces itself. The entire sense seems, then, to be that what is taught by the Church on authority, through the appropriate organs of authority, is equally defended by the Church by reason, through the appropriate organs of reason. The Church as the pillar and ground of the truth commends it to faith; the Church, giving a reason for the faith that is in it, defends it to reason. The Doctor,[68] in other words, is as truly a manifestation of the Church's inherent life as the Bishop himself:

[68] On the "Doctor" in the early church, see Smith and Cheetham, "Dictionary of Christian Antiquities," 1876, i. p. 385a; and Harnack, in his larger edition of the "Didaché," 1884, pp. 131 sq.; and in his "Expansion of Christianity," E. T. i. pp. 444 sq.

reasoning is as inadmissibly her function as authoritative definition. Here is certainly an elevation of authority, properly grounded, as a source of conviction; an elevation of faith, properly placed, as a mode of conviction. But here is no depreciation of demonstration and reason to make way for authority and faith. On the contrary, the two are placed side by side, as joint methods and organs for attaining truth; and the contention is merely that to each its own sphere belongs into which the other cannot intrude.

It has seemed most convenient to present in the first instance Augustine's entire doctrine of faith and reason in concrete form, and in its application to the main problem to which he applied it. But having in this way caught a glimpse of it as a whole and in its ultimate bearings, it seems desirable to pause and to glance in some detail at the main elements which enter into it.

Let us first look at the doctrine in its most general aspects. The fact of primary importance to note here is that with Augustine faith and reason are never conceived as antagonists, contradictories, but always as coadjutants, coöperating to a common end. The thing sought is truth: what Augustine has discovered is that there are two modes of mental action by which truth may be laid hold of. It may be grasped by faith, or it may be grasped by reason. " No one doubts," he tells us, " that we are impelled to the acquisition of knowledge by a double impulse — of authority and of reason." [69] And, though we may be so constituted as eagerly to desire " to apprehend what is true not only by faith but by the understanding "; [70] and may, therefore, give to reason the primacy in rank, yet we are bound to acknowledge for faith a priority in time. [71] Granted that faith may seem to be a mode of conviction more suitable for the ignorant multitude than for the instructed few; yet there is no one who does not begin by being ignorant, and there are many things great and good which we could

[69] " Cont. Acad.," iii. 20. 43, ad fin.; cf. " De ordine," ii. 9. 26, ad init.
[70] " Cont. Acad.," loc. cit.
[71] " De ordine," loc. cit.

never attain were the door not opened to us by faith.[72] Life
is too short to attempt to solve every question for ourselves,
even of those which are capable of being solved. We must be
content to accept many things on faith and leave difficulties
to be dealt with afterwards, or never to be dealt with.[73] And
surely it is the height of folly, because of insoluble difficulties,
to "permit to escape from our hands things which are altogether certain." [74] What is it but pride — which is the destruction of all true knowledge — that leads us to demand that
we shall, as we say, "understand everything"?

Not, of course, as if faith should be lightly or irrationally
accorded. If there is a sense in which faith precedes reason,
there is equally a sense in which reason precedes faith. That
mental act which we call faith is one possible only to rational
creatures; [75] and of course we act as rational creatures in performing it. "If, then," Augustine argues, "it is rational that,
with respect to some great concerns which we find ourselves
unable to comprehend, faith should precede reason; there can
be no question but that the amount of reason which leads us to
accord this faith, whatever that amount may be, is itself an-
terior to faith." [76] Faith is by no means blind: it has eyes of
its own with which, before it completes itself in giving that
assent which, when added to thinking, constitutes it believing,[77] it must needs see both that to which it assents and that
on the ground of which it assents to it. As we cannot believe
without knowing what it is to which we accord our faith, so
we cannot believe without perceiving good grounds for according our faith. "No one believes anything unless he has

[72] *Ibid.*

[73] "Epist." 102 (to Deogratias; 406 or 408 A.D.) chap. 38: "sunt enim in-
numerabiles [quaestiones] quae non sunt finiendae ante fidem, ne finiatur vita
sine fide."

[74] "De musica," vi. 5. 8.

[75] "Epist." 120 (to Consentius) chap. 3. "etiam credere non possemus,
nisi rationales animas haberemus."

[76] *Ibid.*

[77] "De praedest. sanctt." ii. 5: "Believing is nothing else than cum assensione cogitare"; "Enchirid." 20: "But if assent is taken away, faith too
falls; for sine assensione nihil creditur."

before thought it worthy of belief." [78] Reason, therefore, can never be "wholly lacking to faith, because it belongs to it to consider to whom faith should be given." [79] This function of reason, by which it considers to what men or writings it is right to accord faith is then precedent to faith; though faith is precedent to reason in the sense that, an adequate ground of credit having been established by reason, conviction must at once form itself without waiting for comprehension to become perfect.

Our knowledge thus embraces two classes of things: things seen and things believed. The difference between them is this: "with respect to things we have seen or see, we are our own witnesses; but with respect to those which we believe, we are moved to faith by other witnesses." [80] The distinction which Augustine erects between faith and reason, that is to say, is briefly that faith is distinctively that conviction of truth which is founded on testimony as over against that conviction which is founded on sight.[81] All the corollaries which flow from this distinction were present to his mind. He is found, for example, pointing out that all so-called knowledge itself rests on faith, so that in the deepest sense an act of faith precedes all knowledge. And on the other hand — and it is this point which is of most present interest to us — that all faith presupposes reason, and is so far from an irrational act that an unreasonable faith, a faith not founded in a reasonable authority demanding credit on reasonable grounds, is no faith at all, but mere "credulity," while what is thus unwarrantedly believed is mere "opinion." [82] As distinguished from knowledge on the one hand and credulity on the other, faith is that act of assent which is founded on adequate testi-

[78] "De praedest. sanctt." ii. 5.
[79] "De vera religione," xxiv. 45, also xxv. 46.
[80] "Epist." 147. 3. 8.
[81] "Epist." 147. 2. 7; "De Diversis Quaestionibus lxxxiii.," Quaest. 54. In "Retractationes," i. 14. 3 he allows that in such distinctions he is employing the word "knowledge" in a strict rather than a popular sense: in common speech we say "we know" even what rests on testimony.
[82] "De utilitate credendi," 11. 25; "De mendac.," 3.

mony; and the form of conviction which is so called may be free from all doubt whatsoever.[83] So far is faith thus from being a cloak for inexhaustible doubt, that doubt is inconsistent with it and is excluded just in proportion to the firmness of the grounding of faith, or, we may better say, just in proportion as faith fulfills its own idea. Its distinction from knowledge does not turn on the strength of the conviction it describes, but on the ground of this conviction. We know by sight; we believe on testimony.

We turn now to the application of this abstract doctrine of faith to the problem of the Christian religion. In this instance the testimony on which faith rests — on the basis of which that conviction we call faith is formed — Augustine supposed to be the testimony of God Himself. The grounds on which he accepted as such what he took to be a revelation from God may be assailed as insufficient; and the channels through which he considered that what he took to be a revelation from God asserts its authority over us, may be subject to criticism. But we can scarcely refuse to recognize the formal cogency of his reasoning. If it can be established that God, condescending to our weakness, has given us a revelation, then, undoubtedly, that revelation becomes an adequate authority upon which our faith may securely rest; and, as rational beings, we must accept as true what it commends to us as such, even though our reason flags in its attempts even to comprehend it, and utterly fails to supply an immediate rational demonstration of its truth. Here, above everywhere else, faith obviously must precede reason, and prepare the way for reason. It is here accordingly that Augustine's insistence on the priority of faith to reason culminates. It is with this application in mind that he repeats most assiduously that "before we understand it, it behooves us to believe"; [84] that "faith is the starting-point of knowledge"; [85] that we believe

---

[83] "De mendac." 3: "ille qui credit, sentit se ignorare quod credit; quamvis de re quam se ignorare novit, omnino non dubitet; sic enim firme credit. Qui autem opinatur, putat se scire, quod nescit."

[84] "De Trinitate," viii. 5. 8.

[85] *Ibid.* ix. 1. 1.

that we may know, not know that we may believe. Least of all, in this highest application of faith, does he mean that this faith does not itself rest upon reason, in the sense that it is accorded to an authority which is not justified to reason on valid grounds.[86] What he means is rather that the particular truths commended to us on the authority of a revelation from God, validated as such by appropriate evidence, are to be accepted as truths on that authority, prior to the action of our reason upon them either by way of an attempt fully to comprehend them, or by way of an attempt to justify them severally to our logical reason; and that this act of faith is in the nature of the case a preparation for these efforts of reason. The order of nature is, in other words, first, the validation of a revelation as such on its appropriate grounds; secondly, the acceptance by faith of the contents of this revelation on the sole ground of its authority; and, thirdly, the comprehension by the intellect of the contents of the revelation and the justification of them severally to reason so far as that may prove to be possible to us. This order of procedure Augustine defends against the Manichæans — who were the philosophic naturalists in vogue at the time — from every conceivable point of view and with endlessly varied arguments. The gist of the whole, however, is simply that when a revelation has been validated as such, we owe to the truths commended to us by it immediate credit, on the sole authority of the revelation itself, and neither need nor are entitled to wait until each of these truths is separately validated to us on the grounds of reason before we give our assent to it. In a word, the rational ground on which we accept each truth is the proof that the authority by which it is commended to us is adequate, and not a particular verdict of reason immediately passed upon each several truth. The particular verdict of reason on each several truth must wait on the act of faith by which we honor the general verdict of reason on the validity of the authority; and it may wait endlessly without invalidating or weakening the strength of conviction which we accord to the de-

[86] E.g., "Epist." 120. 1. 3 (as quoted above).

liverances of a revelation which has been really validated to us as such.

We may revert, of course, to the prior question, whether the assumed revelation on the authority of which faith is yielded has been soundly validated as such to reason. It is at this point that criticism of Augustine's system of faith becomes possible; and it is at this point that such criticism becomes sharp. We are told that Augustine accepted an alleged revelation on insufficient evidence; and that it is this fact which justifies the suspicion that his acceptance of it and the subjection of his reason to its authority were acts of violence done to his intellect in despair of ever attaining a solid basis in reason for religious conviction. It is quite possible to confuse in such a concrete judgment a number of suggestions, which we should discriminate if we are to form an estimate of the value of the criticism offered. We shall need to ask, for example, if what it is intended to suggest is that the evidence in existence for the reality of the revelation which Augustine accepted as a true revelation from God is insufficient to validate it; or only that the evidence which was actually before Augustine's mind and on which he personally depended in reaching his decision was insufficient. In the latter case we shall need to ask further if what is meant is that the evidence actually before Augustine's mind would be insufficient to convince us — seems to us in itself insufficient to command credit; or that it was actually insufficient to convince Augustine, so that, despite his protestations of conviction, he remained in reality unconvinced and at heart an actual skeptic all his days. It is the last of these propositions, it will be remembered, that Dr. Harnack affirms; although he does not keep it as rigorously separate from the others as would seem desirable. It is surely one thing to say that Augustine is open to criticism for giving credit to the Evidences of Christianity and recognizing the revelatory character of the Christian system; and quite another thing to say that Augustine is open to criticism for the particular conception he entertained of the Christian evidences — the selection he makes of the special items of evidence upon which he personally relies for the validation of the Christian system as a revealed religion; and still quite another thing to suggest that Augustine is open to criticism for his inaccessibility to the evidences of the Christian system as a revelation from God, and for remaining therefore all his life a doubter of the intellect, finding only a precarious peace for his distracted soul in an act of submission to an external authority arbitrarily yielded to in defiance of insatiable skepticism.

It can scarcely be expected that the whole body of the Christian evidences should be subjected to a new critical examination merely because a writer not himself able to look upon them as supplying a satisfactory proof of the divine origin of the Christian religion, blames Augustine for placing upon them a value beyond that which he is himself able to accord. We must be prepared to find those who resist the force of this evidence themselves, despising those who yield to it as superstitious, or even accusing them of intellectual dishonesty. It surely is enough at this point simply to recognize that this not unnatural tendency of the naturalistic mind is not without its influence upon the proneness in some quarters to speak of Augustine as making a sacrifice of his intellect in throwing himself upon authority in matters of religion. One thing is perfectly clear: if Augustine made such a sacrifice he was himself completely unconscious of doing so. He nowhere betrays the state of mind which is here attributed to him. He speaks always in terms of the most complete conviction of the truth of the Christian religion, and rests himself with entire confidence upon the evidences which appealed to him. To go behind his obviously sincere asseverations of security of mind and heart, because we are conscious that, in his place, we should have felt less secure, is to push the biographer's (and critic's) privilege of " imputing himself to his victim " to an unwarrantable extreme. Whatever we may feel Augustine ought to have done; whatever we may feel we, in his place, should have done; it certainly is a matter of historical fact that Augustine confidently accepted the Christian revelation as a genuine revelation, and found for his faith in it abundant justification. No fact in his mental history is more patent, or call it flagrant if you will. When in the closing words of his first Christian composition,[87] in the very act of consecrating himself to a life-long search of truth, he declares that " he certainly would never more give up the authority of Christ, because no stronger could be found," he speaks out of an unmistakably sincere conviction. And the note thus struck so far from fading away swells steadily to the end. Clearly the restless heart had found at last its rest: and rest is the characteristic of his Christian life. A skeptic, intellectual or moral, may be found in any man rather than in Augustine. He who in his despair as, in the crumbling of his former beliefs, he almost gave up hope of ever attaining assurance, yet could not fall in with the Academics because he still knew some things to be indisputably true, and only began to wonder whether the right way to truth was known to man — certainly could not lose his confidence after he had discovered the Way and established himself in it.

It remains a matter of interest of course to determine the nature of the grounds on which Augustine was convinced, or sought to convince others, of the truth of the Christian religion. To do so with any fullness would be, however, to write a section of the history of Apologetics, and would find its importance in that connection. We need not go so far afield in seeking to apprehend Augustine's doctrine of authority in religion. What is of primary importance here is merely to ascertain in a simple manner his conception of the sources, nature, and seat of this authority and the mode of its validation to men. In the Second Article we shall seek to do this with as much completeness as is requisite for our purpose.

[87] " Cont. Acad.," iii. 20. 43. It was the common sentiment of the men of the time: Paulinus of Nola says: " Plurima quaesivi, per singula quaeque cucurri, Sed nihil inveni melius quam credere Christo."

SECOND ARTICLE [88]

IN the First Article we attempted to give a general exposition of Augustine's doctrine of knowledge and authority, which naturally ran up into some account of his doctrine of authority in religion. The more detailed study of this specific subject we were forced, however, to postpone to another occasion. We wish now to take up this topic and to make as clear as possible Augustine's teaching concerning it.

The cardinal facts to bear in mind are that, to speak broadly, with Augustine the idea of authority coalesces with that of revelation, the idea of revelation with that of apostolicity, and the idea of apostolicity with that of Scripture. With him, therefore, the whole question of authority in religion is summed up in the questions whether there is a revelation from God in existence, where that revelation is to be found, and how it is validated to and made the possession of men: while the master-key to these problems lies in the one word apostolicity. Whatever is apostolic is authoritative, because behind the apostles lies the authority of Christ, who chose, appointed, and endowed the apostles to be the founders of His Church; and Christ's authority is the authority of God, whose Son and Revelation He is. The great depository of the apostolic revelation is the Holy Scriptures, and these Scriptures become thus to Augustine the supreme proximate seat of authority in religion. The line of descent is, therefore, briefly, God, Christ, the Apostles, the Scriptures — the Scriptures being conceived as the embodied revelation of God, clothed with His authority as His inspired word, given to us by His accredited messengers, the apostles. Let us see how Augustine expresses himself on each of these points in turn.

On the actual authority of Scripture he certainly expresses himself in no wavering terms. The Holy Scriptures, he tells

[88] *The Princeton Theological Review*, July, 1907, pp. 353-397.

us, have been " established upon the supreme and heavenly
pinnacle of authority " [89] and should therefore always be read
" in assurance and security as to their truth " [90] and all their
statements accepted as absolutely trustworthy.[91] To them
alone among books had he learned to defer this respect and
honor — most firmly to believe that no one of their authors
has erred in any respect in writing: [92] for of these books of the
prophets and apostles it would be wicked [93] to have any doubt
as to their entire freedom from error.[94] " To these canonical
Scriptures only," he repeats,[95] " does he owe that implicit subjection so to follow them alone as to admit no suspicion whatever that their writers could have erred in them in any possible
respect, or could possibly have gone wrong in anything." The
accumulated emphases in such passages, no more than fairly
represent the strength of Augustine's conviction that, as he
puts it in another place, " it is to the canonical Scriptures
alone that he owes unhesitating assent." [96] It is this contention
accordingly in its most positive form which he opposes endlessly to the Manichæans in his long controversy with them.
He points out to Faustus, for example, that a sharp line of
demarcation is drawn between the canonical books of the Old
and New Testaments and all later writings, precisely in point
of authority. The authority of the canonical books, " confirmed
from the time of the apostles by the successions of the bishops
and the propagations of the churches, has been established in
so lofty a position, that every faithful and pious mind submits
to it." Other writings on the contrary, of what sort soever
they may be, may be read " not with necessity of believing

[89] " Epist." 82 (to Jerome), ii. 5: " sanctam Scripturam, in summo et
cœlesti auctoritatis culmine collocatam."

[90] *Ibid.:* " de veritate ejus certus ac securus legam."

[91] *Ibid.:* " veraciter discam."

[92] *Ibid.:* i. 3.

[93] " Nefarium."

[94] *Ibid., ad fin.*

[95] *Ibid.:* iii. 24: " sicut paulo ante dixi, tantummodo Scripturis canonicis
hanc ingenuam debeam servitutem, qua eas solas ita sequar, ut conscriptores
earum nihil in eis omnino errasse, nihil fallaciter posuisse non dubitem."

[96] " De natura et gratia," lxi. 71: " sine ulla recusatione consensum."

but with liberty of judgment." The same truth may indeed be found in some of these which is found in Scripture, but never the same authority, seeing that none of them can be compared with " the most sacred excellence of the canonical Scriptures." From what is said by other books we may accordingly withhold belief, unless indeed it is demonstrated " either by sound reason or by this canonical authority itself "; but " in this canonical eminence of the Holy Scriptures, even though it be but a single prophet, or apostle, or evangelist that is shown to have placed anything in his Scriptures, by this confirmation of the canon we are not permitted to doubt that it is true." [97] Similarly when writing to the Donatist Cresconius,[98] he refuses to treat even Cyprian as indefectible. " For," says he, " we do no injury to Cyprian when we distinguish his books — whatever they may be — from the canonical authority of the divine Scriptures. For not without reason has there been constituted with such wholesome vigilance that ecclesiastical canon to which belong the assured books of the prophets and apostles, on which we do not dare to pass any judgment at all, and according to which we judge with freedom all other writings whether of believers or of unbelievers." In a word, Augustine defends the absolute authority of every word of Scripture and insists that to treat any word of it as unauthoritative is to endanger the whole. This he argues to Jerome [99] and over and over again to the Manichæans, culminating in a most striking passage in which he protests against that subjective dealing with the Scriptures which " makes every man's mind the judge of what in each Scripture he is to approve or disapprove." " This," he sharply declares, " is not to be subject for faith to the authority of Scripture, but to subject Scripture to ourselves: instead of approving a thing because it is read and written in the sublime authority of Scripture, it seems to us written rightly because we approve it.[100]

[97] " Contra Faustum Man.," xi. 5.
[98] II. xxxi. 39.
[99] " Epist." 40. iii. 3.
[100] " Contra Faustum Man.," xxxii. 19.

With no less emphasis Augustine traces the supreme authority which he thus accords to the Scriptures to their apostolicity. Their authority is according to him due in the first instance to the fact that they have been imposed upon the Church as its *corpus juris* by the apostles, who were the accredited agents of Christ in founding the Church. In laying this stress on the principle of apostolicity, he was, of course, only continuing the fixed tradition of the early Church. From the beginning apostolicity had been everywhere and always proclaimed as the mark of canonicity,[101] and apostolicity remained with him the only consciously accepted mark of canonicity.[102] He says expressly that " the truth of the divine Scriptures has been received into the canonical summit of authority, for this reason — that they are commended for the building up of our faith not by anybody you please, but by the apostles themselves." [103] The proper proof of canonicity is to him therefore just the proof of apostolicity: and when it has been shown of a declaration that it has been made by an apostle, that is to give it supreme authority.[104] Though one declaration may be from the writings of one apostle and another " from any other apostle or prophet — such is the quality of canonical authority . . . that it would not be allowable to doubt of either." [105] To say " canonical " writings accordingly is to add nothing to speaking of them as genuine writings of the prophets and apostles.[106] The genuineness of the Christian Scriptures as documents of the apostolic age is, therefore, the point of chief importance for him. " What Scriptures can ever possess weight of authority," he asks with conviction in his voice, "if the Gospels, if the Apostolic Scriptures, do not possess it? Of what book can it ever be certain whose it is, if it

---

[101] This has recently been shown afresh by Kunze, " Glaubensregel, Heilige Schrift und Taufbekenntnis," 1899, pp. 114 *sq.*, 249 *sq.* Cf. Cramer, " Nieuwe Bijdragen," etc., iii. 155.

[102] Cf. Kunze, as cited, p. 302.

[103] " Epist." 82 (to Jerome), ii. 7: " non a quibuslibet, sed ab ipsis Apostolis, ac per hoc in canonicum auctoritatis culmen recepta."

[104] " Contra Faustum Man." xi. 5.

[105] *Ibid.*, 6.   [106] *Ibid.*: " vere.'

be uncertain whether those Scriptures are the Apostles', which are declared and held to be the Apostles' by the Church propagated from those very Apostles, and manifested with so great conspicuousness through all nations? "[107] We are not concerned for the moment, however, with the nature of the evidence relied on to prove these books apostolical: what we are pointing out is merely that to Augustine the point of importance was that they should be apostolical, and that this carried with it their canonicity or authority. Their authority was to him rooted directly in their apostolicity.

How completely Augustine's mind was engrossed with the principle of apostolicity as the foundation of authority is illustrated by a tendency he exhibited to treat as in some sense authoritative everything in the Church for which an apostolic origin can be inferred. The best example of this tendency is afforded by what we may call this doctrine of tradition.[108] This doctrine is, in brief, to the effect that where the guidance of the Scripture fails, the immemorial mind of the universal Church may properly be looked upon as authoritative, on the presumption that what has always been understood by the entire Church is of apostolic origin. Repeated expression is given to this position; for example, in his Anti-Donatist treatise " On Baptism " (A.D. 400) where he is seeking to defend the validity of heretical baptism and is embarrassed by Cyprian's rejection of it on the plea that Scripture is silent on the subject. Cyprian's principle, " that we should go back to the

---

[107] "Contra Faustum Man." xxxiii. 6.

[108] To Roman Catholic writers Augustine's doctrine of tradition seems that of the Church of Rome. Cf. Schwane, " Dogmengeschichte der patrist. Zeit," 1895, § 89.9 (pp. 703 sq.), and, though following Schwane closely, yet somewhat more dogmatically, Portalié in Vacant-Mangenot, " Dictionnaire de théologie Catholique, i. col. 2340. Schwane insists that Augustine joins oral Apostolic tradition to Scripture as necessary both for its completeness and for its interpretation, and that with reference to doctrine as well as usages; yet admits that to Augustine the Scriptures occupy the first place in authority and contain all things necessary to salvation, and that with adequate clearness; and that only the Scriptures are inspired and infallible (cf. loc. cit., pp. 713 sq.). Probably even this is assigning to tradition a much greater rôle than Augustine gave it, particularly with reference to doctrine.

fountain, that is to apostolical tradition, and thence turn the
channel of truth to our own times " he of course heartily accepts; [109] he seeks only to turn it against Cyprian. " Let it be
allowed," he says, that the " apostles have given no injunctions " on this point — that is to say, in the canonical Scriptures. It is not impossible, nevertheless, that the custom (*con-
suetudo*) prevalent in the Church may be rooted in apostolical
tradition. For " there are many things which are held by the
universal Church and are *on that account* (*ob hoc*) fairly
(*bene*) believed to be precepts of the apostles, although they
are not found written," *i.e.*, in the Scriptures: [110] or, as it is put
in an earlier point, " there are many things which are not
found in the letters of the apostles, nor yet in the councils of
their followers, which yet *because they have been preserved
throughout the whole church* (*per universam ecclesiam*) are
believed to have been handed down and commended by
them." [111]

Even when thus arguing for the apostolicity of tradition,
however, Augustine never forgets the superior authority of
Scripture. Perhaps the most instructive passage in this point
of view is one in which he is investigating the value of baptism
of infants. After appealing to the tradition of the universal
Church he proceeds as follows: " And if anyone seeks a divine
authority in this matter — although what is held by the universal Church, and that not as a thing instituted by councils
but as of primitive inheritance (*nec conciliis institutum sed
semper retentum est*) is most properly (*rectissime*) believed
to have been handed down by apostolic authority — we are
able in any case (*tamen*) to form a true conjecture of the
value of the sacrament of baptism in the case of infants from
the circumcision of the flesh . . . " [112] Here, in the very act
of vindicating apostolicity, and therefore authority, for universal primitive custom, language is employed which seems to

[109] " De bapt. contra Donat.," V. xxvi. 37.
[110] *Ibid.*, V. xxiii. 31.
[111] *Ibid.*, II. vii. 12; cf. IV. vi. 9.
[112] *Ibid.*, IV. xxiv. 31.

betray that Augustine was wont to conceive "divine author-ity" (*auctoritas divina*) the peculiar property of Scripture. In another Anti-Donatist treatise — the work against the grammarian Cresconius (c. 406) [113] — we read somewhat simi-larly that "although no doubt no example" of the custom under discussion "is adduced from the canonical Scriptures, the truth of these Scriptures is nevertheless held by us in this matter, since what we do is the *placitum* of the universal Church, which is commended by the authority of these very Scriptures; and accordingly since the Holy Scriptures cannot deceive, whoever is afraid of being led astray by the obscurity of this question should consult with respect to it that Church which without any ambiguity is pointed out by the Holy Scripture."

This care in preserving the superior right of Scripture is not to be accounted for as due to the exigencies of the con-troversy with the Donatists. It reappears in more formal form in purely didactic teaching — in a reply, for instance, which Augustine made to a series of questions addressed to him by a correspondent on matters of ritual observance.[114] Here Augus-tine distinguishes carefully between three varieties of such observances: those prescribed by Scripture, those commended by the practice of the universal Church, those of merely local usage. When an observance is prescribed by the authority of divine Scripture, no doubt can be admitted but that we must do precisely as we read.[115] Similarly also only insane insolence would doubt that we ought to follow the practice of the whole Church, throughout the world.[116] In matters of varying usage in different parts of the Church, on the other hand, we must beware of erecting our own custom into a guide, and should conform ourselves freely to the custom that obtains in the Church where we may chance from time to time to be — in

[113] *Op. cit.*, i. 33. 39.

[114] "Epist." 54 and 55 (to Januarius — the 40th of that name in Smith and Wace, "Dictionary of Christian Biography," — about 400).

[115] "Epist." 54, v. 6: "non sit dubitandum quin ita facere debeamus ut legimus."

[116] *Ibid.;* "quid . . . tota per orbem frequentat ecclesia."

short, follow Ambrose's wise rule of "doing when we are in Rome as the Romans do." [117] There is nothing that Augustine deprecates more than the arbitrary multiplication of ordinances, by which, he says, the state of Christians which God wished to be free — appointing to them only a few Sacraments and those easy of observance — is assimilated to the burdensomeness of Judaism. He could wish therefore that all ordinances should be unhesitatingly abolished which are neither prescribed by the authority of the Holy Scriptures, nor have been appointed by the councils of bishops, nor have been confirmed by the custom of the universal Church [118] — in which sentence the selection of the terms so that "authority" is ascribed to Scripture alone is not unwitting.

Elsewhere, no doubt, Augustine uses the term "authority" more loosely of the other sources of "custom" also. This is true, for example, of the opening paragraphs of these very letters. Here he carefully draws out the threefold distinction among ordinances, which he applies throughout. The fundamental principle of the discussion on which he is about to enter, he tells us, is that our Lord Jesus Christ has subjected us to an easy yoke and a light burden, laying upon us only few Sacraments and those not difficult of observance. He then adds: "But with respect to those not written but traditional matters to which we hold, observed as they are throughout the whole world, what we are to understand is that they are retained as commended and instituted by the Apostles themselves, or by plenary councils, the authority of which in the Church is very useful." [119] The term "authority" happens to be employed here only of what the context tells us is the least weighty of the three "authorities" to the observances com-

[117] *Ibid.*, ii. 3, where a pleasant anecdote is told of Ambrose's advice to Monnica to follow his example in this.

[118] "Epist." 55, xix. 35; cf. 27, where the "authority" of the divine Scriptures and the "consent" of the whole Church are brought together.

[119] "Epist." 54. 1. 1.: "illa autem quae non scripta sed tradita custodimus, quae quidem toto terrarum orbe servantur, datur intelligi, vel ab ipsis apostolis, vel plenariis conciliis, quorum est in ecclesia saluberrima auctoritas commendata atque statuta retineri."

mended by which we should yield obedience: the Scriptures, universal primitive custom arguing apostolic appointment, and counciliary enactment. We may look somewhat roughly, perhaps, upon these three "authorities" as representing to Augustine respectively the authority of "Scripture," the authority of "tradition," and the authority of "the Church"; and if so, then these three "authorities" — the Scriptures, Tradition, the Church — took rank in his mind in that order. First and above all is the "authority" of Scripture, which is just the infallible Word of God, whose every word is to be believed and every precept obeyed just as it stands written. Then comes the "authority" of immemorial universal tradition, on the presumption that just because it is immemorially universal it may, or must, be apostolic; and if apostolic then also of divine appointment. Last of all comes the "authority" of the Church itself, for which no claim is made of divine infallibility, since that is an attribute of Scripture alone — nor even of such constructive apostolicity as may be presumed of immemorial tradition; but only of righteous jurisdiction and Spirit-led wisdom. Neither the individual bishop, nor any body of bishops assembled in council, up to the whole number in the plenary or ecumenical council, though each and all are clothed with authority appropriate to the place and function of each, is safeguarded from error, or elevated above subsequent criticism and correction. This high altitude of indefectible infallibility is attained by Scripture alone.[120]

An appropriate authority is granted of course to bishops,

[120] Cf. Reuter, "Augustin. Studien, p. 329: "There is not, to my knowledge, to be found in Augustine, any statement giving *un*ambiguous expression to this notion [of the infallibility of the Church]. We read, *Contra Cresconium* ii. 33. 39, 'Since Holy Scripture cannot err'; but I have sought in vain for any declaration corresponding to this with reference to the Church. The assertion, 'Outside the Church, there is no salvation' is nowhere complemented by this other one, 'The Church cannot err.'" Reuter proceeds to say that, although this precise formula does not occur, yet "important premises of it" may be found; but here opinions may lawfully differ. On what follows in the text Reuter, pp. 328 *sq.*, 333 *sq.*, may be profitably consulted; cf. also Schmidt, in Liebner's *Jahrbücher für deutsche Theologie* (1861), vi. pp. 197–255, especially 234 *sq.*

each in his proper sphere: but no one of them is free from error or exempt from testing and correction by the Holy Scriptures. Its own appropriate authority belongs similarly to councils of every grade: but no one of them can claim to have seen truth simply and seen it whole. If the Donatists appealed to Cyprian and his council, for example, Augustine, while ready to yield to Cyprian all the deference that was his due, did not hesitate to declare roundly, " The authority of Cyprian has no terrors for me," [121] and to assert that no council is exempt from error. For, he explains at length,[122] no one " is ignorant that the Holy Canonical Scriptures, as well of the Old as of the New Testament, are contained within their own determined (*certis*) limits, and that they are so set above all later letters of bishops that with respect to them it is not possible to doubt or to dispute whether anything that stands written in them is true or right, while all the letters of bishops which, since the closing of the canon have been written or shall be written, are open to confutation, either by the wiser discourses of some one who happens to be more skilled in the particular matter, or by the weightier authority or more learned prudence of other bishops, or by councils — if there chances to be anything in them that deviates from the truth." And as little is anyone ignorant

---

[121] " De Bapt. contr. Donat." ii. 1. 2: " non me terret auctoritas Cypriani." This does not mean, of course, that he denies all authority to Cyprian; but only that he knows the limits of Cyprian's authority. So, when he says, *op. cit.*, iii. 3. 5. *med:* " No authority (nulla auctoritas), clearly, deters me from seeking the truth," he is not proclaiming an abstract indefeasable liberty in seeking the truth, as A. Dorner (" Augustinus," p. 236) appears to suppose (cf. Reuter, *op. cit.*, p. 335, note 4), but means only to say that Cyprian expressly leaves the path open and does not interpose his authority (whatever that may amount to) to shut off free investigation. Accordingly, he repeats at the end of the paragraph more explicitly: " We have then liberty of investigation conceded to us by Cyprian's own moderate and truthful declaration." The assertion of a zeal for truth which takes precedence of all else, apparently wrongly attributed to this passage, may be more justly found in the remark which occurs in the " Contra Epist. Manich. Fundam." iv. 5, to the effect that " if the truth is so clearly proved as to leave no possibility of doubt, it takes precedence of all things which keep me in the Catholic Church." Cf. Schmidt, as cited above.

[122] *Ibid.*, ii. 3. 4.

" that the councils themselves which are held in the several regions and provinces must without any evasion yield to the authority of plenary councils which are assembled from the whole Christian world; and that even the earlier plenary councils themselves are corrected by later ones, when by some actual trial, what was closed has been opened, and what was hidden has come to light." We perceive accordingly that the limiting phrases in the famous passages in which Augustine declares the Holy Scriptures the sole infallible authority in the world are by no means otiose. He means just what he says when he writes to Jerome, " For I confess to your charity that I have learned to defer this respect and honor to those Scriptural books only (*solis*) which are now called canonical, that I believe most firmly that no one of those authors has erred in any respect in writing " ; [123] or again when he says in another place, " In the writings of such authors " — that is to say Catholic writers — " I feel myself free to use my own judgment, since I owe unhesitating assent *to nothing but the canonical Scriptures.*" [124] A presumptive apostolicity may lend to the immemorial customs of the universal Church an authority which only arrogance can resist; and to the Church which was founded by the apostles, and made by them a depository of the tradition of truth, a high deference is due in all its deliverances: but to the Scriptures alone belongs supreme authority because to them alone belongs an apostolicity which coalesces with their entire fabric. They alone present us with what we may perhaps call " fixed apostolicity."

The ground of this conception of apostolicity as the principle of divine authority lies ultimately in the relation in which the apostles stood to Christ. The apostles, as Christ's accredited agents, empowered by His Spirit for their work, are, in effect, Christ Himself speaking. This idea underlies the entirety of Augustine's reasoning, and is very fully developed in a striking passage which occurs at the close of the first book of the Harmony of the Gospels.[125] He tells us here that our

[123] " Epist." 82. 1. 3.   [124] " De natura et gratia," lxi. 71.
[125] " De consensu Evang.," i. 35. 54.

Lord, "who sent the prophets before His own descent, also despatched the apostles after His ascension. . . . Therefore, since these disciples have written matters which He declared and spoke to them, it ought not by any means to be said He has written nothing Himself; for the truth is that His members have accomplished only that which they became acquainted with by the repeated statements of the Head. For all that He was minded to give for our perusal on the subject of His own doings and saying, He commanded to be written by those disciples, whom He thus used as if they were His own hands. Whoever apprehends this correspondence of unity and this concordant service of the members, all in harmony in the discharge of diverse offices under the Head, will receive the account which he gets in the Gospel through the narrative constructed by the disciples, in the same kind of spirit in which he might look upon the actual hand of the Lord Himself, which he bore in that body that He made His own, were he to see it engaged in the act of writing." Apostolicity therefore spells authority because it also spells inspiration: what the apostles have given the Church as its law is the inspired Word of God. The canonical Scriptures are accordingly "the august pen of the Spirit " of God; [126] and in reading them we are, through the words written by their human authors, learning " the will of God in accordance with which we believe these men to have spoken," [127] seeing that it is " the Holy Spirit who with admirable wisdom and care for our welfare has arranged the Holy Scriptures " in all their details,[128] and has spoken in them in perfect foresight of all our needs and perplexities.[129] Accordingly Augustine makes the Lord declare to him, " O man, verily what my Scripture says, I say "; and this is the reason that we may be assured that the Scripture is true — because it is He that is true, or rather the Truth Itself, who has given it

[126] " Confessiones," vii. 21. 27: " venerabilem stilum Spiritus tui."

[127] " De doctrina Christiana," ii. 5. 6.

[128] *Ibid.*, ii. 6. 8.

[129] *Ibid.*, iii. 27. 38: " assuredly the Holy Spirit who through him [the human author] spoke these words, foresaw that this interpretation would occur to the reader. . . ."

forth.[130] Thus the circle of the authority of the Scriptures completes itself. The Scriptures occupy the pinnacle of authority because they are the Word of God, just God's congealed speech to us. We know them to be such because they have been given to us as such by the apostles who were appointed and empowered precisely for the task of establishing the Church of God on earth, and who are therefore the vehicles for the transmission to us of the will of God and the Word which embodies that will.

But have the Scriptures which we have and which have acquired canonical authority in the Church, really been given to us by the apostles as the Word of God? How shall we assure ourselves of these Scriptures that they possess that apostolicity which lends to them their revelatory character and makes them our supreme authority? The answer returned by Augustine to this question has been most variously conceived, and indeed, out of the several interpretations given it, heterogeneous traditions of his teaching have grown up as discordant at the extremes as the formal principles of Romanism and Protestanism. If we could content ourselves with a simple concrete statement, it doubtless would not be far astray to say briefly that Augustine received the Scriptures as apostolic at the hands of the Church; and that this is the meaning of his famous declaration, " I would not believe the Gospel except I were moved thereto by the authority of the Catholic Church." But the question at once arises whether this appeal to the Church is for conclusive testimony or for authoritative decision. Divergent interpretations at once intervene, and we find ourselves therefore little advanced by our concrete response. The precise question that is raised by these divergent interpretations is whether Augustine validated to himself the Scriptures as apostolic in origin and therefore the revealed Word of God by appropriate evidence, more or less fully drawn out and more or less wisely marshaled; or declined all argument and

130 " Confessiones," xiii. 29. 44: " O Domine, nonne ista Scriptura tua vera est, quoniam tu verax et veritas edidisti eam? . . . O homo, nempe quod Scriptura mea dicit, ego dico."

cut the knot by resting on the sheer enactment of the contemporary Church. In the latter case Augustine would appear
as the protagonist of the Romish principle of the supreme authority of the Church, subordinating even the Scriptures to
this living authority. In the former he would appear as the
forerunner of the Protestant doctrine of the supreme authority
of Scripture.

The proper evidence of the apostolicity of the canonical
Scriptures is, of course, historical. Apostolicity is a historical
conception and its actuality can be established only on historical evidence. When Augustine declares of Scripture that it
owes its authority to its apostolicity, he would seem, therefore,
already to have committed himself to dependence for the validation of the authority of Scripture upon historical evidence.
Many others than the Romanists, however, have found Augustine defective in his teaching or at least in his practice at
this point. Neander remarks that Augustine having been
brought by Manichæism into doubt as to which were the true
documents of the Christian religion, and not being prepared
for a historical investigation to determine the truth of the matter, had nothing left him but to fall back upon the tradition
of the Church; [131] and this opinion is echoed by Reuter,[132] and
sharpened by Harnack.[133] It is to be observed, however, that,
when we have suggested that Augustine's dependence was
placed wholly on the " tradition of the Church," [134] as Neander
phrases it, we have not removed the ground of his conviction
out of the sphere of historical judgments. To say " tradition "
is indeed only to say " history " over again. And the question at
this point is not whether the historical evidence which Augustine rested upon was good historical evidence, but whether
he rested upon historical evidence at all, rather than upon the
bare authority of the contemporary Church. It will be useful to

[131] " Katholismus und Protestantismus " (1863), p. 82.
[132] " Augustinische Studien," p. 491, note 1.
[133] " History of Dogma," v. p. 80; cf. Loofs, " Leitfaden zum Studium der
Dogmengeschichte."
[134] " Die Ueberlieferung der kirche."

recall here Augustine's discussion of "tradition" to which we have just had occasion to advert. We will remember that he expressly distinguishes between "tradition" and "Scripture," and decisively subordinates the authority of "tradition" to that of "Scripture." It would certainly be incongruous to suppose him to be at the same moment basing the superior authority of Scripture on the inferior authority of tradition — in any other sense than that in which fact is based upon its appropriate evidence. We should bear in mind, moreover, that his appeal to "tradition" was in the instances brought before us distinctly of the nature of an appeal to testimony, and as such was distinctly discriminated from an appeal to the "Church," speaking, say, through a bishop or a council, and as distinctly preferred to it. His purpose was to validate certain customs prevalent in the Church as incumbent on all. This he does, not directly by asserting as sufficient the authority of the contemporary Church, as if the Church was as such clothed with the right to determine the practice of its adherents by a mere *ipse dixit*. He proceeds, rather, indirectly, by seeking to establish the apostolicity of these customs by an appeal to the immemorial universality of their tradition in the Church. Obviously "tradition" is treated here not as authority, but as evidence; and the "authority" thus validated by tradition is treated as superior to the "authority" of the contemporary Church speaking through whatever channels. It certainly would be incongruous to suppose that he was nevertheless consciously basing the authority of Scripture, which was to him superior to that of even tradition, on the bare authority of the Church, which he defines to be inferior to either. His appeal to the "Church," as by its "authority" moving men to believe the "Gospel" can scarcely be understood otherwise, therefore, than as a broad statement that the Scriptures are validated as apostolic and therefore authoritative in some way by the Church. What is meant, when this is made specific, is, obviously, that the testimony of the whole Church, borne unbrokenly from the beginning, to the apostolicity of the canonical Scriptures is conclusive of the fact.

In his appeals to the " Church " after this fashion Augustine certainly had in mind the Church as a whole, as extended through both space and time; and his fundamental contention is that the testimony of this Church is of decisive weight to the origin of her Scriptures in apostolic gift, and therefore to the authority of the Scriptures as an inspired revelation of the divine will. Such an appeal is distinctly of the nature of an appeal to historical testimony. But the nature of this appeal would not be essentially altered were we to omit consideration of the extension of the Church in time and focus attention on its extension in space alone, as many suppose Augustine to have done. To appeal to the testimony of the universal Church is to adduce historical evidence. Even if we do not accord such weight to this evidence as was obviously accorded to it by Augustine, this difference in our estimate of its conclusiveness should not blind us to its nature. We may smile if we will at the easiness of Augustine's historical conscience, and wonder that he could content himself with testimony so untested. But we ought to recognize that in so doing we are criticising his sense of historical values, not disproving that his resort to the Church was precisely for testimony.

Nor is it very difficult to do serious injustice to Augustine's sense of historical values in a matter of this kind. It is very much a matter of times and seasons. An appeal to the testimony of the universal Church at the close of the nineteenth or at the opening of the twentieth century is not altogether without historical value. But we must not fail to bear in mind that an appeal to the testimony of the universal Church at the close of the fourth or the opening of the fifth century is something very different from an appeal to its testimony at the close of the nineteenth or the opening of the twentieth century. Certainly the testimony of the universal Church at the close of the first or the opening of the second century is still treated in wide circles, as in such a thing as the apostolic gift of the Scriptures, conclusive. And it is not an easy matter accurately to estimate exactly the rate at which the value of this testimony decreases with the lapse of time. Are we so sure that its value had depreciated by the close of the fourth century to such an extent as to render an appeal to the Church as witness-bearer, at that period, absurd? The Church to which the Scriptures were committed by the apostolic college, by whom it was founded and supplied with its corpus juris — is not this Church the proper witness to the apostolicity of the Scriptures it has received from the hands of its apostolic founders? And is it strange that it has always been appealed to for its testimony to this fact? No doubt, as time passed and the years intervening between the commission of the Scriptures to the Church and its witness-bearing to them increased, this testimony became ever weaker as testimony. And no doubt as it became weaker as testimony it naturally took to itself more and more the character of arbitrary authentication. No doubt, further, it was by this slow transmutation of testimony into authentication that the Romish conception of Scripture as dependent upon the Church for its authentication gradually came into being. And no doubt still further the change was wrought practically before it was effected theoretically. Men came practically to rest upon the authority of the Church for the accrediting of Scripture, before they recognized that what they received from the Church was anything more than testimony. The theoretic recognition came inevitably, however, in time. So soon as the defect in the testimony of the Church arising from the lapse of time began to be observed, men were either impelled to cure the defect by an appeal to the Church of the past, that is to say by a historical investigation; or else tempted to rest satisfied with the authority of the living Church. The latter course as the line of easiest resistance, falling in, moreover, as it did, with the increasingly high estimate placed on the Church as mediatrix of religion, was inevitably ultimately taken; and the Romish doctrine resulted. Let it be allowed that in this outline we have a true sketch of the drift of thought through the Patristic Church. It still is not obvious that this development had proceeded so far by the close of the fourth century that Augustine's appeal to the " Church " to authenticate the " Gospel " must be understood as an appeal to the authority strictly so called rather than to the testimony of the Church. On the face of it, it does not seem intrinsically absurd to suppose that Augustine may still at that date have made his appeal to the Church with his mind set upon testimony. And when we come to scrutinize the actual appeals which he made, it seems clear enough that his mind rested on testimony.

Perhaps there is no better way to bring the fact clearly before us than to note the passages quoted by the Romish expositors with a view to supporting their view that Augustine based the authority of the Scriptures immediately upon the dogmatic authority of the Church Thus, for example, Professor E. Portalié writes as follows: [135]

Above Scripture and tradition is the living authority of the Church. It alone guarantees to us the Scriptures, according to the celebrated declaration in the treatise " Against the Epistle of Manichæus called Fundamental," v. 6: " I indeed would not believe the Gospel except the authority of the Catholic Church moved me." Compare " Against Faustus the Manichæan " xxii. 79; xxviii. 2.

We reserve for the moment comment on " the celebrated declaration " from the " Contra Epist. Manich. Fundam.," and content ourselves with observing that if it indeed implies that Augustine based the authority of Scripture on that of the " living " Church, it receives no support from the companion passages cited. They certainly appeal to the " historical " Church, that is to say adduce the testimony of the Church extended in time rather than the bare authority of the Church extended in space. So clear is this in the latter case [136] that Augustine in it sets the testimony of the Manichæans to the genuineness of their founder's writings side by side, as the same in kind, with the testimony of the Church to the genuineness of the Apostolic writings. I believe, he says, that the book you produce is really Manichæus', because from the days of Manichæus until to-day it has been kept in continuous possession

[135] Vacant-Mangenot, " Dictionaire de théologie Catholique," i. col. 2341.

[136] " Contra Faustum Man.," xxviii. 2.

and estimation as his, in the society of the Manichæans: similarly you must believe that the book we produce as Matthew's is his on the same kind of testimony in the Church. To the fixed succession of bishops among the Christians is assigned no different kind of authority than is allowed to the fixed succession of presiding officers among the Manichæans; in both alike this succession is adduced merely as a safeguard for trustworthy transmission. No doubt Augustine represents the testimony of the Church as indefinitely more worthy of credit than that of the Manichæans, but this is a different matter: *gradus non mutant speciem*. Similarly, in the former citation [137] Augustine's appeal is not specifically to the Church of his time, but to the " holy and learned men " who were living in the time of the writers — real or alleged — of the books in question, who, he says, would be in position to know the truth of the matter. Nothing can be clearer in this case either, than that the point of Augustine's argument turns on the validity of the testimony of the Church, not on the dogmatic authority of the Church.

The note struck by these passages is sustained in all Augustine's discussions of the matter and sometimes swells to an even clearer tone. Take for instance the *argumentum ad absurdum* with which he plies Faustus [138] to the effect that we can never be assured of the authorship of any book " if we doubt the apostolic origin of those books which are attributed to the apostles by the Church which the apostles themselves founded, and which occupies so conspicuous a place in all lands." Clearly the appeal to the Church here is for testimony, not for authorization, as is evidenced very plainly in the sequel. For Augustine goes on to contrast the hardiness of the Manichæans in attempting to doubt the apostolicity of books so attested, with their equal hardiness in accepting as apostolic books brought forward solely by heretics, the founders of whose sect lived long after the days of the apostles; and then adduces parallels from classical authors. There are, he tells us, spurious books, in circulation under the

[137] " Contra Faustum Man.," xxii. 79.   [138] *Ibid.*, xxxiii. 6.

name of Hippocrates, known to be spurious among other things from the circumstance " that they were not recognized as his at the time when his authorship of his genuine productions was determined." And who doubts the genuineness of these latter? Would not a denial of it be greeted with derision — " simply because there is a succession of testimonies to these books from the time of Hippocrates to the present day, which makes it unreasonable either now or hereafter to have any doubt on the subject." Is it not by this continuity of the chain of evidence that any book is authenticated — Plato's, Aristotle's, Cicero's, Varro's — or any of the Christian authors' — " the belief becoming more certain as it becomes more general, up to our own day "? Is not the very principle of authentication this: the transmission of information from contemporaries through successive generations? How then can anyone be so blinded by passion as " to deny the ability of the Church of the apostles — a community of brethren as numerous as they were faithful — to transmit their writings unaltered to posterity, as the original seats of the apostles have been occupied by a continuous succession of bishops to the present day? " Are we to deal with the apostolic writings differently from the natural dealing we accord day by day to ordinary ones — whether of profane or religious authors? [139]

The matter is not different when at an earlier place in the same treatise [140] he takes up much the same point on which he is arguing in the famous passage " I would not believe the Gospel, etc." When Manichæus calls himself an apostle, he says, it is a shameless falsehood, " for it is well known that this heresy began not only after Tertullian, but after Cyprian." And what evidence can Manichæus or Faustus bring forward,

[139] Cf. *ibid.*, xxxii. 19: " Why not rather submit to the authority of the Gospel which is so well-founded, so confirmed, so generally acknowledged and admired, and which has an unbroken series of testimonies from the Apostles down to our own day, that you may have an intelligent belief? " Cf. also xi. 2, xiii. 4, xxxiii. 6 and 9. Because Augustine was deeply impressed by the catholicity of the Church's testimony (as e.g., " De morr. eccles. cath.," xxix. 61) is no reason why we should fail to see that he is equally impressed by its continuity — that is, by its historical character.

[140] xiii. 4, 5.

which will satisfy anyone not inclined to believe either their
books or themselves? Will Faustus " take our apostles as witnesses? Unless he can find some apostles in life, he must read
their writings: and these are all against him. . . . He cannot
pretend that their writings have been tampered with; for that
would be to attack the credit of his own witnesses. Or if he
produces his own manuscripts of the apostolic writings, he
must also obtain for them the authority of the Churches
founded by the apostles themselves, by showing that they
have been preserved and transmitted by their sanction. It will
be difficult for a man to make me believe him on the evidence
of writings which derive their authority from his own word,
which I do not believe. . . . The authority of our books,
which is confirmed by the agreement of so many nations, supported by a succession of apostles, bishops, and councils, is
against you. Your books have no authority, for it is an authority maintained by only a few and these the worshippers of
an untruthful God and Christ. . . . The established authority
of the Scriptures must outweigh every other: for it derives
new confirmation from the progress of events which happen,
as Scripture proves, in fulfilment of the predictions made so
long before their occurrence." Of course this is a piece of
polemic argumentation, not a historical investigation: but the
gist of the polemic is simply that the Scriptures of the Christians owe their authority to a valid historical vindication of
them as of apostolic origin, while the Scriptures of the Manichæans lack all authority because they lack such a validation.
Augustine does not think of such a thing as simply opposing
the authority of the Church to the Manichæan contentions;
and much less of course does he take a roundabout way to the
same result, by opposing to them the authority of Scriptures
which owe all their authority to the mere *ipse dixit* of the
Church. If he speaks of authority as given to sacred books
only " through the Churches of Christ," it is clear that this
does not mean that these churches communicate to these
Scriptures an authority inherent in the Churches, but only
that it is by their testimony that that supreme authority

which belongs to the Scriptures from their apostolic origin is vindicated to them, as indeed it is confirmed to them by other testimonies also, those, to wit, of miracles and fulfilled prophecy and the consent of the nations and the succession of apostles, bishops, and councils, to confine ourselves to items enumerated here. Surely it cannot be doubted that here also Augustine's appeal to the Church as authenticating the Scriptures is to the Church as a witness, not as an authorizer.

It is natural to turn from this passage immediately to the closely related one in the treatise " Against Manichæus' Epistle called Fundamental," in which the famous words, " I would not believe the Gospel, etc.," occur. If the passage which we have just had before us is rather a piece of sharp polemics than a historical investigation, much more this. Augustine proposes here to join argument with the Manichæans on the pure merits of the question at issue between them. He wishes to approach the consideration of their claims as would a stranger who was for the first time hearing their Gospel: and as they promise nothing less than demonstration he demands that they give him nothing less than demonstration before asking of him assent.[141] He warns them that he is held to the Catholic Church by many bonds, which it will be hard to loosen: so that their task of convincing him on the ground of pure reason will not be an easy one. He has found a very pure wisdom in the Catholic Church — not indeed attained to in this life by more than a few spiritual men, while the rest walk by faith, but nevertheless shining steadily forth for all who have eyes to see it. He has been deeply impressed by the wide extension of the Church. The authority it exercises — " inaugurated by miracles, nourished by hope, augmented by love, established by antiquity " — has very strongly moved him. The unbroken succession of rulers in the Church possesses for him a great weight of evidence. He confesses that the very name of " Catholic " — retained unchallenged amid so many heresies — has affected him deeply. What have the Mani-

[141] " Contra Epist. Manich. Fundam.," iii. 3.

chæans to offer him which would justify him in setting aside these and such inducements to remain a Catholic? Nothing but the " promise of the truth " (*sola veritatis pollicitatio*). The " promise " of the truth, observe: not " the truth " itself. If the latter — why, Augustine gives up the contest at once. For he allows without dispute, that if they give him truth itself — so clearly the truth that it cannot be doubted — *that* is something that is to be preferred to all these things which he has enumerated as holding him in the Catholic Church — these and all other things that can be imagined as holding him there. For nothing is so good as truth. But he persistently demands that there must be something more than a " promise " of truth before he can separate himself from the Catholic Church — or rather, as he puts it, before he can be moved " from that faith which binds his soul with ties so many and so strong to the Christian religion." It is, then, we perceive, strict demonstration which Augustine is asking of the Manichæans, and he conducts the argument on that basis.

Turning at once to Manichæus' " Fundamental Epistle " as a succinct depository of nearly all which the Manichæans believe, he quotes its opening sentence: " Manichæus, an apostle of Jesus Christ, by the providence of God the Father." There he stops immediately to demand proof — proof, remember, not mere assertion. You have promised me truth, he says — demonstrated truth: and this is what you give me. Now, I tell you shortly, I do not believe it. Will you prove it to me: or will you, in defiance of the whole claim of the Manichæans, that they ask faith of no man save on the ground of demonstration, simply demand of me belief without clear and sound proof? If you propose proof, I will wait for it. Perhaps you will turn to the Gospel and seek there a testimony to Manichæus. But suppose I do not believe the Gospel? Are you to depend for your proof — you who differentiate yourselves from Christians in this, that while they demand faith, you offer them demonstration and ask belief of nothing until you have demonstrated it — are *you* to depend for your proof on this very faith of the Christians? For observe, my faith in the Gospel rests on the authority of the Catholic Church. And moreover, I find myself in this quandary: the same Church that tells me to believe the Gospel tells me not to believe Manichæus. Choose, then, which you will. If I am to believe the Catholics, then I cannot believe Manichæus — for they tell me not to. If I am not to believe the Catholics, then, you cannot use the Gospel, because, it was out of the preaching of the Catholics that I have been brought to believe the Gospel. Or if you say I am to believe them in this one matter and not in the other — I am scarcely so foolish as to put my faith thus at your arbitrary disposal, to believe or not believe as you dictate, on no assigned ground. It was agreed that you should not ask faith from me without clear proof — according to your universal boast that you demand no belief without precedent demonstration. It is clear, then, that to render such a proof you must not appeal to the Gospel. " If you hold to the Gospel, I will hold to those by whose teaching I have come to believe the Gospel; by their instructions I will put no credit in you whatever. And if by any chance you should be able to find anything really clear as to the apostolicity of Manichæus you will weaken the authority of the Catholics for me, since they instruct me not to believe you; and this authority having been weakened I shall no longer be able to believe the Gospel for it was through them that I came to believe it." The upshot of it is that if no clear proof of Manichæus' apostleship is to be found in the Gospel, I shall credit the Catholics rather than you; while if there is such to be found in the Gospel I shall believe neither them nor you. Where then is your demonstration of the apostleship of Manichæus — that I should believe it? Of course I do not mean I do not believe the Gospel. I do believe it, and believing it I find no way of believing you. You can point out neither in it nor in any other book faith in which I confess, anything about this absurd apostleship of Manichæus. But it is certainly evident that your promise to demonstrate to me your tenets signally fails in this case on any supposition.

This is Augustine's argument in this famous passage. Undoubtedly the exact interpretation of its implications with respect to the seat of authority in Christianity is attended with considerable difficulty. And it is not altogether strange that the Romanists have seized upon it as subordinating the " Gospel " to the " Church ": nor even that they have been followed in this, not merely by extreme rationalists predisposed to every interpretation of a Patristic writer which tends to support their notion that the clothing of Scripture with absolute authority was a late and unhistorical dogmatic development,[142] but also by many scholars intent only upon doing complete justice to Augustine's opinions.[143] There are serious difficulties, however, in the way of this interpretation of the passage. One of them is that it would in that case be out of accord with the entirety of Augustine's teaching elsewhere. It is quite true that elsewhere also he speaks of the authority of the Church, and even establishes the Church on the " summit of authority." But in all such passages he speaks obviously of the Church rather as the instrument of the spread of the saving truth than as the foundation on which the truth rests — in a word, as the vehicle rather than the seat of authority.[144] And in general, as we have already seen, Augustine's allusions to the Church as " the pillar and ground of the truth " throw the stress on its function of witness-bearing to the truth rather than found the truth on its bare *ipse dixit*. It is scarcely likely that he has spoken in a contrary sense in our present passage. We must not permit it to fall out of sight that Augustine's point of view in this passage is that of one repelling the Manichæan claim of strict demonstration of the truth of their teaching. His rejoinder amounts to saying that they cannot ground a demonstration upon a Gospel accepted only on faith.

---

[142] Cf. e.g., H. J. Holtzmann, " Kanon und Tradition " (1859), pp. 2, 3.

[143] Cf. e.g., Harnack, " History of Dogma," v. 80; Loofs, " Leitfaden zum Studium der Dogmengeschichte "; Dorner, " Augustinus "; Kunze, " Glaubenslehre," etc.

[144] Portalié, as cited, col. 2413, adduces in proof that Augustine places the Church " above even Scripture and tradition," *De utilitate credendi*, xvii. 35, comparing " Epist." 118, 32.

The contrast at this point is not between the weakness of the basis on which they accept their tenets and the incomparable weight of the authority of the Church on which Christians accept the " Gospel." On the contrary, the contrast is between the greatness of their claims to demonstration and the weakness of its basis — nothing but the " Gospel " which is accepted on " authority" not on " demonstration " — on " faith " not on " reason " — in effect, on " testimony," not on " sight." In a word, the " authority of the Church " is adduced here not as superlatively great — so great that, in the face of it, the Manichæan claims must fall away let them be grounded in what they may; but rather as incongruously inadequate to support the weight the Manichæan must put on it if he is to build up his structure of demonstration. The Manichæan undertakes a demonstration, scorning a faith that rests on authority: and then actually wishes to rest that demonstration on a premise which has no other basis than a faith that rests on authority. He cannot *demonstrate* that Manichæus was an Apostle of Christ on the testimony of a " Gospel" which itself is accepted on the *authority* of the Catholic Church: " authority " being used here in its contrast with " reason," not with " testimony," and in pursuance of Augustine's general contention that all religious truth must begin with faith on authority and not with demonstration on reason. This being the case, so far is the passage from predicating that Augustine esteemed the " authority " of the Church as " the highest of all " as the Romish contention insists,[145] that its very gist is that the testimony of the Church is capable of establishing only that form of conviction known as " faith " and therefore falls hopelessly short of " demonstration."

Such being the case we cannot be surprised that in all ages there has been exhibited a tendency among those more or less emancipated from the Romish tradition to deny that even this famous passage asserts the supreme authority of the contemporary Church. Striking instances may be found

[145] Cf. Portalié, as cited, col. 2341 and col. 2413.

for example in William Occam [146] and Marsilius of Padua [147] in the fourteenth century and in John Wessel [148] in the fifteenth: and examples are not wanting throughout the whole period of papal domination.[149] Of course the early Protestant controversialists take their place in this series. With them the matter was even less than with William Occam and Marsilius a merely academical question. In their revolt from the dogmatic authority of the Church and their appeal to the Scriptures alone as the sole source and norm of divine truth, they were met by the citation of this passage from Augustine. As on its theological side the Reformation was precisely an "Augustinian" revival, the adduction of Augustine's authority in behalf of the subjection of Scripture to the Church, was particularly galling to them and amounted to a charge that they were passing beyond the limits of all established Christianity. They were indeed in no danger, in casting off the authority of the Church, of replacing it with the authority of any single father. Doubtless Luther spoke a little more brusquely than was the wont of the Reformers, in the well-known assertion: "Augustine often erred; he cannot be trusted: though he was

[146] Occam explains that the "ecclesia quae majoris auctoritatis est quam evangelista, est illa ecclesia cujus auctor evangelii pars esse agnoscitur" (Goldasti mon. tom. 1. fol. 402). That is to say, he understands the Church here as projected through time, and as including even Jesus Himself: the historical not the contemporary Church. But he takes "authority" strictly. Cf. Neander, "General History of the Christian Religion and Church," E. T. v. p. 40.

[147] Marsilius explains: "Dicit autem Augustinus pro tanto se credere evangelio propter ecclesiae catholicae auctoritatem, quia suae credulitatis initium inde sumpsit, quam Spiritu Sancto dirigi novit: fides enim quandoque incipit ex auditu" — in which he anticipates the general Protestant position. Cf. (quite fully) Neander, op. cit., E. T. v. pp. 27–28.

[148] De Potestate Ecclesiastica (Opp. p. 759): "We believe in the Gospel on God's account, and on the Gospel's account in the Church and the Pope; not in the Gospel on the Church's account: wherefore that which Augustine says ("Contra Epist. Manich. Fundam.," chap. 6), concerning the Gospel and the Church, originis de credendo verbum est, non comparationis aut praeferentiae. For the whole passage and others of like import, see Gieseler, "Lehrbuch der Kirchengeschichte," 1829, II, part 3, sect. 5, § 153, p. 495; E. T. "Ecclesiastical History," 1868, iii. 468; and cf. Schmidt, Jahrbücher für die Theologie, (1861), vi. 235.

[149] Cf., for example, the instances mentioned by Chamier, below.

good and holy, yet he, as well as other fathers, was wanting in the true faith." But the essential opinion here expressed was the settled judgment of all the Reformers and is by no means inconsistent with their high admiration of Augustine or with their sincere deference to him. The gist of the matter is that though they looked upon Augustine as their great instructor, esteeming him indeed the greatest teacher God had as yet given His Church; and felt sure, as Luther expressed it, that " had he lived in this century, he would have been of our way of thinking "; they yet knew well that he had not lived in the sixteenth century but in the fourth and fifth and that in the midst of the marvelous purity of his teaching there were to be found some of the tares of his time growing only too richly. Ready as they were to recognize this, however, they were not inclined to admit without good reason that he had erred so sadly in so fundamental a matter as that at present before us; and they did not at all recognize that the Romanists had made good their assertion that Augustine in saying that " he would not believe the Gospel except as moved thereto by the authority of the Catholic Church " was asserting the Romish theory that the authority of the Church lies behind and above all other authorities on earth — that, as even Schwane puts it, the Church is the representative of God on earth and its authority alone can assure us of the reality of a divine revelation.

Already at the Leipzig disputation with Eck, Luther had been triumphantly confronted with this statement of Augustine's; and in his "Resolutions" on that debate he suggests that Augustine was only giving what was historically true in his own case.[150] Augustine had himself been led to believe the Gospel through the ministration of the Church; and he adduces this fact only that he might bring to bear upon his heretical readers the impressive testimony of the whole Church, which was, of course, of much more moving weight than his own personal witness could be. As a matter of fact,

[150] See Köstlin, " The Theology of Luther," E. T. ii. pp. 224, 255, and especially i. pp. 320–321.

comments Luther, the Gospel does not rest on the Church, but contrariwise, the Church on the Gospel. It was not Luther's way to say his say with bated breath. This is the way he expresses his judgment in his " Table Talk ":[151] " The Pope . . . to serve his own turn, took hold on St. Augustin's sentence, where he says, *evangelio non crederem*, &c. The asses could not see what occasioned Augustin to utter that sentence, whereas he spoke it against the Manicheans, as much as to say: I believe you not, for ye are damned heretics, but I believe and hold with the Church, the spouse of Christ." It seemed to Luther, in other words, quite one thing to say that the credit of the Church ought to be higher than that of the Manichæans, and quite another to teach that the authority of the Church was needed to give authority to the Gospel. Perhaps the consentient opinion of the Reformers in this matter is nowhere better stated, in brief form, than in the Protestant " Objections " to the Acts of Ratisbon, which were penned by Melanchthon.[152] " Although therefore," we read here, " the conservation of certain writings of the Prophets and Apostles is the singular work and benefit of God, nevertheless there must be recognized that diligence and authority of the Church, by which it has, in part testified to certain writings, in part by a spiritual judgment separated from the remaining Prophetic and Apostolic Scriptures those that are unworthy and dissentient. Wherefore Augustine commends to us the authority of the primitive Church,[153] receives the writings that are approved by the Catholic consent of the primitive Church; (and) repudiates the later books of the Manichæans. Accordingly he says: '*I would not believe the Gospel except the authority of the Catholic Church moved me.*' He means that he is moved by the consentient testimony of the primitive Church, not to doubt that these books were handed down from

---

[151] " Of the Fathers," near the beginning (chap. DXXX.). Augustine's statement is invoked in the bull, *Exsurge Domine,* published by Leo X in 1520 against Luther.

[152] *Corpus Reformatorum,* iv. 350. A French version is given in the Brunswick ed. of Calvin's works, v. 564 (*Corpus Reformatorum,* v. 33).

[153] " Auctoritatem primae Ecclesiae."

the Apostles and are worthy of credit (*fide*)." In a word, according to Melanchthon, Augustine is to be read as appealing to the testimony of the Church not as asserting its authority.

In the same line follow all the Reformers, and much the same mode of statement may be read, for example, in Butzer, or Calvin, or Bullinger, or Peter Martyr. " I will not now remember," writes Bullinger,[154] " how. by manifest words the standard-bearers of that see do write, that the canonical scripture taketh her authority of the church, abusing this sentence of the ancient father St. Augustine, ' I would not have believed the Gospel, if the authority of the holy Church had not moved me.' . . ." How they abused it Peter Martyr tells us more fully: [155] " But they say that Augustine writes ' Against the Epistola Fundamenti,' 'I would not believe the Gospel except the authority of the Church moved me.' But Augustine wished to signify by these words nothing else than that much is to be attributed to the ministry of the Church which proposes, preaches, and teaches the Gospel to believers. For who of us came to Christ or believed the Gospel except as excited by the preaching of the Gospel which is done in the Church? It cannot be inferred from this, however, that the authority of the Gospel hangs on the Church in the minds of the auditors. For if that were true, long ago the Epicureans and Turks had been persuaded. . . ." As was to be expected it was Calvin who gives us the solidest piece of reasoning upon the subject. The gist of what he says is that Augustine was not setting forth the source whence the Gospel derives its authority, but the instrument by which men may be led to recognize that authority. The unbeliever, he remarks, may well be brought to trust the Gospel by the consent of the Church; but the believer's trust in the Gospel finds its authority not in the Church, but in the Gospel itself, and this is logically prior to that of the Church, though no doubt, it may be chronologically recognized last by the inquirer. The Church may thus

---

[154] " Decades," v. 2 (Parker Soc. ed. v. p. 67).
[155] " Loci Communes," Zurich, 1580, i. 251 (iii. 3. 3).

bring us to the Gospel and commend the Gospel to us; but when we have accepted the Gospel our confidence in it rests on something far more fundamental than the Church. Augustine, he insists, " did not have in mind to suspend the faith which we have in the Scriptures on the will and pleasure (*nutu arbitriove*) of the Church, but only to point out, what we too confess to be true, that those who are not yet illuminated by the Spirit of God, are by reverence for the Church brought to docility so as to learn from the Gospel the faith of Christ; and that the authority of the Church is in this way an introduction, by which we are prepared for the faith of the Gospel." Augustine is perfectly right, then, he continues, to urge on the Manichæans the universal consent of the Church as a *reason* why they should come believingly to the Scriptures, but the *ground* of our faith in the Scriptures as a revelation of truth is that they are from God.[156]

The Protestant scholastics, of course, developed what had by their time become the traditional Protestant contention, and defended it against the assaults of the Romish controversialists. Who first invented the philological argument that Augustine uses in this sentence the imperfect for the pluperfect " in accordance with the African dialect " — so that he says, not " I would not believe the Gospel," but, historically, " I would not have believed the Gospel " — we have not had the curiosity to inquire. If we may trust the English version of the " Decades," Bullinger already treats the tense as a pluperfect. Musculus,[157] who devotes a separate section of his *Locus de Sacris Scripturis* to the examination of Augustine's declaration lays great stress on this particular point, that in it *non crederem* is used for *non credidissem;* and Musculus is gen-

[156] " Institutes," i. 7. 3. Calvin very appositely points out that Augustine in the immediately preceding context represents the proper course to be to " follow those who invite us first to believe what we are not yet able to see, that, being made able by this very faith, we may deserve to understand what we believe, our mind being now inwardly strengthened and illuminated not by men but by God Himself." In these words, Calvin remarks, Augustine grounds our confidence in the Gospel on the internal operation of God Himself upon our minds. Cf. below, note 175.

[157] " Loci Communes," Basle, 1560, pp. 181–183 (Locus xxi).

erally cited by later writers upon it. This is true, for example, of both Whitaker and Chamier, who with Stillingfleet may be mentioned as offering perhaps the fullest and best discussions of the whole matter. Whitaker [158] devotes a whole chapter to it, and after adducing the arguments of Peter Martyr, Calvin, and Musculus, affirms that " it is plain that he (Augustine) speaks of himself as an unbeliever, and informs us how he first was converted from a Manichæan to be a Catholic, namely, by listening to the voice of the Church " — in which remark he appears to us to be quite wrong. Chamier's [159] treatment, which also fills a whole chapter, is exceedingly elaborate. He begins by calling attention to the singularity of the passage, nothing precisely to the same effect being adducible from the whole range of Augustine's writings. Then he cites the opinions of eminent Romanists divergent from the current Romish interpretation — those of John, Cardinal of Torre Cremara, Thomas Valden, Driedo, Gerson, who represent Augustine as assigning only a *declarative* authority to the Church, or as speaking not of the "living" but of the "historical" Church. " Augustine," says Driedo, " speaks of the Catholic Church which was from the beginning of the Christian faith ": " by the Church," says Gerson, " he understands the primitive congregation of those believers who saw and heard Christ and were his witnesses." All these are good staggers towards the truth, says Chamier: but best of all is the explanation of the passage which is given by Petrus de Alliaco, himself a cardinal, " in the third article, of the first question on the first of the sentences." In the judgment of this prelate Augustine's meaning is not that the Church was to him a *principium theologicum*, by which the Gospel was theologically proved to him to be true, but only a " moving cause " by which he was led to the Gospel — much " as if he had said, ' I would not believe the Gospel unless moved thereto by the holiness of the Church, or by the miracles of Christ: in which (forms of statement) though

[158] " Disp. on Holy Scripture " (1610), iii. 8 (Parker Society, E. T. p. 320).
[159] " Panstrat. Cathol." (Geneva, 1926), i. pp. 198 *sq.* (I. i. 7. 10).

a cause is assigned for believing the Gospel, there is no *principium prius* set forth, faith in which is the cause why the Gospel is believed." In a word, as it seems, Petrus de Alliaco is of the opinion that Augustine's appeal to the Church is to its testimony rather than to its authority. This opinion, now, continues Chamier, is illustrated and confirmed by weighty considerations brought forward by Protestant writers — whereupon he cites the arguments of Peter Martyr, Calvin, Musculus, Whitaker, and through them makes his way into a detailed discussion of the passage itself in all its terms. Rivaling Chamier's treatment in fullness if not equaling it in distinction is that given the passage in Stillingfleet's " Rational Account of the Grounds of the Protestant Religion," [160] under the three heads of (1) the nature of the controversy in which Augustine was engaged; (2) the Church by whose authority he was moved; and (3) the way and manner in which that Church's authority moved him — certainly a logically complete distribution of the material. The whole argument of scholastic Protestantism is brought before us in its briefest but certainly not in its most attractive form, however, in the concise statement given in De Moor's Commentary on John Marck's Compend.[161] According to this summary: (1) The Papists in adducing this passage to support their doctrine of the primary authority of the Church deceive themselves by a twofold fallacy — (A) They draw a general conclusion from a particular instance: it does not follow that because Augustine did not believe the Gospel except as moved by the authority of the Church, therefore no one can believe the Gospel whom the authority of the Church does not move; (B) They misunderstand Augustine, as if he were speaking of himself at the time of his writing, instead of at the time of his conversion. " For where he says, ' I would not believe were I not moved ' he is employing, as the learned observe, an African mode of speech, familiar enough to Augustine, in which the

[160] i. 7; " Works " (1709), iv. pp. 210 *sq.*
[161] " De Moor in J. Marck. Compend.," (1761), i. p. 160 (chap. ii. 7. *ad fin.*).

imperfect form is used for the pluperfect." . . . " His meaning then is not that believers should depend on the authority
. of the Church, but that unbelievers should take their start
from it "; and in this sense he elsewhere speaks often enough.
(2) Augustine is not speaking here of *auctoritas praecipiens,
juris et imperii* (injunctionary authority, with a legal claim
upon us for obedience) " as the Papists insist, — as if Augustine would have believed solely because the Church pronounced
belief to be due ": but of *auctoritas dignitatis* (the authority
of observed desert), "which flows from the notable manifestations of Divine Providence observable in the Church, —
such as miracles, antiquity, common consent (chap. iv.), and
which may lead to faith though it is incapable of implanting
it in the first instance." (3) " What is noted here, then, is the
external motive of faith, but not at all the infallible *principium
credendi,* which he teaches in the fourth chapter is to be sought
in the truth alone. . . . And it is to be noted that the fathers
elsewhere rightly hold that the Holy Scriptures are superior
in authority both *in se* and *quoad nos* to the Church. . . ."

Of course it is observable enough from this survey, that
the interest of the Protestant scholastics was far more in the
dogmatic problem of the seat of authority in Christianity,
than in the literary question of the precise meaning of Augustine's words. We must bear in mind that the citations we have
made are taken not from studies in literary history but from
dogmatic treatises; and that their authors approach the particular question upon which we are interrogating them from
a dogmatic point of view, and in a doctrinal interest. There
would be a certain unfairness in adducing these citations in
a connection like the present, therefore, were there any real
occasion to defend the tone in which they are couched. This
is by no means the case. We need not hesitate to recognize
nevertheless at once that some of the reasoning employed
by them to support their interpretation will scarcely bear
scrutiny. It is a counsel of despair, for example, to represent
Augustine as employing — " in accordance with the usage of
the African dialect " — the imperfect in a pluperfect sense.

We may readily confess that the supposition does violence to the context of the passage itself, which requires the imperfect sense; it seems clearly to be the offspring of a dogmatic need rather than of a sympathetic study of the passage. And we are afraid the same must be said of the general conception of the meaning of the passage which has probably given rise to this philological suggestion — viz., that it is a historical statement of Augustine's own experience and means merely that he himself was led by the Church's authority to the Gospel. He is not writing his autobiography in this passage, but arguing with the Manichæans; and he is not informing them of what had been true of his own manner of conversion but confounding them by asserting what in a given case he, as a reasonable man, would do. There are elements enough of doubtful validity in the argument of the Protestant scholastics, therefore — as there could not fail to be in the circumstances. But it is quite another question whether their general conception of the passage is not truer than that of their Romish opponents, and whether they do not adduce sound reasons enough for this general conception to support it adequately. It is a matter of common experience in every department of life — and not least in judicial cases, where the experience has been crystallized into a maxim to the effect that it is best to announce decisions and withhold the reasons — that the decisions of men's judgment are often far better than the reasons they assign for them: and it may haply prove true here too, that the position argued for by the Protestant scholastics is sounder than many of the arguments which they bring forward to support it.

It must be confessed, meanwhile, that modern Protestant opinion does not show so undivided a front as was the case during the scholastic period. The majority of Protestant scholars, historical investigators as well as dogmatic systematizers, do, indeed, continue to defend the essential elements of the interpretation for which the Protestant scholastics contended; but even these ordinarily adopt a different line of argument and present the matter from a somewhat different point of

view; and there are many recent Protestant scholars, and they
not invariably those deeply affected by the rationalism of
the day, who are inclined to revert more or less fully to the
Romish interpretation. Even Dr. W. G. T. Shedd, who reproduces more of the scholastic argument than is now usual,[162]
shows the effect of the change. Even he quotes Hagenbach [163]
approvingly to the effect that Augustine " merely affirms " " a
subjective dependence of the believer upon the authority of
the Church universal, but not an objective subordination of
the Bible itself to this authority "; though he proceeds to
weaken the " subjective dependence of the believer upon the
authority of the Church " so as to leave room for a " private
judgment." What in his view Augustine is asserting is the
duty of the individual to respect the authority of the Church,
because the " Church universal had an authority higher than
that of any one member," and it is therefore unreasonable
for the individual, or a heretical party, to "oppose their private judgment to the catholic judgment." Or rather, what he
supposes Augustine to affirm is — as he fortunately weakens
the statement in the next sentence — " the greater probability
of the correctness of the Catholic Mind, in comparison with
the Heretical or Schismatic Mind, and thereby the *authority*
of the Church in relation to the individual, without dreaming,
however, of affirming its absolute *infallibility*, — an attribute
which he confines to the written revelation." Augustine's notion of " ecclesiastical authority " is by this expedient reduced
to "the natural expectation of finding that the general judgment is a correct one," coupled with " the right of private
judgment; the right to examine the general judgment and
to perceive its correctness with his own eyes." Thus, Dr. Shedd
supposes, " Augustine adopts the Protestant, and opposes the
Papal theory of tradition and authority." " The Papist's
method of agreeing with the catholic judgment," he explains,
" is passive. He denies that the individual may intelligently

---

[162] " History of Christian Doctrine," i. pp. 144–150. Cf. S. Baumgarten:
" Untersuchung. theol. Streitigkeiten," iii. pp. 2, 8.
[163] " Dogmengeschichte," § 119.

verify the position of the Church for himself, because the Church is *infallible,* and consequently there is no possibility of its being in error. The individual is therefore shut up to a mechanical and passive reception of the catholic decision. The Protestant, on the other hand, though affirming the high probability that the general judgment is correct, does not assert the infallible certainty that it is. It is conceivable and possible that the Church may err. Hence the duty of the individual, while cherishing an antecedent confidence in the decisions of the Church, to examine these decisions in the light of the written word, and to convert this presumption into an intelligent perception, or else demonstrate its falsity beyond dispute. ' Neither ought I to bring forward the authority of the Nicene Council,' says Augustine (" Contra Maximianum Arianum " II. xiv. 3), 'nor you that of Ariminum, in order to prejudge the case. I ought not to be bound (*detentum*) by the authority of the latter, nor you by that of the former. Under the authority of the Scriptures, not those received by particular sects, but those received by all in common, let the disputation be carried on, in respect to each and every particular.' " [164]

What strikes one most in these remarks of Dr. Shedd is that they begin by attributing to Augustine a doctrine of the authority of the Church universal over the individual, which forbids the individual to oppose his private judgment to the catholic judgment: proceed to vindicate to the individual a private judgment in the sense of a right to examine the general judgment that he may perceive its correctness with his own eyes — that is to say to an active as distinguished from a merely passive agreement with the catholic judgment: and end by somehow or other supposing that this carries with it the right to disagree with and reject the catholic judgment on the basis of an individual judgment. The premise is that it is not reasonable to erect the individual judgment against the catholic judgment: the conclusion is that it is the duty of the individual to subject the catholic judgment to his per-

[164] *Op. cit.,* pp. 148–149.

sonal decisions: the connecting idea is — that the individual
ought to be able to give an active and not merely a passive reception to the catholic decision. The logic obviously halts.
But it seems clear that what Dr. Shedd is striving to do is to
give due validity to what he considers Augustine to assert in his
famous declaration, viz., this, that the individual is subjectively under the authority of the Church; and yet at the same
time to vindicate for Augustine a belief in the right of private
judgment. He wishes to do justice to the conception of " authority " which he supposes Augustine to have had in mind in
this expression, without doing injustice to Augustine's obvious
exercise of freedom of opinion under the sole authority of the
Scriptures. It cannot be said that he has fully succeeded,
although there is much that is true in his remarks, considered
as an attempt to give a general account of Augustine's estimate of the authority of the Church. But it is of no great
importance for our present inquiry whether he has fully succeeded in this particular effort, or not; since, as has already
been pointed out, Augustine does not seem to intend in this
passage to place the individual subjectively under the " authority of the Church "; but appears to employ the term
" authority " in an entirely different sense from that which it
bears in such phrases — the sense namely in which it is the
synonym of " testimony " and the ground of " faith," in distinction from the " demonstration " of " reason " which is the
ground of that form of conviction which he calls " knowledge."

   From another point of view of importance Dr. Shedd's instinct has carried him very near to the truth. We refer to the
recognition that informs his discussion that Augustine did
make more of the Church and of the authority of the Church
than the Protestant scholastics were quite ready to admit.
It is probably the feeling that this is the case which accounts
for much of the tendency among recent scholars to concede
something to the Romish interpretation of Augustine's doctrine of the authority of the Church. It certainly cannot easily
be denied that Augustine does declare in this passage, that
the credit we accord the Gospel hangs on the credit we give

the Church. In this particular passage, this no doubt means
no more than that we are dependent on the Church to accredit
to us the Gospel; that it is from the Church's hands and on
her testimony that we receive the Gospel as apostolic and
divine. But, if we raise the broader question of Augustine's
attitude towards the Church in its relation to the reception
of the truth it cannot be successfully contended that it was
solely as a *motivum credibilitatis* that he reverenced the
Church. To him the Church was before all else the institute
of salvation, out of which there is no salvation. And although
it may be difficult to find expressed in language parallel to
this crisp *extra ecclesiam nulla salus,* that outside of the
Church there can be no right knowledge of God, it nevertheless
certainly belongs to the very essence of his doctrine that outside of the Church there can be no effective knowledge of
God. The Scriptures may be the supreme authority for faith,
and it may be true, therefore, that wherever the Scriptures go,
the salvatory truth will be objectively conveyed; but it is
equally true that with Augustine this Word of truth will exert
no saving power save in and through the Church.[165] As the
Church is the sole mediatrix of grace and that not merely in
the sense that it is through her offices alone that men are
brought once for all to God, but also in the sense that it is
through her offices only that all the saving grace that comes
to men is conveyed to them — so that we are with Christ
only when we are with His body the Church, and it is only
in the Church that communion with God can be retained as
well as obtained — it follows that the Word, however well
known it may be and however fully it may perform its function of making known the truth of God, profits no man spiritually save in the Church.[166] It seems to be implicated in this
that it is part of Augustine's teaching that the revealed truth
of God, deposited in the Holy Scriptures, will not profit men

165 The distinction between " habere " and " utiliter habere " or " salubriter
habere " was made to do yeoman's service as regards baptism, in the Donatist
controversy.

166 Cf. A. Dorner, " Augustinus," pp. 233 *sq.,* and H. Schmidt, in *Jahrbücher
für die Theologie* (1861), vi. 233.

even intellectually so that they may come by it to know God
save in communion with the Church. Certainly he would never
allow that an adequate knowledge could be obtained of that
truth which must be chastely and piously sought and the key
to which is love — access to which is closed to all but the
spiritual man — outside the limits of that Church the supreme
characteristic of which is that in it and in it alone is the love
of God shed abroad in our hearts by the Holy Spirit which
He has given unto us.[167]

The reverence which Augustine accordingly shows to the
teaching of the Church is both great and sincere. It is no
meaningless form when he opens his treatise on the "Literal
Interpretation of Genesis"[168] or his great work on "The Trinity"[169] with a careful statement of the faith of the Church on
the topics to be dealt with, to stand as a norm of teaching
beyond which it would be illegitimate to go[170] — declaring
moreover with complete simplicity, "This is my faith, too,
since it is the Catholic faith."[171] There can be no question
therefore that he accorded not merely a high value but also
a real authority to the teaching of the Church, an authority
which within its own limits may well be called a "dogmatic
authority." But it needs also to be borne in mind that the
organs of this authority were not conceived by him as official
but vital — those called of God in the Church to do the thinking and teaching for the Church;[172] that the nature of this
authority is never conceived by him as absolute and irreform-
able but always as relative and correctible — no teaching
from any source is to be accepted unhesitatingly as above
critical examination except that of the Scriptures only; and
that as to its source this authority is not thought of by him

[167] "De unitate eccles." ii. 2: "The members of Christ are linked together
by means of love that belongs to unity, and by means of it are made one
with their Head."

[168] "De Gen. ad Lit. imperf.," ad init.   [169] "De Trinitate," i. 4. 7.

[170] "De Gen. ad Lit. imperf.," i. 1: "catholicae fidei metas; . . . praeter
fidem catholicae disciplinae"; 2: "as the Catholic discipline commands to be
believed."   [171] "De Trinitate," i. 4. 7, ad fin.

[172] "Epist." 118, v. 32: "armed with the abundant weapons of reason, by
means of a comparatively few devoutly learned and truly spiritual men."

as original but derived, dependent upon the Scriptures upon which it rests and by which it is always to be tested and corrected. The Catholic faith as to the Trinity, for example, which is also his faith because it is the Catholic faith, is the faith that has been set forth, not by the organized Church on its own authority, but by " the Catholic expounders of the Divine Scriptures," intent upon teaching " according to the Scriptures " [173] and therefore only on the authority of these Scriptures. If there can be no question, therefore, that Augustine accorded a " dogmatic authority " to the Church, there can be no question either that the " dogmatic authority " he accorded to the Church was subordinated to the authority of the Scriptures, and was indeed but the representation of that authority in so to speak more tangible form. This, it is obvious, is in complete harmony with what we have already had occasion to note, in the matter of Christian observances, as to the relative authority Augustine accorded to the Scriptures, Tradition, the Church — in descending series. Only, it is to be noted that the dogmatic authority of the Church of which we are now specifically speaking expresses itself not merely, and not chiefly, through conciliar decrees, but rather through the vital faith of the people of God, first assimilated by them from the Scriptures, and then expressed for them by the appropriate organs of the expression of Christian thought, which in general are the Doctors of the Church. Such being the case, there can no question be raised whether or not the Church may be conceived as the supreme seat of authority in the dogmatic sphere. In many cases the proximate seat of authority it doubtlessly is; but never the ultimate seat of authority. That belongs with Augustine ever and unvaryingly to the Holy Scriptures,[174]

---

[173] " De Trinitate," i. 4. 7, *ad init.*

[174] " Epist." 164, iii. 6, offers a typical mode of statement: " And with respect to that first man, the father of the human race, that [Christ] loosed him from hell almost the whole Church agrees; and it is too considered that the Church does not believe this in vain — whencesoever it has been handed down, although the authority of the Canonical Scriptures is not expressly adducible for it (etiamsi canonicarum Scripturarum hinc expressa non proferatur auctoritas)."

witnessed to by the Church as given to it by the apostles as the
infallible Word of God, studied and expounded by the Church
for its needs, and applied by it to the varying problems which
confront it with the measure of authority which belongs to it
as the Church of God, the pillar and ground of the truth.

It is, however, in a deeper sense than even this that Augustine thought of the Church in relation to the acquisition
of the knowledge of the truth. With Augustine the Church as
it is the mediatrix of divine grace, is also the mediatrix of divine knowledge. As such the Church holds a position of the
very highest significance between the supreme seat of authority, the Holy Scriptures, and the souls of men. Only in and
through the Church can a sound as well as a saving knowledge
of the contents of the Scriptures be hoped for; only in and
through the Church can the knowledge of God enshrined in the
Holy Scriptures avail for the illumination of the intellect with
true knowledge of God, no less than for the sanctification of
the soul for true communion with God. But, it must be remembered that in speaking thus, Augustine is thinking of the
Church not mechanically as an organized body acting through
official organs, say the hierarchy, but vitally, as the *congregatio
sanctorum* acting through its vital energies as a communion of
love. The Church in which alone according to Augustine true
knowledge of God is to be had is fundamentally conceived as
the Body of Christ. And this is as much as to say that the essence of his doctrine of the authority of the Church would
not be inaptly expressed by the simple and certainly to no
Christian thinker unacceptable formula, that it is only in Jesus
Christ that God can be rightly known. The Church of Christ
is the Body of Christ, and this Body of Christ is the real subject of the true knowledge of God on earth: it is only therefore
as one is a member in particular of this Body that he can
share in the knowledge of God, of which it is the subject. This
is the counterpart in Augustine of that doctrine of the *Testimonium Spiritus Sancti* which was first formulated by Calvin and
from him became the corner stone of the Protestant doctrine
of authority: and it differs from that doctrine only because

and as Augustine's doctrine of " the means of grace " differs from the Protestant.[175]

Augustine's doctrine of the Church is a fascinating subject on which it is difficult to touch without being carried beyond the requirements of our present purpose. Perhaps enough has already been said to indicate sufficiently for the end in view the place which the Church holds in Augustine's doctrine of authority. In the sin-bred weakness of humanity, the Church mediates between the divine revelation deposited in the Holy Scriptures and the darkened mind of man; and thus becomes a paedagogue to lead men to the truth. It is in the Church that the truth is known; and this not merely in the sense that it is in the hands of the Church that the Scriptures are found, those Scriptures in which the whole Truth of God is indefectibly deposited; but also in the sense that it is in the Church alone that the mysteries of the faith, revealed in the Scriptures, are comprehended: that it is only in the participation of the graces found in her that men may hope to attain to the vision which is the possession solely of saints. The true knowledge of God belongs to the fellowship of His people, and out of it cannot be attained. And therefore, although Augustine knows of many things which bind him to the Catholic Church and the adduc-

[175] On Augustine's conception of the Church as a communion of saints, see the fifth of Reuter's " Augustinische Studien "; and compare Schmidt as above cited, especially from p. 233. On Augustine's relation to the Protestant doctrine of the " testimony of the Holy Spirit " see Pannier, " Le Témoignage du Saint-Esprit " (1893), pp. 67–68. After citing " Tract. iii. in Ep. Joan. ad Parthos," ii. 13; " De Trinitate," iii. 1–2; " Confessiones," vi. 5, and xi. 3, he adds: " There certainly is not yet here the whole of the witness of the Holy Spirit. . . . But St. Augustine has the intuition of a mysterious work which is wrought in the soul of the Christian, of an understanding of the Bible which does not come from man, but from a power external to him and superior to him; he urges the rôle which the direct correspondence between the Book and the reader must play in the foundation of Christian certitude. In this, as on so many other points, Augustine was the precursor of the Reformation, and a precursor without immediate continuers." In point of fact Augustine is just as clear as the Reformers that earthly voices assail only the ears, and that cathedram in coelo habet qui cordia docet (" Tract. iii. in Ep. Joan. ad Parthos," ii. 13). He differs from them only in the place he gives the Church in communicating that grace out of which comes the preparation of the mind to understand, as well as of the heart to believe, and of the will to do.

tion of which as undeniable credentials giving confidence to those who hold to that Church, he thinks should impress any hearer — such as the consent of peoples and nations, the just authority it enjoys among men, the unbroken succession of its rulers from the beginning, and the very name of Catholic — yet the real thing which above all others held him to the Catholic Church was, as he was well aware, that there was to be found in it "the purest wisdom" (*sincerissima sapientia*). He needs indeed to confess that to the knowledge of this wisdom only a few spiritual men (*pauci spirituales*) attain in this life, and even they (because they are men) only very partially (*ex minima quidem parte*), though without the least uncertainty (*sine dubitatione*).[176] The crowd (*turba*) meanwhile walk even in the Church, by faith — since their characteristic is, not vivacity of intellect, but simplicity in believing — the Church performing its function to them in holding out the truth to them to be believed. So that even the crowd are made in the apprehension of faith — each according to his ability — to share in the truth of which the Church is the possessor. All the time, however, there is in the Church and in it alone for the few spiritual men both the fullness of truth to be known and the opportunity to know it. The underlying idea is clearly that for the knowledge of the truth there are requisite two things — the revelation of the truth to be apprehended and the preparation of the heart for its apprehension: and that these two things can be found in conjunction only in the Church. Our thought reverts at once to Augustine's fundamental teaching that the remedy for the disabilities of sinful men is to be found in the twofold provision of Revelation and Grace. In the Church these two provisions meet, and it is therefore only in the Church that the sin-born disabilities of men can be cured: and only in the Church that men, being sinful, can attain to that knowledge of divine things in which is life.

By this construction, it will not fail to be perceived, Augustine sets the Church over against the world — or, as he would have phrased it, the glorious city of God over against

[176] "Contra Epist. Manich. Fundam.," i. 4, 5.

the earthly city — as the sole sphere in which true knowledge (*sapientia*) is found. Thus there is introduced a certain dualism in the manifestation of human life on earth. Two classes of men are marked off, separated one from another as darkness is separated from light. In the one, at the best only broken lights can play; because it is the natural development of sin-stricken humanity alone that it can offer. In the other may be found the steady shining of that true light which shall broaden more and more to the perfect day. The dualism of this conception of human life is resolved, however, by two considerations. In observing human life in its dualistic opposition we are observing it only in its process of historic development. The dualism is constituted by the invasion of the realm of darkness by the realm of light: and it exists only so long as the conquest of the darkness by the light is incomplete. A temporary dualism is the inevitable result of the introduction of any remedial scheme which does not act immediately and all at once. In the city of God — the Church of God's saints — we perceive the progress of the correction of the sin-born disabilities of men. Again the opposition of nature and the supernatural as the principles of the opposing kingdoms, must not be pressed to an extreme. With Augustine, as we have seen, all knowledge, even that which in contrast with a higher supernatural, may rightly be called natural knowledge, is in source supernatural: all knowledge rests ultimately on revelation. The problem to him was not, therefore, how to supplant a strictly natural knowledge by a strictly supernatural knowledge: but how to restore to men the power to acquire that knowledge which we call natural — how to correct sin-bred disabilities so that the general revelation of God may be reflected purely in minds which now are blinded to its reflection by sin. For this end, a special revelation, adapted to the needs of sin-disabled minds, is called in. Special revelation is not conceived here, then, as a substitute for general revelation, but only as a preparation for its proper assimilation. The goal is still conceived as the knowledge of God by direct vision; and special revelation is presented only as spectacles through which

the blind may trace out the way to the cure. The intervention
of God by a special revelation works, therefore, harmoniously
into the general scheme of the production of knowledge of God
through general revelation. The conception is that man being
a sinner, and unable to profit by general revelation, God intervenes creatively by special revelation and grace — by special
revelation enabling him to walk meanwhile until by grace he
is once more prepared to see the Light in its own light. Special
revelation, given through the prophets and apostles, is embodied in the Scriptures and brought to bear on man by the
Church, in which is found the grace to heal men's disabilities.
The Church therefore sets up in the world a city of God in
which, and in which alone, man may live free from the disabilities that clog all action in the earthly city.

If we cry out that the remedy is incomplete, the answer
is that it were better to say that the cure it is working is as
yet uncompleted. So long as grace has not wrought its perfect
work in our souls, there remains a dualism in all the functioning of our souls; so long as grace has not wrought its perfect work in the world there will remain a dualism in the
world. But when grace has wrought its perfect work, then, as
sin has been removed, the need of special revelation falls away,
nay the need of all the instrumentalities by which grace is
wrought falls away — the Church, the Scriptures, Christ the
Mediator Himself — and God alone suffices for the soul's requirements. The end to which all is directed and in which all
issues is not the destruction of nature but the restoration of
nature: and when nature is restored, there is no longer need of
the remedies. "There is nothing," says Augustine with emphasis, "that ought to detain us on the way" in our aspiration to God, in whom alone can we find our rest. And to put
the sharpest possible point upon the remark he at once proceeds to apply it to our Lord Himself, who, says he, " in so far
as He condescended to be our Way," wished not " to hold us "
— the reference being possibly to Jno. xx. 17 — " but rather to
pass away, lest we should cling weakly to temporal things,
even though they had been put on and worn by Him for our

salvation, and not rather press rapidly through them and strive to attain unto Himself who has freed our nature from the bondage of temporal things and set it down at the right hand of His Father." [177] The whole soteriological work of our Lord, in other words, is viewed by Augustine as a means to the end of our presentation, holy, and without spot, to the Father, and therefore as destined to fall away with all means when the end is attained.[178] When the Mediatorial Christ is viewed thus as instrument, of course the lower means also are so considered. Augustine, even, in a passage in the immediate neighborhood of what we have just quoted, speaks as if a stage of development might be attained even in this life in which the Scriptures, say, might fall out of use as a lame man healed would no longer need his crutch. " A man," says he,[179] " supported by faith, hope and love, and retaining these unshakenly, does not need the Scriptures except for instructing others." He adduces certain solitaries as examples: men in whom I Cor. xiii. 8 is already fulfilled — who "by means of these instruments" (as they are called) have had built up within them so great an edifice of faith and love that they no longer require their aid. So clear is it that by him all the means put in action by grace to cure the sin-bred disabilities of man were strictly conceived as remedies which, just because they work a cure, provide no substitutes for nature but bring about a restoration of nature.[180]

[177] " De Doctrina Christiana," i. 34, 38.

[178] Th. Bret, " La Conversion de S. Augustine " (Geneva, 1900), p. 64, generalizes as follows " We remark, however, that Augustine is affirmative only in what concerns the activity of Christ as reconciler. The rôle of eternal mediator, of perpetual friend, between the individual and God, was never clearly understood by Augustine. For him Christ came to restore man to his true condition, but, that once attained, the rôle of Saviour passed into the background. The sinner once cleansed of his sins, and placed in an atmosphere of the grace of God, found himself directly united with the Father without the intervention of the Son." This is only very partially correct; and its incorrectnesses touch on some important elements of Augustine's teaching. But it contains the essential matter.

[179] " De Doctrina Christiana," i. 39. 43.

[180] The general conception — but guarded from the fancy that attainment in this life can proceed so far as to be freed from the necessity of means

Augustine's whole doctrine thus becomes a unit. Man is to find truth within himself because there God speaks to him. All knowledge rests, therefore, on a revelation of God; God impressing on the soul continually the ideas which form the intellectual world. These ideas are taken up, however, by man in perception and conception, only so far as each is able to do so: and man being a sinner is incapacitated for their reception and retention. This sinful incapacity is met in the goodness of God by revelation and grace, the sphere of both of which is the Church. The Church is therefore set over against the world as the new Kingdom of God in which sinful man finds restoration and in its gradual growth we observe the human race attaining its originally destined end. The time is to come when the Kingdom of God shall have overspread the earth, and when that time comes, the abnormalities having been cured, the normal knowledge of God will assert itself throughout the redeemed race of man. Here, in a single paragraph, is Augustine's whole doctrine of knowledge and authority.

— is among the inheritances of Augustinians until this day. Cf., e.g., A. Kuyper, "Encyc. of Sacred Theology," E. T. pp. 368 *sq.*; and especially H. Bavinck, "Gereform. Dogmatiek," i. pp. 389 *sq.*, where the necessary cautions are noted. The misapprehensions of Harnack ("History of Dogma," E. T. v. pp. 99–100) will be obvious.

APPENDIX

JOHN CALVIN THE THEOLOGIAN

THE subject of this address is "John Calvin the Theologian," and I take it that what will be expected of me is to convey some idea of what manner of theologian John Calvin was, and of his quality as a theological thinker.

I am afraid I shall have to ask you at the outset to disabuse your minds of a very common impression, namely, that Calvin's chief characteristics as a theologian were on the one hand, audacity—perhaps I might even say effrontery—of speculation; and on the other hand, pitilessness of logical development, cold and heartless scholasticism. We have been told, for example, that he reasons on the attributes of God precisely as he would reason on the properties of a triangle. No misconception could be more gross. The speculative theologian of the Reformation was Zwingli, not Calvin. The scholastic theologian among the early Reformers was Peter Martyr, not Calvin. This was thoroughly understood by their contemporaries. "The two most excellent theologians of our times." remarks Joseph Scaliger, "are John Calvin and Peter Martyr, the former of whom has dealt with the Holy Scriptures as they ought to be dealt with—with sincerity, I mean, and purity and simplicity, without any scholastic subtleties. . . . Peter Martyr, because it seemed to fall to him to engage the Sophists, has overcome them sophistically, and struck them down with their own weapons."

It is not to be denied, of course, that Calvin was a speculative genius of the first order, and in the cogency of his logical analysis he possessed a weapon which made him terrible to his adversaries. But it was not on these gifts that he depended in forming and developing his theological ideas. His theological method was persistently, rigorously, some may even say exaggeratedly, *a posteriori*. All *a priori* reasoning here he not only eschewed but vigorously repelled. His instrument of research was not logical amplification, but exegetical investigation. In one word, he was distinctly a Biblical theologian, or, let us say it frankly, by way of eminence *the Biblical theologian of his age*. Whither the Bible took him, thither he went: where scriptural declarations failed him, there he stopped short.

It is this which imparts to Calvin's theological teaching

the quality which is its prime characteristic and its real offence in the eyes of his critics—I mean its positiveness. There is no mistaking the note of confidence in his teaching, and it is perhaps not surprising that this note of confidence irritates his critics. They resent the air of finality he gives to his declarations, not staying to consider that he gives them this air of finality because he presents them, not as his teachings, but as the teachings of the Holy Spirit in His inspired Word. Calvin's positiveness of tone is thus the mark not of extravagance but of sobriety and restraint. He even speaks with impatience of speculative, and what we may call inferential theology, and he is accordingly himself spoken of with impatience by modern historians of thought as a "merely Biblical theologian," who is, therefore, without any real doctrine of God, such as Zwingli has. The reproach, if it be a reproach, is just. Calvin refused to go beyond "what is written"—written plainly in the book of nature or in the book of revelation. He insisted that we can know nothing of God, for example, except what He has chosen to make known to us in His works and Word; all beyond this is but empty fancy, which merely "flutters" in the brain. And it was just because he refused to go one step beyond what is written that he felt so sure of his steps. He could not present the dictates of the Holy Ghost as a series of debatable propositions.

Such an attitude towards the Scriptures might conceivably consist with a thoroughgoing intellectualism, and Calvin certainly is very widely thought of as an intellectualist *à outrance*. But this again is an entire misapprehension. The positiveness of Calvin's teaching has a far deeper root than merely the conviction of his understanding. When Ernest Renan characterised him as the most Christian man of his generation he did not mean it for very high praise, but he made a truer and much more profound remark than he intended. The fundamental trait of Calvin's nature was precisely —religion. It is not merely that all his thinking is coloured by a deep religious sentiment; it is that the whole substance of his thinking is determined by the religious motive. Thus his theology, if ever there was a theology of the heart, was distinctively a theology of the heart, and in him the maxim that "It is the heart that makes the theologian" finds perhaps its most eminent illustration.

His active and powerful intelligence, of course, penetrated to the depths of every subject which he touched, but he was incapable of dealing with any religious subject after a fashion which would minister only to what would seem to him the idle curiosity of the mind. It was not that he restrained himself from such merely intellectual exercises upon the themes of religion, the force of his religious interest itself instinctively inhibited them.

Calvin marked an epoch in the history of the doctrine of the Trinity, but of all great theologians who have occupied themselves with this soaring topic, none have been more determined than he not to lose themselves in the intellectual subtleties to which it invites the inquiring mind; and he marked an epoch in the development of the doctrine precisely because his interest in it was vital and not merely or mainly speculative. Or take the great doctrine of predestination which has become identified with his name, and with respect to which he is perhaps, most commonly of all things, supposed to have given the reins to speculative construction and to have pushed logical development to unwarrantable extremes. Calvin, of course, in the pellucid clearness and incorruptible honesty of his thought and in the faithfulness of his reflection of the Biblical teaching, fully grasped and strongly held the doctrine of the will of God as the *prima causa rerum*, and this too was a religious conception with him and was constantly affirmed just because it was a religious conception—yes, in a high and true sense, the most fundamental of all religious conceptions. But even so, it was not to this cosmical predestination that Calvin's thought most persistently turned, but rather to that soteriological predestination on which, as a helpless sinner needing salvation from the free grace of God, he must rest. And therefore Ebrard is so far quite right when he says that predestination appears in Calvin's system not as the *decretum Dei* but as the *electio Dei*.

It is not merely controversial skill which leads Calvin to pass predestination by when he is speaking of the doctrine of God and providence, and to reserve it for the point where he is speaking of salvation. This is where his deepest interest lay. What was suffusing his heart and flowing in full flood into all the chambers of his soul was a profound sense of his indebtedness as a lost sinner to the free grace of God his Saviour. His zeal in asserting the doctrine of two-fold pre-destination is grounded in the clearness with which he perceived—as was indeed perceived with him by all the Reform-ers—that only so can the evil leaven of "synergism" be elimin-ated and the free grace of God be preserved in its purity in the saving process. The roots of his zeal are planted, in a word, in his consciousness of absolute dependence as a sinner on the free mercy of a saving God. The sovereignty of God in grace was an essential constituent of his deepest religious consciousness. Like his great master, Augustine—like Luther, Zwingli and Butzer (Bucer), and all the rest of those high spirits who brought about that great revival of religion which we call the Reformation—he could not endure that the grace of God should not receive all the glory of the rescue of sinners from the destruction in which they are involved, and from which, just because they are involved in it, they are unable to do anything towards their own recovery.

The fundamental interest of Calvin as a theologian lay, it is clear, in the region broadly designated soteriological. Perhaps we may go further and add that, within this broad field, his interest was most intense in the application to the sinful soul of the salvation wrought out by Christ,—in a word in what is technically known as the *ordo salutis*. This has even been made his reproach in some quarters, and we have been told that the main fault of the *Institutes* as a treatise in theological science, lies in its too subjective character. Its effect, at all events, has been to constitute Calvin pre-eminently *the theologian of the Holy Spirit*.

Calvin has made contributions of the first importance to other departments of theological thought. It has already been observed that he marks an epoch in the history of the doctrine of the Trinity. He also marks an epoch in the mode of present-ing the work of Christ. The presentation of Christ's work under the rubrics of the three-fold office of Prophet, Priest and King was introduced by him; and from him it was taken over by the entirety of Christendom, not always, it is true, in his spirit or with his completeness of development, but yet with large advantage. In Christian ethics, too, his impulse proved epoch-making, and this great science was for a generation cultivated only by his followers.

It is probable however that Calvin's greatest contribution to theological science lies in the rich development which he gives—and which he was the first to give—to the doctrine of the work of the Holy Spirit. No doubt, from the origin of Christianity, everyone who has been even slightly imbued with the Christian spirit has believed in the Holy Spirit as the author and giver of life, and has attributed all that is good in the world, and particularly in himself, to His holy offices. And, of course, in treating of grace, Augustine worked out the doctrine of salvation as a subjective experience with great vividness and in great detail, and the whole course of this salvation was fully understood, no doubt, to be the work of the Holy Spirit. But in the same sense in which we may say that the doctrine of sin and grace dates from Augustine, the doctrine of satisfaction from Anselm, the doctrine of justification by faith from Luther,—we must say that the doctrine of the work of the Holy Spirit is a gift from Calvin to the Church. It was he who first related the whole experience of salvation specifically to the working of the Holy Spirit, worked it out into its details, and contemplated its several steps and stages in orderly progress as the product of the Holy Spirit's specific work in applying salvation to the soul. Thus he gave systematic and adequate expression to the whole doctrine of the Holy Spirit and made it the assured possession of the Church of God.

It has been common to say that Calvin's entire theological work may be summed up in this—that he emancipated the soul from the tyranny of human authority and delivered it from the uncertainties of human intermediation in religious things: that he brought the soul into the immediate presence of God and cast it for its spiritual health upon the free grace of God alone. Where the Romanist placed the Church, it is said, Calvin set the Deity. The saying is true, and perhaps, when rightly understood and filled with its appropriate content, it may sufficiently characterise the effect of his theological teaching. But it is expressed too generally to be adequate. What Calvin did was, specifically, to replace the doctrine of the Church as sole source of assured knowledge of God and sole institute of salvation, by the Holy Spirit. Previously, men had looked to the Church for all the trustworthy knowledge of God obtainable, and as well for all the communications of grace accessible. Calvin taught them that neither function has been committed to the Church, but God the Holy Spirit has retained both in His own hands and confers both knowledge of God and communion with God on whom He will.

The *Institutes* is, accordingly, just a treatise on the work of God the Holy Spirit in making God savingly known to sinful man, and bringing sinful man into holy communion with God. Therefore it opens with the great doctrine of the *testimonium Spiritus Sancti*—another of the fruitful doctrines which the Church owes to Calvin—in which he teaches that the only vital and vitalizing knowledge of God which a sinner can attain, is communicated to him through the inner working of the Spirit of God in his heart, without which there is spread in vain before his eyes the revelation of God's glory in the heavens, and the revelation of His grace in the perspicuous pages of the Word. And therefore, it centres in the great doctrine of Regeneration,—the term is broad enough in Calvin to cover the whole process of the subjective *recovery* of man to God—in which he teaches that the only power which can ever awake in a sinful heart the motions of a living faith, is the power of this same Spirit of God moving with a truly creative operation on the deadened soul. When these great ideas are developed in their full expression—with explication of all their presuppositions in the love of God and the redemption of Christ, and of all their relations and consequents—we have Calvin's theology.

Now of course, a theology which commits everything to the operations of that Spirit of God who "worketh when and where and how He pleases," hangs everything on the sovereign good-pleasure of God. Calvin's theology is therefore, predestination to the core, and he does not fail, in faithfulness to the teachings of Scripture and with clear-eyed systematizing genius, to develop its predestinarianism with fulness and with emphasis; to see in all that comes to pass the will of God fulfilling itself, and to vindicate to God the glory that is His due as the Lord and disposer of all things. But this is not the peculiarity of his theology. Augustine had taught all this a thousand years before him. Luther and Zwingli and Martin Butzer, his own teacher in these high mysteries, were teaching it all while he was learning it. The whole body of the leaders of the Reformation movement were teaching it along with him. What is special to himself is the clearness and emphasis of his reference of all that God brings to pass, especially in the processes of the new creation, to God the Holy Spirit, and the development from this point of view of a rich and full doctrine of the work of the Holy Spirit.

Here then is probably Calvin's greatest contribution to theological development. In his hands, for the first time in the history of the Church, the doctrine of the Holy Spirit comes to its rights. Into the heart of none more than into his did the vision of the glory of God shine, and no one has been more determined than he not to give the glory of God to another. Who has been more devoted than he to the Saviour, by whose blood he has been bought? But, above everything else, it is the sense of the sovereign working of salvation by the almighty power of the Holy Spirit which characterizes all Calvin's thought of God. And above everything else he deserves, therefore, the great name of *the theologian of the Holy Spirit.*

THE THEOLOGY OF CALVIN

THE subject of this address is the theology of John Calvin and I shall ask leave to take this subject rather broadly, that is to say, to attempt not so much to describe the personal peculiarities of John Calvin as a theologian, as to indicate in broad outlines the determining characteristics of the theology which he taught. I wish to speak, in other words, about Calvinism, that great system of religious thought which bears John Calvin's name, and which also—although of course he was not its author, but only one of its chief exponents—bears indelibly impressed upon it the marks of his formative hand and of his systematizing genius. Of all the teachers who have wrought into it their minds and hearts since its revival in that tremendous religious upheaval we call the Reformation, this system of thought owes most perhaps to John Calvin and has therefore justly borne since then his name. And of all the services which Calvin has rendered to humanity—and they are neither few nor small—the greatest was undoubtedly his gift to it afresh of this system of religious thought, quickened into new life by the forces of his genius, and it is therefore just that he should be most widely remembered by it. When we are seeking to probe to the heart of Calvinism, we are exploring also most thoroughly the heart of John Calvin. Calvinism is his greatest and most significant monument, and he who adequately understands it will best understand him.

It was about a hundred years ago that Max Göbel first set the scholars at work upon the attempt clearly to formulate the formative principle of Calvinism. A long line of distinguished thinkers have exhausted themselves in the task without attaining, we must confess, altogether consistent results. The great difficulty has been that the formative and distinctive principles of Calvinism have been confused, and men have busied themselves rather in indicating the points of difference by which Calvinism is distinguished from other theological tendencies than in seeking out the germinal principle of which it itself is the unfolding.

The particular theological tendency with which Calvinism has been contrasted in such discussions is, as was natural, the sister system of Lutheranism, with which it divided the heritage of the Reformation. Now undoubtedly somewhat different spirits do inform Calvinism and Lutheranism. And equally undoubtedly, the distinguishing spirit of Calvinism is due to its formative principle and is not to be accounted for by extraneous circumstances of origin or antecedents, such as for example, the democratic instincts of the Swiss, or the superior humanistic culture of its first teachers, or their tendency to intellectualism or to radicalism. But it is gravely misleading to identify the formative principle of either type of Protestantism with its prominent points of difference from the others. They have vastly more in common than in distinction. And nothing could be more misleading than to trace all their differences, as to their roots, to the fundamental place given in the two systems respectively to the principles of predestination and justification by faith.

In the first place, the doctrine of predestination is not the formative principle of Calvinism, it is only its logical implication. It is not the root from which Calvinism springs, it is one of the branches which it has inevitably thrown out. And so little is it the peculiarity of Calvinism, that it underlay and gave its form and power to the whole Reformation movement —which was, as from the spiritual point of view a great revival of religion, so from the doctrinal point of view a great revival of Augustinianism. There was, accordingly, no difference among the Reformers on this point; Luther and Melanchthon and the compromizing Butzer were no less zealous for absolute predestination than Zwingli and Calvin. Even Zwingli could not surpass Luther in sharp and unqualified assertion of this doctrine; and it was not Calvin but Melanchthon who paused, even in his first preliminary statement of the elements of the Protestant faith, to give it formal assertion and elaboration.

Just as little can the doctrine of justification by faith be represented as specifically Lutheran. It is as central to the Reformed as to the Lutheran system. Nay, it is only in the Reformed system that it retains the purity of its conception and resists the tendency to make it a doctrine of justification on account of, instead of by, faith. It is true that Lutheranism is prone to rest in faith as a kind of ultimate fact, while Calvinism penetrates to its causes, and places faith in its due relation to the other products of God's activity looking to the salvation of man. And this difference may, on due consideration, conduct us back to the formative principle of each type of thought. But it, too, is rather an outgrowth of the divergent formative principles than the embodiment of them. Lutheranism, sprung from the throes of a guilt-burdened soul seeking peace with God, finds peace in faith, and stops right there. It is so absorbed in rejoicing in the blessings which flow from faith that it refuses or neglects to inquire whence faith itself flows. It thus loses itself in a sort of divine euthumia, and knows, and will know nothing beyond the peace of the justified soul. Calvinism asks with the same eagerness as Lutheranism the great question, "What shall I do to be saved?" and answers it precisely as Lutheranism answers it. But it cannot stop there. The deeper question presses upon it, "Whence this faith by which I am justified?" And the deeper response suffuses all the chambers of the soul with praise, "From the free gift of God alone, to the praise of the glory of His grace." Thus Calvinism withdraws the eye from the soul and its destiny and fixes it on God and His glory. It has zeal, no doubt, for salvation but its highest zeal is for the honour of God, and it is this that quickens its emotions and vitalizes its efforts. It begins, it centres and it ends with the vision of God in His glory and it sets itself, before all things, to render to God His rights in every sphere of life-activity.

If thus the formative principle of Calvinism is not to be identified with the points of difference which it has developed with its sister type of Protestantism, Lutheranism, much less can it be identified with those heads of doctrine—severally or in sum—which have been singled out by its own rebellious daughter, Arminianism, as its specially vunerable points. The "five points of Calvinism," we have no doubt learned to call them, and not without justice. They are, each and every one of them, essential elements in the Calvinistic system, the denial of which in any of their essential details is logically the rejection of the entirety of Calvinism; and in their sum they provide what is far from being a bad epitome of the Cavinistic system. The sovereignty of the election of God, the substitutive definiteness of the atonement of Christ, the inability of the sinful will to good, the creative energy of the saving grace of the Spirit, the safety of the redeemed soul in the keeping of its Redeemer,—are not these the distinctive teachings of Calvinism, as precious to every Calvinist's heart as they are necessary to the integrity of the system? Selected as the objects of the Arminian assault, these "five-points" have been reaffirmed, therefore, with the constancy of profound conviction by the whole Calvinistic world. It is well however to bear in mind that they owe their prominence in our minds to the Arminian debate, and however well fitted they may prove

in point of fact to stand as a fair epitome of Cavinistic
doctrine, they are historically at least only the Calvinistic
obverse of "the five points of Arminianism." And certainly
they can put in no claim, either severally or in sum, to announce
the formative principle of Calvinism, whose outworking in
the several departments of doctrine they rather are—though
of course they may surely and directly conduct us back to
that formative principle, as the only root out of which just
this body of doctrine could grow. Clearly at the root of the
stock which bears these branches must lie a most profound
sense of God and an equally profound sense of the relation
in which the creature stands to God, whether conceived
merely as creature or, more specifically as sinful creature. It
is *the vision of God and His Majesty*, in a word, which lies at
the foundation of the entirety of Calvinistic thinking.

The exact formulation of the formative principle of
Calvinism, as I have said, has taxed the acumen of a long
line of distinguished thinkers. Many modes of stating it
have been proposed. Perhaps after all, however, its simplest
statement is the best. It lies then, let me repeat, in a profound
apprehension of God in His majesty, with the poignant
realization which inevitably accompanies this apprehension,
of the relation sustained to God by the creature as such, and
particularly by the sinful creature. The Calvinist is the man
who has seen God, and who, having seen God in His glory,
is filled on the one hand, with a sense of his own unworthiness
to stand in God's sight as a creature, and much more as a
sinner, and on the other hand, with adoring wonder that
nevertheless this God is a God who receives sinners. He
who believes in God without reserve and is determined that
God shall be God to him, in all his thinking, feeling, willing—
in the entire compass of his life activities, intellectual, moral,
spiritual—throughout all his individual, social, religious
relations—is, by the force of that strictest of all logic which
presides over the outworking of principles into thought and
life, by the very necessity of the case, a Calvinist.

If we wish to reduce this statement to a more formal
theoretical form, we may say perhaps, that Calvinism in
its fundamental idea implies three things. In it, (i) objectively

speaking, theism comes to its rights ; (ii) subjectively speaking, the religious relation attains its purity ; (iii) soteriologically speaking, evangelical religion finds at length its full expression and its secure stability. Theism comes to its rights only in a teleological view of the universe, which recognizes in the whole course of events the orderly working out of the plan of God, whose will is consequently conceived as the ultimate cause of all things. The religious relation attains its purity only when an attitude of absolute dependence on God is not merely assumed, as in the act, say, of prayer, but is sustained through all the activities of life, intellectual, emotional, executive. And evangelical religion reaches its full manifestation and its stable form only when the sinful soul rests in humble, self-emptying trust purely on the God of grace as the immediate and sole source of all the efficiency which enters into its salvation. From these things shine out upon us the formative principle of Calvinism. The Calvinist is the man who sees God behind all phenomena, and in all that occurs recognizes the hand of God, working out His will; who makes the attitude of the soul to God in prayer the permanent attitude in all its life activities; and who casts himself on the grace of God alone, excluding every trace of dependence on self from the whole work of his salvation.

I think it important to insist here that Calvinism is not a specific variety of theistic thought, religious experience, evangelical faith, but the perfect expression of these things. The difference between it and other forms of theism, religion, evangelicalism, is a difference not of kind but of degree. There are not many kinds of theism, religion, evangelicalism, each with its own special characteristics, among which men are at liberty to choose, as may suit their individual tastes. There is but one kind of theism, religion, evangelicalism, and if there are several constructions laying claim to these names they differ from one another, not as correlative species of a more inclusive genus, but only as more or less good or bad specimens of the same thing differ from one another.

Calvinism comes forward simply as pure theism, religion. evangelicalism, as over against less pure theism, religion. evangelicalism. It does not take its position then by the side of other types of these things, it takes its place over them, as what they too ought to be. It has no difficulty thus, in recognizing the theistic character of all truly theistic thought, the religious note in all really religious manifestations, the evangelical quality of all actual evangelical faith. It refuses to be set antagonistically over against these where they really exist in any degree. It claims them in every instance of their emergence as its own, and seeks only to give them their due place in thought and life. Whoever believes in God, whoever recognizes his dependence on God, whoever hears in his heart the echo of the *soli Deo gloria* of the evangelical profession—by whatever name he may call himself, by whatever logical puzzles his understanding may be confused—Calvinism recognizes such as its own, and as only requiring to give full validity to those fundamental principles which underlie and give its body to all true religion to become explicitly a Calvinist.

Calvinism is born, we perceive, of the sense of God. God fills the whole horizon of the Calvinist's feeling and thought. One of the consequences which flow from this is the high supernaturalism which informs at once his religious consciousness and his doctrinal construction. Calvinism indeed would not be badly defined as the tendency which is determined to do justice to the immediately supernatural, as in the first so in the second creation. The strength and purity of its apprehension of the supernatural Fact (which is God) removes all embarrassment from it in the presence of the supernatural act (which is miracle). In everything which enters into the process of the recovery of sinful man to good and to God, it is impelled by the force of its first principle to assign the initiative to God. A supernatural revelation in which God makes known to man His will and His purposes of grace; a supernatural record of the revelation in a supernaturally given Book, in which God gives His revelation permanence and extension,—such things are to the Calvinist matters of course. And above all things, he can but insist with the utmost strenuousness on the immediate supernaturalness of the actual work of redemption; this of course, in its impetration. It is no strain to his faith to believe in a supernatural Redeemer, breaking His way to earth through a Virgin's womb, bursting

the bonds of death and returning to His Father's side to share
the glory which He had with the Father before the world was.
Nor can he doubt that this supernaturally purchased redemption is applied to the soul in an equally supernatural work of
the Holy Spirit.

Thus it comes about that monergistic regeneration—
"irresistible grace," "effectual calling," our older theologians
called it,—becomes the hinge of the Calvinistic soteriology,
and lies much more deeply imbedded in the system than many
a doctrine more closely connected with it in the popular mind.
Indeed, the soteriological significance of predestination itself
consists to the Calvinist largely in the safeguard it affords to
the immediate supernaturalness of salvation. What lies at the
heart of his soteriology is absolute exclusion of creaturely
efficiency in the induction of the saving process, that the pure
grace of God in salvation may be magnified. Only so could he
express his sense of men's complete dependence as sinners on
the free mercy of a saving God; or extrude the evil leaven of
synergism, by which God is robbed of His glory and man
is encouraged to attribute to some power, some act, some
initiative of his own, his participation in that salvation which
in reality has come to him from pure grace.

There is nothing therefore, against which Calvinism sets
its face with more firmness than every form and degree of
auto-soterism. Above everything else, it is determined to
recognise God, in His son Jesus Christ, acting through the
Holy Spirit whom He has sent, as our veritable Saviour. To
Calvinism, sinful man stands in need, not of inducements or
assistance to save himself, but precisely of saving; and Jesus
Christ has come not to advise, or urge, or woo, or help him
to save himself, but to save him; to save him through the
prevalent working on him of the Holy Spirit. This is the root
of the Calvinistic soteriology, and it is because this deep sense
of human helplessness and this profound consciousness of
indebtedness for all that enters into salvation to the free grace
of God is the root of its soteriology, that election becomes to
Calvinism the *cor cordis* of the Gospel. He who knows that
it is God who has chosen him, and not he who has chosen
God, and that he owes every step and stage of his salvation

to the working out of this choice of God, would be an ingrate indeed if he gave not the whole glory of his salvation to the inexplicable election of the Divine love.

Calvinism however, is not merely a soteriology. Deep as its interest is in salvation, it cannot escape the question —"Why should God thus intervene in the lives of sinners to rescue them from the consequences of their sin?" And it cannot miss the answer—"Because it is to the praise of the glory of His grace." Thus it cannot pause until it places the scheme of salvation itself in relation with a complete world-view in which it becomes subsidiary to the glory of the Lord God Almighty. If all things are from God, so to Calvinism all things are also unto God, and to it God will be all in all. It is born of the reflection in the heart of man of the glory of a God who will not give His honour to another, and draws its life from constant gaze upon this great image. And let us not fail punctually to note, that "it is the only system in which the whole order of the world is thus brought into a rational unity with the doctrine of grace, and in which the glorification of God is carried out with absolute completeness." Therefore the future of Christianity—as its past has done—lies in its hands. For, it is certainly.true, as has been said by a profound thinker of our own time, that "it is only with such a universal conception of God, established in a living way, that we can face with hope of complete conquest all the spiritual dangers and terrors of our times." "It, however," as the same thinker continues, "is deep enough and large enough and divine enough, rightly understood, to confront them and do battle with them all in vindication of the Creator, Preserver and Governor of the world, and of the Justice and Love of the divine Personality."

This is the system of doctrine to the elaboration and defence of which John Calvin gave all his powers nearly four hundred years ago. And it is chiefly because he gave all his powers to commending to us this system of doctrine, that we are here to-day to thank God for giving to the world the man who has given to the world this precious gift.

THE PRESENT DAY ATTITUDE TOWARD CALVINISM
ITS CAUSES AND SIGNIFICANCE

THE subject of this address involves the determination of a matter of fact, about which it is not easy to feel fully assured What is the present-day attitude towards Calvinism? The answer to this question is apt to vary with the point of sight of the observer, or rather with the horizon which his eye surveys.

Our learning today is "made in Germany", our culture comes to us largely from England. And the German learning of the day has a sadly rationalistic *tendency; which is superposed, moreover, on a Lutheran foundation that has an odd way of cropping up and protruding itself in unexpected places. Similarly, English culture is not merely shot through, but stained through and through with an Anglican colouring. Lutheranism was ever intolerant of Calvinism. Anglicanism was certainly never patient of it. Naturalism is its precise contradictory. He who breathes the atmosphere of books, therefore—whether books of erudition or books of pure literature—is apt to find it stifling to his Calvinism.

There is, of course, another side to the matter. There may very likely be more Calvinists in the world to-day than ever before, and even relatively, the professedly Calvinistic Churches are no doubt holding their own. There are important tendencies of modern thought which play into the hands of this or that Calvinistic conception. Above all, there are to be found everywhere humble souls, who, in the quiet of retired lives, have caught a vision of God in His glory and are cherishing in their hearts that vital flame of complete dependence on Him which is the very essence of Calvinism.

On the whole however, I think we must allow, especially when we are contemplating the trend of current thought, that the fortunes of Calvinism are certainly not at their flood. Those whose heritage it was, have in large numbers drifted away from it. Those who still formally profess it do not always illustrate it in life or proclaim it in word.

* The Rationalism here spoken of in 1909 opened the way for the materialism of a Hitler and devastated the world in two mighty wars; but Calvinism goes on!—Ed.

There remains, however, undoubtedly a remnant according
to the election of grace. But the condition of a remnant,
while it may well be a healthful one—bearing in it, as a fruitful
seed, the promise and potency of future expansion—is little
likely to be a happy one. Unfriendly faces meet it on every
side; if doubt and hesitation are not engendered, at least an
apologetical attitude is fostered, and an apologetical attitude is
not becoming in Calvinists, whose trust is in the Lord God
Almighty. In such a situation, Calvinism seems shorn of its
strength and is tempted to stand fearful and half-ashamed
in the marts of men. I have no wish to paint the situation in
too dark colours; I fully believe that Calvinism, as it has
supplied the sinew of Evangelical Christianity in the past,
so is it its strength in the present and its hope for the future.
Meanwhile, does it not seem, in large circles at all events, to
be thrown very much on the defensive? In the measure in
which you feel this to be the case, in that measure you will be
prepared to ask with me for the causes and significance of
this state of things.

We should begin, I think, by recalling precisely what
Calvinism is. It may be fairly summed up in these three
propositions. Calvinism is (i) Theism come to its rights.
Calvinism is (ii) Religion at the height of its conception.
Calvinism is (iii) Evangelicalism in its purest and most stable
expression.

(i) *Calvinism, I say, is Theism come to its rights.* For in
what does Theism come to its rights but in a teleological view
of the universe? For, though there be that are called gods,
whether in heaven or on earth—as there are gods many and
lords conceived by men—yet to the Theist there can be but
one God, of whom are all things and unto whom are all things.
You see, we have already slipped into the Calvinistic formula,
"The will of God is the cause of things." I do not say, you will
observe, that Theism and Calvinism have points of affinity,
lie close to one another; I say they are identical. I say that the
Theism which is truly Theism, consistently Theism, all that
Theism to be really Theism must be, is already in principle
Calvinism; that Calvinism in its cosmological aspect is
nothing more than Theism in its purity. To fall away from

Calvinism is to fall away, by just so much, from a truly Theistic conception of the universe. Of course then, to fall away in any degree from a pure Theism in our conception of things is just by that much to fall away from Calvinism. Wherever in our view of the world an imperfect Theism has crept in, there Calvinism has become impossible.

(ii) *Calvinism*, I have said, *is religion at the height of its conception*, for, whatever else may enter into the conscious religious relation,—a vague feeling of mystery, a struggling reaching out towards the infinite, a deep sentiment of reverence and awe, a keen recognition or dull apprehension of responsibility,—certainly its substance lies in a sense of absolute dependence upon a Supreme Being. I do not say, you will observe, an absolute feeling of dependence, which, in the Schleiermacherian meaning at least of a feeling without intellectual content, were an absurdity. What I say is, that religion in its substance is a sense of absolute dependence on God and reaches the height of its conception only when this sense of absolute dependence is complete and all-pervasive, in the thought and feeling and life. But when this stage is reached we have just Calvinism.

For what is Calvinism but the Theistical expression of religion, conceived as absolute dependence on God? Wherever we find religion in its purity, therefore, there Calvinism is implicit. I do not say, observe again, that an approach to Calvinism is traceable there, in less or greater measure. I say, there Calvinism is—implicit indeed, but really present. Religion in its purity is Calvinism in life, and you can fall away from Calvinism only by just in that measure falling away from religion; and you do fall away from Calvinism just in proportion as you fall away from religion in its purity. It is however, dreadfully easy to fall away from religion at the height of its conception. We may assume the truly religious attitude of heart and mind for a moment; it is hard to maintain it and give it unbroken dominance in our thought, feeling, and action. Our soul's attitude in prayer—that is the religious attitude at its height. But do we preserve the attitude we assume in prayer towards God, when we rise from our knees? Or does our Amen! cut it off at once, and do we go on about our affairs in an entirely different mood? Now, Calvinism means just the preservation, in all our thinking and feeling and action, of the attitude of utter dependence on God which we assume in prayer. It is the mood of religion made determinative of all our thinking and feeling and willing. It is therefore *con*terminous with religion in the height of its conception. Wherever religion in any measure loses hold of the reins of life and our immanent thought has slipped away from its control,—there Calvinism has become impossible.

(iii) I have said too, that *Calvinism is evangelicalism in its pure and only stable expression.* When we say evangelicalism we say sin and salvation. Evangelicalism is a soteriological conception, it implies sin, and salvation from sin. There may be religion without evangelicalism. We may go further: religion might conceivably exist at the height of its conception and evangelicalism be lacking. But not in sinners. Evangelicalism is religion at the height of its conception as it forms itself in the hearts of sinners. It means utter dependence on God for salvation. It implies therefore, need of salvation and a profound sense of this need, along with an equally profound sense of helplessness in the presence of this need, and utter dependence on God for its satisfaction. Its type is found in the publican who smote his breast and cried, "God, be merciful to me a sinner!" No question there of saving himself, or of helping God to save him, or of opening the way to God to save him. No question of anything but, "I am a sinner, and all my hope is in God my Saviour!" Now this is Calvinism; not, note once more, something like Calvinism or an approach to Calvinism, but just Calvinism in its vital manifestation. Wherever this attitude of heart is found and is given expression in direct and unambiguous terms, there is Calvinism. Wherever this attitude of mind and heart is fallen away from, in however small a measure, there Calvinism has become impossible.

For Calvinism, in this soteriological aspect of it, is just the perception and expression and defence of the utter dependence of the soul on the free grace of God for salvation. All its so-called hard features—its doctrine of original sin, yes, speak it right out, its doctrine of total depravity and the entire inability of the sinful will to good; its doctrine of election, or, to put it in the words everywhere spoken against, its doctrine of predestination and preterition, of reprobation itself—mean just this and nothing more. Calvinism will not play fast and loose with the free grace of God. It is set upon giving to God, and to God alone, the glory and all the glory of salvation. There are others than Calvinists, no doubt, who would fain make the same great confession. But they make it with reserves, or they painfully justify the making of it by some tenuous theory which confuses nature and grace. They leave logical pitfalls on this side or that, and the difference between logical pitfalls and other pitfalls is that the wayfarer may fall into the others, but the plain man, just because his is a simple mind, must fall into those. Calvinism will leave no logical pitfalls and will make no reserves. It will have nothing to do with theories whose function it is to explain away facts. It confesses, with a heart full of adoring gratitude, that to God, and to God alone, belongs salvation and the whole of salvation; that He it is, and He alone, who works salvation in its whole reach. Any falling away in the slightest measure from this great confession is to fall away from Calvinism. Any intrusion of any human merit, or act, or disposition, or power, as ground or cause or occasion, into the process of divine salvation,—whether in the way of power to resist or of ability to improve grace, of the opening of the soul to the reception of grace, or of the employment of grace already received—is a breach with Calvinism.

Calvinism is the casting of the soul wholly on the free grace of God alone, to whom alone belongs salvation. And, such being the nature of Calvinism, it seems scarcely necessary to inquire why its fortunes appear from time to time, and now again in our own time, to suffer some depression. It can no more perish out of the earth than the sense of sin can pass out of the heart of sinful humanity—than the sense of God can fade out of the minds of dependent creatures—than God Himself can perish out of the heavens. Its fortunes are bound up with the fortunes of Theism, religion, evangelicalism; for it is just Theism, religion, evangelicalism in the purity of their conception and manifestation. In the *purity* of their conception and manifestation—there is the seat of the difficulty. It is proverbially hard to retain, much more to maintain, perfection. And how can precisely these things be maintained at their height? Consider the currents of thought flowing up and down in the world, tending—I do not now say to obliterate the perception of the God of all; atheistic naturalism, materialistic or pantheistic evolutionism—but to blunt or obscure our perception of the Divine hand in the sequence of events and the issues of things. Consider the pride of man, his assertion of freedom, his boast of power, his refusal to acknowledge the sway of another's will. Consider the in-grained confidence of the sinner in his own fundamentally good nature and his full ability to perform all that can be justly demanded of him.

Is it strange that in this world, in this particular age of this world, it should prove difficult to preserve not only active, but vivid and dominant, the perception of the every-where determining hand of God, the sense of absolute depen-dence on Him, the conviction of utter inability to do even the least thing to rescue ourselves from sin—at the height of their conceptions? Is it not enough to account for whatever depression Calvinism may be suffering in the world to-day, to point to the natural difficulty—in this materialistic age, conscious of its newly realized powers over against the forces of nature and filled with the pride of achievement and of material well-being—of guarding our perception of the governing hand of God in all things, in its perfection; of maintaining our sense of dependence on a higher power in full force; of preserving our feeling of sin, unworthiness, and helplessness in its profundity? Is not the depression of Calvinism, so far as it is real, significant merely of this, that to our age the vision of God has become somewhat obscured in the midst of abound-ing material triumphs, that the religious emotion has in some measure ceased to be the determining force in life, and that the evangelical attitude of complete dependence on God for salvation does not readily commend itself to men who are accustomed to lay forceful hands on everything else they wish, and who do not quite see why they may not take heaven also by storm?

Such suggestions may seem to you rather general, perhaps

even somewhat indefinite. They nevertheless appear to me to embody the true, and the whole, account of whatever depression of fortunes Calvinism may be suffering to-day. In our current philosophies, whether monistic evolutionism or pluralistic pragmatism, Theism is far from coming to its rights. In the strenuous activities of our materialised life, religion has little opportunity to assert itself in its purity. In our restless assertion of our personal power and worth, evangelicalism easily falls back into the background. In an atmosphere created by such a state of things, how could Calvinism thrive?

We may, of course, press on to a more specific account of its depressed fortunes. But in attempting to be more specific, what can we do but single out particular aspects of the general situation for special remark? It is possible, indeed, that the singling out of one of these aspects may give clearness and point to the general fact, and it may be worth while, therefore, to attend to one of these special aspects for a moment.

Let us observe then, that Calvinism is only another name for consistent supernaturalism in religion. The central fact of Calvinism is the vision of God. Its determining principle is zeal for the Divine honour. What it sets itself to do is to render to God His rights in every sphere of life-activity. In this it begins, and centres, and ends. It is this that is said, when it is said that it is Theism come to its rights, since in that case everything that comes to pass is viewed as the direct outworking of the Divine purpose—when it is said that it is religion at the height of its conception, since in that case God is consciously felt as Him in whom we live and move and have our being —when it is said that it is evangelicalism in its purity, since in that case we cast ourselves as sinners, without reserve, wholly on the mercy of the Divine grace. It is this sense of God, of God's presence, of God's power, of God's all-pervading activity—most of all in the process of salvation—which constitutes Calvinism. When the Calvinist gazes into the mirror of the world, whether the world of nature or the world of events, his attention is held not by the mirror itself (with the cunning construction of which scientific investigations may no doubt very properly busy themselves), but by the Face of God which he sees reflected therein. When the Calvinist contemplates the religious life, he is less concerned with the psychological nature and relations of the emotions which surge through the soul, (with which the votaries of the new science of the psychology of religion are perhaps not quite unfruitfully engaging themselves), than with the divine Source from which they spring, the divine Object on which they take hold. When the Calvinist considers the state of his soul and the possibility of its rescue from death and sin, he may not indeed be blind to the responses which it may by the grace of God be enabled to make to the divine grace, but he absorbs himself not in them but in it, and sees in every step of his recovery to good and to God the almighty working of God's grace.

The Calvinist, in a word, is the man who sees God. He has caught sight of the ineffable Vision, and he will not let it fade for a moment from his eyes—God in nature, God in history, God in grace. Everywhere he sees God in His mighty stepping, everywhere he feels the working of His mighty arm, the throbbing of His mighty heart. The Calvinist is therefore, by way of eminence, the supernaturalist in the world of thought. The world itself is to him a supernatural product, not merely in the sense that somewhere, away back before all time, God made it, but that God is making it now, and in every event that falls out. In every modification of what is, that takes place, His hand is visible, as through all occurrences His "one increasing purpose runs." Man himself is His—created for His glory, and having as the one supreme end of his existence to glorify his Maker, and haply also to enjoy Him forever. And salvation, in every step and stage of it, is of God. Conceived in God's love, wrought out by God's own Son in a supernatural life and death in this world of sin, and applied by God's Spirit in a series of acts as supernatural as the Virgin Birth and the Resurrection of the Son of God themselves— it is a supernatural work through and through. To the Calvinist, thus, the Church of God is as direct a creation of God as the first creation itself. In this supernaturalism, the whole thought and feeling and life of the Calvinist is steeped. With-

out it there can be no Calvinism, for it is just this that is
Calvinism.

Now the age in which we live is anything but supernaturalistic; it is distinctly hostile to supernaturalism. Its
most striking characteristic is precisely its deeply rooted and
wide-reaching rationalism of thought and sentiment. We
know the origin of this modern naturalism; we can trace its
history. What it is of more importance to observe, however,
is that we cannot escape its influence. On its rise in the latter
part of the seventeenth century a new era began, an era in
which men have had little thought for the rights of God in
their absorption in the rights of man. English Deism, French
Encyclopaedism, German Illuminism—these are some of the
fruits it has borne in the progress of its development. And now it
has at length run to seed in our own day in what arrogates to
itself the name of the New Protestantism—that New Protestantism which repudiates Luther and all his fervid ways, and turns
rather for its spiritual parentage to the religious indifferentism
of Erasmus. It has invaded with its solvent every form of
thought and every activity of life. It has given us a naturalistic
philosophy (in which all "being" is evaporated into "becoming"), a naturalistic science (the single-minded zeal of which
is to eliminate design from the universe); a naturalistic
politics (whose first fruits was the French Revolution, and whose
last may well be an atheistic socialism); a naturalistic history
(which can scarcely find place for even human personality
among the causes of events); and a naturalistic religion,
which says, "Hands off" to God—if indeed it troubles itself
to consider whether there be a God, if there be a God, whether
He be a person, or if He be a person, whether He can or will
concern Himself with men.

You, who are ministers of the Gospel, have been greatly
clogged by this naturalism of current thought in the prosecu-
tion of your calling. How many of those to whom you would
carry the message of grace do you find preoccupied with a
naturalistic prejudice! Who of your acquaintance really
posits God as a factor in the development of the world? How
often have you been exhorted to seek a "natural" progress
for the course of events in history? Yes, even for the history

of redemption. So, even in the region of your own theological science a new Bible has been given to you—not offered to you merely, but violently thrust upon you, as the only Bible a rational man can receive—a new Bible reconstructed on the principle of natural development, torn to pieces and rearranged under the overmastering impulse to find a "natural" order of sequence for its books, and a "natural" course of development for the religion whose records it preserves. But why stop with the Bible? Your divine Redeemer Himself has been reconstructed, on the same naturalistic lines. For a century and a half now—from Reimarus to Wrede—all of the resources of an age pre-eminent for scholarship have been bent to the task of giving you a "natural" Jesus. Why talk here of the miracles of the Old Testament or of the New? It is *the* Miracle of the Old Testament and of the New which is really brought into the question. Why dispute as to the Virgin Birth and the Resurrection of Jesus? It is the elimination of Jesus himself, as aught but a simple man of His day—in nothing, except perhaps an unusually vivid religious experience, differentiated from other Galilean peasants of His time—that the naturalistic frenzy of our age is set upon. And so furiously has the task been driven on, that the choice that is set before us at the end of the day is, practically, between no Jesus at all or a fanatic, not to say a paranoiac Jesus.

In this anti-supernaturalistic atmosphere, it is strange that men find the pure supernaturalism of the Calvinistic confession difficult—that they waver in their firm confidence that it is God who reigns in heaven and on earth, that in Him we all live and move and have our being—that it is He, and not ourselves, who creates in us every impulse to good—and that it is His almighty arm alone that can rescue us from sin and bring to our helpless souls salvation? Is it strange that here, too, men travel the broad road beaten smooth by many feet—that the Calvinistic gate seems narrow so that few there be that find it, and the Calvinistic way so straitened that few there be who go in thereat?

But let us make no mistake here. For here, too, Calvinism is just Christianity. The supernaturalism for which Calvinism stands is the very breath of the nostrils of Christianity;

without it Christianity cannot exist. And let us not imagine that we can pick and choose with respect to the aspects of this supernaturalism which we acknowledge—that we may, for example, retain supernaturalism in the origination of Christianity, and forego the supernaturalism with which Calvinism is more immediately concerned, the supernaturalism of the application of Christianity. Men will not believe that a religion, the actual working of which in the world is natural, can have required to be ushered into the world with supernatural pomp and display. These supernaturals stand or fall together.

A supernatural Redeemer is not needed for a natural salvation. If we can, and do, save ourselves, it were grossly incongruous that God should come down from heaven to save us, trailing clouds of glory with Him as He came. The logic of the Socinian system gave us at once a human Christ and an auto-soteric religion. The same logic will work to-day, and every day till the end of time. It is only for a truly supernatural salvation that a truly supernatural redemption, or a truly supernatural Redeemer, is demanded,—or can be believed in. And this reveals to us the real place which Calvinism holds in the controversies of to-day, and the service it is to render in the preservation of Christianity for the future. Only the Calvinist is the consistent supernaturalist, and only consistent supernaturalism can save supernatural religion for the world.

The supernatural fact, which is God; the supernatural act, which is miracle; the supernatural work, which is the revealed will of God; the supernatural redemption, which is the divine deed of the divine Christ; the supernatural salvation which is the divine work of the divine Spirit,—these things form a system, and you cannot draw one item out without shaking the whole. What Calvinism particularly asserts is the supernaturalism of salvation, as the immediate work of God the Holy Spirit in the soul, by virtue of which we are made new creatures in Christ our Redeemer, and framed into the sons of God the Father. And it is only he who heartily believes in the supernaturalism of salvation who is not fatally handicapped in meeting the assaults of that anti-supernaturalistic world-view which flaunts itself so triumphantly about us. Conceal it from ourselves as we may, defeat here lies athwart the path of all half-hearted schemes and compromising constructions. This is what was meant by the late Dr. H. Boynton Smith, when he declared roundly: "One thing is certain,— that Infidel Science will rout everything excepting thoroughgoing Christian orthodoxy. . . . The fight will be between a stiff thoroughgoing orthodoxy and a stiff thoroughgoing infidelity. It will be, for example, Augustine or Comte, Athanasius or Hegel, Luther or Schopenhauer, J. S. Mill or John Calvin." This witness is true.

We cannot be supernaturalistic in patches of our thinking and naturalistic in substance. We cannot be supernaturalistic with regard to the remote facts of history, and naturalistic with regard to the intimate events of experience. We cannot be supernaturalistic with regard to what occurred two thousand years ago in Palestine, and simply naturalistic with regard to what occurs to-day in our hearts. No form of Christian supernaturalism can be ultimately maintained in any department of life or thought, except it carry with it the supernaturalism of salvation. And a consistent supernaturalism of salvation is only another name for Calvinism.

Calvinism thus emerges to our sight as nothing more or less than the hope of the world.

SOL DEO GLORIA